Society and Education

third edition

Society and Education

third edition

ROBERT J. HAVIGHURST

and

BERNICE L. NEUGARTEN

ALLYN AND BACON, INC.   BOSTON

Third printing . . . March, 1968

Library of Congress Catalog Card Number: 66–27001

Printed in the United States of America

Preface

To be a teacher in America requires not only a competence in teaching children the school subjects, but also an understanding of how the school fits into the society and what its tasks are. This book aims to help teachers gain some of this understanding.

The quickening pace of social change has given the schools more opportunities and more problems. The new patterns of work and leisure, metropolitan development and the urban crisis, the Negro "revolution," the enormously expanded functions of the federal government in the field of education, the emergence of a serious problem of unemployed and out of school youth—these are some of the social changes that require new ideas in education and new ways of teaching.

A book on the sociology of education must keep up with the quantity of new empirical studies and new interpretations that sociologists and social psychologists contribute. Some selection is necessary and some topics from sociology must be omitted. We have included what we feel will be of greatest use to classroom teachers and to other readers interested in education. This is our sociological interpretation of education.

As we have rewritten this book for the second time in less than ten years, we are impressed with the ways in which social change in America has increased and made more complex the knowledge that teachers should have about the society in which and for which they work. We have had to revise every chapter in order to take into account new

v

research that has been published within the past five years. The chapter dealing with the education of Negro children is completely new. The chapter on metropolitan development has been expanded to give more attention to the relations of suburbs and central cities in the metropolitan areas.

In this edition the schools are seen more clearly as an agent for social urban renewal, now the major domestic problem of our country. A new chapter on the relations of school systems with other social systems presents a basis for thinking about the cooperation that is developing between schools and other social institutions.

In Part One, we examine the school and the college in the social structure, particularly in the social class structure, seeing how the schools reflect both the hierarchical structure and the social pluralism of the modern democratic society and how they provide for social mobility.

In Part Two, we consider the school as a relatively self-contained social system and discuss its relationships to certain other social systems, primarily the family and the peer group, as they operate together as socializing agencies in the lives of children and adolescents.

In Part Three, the school is seen in the context of the local community, particularly the metropolitan community consisting of suburbs and central city that has become increasingly the focus of interest of citizens and the civic leaders who work for the "social renewal" of urban America.

Part Four deals again with the school in the wider society, as it affects and is affected by changing industrial patterns, population growth, race relations, juvenile delinquency, and the altered relations between local, state, and federal government in the educational enterprise.

In Part Five the focus is upon the teacher: the various roles of the teacher in the classroom and in the community, the career of the teacher as a member of the largest professional group in modern society, and upon the new professionalism in teaching.

Throughout the book we have attempted to rest our interpretations upon empirical findings and thus to maximize the social science base on which educational policies and practices depend. At the same time a sociological interpretation of education is bound to deal with controversial issues and to involve value judgments. We have not avoided such issues, although we have attempted to make clear where our interpretations are supported by research findings and where they rest upon value judgments.

Full data on all references cited in the text and in the suggested readings at the end of each chapter appear in the Bibliography. To make this section of maximum value, we have placed in parentheses after each reference the page numbers where the reference has been cited in this book.

We are indebted to a number of persons who have assisted us in various ways in writing the first and subsequent revisions of this book. We should like particularly to acknowledge the influence of our longtime friend and colleague, Professor W. Lloyd Warner, whose research and writing have had a major effect upon our thinking about social structure in America. We are indebted to our many graduate students who contributed illustrative materials and who have made many useful suggestions in the light of their own experience as classroom teachers. We have had again the invaluable assistance of Miss Jacqueline Falk who worked with us on the earlier editions; and finally we are indebted to Mrs. Elizabeth Garber for her editorial assistance in the preparation of the manuscript.

ROBERT J. HAVIGHURST

BERNICE L. NEUGARTEN

Contents

Influence of the Peer Group. Status in the Peer Group. The Peer Group and the School.

The Culture of the School. The School as a Social Organization.

PART 3
The School in the Community

What Is a Community? A. The Traditional School. B. The School as a Model of the Community. C. The Community School. Schools in Differing Metropolitan Neighborhoods.

Forces Causing Urbanization. Metropolitanism and the Schools. Increased Socioeconomic and Racial Stratification. Effects of Stratification on the Schools. Urban Renewal.

Social System Defined. Role Analysis. Relations Among Educational Sub-Systems. Inter-system Relations in the Metropolitan Area. The "Independent" School System. Cooperative Planning by Social Systems. Salient Roles in Changing Social Systems. Role Relations. Conclusions.

PART 4
The School in the Wider Society

Federal Government and Education.   Policy Makers in Education.

PART 5
The Teacher

The Choice of Teaching as an Occupation.   Social Mobility Among Teachers.   Social Origin as a Factor in Teaching Performance.

The Teacher in the Community.   The Teacher in the School. Fulfilling the Roles of the Teacher.

The Teacher as a Socializing Agent.   Leadership in the Classroom.

The Career Pattern.   The Economic Status of the Teacher. Professionalization.

PART 1

THE SCHOOL IN
THE SOCIAL STRUCTURE

1 / Social Structure in America

The society in which American children grow up is highly diversified and complex. It consists of many different groups of people with characteristically different ways of life. Schools differ because the people who inhabit the neighborhoods served by the schools are different. The fact that children, schools, and teachers all reflect this diversity can be seen from the following descriptions of three fifth-grade classrooms:

A Fifth Grade in a Metropolitan Area

Mrs. Gordon stood at the girls' entrance to the grimy, red-brick school making sure that the girls formed an orderly line ready to march inside when the buzzer sounded. She heard a scuffle behind her and a big eighth-grade girl landed on the ground beside her. "Damn you!" the girl shouted, and then looking up at Mrs. Gordon she said, "Teacher, they pushed me."

"Get back in line," said Mrs. Gordon. "How can we make the little children behave when you big girls act like that?" By this time the lines were moving into the building. Mrs. Gordon followed them in and up to her own fifth-grade room on the third floor. There was a lot of noise coming through the open door but it died down as she strode into the room and with a strong voice said, "Good morning, boys and girls."

Forty boys and girls stood beside forty desks in five rows, and, placing their hands over their hearts, they repeated the pledge of allegiance to the flag, "and to the Republic, for which it stands." Mrs. Gordon liked this ceremony. It was a symbol of unity in a variegated group which she sometimes called her "United Nations." About half of the youngsters were Negroes, mostly very dark-skinned, but some light brown and yellow, barely distinguishable from several Mexicans in the class. There were four Puerto

3

Ricans. Several children with Polish names and three or four with Scotch names, who spoke a hillbilly English from Kentucky, were the only blondes in the room.

Mrs. Gordon had been teaching in the John T. McManus School in the Canalport district of Metropolis for 15 years. Previously she had taught in two schools which were known among teachers as "better schools," because the children came from families of professional men and lived in better houses. Most teachers liked these other schools, but Mrs. Gordon had not liked either the children or the parents in those schools. The children had been argumentative with her—they would quote their fathers or mothers, or bring to school something they had read that didn't agree with her statements. As for the parents, she thought they were always criticizing. They found fault with everything and everyone from the Superintendent of Schools down to the janitor. So when she heard of a vacancy in the McManus school, where there was a principal who was known as a good one to work under, Mrs. Gordon had applied for the transfer.

The John T. McManus school had been tutor to thirteen thousand children during its 75 years of existence. About half the children had been pupils for the full eight years, while the others stayed shorter terms. At first they were children of Irish immigrants. Then the Irish moved out of Canalport to better houses farther from the factories of the neighborhood, and the Bohemians and Hungarians moved in. Their children were followed by Italian and Polish children, and more recently these families were moving out, and Negroes, Mexicans, and Puerto Ricans were coming in. The McManus school had some distinguished graduates, including three state senators and the present sheriff. At present it had the best eighth-grade basketball team in the city.

Mrs. Gordon knew all these things, and was proud of them. Her own two children had gone to school in the "good" residential district where she and her husband lived before her husband's death and her sons were now in college. Having raised her own, she never had any doubts about her ability to handle other people's children. The children felt that she was a fair teacher, although a strict one, and many of them in later years looked back to their year with her in the fifth grade as the year they learned how to work, and they thanked her for it.

There were all types of children in her room, Mrs. Gordon thought. Of course, many were slow about learning, like their parents. They would drop out of school as soon as they reached the age of 16. But she could teach them a little more than their parents knew. There were a few bad ones. She was keeping her eyes on John Washington, a tough, over-age Negro boy with a sullen expression. One day he had been annoying the boy sitting in front of him, and the boy had turned his head sharply and rammed it into Washington's open knife. The gash in his cheek had required five stitches. The principal had warned the Washington boy that if he ever came to school with a knife again he would be sent to the special school for delinquent boys. Mrs. Gordon knew that McManus had graduated some hoodlums and thieves as well as three state senators, and she regarded it as her job to reduce delinquency by firm control of her pupils.

There were a few children in her room who would make good—maybe even in a big way, Mrs. Gordon thought. There was Maria, the Puerto Rican girl who had the looks and possibly the talent to become a great dancer. Mrs. Gordon personally took Maria to the settlement house in the neighborhood and asked the Director to place the girl in a dance group. She told Maria's mother that the girl had talent and must be kept in school until she had learned enough English and enough manners to be accepted by the people she would have to work with if she became a dancer. There was also David Widder, the Negro boy who scored the highest in the class on an intelligence test. He was a good reader and good at arithmetic, and she thought he might become a scientist or a doctor. She told him this, and she told it to his father and mother whom she summoned to school. She told them about Donald Matthews, the highest ranking boy in her first class at McManus, also a Negro, who had just won a fellowship for graduate work in chemistry at the State University.

Mrs. Gordon knew that the great majority of her pupils would grow up to be hard-working, respectable people, and she was sure that they needed patient teaching and firm handling from her.

A Fifth Grade in a Small City

Miss Johnson stood in the hallway beside the door of her fifth-grade classroom in Center School in Homeville as the boys and girls marched in. She closed the door, then walked to her desk in front of the room, where she took out her attendance record and checked off the names of the children as they came from the coat room. They stood and repeated in unison the pledge of allegiance to the flag. Then they took out their arithmetic books and began to work the problems she had listed on the blackboard.

She knew her class pretty well by now, two months after the beginning of school. They came from all over Homeville, these fifth-graders, after spending the first four grades in neighborhood schools.

As she walked up and down the rows of seats, Miss Johnson stopped occasionally to help someone who was having difficulty. She leaned over to see what Bob Wilson had written on his paper, and she noticed his dirty hands. His hands were always grimy, she thought, and she must remind him at recess time to wash them—but not now, because he would have an excuse to go to the washroom and leave his work behind. He was the third Wilson child she had taught, and they had all been slow pupils. Still, she thought, they could probably read better than their father, who worked on the crew that cleaned the streets.

The first one to finish with the lesson was Sidney, the Jewish boy whose father ran the Army store. Sidney had told Miss Johnson that he was going to be a doctor when he grew up, and he worked hard in school.

Patricia Morgan raised her hand and asked for help on a problem in long division. It was a pleasure to help Patricia. Miss Johnson thought she was the most attractive child in the room. In another three or four years the girl would be sent to a private school in the East, and then to Vassar, where her mother had graduated. Patricia's father was a lawyer, and her mother was the daughter of the bank president. Her grandfather had been one of the first settlers in the county and had acquired a thousand acres of the best corn land to start the biggest fortune in Homeville. Patricia was just an average scholar, but she worked steadily, and her mother had told the teacher that she was not to be favored over the other children.

A Fifth Grade in a Suburb

Miss Bond was seated at her desk in a corner of the room as her fifth-graders came in from the schoolgrounds. They went first to the coat room to hang up their coats and then to their seats. A few gathered in little groups, talking to one another. Looking out the window Miss Bond could see other children arriving, many of them in automobiles driven by their mothers, with occasionally a child coming in a long black Cadillac driven by a chauffeur. Other children walked from nearby houses.

She could see the sloping curve of the landscaped grounds. The children played in the large field on the other side of the building. Now the last boy sauntered in, and the class was slowly getting to work, most of them at their desks grouped in one half of the room, while a few were sitting at worktables using reference books. It was a large, light, airy room, with green blackboards and green-colored bulletin boards on which brightly colored posters were mounted. The fluorescent lights were not needed this morning, but it was cool, and the floor was comfortably warmed by inlaid heating coils.

Forest Park School was a show place, and Miss Bond felt fortunate to be able to work in such a fine building, in the finest suburb of the metropolis. For five years now she had taught in this school, after ten years at Homeville. She had fewer pupils than she had had in Homeville, and this school had much better equipment with which to work.

The children were all engrossed in work now, most of them on arithmetic, though one small group worked at a table getting together a report about the first Thanksgiving. They were a good-looking lot, clean and sweet-smelling; as though, Miss Bond thought, they had come out of scented bedclothes. There was Estelle Woodford, taking charge of the committee, acting just like her mother who was President of the Garden Club and who had been PTA president last year. Tommy Beauregard raised his hand to ask for help. He was a plodder, certainly not one of the stars in the class, but he kept at his work. She knew that he would work hard through high school and then through an Ivy League college, and then probably work up into the management of the industrial machinery company of which his father was president.

Helen Fischer sat in a corner, studying from a sixth-grade arithmetic book. She had finished the fifth-grade book and was going ahead on her own. The girl was too much on her own, thought Miss Bond. Dr. Fischer was a psychiatrist who had just bought a big house and moved his family out from the city. Neither the girl nor her mother seemed to have made friends yet, as far as Miss Bond could tell. She would like to help Helen get on more friendly terms with the other children but she hardly knew how to go about it. If this had been Homeville, she would have spoken to some of the mothers and suggested that they invite Helen to their daughters' parties. But in Forest Park she did not know how to do this. She supposed the little girls had parties, but she knew nothing about them. She had thought of speaking to Mrs. Fairbairn, her PTA room mother, but Mrs. Fairbairn seemed so occupied with her own plans for the year's activities and so sure of how Miss Bond should fit into them that the teacher felt there was no room for her to make suggestions about the welfare of Helen Fischer.

Her relations with the mothers were different from what she had known in Homeville. She felt that she had an accepted place with Forest Park mothers, and a respected place, but that she should not step out of it. Only twice had she been in the home of any of her pupils—and then on the occasion of a tea to plan a school program. On these occasions she had been uncertain about what kind of dress to wear, and whether to wear gloves, and she had been uncomfortable. The women spoke of the Eastern colleges they had attended, and Miss Bond was afraid they would ask her where she had gone to college. Suddenly the state teachers' college which had meant so much to her had become something to keep quiet about.

When taken as a whole, each classroom is different from others and reflects the community of which it is a part. Mrs. Gordon, teaching in what is often called a slum school, has a fairly homogeneous group in terms of socioeconomic characteristics. Miss Johnson teaches in a small Midwest city, where in the same classroom there are children coming from all parts of town and from a fairly wide range of social backgrounds. Miss Bond in her exclusive suburb has a group that comes from "good" homes where great importance is placed upon the quality of education and preparation for college.[1]

[1] Some people, when they first become acquainted with the idea of social classes, tend to deny their existence in America because they feel they are undemocratic. Yet all of us are aware that differences in social rank exist in any

These three teachers, all of them good teachers, will have quite different experiences and will derive different kinds of satisfactions from their work. This is true not only because they are teaching children from different social groups, but because they themselves have come from somewhat different social backgrounds and are different in personality and in their attitudes toward children.

Culture and Subcultures

When a social group shares certain ways of behaving and believing, it is said to share a culture or a subculture.

By a culture, we refer to the patterns and products of learned behavior: the etiquette, language, food habits, religious and moral beliefs, systems of knowledge, attitudes, and values; as well as the material things and artifacts produced—the technology—of a group of people. Culture refers, in short, to the patterned way of life of a society. (The term society refers to the persons who share a given culture, and to the network of relationships that exists among the members of the group. A human society does not exist apart from a culture.)

Culture is a human production, and man differs from animals because he creates culture, and because he transmits what he has learned and what he has created from one generation to the next.

A complex society such as that of modern America has both an overall culture, a way of life shared by all Americans; and a set of subcultures, ways of life that differ from one subgroup to another. Whenever a smaller group of people within a society have certain ways of behavior, certain attitudes and beliefs that constitute a variant of the culture, we say they have a subculture of their own. For example, nearly

---

community, whether or not we use the term "social class" in describing them. The reader can refer to his own community and will recognize that there are certain people in it who are considered "the best families" or "the elite," others who are "the leaders" or "pillars of the community," others who are "just nice, respectable people" or "the working people," still others who are "poor, but honest" or "good people, but nobody," and still others who are "bottom of the heap." We Americans speak of people who have "gone a long way up," or "climbed the social ladder," or of people who have "dropped a notch." We speak, too, of marrying "above" or "below" one's own position and of having made "good" or "poor" marriages.

Whatever the terms used in a particular group, such expressions refer clearly to a social organization characterized by different levels of rank and prestige.

all Americans share a common language; use the same systems of money, weights, and measures; dress somewhat alike; and have certain political principles in common. These ways of life, shared by nearly all Americans, make up the American culture.

At the same time, within the American culture, there are a number of subcultures that are characteristic of subgroups. There are subgroups based upon ethnicity, or country of origin—German, Polish, Italian. There are subgroups based upon race—Negro, Oriental, white. We can distinguish ways of life according to where people are located—in rural or in urban areas or in different parts of the country such as the West Coast, New England, the Deep South.

Members of such groups share a certain subculture when they have in common certain practices, beliefs, or attitudes that are not held by other American groups.

Social Classes as Subcultures

Another type of social grouping that cross-cuts ethnic, racial, and religious subcultures and is of particular importance to educators is the social class. There are middle-class (as well as upper- and working-class) Catholics, Protestants, Jews, German-Americans, Italian-Americans, Negroes and whites.

Social classes constitute subcultural groups. When people from the same social class meet and converse they soon find they have much in common, even though they may come from different ethnic or religious backgrounds or from different sections of the country. They will find that they live in much the same kinds of neighborhoods, have similar eating habits, dress in pretty much the same ways, have rather similar tastes in furniture, literature, and recreation, and have about the same amount of education.

Social-Class Membership

A social-class group consists of people who have similar social habits and values. One of the tests of membership in a social class is that of association, actual or potential. In a small community, the members of a particular social class tend to belong to the same social organizations and to entertain one another in their homes. If they live in a big city, their numbers are so large that only a few can actually associate with one another; yet, even in large cities, if members of the same social class meet as strangers they soon recognize a good deal of similarity in their ways of life, and recognize each other as social equals.

Subcultural differences based upon ethnic or religious factors can effectively separate members of a given social class. For example, social visiting and entertaining is not common between working-class German Lutherans and working-class Italian-Americans. Yet, even in those instances in which there are barriers to social intercourse, members of a given social class share a common subculture. In many respects, working-class Negroes and whites are more alike in their way of life than are working-class and middle-class Negroes; in the same way, middle-class Protestants and Catholics are more alike than are working-class and middle-class Protestants.

Education and Social Class

Any concept of group membership is of value if it predicts with a fairly high degree of accuracy some important characteristics of the members of the group. Among the various social group concepts—ethnicity, race, religion, geographical region—social class is probably the most useful for educators. As we shall see in the chapters that follow, by knowing the social-class composition of a school or a classroom, a teacher can anticipate such important characteristics of the group as these: (1) The general level of educational achievement; (2) the educational aspirations, (for example, whether the majority will be interested in job training, or in college entrance); (3) the drive for achievement, and the willingness to postpone gratification (that is, to do things that are difficult or uncomfortable in the expectation that they will bring future gain); (4) some of the experiences the child will have had in his family before he entered school as well as some of the experiences in the family and the neighborhood that he is likely to have during his school years. For example, children from one social class can be expected to have had a different kind of intellectual stimulation during the pre-school years than children from other social classes. While we shall consider the family in greater detail in Chapter 6, at this point it may be said that, compared with race, religion, or ethnicity, social class is in most instances the main determinant of family experiences that contribute to or hinder a child's mental development and that will affect a child's progress in school.

Before we consider the relations between schools and social-class differences in children, however, we shall describe briefly the social-class structure in America, the subcultures of the various social classes, and some of the methods by which the social structure has been studied by sociologists.

The Social-Class Hierarchy

The various social groups that are found in America are organized into one functioning society, a society with an intricate pattern of inter-relationships between groups, but one in which an overall hierarchical structure can be described.

Most persons recognize that they occupy a position on a social scale. They acknowledge that there are other people and other groups that have more or less economic and political power and social prestige than their group. Within a particular community people can rank themselves and their neighbors according to power or prestige; that is, they can assign different individuals to particular positions on a "social ladder."

All societies, large or small, primitive or modern, show this phenomenon of rank: the leaders and people of high prestige occupy positions at the top; others occupy intermediate positions; and still others are at the bottom of the social scale. This is true regardless of the political form of government. A democracy has rank; so does an absolute monarchy; so also does a communist society such as the Soviet Union. While the king and the nobility are at the top in a monarchy, the top people in the Soviet Union are the leaders of the Communist Party and the high government and military officials. In a democracy the people at the top are those who have earned or inherited economic power or social prestige.

Dimensions of Social Class

In speaking of social classes, such terms as "structure," "hierarchy," and "rank" are often used, but the sociologist also uses the more general term, "social stratification." Social stratification has been studied in many countries, and constitutes an important area in sociological research and theory.

Kahl (1957) has delineated the major *dimensions* that underlie the American social-class structure (and that sociologists measure when they undertake empirical studies of stratification) as follows:

1. Prestige. Some people in the community have more personal prestige than others, and are regarded by others with respect and deference.
2. Occupation. Some occupations are considered "higher" than others, partly because they are more important to the welfare of the community, partly because they require special talents, and partly because they pay high rewards.
3. Possessions, or wealth, or income.
4. Social interaction. In a large community, everyone cannot interact with everyone; patterns of differential contact arise; and people are most comfortable with "their own kind."
5. Class consciousness. The degree to which people at given levels are aware of themselves as distinctive social groupings. Americans are said to be less class conscious than Europeans; yet Americans, too, think of themselves as "working-class" or "middle-class"; and a large proportion identify "on the side of management" or "on the side of labor."
6. Value orientations. People differ about the things they consider good or important; and groups of people come to share a limited number of abstract values or value systems.
7. Power, or the ability to control the actions of other people. Kahl points out that this variable, while it is important in determining social class, cannot be measured directly. It can be studied indirectly, however, by delineating the cliques of important people in a community; or by studying the people who control the capital wealth of a community.

Although each of the first six dimensions may be considered independently, all seven are interdependent; they interact to form the basis of the social-class structure. Thus, for example, a person is often granted prestige only on the basis of his occupation. Similarly, people with high incomes tend to be persons within certain occupational groupings; they tend to interact with people in the community who are like themselves; they are accorded considerable prestige; and they tend to occupy powerful positions with regard to community organizations, civic, political, or economic. In somewhat different words, persons who are high (or low) on one dimension tend to be high (or low) on the others and they constitute a social class.

Studying the Social Structure

Although various sociologists have chosen to highlight one or another of the dimensions listed above in undertaking studies of social stratification, we are primarily concerned with a number of studies of American communities made by sociologists and social anthropologists since about 1930 according to the methods developed by W. Lloyd Warner and his associates (Warner, Meeker, and Eells, 1960). These investigators have stressed the dynamics of community organization; that is, they focused upon the prestige of individuals and families and the patterns of social interaction that constitute the social life of a community.

The usual procedure in these studies was for the social scientist to move into the community and live there for a time, visiting and conversing with people and observing the social scene. By such means he discovered the social groups that existed. He talked with the members of various social groups and asked about the social structure of the community. He learned who associated with whom, who were considered the "top" people, who the "bottom," and why. Gradually he pieced together a picture of the community as it was viewed by its members. Seldom did any one citizen see the whole structure of his community clearly, but the social scientist combined the views of many people into a single composite picture representing the consensus. This picture showed groups of people arranged in a network, but arranged also on a social scale from top to bottom in terms of the status assigned them by their fellow-citizens.

After the major lines of the social structure had been delineated; and after the positions of a few key people had been agreed upon, it was possible to locate other people in relation to the original persons. Eventually the majority of the population could be located on the social map in this way.[2]

2 This method of mapping the social system and of discovering the social class of a particular person is called the "method of evaluated social participation," often abbreviated as E.P. First, by interviewing members of the community the major lines of social structure were ascertained, and the names obtained of a few people who interviewers agreed occupied given positions in the structure. It was then noted with whom these people associated in social clubs, informal social cliques, service clubs, church associations, and so on. Thus other people were placed in relation to the original group. Eventually the majority of the population was placed in this way. Then, if the social scientist wished to know the social status of Mr. X, whose name had not previously been brought into the study, he asked who Mr. X's friends were, what clubs or associations he belonged to, and

This method, of course, worked well only in small communities, where it was possible to meet with, or at least find out about, practically every adult inhabitant. Somewhat different methods had to be devised for use in metropolitan areas, as will be described later on in this chapter.

Social Structure in America

The results of a score of community studies enabled social scientists to draw certain general conclusions about social structure in the United States. In general, there is a basic five-class structure. (See Figure 1.3, page 19.) The proportion of people in each class varies depending upon the size, the age, and the economic character of a given community. Thus, in comparison with the country as a whole, a community in a coal-mining or steel-mill area is likely to have a higher proportion of working-class people, while a community with a college or university is likely to have a higher proportion of upper-middle-class people. If the economic situation of a community changes drastically, the social structure of that community is likely to change also.

Small Communities

It is very common for Americans, particularly if they live in small, self-contained communities (that is, communities that are not satellites of big cities) to stress equalitarianism and to play down, or deny, the existence of social classes. At the same time they recognize that there are different "types" of people in their community. As a respected citizen of Jonesville, a city of 6,000, explained:

> Almost everyone in this town is rated in some way; people can rate you in just a few minutes by talking to you. It's remarkable how you can size people up in a hurry—suppose I use a rating scale of zero to 100 and rate people on it. You can be sure this is not a hypothetical thing either. Not to the people of Jonesville. People like the Caldwells and Volmers . . . rate 100. The Shaws would be up there, too. People like me, oh, a 70 maybe, and

---

then found that Mr. X was close to one of the groups already defined on the social map. Mr. X's social participation was thus *evaluated* in relation to that of others in the community, and his place in the social structure *was determined*.

people like John (a janitor) about a 40, no better than that. Remember, this is the social rating. If we rated them financially, some of them would rank differently. (Warner and associates, 1949, p. 22.)

This man did not speak of social classes as such; however, he recognized that his community reflected a social hierarchy.

THE SMALL RURAL COMMUNITY. Studies of extremely small communities, villages ranging from a few hundred in population up to about 1,500, generally showed a three-class structure consisting of an upper-middle class, a lower-middle class, and a few families at the very bottom. Class lines in these communities were relatively indistinct as compared to larger communities, and there was more social intercourse between classes (Barker and Wright, 1954; Havighurst and Morgan, 1951; Bailey, 1953).

CHANGE IN A SMALL RURAL COMMUNITY. Plainville, an Ozark community, deserves special mention because unlike most communities, it was studied twice, and also because it demonstrates that profound changes in social structure can take place in a relatively short time. When West studied the community in 1939, he found two distinct social classes with practically no movement between them. The upper class was associated with residence on the prairie; they used modern commercial farming practices, and their style of life was maintained by proceeds from cash crops (West, 1945). Members of this class were called "honest, self-respecting people"; a few were "upper crust." The lower class was associated with residence in the hill country and with subsistence farming. Lower-class people included some "good" people, but also a "lower element" with, at the very bottom, a few "who lived like animals."

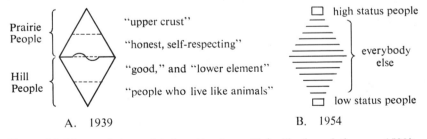
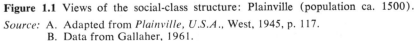

Figure 1.1 Views of the social-class structure: Plainville (population ca. 1500).
Source: A. Adapted from *Plainville, U.S.A.*, West, 1945, p. 117.
B. Data from Gallaher, 1961.

West's study, was undertaken just at the time that the Department of Agriculture was beginning its demonstration programs in the Ozarks. During the next few years, modern commercial farming became increasingly the standard practice, while the timber market, upon which many subsistence farmers had depended for their cash needs, dwindled. Many hill farmers quit farming and either went to the city or retired in town on Old Age Assistance payments. Farms were consolidated into larger units and mechanization spread.

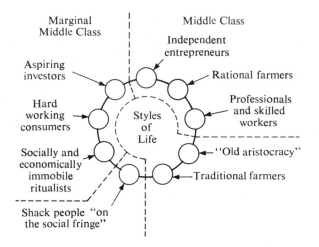

Figure 1.2 Views of the social-class structure: Springdale, 1952 (population ca. 2500).

Source: Data from Vidich and Bensman, 1958.

Fifteen years after the original study, Gallaher (1961) found that "hill" and "prairie" were merely geographical expressions in Plainville, now unrelated to social status or to style of life. Everyone, including the lowest-status people, had raised their standard of living; and social-class boundaries had shifted dramatically. (See Figure 1.1.) While such drastic changes are unlikely to occur in larger towns that include some industry, and while they probably have little effect upon the proportions of different classes in the country as a whole, it is important to keep in mind that the class structure is a dynamic, shifting set of relationships in a given community. Changes are occurring rapidly in large cities as well as in small towns, a point to which we shall return especially in the chapter on metropolitan development.

The Small City

Cities with a population from about 5,000 to 15,000 tended to exhibit a five-class structure. A good example is a midwestern community that was described under the names of Jonesville, Elmtown, and Midwest. (Warner and associates, 1949; Hollingshead, 1949; Warner, Meeker, and Eells, 1960.) This city had a population of about 6,000, and represented the most common type of small city in the north central states—a county seat, with both an industrial and an agricultural population.

In this community, the upper class constituted about three percent of the population. Some of them were the descendants of a pioneer settler who, a hundred years earlier, had acquired large tracts of farmland which had now become the best real estate in the city. Others were executives of a small factory, or they were the owners of the banks, the largest farms, and the most profitable businesses.

The upper-middle class contained about 10 percent of the population and consisted mainly of professional men, business executives, and owners of businesses and of large farms. The lower-middle class, about 30 percent of the whole, consisted mainly of white-collar workers, owners of small retail businesses, a few foremen and skilled manual workers, and the bulk of the prosperous farmers. These people were said by those in the classes above them to be "nice people," but social "nobodies."

The working class, numerically the largest group with 35 to 40 percent of the population, were described as "poor but honest" people who worked as skilled and unskilled laborers or as tenant farmers.

The lowest class, about 15 percent, consisted partly of people who were working hard to maintain a respectable kind of poverty and partly of people who seemed to the rest of the community to be generally immoral, lazy, and defiant of the law.

After the Jonesville studies were made, two other midwestern communities, one of 40,000 and one of 100,000, were studied. In these communities essentially the same picture of social structure emerged (Havighurst *et al.,* 1962; Eells *et al.,* 1951).

A somewhat more complicated six-class social structure had been found, however, in a New England community of about 17,000 called "Yankee City," the first community to be studied by these methods (Warner and Lunt, 1941). In that community, there were two upper-class groups: an "upper-upper," consisting of families who traced their lineage back to colonial times and who had had wealth and high social position for several generations; and a "lower-upper" group or *nouveaux riches,* families who had moved into the community more recently, and whose money had been acquired for the most part in the present generation or in the one just preceding. There was a clear separation between these two groups in terms of their social participation.

The Large City

In a large city it is impossible for the sociologist to analyze social-class differences on the basis of actual social participation (who associates with whom), for only a handful of people are known to each other and any given pattern of face-to-face interaction can involve only a small number of the total population.

In attempting to study the social structure of the metropolitan area of Kansas City in the late 1950's, however, investigators found that residents made consistent evaluations of various *symbols* of status (Coleman and Neugarten, 1967). Kansas Citians had a highly-developed awareness of the status hierarchy in their community; and, although the average citizen could name only some of the persons who were at the top and some who were at the bottom of the social ladder, he nevertheless ranked his fellow residents on the basis of such dimensions of status as area of residence, quality of housing, occupation, club-membership, ethnic identification, and so on. Thus, for example, Kansas Citians were particularly aware of the prestige ranking of various neighborhoods and tended readily to "locate" persons on the social ladder according to their home addresses.

As anticipated, the heterogeneity and complexity of the large city produced a much more highly differentiated social structure than in a small town. Thirteen different social strata were visible, each stratum representing a gradation on the social scale. At the same time, the basic five-class system seemed applicable. There were five "core" groups of people, readily distinguishable on the basic social characteristics mentioned above; with each of the other eight groups forming a variant of one of the basic patterns; and with greater differences appearing between the five larger groups than between the 13 smaller ones.[3]

[3] The study of Kansas City stands midway, in a sense, between studies of social structure in smaller communities based upon the method of E.P. (see footnote, page 13), and studies of social stratification based on particular indices of

Large cities then can be described in terms of the basic five-class structure, granted that there will be many subgroups. The proportions of people in the five classes are probably roughly the same as those for small cities. In Kansas City, for instance, the percents of the population in the five social classes were estimated to be, from upper to lower, 2.5, 11, 32, 40, and 14, proportions which agree quite closely with the proportions in smaller communities as shown in Figure 1.3.

In the same way, Hodges (1963) after studying the "Peninsula" area of California (from San Francisco through San Jose) and after studying data obtained from almost 2,000 heads of households in the area, summarized the social structure as a five-class structure.

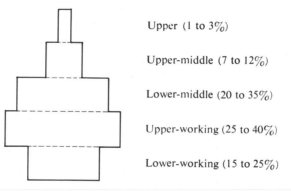

Upper (1 to 3%)

Upper-middle (7 to 12%)

Lower-middle (20 to 35%)

Upper-working (25 to 40%)

Lower-working (15 to 25%)

Figure 1.3 A national view of the social-class structure.

Source: The percentages presented are derived from a number of studies of the social structure made in communities ranging from 5,000 to 500,000 in population; the percentage ranges show how a given class varies in size.

The Metropolitan Area

In huge metropolitan areas such as New York, Chicago, or Los Angeles, a large proportion of residents will neither be sufficiently acquainted with various neighborhoods (except in very gross terms) nor with

---

socioeconomic status such as level of education or occupation. The essential difference lies in the fact that neither social participation itself, nor the objective indices themselves, but the *evaluations* of these *indices* as made by the residents of the community formed the basis of the study. Thus, as one of the dimensions of status, persons were not ranked according to the economic value of their houses but according to the prestige assigned *by fellow* residents to the neighborhood in which the house was located.

particular clubs and associations to assign them prestige ranks; and some of the other dimensions of status used in Kansas City will not be applicable. It is relatively useless to attempt to study the status structure of the large metropolitan area on the basis of patterns of social participation or evaluated symbols of status. Instead, the sociologist relies on socioeconomic indices such as occupation, level of education, or income —indices that have been shown to be highly related to social status positions in smaller communities (Warner, Meeker and Eells, 1960).

The same is true in making generalizations concerning the social structure of the society at large; sociologists for the most part must use socioeconomic variables as indices of social status and social classes are defined most frequently as groups that vary according to occupation or according to educational levels. We shall return to this point shortly, after describing social classes as subcultures, but it should be pointed out that there is good empirical evidence to show that, in this as in other industrialized countries, occupations and/or levels of education follow a consistent prestige ranking. In other words, to know a man's occupation is to enable one to predict, with a large degree of accuracy, his social status in his own community and in the society at large.

In the chapters to follow in this book we shall be referring to social classes that have been differentiated on the basis of socioeconomic indices rather than on the basis of direct evidence of status or of evaluated participation. As will be seen from the following descriptions, however, the concept of a social class refers primarily to a way of life and a set of attitudes and values that are common to members of the group, ways of life that are only approximated by discrete items of information such as occupation, education, or income.

Subcultures of the Social Classes

Finding that people can be described as belonging to different classes is only a first step. How do the class groups differ in behavior, in beliefs, in attitudes, in values? In other words, what is the subculture that characterizes each of the social-class groups?

In describing subcultures we will make use of the five-class structure that has been found to be characteristic of American communities, even though this is an oversimplification, especially of the complex metropolitan area. The following descriptions are based upon studies carried out in large cities (such as Kansas City) and larger geographical areas (such as the San Francisco peninsula) as well as in smaller communities. While they are only thumbnail sketches and thus cannot do justice to the variety of patterns to be found at each class level, they should suffice to point up the most salient differences in styles of life as these differences bear upon educational system.

It should be remembered that the classes are in many respects more alike than they are different. People of all classes, for instance, share the modern American mass culture; that is, to a great extent they read the same newspapers, go to the same movies, listen to the same music, watch the same television programs and commercials. Many social scientists such as Riesman (1950) and Hodges (1963) believe that the mass culture is obliterating class differences, particularly between the lower-middle and the working classes.

The following descriptions apply to the majority of people in a given social class, but not to every person in the class. There are many people who share the major socioeconomic characteristics of a given social class, but who do not follow its way of life in all respects. There are also large numbers of persons who will show "status discrepancies," or inconsistencies; that is, they will rank higher on some of the dimensions of status than on others.

Upper Class

Upper-class people generally have inherited wealth, and usually have a family tradition of social prominence that extends back several generations. A few may not be wealthy, but as the respected cousins, nieces, or nephews of upper-class families, they also belong in the upper class. All these people will be listed in the *Social Register* (if the community has one) and will belong to the most exclusive social clubs. They are likely to be well-versed in family history.

Upper-class people belong to the boards of directors of art museums, of symphony and opera associations, or of Ivy League colleges. They tend to support charitable organizations, chambers of commerce, and the Republican Party (in the North). In older New England communities, their support was often silent ("the power behind the throne") and they left the offices in these organizations to be filled by upper-middle-class people. In newer and in larger cities, however, they are likely to be indistinguishable from upper-middles in this respect and are visible as community leaders. Upper-class people usually belong to the Protestant Episcopal, Presbyterian, or Congregational churches in the Midwest, or to the Unitarian or Congregational churches in New England. Relatively few are Catholics or Jews.

Only rarely do upper-class people indulge in conspicuous consumption—showy parties, ostentatious mansions with numerous servants, jewels, and furs. Their houses, gardens, summer places, automobiles, and clothes are more likely to be conservative and inconspicuous (but in "the best of taste").

In the eyes of upper-class people, education is a matter of proper rearing; formal schooling is no more important in this connection than are other aspects of training that children need if they are to fill their adult roles properly. Training for an occupation is not of primary importance, since these children will inherit high status and cannot go any higher by occupational success. Nevertheless, the occupation must be of the "right" type for the upper class. Young men go into business or into one of the higher status professions such as architecture, medicine, law, and (infrequently) the ministry in an upper-status denomination. Boys and girls generally attend private schools and the prestige Ivy League and selective women's colleges.

Joseph Kahl in his book, *The American Class Structure,* discussed at some length the dominant value orientations of the various social classes, as he perceived them in the late 1950's, and he chose a single word or phrase that, in his opinion, expressed the distinctive quality of life at each social level. For the upper class, this phrase was "graceful living." He said:

> The upper class, in short, can be described as a group who believe in tradition, in continuity of behavior with the past; they emphasize familism and lineage, which is cemented by the family fortune either as something inherited from the past or to be passed along in the future; they favor the skills of graceful living and dilettantism, and tend to value the man more than the accomplishment. They are conservative, both in the sense they want to preserve the system which put them on top, and because they revere the relics of the past which gave them a personal link to those forces and people who legitimate their claim to superiority. Yet they often are also liberal, for their family position guarantees enough security to permit individualistic expression and variation. And although they feel superior, they also vaguely recognize that much of the nation is suspicious of their right to do so; they are defensive, for the American values of equalitarianism and of prestige through accomplishment are at variance with inheritance and dilettantism. (Kahl, 1957, pp. 192–193.)

Some observers of the current social scene would take issue with Kahl's ascription of dilettantism, taking cognizance of an increasing frequency of upper-class people in positions of political and business prominence, and of the participation of upper-class college youth in political and civil rights activities in the 1960's alongside youth of lower class levels. Few would quarrel, however, that the term "graceful living" is still appropriate.

Some of the parents of the children in Miss Bond's class in Forest Park are in the upper class. Living in an exclusive suburb, they may send their children to the public school, at least for the first few years. If they live in a more heterogeneous community, they may send their children to the local public school until the children are old enough, at 12 or 14, to go away from home to a private school.

Upper-Middle Class

About half of the adult members of this class have climbed to their present status from lower beginnings. Hence this class seems to be made up largely of active, ambitious people. The men are business executives and professional men; the women are active in home-making, club work, PTA, and civic organizations. The members of this class do not have aristocratic family traditions. Although some are interested in building up such traditions, the typical comment is, "We do not care about our ancestors. It isn't *who* you are, but *what* you are."

The great bulk of positions of leadership in civic, business, and professional organizations are held by upper-middle class people— organizations such as Rotary and Kiwanis clubs, the League of Women Voters, the Chamber of Commerce, the Medical Society, the Ministerial Association, the Bar Association, and the National Association for the Advancement of Colored People.

Hodges (1963) has labelled these people the "Americans of 'tomorrow,'" pointing out that they have been the first group to accept many now-standard innovations and gadgets, such as the split-level home, the Ivy-League style in men's clothing, the sport car, the back-yard barbecue, and hi-fi music. Their homes are medium to large in size, neat and well kept; houses usually have a flower garden or lawn that is cared for by the family, and a recreation room or a wood-working shop in the basement; apartments will be large and located in good residential areas of the city.

The upper-middle-class family is conscious of the importance of money. It may be a quite wealthy family, with money earned in the present generation; more usually the income is "adequate," enough to pay for a comfortable home, a new automobile every few years, a fair-sized insurance and pension plan, college education for the children, and some left over for modest investment in stocks and bonds.

Most such families take a summer vacation and sometimes a winter vacation also. They are likely to travel by automobile, to go to a summer cottage on a lake, or to go abroad. They patronize the theater and the symphony concerts, and they read such periodicals as *Harper's Magazine,* the *Atlantic Monthly,* and the *New Yorker.*

Almost every family is affiliated with a church, and active church leaders come mainly from this class. The favored churches are Presbyterian, Congregational-Christian, Methodist, Baptist (in the Middle West) and Unitarian (in New England). There are also numerous Roman Catholic, Lutheran, and Jewish upper-middle-class people. Nearly all of the members of this class are native-born Americans, and most of them have native-born parents and grandparents.

Upper-middle-class people stress harmonious relations with others; they tend to be flexible, tolerant, and non-dogmatic. In the California suburban area studied by Hodges (1963), the upper-middle parents were found to be less anxious and more easy-going in rearing their children than lower-middle and working-class parents.

Education is extremely important to people in this group. Many of them have risen into this class through professional careers, and they feel that it is almost essential that their children secure a college degree if they are to maintain upper-middle status in the next generation. The children generally go to public schools, and then to the State University or to privately supported liberal arts colleges including Ivy League colleges in the East.

The central value orientation for the upper-middle class is, in Kahl's terms, "career."

What do they believe? Primarily, they believe in themselves and in organization. They stress individual initiative combined with smooth group functioning. They have faith that anything can be accomplished by this combination. They say that a man must be smart, must be educated, must be energetic, but at the same time he must be cooperative, must not stand out too much from his crowd of equals, must not be eccentric or "controversial." These are the values of the upper levels of most bureaucratic structures. They are very effective in their proper situation; they may not produce great art or literature or scientific theory, but they certainly produce efficient organizations.

The upper-middle class believe in themselves and in the American way of life, and they are devoted to their careers. They stress planning for the future and not too much regard for the past; they stress activity, accomplishment, practical results; they stress individualistic achievement within the framework of group cooperation and collective responsibility. They are not much interested in tradition, in art, in any sort of theory for its own sake. They always ask of an idea, "What good is it; how can you use it?" They are on the move, "on the make," and they have the zest of winners (though the tensions of racers). (Kahl, 1957, p. 201.)

The new and exclusive suburbs of the big cities are populated largely by upper-middle-class people. They are, for instance, most of the parents of Miss Bond's Forest Park school. They live also in "good" residential sections of Homeville and every other town or city, small or large. (Miss Johnson has several upper-middle-class children in her Center School class, but Mrs. Gordon left this group behind when she transferred to the McManus school in a slum neighborhood.)

Lower-Middle Class

This large group is often called the "common man" group by those above them in the social scale, although they themselves think of working-class people as being the "common man."

The lower-middle class consists of white-collar clerical and sales workers. Some are factory foremen or members of the "labor aristocracy" such as railroad engineers, conductors, photo-engravers; some are small building, electrical, and plumbing contractors. Most farm owners who operate their own farms are also in this class. These people tend to be at the "national average"; their income is at about the middle of the national income range, and the magazines, sports, TV programs, movie stars and comic strips that they prefer tend also to be the national favorites.

Lower-middle-class people stress thrift and are proud of their economic independence (although Hodges found that lower-middle-class people in suburbia were likely to be living above their means). Their houses are usually comfortably furnished and well kept, but small to medium in size and located nearer the "wrong part of town," or in inexpensive suburban tracts. Occasionally a young doctor or teacher coming into a new community will buy a house in a lower-middle-class area and his older associates will shake their heads and say, "He made a mistake to buy in that area."

The members of this group travel widely in this country by automobile, but almost never go abroad, as do people in the classes above them. They make up the bulk of members of fraternal organizations such as the American Legion; their wives are active in the women's auxiliaries. They are fairly active in the PTA, and they furnish the bulk of membership in the Protestant and Catholic Churches. They also furnish the lay leadership of some churches, especially the Baptist, the Lutheran, and in many places the Methodist churches. Many lower-middle-class people are Catholics, and some are Jews. This class has in it appreciable numbers who are children or grandchildren of immigrants.

Most members of the lower-middle class finished high school, and a third to a half of their children go on to college, generally a junior college. Schooling is considered essential for a good job, and the children are expected to be obedient pupils. (Some of the hardest-working and brightest pupils in Miss Johnson's room in Homeville are lower-middle class, and she likes to work with them. They are seldom discipline problems.)

Financially, the lower-middle class has not fared as well as the upper-middle or the working classes. From 1950 to 1960 the real income of this class shrank, making it more difficult for these people to maintain what they feel is a comfortable style of life. In the suburbs, lower-middle-class and working-class people often live in the same developments and have many characteristics in common. In time, the two classes may become enough alike to be considered together as the "common man" group.

For Kahl, the term "respectability" is the key to the value orientations of the lower-middle class. Respectability is expressed in various ways: in the high value placed upon education; in religion (the lower-middles are the most regular churchgoers in our society); in home ownership as a symbol of stability and family solidarity. Kahl goes on to say:

Respectability has its price. Particularly when the rewards are minimal, when the consumption pleasures and prestige returns are slim by comparison to the upper-middle class, the white-collar man may come to feel that he is bound by a very stiff collar. The successful blue-collar worker enjoys his respectability much more, for he tends to compare himself to the run-of-the-mill workers who stand immediately below him. But the petty white-collar worker looks up; he feels that he is constantly holding his impulses in check in order to be liked by his boss, by his customers, by his neighbors. He has to sell his personality as well as his labor. . . . Our recent literature, both scientific and fictional, has tended to emphasize the extremes of lower-middle-class life, perhaps because the values there expressed are so diametrically opposed to those of the intellectuals who write books. The intellectuals portray little people with restricted lives, tight and authoritarian personalities. . . . I do not doubt that when the lower-middle-class way of life goes to extremes it produces just such reactions. The extreme version of upper-middle-class values is snobbery; that of lower-middle-class, respectability, prudery. But must we judge each group by its extremes? For many the lower-middle-class way of life is quietly satisfying; it connotes the accomplishment of moderate education and moderate educational achievement; it means successful Americanization from not-too-distant ethnic roots; it brings a strong, stable, family-centered life; especially in the smaller towns and cities, it brings a degree of public recognition as solid citizens. (Kahl, 1957, pp. 204–205.)

Upper-Working Class[4]

The "respectable working people," the skilled and semi-skilled "blue-collar" (as opposed to "white-collar") workers, make up the working class. This group contains a large number of people whose parents were immigrants. They are often Catholics, but there are also considerable numbers in the fundamentalist Protestant denominations such as the Assembly of God, the Pentecostal, and Holiness churches. They are also frequently Baptists and Methodists and, in the big eastern cities, Jews. At the same time, a considerable minority of this group are not church members, and some are hostile to churches.

Working-class people in small towns and cities live "across the tracks" or "on the wrong side of town" in small houses that are often well kept and sometimes have additions built by the owner in his spare time. The working class has, however, enjoyed a considerable increase in

[4] In earlier studies of social structure undertaken by Warner's methods, this social class was referred to as "upper-lower," and the bottom class as "lower-lower." While it is not easy to find substitute terms which are free of implied derogation, the present authors have chosen the terms "working class" and "lower-working class" as at least somewhat less biased, and as reflecting more accurately the fact that most persons at the lowest social level are also workers. At the same time, to do as certain other sociologists have done and to draw no distinctions within the working class is to obliterate some very significant differences between the large group of stable, blue-collar workers at the "common-man" level and the smaller group who in many respects stand apart from all the other levels of society by virtue of poverty and other social and economic deprivations.

real income in recent years, particularly in the big cities, which has enabled increasing numbers to buy homes in inexpensive suburban tracts. Working-class people are as fond of labor-saving gadgets as middle-class people, and frequently show concern about "keeping up with the Joneses" by buying more household equipment, newer and bigger cars, and by frequently remodeling their homes. Wives expect to add to the family income by working, when they are not tied down with children.

Working-class people seldom join civic organizations. The men belong to veterans' organizations and occasionally to fraternal orders. Their wives join the ladies' auxiliaries and are often members of PTA when the children are small. The men enjoy hunting and fishing; but most working-class people spend their leisure time at home, watching TV, working in the vegetable garden, or "fixing up around the house." They seldom read more than the local newspaper and one or two magazines.

Typically, working-class adults did not complete high school. They put little value upon learning for learning's sake, but they recognize that education is the key to a good job, and they want their children to go further in school than they themselves have gone. At present about half of the children from this social class complete high school, and a few go on to college. (Miss Johnson has a large number of these children in her room, as does Mrs. Gordon.)

Kahl, in discussing the semi-skilled factory operative as the typical representative of this class, says:

A worker is not greatly concerned about his public reputation. He expects to move from one routine job to another as opportunities expand and contract, and he knows that he will be hired as an anonymous person. He need not sell his personality, his family background, his consumption skills; all he needs is a pair of willing hands. His work has little intrinsic interest; he learns to adjust, to lower his aspirations, to become adroit at working without thinking and without dreaming of future advancement. As he retreats from work as a thing of inner importance, he turns to his family and to consumption pleasures. He cannot live extravagantly, but in our productive economy he can live comfortably and can expect his home slowly to add one gadget to another. He takes pride in this method of "getting ahead." He and his family learn to be amused by the mass media of entertainment—most predominantly, television. In smaller towns . . . he devotes an extraordinary amount of time to fishing. He does not participate much in community life nor in active group recreations. He is a spectator in recreation just as he is in work. (Kahl, 1957, p. 210.)

Lower-Working Class

Most of society looks down on this group, using such terms as "river rats," "the lower element" or "people of the slums." It is generally believed that most of the delinquency, crime, and sexual promiscuity is found in this class.

Lower-working-class people are easy to stereotype because they live in highly visible and often shockingly poor quarters—big city slums or the low-income public housing developments that are now replacing the slums; flimsy shacks on "the flats" at the edges of cities; or tenant farmers' cabins. Sometimes the stereotype holds true, but frequently it does not. Miller (1964), for example, has distinguished four groups within this class: the "stable poor," unskilled workers who have steady jobs and a stable family life; the "strained," who have steady jobs but who have major family or personality difficulties; "the copers," people who have economic difficulties but strong family relations, and who manage to get along most of the time; and the "unstable," people who have both financial and familial or personal problems and who may, at some period, end up on the welfare rolls as "multi-problem" or "hard-core" cases.

According to origin, lower-class people may be divided into at least two groups. There are those who have been at the bottom of the social structure for several generations and seem destined to stay there (except for an occasional mobile son or daughter who climbs up and then out of the family's sight). There are also the newest immigrants who perform the most menial tasks of the society while they are learning American ways of life. In the past, such people were frequently Irish, German, Swedish, or Polish. Today they are primarily Puerto Ricans, Mexican-Americans or Negro and white tenant or marginal farmers from the poorer rural areas, who have moved to the city and who must learn new skills to succeed in modern industrial society. Most migratory farm laborers also belong to this class.

Lower-working-class people have few skills and frequently have less than a grade-school education. Many have difficulty finding jobs because of their color. Because they are "the last to be hired and the first to be fired" they have difficulty acquiring job seniority. A business recession that has only a slight effect upon the other classes will put many lower-working-class people out of work, swelling the relief rolls. Many people in this class spend a great deal of time seeking work—

work that will not bring personal satisfaction, but will provide a meal ticket for the family and an opportunity to buy "on credit." Many families are constantly in debt. It is not surprising that many of these people believe that diligence and thrift has little to do with getting ahead, and that only by "luck" or "connections" will they ever better themselves.

These people often distrust persons with unfamiliar skills, strangers, or persons who represent government agencies. For insurance against trouble they look to their network of mutual-help relationships with relatives. Lower-class people in suburbia were found by Hodges (1963) to visit their relatives more often than the members of any other class. For many, welfare is seen as a last resort.

Some lower-working-class people are members of fundamentalist Protestant churches, some are Catholics, but many are unattached to any church. They seldom belong to formal organizations, except occasionally to a labor union. It is as though, being unsuccessful in the wider society, many find social recognition and satisfactions exclusively within kin and informal friendship groups.

This group began to draw a great deal of attention in the mid-1960's with the "war on poverty," and the large-scale government programs organized under the Office of Economic Opportunity. Its size has been variously estimated. All thoughtful observers agree, of course, that all poor people are not of low social status, in the sense that the term "lower-class" is often used. For example, there are large numbers of older people in the population whose reduced incomes place them in the "poverty" group; and there are the differentiations made by Miller (1964) and others between various types of "respectable" and "unrespectable" poor. Nevertheless, with estimates of the poor ranging as high as 25 or 30 percent of the American population (Harrington, 1962); and with the evidence that the gap in income—at least in the early 1960's—was not narrowing between the poor and the rest of society, this group is by no means an insignificant minority.

Families of this class produce a large share of "problem" children in the schools: the slow learners, the truants, the aggressive, and the delinquent. (Mrs. Gordon has taught many of these children at the McManus school, and Miss Johnson knows them, too.) These children draw a good deal of attention from the educational authorities. In city school systems, some of these children are placed in "ungraded" rooms or "opportunity classes." Identified as needing "compensatory education," some get considerable help from remedial reading specialists, counselors, truant officers, and more recently, volunteer tutors. In small towns, where there are fewer specialized school services, teachers may give such children less attention than other children, although it is probably fair to say that there has been a growing sensitivity to the needs of such children on the part of all American educators in the past five to ten years.

Social Structure: A Nationwide View

Not all sociologists agree that the social structure of the United States is fairly represented by the five-class hierarchy shown in Figure 1.3. For one thing the economic and technological changes occurring in American society are producing raised standards of living and changed relationships between various classes. From certain perspectives, the differences between classes are becoming obliterated. For instance, the lines between upper class and upper-middle class seem to be disappearing, with less emphasis given to lineage in all but the oldest and most conservative communities, and with upper-status people taking active leadership roles in community affairs. To take another example mentioned earlier, blue-collar workers have had greater relative gains in income over the past two decades than white-collar workers, and patterns of buying and spending have become more similar between the two groups.

From other perspectives, the differences between social classes are becoming sharpened—as, for instance, between the group on public assistance in metropolitan and rural areas and all the other groups in the society.

Some observers describe the American social-class structure as one in which there are three major class divisions appearing: not the old alignments of upper, middle, and lower, with their subdivisions and their changing proportions but a three-class system in which there is a growing upper-middle class that encompasses the old upper class; then a huge, increasingly undifferentiated "common-man" or blue-and-white-collar working class; and a "lower" class of unskilled, public-assistance families, sometimes referred to as the "hopeless" class. Mayer (1963) for one, describes the changing social class outlines of America not as a pyramid, but as approximating a diamond in which there are small groups of non-mobile people at both the top and the bottom, with all the rest of society in between, and in which gradations in the undifferentiated middle are so numerous and so gradual that class lines are relatively obliterated—a picture that approximates Figure 1.1B rather than Figure 1.3.

Other sociologists go further. While they do not deny differences in rank, they feel that class lines cannot be drawn at all in an "open" society like our own, where there is so much movement or mobility up and down; where networks of informal social interaction overlap friendship, clique and membership groups to form a series of gentle gradations; and where, accordingly, the concept of social class itself lacks meaning.

Social classes can be thought of, however, as *conceptually* discrete, even though, in an increasingly urbanized society, the social scientist finds it difficult to establish empirically the boundaries between classes. In this view, social classes can be described in terms of averages; classes differ, *on the average,* by income, by occupational level, by attitudes toward education, and by other value systems that we have been describing. In terms of typical, or average characteristics (for example, in saying that an upper-middle-class person is a college graduate who makes ten thousand dollars a year; and that a lower-middle-class person is a high school graduate who makes seven thousand dollars a year), it must be kept in mind that such descriptions can be misleading. People who rank high on one class indicator such as education will *tend* to rank high on others such as occupation or income; yet there will be many exceptions. Probably everyone has met at least one such exception: a successful businessman who never completed high school; a Pullman porter who has a college degree; a social worker who lives in the slum neighborhood in which he works; a graduate student who is scraping along on a very meager income.

Such inconsistencies are not at all unusual. Nam and Powers (1965), in ranking a national sample on education, income, and occupation, found inconsistencies, or "status discrepancies," in about two-thirds of their cases. People can be members of one class and still have some characteristics in common with members of another class.

On the other hand, people whose characteristics are very different from the average on many characteristics of their class will be very possibly in the process of moving into the class immediately above or immediately below their own. As we shall show in the next chapter, there is a great deal of movement between classes. A modern democratic society always has open social classes; that is, people are able to move from one to another class according to their ability and effort.

Socioeconomic Characteristics of the Social Classes

The preceding descriptions have dealt mainly with the common ways of behaving and believing, the habits and values of the several social classes.

It should be clear, from what has been said thus far, that social-class differences are broader in nature and more inclusive than socioeconomic differences. To reiterate, social classes, as we have been describing them, are based upon factors of social participation, with members of a given class feeling on an equal basis with members of the same class, and with members of the same class sharing a common culture or a common way of life—including not only similarities in the amount of income and type of job, but also in such matters as etiquette, dress, speech, attitudes toward education, civic responsibility, religious participation, and so on.

It is nevertheless true, as indicated in the foregoing descriptions, that socioeconomic factors are highly correlated with social-class placement. Although there are many individual exceptions, upper-class people are generally the most wealthy, and lower-working-class people, the least wealthy; upper-status people are engaged in one set of occupations and lower-status people in another; middle-class people live in bigger and more comfortable houses than do working-class people; and upper- and middle-class people have more education.

Social Classes in the Negro Society

Although the position of the Negro in American society has changed rapidly in the past decade, it is nevertheless true that in most communities there is a line of demarcation in social participation between Negroes and whites, with Negroes still forming a caste-like group. A group may be called a caste when it is separated from other groups by a barrier that prevents movement into other groups, when intermarriage is discouraged, and when this status is passed from parent to child. Negroes and whites of the United States are caste-like groups with barriers of custom, rather than law, now operating to separate them.

Within a caste-like group there is likely to be a social-class structure if the group is large, and if there has been sufficient opportunity for some of its members to secure property or occupations that confer leadership and prestige so that variations in socioeconomic status can occur. This has happened among Negroes, who comprise by far the largest nonwhite group in the United States. (As of 1960, the racial composition of the United States was: white, 88.6 percent; Negro, 10.5 percent; other nonwhite, 0.9 percent.)

It can be seen from Figure 1.4 that the *range* of socioeconomic status is the same for both whites and nonwhites (92 percent of whom are Negro), although there are fewer nonwhites at the upper end of the scale and more at the lower. This difference reflects an earlier, more rigid caste structure in which Negroes were systematically subordinated. It will be seen also that the two distributions are more like each other in metropolitan areas than in small town and rural areas. As *groups,* both whites and nonwhites are better off in metropolitan areas; but for nonwhites, the difference in status within and without metropolitan areas is dramatic. In the rural South, where the caste line is relatively strict, only small Negro upper and upper-middle classes have developed. In northern industrial cities, on the other hand, there has been a rapid increase in the size of the Negro middle class. If present trends continue, it is probable that the socioeconomic distribution of the nonwhite part of the society will become in time very similar to that of the white.

Exercises

1. A person's social position as measured by socioeconomic indices (occupation, income, level of education, and so on) does not always coincide with his social position as evaluated by the status assigned him by the people in the community. (For example: a poor, but upper-class woman; or a wealthy, but lower-class businessman; or a politically powerful person who has been refused membership in the country club.) Have you known such a person? Describe him briefly. What does his (or her) case illustrate about the bases of rank in his community?

2. Obtain a map of your community. Interview a few people, and ask them to point out the areas that are "best," "average," and "worst" neighborhoods. (One of the best persons to interview will be a real-estate man.) How much agreement do you find among your informants? On what kinds of factors are their judgments made?

3. Select an elementary school in your community (if you are presently teaching, take your own school), and make an informal investigation of

WHITE   NONWHITE

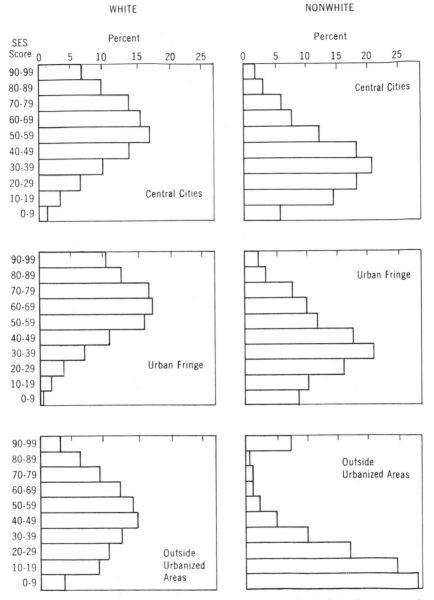

Figure 1.4 Socioeconomic status of family heads in the U.S.A. by race and residence: 1960.

Socioeconomic status scores are based on education, family income, and occupation. The higher the score, the higher the status.

Source: Nam and Powers, 1965. Based on data from the 1960 Census of Population. Courtesy of the American Sociological Association.

the community from which it draws its pupils. Walk up and down the streets of the neighborhood, observing the houses, lawns, alleys; look at the names on doorbells for information regarding ethnic backgrounds; go into the stores and notice what kinds of food, clothing, and other goods and services are sold; and so on. What kinds of activities do children and adults seem to be engaged in? Where do children play, and with what kinds of play equipment? Then write a summary of what you have learned about the social backgrounds of the children attending the school. From what social classes would you say the school draws? How heterogeneous is the neighborhood?

4. The pamphlet by Louis E. Raths and Stephen Abrahamson, "Student Status and Social Class," has been written for teachers, and demonstrates how to determine the social class positions of pupils by use of Warner's ISC.* Use this method on a classroom group (if you are presently teaching, use your own pupils). Remembering that this ISC is based upon studies of a small midwestern city (and may not be altogether accurate when applied to large cities), how valuable do you find this technique to be? How does it compare, in your opinion, with the second method of social-class placement, that of teacher judgment, described by Raths and Abrahamson?

5. Think about the community in which you grew up. (If it was a large city, interpret this to mean your neighborhood.) Write a four- or five-page description of that community in terms of its social class structure. Include information on the following points: How many social classes do you think there were? Were class lines clearly drawn? What kinds of people occupied positions of highest status? Of lowest status? What were some of the terms or phrases used to describe the people at the top, in the middle, at the bottom? In thinking back upon it, does it make sense to you to think of your community as a system of social classes? Why or why not?

Suggestions for Further Reading

1. There are a number of studies of social structure in various American communities. The first and most elaborate study was of a New England community, reported in a series of volumes called the Yankee City Series. Volume I of the series, *The Social Life of a Modern Community,* by W. Lloyd Warner and Paul S. Lunt is the most appropriate for students of education. For a description of a community in the South, see *Deep South,* by Allison Davis, Burleigh B. Gardner, and Mary R.

* For each of these references, see Bibliography for facts of publication.

Gardner. A midwestern community is reported in *Democracy in Jonesville,* by W. Lloyd Warner and associates. A small agricultural town in a border state is described in *Plainville, U.S.A.,* by James West; the same community studied again is described in Gallaher *Plainville Fifteen Years Later.* The social structure of the San Francisco peninsula is described in Hodges, *Peninsula People.* For a discussion of the social-class structure in America at large (rather than a study of a particular community), read *American Life: Dream and Reality,* by W. Lloyd Warner.

2. Several studies have been made of the social-class system and of the effects of class and caste upon the personalities of Negroes. Among them are *Children of Bondage,* by Allison Davis and John Dollard; *Caste and Class in a Southern Town,* by John Dollard; *Color, Class and Personality,* by Robert L. Sutherland; *Color and Human Nature,* by W. Lloyd Warner, Buford H. Junker, and Walter A. Adams; and *Black Metropolis,* by St. Clair Drake and Horace R. Cayton. The last is a study of the Negro community of Chicago. (See also the suggested readings given at the end of Chapter 14 in this book.)

3. The student who wishes to explore further the methods of investigating and measuring social status should consult *Social Class in America,* by W. Lloyd Warner, Marchia Meeker, and Kenneth Eells; and Chapters 1 and 2 in Kahl's book, *The American Class Structure.* Also, *Class, Status and Power: A Reader in Social Stratification* edited by Reinhard Bendix and Seymour M. Lipset is a good reference for the student who wishes to explore further the theoretical issues of social structure, or to study different theories of stratification.

4. Changes in the value orientations of Americans are described in books of sociological essays that became best-sellers: *The Lonely Crowd* by David Riesman and others; *The Organization Man* by William H. Whyte, Jr.; and *The Affluent Society* by John K. Galbraith.

5. There are a number of books that analyze value patterns and life styles of particular social classes. For example, C. Wright Mills' book, *White Collar,* is a penetrating analysis of the American middle class. *The Exurbanites* by Auguste C. Spectorsky describes the lives of upper-middle-class suburbanites. *Automobile Workers* and the *American Dream* by Ely Chinoy, *The Man on the Assembly Line* by Charles R. Walker and R. H. Guest, *Workingman's Wife* by Lee Rainwater, Richard P. Coleman and Gerald Handel are interesting studies of the working class, and *Blue Collar World,* edited by Arthur B. Shostak and William Gomberg is a recent compilation of research findings on working-class life prepared by various authors.

6. Brief descriptions of the values and attitudes of various social-class groups in a metropolitan area appear in the article by Hodges in *Society and Education: A Book of Readings,* by Havighurst, Neugarten, and Falk. In that same book the Choate article describes upper-class life among elite Chicago families; the Hammer and Heise articles report life in the slum worlds of New York and Chicago; and the Barber and Lobel article shows how status and social mobility are reflected in women's fashions.

7. The selection by Mayer in *Society and Education: A Book of Readings,* (Havighurst, Neugarten, and Falk), discusses the general theoretical issue of the "shape" of the American class structure and how it may be changing; while the selection by McKinley describes the dominant cultural themes and values of American society from a historical perspective.

8. Ruth Landes' book, *Culture in American Education,* describes an experimental teacher-training program based on anthropology and education, aimed at helping teachers understand cultural traits of California minorities, especially Negroes and Mexican-Americans.

9. The selection by Lenski in *Society and Education: A Book of Readings* (Havighurst, Neugarten, and Falk) shows the importance of the factor of religion in American society and proposes that religious groups are becoming more rather than less important in American life. In the same book, the paper by Rossi and Rossi discusses the effect of the parochial school system upon the attitudes and beliefs of Catholics. Gordon's *Assimilation in American Life* is a recently published book that deals with religious as well as ethnic factors. Greeley's book, *Religion and Career* is a study of differences between Catholics, Protestants, and Jews in a large sample of college graduates.

10. A number of recent books focus attention upon problems of poverty in modern America, among them Harrington's *The Other America;* Bagdikian's *In the Midst of Plenty: The Poor in America;* Miller's *Rich Man, Poor Man;* the report of the Conference on Economic Progress, *Poverty and Deprivation in the United States.*

11. The heterogeneity of suburban life is described in Berger's book, *Working Class Suburb;* and in Dobriner's *Class in Suburbia.*

12. *The Schoolchildren: Growing Up in the Slums* by Greene and Ryan is the true story of a group of children in an elementary school in Harlem, narrated by a teacher at that school. The book records what the children themselves said about their lives and the world they live in.

2 / Mobility in the Social Structure

One essential characteristic of a complex democratic society is that a considerable degree of movement upward from one social class to another is encouraged. This movement is implied by the ideal of equality of opportunity. The term social mobility, as we shall use it, refers to the movement of an individual from one position to another in the social hierarchy.

Mobility may occur in only one phase of life, such as in occupation (when a man moves from the position of factory worker to that of factory foreman) or in living arrangements (when a family moves from a small house in one part of town to a larger house in a "better" part of town). More typically, however, the term social mobility means movement from one social class to another, involving the *consolidation* of the various elements of the new social position, including occupation, income, type of house, neighborhood, new friends, and new organizational memberships.

Mobility is an intrinsic element of the American social system where social classes are open and where each group gains members and loses members.

Upward Mobility as Social Learning

Because the various social classes have somewhat different subcultures, a person moving up on the social scale must learn the subculture of the class into which he is moving. The amount that must be learned will, of

Figure 2.1 There is both upward and downward mobility in the social structure.

course, vary according to the particular circumstances of the family into which the person was born, as well as the social distance he travels.

Mobile people are most likely to move into the class immediately above the one of their parents. Only very rarely does a person move "from rags to riches." However, to illustrate the kinds of things a person may need to learn when moving up the status ladder, we shall look at a relatively extreme case, such as that of a man who at age eight worked with his parents in the fields as a migrant farm laborer but who by age 45 had risen to the position of assistant division manager in a large corporation. During his rapid rise this man would have found it necessary to learn a great deal besides the techniques and information necessary for his occupation. A list of such things would almost certainly include:

1. How to speak middle-class English; that is, with good grammar and with the appropriate vocabulary, intonation, and inflections of speech.
2. How to dress appropriately for both formal and informal occasions.
3. How to converse with business associates and other upper-middle-class men; how to agree and disagree with them.
4. How to choose a home in a "good neighborhood" and furnish it in the proper style.
5. How to discuss matters often foreign to the world in which he grew up, matters such as current books, theater, art, tennis, golf.

6. The etiquette and "little" social skills of middle-class life: for example, how to meet strangers and introduce them to one's friends; how to converse with women; how to check one's coat and hat, order a meal, and tip the waiter at a first-class restaurant or club.

7. How to participate in professional or business associations, as well as charitable and civic associations.

A man who began life as an unskilled laborer would find the learning of these tasks difficult but not impossible. First, he would probably have spent a relatively long apprenticeship in school and at work, during which time he would gradually have acquired the ways of the new class (by watching and imitating friends and acquaintances who possessed the desired attributes, by reading, and by traveling and observing the ways other people act in new situations).

Second, he would probably have had help from others. Once a person has moved into a higher-status *occupation* and has proved his worth, his colleagues will help him to fit into his new *social* world. They may, for example, suggest a good neighborhood in which to live, tactfully point out a good place to buy his clothes, or sponsor him for membership in a club. Third, such a man is likely to have married a woman of higher status or one who was sensitive to status points, and he probably learned from her.

Such a man need not absorb every bit of the culture of his new class. He might keep on feeling awkward at cocktail parties; and he might continue to stumble a bit in vocabulary. However, particularly if he lived in a metropolitan area, the acquisition of a few major symbols of status such as an apartment with a "good address" or the high-status occupation itself would indicate to the vast majority of observers that he was a bona-fide member of the class into which he has moved. The small group who know him personally may think of him as "a rough diamond," but they are likely to respect and prize him for the qualities that brought him to the top, and they are likely to take a proprietary interest in "polishing off the edges."

Mobility as Changing Social Interaction

As implied in the description of social status in the preceding chapter, mobility has occurred when the individual's pattern of social interaction has changed.

It involves the individual's easy *participation* with persons already initiated in the new position, and the *reputation* of such participation as assigned by others. The implication is that "arrival" is both a state of mind and a pattern of participation, with conventional symbolic and objective evidence observable in the life of the arrived person. Simultaneously, arrival also implies an integration into the social lives of others which is manifested in the acceptance by others of the "right" of the mobile person to such participation.

The many variations on this classic pattern hinge upon the principal routes used by the individual. These routes may be divided into such categories as: *occupation, personal talents* (including beauty and specialized skills with social implications), and *social techniques*. In the final analysis, all of these may be involved in varying proportions, with the weight going to personal talents and social techniques in the case of the female and to occupations and social techniques in the case of the male.

For the male, the *occupational route* is always a necessary component of successful mobility, and concentration upon advanced positions in business or professional life may be the principal and almost sufficient route. This route can exclude personal talents, such as charm, or attention to social techniques, in the sense of deliberate attempts on the part of the male to integrate his social participation. The wealthy vice-president can thus almost always consolidate his *social participation after* the fact of occupational mobility. . . .

The *personal talent route* is more characteristic of the woman, at all phases; and of both sexes, it is characteristic at the earlier phases of mobility. The football hero has only to avoid being a boor in order to become socially successful—at least during his playing years. The beautiful woman, with a talent for dress and presentation of self, can go far, even without using these attributes for marriage to a higher status—or mobile—man. Similarly, highly skilled *social techniques* can serve to integrate a person, man or woman, within a clique or larger social scene, in such a manner that lagging occupational status, or low income, or absence of notable personal talents remains unnoticed in the total picture. (Henry, 1965, pp. 31–32.)

Examples of Upward Mobility

A socially valued talent assists a person to move up the social scale. A working-class girl with intellectual ability, for example, can become mobile either by learning a skill that is useful in business or by studying for a profession. Emma Weaver did both of these things.

EMMA WEAVER

Emma was born the youngest of six children in the family of a Missouri tenant farmer. The children attended a one-room rural school, where they did about the same quality work as the other children, except for Emma, who seemed to take naturally to books. She read everything she could borrow from the teacher, for there were no books except the Bible in her own home. By the time she was nine, she was reading with the eighth-grade boys and girls.

Just at that time Emma's mother became ill and died. The family welcomed the offer by Emma's aunt to take the girl to live with her in Bluff City, a city of 30,000, where she lived in an area of old and somewhat run-down houses.

To Emma the big new school was a great experience. After hearing her read, the principal put her in the sixth grade, saying, "The other pupils will be a bit older than you, but I think you'll get along. You look older than you really are."

School was pleasant, but the Carnegie Library in the Courthouse Square was a palace. The librarian came to know her very well, and soon introduced her to the "stacks" in the adult part of the library, telling Emma that she could choose books there if she wanted to.

The aunt and uncle, whose own children had already finished school and gone to work, were at first somewhat concerned about Emma, for she was so different from their own children. She seemed to know just what she wanted and just how to get it, so after a time they concluded they would trust her to direct herself. She spent most of her afternoons at the library and brought books home to read in the evenings.

Emma graduated from high school at sixteen, salutatorian of her class, and editor of the high school annual. She was now a plain looking young woman although her English teacher told her once that she could make herself into a pretty girl if she would only try.

During her last year in high school Emma got a job as clerk on Saturdays in a small department store. Soon she became a bookkeeper at a salary that was as much as the wages her uncle was making.

For a year and a half Emma kept books for the business, but the best part of her life was her reading, and best of all was the week's vacation she took in Chicago, where she saw her first theater performance. She went one day to Evanston to call on her former English teacher, who was studying for a master's degree at Northwestern University. Miss Ward took her into the university library, and also to a class where Emma heard a lecture on the teaching of reading. The professor made a tremendous impression upon her. She thought he was both handsome and brilliant. When she returned home she said to her aunt, "I'm going to college next year. I'm going to become a teacher."

The aunt could not understand how Emma could give up a good-paying job. "But, Emma," she said, "you're already earning a good salary. Why don't you look around for a young man and get married? You can use your savings to help pay on a house."

"There's no man in Bluff City for me," Emma replied, "and anyway I've got to get an education."

Emma enrolled at Averill College in Bluff City. She kept a Saturday job, carried a heavy load of college studies, and at first took little part in college life. By taking summer-school work she graduated in three years with an excellent record.

Emma had several offers of teaching positions, and she took one in Omaha teaching fourth grade. She could have taught English in Bluff City High School, but she preferred to go to a larger city. She enjoyed teaching, and she liked Omaha. There was a good public library, and Emma formed pleasant associations with other teachers and with people whom she met at lectures and education association meetings.

Toward the close of her second year Emma decided that she could not go ahead without a master's degree, and she enrolled at Northwestern. There she met other teachers, most of them older than she, who were well established in teaching careers. Her good work drew the attention of the faculty. They made her see clearly how important the teaching profession was and convinced her that she had found the right career.

She went back to Omaha, this time to teach English in high school. She gained the reputation with students of being a fair-minded teacher who expected them to work hard; and with her fellow-teachers, of being a responsible and capable person, devoted to her work. She soon found herself quite active in professional work, as chairman of teachers' committees, and as delegate to state meetings.

After five years of high school teaching Emma decided that she needed more graduate work. Now she was almost thirty years old and felt she would have to choose between being a classroom teacher all her life or moving into some kind of supervisory or administrative work. A career in administration was attractive, and she started to study at the state university in the field of curriculum.

At State she enjoyed pleasant relations with other graduate students and with faculty. There she met Harvey, a graduate student in chemistry. After a couple of weeks she found that she was seeing him regularly on weekends.

It was two months after their first meeting that Harvey asked her to marry him. He told her about the college town where he expected to teach next year, and talked about the kind of house he wanted, and the children he wanted. That evening she said to him, "Harvey, I want to have time to think about it. I think I love you, but I've had plans for my career all these years, and I have to think about them, too." She had her heart set on getting her doctor's degree, she said, and this would take another year and a half. Couldn't they just be friends for a while, and see how they felt about marriage in a year or so?

In another month Emma was back into the swing of her studies and by the end of the summer, Harvey was just an old friend. Emma passed her examinations with good grades and began the research for her doctor's thesis. The next year she got an offer of a job as supervisor of elementary school reading in a large city, and she moved into an office of the Board of

Education with her name, "Dr. Weaver," on the door. She found a small apartment in a neighborhood where rents were high; she made friends with other professional people, most of them educators; and that summer she took a long-dreamed-of trip to England. In a few years she was promoted to be Assistant Superintendent in charge of Elementary Curriculum.

Emma Weaver, with intellectual talent and a single-minded ambition, moved from working- to upper-middle-class status, utilizing higher education and a professional career as the channels of upward mobility.

Another example of ambition and talent leading to dramatic upward mobility is the instance of a Negro man recently appointed a regional director of the Office of Economic Opportunity.

ERNEST SMITH

Ernest Smith was born in a midwestern state, a few months after the death of his father in a farming accident. His mother moved back to her family on a farm in another state; then moved to Chicago when Ernest was ready for school. She found a manual job, and the boy went to school in a poor neighborhood in the city. He delivered newspapers and later worked part-time in a neighborhood store, where he learned, among other things, that a part-time accountant earned as much as the store owner.

After graduating with a good record from an all-Negro high school in the inner city, he entered the school of business at the state university. He finished in the early 1930's, just at the time of the Great Depression.

Unable to find work at first, he and his mother were forced on relief for several months. He then found a job clerking and keeping books. Later he was a caseworker for the county, dealing with families on public assistance. Next, he began an accounting business. By the early 1940's he was working in Washington as a budget officer for the federal Fair Employment Practices Commission.

Returning to Chicago in the mid-1940's, Smith took a position with an insurance firm, and over the years he moved up to become senior vice-president and general manager. At the time of his appointment to OEO, when he was 50, he was president-elect of the firm. He lived with his wife, who was a social worker, in a mixed Negro-white upper-middle-class neighborhood; one child had just finished college and was beginning graduate study; the other was in college on the West Coast. He owned a large boat and was one of the first Negroes admitted to the local yacht club.

The newspapers described Smith as having filled a succession of civic and public offices: he had served as a member of the state parole board, as a member of the state Public Aid Commission, as a board-member of a national child welfare association, as a member of a national committee on equal opportunities in housing, and as president of the local chapter of the National Association for the Advancement of Colored People. He was presently a member of the board of trustees of the university from which he had graduated some thirty years earlier.

Other Patterns of Mobility

In the two cases just described, the individuals had high intellectual ability as well as ambition. Other types of talents and personal assets are also good bases for mobility. A working-class boy with dramatic ability develops his talents in high school, may obtain a scholarship in dramatics at a college, and may get a tryout in a Broadway show. If he makes good, his rise in the social scale is almost certain.

Even though most upward social mobility today occurs through education, there are other channels. The self-made businessman who marries a wife who guides him up the social ladder is one example of an alternative pattern of mobility. A girl with unusual beauty may make a "good" marriage. She may marry a man of much higher status than her own; then, if she is skillful, she learns the ways of her husband's social class and finds a secure position in it.

Athletic prowess in a boy often provides a good base for mobility, as in the instance when a boy becomes a professional baseball or football player. Although there are notable exceptions, in most such cases athletic ability is also combined with a college education if the young man is to become a successful middle-aged man.

Examples of Unattained Mobility

For both Emma Weaver and Ernest Smith, upward mobility hinged to a large degree upon education and upon success in high school and college. Good academic records do not, of course, always lead to successful careers, much less to such dramatic examples of upward mobility as in these two instances.

Even more frequent are the instances in which young people do not succeed in high school; or others who do not succeed in college, despite promising high school records; or others who drop out of school or college for reasons other than academic difficulty. Two brief cases are illustrative:

DONALD LEWIS

Donald Lewis graduated 10th in a class of 110 in an all-Negro high school. With an IQ of 112, and scoring at the 83rd percentile of the College Aptitude Test, he had done consistently superior work in science and mathematics. His father and mother were both high-school graduates; his father had a stable job as a maintenance man; and they thought Donald had made a good choice when he entered the school of engineering at the state university.

Donald wrote, as a high school senior:

"For as long as I can remember, I have always wanted to go to college and become a mechanical engineer. My family is behind me one hundred percent.

"I attend the AME Church where I help teach a young boys' class in Sunday School. I get joy from being able to share my knowledge with them. I enjoy reading and working difficult mathematical problems. My hobby is tinkering with motors of all kinds."

His teachers recommended him highly, though one of them commented, "With a little more aggressiveness, Donald could develop into an outstanding college prospect."

Donald got all C's and D's in his first year at the university and was placed on scholastic probation. The next year he repeated a mathematics course, but did not get a good start and he withdrew from school until the second semester, when he started again. This time he withdrew after only six weeks. Donald, thereupon, gave up on his college career. He took a civil service examination and got a job in an office in the city government.

Although it appears likely that Donald will move into a lower middle-class occupation and that accordingly he will rise above his parents' level in socioeconomic status, nevertheless his failure to complete college is a puzzle to his high school teachers. Donald looked like a good risk for college graduation; he was a conscientious student, with a very good high school record; yet he fell down when he met the standards of a first-class university. It is this kind of experience that leads some educators to argue that a segregated Negro school in the mid-1960's may not maintain scholastic standards high enough to prepare even their best students for the competition of a good university. They feel that failures like Donald's are to be blamed upon poor schools, not upon lack of ability or motivation in the student. (We shall return to these issues in later chapters in this book.)

LAURA CARTER

Laura Carter's home room teacher in the 12th grade wrote:

"This girl ranks high in scholastic ability and she has a burning desire for a college career. I feel she would be quite successful in college."

Laura is next to the oldest in a family of ten children. Her father, who did not go beyond the eighth grade, is disabled and receives income from a disability pension; her mother, who is a high school graduate, stays at home and looks after the big family. They lived on an income of $220 a month when Laura was in high school.

Laura was a school leader and was president of her Honor Society. She was active in church work, and a member of a Junior Achievement program.

Her ambition was to become a research scientist. Her aptitude tests indicated a strong interest in scientific work; her IQ was 108; and she scored at the 75th percentile of the College Aptitude test. On the basis of her course grades, she ranked second in a high school class of 200. Her counselor commented that she was "a hardworking girl who strives for perfection."

Laura seemed to have the qualities for success in college, and she was given a full scholarship to the state university.

In her first semester she made the Dean's list, with a fairly easy program of only 12 hours. Then she started into a heavy program of science and mathematics, her grades going down to only average. During her second year she joined a sorority. At the end of that year, she wrote the following letter to her scholarship sponsor:

Dear Mr. Roberts:

This letter should have come to you much sooner and I apologize. I think I have been postponing it because I know you would not be entirely pleased with the news. I am planning to be married in August and do not plan to return to school in the fall. It is not a matter of money but rather a matter of the way I feel about school at present. I am tired of all the studying and the hard work with no success. Perhaps someone else would be pleased with my grades but it is hard for me to accept the fact that I am only average in the field I have chosen.

I could continue with school after being married; I have seen other women do it. But I no longer have the desire to put in the time and effort for only mediocre results.

This last semester was better than the first. I have five hours of C in Calculus, three hours of C in German, five hours of C in Qualitative Analysis and two hours of A in English History. And I can honestly say I tried my hardest this semester.

I'm sorry I have not done better because I know everyone thought I would. But I'm not sorry I tried. Those two years in Chemistry will enable me to get a job as a lab technician at a decent salary. College has also, as it does for everyone, broadened my views and made me more aware of people. I also do not regret joining the sorority; the experience there was well worth the money and time spent on it.

I'm looking forward with great eagerness to marriage, as for me this signifies the beginning of life as an adult. I have always felt too sheltered in college, too cut off from what I consider to be the world. College is really a different world and I no longer want to be a part of it.

Yours truly,

Laura Carter

There is no question of Laura's ability to complete a satisfactory college record, but she was caught in a situation that is typical for many girls. The first person in her family to go beyond high school, she was headed for a career in a middle-class occupation. But the boy whom she was dating wanted to be married. Laura would probably not have been able to have her post-college career as a research scientist, even if she had postponed marriage until graduation.

Downward Mobility

Downward mobility is less frequently observed than upward mobility. There are several types of downward mobility. One is relatively dramatic, in which a man may lose his job and may suffer a marked loss of economic and social status in the succession of poorer jobs that follows. There is not only loss of money but loss of friends. Sometimes alcoholism is involved or some other form of personal maladjustment. Such a man may drop a level or two in the social scale.

Other instances involve intergenerational mobility: the son of a high-status family does poorly in school, rebels against the family's expectations and may settle for an occupation of lower status. In one such family, for example, the father was a successful businessman, the oldest son is a practising surgeon living in an expensive home in a fashionable suburb; the second son is beginning an academic career as a college instructor; but the youngest son has been downward mobile. He rejected his family's style of life, dropped out of high school, and is an electrician, supporting a wife and two children in a working-class suburb of the city.

To take another example, a girl whose father was an upper-middle-class professional man found high school somewhat boring and decided to marry an attractive young man who was a clerk in a supermarket. Soon there were children, and she settled down to a more or less contented life as the wife of a husband who will probably remain at a working- or lower-middle-class level. The girls' parents say that she married "beneath" her and made a "poor" marriage; the social scientist says she has been downward mobile.

A more frequent type of downward mobility is the slow and almost imperceptible downward movement that may come to people who do not manage to keep up with the rising standards of living. For instance, an upper-middle-class youth who does poorly in college and then does only an average job in his occupation may find himself, after ten years of adulthood, falling behind his associates as they are promoted. He cannot afford to move to a better neighborhood, as they do; he does not get invited to the "right" clubs nor to work on civic committees. His wife may not make a good impression on the wives of his associates or upon those who are above him in the business hierarchy. Thus he gradually drops in social status.

Characteristics of Upward Mobile People

In addition to the various abilities we have described, upward mobile people usually have a strong desire to better themselves, are quick learners, and are willing to work hard. Not all ambitious, intelligent, and hard-working people, however, want to adopt a new way of life. Those who do not are likely to become very successful members of the class into which they were born, rather than newcomers to a higher class.

It is also true that, in a rapidly changing technology, the demand for personnel in certain fields makes mobility relatively easy. For instance, once a boy whose father is an unskilled laborer takes the first steps toward being trained as a machinist or an electrician, he is likely to be moved quickly along and to gain relatively early in life a secure position in the upper-working class. Similarly, a working-class boy with the requisite abilities who chooses, say, to become a physicist rather than a physician may reap certain immediate advantages through scholarships and fellowships in graduate school and because of relatively high salaries in the very first stages of his work career.

Characteristics of Young Adults

Teachers and other observers often feel confident that they can spot the talented or the ambitious boys and girls, and that they can predict which ones will and which ones will not get further in life than their parents. At the same time there are relatively few studies in which a large group of youngsters has been followed to find which ones actually do, in adulthood, follow patterns of upward mobility and, in this way, to identify the characteristics leading to mobility.

One such study was carried out on a group of boys and girls who in 1951–52 constituted all the sixth-graders in the public schools of a community called River City, and who were then followed until 1964 when they were approximately 23 years old. Some of the original 450 left the city and were lost to the study, but fairly adequate data are available on almost four hundred of the group.

Table 2.1 shows the social and intellectual characteristics of the group when studied at age 23. By this time almost all of those who expected to go to college had at least started. Of those who had not gone to college, the men and some of the women had been working for four to seven years. Most of the women had married and were home-makers.

Each person in the group was evaluated in comparison to his

Table 2.1   Characteristics of Mobile and Stable 23-Year-Olds in River City (N = 399)

		Mean percentile scores[a]		
	N	IQ[b]	HIGH SCHOOL GRADES	SOCIAL EFFECTIVE-NESS[c]
Upward mobile:				
Men	52	71	59	70
Women:				
Not married	11	75	75	77
Married between ages 21 & 24	18	65	75	77
Married by age 20	36	50	51	64
Total	117			
Stable:				
Men	101	42	45	42
Women:				
Not married	10	86	66	80
Married between ages 21 & 24	17	59	71	57
Married by age 20	72	42	47	46
Total	200			
Downward mobile:				
Men	44	28	26	40
Women:				
Not married	4	42	41	44
Married between ages 21 & 24	4	34	52	—
Married by age 20	30	50	48	42
Total	82			

[a] Based on the entire group of students.
[b] Based on a number of tests given in sixth grade.
[c] A combination measure including popularity, friendliness, and leadership as evaluated by both teachers and peers.

family of origin with regard to educational level, occupation, occupational performance, and reputation in the community; then on this basis
he or she was identified as upward mobile, stable, or downward mobile.
(The women who had married were assigned the status of their husbands; those who had not married were evaluated in the same way as
the men.)

The data on *intelligence* are based on a battery of tests administered when the group was in the sixth grade. The data on *social
effectiveness* came from sociometric tests and teachers' descriptions
obtained when the boys and girls were in the sixth grade and again when
they were in the ninth grade. The combination measure shown in Table
2.1 includes popularity, friendliness, and leadership as evaluated by
both teachers and peers.

Among the men the upward mobile as compared to the socially
stable had been markedly superior in high school on measures of
intelligence, school grades, and social effectiveness. The downward
mobile had been the poorest on these measures. Thus, a teacher who
knew this group of students could have predicted with considerable
accuracy which of the boys would be upward mobile and which would
be downward mobile.

For the women, however, predictions would have been more
difficult. In general, the upward mobile women had been superior in
high school to the stable and to the downward mobile on all three
measures of intelligence, school grades, and social effectiveness (Moorefield and Havighurst, 1964). This was true whether their upward mobility came through marriage or through college and career. The patterns
for women, however, were complicated by differences related to age at
marriage. With a few exceptions, in the stable and upward mobile groups
of women, the late-marrying (those who had not yet married by age 23)
had been superior to those who married between 21 and 24; the latter,
in turn, had been superior to those who married early (before age 20).

At the same time, the girl who was upward mobile as the result of
an early marriage to a higher-status man was higher on social effectiveness than other early-marrying women, though not higher in intelligence
or school grades. The early-marrying downward mobile girls had the
same IQ as the early-marrying upward mobile girls. In short, social
effectiveness, but not IQ, differentiated between early-marrying girls
who married "above" and early-marrying girls who married "below"
their own social status levels.

All in all, the River City study showed clearly two main paths of
social mobility. Boys, and a few girls, will climb the social ladder by

making use of superior intelligence and superior social effectiveness to succeed in school and college and on the job. The more frequent path for girls will be by marrying a relatively successful young man.

Intelligence, Education, and Mobility

As we have seen, one of the principal means to social mobility is through a good education, which implies the possession of above-average intelligence, even though in some cases other factors appear to be more important. Some persons have argued that intelligence itself is a major cause of upward or downward mobility, while others have argued that education is the principal factor.

According to Himmelweit (1961), intelligence not only permits a person access to higher education, but also helps to make him upward mobile by influencing his *motivation*. Thus, Jayasuria, who worked with Himmelweit, found that the vocational aspirations of early adolescent boys and girls in England were more dependent upon intelligence than upon social class. Jayasuria interpreted this finding to mean that:

> Intelligence acts as a kind of energy arouser which greatly influences the individual's desire to experiment, affects his belief in himself, his desire to excel in all areas, not only in those related to school or to scholastic performance. Greater intelligence thus provides the motivational conditions needed for mobility. This factor is subsequently reinforced by differential educational experience, rather than created by it. (Jayasuria, 1960.)

Of the upward mobile River City boys mentioned earlier, 24 of the 52 were in the upper quarter of their class in intelligence and only 4 were in the bottom quarter. Of the downward mobile boys, 21 of the 44 were in the lower quarter in intelligence and only 6 in the upper quarter. Among the girls the difference was not so striking because girls who are upward mobile by early marriage are not more intelligent on the average than girls who are downward mobile by early marriage. For boys, then, but not for girls, the River City data support the views of Himmelweit and Jayasuria concerning intelligence.

How important is education for upward social mobility? In River City, the investigators estimated that about 20 percent of upward mobile youth (6 percent of the total group) were relying primarily upon intellectual ability and intellectual training. There is no way of estimating how many of these youth would have moved up the social scale if they had not had access to higher education.

Another 50 percent of the upward mobile (15 percent of the total group) were relying primarily on their social skills or on their drive and ambition. Their mobility was achieved through performance in their work. Many of this group used education as a means of obtaining certain useful skills or knowledge, but they would probably have been upward mobile without much education if they lived in a society in which higher education was not so easily accessible.

Finally, 50 percent of the upward mobile girls (9 percent of the total group) had made "favorable marriages." These girls would probably not have been upward mobile on any other basis. They had married while relatively young, and they did not have outstanding intellectual ability. Some of them rejected education.

On the whole it seems that education is less a *cause for* than a *means of* upward social mobility. Where education is as available as it is in the United States, boys and girls with intelligence and ambition will find it a ready means for self-improvement.

On the other hand, the lack of educational opportunity has little relation to downward mobility. Most downward mobile individuals in River City were school dropouts or persons who did not go beyond high school, but the reason was not lack of opportunity for more education. Of the downward mobile group, 40 percent were girls who were downward mobile by marriage; 25 percent (5 percent of the total group) were probably downward mobile primarily because of low intelligence. Another 15 percent (4 percent of the total group) lacked drive or ambition. The rest (19 percent of the downward mobile and 4 percent of the total group) had defects in moral character.

Family Factors in Mobility

There is at present little empirical evidence that will aid in predicting which families are likely to produce upward mobile children. One such study (Krauss, 1964), based upon questionnaires administered to high school seniors in the San Francisco Bay Area, suggests that those working-class boys and girls who are most likely to move up into another class (as indicated by the desire to go to college) are those with families that are in some ways not typical working-class families. A student, for example, was more likely to want to go to college if his mother held a non-manual than a manual job; if one parent had had some college (particularly if the mother had been to college while the father had not); if the father held an unusually good job, as a craftsman or foreman; if there had been a grandparent who had been in a non-manual occupation; or if older brothers and sisters, or friends of the family, had attended college. In school, these students tended to associate primarily with others who were also interested in college. There was no way of predicting in this study how many of these students would actually in later life move into a higher class. It appeared likely, nevertheless, that for many, social mobility has its roots in status discrepancies within the family and is fostered by association with like-minded peers.

Group Mobility

We have been considering the phenomenon of individual social mobility, one mark of democracy in the American social-class system. Group mobility also affects and qualifies individual mobility.

Group mobility occurs when a social group moves as a whole in relation to other groups. The mobile group may be a large or a small one. For example, skilled workers in America have gained greatly in economic status relative to minor white-collar workers and relative to farmers. The wages of electricians, plumbers, railroad men, and others of the "aristocracy" of labor have risen more since 1900 than have the incomes of clerical and retail salesworkers, teachers, farmers, and other groups. This economic gain has enabled many of these blue-collar workers to move up, using their money to purchase the symbols of lower-middle-class living.

Upward group mobility tends to favor upward individual mobility of members of the group, but the two movements are not identical. Thus, as the American standard of living has risen, working-class people in America have come to enjoy fancy automobiles, the newest home appliances, high school educations, and paid vacations, all of which would have marked them as middle class in 1920. Indeed this phenomenon has caused some foreign observers to refer to America as a nation of middle-class people. However, those working-class people who in 1965 possessed certain material and nonmaterial goods that in 1920 would have symbolized middle-class status have not thereby been turned into middle-class people. This is true because many of the symbols of middle-class status have changed in the interim. By 1965, middle-class people quite generally have a college education rather than the high school education that was characteristic of the middle class in 1920. A great many belong to country clubs. They buy high-fidelity and stereophonic phonographs and read the *New Yorker* magazine. Quite a few travel to Europe. These things have now become symbols of a middle-class life-style, a life-style which is not shared by working-class people.

Thus the system of rank continues in a changing society even though the *bases* or signs of rank are shifting.

Mobility of Ethnic and Religious Groups

There has been a great deal of group mobility among the various ethnic and religious groups that have come to this country. At first, during the Colonial period of American history, immigrants set up colonies with names like New England, New France, New Sweden, New Amsterdam. In time these were blended into a new American culture.

Then came waves of immigrants—Irish, German, Scandinavian, French, English, Dutch, Polish, Hungarian, Italian, Bohemian, Serbian, Roumanian, Armenian, Chinese, Japanese and Spanish-American. People came in groups and made settlements either in the new lands on the frontier or in the old cities. Gradually they joined the main cultural stream of American life, dropping their native languages and many of their ethnic ways and contributing to the new American culture. The schools hastened this process by teaching American ways to their children.

NINETEENTH CENTURY IMMIGRANTS. Generally a new immigrant group started at the bottom of the social scale and worked up. The Irish, the lowest-status group in the mid-nineteenth century, were employed in digging canals and building railroads in the expanding country. They moved up, leaving room at the bottom for Scandinavians, Italians, and Bohemians, who in turn worked their way up. (The roll of the McManus School where Mrs. Gordon teaches could tell this story. The first names on it were Irish; then Bohemian names appeared, then Polish and Hungarian and Italian, as group after group of immigrants came to the slums around the McManus School and reared their families. As the children acquired better jobs and more knowledge of American ways, the families were able to move to better districts.)

Some immigrant groups came into the American social system at a level above the bottom, either because they possessed capital, or because they brought with them a culture which was enough like that of the American middle class to enable them to participate at once at that level. For example, numerous Germans came to America after 1848 because of political unrest and persecution in Germany. Some of them were middle-class people who brought capital with them. Such people started businesses and built up cities such as Milwaukee, St. Louis, and Cincinnati. Other Germans had vocational skills, work habits, and religious habits that enabled them to join native-born Americans on the frontier (which had by then reached the Mississippi) and to take a place in the new middle class that developed there.

THE JEWISH PEOPLE. The Jews came with their religion and with a compound Jewish ethnic culture from Holland, France, Germany, England, Poland, and Russia. Some, with business skills and a willingness to go alone into new communities, moved into small towns and cities where they rapidly rose to middle-class status, though their religious culture set them apart from other middle-class people. Many others remained in big cities where, although they now occupy a wide range of social class positions, a large proportion work mainly as factory workers. Today the Jewish people themselves comprise a variegated set of cultural subgroups, some much more a part of general American culture than others. Some have become "liberal" in their religious views and have stopped observing the orthodox food practices and the holidays. Others have remained orthodox in religion and have retained a good deal of their Jewish culture.

The Jews who came to this country first—from Spain (by way of Holland and England), from Germany, and from France—in general moved further up the American social scale; most of them are now middle class and a few are upper class. While the latest immigrants from Eastern Europe are, in general, lower on the social scale (working- and lower-middle), social mobility has been rapid for this group, too. The Jews have probably made more use of education as a means of moving up in the American social class structure than has any other immigrant group, although education alone does not account for their mobility. According to studies by Fauman (1958) and Glazer (1958), even when education is held constant, Jews as a group still outdistance non-Jews in occupational mobility.

POST-WORLD WAR II IMMIGRANTS. Japanese immigrants who settled on the Pacific coast and who had lived in "islands" of Japanese culture were dispersed by the relocation measures of World War II. Possessing personal habits that were acceptable to middle-class Americans and having work skills that were valuable, they moved into the cities of the Midwest at lower-middle- and upper-working-class levels.

The displaced persons who fled into Germany at the close of World War II from Lithuania, Estonia, and Latvia, and who later came to the United States, were mainly middle-class people. So also were the Hungarian refugees of the mid-1950's. Although they took whatever working-class jobs they could get, they quickly integrated themselves into the American culture. Their children adopted American middle-class ways of life relatively quickly.

Differences in Group Mobility

Various ethnic groups in America have differed in the rates with which they have moved up the social scale. Among immigrant groups in the northeastern section of the United States, for instance, the Greeks as well as the Jews attained middle-class status more quickly than French-Canadians or southern Italians (Strodtbeck, 1958; Rosen, 1959). There are probably several reasons for such differences in rates of mobility. One is the extent to which the immigrant group possesses certain work skills that are valuable in the economy; another is the degree to which the dominant group is willing to permit newcomers equal access to jobs, housing, and schooling. In addition, part of the differences are probably due to differences between the immigrant groups in psychological and cultural orientations toward achievement. In a study of six ethnic and racial groups (Rosen, 1959), historical and ethnographic data showed that differences between the groups in achievement motivation, values, and aspirations existed before these groups arrived in the United States, and that these differences tend to persist into the present. The differences are related to the variations among the groups in rates of upward mobility.

Recent data shown in Table 2.2 indicate how the Negroes and Oriental groups in the United States have fared in socioeconomic status in the last two decades. While the Japanese and Chinese have gained greatly relative to whites, the Negroes have not done so.

Table 2.2   Socioeconomic Status of Nonwhite and White Male
Population: 1940–1960

*Percent of employed nonfarm male population
in white-collar jobs*

	1940	1950	1960
Japanese	45	36	56
White	39	39	42
Chinese	35	42	51
Negro	9	11	14

*Percent of male population, aged 25+, with four years
of high school and over*

Japanese	34	57	69
White	24	34	42
Chinese	11	27	40
Negro	7	12	18

Source: Schmid and Nobbe (1965). Courtesy of the American Sociological Association.

Extent of Mobility in the United States

In a complex and culturally heterogeneous society, both individual and group mobility indicate the extent to which equality of opportunity exists, as well as the extent to which economic expansion and industrialization are occurring.

The extent of individual social mobility in this country can be studied by measuring the degree and kinds of mobility that have occurred in the lives of adults. Such studies have been carried out with several samples of the population in recent years, with generally similar findings. Using a five-class system as the frame of reference, social scientists estimate that about one in every four or five persons climbs one step in the class system during his lifetime. (It is only the rare individual who climbs more than one step.)

In the data already presented from River City (see Table 2.1), of the total number of young people followed from the time they were in the sixth grade, almost 30 percent were upward mobile by the age of 23. This figure is probably an underestimation, for undoubtedly some of these young people are late starters. Further changes are likely to occur

by the time the group reaches their middle 40's when most people reach
the peak of their careers.

In a study of middle-aged adults in the metropolitan area of Kansas
City, it was found that 37 percent had been upward mobile at least one
social level, while 13 percent had been downward mobile. (Coleman
and Neugarten, 1967). In that study, a representative sample of men
and women aged 40 to 70 were interviewed, and their current status as
well as the status of their parents was determined. Thus it was possible
to construct Table 2.3, which shows the present social class of the adults
in relation to their social class at birth. While similar studies are needed
for other parts of the country, the Kansas City study indicates a relatively high degree of fluidity in the society.

Table 2.3   Amount of Mobility in Kansas City Adults

Parents' Status	*Current Status*			
	UPPER AND UPPER-MIDDLE	LOWER-MIDDLE	UPPER-WORKING	LOWER-WORKING
	(in percent)			
Upper and Upper-middle	5.8	3.4	.6	.0
Lower-middle	7.1	15.7	5.3	.2
Upper-working	2.1	14.0	24.5	3.1
Lower-working	.0	2.0	10.2	6.0
Total	15.0	35.1	40.6	9.3
Total, upward mobile	37			
Total, nonmobile	50			
Total, downward mobile	13			

Note: The table is to be read as follows: 5.8 percent of the total sample are currently of upper-middle-class status and were born into upper-middle-class families;
7.1 percent of the total sample are currently of upper-middle status, but were
born into lower-middle families; and so on.

Source: Coleman and Neugarten, 1967.

Business Leaders

One of the most interesting studies of mobility is an earlier one concentrated on business leaders—the owners and executives of the large

business concerns of the country. In 1952, Warner and Abegglen made a study of the social origins of business leaders, similar to an earlier study made in 1928 by Taussig and Joslyn (Warner and Abegglen, 1955). By combining the two studies it is possible to see how the occupations of fathers of the business elite had changed since 1900. Table 2.4 gives the data, showing that the proportion of business leaders whose fathers were laborers, farmers, or minor white-collar workers had increased from 36 percent in 1900 to 43 percent in 1950. This is one type of evidence that the amount of social mobility is not decreasing but has, perhaps, increased in the past 50 years.

Table 2.4   Long-Range Trends in Mobility in American Business

Occupation of Father	*Approximate Date of Leadership in Business*			
	1900	1920	1930	1950
Laborer	7	10	11	15
Clerical and sales				
(Minor white collar)	5	7	12	19
Farmer	24	21	12	9
Professional	11	10	13	14
Owner small business	19	23	20	18
Owner large business	17	16	14	8
Major executive	15	13	17	15
Other	2	0	1	2
Total	100%	100%	100%	100%

Source: Warner and Abegglen, 1955, p. 33.

Other Occupations

Using occupation as the single index of social mobility, but using data from nationwide surveys, Lipset and Bendix (1959) studied intergenerational shifts between manual and nonmanual occupations—that is, the extent to which sons of manual workers follow nonmanual occupations. This is a relatively gross index even of occupational mobility alone, since it does not take into account the shifts *within* the two broad categories of occupations. Nevertheless, these investigators estimated that for all nonfarm workers, the total vertical mobility in the United States over the past few decades had been about 30 percent. This includes both upward and downward mobility. That is, roughly one out of three urban males had either fallen into a manual position from his father's nonmanual position or had risen from his father's working-class occupation into a middle-class one.

It is an interesting fact, in this connection, that similar data on Germany, Sweden, Japan, and France yielded the unexpected finding that all these countries have about the same rate of *total* mobility as is true for the United States, although there is considerable variation among countries in rates of upward or downward mobility when the latter are analyzed separately.

Kahl (1957), in a somewhat similar approach, assessed the extent of occupational mobility between 1920 and 1950 in the United States but used a more refined breakdown of occupational categories. He estimated that two-thirds of the labor force (67 percent) in 1950 had been mobile relative to their fathers.

The differences in estimated rates of mobility between various studies such as that of Lipset and Bendix, on the one hand, and Kahl, on the other, show that such percentages have no absolute meanings since they differ according to the system of classifying occupations—the greater the number of categories, the greater the rate of occupational mobility.

It may be generally concluded, however, from such studies of occupational mobility, as well as from studies that focus directly upon social class, that the social structure in the United States is by no means "hardening" in the sense that class lines have become more tightly drawn or that barriers between class levels have become more difficult to surmount. On the contrary, our social-class system may have become even more fluid during the twentieth century than earlier. If the "war on poverty" of the mid-1960's and 1970's is successful, it will mean a lessening of the social and economic distance between the lowest-status group in American society and the rest of the working class, with simultaneously increasing proportions of men and women moving up from the bottom. These will be largely Negro people, although there will also be Puerto Ricans, Mexicans, and others. Mobility upward from blue-collar working class to lower-middle and from lower-middle to upper-middle is also likely to continue at a high rate if the present needs for technical and professional workers in the society continue to exist. (We shall return to this point in Chapter 12, in discussing economic and technological trends in relation to population.)

Factors That Promote Mobility

Among the factors that tend to promote upward mobility in the United States are the expanding economy and increasing industrialization. Not only is economic production in America increasing, but the economy is changing in the direction of increasing the proportion of highly trained people. There are fewer unskilled laborers in relation to skilled; there are more jobs in the professions and in the managerial and technical occupations, jobs which carry with them middle-class status.

Lipset and Bendix (1959), from their study of mobility in the United States and in various European countries, concluded that industrialization rather than economic expansion is the major factor here. The social mobility rate becomes relatively high once the industrial, and hence the economic, expansion in a society reaches a certain level. (Thus we would not expect to find such high rates in less industrialized countries, even though, as is true in underdeveloped areas of the world, these countries may be undergoing rapid economic development.)

Another factor influencing rates of social mobility is that of differential birthrates among the various social classes. The upper and upper-middle classes have not been producing enough children to fill their places. As a consequence, children from the lower classes grow up and move into middle- and upper-class economic positions.

Kahl (1957) has analyzed the causes of mobility when seen from this broader perspective of the society at large (rather than from the point of view of the mobile individual or group). As he points out, the man who has advanced in the world as compared with his father may have no idea which of the social forces made it possible for him to get ahead, and he might not care if he were told. But for the social scientist who looks at the society as a whole, it is relevant to study the *causes* or the forces within a society that promote or impede mobility as well as the *patterns* of mobility followed by individuals or groups. From this point of view, Kahl has weighed the relative importance of four factors:

1. Individual mobility, or the fact that some people slip down and make room for others to move up.
2. Immigration mobility, or the fact that immigrants do not enter the system at all levels in proportion to the numbers already there.
3. Reproductive mobility, or differential birthrates, whereby people at the top levels have smaller families than those at lower levels, thus making room at the top.

4. Technological mobility, whereby changes in the economy and occupational distribution result in an upgrading of the work force and in creating new jobs at the upper levels.

By analyzing census and other nationwide data, and by comparing numbers of men in specific occupational categories against the numbers that might have been expected under varying conditions, Kahl arrived at certain conclusions regarding the relative importance of these factors. As already stated, he described some 67 percent of the labor force in 1950 as having been mobile. Of this 67 percent, 20 percent were mobile by virtue of technological changes in the society; 7 percent because of reproductive mobility (see Chapter 12, pp. 306–311, for further discussion of the effects of differential rates of reproduction upon social mobility); and 40 percent because of individual mobility. While immigration had a greater effect in earlier periods, its effect on the generation just preceding 1950 was almost nil.

The Influence of Economic Factors Upon Individual Mobility

In an open society with relatively free educational opportunity and with a tradition favoring social mobility, the amount of individual mobility is relatively high. This is the situation in the United States, Great Britain, and the Soviet Union. Upward and downward mobility, considered together, may be called *exchange mobility*. The amount of one kind of mobility over the other may be called *net mobility*.

A society may have considerable exchange mobility and yet, if industrialization is not rapid and if upward and downward mobility are approximately equal, there may be very little *net* upward mobility. Glass (1955) found this condition to exist in Great Britain between 1920 and 1950. During that time, given the more rapid economic and industrial expansion in the United States, it probably required less intelligence, drive, and social effectiveness to be upward mobile in the United States than it required to be upward mobile in Great Britain. For the same set of reasons, those who were downward mobile in the United States were probably less able and less ambitious that those who were downward mobile in Great Britain.

Equality of Opportunity

Both rates of mobility and the relative importance of the factors that produce these rates fluctuate through time. In a complex and culturally heterogeneous society, the degree of mobility is often regarded as an indicator of the social health of a democracy, because it is taken to signify the extent that equality of opportunity exists. A low degree of mobility is interpreted as a hardening of the social structure and a lessening of opportunity. On the other hand, too high a degree of mobility may indicate a revolutionary or chaotic quality in the society. This is unhealthy because people cannot count on holding and passing on to their children the gains they have made. No one can say what degree of individual mobility would be most desirable in a modern society, but there would probably be general agreement among Americans that the present amount of mobility in the United States should not decrease.

Belief in Opportunity

In this chapter we have been discussing social mobility without direct reference to the effects created by our democratic institutions and value orientations. These are factors which also influence rates of mobility. Earlier, we referred to the finding that in recent decades overall rates of occupational mobility from manual to nonmanual levels have been about the same in various European countries as in the United States. It is probably true, nevertheless, that the United States differs from these other countries in that *more* Americans than the facts might warrant *believe* their children can be mobile and get further in life than they themselves; and in other countries probably *fewer* people believe this than the facts warrant. This difference in beliefs between Americans and Europeans may be connected with the great wealth of the United States which makes for a more "open" society with regard to styles of life.

It is also very likely that, as Noel (1962) suggests, criteria and strategies for social mobility are less clearly perceived in the United States because they are less formal, less explicit, and less objective than is true in European countries, where there is a more formal sorting and selecting function performed by the educational system. In the United States, upward mobility is less often directly dependent upon decisions regarding choice of school program in the early school years. Turner

(1960) has dealt with this point at some length in comparing the English and the American patterns of mobility. He refers to the American as "achieved" mobility, in which the individual competes directly for the "prize" of higher status; and to the English, as "ascribed" mobility, in which the most able youngsters are *selected* by the present elite groups in the society, then sponsored in various formal ways through the period of their schooling and preparation for occupational careers.

While these factors are operating, nevertheless the *belief* in upward mobility is itself a salient factor when we consider the social structure and the degree to which it is an open system. "The American dream" probably operates as an added and somewhat independent factor in promoting overall mobility in this country.

Social Mobility in a Changing Society

Finally, in addition to all the factors we have been mentioning as influencing the rates and patterns of mobility in the United States, there is the encompassing factor of rapid social change itself, which produces increasing differentiation in styles of life. Warner, in commenting upon the increasing heterogeneity of the society, says,

. . . given the needs of a fluid and flexible society, fixed status is no longer adaptive, creates conflict, and consequently is rapidly changing toward open status, where there is greater freedom for the individual and his family to move unfettered and thus be available for use in a changing world. All the evidence of our research suggests that color castes, closed systems of class, and other forms of rank that permanently fix the place of an individual and his family cannot continue to survive. (Warner, 1962, p. 5.)

Exercises

1.   Make a list of things that a girl, born the daughter of a factory worker, would have to learn if she were to become the wife of the executive vice-president of the company that employed her father.

2.   Describe the group mobility of one subgroup in your own community during the past 100 years.

3.   From among your acquaintances, describe briefly three who have been upward or downward mobile. Try to think of people who have experienced mobility for different reasons, and by different channels.

4. Do you think that upward mobility requires that a person should have a certain set of personality characteristics? What characteristics seem to have been common to the mobile people you know or have read about?

Suggestions for Further Reading

1. One of the most dramatic examples of intergenerational mobility is provided by President Kennedy's family, where within three generations (the President's great-grandfather to his father) the family moved from the lowest to the highest rungs of the social ladder. This family history is, of course, described in various biographies of John F. Kennedy; one, written in colorful terms, constitutes the first chapter of *John Kennedy: A Political Profile* by James MacGregor Burns. Whalen's *The Founding Father* is a biography of the President's father, Joseph P. Kennedy.

2. *Social Mobility in Industrial Society* by Seymour M. Lipset and Reinhard Bendix is an important treatment of the topic of mobility; it summarizes a number of different studies based on national and international data. See also Chapter 9 in Joseph A. Kahl's book, *The American Class Structure*.

3. Read *Big Business Leaders in America* by W. Lloyd Warner and James Abegglen for an interesting analysis of the social origins of business executives, and for a discussion of mobility in America.

4. Novelists have described social classes in America and various types of social mobility. Among the many examples: Christopher LaFarge's *The Wilsons* describes upper-class behavior in a Rhode Island community. John Marquand's *The Late George Apley; H. M. Pulham, Esquire; Wickford Point* and *Point of No Return* are penetrating observations of upper-class New England. Sinclair Lewis' *Elmer Gantry, Babbitt,* and *Main Street* deal with middle-class and upper-class people. Budd Schulberg's *What Makes Sammy Run?* describes the rapid rise of a New Yorker who goes to Hollywood; and his *The Harder They Fall* is a "success" story of a prize-fighter.

5. There are a number of autobiographies of immigrant youth that give different versions of upward mobility, such as *The Americanization of Edward Bok* by Edward W. Bok, and *From Immigrant to Inventor* by Michael Pupin. Others are Eugene Lyons' biography of *David Sarnoff* and Carl Rowan's autobiography. Perhaps the best known fictionalized account told as an autobiographical narrative of an immigrant's mobility is *The Rise of David Levinsky,* by Abraham Cohan.

6. The article by Coleman and Neugarten, in *Society and Education: A Book of Readings* (Havighurst, Neugarten, and Falk) is an empirical study of the rates and the patterns of social mobility in a large midwestern city.

7. For a description of ethnic group differences in America, see the book by Glaser and Moynihan, *Beyond the Melting Pot;* or Gordon's book, *Assimilation in American Life;* or Lieberson's, *Ethnic Patterns in American Cities.* Handlin's *The Newcomers* is an interesting written account of the problems of assimilation in various immigrant groups. Ganz's book, *The Urban Villagers,* is a study of an Italian community in the metropolitan area. Two recent studies of Puerto Rican immigrants are reported in Patricia Sexton's *Spanish Harlem* and in Padilla's *Up from Puerto Rico.*

$\mathcal{3}$ / The School as a Sorting and Selecting Agency

Since the landing of the pilgrims in Massachusetts more than three hundred years ago, America has been a land of opportunity. Of the people who came to these shores, many had been victims of political oppression or religious persecution, many wanted freedom to live according to their personal convictions and opportunity to build a good life. The oppressed and the poor came from the countries of Europe and later from East Asia and Latin America.

Their faith in the new country was justified. During the eighteenth and nineteenth centuries there was good land to be had at low prices, and there were jobs available in the expanding economy. New cities were being built and new industries were being established. A young man could start without capital and become a wealthy merchant, banker, factory owner, or farmer.

Education Becomes the Avenue of Opportunity

Then the good free land gave out and the frontier society disappeared. Since 1900 the areas of economic opportunity in America have shifted to expanding industry and to the expanding technical and service professions.

The amassing of great private fortunes is perhaps less frequent or less visible now than in the nineteenth century, yet the evidence points to the existence of as much overall economic opportunity in this country today as there was a century ago. In the technical and service professions there has been an enormous increase in numbers since 1900, an increase that far exceeds the increase in population. For instance, the number of engineers doubled in just the ten years from 1940 to 1950, while the numbers of industrial research workers and chemists increased by 50 percent during the same period.

These increases continued during the 1950's and 1960's, a period in which the demand for teachers increased tremendously due to the rapid rise in school enrollments. Industry and trade have also expanded more rapidly than the population, thus creating a greater proportion of executive positions than existed in earlier generations. These are middle-class occupations, and children of middle-class families tend to enter them. At the same time, the numbers of these positions have increased so rapidly that there are not enough children born in middle-class families to fill them.[1] Consequently some of these positions must be filled by youth from lower-status levels.

These occupations require higher education. The professions all require at least a college degree, and executive positions in business and industry are awarded more and more to young men and women who have graduated from college. One recent study showed, for instance, that 57 percent of business executives were college graduates in 1952, as compared with 32 percent in 1928 (Warner and Abegglen, 1955).

A recent study by Anderson (1961) demonstrates the need for caution in assuming that upward mobility is closely dependent upon formal schooling. Comparisons based on educational levels and occupational levels attained by fathers and their sons showed that mobility independent of schooling occurred at a high rate in recent decades in Sweden, England, and the United States. The implication is that intelligence and motivation are also important factors which, to some extent at least, operate independently of formal schooling. Nevertheless, education is probably more closely related to mobility in the United States than in other countries; and on the whole, it is probably true that the school provides the best single channel through which ability and motivation can be demonstrated across the population of boys and girls.

Thus education has become the principal avenue of opportunity in twentieth-century America: college education for upper-middle-class occupations, and high-school education for such lower-middle-class occupations as clerical work, sales work, and skilled technical work. Realizing that the avenue of opportunity is provided by the educational system, parents have encouraged their children to go further and further

[1] Differences in birth rates among various social classes are discussed in more detail in Chapter 12.

in school and college. Since 1890 the proportion of young people attending high school has multiplied twelvefold, while the proportion attending college has multiplied elevenfold. Table 3.1 shows the increase in high school and college attendance since 1910.

Table 3.1 Change in the American Educational System as a Selecting Agency

Number Out of Every Thousand of a Given Age Who Reach a Given Educational Level	Year			
	1910	1938	1960	1965
First year high school (age 14)	310	800	904	937
Third year high school (age 16)	160	580	746	810
Graduation from high school (age 18)	93	450	621	710
Entrance to college or a similar educational institution	67	150	328	370
Graduation from college (Bachelor's degree)	22	70	170	180
Master's degree	1.5	9	34	42
Doctor of Philosophy degree	0.2	1.3	4.7	6.7

Source: Estimates by the authors, based on studies of educational attainment in various parts of the country.

Amount of education has now become a good indicator of socio-economic status, from lower-working up through upper-middle class, for education leads to economic opportunity. Young people, through education, secure higher-status jobs than their fathers had. With greater incomes, young adults from lower-status families tend to associate with persons of higher status and learn and adopt their ways. It may be concluded, consequently, that education provides the channel not only to better socioeconomic status, but also to social mobility in the broader sense.

The School as a Sorting and Selecting Agency

The American educational system provides opportunity for social and economic mobility by selecting and training the most able and industrious youth for the higher-status positions in society. Insofar as the school system does this job efficiently and fairly, it equips youth to be qualified for career opportunities and contributes to the success of democracy.

The degree of selection can be observed in Table 3.1, which shows the number of boys and girls out of a thousand born in a given year who reach various levels of the educational ladder. It will be seen that the

The educational system as a selecting agency in 1965

Figure 3.1 The educational system as a selecting agency in 1965.

high school is much less selective than it was forty or fifty years ago, but that the college, while graduating increasing numbers, still operates as a highly selective agency.

The process of selection is not carried on in a formal sense by the school alone. Several factors determine how far a boy or girl goes in school: the parents' wishes, the individual's aspirations and ability, the financial status of the family, as well as the school's system of encouraging some students and discouraging others. The end result, however, is selection, with the school playing a major part in the process.

This selection process can be seen from the findings of Project TALENT, a large-scale research undertaking in which nearly a half-million boys and girls who were in 9th, 10th, 11th, and 12th grades in 1960 were given a large battery of achievement and ability tests; they are being followed up at one, five, ten and twenty years after graduation from high school. In the 1961 follow up of students who graduated in 1960, 42 percent entered a recognized two-year or four-year college within a year after leaving high school. Of these about 22 percent dropped out during or at the end of the freshman year, the great majority to take jobs or because of financial difficulties. Among girls, marriage accounted for 23 percent of the dropouts; among boys, 22 percent reported that they had failed in their academic work (Flanagan, 1964).

One may ask whether or not the educational system does an efficient and fair job of selecting able and industrious youth. This is not an easy question to answer, because it is not easy to determine who are the ablest and most industrious youth. The ablest in terms of intellectual ability (at least in terms of IQ) can be discovered more easily than the most industrious. Intelligence tests are fairly good measures of intellectual ability, even though they do not measure artistic, musical, or social leadership ability. Furthermore, the ordinary paper-and-pencil test of intelligence probably underestimates the abilities of lower-class youth, a point we shall return to presently.

Intellectual Ability

With these qualifications, we may consider first the question, How well does the educational system select and carry along the ablest youth? The answer is that the abler youth in general go further in school and college, but a considerable proportion of able youth do not enter college, and some do not even finish high school.

Most of the boys and girls who drop out of school are below average in academic ability, but a considerable proportion are above average. Table 3.2 shows the IQ distribution of those who dropped out of school before high school graduation in the class of 1958 in River City, a midwestern city of 45,000 population. About 5 percent of the dropouts were in the top quarter of intelligence, while 40 percent were in the bottom quarter. These data, although they come from one particular city, confirm the findings from other studies of school dropouts. Studies which show that on the average about 5 percent of the dropouts are in the top fifth in intelligence, while about 33 percent are in the bottom fifth.

Table 3.2   Intelligence and Social Class in Relation to Progress Through School in River City

	Boys			*Girls*		
	H.S. DROP- OUT	H.S. GRADU- ATION ONLY	COLLEGE AND POST- H.S.	H.S. DROP- OUT	H.S. GRADU- ATION ONLY	COLLEGE AND POST-H.S.
IQ:						
IV (high)	4	13	27	3	23	36
III	18	17	22	12	24	18
II	25	25	7	27	26	3
I	37	15	3	26	17	4
Social Class:						
Upper and						
upper-middle	1	4	15	1	2	18
Lower-middle	9	22	27	10	28	22
Upper-working	38	25	15	23	46	20
Lower-working	36	19	2	34	14	1
Total number	84	70	59	68	90	61

Source: Data from the River City study.

Table 3.3 presents recent data on the "holding" power of the public schools in Philadelphia. In comparing Negro with white children, it should be kept in mind that the socioeconomic status of the two racial groups is not the same, and that a much higher proportion of the Negro children come from low socioeconomic status than is true of the white children. It is nevertheless of interest to compare girls with boys in both racial groups, and to note the relationship between IQ and rates of dropouts (the IQ groups in the table have not been controlled for race *or* socioeconomic status).

Table 3.3   Educational History of the School Class That Entered Philadelphia Schools in the First Grade in 1949

	Percentage who graduated from high school
All pupils	70
All girls	76
All boys	66
All whites	79
All Negroes	56
White girls	83
White boys	75
Negro girls	65
Negro boys	48
IQ groups:	
Top Quartile	91
Second Quartile	79
Third Quartile	72
Fourth Quartile	35

Source: Adapted by the authors, based on data published in Odell (1965), pp. 40–47.

A more general indicator than the number of high school dropouts is an overall tendency for youth of higher ability to stay longer in school and in college. This is shown in Table 3.4, where the estimates are based upon recent studies undertaken in various parts of the country. At the same time, many boys and girls of only average ability also finish high school and enter college. Only those in the lowest quarter of scholastic ability are effectively eliminated from the educational system by the time they pass the high-school graduation mark.

Table 3.4   Amount of Education in Relation to Intelligence

IQ QUARTILE	Percentage in Each IQ Group Achieving a Given Educational Level in the U.S.A. (1965)			
	ENTER HIGH SCHOOL	GRADUATE FROM HIGH SCHOOL	ENTER COLLEGE	GRADUATE FROM COLLEGE
IV (high 25% of population by IQ level)	98	95	80	53
III	96	84	45	15
II	92	65	18	4
I (low 25% of population by IQ level)	88	40	6	0

Source: Estimates by the authors, based on recent studies in various parts of the country of college attendance and educational attainment.

Intellectual Ability and Social Class

Although ability alone is a major factor in determining level of education, the general picture is greatly modified when we consider the additional factor of social status. Youth from upper-middle-class families are likely to go to college even though they have only average ability, while youth from lower-status families have less chance of entering college, even when they have high ability. It is clear that social class as well as intelligence determines who shall finish high school and who shall go to college.

Table 3.5 is based on information from a number of different studies concerning the educational experience and social status of boys and girls who are in the upper quarter of the population in intellectual ability, those with IQ's of 110 or above. Under the conditions existing in 1965 about 53 percent of the ablest quarter of youth completed a four-year college program, while about five percent of these able youth did not finish high school.

It is clear that the educational system selects and carries along most of the ablest youth of upper and upper-middle status, but that able youth of working-class status tend to stop their formal education at the end of high school. The reasons for this lie partly in the inability of

Table 3.5   Level of Education in Relation to Social Class of Youth in the Upper Quarter of Intellectual Ability

	Social Class			*Totals*
	UPPER AND UPPER- MIDDLE	LOWER- MIDDLE	WORKING CLASS	
COMPOSITION OF GROUP (%)	20	42	38	100
Do Not Finish High School (%)	0	1	4	5
High School Graduates. Do not Enter College (%)	2	4	9	15
Enter College but Do Not Finish (%)	2	11	14	27
Complete a 4-Year College Program (%)	16	26	11	53

many working-class youth to pay for a college education, and partly in the lack of motivation for higher education. This lack of motivation is illustrated in the following statement made in an interview by Kenneth Walters, a filling station attendant. Kenneth had been doing quite well in school when, a few months before his sixteenth birthday, he quit school and went to work. Ten years later, he was asked by an interviewer why he had not continued. He answered:

Well, there was quite a few of us. At the time I quit school there was five of us children at home. My mother and father never got along very well. They broke up and, well, my brother and I quit school and went to work. We kept our two sisters going to school. But at that time—I'll be honest with you—it didn't make me very mad, because I didn't like school very well anyway. I was kind of fickle about the whole thing. 'Course now being a little older, I wouldn't mind going a little further. One funny thing—the same year I quit school I went to work up at the mill and that summer my grammar-school principal—he was a very nice fellow—well, he worked up at the mill too. So there was me, the dumbbell, and him just as high as you can go, I guess, in education—both of us working at the mill. As a matter of fact I think I was makin' a little more than he was. He was just up there for the summer months you know. So he gets all that education—all filled up—and for what?

Not all working-class youth share Kenneth's attitudes, of course. David Borgeson, for instance, son of a janitor, was a boy who took readily to school. He was a favorite of his teachers because of his eagerness for what the school gave him. While David was in high school, he and his classmates answered a question which read as follows, "What is the best thing that could happen to you?" David wrote: "The best thing is that somehow I should be able to go to college and to enter the profession I have in mind." After his military service David obtained a scholarship to go through college, and by his good work in college he won a sizable fellowship for graduate study.

We shall return, in the next chapter, to a further discussion of motivation as a factor in college attendance. At this point in summarizing the facts it is clear that the educational system does tend to select and retain the more able pupils, but that it operates much less effectively in this respect with children from the lower social classes than with children from the upper-middle and upper classes.

Intelligence in Relation to Social Class and Color

The performance of the school system as a sorting and selecting agency must be directed with skill and wisdom in a democratic society. It could be done more or less mechanically if there were a close relationship between intellectual ability and social status, or between intellectual ability and ethnicity or skin color. Until recently it was widely believed that there was an inborn intellectual inferiority in people of lower-class status and in people of nonwhite skin color. Some white people developed the idea that whites had the highest innate intelligence and that other races followed in the order of their departure from white color, with the blackest-skinned Negroes lowest in the scale of intelligence. This idea was supported by some of the earlier intelligence test studies, in which it was found that American Negro children scored lower than American white children, with children of mixed white and Negro parentage scoring between the two groups.

However, more critical studies of intelligence testing (Eells *et al.,* 1951) have shown that the ordinary intelligence tests favor children whose parents are of middle- or upper-class status. The problems in the tests are ones for which life in an upper-class or middle-class home give superior preparation.

For example, in the following test item,

A symphony is to a composer as a book is to what?
(   ) paper   (   ) sculptor   (   ) author   (   ) musician   (   ) man

the problem is probably easier for middle-class children. They are more likely to have heard their parents talking about symphonies than are working-class children.

On the other hand, the following item is probably as difficult for high- as for low-status children:

> A baker goes with bread the same way as a carpenter goes with what?
> (   ) a saw (   ) a house (   ) a spoon (   ) a nail (   ) a man

The ordinary intelligence test contains many items of the first type. As a consequence, the test, by bringing in words that are less familiar to him, tends to penalize the child of low socioeconomic status.

Furthermore, children of upper- and middle-class families are more often pushed by their families to do good work in school. School training itself helps one to do well in most intelligence tests. Therefore it is now thought that the differences in intelligence test performance between Negro and white children are mainly due to the fact that more Negro children are working-class. When middle-class Negro children are given intelligence tests, they do about as well as middle-class white children.

Most anthropologists and psychologists now believe that there is no innate difference in intelligence between racial or ethnic or religious groups. There are innate differences between *individuals* within these groups, but the average intelligence of the *groups* is the same, it is thought, if the groups have equal opportunity and similar training in solving the ordinary problems of life. These conclusions are summed up in a statement issued in 1950 on behalf of UNESCO (the United Nations Educational, Scientific and Cultural Organization) by a committee of psychologists and anthropologists from seven countries, entitled "The Scientific Basis for Human Unity." One paragraph of their summary reads as follows:

> According to present knowledge, there is no proof that the groups of mankind differ in their innate mental characteristics, whether in respect of intelligence or temperament. The scientific evidence indicates that the range of mental capacities in all ethnic groups is much the same (*UNESCO Courier*, 1950, p. 1).

Such group differences as are actually found in studies based on intelligence tests are believed to result from several factors—differences in experience with the particular types of problems that make up the tests, differences in motivation to do one's best on the tests, and possibly differences in experience during the pre-school years.

Social Mobility and Success in School

When the school system is viewed as a sorting and selecting agency, it becomes apparent that the sorting helps those who are successful in school to move into favored social and economic positions as adults. The child who succeeds in school tends to stay on through high school and to go on to college. In doing so, he gets a kind of training which (a) prepares him for a high-status occupation and (b) gives him social knowledge and social skills that enable him to associate easily with people of middle-class status. If he is already in a middle-class family, he stays at that level or moves from lower-middle to upper-middle class. If he is in a working-class family, he moves up the social scale.

Unpublished data from the River City study illustrate this process. Of the 409 boys and girls who were studied from the time they were in the 6th grade until they were 23 years old (in 1965), 123 were upward mobile, 209 were stable, and 82 were downward mobile. Their mobility was determined by comparing the socioeconomic status of their families when these boys and girls were in the 6th grade with their "initial adult status," determined when they were 23 years old.

As described in Chapter 2, (see page 50 ff), success in school in the River City study was measured in two ways, by *school grades* and by *social effectiveness*. Intelligence was measured by a battery of intelligence tests.

Table 3.6 shows how the three mobility groups compare on these measures of success in school. (This table is a simplified form of Table 2.1, p. 51.) The members of the upward mobile group are clearly superior to those in the stable group, and the members of the stable group are clearly superior to those in the downward mobile group on all three measures. For instance, the average percentile rank of upward mobile boys in *school grades* was 59, while the downward mobile boys averaged 26. On *social effectiveness,* the upward mobile boys averaged the 70th percentile, and the downward mobile boys were at the 40th percentile. (The correlation coefficient between school grades and social effectiveness was about .4.)

The two forms of success in school each contribute to success in adult life, if upward social mobility is taken as an indication of success.

Girls did not show much striking differences between mobility groups as boys, because most girls are married by the age of 23 and get their adult status rating from their husbands' status. Those girls who

Table 3.6   Comparison of Mobile and Stable Students in River City

	Number of Cases	Mean Percentile Scores[a]		
		IQ	HIGH SCHOOL GRADES	SOCIAL EFFEC- TIVENESS
Upward Mobile:				
boys	52	71	59	70
girls	65	59	65	70
Stable:				
boys	101	42	45	42
girls	99	50	55	54
Downward Mobile:				
boys	44	28	26	40
girls	38	46	47	42

[a] In this Table the boys and girls are combined in computing percentile scores.
Source: Unpublished data from the River City study.

were upward mobile due to marriage were nearly equal in IQ and school grades to those who were downward mobile due to marriage. In social effectiveness, however, the upward mobile girls were clearly superior to those who were downward mobile.

How the School Operates as a Selecting Agency

The school system attempts to treat children in accordance with their intellectual ability on the ground that children of different kinds of intellectual ability need somewhat different educational experience. At the same time, the system tends to treat children of higher social status as though they had higher intellectual ability. This differential treatment in relation to social class is not intentional on the part of most school systems; it results primarily from the cultural differences between social classes.

One can see the school system operating to encourage children of higher social status and to discourage children of lower social status in nearly every aspect of the school program, formal and informal.

Ability Grouping

In many schools where there is more than one classroom per grade there is "ability grouping" or "homogeneous grouping," whereby pupils of the same general academic level are supposed to be grouped together. This is aimed at facilitating the work of the teacher, who can then expect all her pupils to do work at about the same level. Whenever there is "homogeneous grouping" in a school that draws from a socially diverse population, however, the groups tend to become homogeneous for social class as well as homogeneous for mental ability.

The pattern of grouping children varies from community to community. Small schools with only one classroom per grade do not, of course, group children except by age. In some schools, ability groups are formed only in particular subject-matter areas, as when those children in a grade who are poor in reading, or those who are particularly good in science, are given special instruction as a group. In such schools, the child may spend only one period a day with a "special" group; the rest of the time, with his regular and heterogeneous grade group. This modification of "homogeneous grouping" tends to counteract the possible social-class biases that may otherwise operate.

To take another example, schools in homogeneous parts of a large city, where the school population is drawn from one or two social classes, may use a scheme of sectioning by ability that brings together those children with the most motivation for education. The children who consistently work hard often seem to teachers to be the abler ones and will tend to be grouped together.

In a large city (while there are many exceptions) there is a tendency for boys and girls of a given social level to be found together in elementary school because the neighborhood around the school tends to be homogeneous with regard to social class.

In the 1960's, with increasing national attention being given to the identification and utilization of talent, there is probably an overall decrease in the extent to which social status influences homogeneous groupings in school. Teachers and administrators are increasingly sensitive to the need for selecting able students, no matter what their social backgrounds may be, and of placing them in "accelerated" or "honors" sections. Nevertheless, it continues to be true that by far the highest proportions of children and adolescents in such accelerated groups are from middle- rather than working-class families.

High School Curricula

In the high school there appears a new basis for grouping pupils: by type of curriculum. The typical American high school is of the "comprehensive" type, with several different curricula or courses of study. There is the college preparatory curriculum; the commercial; the vocational, which may include agricultural and home-economics programs; and the "general" curriculum for those whose vocational aim is not clear and whose ability is not high enough to warrant entrance to the college preparatory program. (The general curriculum does not usually include mathematics or a foreign language, and thus differs from the college preparatory.)

The several curricula tend to draw differentially from the social classes, with the college preparatory curriculum enrolling higher-status pupils and the general and vocational curricula those of lower status.

The several curricula are seen by students and faculty alike as having differing social-status value. At the top is the college preparatory course. The commercial course is generally next, followed by other vocational courses. The general curriculum is usually at the bottom.

Type of Secondary School

In large city school systems, high schools themselves are often of various types (as differentiated from comprehensive high schools in which several curricula are offered within the same school building). Usually there are the "academic" or "general" high schools, and the "trade" or technical schools, each of which in turn may be public, parochial, or private.

A recent study of white eighth-grade graduates in St. Louis concerned the relationships between choice of secondary school, academic ability, and socioeconomic status of the child's family. Increases were found in both average socioeconomic and ability scores for both boys and girls, starting with those who did not attend any high school, and followed in order by those who attended public technical, public and parochial general, private parochial, and other private high schools. For both sexes, socioeconomic status was found to be a more important factor in the choice of secondary school than was academic ability. The author concluded:

In view of the fact that the several types of secondary schools in St. Louis place a varying emphasis on college preparation and tend to direct their pupils into certain occupational levels, the findings of this study are significant in that they indicate a definite limitation on the role of education in promoting social mobility. Although it is not possible to generalize from the findings in one community, and although the specific pattern of school types may vary for other cities, there is reason to believe that similar relationships exist elsewhere. (Pohlmann, 1956, pp. 396–397.)

In the majority of large cities, the general or comprehensive schools have attendance districts of their own, and all students living in a given district are expected to attend the school from that district unless they go to a vocational or other special school. The attendance districts served by high schools tend to be fairly homogeneous in the social class of their residents. There will be middle-class communities with middle-class schools, and working-class communities with working-class schools.

The differences among such schools are indicated in Table 3.7 which reports data on comprehensive high schools in Chicago. The schools are ranked according to the socioeconomic ratio (SER) of occupations of adult males in the school attendance area. The average achievement level is shown to be closely related to socioeconomic level, as is the proportion of students of low reading ability. These comprehensive schools practice ability grouping, with as many as five levels or "tracks," aimed at adjusting the methods of teaching and the difficulty level to the ability of the students. However, a school located in a low-status neighborhood with a generally low achievement level has difficulty in motivating the abler students to work as effectively as does a school with a generally high achievement level located in a middle-class area.

The grades or marks secured by pupils reflect social class differences in the communities served by the schools. Thus, in a study of eight high schools in Oakland, California, a much higher proportion of students in the middle-class schools obtained "A's" and "B's" than did those in the working-class schools (Wilson, 1959). This is not to say that teachers necessarily show favoritism to upper-status pupils. The study habits, the educational motivation, and the scholastic intelligence of the higher-status pupils are likely to be superior to those of lower-status pupils, on the average. Neither does the relationship between school grades and social class position hold true equally in all communities. As Udry (1960) found, this relationship is less striking in a new community where social class lines are less recognizable or have had less chance to crystallize; or in a school where teachers are particularly sensitive to social class differences and have learned how to minimize their own biases in this respect in evaluating students' performance.

Table 3.7 Socioeconomic Factors in School Achievement in High Schools of a Big City

School number	SER[1]	Achieve-ment[2]	Low read-ing level[3]	Say will enter college[4]	Percent Negro Enroll-ment
1	290	52	0	94	0
3	199	54	0	91	0
5	123	40	12	71	26
7	97	36	0	74	0
9	82	29	22	55	21
11	79	36	5	74	0
13	74	41	0	49	0
15	68	33	14	52	0
17	66	28	4	48	0
19	54	11	16	46	28
21	53	21	15	76	88
23	53	25	12	42	19
25	50	23	0	41	0
27	39	22	4	38	1
29	27	27	0	44	0
31	23	11	16	36	9
33	22	4	56	53	94
35	20	14	29	39	44
37	17	4	37	51	91
39	11	6	41	53	100

[1] Socioeconomic ratio of adults in the school's attendance area in 1960. See p. 249 for a description of the SER. Certain schools are not representative of the adult socioeconomic distribution because there is a selective factor in attendance at public schools.

[2] Percent of ninth and eleventh graders in top three stanines on standard tests of reading. (For city as a whole, 23 percent are in the top three stanines.)

[3] Percent of ninth-grade English classes in Basic English. Pupils are below sixth-grade level in such classes. In some high schools there are too few such pupils to form a class, though almost every high school has at least a handful of such pupils.

[4] Students who will graduate in June are asked in the spring whether they expect to go to college. (Composite of data from 1962, 1963, and 1964.)

Source: Adapted from Havighurst (1964), *The Public Schools of Chicago*, pp. 208–9.

Private Schools

The parochial type of private school is usually quite similar to a public school in its relation to social class. Most parochial schools are Roman Catholic, and the Catholic Church in most communities is fairly representative of the total population as regards social class. In a large city the Catholic parishes are likely to be differentiated along social class as well as along ethnic lines, thus producing variation from one elementary school to the next. The parochial high schools are generally of the comprehensive type and draw from all social groups.

The "independent" private schools cater to families of upper and upper-middle class and perform special functions in relation to the social structure. Boys and girls of upper-middle-class families may learn social skills and may make friendships that will help them later to rise to upper-class positions. The social and academic atmosphere in most private schools is rather different from that of a public school, even when the public school draws pupils from an upper-middle-class area of a city. A study of the personalities of boys in public and in private schools supports this statement (McArthur, 1954). It was noted that public school boys are "Doing" boys, while those in private school are "Being" boys. The latter do not strive so hard to get ahead with vocational plans.

The School and the Social Class

The conclusions to be drawn from these pages may be summed up in the words of Professor W. W. Charters,

It is proper to conclude that pupils of the lower classes will experience frustration and failure and pupils of the higher classes will experience gratification and success in their educational experiences. The evidence supporting this conclusion is overwhelming.

To categorize youth according to the social class position of their parents is to order them on the extent of their participation and degree of "success" in the American educational system. This has been so consistently confirmed by research that it now can be regarded as an empirical law. It appears to hold, regardless of whether the social class categorization is based upon the exhaustive procedures used in Elmtown (Hollingshead, 1949) or upon more casual indicators of socioeconomic status such as occupation or income level. It seems to hold in any educational institution, public or private, where there is some diversity in social class, including universities, colleges, and teacher-training institutions as well as elementary and secondary schools. Social class position predicts grades, achievement and intelligence test scores, retentions at grade level, course failure, truancy, suspensions from school, high school drop-outs, plans for college attendance, and total amount of formal schooling. It predicts academic honors and awards in the public school, elective school offices, extent of participation in extra-curricular activities and in social affairs sponsored by the school, to say nothing of a variety of indicators of "success" in the formal structure of the student society. Where differences in prestige value exist in high school clubs and activities, in high school curricula, or in types of advanced training institutions, the social class composition of the membership will vary accordingly.

The predictions noted above are far from perfect. Inasmuch as the social class position rarely accounts for more than half the variance of school "success," the law holds only for differences in group *averages*, not for differences in individual success. (Charters, 1963, p. 739–740.)

The School, Social Stability, and Social Fluidity

In a democratic society the school system is called upon to work toward two somewhat different goals: one, of improving society and promoting social change; the other, of stabilizing society and preserving the *status quo*. When the school system acts as a sorting and selecting agency it promotes movement or fluidity in the social structure by selecting some people for upward social mobility. At the same time the school maintains stability of society by some of the ways it helps to keep children in the same social class levels as their parents, as, for instance, in its ways of grouping pupils.

The two goals of education, social fluidity and social stability, must be sought within the framework of certain basic realities about society and about human beings.

One reality is that the structure of society is based on a *division of labor*. This means that there are positions of greater and lesser responsibility and prestige, positions requiring greater and lesser ability and energy. The social structure is changing due to powerful technological forces, with a relative increase in those positions that give generally greater rewards and that require greater ability and training.

Another of these realities is that of *individual differences* in abilities and temperament. While some types of ability are more socially valuable than others, children with all types of ability are born to parents of low as well as high status. According to generally accepted social ideals in America, a good educational system helps people to develop their socially valuable abilities and to find the positions in society where they can contribute most to the general welfare. Enough has been learned about the distribution of ability to know that we still have a long way to go in America before we reach the place where we are making the best use of all people's abilities. This is a job in which the educational system plays an important role.

There are also many people with mediocre abilities and with temperaments that enable them to fit well into the less creative and less prestigious positions of the society. The educational system can help these people to find their appropriate places, to enjoy their lives, and to know they are worthwhile and productive members of the society.

It will be possible for the people of each new generation to find the places for which they are best fitted, only if the society remains in a fairly fluid state. There must be a good deal of movement of young people from the social positions established for them by their parents to new social positions that they establish for themselves. The educational system helps in this process, while educating the society at large to welcome such fluidity.

Some kind of upper-status group is present in any complex society. The society will be served best if it seeks out and trains the most able people to become the elite, and if it rewards them by giving them prestige. At the same time, the society must have enough stability so that parents with high social status can give their children a favored start in life, since they will insist on passing on to their children some of the rewards they themselves have gained.

Thus a successful democracy should have enough fluidity in its social structure to permit able and industrious persons to move from low-status positions to higher-status positions; at the same time, it must have enough stability for higher-status people to pass on their advantages to their children. In other words, those at the top must have some assurance that their children will have a good chance to remain at the top; but those at the bottom must have a chance to compete with those above them for good positions.

We have already indicated certain features of the educational system that promote social stability and others that promote social fluidity. Still other procedures work toward stability and fluidity at the same time.

Homogeneous Grouping

The experience with homogeneous grouping shows that it tends to place children of similar social status together. This is true partly because there is a relationship between social status, school grades, and intelligence test scores, and this relationship itself operates to place pupils of high social status with other pupils of high social status. This result occurs also in part because of the informal and unofficial exceptions that are made, the exceptions in which high-status children are placed with other high-status children, whether or not their ability warrants it.

If homogeneous grouping by ability or achievement tends to make for homogeneous grouping by social class, then the children of lower social class tend to grow up together and to learn to expect to go through life together. Furthermore, the learning ability of some of these children may be mistakenly rated as low, and they may be taught in such ways that they are not motivated to work hard. In turn, they may do poorly in high school and may not find their way into college preparatory courses. In these ways, homogeneous grouping may operate toward social stability.

On the other hand, homogeneous grouping is bound to place at least a few bright lower-status children in the rapid-learning groups, where they associate with higher-status children and learn from them the skills necessary for mobility. These lower-status children are given school programs that prepare them for college and for the mobility that is likely to come with a college education.

The Single-Track School System

The single-track school system is one in which there is one general pathway from the first to the last year of school, a track that leads from the first grade to the terminus of the university. All pupils continue in the same pathway until they leave school, whether they drop out as soon as the law allows or whether they go on beyond this point.

By contrast, a multiple-track school system is one in which pupils start out together at the elementary level, but where they are later shunted to one or another track—one leading to the university, another leading to the teacher-training institution, another to the vocational school, and so on.

While in reality both American and European educational systems

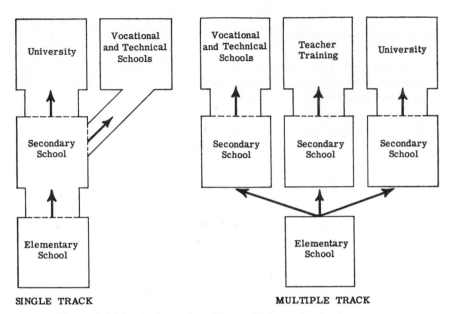

SINGLE TRACK   MULTIPLE TRACK

Figure 3.2 The single-track and the multiple-track school systems.

provide more than one track, it is customary to speak of European systems as multiple-track systems, with elementary schools that lead to commercial, teacher-training, or trade schools, and with only a minority of pupils shifting over at the age of eleven, twelve, or thirteen to secondary schools leading to the university.

The system in the United States, with the majority of pupils following the track that can lead to the university, is usually spoken of as a single-track system. Certainly the single track has been carried further in America than in other countries, with the choice of pathway, when it occurs at all, being postponed until at least the ninth, and usually until the tenth or eleventh grade, and with the possibility for a pupil to move back and forth from one pathway to another.

The single-track system promotes social fluidity by keeping the way open to higher education for practically all young people up to the age of seventeen or eighteen. This provides time for boys and girls, with the aid of teachers, guidance officers, and age-mates, to explore the possibilities of higher education. Many young people of working-class status, if required at an early age to choose between a college-preparatory or a noncollege-preparatory course, as in the multiple-track system, would choose (or their parents would choose) a noncollege course. They might later regret the choice, at a time when it was too late to change.

On the other hand, the single-track system may discourage some working-class pupils from developing their abilities by forcing them into a verbal, academic curriculum, one that they dislike and which may cause them to drop out of school altogether.

Whether the single-track system promotes social fluidity, then, depends upon the particular school. One school may be so heavily dominated by the traditional college-preparatory requirements of mathematics and foreign languages that it alienates the alert and active-minded working-class youth. Another school, still within the single-track system, may offer a variety of alternative curricula, and may provide easy transfer arrangements, so that a boy or girl who starts in a commercial or vocational course can readily shift his program to get enough academic subjects to qualify for college entrance.

The Comprehensive High School

The American high school of the so-called comprehensive type carries the single-track system furthest toward the goal of social fluidity, since it contains a variety of curricula under one roof and permits transfers from one curriculum to another fairly easily. Furthermore, this type of school usually brings youth from all social levels together in classrooms and in extracurricular activities, thus encouraging the potentially mobile lower-status youth to learn social skills from middle-class age-mates.

The comprehensive high school may, however, operate to limit mobility. Students choose one curriculum rather than another in line with their social class positions. Thus, the boys who take an auto-mechanics course or a printing-trades course tend to find themselves with other boys of their own social background, and they may learn to fit into the adult social structure accordingly.

A comprehensive high school, if it is run like a set of parallel schools, may do little in actuality to promote social fluidity. If it is run with a minimum of barriers between curricula, it may do much to promote fluidity.

Special Classes for the Gifted

Schools in some communities offer a program of special classes for gifted children. This is a kind of homogeneous grouping, but one that provides for only those children with very high abilities of various kinds.

This kind of program will encourage social fluidity if talented youth in the lower social groups are searched out; and if those lower-status youth who fall just short of being "superior" (when "superior" is defined in the currently accepted fashion) are given the benefit of the doubt and are included in the talented groups.

A program of special education for talented children will, however, leave the great bulk of lower-status children in "average" classrooms. There they may lack some of the stimulation they might otherwise gain from being in classrooms with a few very bright children.

Extracurricular Activities in High School

A high school with an active program of clubs, special interest groups, and social affairs may promote social fluidity by bringing lower-status youth into intimate social contact with upper-middle-class youth. Thus lower-status boys and girls may learn skills and attitudes useful for upward mobility.

In the typical high school, however, the cliques who dominate the social life of the school consist mainly of higher-status youth. Although a few lower-status boys and girls, usually those who are already oriented toward upward mobility, may occupy positions of leadership, most lower-status youth do not participate in many extracurricular activities. Some, feeling excluded and unhappy, drop out of school altogether, thus losing opportunities for mobility.

Public and Private Schools

Where most youth of a community attend a public school system, and where this system offers the same kind of education for everybody, social fluidity is encouraged. In this situation, children of all social classes study and play together, and lower-status children get a maximum of opportunity to learn from and to compete with higher-status children. When, however, the public school in a community is supplemented by private schools that draw off most upper-status children, then the public school may consist largely of lower-middle- or working-class pupils. It may then become part of a system that promotes rigidity in the social structure.

Private schools that attract children of upper-class families in general make for rigidity in the social structure. However, even the most exclusive private schools today include a few upper-middle-class boys and girls, both Negro and white, and they thus provide for mobility for a few children who will make their way into the upper class. A few such schools also have scholarship programs aimed to bring in a few working-class youth; where these programs operate successfully, they also foster a limited amount of mobility.

The private parochial schools are usually much like the public schools in their range of social class membership. The Catholic parochial school system in a big city, for example, generally operates for and against social mobility in about the same ways as does the public school system. Parochial schools, although they tend to preserve the separation of society into religious and cultural groups, do not generally make for rigidity of social class structure.

Exercises

1. In a school to which you have access, make a list of the children in a given classroom. Estimate their socioeconomic positions. Compare these positions with such things as their school grades, their extracurricular activities, and their vocational goals.

2. Study the life and functioning of a high school, to find out how it fits into the social structure of the community it serves. To what extent does it encourage upward social mobility? To what extent does it fit boys and girls for social positions similar to those of their parents?

3. Read the section on the American high school in Denis Brogan's *The American Character*. Summarize the argument presented by this British observer of American society. State your reaction to it.

4. Interview several high school students of different social backgrounds, to find out what their attitudes are toward the school and its various curricula.

5. Outline the kind of school-parent relationship that you think would be best in an elementary school situation in a working-class area of the city. How might this relationship differ from what would be best in a middle-class area? What would you try to accomplish through the school-parent relationship in the one and the other type of community?

6. How would you go about improving the extracurricular program in a high school where these activities have long been monopolized by a small fraction of the students?

Suggestions for Further Reading

1. The effect of the social-class structure upon education is treated at
    length in *Elmtown's Youth* by August B. Hollingshead; in *Children of
    Brasstown* by Celia B. Stendler; and in *Social-Class Influences upon
    Learning* by Allison Davis. For a somewhat different perspective on the
    role of the school in relation to the social and economic structure of the
    society, see the book by Kimball and McClellan, *Education and the
    New America.*

2. Roger G. Barker *et al.,* in their study of a small midwestern town, report
    they found no class bias in the school there. See their article, "There
    Is No Class Bias in Our School." (This article has been reprinted on
    pp. 258–261 of *Social Foundations of Education* by William O. Stanley
    et al.)

3. A summary and analysis of the special summer program undertaken in
    1963 to combat school dropouts in over 60 cities is given in the
    pamphlet, "The 1963 Dropout Campaign," published by the Office of
    Education in 1964.

4. A good summary of the issues and of the research program that at-
    tempted to create "culture-fair" tests of intelligence (tests that would
    not penalize boys and girls from lower socioeconomic level) is given in
    "Social Class and Intelligence Tests" by W. W. Charters, Jr. that appears
    in *Readings in the Social Psychology of Education.*

5. For the student who is interested in the sociology of education as a
    field, and in knowing something of the history of this field, read the
    book by Brim, *Sociology and the Field of Education,* or the chapter by
    Gross, "The Sociology of Education," in *Sociology Today* (edited by
    Merton, Broom and Cottrell, Jr.). Also, Chapter 3, "The Sociological
    Study of Education," in Corwin, *A Sociology of Education* is a good
    brief overview of the issues.

6. A recent extensive study of high schools in a sample of cities throughout
    the country has been reported by Herriott and St. John. Their book,
    Social Class and the Urban School documents the discussion in this
    chapter.

4 / The College in the Social Structure

Increasing numbers of Americans during the present century have come to look upon a college education as a necessity. The vast majority of upper-middle-class vocational positions are now occupied by college-educated men and women, and the number of these positions is increasing rapidly. As a consequence, there is need not only for young people born in middle-class families, but also for young people from lower-middle and working-class families, to obtain college educations. College is the avenue of upward mobility for growing numbers of young people.

Factors Related to College Attendance

If the college system is to work efficiently in providing opportunity, the ablest young people should attend college. As shown in the preceding chapter abler youth (in terms of IQ) are more likely to go to college than are those of lesser ability.

For example, a recent report from Project Talent (1964) concerning high school graduates of 1960 showed this general picture, although the actual percentages were a bit different from those given in Table 3.4 in the preceding chapter. The Project Talent report showed that, 18 months after high school graduation, 94 percent of the top quarter of high school graduates had entered college. Of those above average but below the top quarter, 53 percent had entered college. A study of high school graduates of 1961 in Minnesota showed that 88 percent of the top 10 percent entered college (Hood and Berdie, 1964).

ACADEMIC ABILITY. The present authors estimate that 80 percent of the youths who are in the top quarter in scholastic ability now enter college. This leaves 20 percent of the top quarter, or 5 percent of the total age group, who ought to go to college if scholastic ability were the major determinant. Who are these young people, and why do they not go to college today? The majority of them come from working-class homes or from lower white-collar homes. The majority of them are girls. If they are to go to college, most of them will need financial assistance, and many, if not most, will need substantially more motivation for higher education.

Of the third highest quarter in intellectual ability, some 45 percent now enter college. The remaining 55 percent of this ability group come mainly from working-class and lower-middle class families and a good many of them are Negro, Puerto Rican, or Mexican, whose IQ scores probably underestimate their true learning ability. Also, more than half of them are girls. If the schools undertook a major program of financial aid and of motivation aimed at this particular group, perhaps as many as a third to a half of them might be persuaded to enter college, or another 5 percent of the total age group.

The great increase of college enrollments since World War II has not lowered the scholastic ability of students who are in college. Thus Berdie, who studied the scholastic ability of college freshmen in Minnesota between 1930 and 1960 says, "The intellectual ability of the Minnesota college students today is no different from what it was thirty years ago (Berdie *et al.,* 1962, p. 39). In spite of a tremendous increase in the absolute and relative numbers of students attending college, the mean ability scores of these students have remained remarkably constant. Similarly, Darley (1962) summarized the data from a national sample of 167 colleges and found that the average scholastic aptitude of college entrants did not change significantly between 1952 and 1959.

The relation between ability and college attendance is not always consistent. There are various factors besides ability that determine whether or not a person goes to college.

SEX. One of these factors is sex. Whereas more girls graduate from high school (in the ratio of about 51 to 49), more boys enter college. Roughly 58 percent of entering college students are men and 42 percent are women, and this ratio is about 60 to 40 for college graduates.

RACE AND RELIGION. Ethnic and religious groups differ in the number of young people who attend college. In general, fewer boys and girls of recent immigrant groups go to college. In a study of Connecticut high school graduates it was found that 57 percent of the Catholic, 63 percent of the Protestant, and 87 percent of the Jewish boys and girls applied for college (Stetler, 1949).

Smaller proportions of Negro youth go to college than is true of the population. However, total differences between white and nonwhite groups will probably become less marked as Negroes gain more economic and social opportunity.

SOCIOECONOMIC STATUS AND ABILITY. Young people from high-status families usually have both the financial means and the motivation to attend college.

The relationships between aspirations for college attendance and social class are shown in a study by Cutright (1960) of over 1,000 seniors in nine Illinois high schools. Cutright found that although over 50 percent intended to enter college, a year later only 33 percent actually were found in college; or, as would be anticipated, that it was easier to want to go to college than actually to attend. In a careful attempt to weigh the influence of various factors upon college entrance, he found not only that social class was a very good predictor of college attendance, but that, even more, it was a better predictor than intentions themselves. In other words, if the investigator knew the social class of the student, he could predict better whether or not that student would be in college the next year than if he knew what the student himself said about his plans, even as late as the spring of the student's senior year in high school.

It is often contended that social class may determine who enters college but that intellectual ability becomes the decisive factor thereafter; and that ability, not social class, determines who will graduate. Eckland (1964), however, has gathered evidence which shows that the higher a student's social class, the greater his probability of graduating from college once he has entered.

Basic facts from many studies such as the ones just cited concerning social status and college attendance are shown in Table 4.1, where data are presented concerning the social class origins of college entrants. Since 1920 the proportions of working-class youth who enter college have risen markedly; but so, also, have the proportions of upper- and middle-class youth.

If the factor of intellectual ability is added to this general picture, the three-way relationship between intellectual ability, socioeconomic status, and college attendance becomes clear, as stated in the preceding

Table 4.1   Social Class Origins of College Entrants

Social Class	1920	1940	1950	1960	1965	
					MALES	FEMALES
Upper and upper-middle	40	70	75	80	90	80
Lower-middle	8	20	38	50	62	45
Upper-working	2	5	12	25	35	24
Lower-working	0	0	2	4	8	4
Percent of total age group entering college	6	16	22	33	43*	32*

* When 1965 figures for males and females are averaged, the percent of the total age group who enter college is approximately 37.

Sources: 1920—estimated by the authors from scattered data.
1940—estimated by the authors on the basis of several studies of the occupations of fathers of college students.
1950, 1960 and 1965—composite figures from several studies of social class and college attendance.

chapter. With relatively few exceptions, the boys and girls who are both high in intellectual ability and high in social status go to college. The proportion who go to college is considerably lower, however, in groups who are lower on one or both characteristics.

Who Will Go to College?

While the factors we have been discussing are related to college attendance in overall terms, the question of who does and who does not go to college can also be considered from the point of view of the young person himself. The probability that a particular boy or girl will go to college depends upon four factors: (1) mental ability, (2) financial ability, (3) propinquity to college, and (4) individual motivation. In other words, a young person will or will not attend college depending upon the extent to which one or more of these four factors determine his decision.

Of the four, mental ability is the factor that can be influenced least. Still, there is evidence that ability to do college work is influenced by school preparation as well as by family experience. The intelligence tests used to measure mental ability do not measure innate ability as such, but the result of innate ability combined with experience and training.

The "mental ability" of many children can probably be increased as elementary and secondary schools find better methods of instruction. (We shall return to this point in Chapter 5.) As schools become better from this point of view, more boys and girls are able to succeed in college.

Financial ability has greatly increased in this country during the past hundred years, so that a higher proportion of families can now afford to send children to college than ever before. Furthermore, as will be seen from the discussion in Chapter 15, a substantial increase in scholarships in recent years has had the effect of sending more young people to college.

Propinquity to college has also increased for a great many people. Not only has urbanization operated to give more people easy access to colleges and universities, but more institutions, such as junior colleges and branches of state universities, have become available.

Motivation for College

The most important factor in determining who will go to college is that of motivation, the individual's desire for a college education. Low motivation is actually more of a deterrent than low financial ability in preventing able young people from entering college. Studies of high school seniors in various parts of the country have made this clear (Barker and Wright, 1954; Conger, 1950; Phearman, 1949; Roper, 1949; Stivers, 1958, 1959). When boys and girls are asked whether or not they intend to go to college and, if not, why not, the majority of those who do not intend to go reply that they are not interested in going. Only a minority indicate that financial need is the main obstacle.

Motivation or personal incentive for a college education arises from the following four factors:

1. *Need for achievement.* There seems to exist in some people a basic need for achievement that drives them toward accomplishing as much as they can in almost everything they undertake. McClelland *et al.* (1953), Rosen and D'Andrade (1959) and others have defined the concept of *need for achievement,* and have worked out tests by which to measure it. This need for achievement is a deep and possibly unconscious drive. Not only may the person be unaware of the extent to which this need operates within him, but the extent of the drive may not always be apparent in the person's school record.

2. *Identification with persons who have gone to college or done well in school.* It is likely that a boy or girl will do his best in school if he has identified closely with another person, usually a parent, who has done well in school. The process of psychological identification is well known whereby a child takes an older person for his model and tries to do and to be all the things that model represents to him. The child therefore attempts to do well in school if he sees school achievement as important in the life of the person with whom he identifies.
3. *Social pressure.* In addition to the unconscious pressure that stems from identification, there are also a number of social pressures upon an individual of which he is fully aware. Family members, friends, teachers, and other persons in the community have expectations concerning school achievement, high school graduation, and college attendance, and these expectations act as pressures upon the individual.
4. *Intrinsic pleasure in learning.* A person who enjoys studying and learning will do as well in school as his ability permits. Probably intrinsic pleasure is a more important factor in artistic and musical achievement than in school achievement at the elementary and secondary school levels. It is likely, however, that intrinsic pleasure in learning is a factor of some importance when it comes to making decisions about entering college and in achievement in college.

Stivers (1958, 1959) studied the motivation for college in students who were in the upper quarter of intellectual ability. (Stivers' data are also reported in Havighurst *et al.,* 1962.) Comparing boys in the study group who went to college with those who did not go to college, Stivers found that those who did go had a higher score on McClelland's test of need for achievement. Also operating in the lives of these boys was a significantly greater set of social pressures by parents, teachers, and friends which pushed them toward college. Those who went to college had received higher marks in high school than those who did not, and they had more academic interests and hobbies, indicating that these boys got more pleasure out of studying and doing things related to school than did the other boys.

The girls in Stivers' study presented a somewhat different picture. Those who went to college had greater social pressure to do so than those who did not, and they got better marks in high school. However, they did not have higher scores on the test of need for achievement. The explanation for this difference between the girls and the boys who were motivated for college may be an artifact of the test itself, since the test situations may be less appropriate for girls than for boys. Another possibility is that the achievement drive in able girls can be satisfied either by going to college or by getting married and raising a family. It seems clear that many high school girls perceive some conflict between the goals of college and a career on the one hand, and marriage and family on the other.

Some of the differences between boys and girls of superior ability who attend or do not attend college are illustrated by the following cases:

Ralph, an upper-working-class boy with a high score on the test of need for achievement, planned to attend the university, to be a musician and a music teacher. In elementary school he had little competition and did well with scarcely any effort. His divorced mother had high hopes for him; both she and his older brother were proud of Ralph's success. In high school, apart from some difficulty in geometry, he continued to do well, especially in music. His mother and brother occasionally suggested college to him, and several of his best friends planned to go, but his greatest sources of encouragement were his music teachers and his own accomplishments in music.

"I once wanted to be a farmer. Father was one, and also a couple of uncles. But when we moved into town my grandfather, a musician, prophesied that I'd be one, too. I didn't get interested, though, until the seventh grade, when I started my private music lessons. My present teacher especially has had a tremendous effect on me. With him, I built up my interest in music. He has talked to me many times about going into music, and he told me that I'd have to choose between professional music and teaching. He built me up, maybe too much. After all, I'm no child prodigy; neither am I an idiot. To sum up, my teachers have influenced me to become as good as they are. And my ability to play and strive to perfect music and my understanding of music is an influence on me."

On the other hand, Tom, with a below-average score on need for achievement, plans "to help Dad on the farm for awhile, probably, then get a job in town. I'm not sure what kind. Then I'll try for something better and advance as much as I can." Tom's elementary school years were spent in rural school, where he did good work. In high school he did fairly well, though his teachers thought that he should do better. "I usually don't do as well in English as in other subjects," he said. His mother used to talk about college but has not mentioned the subject for several years. No other adult ever suggested that he attend college, and none of his close friends was going.

"We've lived on a farm since I was five, so I got kind of interested in farming. And Barry (Tom's best friend) belonged to the Future Farmers last year and told me about it, so I got interested in it. But when I first came to high school I took industrial arts, and down in electric shop I kind of got interested in that. So I joined the 4-H Club and went to electricity training school. My Dad thinks that I should get a job in town after high school; I don't know exactly what kind. Mother thinks so too; maybe some kind of carpentry work, because my father does a lot of that."

Among girls the motivation for college seems to depend more upon social pressures, as is seen in the following two cases:

Louise, a lower-middle-class girl with an average score on need for achievement, planned to go to a teachers college. "I want to get my master's degree and teach English," she told the interviewer. When she was a child, two of the most important people in her life were teachers. "They were wonderful persons. They expected good things of me—excellent marks—and put me in the limelight frequently." Her parents also expected her to get excellent marks. "They placed a high value on study and mentioned it often. I think my grandmother mentioned it often, too. She didn't have the opportunity to finish high school and college, and she was always sorry."

In high school Louise found another teacher with whom to identify. "My English teacher is a wonderful person and does what I want to do. I see my old English teacher occasionally, too, and I would like to be a teacher just like her. I know they both expect good things from me. I made almost straight A's in their classes. English is a natural for me. I've told them of my ambition, and they've encouraged me."

On the other hand, Susan, a lower-middle-class girl with an extremely high need for achievement, planned to get a secretarial job after graduation from high school. "I will work through the summer until around November. Then I plan to get married," she told the interviewer. During her earliest years in elementary school she received only above-average marks, and some of her teachers felt that she could get top marks in all subjects if she tried. Until she entered junior high school, however, no one else set high standards for her. "In the seventh grade I started to run around with Judy. She liked to get good grades, and she was jealous of mine. I didn't care at first, but in the end I tried to beat her, and I did." Through grade school and into high school, her parents' attitude did not change a great deal. "They're like me. They want me to get A's and B's, but if I get a C it doesn't bother them much."

Other personal influences in her life did change, though. In high school, her best friend made only average marks. Of the boy to whom she became engaged she said with a laugh, "Well, he gets average and sometimes maybe a little lower marks. He doesn't hate school or anything, but he enjoys himself while he's here."

A study of Boston boys showed the influence of family social pressures on motivation for college (Kahl, 1953). Of the boys in the upper 20 percent in ability whose fathers were minor white-collar workers or skilled or semi-skilled manual workers, about half expected to go to college. When interviews were held with twelve boys in this group who expected to go to college and with twelve who did not, it was found that the principal difference between the two groups lay in the amount of parental pressure exerted.

The following case illustrates how parental attitudes may depress motivation for college:

Case B: The father is a bread salesman; he has five children. He is a high school graduate. "I was never a bright one myself, I must say. The one thing I've had in mind is making enough to live on from day to day; I've never had much hope of a lot of it piling up. However, I'd rather see my son make an improvement over what I'm doing and I'm peddling bread. . . . I think he's lazy. Maybe I am too, but I gotta get out and hustle. . . . I don't keep after him. I have five kiddos. When you have a flock like that it is quite a job to keep your finger on this and the other thing. . . . I really don't know what he would like to do. Of course, no matter what I would like him to do, it isn't my job to say so, as he may not be qualified. I tried to tell him where he isn't going to be a doctor or lawyer or anything like that, I told him he should learn English and learn to meet people. Then he could get out and sell something worth while where a sale would amount to something for him. That is the only suggestion that I'd make to him. . . . I took typing, short-hand, bookkeeping and we had Latin, French, Geometry. We had everything. But anything I would know then I've forgotten now. . . . I suppose there are some kids who set their mind to some goal and plug at it, but the majority of kids I have talked to take what comes. Just get along. . . . I don't think a high school diploma is so important. I mean only in so far as you might apply for a job and if you can say 'I have a diploma,' it might help get the job, but other than that I don't see that it ever did me any good." (Kahl, 1953, pp. 194–195.)

The boys in this study could be divided into two main groups: those who believed in "getting by" and those who believed in "getting ahead." This basic split was reflected in their more specific attitudes toward the details of schoolwork, after-school recreation, and jobs. The boys who believed in just "getting by" were generally bored with school, anticipated some sort of job at the level of the common man, and found peer group activity to be the most important thing in life.

Types of Colleges

There is great variety among the 2,150 colleges and universities of the United States, not only in the nature of their educational programs, but also in the social composition of their student bodies. It is possible to categorize colleges and universities into several main types. No given institution will fit in every respect one of the following types, nor is this an exhaustive list, but the types are useful in considering how colleges vary in the ways in which they fit the social structure.

Cosmopolitan University

This University is either a midwestern or western state university or a large municipal university. It charges little tuition. Although it has a liberal admission policy, it maintains fairly high academic standards by failing a large proportion of the freshman class every year. In socioeconomic status its students, as shown in Table 4.2 (page 107), come from almost the whole range of social levels. Campus life tends to be dominated by upper-middle and a few lower-middle-class students. A large and growing group of boys and girls from working-class families contributes to the relatively inarticulate mass of youngsters who follow the social patterns set by campus leaders.

The social life of this campus is extraordinarily diverse. There are conventional fraternities and sororities that draw upper-middle-class youth and a few mobile youth from lower-middle- and working-class homes. The church foundations provide social centers for those young people of all status levels who do not care for the activities of the more sophisticated social organizations. A Student Union offers organized activities and informal recreation for boys and girls of all degrees of social affiliation and sophistication.

State College

This type of college is supported by state funds or by local funds of a large city and is found in all parts of the country. It charges little tuition. State College started years ago as a college for the training of teachers; it expanded by adding a liberal arts program and then other elements of a university, such as a program of graduate work leading to a master's degree. The majority of the student body comes from lower-middle-class families, with the remainder about evenly divided between upper-middle and upper-working class. The trend at present is for increasing numbers of students to come from working-class families. This college has more boys and girls from farm families than does any other type. The social life of the students centers around the dormitories, student unions, and sometimes fraternities and sororities. Many boys and girls return to their homes most weekends and keep their hometown friendships active.

Opportunity College

This college appears in several versions, always characterized by low costs, easy admission standards, and a predominance of students from working-class families. It may be a city junior college, with all its students commuting to school. Or it may be a small "self-help" college, with a number of cooperative work enterprises in which students earn their board and room.

This college tends to draw ambitious youngsters, usually of high average but seldom of superior academic ability. The sons and daughters of salespeople, office clerks, railway brakemen, construction workers, factory workers, and tenant farmers predominate. Opportunity College is primarily a place for youth who hope to be socially mobile by learning middle-class vocational skills more than by learning middle-class social skills. (A case study of this type of college is given by Clark, 1960.)

Ivy College

This is the generic name for the high-status colleges with long and respected tradition, which are highly selective in their admission policies. They are likely to be colleges for men or women only, but occasionally they are coeducational. Ivy College may be an eastern school that ranks at the top of the liberal arts hierarchy; or a midwestern church-related college where there is a long waiting list. Both types have fine records of sending students on to graduate work.

Ivy College is the only type in America that has a literal majority of students from upper- and upper-middle-class families. Added to these are a minority of ambitious, hard-working boys and girls from lower-middle-class families and a scattering of working-class youth who are strongly motivated for academic and professional success. Social life centers around clubs, fraternities, and informal dormitory activities. The social interests of most students are not altogether focused upon campus activities, since many go back and forth to winter and summer homes and maintain close ties with family and with friends in other colleges.

For the minority of upward mobile youth in Ivy College there are tremendous learning opportunities, both intellectual and social. The intellectual opportunities are open to all, through a stimulating academic program and through personal relationships with competent scholars. The social opportunities tend to be more restricted for these mobile young people, with only those of attractive social talents, or with special artistic or athletic abilities becoming members of the prestigious campus cliques and organizations. Many of the highly intelligent but less scintillating students fail to find their way into the prevailing social life of the campus.

Warnell College

There are several hundred Warnells, a generic name used to represent those liberal arts colleges found in cities of 10,000 to 100,000, where they are regarded as the chief cultural asset of the community. Most of these colleges are church-related, either now or in the past. They are essentially middle-class institutions, as much lower-middle as upper-middle. By location and by tradition they tend to remain culturally homogeneous. They may be largely Methodist, or Presbyterian, or Baptist, or Lutheran, or Catholic. There are some Negro Warnells in the South, and a small but increasing number of Negro students attend the northern Warnells. Jewish students are present, but in a small minority.

Warnell is a much more comfortable place than Ivy College for boys and girls of lower-middle- and working-class status. It is the easiest kind of college in which to learn upper-middle-class social skills. Lower-status youth can make their way into fraternities and clubs fairly easily, but they can also feel comfortable and accepted if they belong instead to eating clubs, church groups, and local fraternities.

Composition of Student Bodies

Table 4.2 represents the estimated proportions of young people from different social classes who make up the student bodies in these various types of colleges and universities. The estimates have been arrived at on the basis of a variety of studies, both formal and informal, relating to occupational and social-class levels of students in attendance at various institutions, admission policies, dropouts, educational standards, and so on. (Examples of such studies are Clark, 1960; Sanford, 1962; Berdie *et al.,* 1962; Astin, 1964.)

Table 4.2   Estimated Social Class Composition of Students in Various Types of Higher Institutions

Family Status	Cosmo-politan University	Ivy College	Opportunity College (*in percent*)	Warnell	State College
Upper and Upper-middle	30	75	5	40	20
Lower-middle	45	20	40	50	50
Working	25	5	55	10	30

The American college system is adapted to a fluid and variegated social structure and to a society in which a relatively high proportion of young people go to college. The diversity and fluidity of the society are reflected in the colleges. Some colleges contribute to the economic mobility of lower-status youth by training them for middle-class occupations, but they cannot offer much training in the social skills because their students are mainly working- and lower-middle class. Other colleges are of greater service in aiding the mobility of the very few lower-status youth who gain entrance to them, because they enroll predominantly upper- and upper-middle-class students.

Empirical studies of college characteristics supplement the descriptions just given. Stern (1963) identified the following six factors in the college environment which are related to student characteristics: intellectual orientation, social effectiveness, play, friendliness, constraint, and dominance-submission. Astin (1962, 1964) analyzed data on college characteristics and reported six underlying dimensions on which colleges vary: affluence, size, private versus public, proportions of male students, homogeneity of environment, and realistic (technical) emphasis. Thus the studies of colleges and of the students who attend them have shown, as McConnell (1961) concluded, that colleges tend to select students on the basis of their aptitude, interests, values, social status, and intellectual disposition, and students select a college in relation to their own personal characteristics.

How Many Should Go to College?

A much larger percentage of the youth of the United States attend college than of any other country—at least twice as many as Canada or New Zealand, and many times that of other countries. The proportion is increasing in the United States, giving rise to a question, "In relation to the welfare of the society and the happiness of its youth, how many young people should go to college? Is there danger that too many may go?" (For further figures on number of college students, see Chapter 12, Table 12.1.)

Three Answers to the Question

A number of educational commissions have tried to answer the question of how many should go to college, and three major alternatives have been proposed:

1. *Half of the population for two years: one third for four years.* The President's Advisory Commission on Higher Education in 1947 urged that a national policy be adopted that would bring all boys and girls of average intelligence or higher into college for two years, and keep a third of the total age group in college throughout a four-year course (The President's Advisory Commission, 1948). This is the most expansive proposal yet made by a responsible and influential group of people.
2. *Those who are in the upper half of the population in intellectual ability and who want to go to college.* This answer takes account of the fact that many able boys and girls do not wish to go to college. About three out of ten in the top quarter of ability do not have a strong desire to go; and motivation for college attendance becomes lower as we go down the scale in intellectual ability. This would bring about 35 percent of the age group into college.
3. *Those in the upper quarter of intellectual ability who possess a strong and clear motivation for college education.* Again, taking account of the facts of motivation for college-going, this proposal would bring at the most 15 percent of the age group into college and would graduate about 12 percent.

The situation in 1965 was close to the second of these alternatives. About 37 percent of the age group entered college; many dropped out after one or two years, and approximately 18 percent graduated with a bachelor's degree after four years.

The Socioeconomic Functions of Colleges and Universities

During the twentieth century colleges and universities in the United States have grown rapidly in order to keep pace with the development of a modern economy.

The modern technological society depends on the work of a large number of people in such occupations as research chemist, industrial engineer, accountant, laboratory technician, nurse, physician, teacher, banker, and specialist on computing machines. These are called "tertiary occupations" to distinguish them from the primary occupations of agriculture and mining and the secondary occupations of manufacturing and construction. They are service occupations in which the worker receives a salary or fee rather than an hourly or weekly wage, or profits.

Table 4.3 shows how these occupations have increased since 1910 in the United States and how they will probably increase during the next two decades. In this table it can be seen that the biggest increases are in categories 2 and 3, where most of the tertiary occupations are located, and in category 6, which contains factory workers. This increase has been paralleled by decreases in the number of unskilled workers. The important thing about the changes in the occupational distributions shown in Table 4.3 is that the occupations of categories 2 and 3, which are growing rapidly, require a college education, or at least a secondary school education; while those that have been decreasing in numbers do not require formal schooling.

Schultz (1961) attributes a large part of the economic growth of the United States to the increased knowledge and skill obtained through education by the people in the working force. He believes that, in expanding per capita production, the development of human capital through education is as important or more important than the development of physical capital such as factories, steel mills, power plants, and highways. The college and university may be seen as an investment made by a modern society with the aim of increasing economic production.

Since about 1920 the colleges of the country have been increasingly regarded by business and industry as agencies for recruiting and training the people who will occupy their most important positions. Major

Table 4.3   Occupational Distribution in the United States, 1910–1980

Occupational Class	Percent of Males					Percent of Females			
	1910	1930	1950	1960	1980	1910	1930	1950	1980
1. Architects, physicians, lawyers, etc.	1.2	1.5	1.4	1.5	1.5	0.2	0.4	0.3	0.4
2. Proprietors, officials, and managers in manufacturing; bankers, stockbrokers, engineers, scientists, clergymen, college teachers, state and federal government officials, etc.	11.9	11.5	17.4	19.0	23.0	13.1	16.8	15.1	15.0
3. School teachers, musicians, other professions, trained nurses, real estate and insurance agents, retail merchants, salesmen, city and county officials, other proprietors and managers, semi-professional occupations, owners of large farms, etc.	2.4	2.7	4.8	6.5	9.0	0.9	1.6	1.9	2.0
Sub-total of Classes 1, 2, 3	15.5	15.7	23.6	27.0	33.5	14.2	18.8	17.3	17.4
4. Clerks and salespeople in offices and stores, stenographers, foremen, locomotive engineers, restaurant and tavern owners, owners of medium-sized farms, etc.	17.2	19.4	15.8	15.0	14.5	16.9	31.6	35.2	35.1
5. Skilled workers, policemen, firemen, mail clerks and carriers, delivery men, cooks, farmers with mortgages, small farm owners, tenant farmers, etc.	25.2	25.6	24.7	23.5	19.5	18.3	11.7	7.3	7.0
6. Semi-skilled workers, factory operatives, truck drivers, miners, etc.	18.0	18.8	29.5	28.5	27.5	15.7	18.6	30.5	30.5
7. Unskilled laborers, farm laborers, domestic workers, etc.	24.1	20.7	6.5	6.0	5.0	34.9	19.4	9.8	10.0

Source: Havighurst, 1960. This table represents ages 21–44 for 1910 and ages 25–34 for the later years. It is based on analysis of census data and on projections of the labor force published by the U.S. Bureau of Labor Statistics.

corporations maintain a corps of "talent scouts" who visit colleges and universities to find and employ the young men and women who will carry on the technological development of the society. The highly educated person has become the central figure and the principal resource of modern society.

The vast and rapid economic growth of the United States has been both the cause and the result of the vast expansion of secondary and higher education during the twentieth century. At the same time, the expansion of education and of the economy has made possible a very large degree of upward social mobility. Working-class youth have made a major and increasing use of secondary and higher education as a means of achieving economic advancement. The selective process in American secondary schools and colleges has worked to recruit very large numbers of poor but able youth and to promote them into a new American elite.

Manpower Needs and College Enrollment in the Future

Technology and economic growth have required expansion of secondary and of higher education; and in accordance with those demands, rates of college enrollments have risen sharply. But will the technology of the next twenty years require further expansion of college enrollments from the 1965 level? This question is very frequently discussed at present, and two points of view on the subject have emerged. Both assume some further expansion of college enrollments, but they differ with regard to the degree of growth that may be expected.

THE EXPANSIONIST VIEW. This view is that the rate of increase of college enrollments that existed during the 1960's will continue for another ten or even twenty years. Projecting this rate into the future, we can estimate that enrollments which rose from 3.6 million in 1960 to 5 million in 1965, will go to 7 million in 1970, and 9 million in 1980. This increase consists partly of an increase in the *proportion* of the age group who go to college and partly of increases in the *number* of people within an age group, the latter, in turn, due to increase of the birthrate between 1940 and 1950.

When asked how the American labor force can continue its increasing intake of college graduates between 1960 and 1970 (as is implied by a doubling of the college enrollment), the expansionist answers that the economic growth of the country will create many more new middle-class positions in the labor force; and that, in any case, a college education will be a good thing for a larger part of the population even though its members may not all secure middle-class jobs. The expansionist says that some college education will make a better citizen out of a garage mechanic or a service-station operator, even though his job does not specifically require it.

McConnell, an effective spokesman for the expansionist group, states:

> Educators might as well face the fundamental fact that it will not be up to them alone to determine how many young people will go to college in the future. In the long run, society will make that decision. In the United States the decision will be to educate the many rather than the few, to send a greater percentage rather than a smaller one to some kind of higher institution. Mass education is here to stay. American higher education will become more rather than less inclusive. This means that the educational system will have to serve an enormously diverse population, a student body certainly no less heterogeneous than the one we have now. (McConnell, 1962, p. 18.)

A CONSERVATIVE VIEW. It is possible to compare these figures on college enrollments with figures regarding the demand for college graduates in the labor force, with the latter based on the projections shown in Table 4.3. Havighurst (1960) has published a comparison of this type. Although the comparison rests upon several assumptions which may prove to be in error, a more conservative estimate of future college enrollments leads to the prediction that the supply of college graduates will slightly exceed the labor-force demand for them after about 1965. (If the expansionist estimate of college enrollments is used, the supply of college graduates will far exceed the labor-force demand for them.)

Consideration of these facts and these estimates raises some serious questions about college enrollment policies for the coming two decades. In the past the policy of rapid expansion of college enrollments has been encouraged by the needs in the American economy for more college graduates. This policy has worked quite successfully in the opinion of most educators and social philosophers. Some critics have argued that the intellectual standards of American colleges have been dangerously lowered by these practices. Others have argued that, although it is possible for mediocre students to enter certain colleges in the United States and to graduate with relatively low quality of work, the best American college students do as good or better quality work than the best university students in any other country.

The fact that the educational system is a system of selection for positions of higher social and economic status makes it advisable to gear the selecting machinery to meet the capacity of the social structure. If too few people are selected and promoted through the educational system, the upper levels of the society will be filled in other ways, perhaps by people who are not well equipped by skill and training for these positions. If too many people are selected and pushed up through the educational system, competition for the higher-level jobs will become intense; some people will have to take positions below the level for which they have been trained; and this will create dissatisfaction with the social order.

Increasing Selectivity in College Admissions

Whatever may be the attitude of educators and of the public concerning college enrollment policy, it became clear in the late 1950's and early 1960's that competition for entrance to the more favored colleges was increasing, and that colleges were becoming more selective in their entrance requirements. The reasons were the increasing numbers of young people of college age and the rising cost of maintaining a college. These factors operated to keep private colleges from expanding to any great degree and forced public-supported institutions to take most of the increased enrollment. Although it is possible for any boy or girl who has average ability to get into a college, it is much more difficult than formerly for the person with average ability to get into one of the growing number of selective colleges. Even the state universities are establishing strict entrance requirements, whereas most of them in 1940 were admitting any student in the state who had a high school diploma.

The end result of the increasing selectivity, if it is intensified, may be to create a kind of bimodal distribution of higher institutions. In one group there will be the more selective private colleges and universities, whose students average at about the 85th percentile or above on scholastic aptitude. There will be a few students in these colleges whose intellectual abilities are only average for all college students, but who have other special abilities which make them desirable. In the other, larger group, will be most of the state and municipal colleges and universities, together with the less selective private institutions. Their students will average between the 60th and 70th percentile in scholastic aptitude, with no more than 15 or 20 percent of them above the mean of students in the more selective institutions.

Admission Criteria

Selectivity is being stepped up at present by two devices. First, the scholastic-aptitude and academic-achievement requirements are being pushed upward by the selective colleges and universities. Second, tuition fees and cost-of-living expenses are rising.

If these methods were to continue without being compensated for in any way, the college students of the late 1960's would be drawn increasingly from the upper half of high school graduates in terms of academic ability and socioeconomic status. (During the 1950's there were compensations for these trends. Due to the rising real income of working-class families, the veterans' educational-benefit programs, and the substantial scholarship programs funded with government and private money, the socioeconomic distribution of college students was pushed down, rather than up. At the same time, the average scholastic aptitude of entering college students was not raised.)

Selection of students from among large numbers of applicants requires a value judgment as to what kinds of students are desirable in the composition of a given college, and what kinds of people in general should go to college. The use of aptitude and achievement tests represents one kind of value judgment. Another value is served by selecting the "rounded man" college applicant. In the latter case, the candidate's non-intellectual interests and talents are given weight, and the candidate may be given preference because of his activities in music, creative art, or writing, or because of his leadership in student affairs. Some colleges are likely to select students with specific personality patterns, such as liberalism, or scientific abilities, or aesthetic interests.

One of the principal issues concerning college admission will probably have to do with policy toward boys and girls from working-class families, Negro or white, whose scholastic aptitude and rank in high school class tend to be depressed by their lack of cultural privileges at home. These students will have increasing difficulty in gaining admission to the more highly selective colleges unless these colleges develop deliberate policies of favoring a number of such applicants over others who come from more privileged homes and who have superior academic records.

The question will probably remain, also, of differential admission policies for students from certain minority groups. Some colleges will deliberately encourage Negro students, while others will discourage them. The question of admission policy with respect to numbers of Jewish students will probably remain a live issue.

The question, Who should go to college? is a complicated one because the colleges have several functions to perform for society—to maintain social stability, yet to promote social fluidity; to aid economic growth, yet to enhance non-economic values.

The 1965–1970 Crisis

The answers to the questions—How many should go to college? and Who should go to college?—are being worked out in the critical 1965–1970 period primarily by the national Congress and the state legislatures, because it is clear that privately supported colleges and universities cannot meet the growing demand for higher education.

The demand is due partly to the needs of the labor force for increasing proportions of college-trained people; partly to the increasing desire of American parents to send their children to college; and partly to the sharp increase of college-age youth resulting from the rise of the birthrate after World War II. (The latter topic is discussed in Chapter 12.) The numbers of youth in the age group from 18 through 21 will increase from 11.2 million in 1964 to 14.4 million in 1969, and then increase more slowly. If the proportion of young people in college is not reduced between 1965 and 1970, the colleges must expand at least 30 percent.

For the minimum expansion of 30 percent (which is needed merely to maintain the present proportional level of college attendance) the state legislatures and the national Congress are appropriating hundreds of million dollars annually. These appropriations are being made for the most part on the assumption that the students now in college, who are mainly from middle-class families, will be able to pay their way with the same extent of help from scholarship and loan funds as was available in the early 1960's.

If the *proportions* of youth who attend college are to be increased, however, there must be substantial scholarship funds, loan funds, and building of colleges in the home towns of the students. These additional students will generally have little or no financial support from their families, and they will need a great deal of encouragement.

The Higher Education Act of 1965

The Higher Education Act of 1965 placed the federal government squarely in the position of the major resource for student support. The government first came into the student assistance field in 1959 with loans under the National Defense Education Act. Added to this was government-financed employment in a work-study program on socially useful projects under the Economic Opportunity Act of 1964. The 1965 Act also provided federal-supported scholarships for undergraduate students, an innovation which had been debated for some years earlier. (The federal government has provided stipends or scholarships for certain categories of graduate students since about 1955.)

According to estimates presented by government officials to the U.S. Congress (1965) the new scholarship program will aid about 140,000 students once it becomes fully operative. The number may go up to 200,000 students after a few years. The total number of full-time undergraduate students receiving some form of financial assistance was estimated at 1.4 million in 1966, out of approximately 4.6 million full-time undergraduate students. For 1963–64, it was estimated that 24 percent of undergraduate students received some form of financial assistance. The federally-supported work-study program and the new scholarships were estimated to add about 6 percent of the total college age group to the numbers receiving assistance in 1966. Table 4.4 shows the data on student financial assistance from federal, state, and college sources.

It was anticipated by Congress that the new undergraduate scholarships would go principally to young people who could not otherwise attend college. The scholarships would range from $200 to $800 per year and be limited to students from low-income families. They would need to earn money in addition, or to borrow money, unless they were living at home and attending a tuition-free college. The Congress and the colleges are watching the situation closely to find out whether this procedure will actually increase the proportion of young people going to college or if it will simply make it easier for some of them to attend college who would get there anyway.

In effect, the Higher Education Act of 1965 says that it shall be public policy to increase the college attendance rate by 5 or 6 percent of the college-age group, the new students being intellectually able but financially poor.

Table 4.4   Undergraduate Student Financial Assistance in 1966

	No. of Students Served	*Net No. Allowing for Packaging**
Federal Govt. Programs		
National Defense Education Act loans	450,000	
College work-study	300,000	
Undergraduate scholarships	140,000	
Total	890,000	590,000
State Govt. Programs		
Guaranteed loans	79,000	
Scholarships and grants	225,000	
Total	304,000	179,000
College and University Programs		
Loans	175,000	
Student employment	435,000	
Scholarships	425,000	
Total	1,035,000	650,000
GRAND TOTAL		1,419,000

* "Packaging" is a combination of types of assistance used by a student.

Source: United States 89th Congress: *Hearings on the Higher Education Act of 1965.* Exhibit 15, p. 107.

Scholarships and Social Fluidity

The extent to which scholarships and loans promote social fluidity depends on the extent to which financial need, as well as ability, is taken into consideration. A considerable proportion of scholarship awards made before 1955 went to middle-class youth who would have gone to college anyway. The winner of a Harvard National Scholarship, for example, was often an upper-middle-class boy who used the scholarship to go to Harvard instead of to his own state university where the expenses would have been less.

The scholarship award situation changed slowly during the 1950's, as major scholarship funds began to stress the policy of aiding youth who needed financial help. By 1960 a concerted effort was being made to award scholarships on the basis of family income. The National Merit

Scholarship Corporation awarded its scholarships on the basis of ability, but regulated the amount of the award according to the student's family income, with students from wealthy homes getting a Scholarship Certificate which had no money value. The colleges which offered the most valuable scholarships introduced the practice of requiring the parent of a scholarship applicant to fill out a form indicating the amount of his current income, the value of his insurance, capital assets, etc. As a result, very few students from families whose incomes were over $10,-000 were given scholarships of much value, and the majority of awards went to young people from lower-middle-class families whose incomes were at or slightly above the median level for all American families.

Data from the National Merit Scholarship Corporation on the family incomes of the 12,418 finalists who graduated from high school in 1964 throw some light on the effects of a highly selective scholarship program on educational opportunity for youth of low-income families. Nichols (1965) reported that Merit Finalists numbered 0.6 percent of high school graduates in 1964. Of this group, 1.8 percent reported family incomes less than $3,000; 3.8 percent less than $4,000; 11.1 percent reported less than $6,000; and 22.9 percent reported less than $8,000. The median family income in the United States was about $6,000. Thus about 1,300 young people from families below the median income won Merit Scholarships. Eighty-nine percent of the scholarships went to boys or girls from families with income above the median. Many of them were awarded only a token stipend because they did not need the money.

Financial Resources

The crisis in higher education is being met by major outlays by state and federal governments. The cost of operating the 2,150 colleges and universities is met from three major sources: in 1962, students paid 25 percent of the cost in tuition fees; voluntary gifts and endowment income accounted for about 12 percent; and government—city, state, and federal—paid the remaining 63 percent.

More than double the 1962 outlay of money is required by 1970 if higher education is to expand to keep pace with the demand. The American Council on Education, representing both private- and public-supported colleges and universities, issued a statement in 1961 calling on the federal government to pay for a part of this expansion. The recommendations of the Council were:

1. The Federal Government can and should provide greater financial assistance to approved institutions of higher learning for expansion and improvement of facilities.
2. The Federal Government can and should provide greater assistance in increasing the supply and improving the quality of college teachers.
3. The Federal Government can and should provide greater assistance in removing financial barriers to higher education for qualified students.

The Higher Education Act of 1965 was at least a partial response to these recommendations.

Exercises

1. Select a college you know. Analyze the student body in terms of socioeconomic backgrounds. What is the relation of socioeconomic background to fraternity membership, participation in athletics, scholarship awards, participation in church organizations, and enrollment in various curricula or courses of study?

2. Of the four factors which determine whether or not a person shall go to college, which ones can be most easily changed in your home community? How would you go about changing them?

3. To what extent do you believe that there is danger of too many people going to college in the United States? What arguments can you use to support your position?

4. Suppose you were counseling a high school boy of about 110 IQ, who was not certain whether or not he should go to college. What advice would you give him, and how would you support your argument?

5. Assume that the state university and the private colleges of your state will receive applications for admission from 100 percent more youth in 1970 than in 1955. Suppose you were a member of a State Commission on Higher Education. What admission policies would you favor for the private colleges? For the state university? Why?

Suggestions for Further Reading

1. For an understanding of the present manpower needs and manpower shortages in the United States and how education might be brought to bear on this situation, read *America's Resources of Specialized Talent*

by Dael Wolfle or *Manpower and Education* by the Educational Policies Commission, National Education Association, and *Womanpower,* by the National Manpower Council. See also *Occupational Planning for Women* by Marguerite W. Zapoleon; and *Cybernation: The Silent Conquest* by Donald Michael.

2. For further consideration of the student composition of American colleges in relation to American social ideals, read *Who Should Go To College?* by Byron S. Hollinshead.

3. There have been a number of recent studies of the nature of college students and their motivation for attending college. Some of these are: *The American College* edited by Nevitt Sanford; *Who Goes to College?* by Ralph Berdie *et al.; A General Pattern for American Higher Education* by T. R. McConnell; *Factors Affecting Admission of High School Seniors* by Elmo Roper; *Changing Values in College* by Philip E. Jacob; and *Encouraging Scientific Talent* by Charles C. Cole, Jr.

4. A useful set of readings on the relations between technological change, social change, and educational change, *Education, Economy, and Society,* has been edited by A. H. Halsey, Jean Floud, and C. Arnold Anderson.

5. For a recent and thoughtful book addressed to the problem of how standards of excellence can be achieved in a democratic society which subscribes to equalitarianism ("everyone has a right to go to college"), read John W. Gardner's book, *Excellence.*

6. Bernard Berelson's *Graduate Education in the United States* is a readable book which describes the history of graduate education, the issues that have developed through time, and those that are currently controversial. (Included also is a discussion of the problems surrounding the preparation of college teachers.)

PART 2

THE SCHOOL AS A
SOCIALIZING AGENCY

5 / Socialization and the Child's Social Life Space

In the first section of this book we focused attention upon the social structure of the society and upon the way the school functions within the social structure to promote both social stability and social mobility.

In this section we move to the function of the school as a socializing agency in the life of the child, and give attention to ways in which the school relates to other socializing agencies, particularly the family and the peer group, in molding the behavior of the child and in providing him the experiences by which he gradually learns to take his place in the society as a participating member.

The Influence of the Social Environment

The mind and the personality of the child develop, not according to immutable processes inherent in the child's genetic endowment, but according to the influences that particular social experiences have upon him. While normal development of mind and personality requires a normal physique (body, brain, and nervous system), the kinds of intellectual and social traits that develop depend primarily upon the interaction between the social environment and the child's biological potentials, upon what the child learns, and upon what he experiences from social interaction.

The effect of the social environment upon the child's social development may perhaps be highlighted by asking, "How would a child behave if he had been deprived of interaction with other human beings?"

The question is an academic one, of course, since human beings die in infancy unless they are cared for by other people and we cannot observe behavior that has not been socially influenced. It is true that there have been occasional cases reported in various parts of the world of children reared by animals, but it is not likely that these reports are valid. They have probably been devised to explain what appeared to be "non-human" behavior in children who were severely retarded intellectually or severely disturbed mentally (Bettelheim, 1959).

Effects of Social Isolation

There is other evidence, however, pointing to the conclusion that very little of the behavior that is regarded as "human" would develop if a child were raised in social isolation. One illustration, while less dramatic than others that have been reported, is of special interest because the abnormal behavior was corrected. It is therefore certain that neither feeble-mindedness nor psychosis was the cause of the "non-human" behavior. The case has been described by the sociologist, Kinsley Davis:

A girl, Isabelle, who was discovered in November, 1938, was judged to be approximately six and a half years of age. She was an illegitimate child who had been kept in seclusion for that reason. Her mother was a deaf-mute, and she and Isabelle had spent most of their time together in a dark room shut off from the rest of the family. As a result Isabelle had no chance to develop speech, but communicated with her mother by means of gestures. When first seen by professional persons, her behavior was described as almost that of a wild animal. She showed great fear and hostility; and instead of speech she made only a strange croaking sound. At first it was even hard to tell whether or not she could hear, since many of her actions resembled those of deaf children. She was thought to be feeble-minded and the general impression was that she was wholly uneducable.

Yet the individuals in charge of Isabelle removed her from her home and launched a program of training. "The approach had to be through pantomime and dramatization, suitable to an infant. It required one week of intensive effort before she even made her first attempt at vocalization. Gradually she began to respond, however, and after the first hurdles had at last been overcome, a curious thing happened. She went through the usual stages of learning characteristic of the years from one to six not only in proper succession but far more rapidly than normal. In a little over two months after her first vocalization she was putting sentences together. Nine months after that she could identify words and sentences on the printed page, could write well, could add to ten, and could retell a story after hearing it. Seven months beyond this point she had a vocabulary of 1,500–2,000 words and was asking complicated questions. Starting from an educational level of between one and three years, she had reached a normal level by the time she was eight and a half years old. In short, she covered in two years the stages of learning that ordinarily require six. Or, to put it another way, her I.Q. trebled in a year and a half. . . . Today she is over fourteen years old and has passed the sixth grade in a public school. Her teachers say that she participates in all school activities as normally as other children. Though older than her classmates, she has fortunately not physically matured too far beyond their level" (Davis, 1947, pp. 436–437).

Cases such as Isabelle's provide evidence that the individual becomes "human" as a result of his social relationships. Without an opportunity to live with other people, his human potentialities remain unrealized.

The typical child, from the very moment of his birth, is continually influenced by the society of which he is a member and by the ways of life of the people around him. A newborn infant may be washed in water, or rubbed with oil; he may be placed at once at the mother's breast, or he may be whisked away to an antiseptic nursery. These immediate experiences, like most of his experiences to follow, are determined by the society and the culture into which he is born. The child's social experiences, in turn, are crucial in forming his behavior and in influencing his personal and social development. How the child handles his body, his posture, gesture, and gait; how he thinks and talks; how he expresses his emotions; how he relates to other people; all these are learned behaviors, and they are learned as a result of social interaction.

Socialization

There are two major aspects of social development that are of special importance to educators. The first is the general process of social learning, whereby the child learns all the many things he must know and all the things he must do or not do to become an acceptable member of society. We refer to this process as the socialization process; we say that the child is gradually "socialized" (that is, he becomes a member of the group and takes on the ways of life that are the group's ways); and we say that society, through its agents (parents, teachers, and other persons), acts to "socialize" the child.

The second aspect of social development is the formation of social values and social loyalties in the child: his feeling of allegiance to the various groups of which he is a member; his desire to collaborate with others; and the merging of his self-interest with group-interest.

Social Learning

Biologically the human organism is predisposed toward social living and social learning. Because of his biological immaturity and his long-extended growth period, the infant is dependent upon other people. The human organism is also characterized by adaptability and by intelligence; by the ability to learn a great variety of modes of behavior, to benefit from experience, to change and to organize behavior in countless ways. Indeed, it is this great adaptability that makes the human infant different from the animal infant.

The human infant is capable of learning any one of a great variety of cultures and subcultures. Any child born and reared in America learns the general American culture, but he also learns the particular customs and values of his group. Thus the child born to a Protestant family learns something different from the child born to a Catholic or Jewish family; the child of Polish immigrants learns something different from the child of Mexican immigrants; and the child born into an upper-class family learns different behaviors and attitudes from those of a child born into a working-class family.

The Socialization Process

Socialization has facetiously been referred to as the lifelong process of "housebreaking." While the term is often applied to learning experiences that occur within the first years of life, to patterns of feeding, sleeping, toilet-training, control of aggression, and sexuality, it is more accurate to think of socialization as a lifelong process. The child who learns in school how to read and write, the adolescent who learns to speak the slang used by his peers, the woman who learns how to behave as a mother and the man who, at 65, learns how to retire from work "gracefully" are all being socialized. Various social groups constantly provide new learning situations and expect new responses from the individual; all through life the individual is constantly fitting his behavior to social expectations.

While the term "housebreaking" is in some ways applicable to the socialization process, it serves to highlight only one aspect of the process, for it implies that socialization is a matter of controlling, restricting, or hindering the child's behavior. Socialization has also active and constructive aspects; it produces growth; it encourages, nurtures, stimulates and motivates; it produces an infinite variety of desires and strivings in the individual; it leads to development and to achievement of all kinds.

Socialization is thus both a molding and a creating process, in which the culture of the group is brought to bear upon the infant, and in which the individual's thought, feeling, and behavior gradually develop in accordance with the values set by the social groups to which he belongs.

Social Roles

Utilizing various processes of social learning, every individual becomes socialized by learning a set of social roles. A social role may be defined as a coherent pattern of behavior common to all persons who fill the same position or place in society and a pattern of behavior *expected* by the other members of society. The pattern may be described without reference to the particular individuals who fill the role. Thus, for example, all women behave in certain patterned ways when they fill the role of mother, so we speak of the social role of mother. All teachers are expected to behave in certain ways within the school room, regardless of how they may behave when school is over and when they are filling other roles such as father or mother, husband or wife, friend, or church member.

The growing child takes on a series of social roles and incorporates the expected behavior into his personality. A very young child learns first how to behave in the role of child; he learns that his parents take care of him and make decisions for him; that he may behave in certain ways, but not in other ways. Soon he learns to differentiate other social roles: that of brother or sister, then playmate, then pupil.

As he grows older and as his circle of social interactions widens in scope, he takes on an ever-increasing number of social roles and incorporates the role behaviors into his personality. (See Figure 5.1.) In this sense, the social self consists, in large part, of the behavior the individual expresses in his various social roles. In this sense, too, the

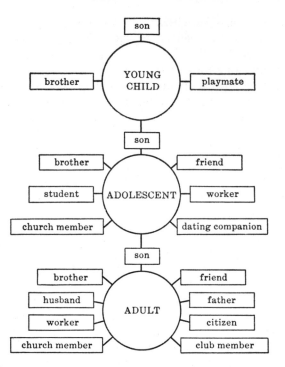

Figure 5.1 Social roles increase with age.

well-socialized individual is one who fills his various roles successfully. While every person has his idiosyncratic pattern of role behaviors (thus no two persons fill the role of teacher in exactly the same ways), still the well-socialized person is one whose behaviors are appropriate to the expectations set by the social groups with which he interacts.

Socializing Agencies

The major socializing agencies in the life of the child are the family, the peer group, the school, the church, the youth-serving organizations, political and economic institutions, and the mass media. Some of these agencies are formal and some informal. The school is an example of an agency formally organized for the purpose of inducting the child into his society; the peer group is an example of an agency that is informally organized. Before looking more closely at each of these agencies and the ways they interrelate, let us look further at the general course of socialization, especially with regard to the timing of significant experiences in intellectual growth.

Socialization in the Early Years of Life

Although individuals keep learning new ways of behavior all through their lives, it is also true that early learnings tend to be crucial ones because they set the pattern for subsequent learnings.

Educators in particular have long been concerned with the timing of different kinds of socialization: at what age, for example, the child is "ready" to be taught to read; whether there are natural sequences that should be followed in providing particular learning experiences; how much can early experience be "undone" by specially-planned education or retraining; at what point in the child's development are certain types of teaching most strategic or most economical in achieving desired educational outcomes. These questions have taken on new urgency in recent years as, on the one hand, educators and social scientists seek new ways of producing excellence in young people who pursue intellectual and scientific careers; and, on the other hand, as the educational system has been increasingly urged to provide "compensatory" education for disadvantaged groups in the society.

There has been an upsurge of research in child psychology and child development with regard to growth in cognition, curiosity behavior, and creativity, and with the effects of early stimulation upon cognitive development. At the same time there has been a great multiplication of educational experiments in schools all over the country. To take but one example, the program called "Head Start," initiated in 1965, in which special educational opportunities are being provided to four-year-olds of poor socioeconomic background, is predicated on the assumption that, to have maximum effects upon subsequent intellectual development, it is important to enrich the experiential environments of children as early as possible. Some educators question this approach, on grounds that perhaps more can be accomplished if special educational experiences are provided at later ages when children are more mature and presumably more able to benefit.

Still others point out that the quality of the social environment is important at both early and later years of the child's life, and that special enriched programs at the preschool level need to be followed by special programs in successive school years. For example, a number of investigators who have worked with children of preschool age (Deutsch, 1965; Gray and Klaus, 1965; and others) have produced improvement in intellectual and cognitive behavior, but the problem lies in maintaining this improvement and preventing fall-back, as when children who have had compensatory educational opportunities are returned to traditional school programs at kindergarten or first grade level. As S. M. Miller (1964) has pointed out: "Preschool programs should not be used as a substitute for interventions at later stages of the school life-cycle. The best guess today is that interventions at the later stages can be effective without interventions at the early, but that interventions at the early stages without intervention at the later will have very limited payoff."

It is too soon to evaluate the outcomes of such educational experiments as Head Start, or to settle the differences in opinion just described, but outside the school setting itself evidence is accumulating which points to the overwhelming importance of early socialization upon later development and learning.

Bloom (1964), for example, after analyzing the data from approximately 1,000 different studies dealing with the development of various human characteristics from infancy to adulthood, concluded that variations in the environment have the greatest effect during the early years of life—that is, during the period when the child is growing and changing at his most rapid rate. On many different physical, mental, and social measures the course of development seems relatively fixed after early childhood; and, by implication, drastic changes in environment are required at successive ages if changes in the direction of growth are to be produced. With regard to mental growth, in particular, it is likely that many of the children who in the past were considered "dull" or even retarded were, in effect, made so in early life by restricted environments, to the extent that they were never able to succeed at the tasks expected of normal individuals. To put it another way, we have in the past been prone to blame the effects of heredity without first taking a close look at the effects of environment; and we have been prone to underestimate, in particular, the effects of early environment upon later achievement.

Differences in Early Environments

A dramatic illustration of this point is provided by a recent follow-up of a group of children first studied in the 1930's by Skeels and Dye (1939).

Thirteen infants ranging in age from 7 to 30 months who were considered unfit for adoption because of mental retardation (mean IQ, 64.3) were removed from an orphanage and placed in an institution for the feebleminded. Another group of 12 children who came from comparable family backgrounds but who seemed of better intellectual endowment (mean IQ, 90.0) remained in the orphanage where they were periodically observed and tested. Because there are few follow-up studies of this type yet available and because the findings have been so startling, this study is worth describing in some detail.

The orphanage nursery, as it was being operated prior to the study, was limited to a rather small play room with additional dormitory rooms. . . . The children were cared for by two nurses assisted by one or two girls aged ten to fifteen. . . . Contacts with adults were largely limited to feeding, bathing, dressing, and toilet details. . . . The girls who assisted the nurses accepted the work as a necessary evil and took little personal interest in the children as individuals. Few play materials were available and little attention was given to the teaching of play techniques. The children were seldom out of the nursery room except for short walks for fresh air.

At two years of age the children moved on to "cottages," where thirty to thirty-five children of the same sex under six years of age lived in charge of one matron and three or four untrained girls aged thirteen to fifteen. The waking hours of these children were spent (except during meal times and a little time outdoors) in an average sized room approximately fifteen feet square, a sun porch of similar size, and a cloak room. . . .

The duties falling to the matron were not only those involved in the care of the children but also those related to clothing and cottage maintenance, cleaning, mending, and so forth. . . . With so much responsibility centered on one adult, the result was a necessary regimentation. The children sat down, stood up, and did many things in rows and in unison. They spent considerable time just sitting on chairs for, in addition to the number of children and the matron's limited time, there was the misfortune of inadequate equipment. . . .

The experimental situation in the school for the feebleminded provided quite a different environment. Generally one, and no more than two, of the experimental children were placed in wards that contained only older, brighter girls. The attendants and the older girls became very fond of the child placed in their ward and took great pride in the child's achievement. In fact, there was considerable competition between wards to see which one would have "their baby" walking or talking first. The girls would spend a great deal of time with the children, teaching them to walk, talk, play with toys. . . . They would spend their small allowances to buy them special foods, toys, picture books, and materials for clothing.

Similarly, attendants gave of their time, money, and affection, and during their free hours frequently took the children on excursions, car rides, and trips. In addition, it was the policy of the matron in charge of the girls' school division to single out certain of these children whom she felt were in need of individualization, and permit them to spend a portion of time each day visiting her office. This furnished new experiences, including being singled out and given special attention and affection, new play materials, additional language stimulation, and contacts with other office callers. . . .

The children were sent to the school kindergarten as soon as they could walk. . . . As a part of the school program, the children each morning attended fifteen minute chapel exercises, including group singing and music by the orchestra. The children also attended the dances, school programs, moving pictures, and Sunday chapel services. (Adapted from Skeels and Dye, 1939.)

Findings: The results of this experiment were unexpected. All the experimental children (who had been considered mentally retarded by the trained members of the orphanage staff as well as by a psychiatrist) achieved the normal range of intelligence within 6 to 52 months. The average gain in IQ was 27.5 points, with three children gaining 45 points or more. A year after the experiment ended, two of these children were above average in intelligence and only one had an IQ below 80.

The children who remained in the orphanage, on the other hand, fell increasingly behind in intellectual development. Except for one child who gained 2 IQ points, all suffered losses ranging from 8 to 45 points, with an average loss of 26.2 IQ points. (There was little doubt in the investigators' minds that had the experimental children remained in the orphanage, they would have suffered the same fate.)

The radical improvement in the experimental children cannot, however, be attributed solely to environmental enrichment. Nine children who became greatly attached to one or two adults gained an average of 34 IQ points, while the four children who did not develop close personal attachments to an adult made an average gain of only 14 points. A parent surrogate whom the child learns to love and imitate is apparently an important factor in optimum development.

When these results became known, the orphanage staff made heroic efforts to improve conditions by adding more personnel to the staff, cutting down the numbers of children in the cottages, and initiating a preschool program in the nursery. Nevertheless, the damage to the orphanage group could not be undone; and the differences persisted between the children who had received special attention in infancy and the children who had not.

Follow-up: Twenty-one years later all the children were located and re-studied (Skeels, 1966). Every one of the thirteen children of the experimental group had eventually been placed in a family and was now found to be living a normal life. They had completed, on the average, 12th grade; four had entered college, and one had received a B.A. Eleven had married, and nine of these had children.

In contrast, of the orphanage group (originally the better endowed), one had died in adolescence after prolonged institutionalization for mental retardation, and three others were still inmates of such institutions. One was in a mental hospital. Of the two who had married, one was divorced. In conformity with state law, three girls, classified as retarded, had been sterilized before they had been permitted to leave the institution. On the average, this group had completed less than third grade in school. Half were unemployed; and of those who were working, all but one held the lowest of menial jobs.

While the Skeels findings are dramatic, they should be interpreted cautiously since they do not themselves prove that the effects of early enrichment are permanent. The two groups studied by these investigators were not only different in early childhood experiences, but they were different also with regard to the experiences which intervened between early childhood and the time of follow-up some 20 years later.

As already suggested, the question of the long-term effects of early deprivation or early enrichment is controversial; and there is little clear scientific evidence by which to decide the long-range effects of early childhood education. Still the Skeels findings are in line with other sets of evidence which warrant these conclusions: the child's social and intellectual development is a direct reflection of the environment in which he grows up; the quality of the social environment in the first years of life is of particular importance; it is difficult to overcome the effects of early social and intellectual deprivation on later intellectual development.

The Development of Social Loyalties and Social Values

The case for the significance of early experience is less clear-cut when we move from intellectual development to the development of social values and social loyalties, although the latter also develop throughout life concomitant with socialization itself. In one important sense, the socialization process may be regarded as having been successful when the individual seeks to become a member of groups that are approved by society, when he develops appropriate feelings of belonging, and when he develops allegiance to the various groups of which he is a member. The typical individual, as he goes from childhood to adulthood, develops feelings of loyalty to his family, then to his play group, his church, his school, his ethnic group, his local community, his occupational group, and his nation.

The Bases of Social Loyalties

Feelings of loyalty have their bases in simpler forms of social participation, the processes of communication and collaboration. A normal baby comes to anticipate satisfaction when the mother's voice is heard. Soon, by gesture and by sound, the mother and child develop a language in which they communicate. After a short time, the child not only communicates with the mother, but he collaborates with her, as in feeding and dressing. Out of such rudimentary forms of communication and collaboration the child moves on to more complicated forms, not only in relation to the mother, but also to the father, to siblings, and later to persons outside the family.

The child usually develops affection for those persons who help him to gratify his needs. For such persons the child feels a close bond, a willingness to cooperate, and, eventually, a willingness to make sacrifices for the other person's welfare. Involved also is the process of identification, in which the child tries to *be* another person. There are differing theories regarding the basis for early identification. Some psychologists believe that the young child identifies first with the person who gratifies his needs; others believe the child identifies with the person whose status he envies and who withholds from him the things he wants (Kagen, 1958; Bronfenbrenner, 1960; Burton and Whiting, 1961.) In any case the child imitates, consciously and unconsciously, the behavior of the person with whom he identifies; he takes on that person's attitudes, values, and ideals. As he grows older, the child identifies not only with family members, but with persons outside the family, and identifies his own interests with those persons' interests.

These, then, are the elements from which feelings of group allegiance develop: communication, collaboration, affection, identification, and the merging of one's own interests with those of another.

Expanding Social Allegiances

Having learned to collaborate with others in the family situation, the child moves into the neighborhood play group and into the schoolroom group. Here he learns to communicate and collaborate with age-mates and, if these experiences are satisfying, he develops feelings of loyalty to these groups. This basic pattern repeats itself in more complex forms in the formation of loyalty to church, ethnic group, school, and community.

Social groups build upon this pattern, with or without awareness, in inculcating feelings of loyalty in their members. Formal and informal rituals are used in most social groups to promote feelings of group solidarity. Among age-mates there are the initiations, the secret passwords, and the oaths of loyalty—all of them ceremonies and symbols of social collaboration and identification. Schools have their own symbols and rituals, among them school songs, school colors, school assemblies, convocations, and homecoming day.

Churches have religious holidays, music, holy communion, baptism, and confirmation, as well as the rituals of the weekly services. Fraternal orders such as the Masons, the Elks, the Eagles, and the Knights of Columbus have their symbols, their initiation ceremonies, and their rituals. Our nation celebrates Independence Day, Thanksgiving Day, and Washington's Birthday. We have our national heroes, our patriotic songs, and our pledge of allegiance to the flag.

Loyalty to Secondary Groups

The family, the play group, the school group, and the local church are *primary* groups; that is, groups in which interaction between members is directed. The maturing individual also develops loyalty to *secondary* groups whose members may be spatially separated and who may never meet, but who nevertheless share common experiences and common interests. Occupational groups, ethnic groups, religious groups, political groups, and other national and international groups are examples of secondary groups. A teacher, for example, develops strong feelings of loyalty to the teaching profession, even though he is personally acquainted with only a handful of other teachers. Similarly, an American feels loyal to other Americans.

There has been comparatively little study of how secondary loyalties are developed, but presumably imitation, identification, and rational thought processes become increasingly important with the age of the individual. The socialization of political attitudes in children and adolescents, for example, has been relatively neglected by social scientists; but a study by Hess and Easton (1960) suggests that there is a developmental process in the formation of political attitudes and political loyalties that occurs in early and middle childhood. Attitudes toward figures such as the President may initially be reflections of attitudes toward authority figures in the family. Only later do the images of governmental figures become differentiated as the child gains more knowledge of the functions of various governmental offices and of the particular persons who occupy given offices. The majority of Americans maintain allegiance to the same political party throughout their lives, following the political choices of their parents (Lane, 1959).

Rational and abstract learnings become increasingly important in reinforcing earlier emotional experiences. A teacher (or a lawyer or a doctor) decides that his own welfare and the general welfare are served by promoting his professional group, and thus he forms new stronger feelings of loyalty to this secondary group.

A Contrast in Social Loyalties

These generalizations we have been putting forth may be illuminated by contrasting two classmates, Curt and Roy, and seeing how their socialization experiences within the family and the peer group produced two very different patterns of social development and social allegiances. Although the descriptions do not deal with these boys' experiences in school, the educator may well keep in mind the questions, "What was the school's role? Could or should it have been different?"

Curt and Roy were born in the same midwestern community of about 10,000, in which they later attended school. Both boys had high intelligence. Curt was near the top of the class on the intelligence test; Roy, in the upper 20 percent.

Experience in the family. Curt's father was a minor executive in a factory. Both his parents were very active in community affairs. The county judge said about Curt's father: "He is one of the finest men we have in town. He has an excellent community attitude."

Because of illness, Curt's father was out of work for several years and the family had hard sledding. The parents gave up some of their outside social life. The family drew together and became very close, and the children became rather defensive about family affairs. Curt, the oldest child, was especially sensitive about the family finances, even though he was only ten or twelve at the time.

Curt did a great many things with his father. They used to take long walks together; and during his high school years they hunted and fished together nearly every weekend. On a questionnaire asking about his relations with his family, filled out in his junior year, Curt said that he felt happy at home, and that his parents had confidence in him.

Roy's father was a traveling man. He made a good salary, and Roy, the only child, had plenty of nice clothes and toys. But the father and mother did not get on together. They quarreled a good deal during the brief periods when the father was at home. Finally, when Roy was eight years old, they were divorced. His mother went to work in an office, and she and Roy lived with her older brother and his wife, who were childless.

When Roy was eighteen years old, he was asked by the interviewer to fill out a questionnaire which contained, among other items, the following: "Describe briefly some conditions or situations in which you had a lot of unpleasantness or disappointment." He said, in answer to this, "About the only one I can remember is when my folks separated." When a junior, Roy reported that he had no recreation with his family and did not eat regularly with them. He said they often nagged and were suspicious of him. In his last year in high school, Roy became "fed up" with the nagging he got at home and he moved out, sleeping in the back room of the store where he was employed.

Comparing the two young men, we see a marked contrast in their family experiences. Curt had many satisfactions in his home. Roy, on the other hand, never had much family life. His father dropped out of his life almost completely after he was eight years old. His uncle and aunt treated him impersonally, expecting him to behave like a man, and paying attention to him only when he did something wrong. His mother was busy outside the home.

Curt's experiences with the peer group. Curt was not a particularly sociable boy; in elementary school, he was thought of by his teachers as rather reserved and even sullen. Nevertheless, he got along reasonably well with the other boys, went to Sunday School and Junior League on Sundays, and joined the Boy Scouts when he was twelve. He enjoyed the Scouts a great deal. He worked for merit badges, went to Scout Camp every summer, and continued to be active until he was sixteen. He gradually became more sociable and more popular as he progressed through high school. He joined school clubs, made the football team, and in his senior year was elected president of his class. When the interviewer asked Curt to describe some situations which had been unpleasant, he wrote, "Last year in the junior play. Some of the kids started getting mixed up in their lines so that it was just simply awful. We got in at the wrong time and nothing went right. That was pretty bad and I still remember it."

When asked to describe some things he had done that were fun, he named: "Playing on the football team, class plays, school parties."

Curt became so wrapped up in the life of his peer group that he made a considerable sacrifice to remain with it. He was offered an all-expense scholarship to a very good private school for the last year of high school but he refused this offer because he wanted to finish school with his class.

Roy's experiences with the peer group were very different. As a little boy, he was thought well of by his teachers, and he was quite popular with other boys. He belonged to the same Sunday School class as Curt and joined the Boy Scouts at the same time.

However, he gradually drifted out of the group during his early adolescence. When he was 17 he told the interviewer, "When I was growing up, I used to run around with a bunch of kids, and their folks are respectable and pretty well-to-do and everything, and then I stopped going around with them and began to go around with another bunch of kids that didn't amount to much. My mother can't understand it. She always wants to know why I don't go around with those good kids anymore."

He said he didn't know himself what had been responsible for the change—it just happened. Actually, Roy never joined any group of boys, even a disreputable group. He made a few individual friends, mostly boys with poor reputations, but these boys did not form a cohesive group.

Roy got into trouble with the school authorities when he was about 14 because he would go to the elementary school playground at night and tie knots in the swings so that the little children could not get them down. Later, when he was 16 or 17 he could usually be seen in the evening sitting alone on the steps of stores on the main business street, idly watching the passersby.

By the time he was a junior in high school, Roy had a reputation for being antisocial and unfriendly. He did not belong to any high school organization. On an interest inventory he was the lowest in his class in his liking for both school activities and out-of-school activities. When invited by the interviewer to a picnic she was giving for his class, he said, "I never go to any of the high school social affairs."

The contrast between Curt and Roy is brought out clearly in responses of the two boys to a test of social attitudes. A few of the items (to which students indicated "agree," "disagree," or "uncertain") were these:

STATEMENT

		Curt	Roy
1.	If your homeroom or class decides to do something which they know you do not care to support, you have the right to refuse to help them.	D	A
2.	Students who do not attend the school games, plays, and parties are poor citizens.	A	D
3.	A busy person has the right to refuse to do a job which will benefit a club to which he belongs, but which will not benefit himself.	D	A

4. Students who are not willing to do the minor and somewhat boring tasks to help the school and the teachers are not really good citizens of the school.   A   D
5. A club should not expect you to do tasks which you are not willing to do.   U   A

The interviewer, who liked Roy, once said to him at the close of an interview, "You don't seem like a happy person."

Roy answered, "Well, sometimes I am and sometimes I'm not. But anyway, the way I am now, nobody's going to hurt me any. If they want to treat me okay, all right; if not, all right; it's not going to bother me any. I don't show no consideration for other people—not as much as I should, I guess, but if they want to be nice to me, I'll be nice to them. Otherwise, what difference does it make?"

It is difficult to see Roy collaborating in social groups as he grows older. He has learned to protect himself from what he expects will be hostility or indifference from other people; for he has had few experiences of receiving affection and support from a social group in return for loyalty to that group.

Curt, on the other hand, has a solid foundation of satisfactory experience with family and peer group. He knows what it is to be loved and helped by others in a social group, and he has responded with strong feelings of loyalty. It is likely that Curt will grow up to be a man who believes in his community and who will be ready to make sacrifices for its social welfare.

The Concept of Life Space

From another point of view, socialization can be seen as learning to participate in an ever-expanding social environment. The social environment, in turn, can be viewed in terms of the life space in which a child or an adolescent lives and grows. The concept of life space, as it is used here, involves three different elements: physical space, the objects contained within that space, and the people who inhabit that space. All three elements are socially determined.

For instance, the objects within an individual's life-space are, to a large extent, the products of social living. The chairs and tables, the books and toys, the buildings and automobiles that are present in the child's life-space are the products of the culture and are thus social products. The child learns to use objects in ways defined by his society—chairs are to sit on, not to climb on; books are to be read, not to be chewed. Even the natural objects of the environment are to be used in socially-defined ways. Depending upon the community setting, trees are or are not to be climbed; grass may or may not be walked on; and animals of various kinds may or may not be played with.

The Physical Life Space

From the same point of view, physical space itself takes on socially-defined limits and uses. Thus a child may live in certain rooms in the house, but perhaps not in others. He may, if he grows up in a small town or on a farm, be free to explore hills and fields; or he may, if he grows up in a city, be confined to the backyard or to the block on which he lives. The family, the peer group, the school, the local community, all of them social groups, thus define for the child even the physical aspects of his life-space.

The life space of the growing individual expands—from the crib, to the living room, to the street in front of the house, to the neighborhood, and then to selected streets and areas of the community. From here it enlarges partly through the child's travel experience and partly through his vicarious experience by way of moving pictures, television, magazines, books, maps, and geography lessons.

The child's physical life space may be defined more objectively as the space in which he moves about on his own responsibility, the space that he covers alone or with playmates.

THE SMALL CITY. In a study of the living space of children in a midwestern community of about 6,000 population, called Prairie City, it was found that eleven-year-olds were pretty much limited to their home areas, although the actual area known to the children varied from 10 square blocks to 142. One boy was not only familiar with the routes leading to school, the neighborhood grocery, church, community swimming pool, and the homes of three friends, but in addition, because he delivered newspapers, he was familiar also with a large part of the town. Another boy, with a small life space, knew only the area immediately around his home and the streets leading to a playground, the school, and the store where his brother worked. Half of the eleven-year-old children were familiar only with their home area and the route to school (Volberding, 1948, 1949).

In the same study it was found that boys, on the average, had a physical life space larger than that of girls. The children from the middle-class and working-class homes had about the same size life space, but the children of the lowest socioeconomic class moved about within much smaller areas. The latter was an unexpected finding, since it is generally thought that it is the children of the lowest social class who, less controlled by their parents, "run all over town." Perhaps the explanation is that a considerable number of these children are insecure and intimidated. Even though their parents may not supervise them carefully, they may be fearful of moving far from home, and some of these children lack the enterprise to do so.

THE LARGER CITY. What is true for the small town like Prairie City seems true also in large cities with respect to life-space in relation to social class. While less true now than in former years, it is not unusual today to find a lower-class adolescent in the city, especially a girl, whose whole life has been circumscribed by the local neighborhood in which she has grown up. Middle-class children generally have the wider range at all ages above the primary grades.

In a study of families who live in a large public housing project in Chicago, mothers often reported to the interviewers that their ten-year-olds were not allowed out of the apartment alone, except to go back and forth from school; or they were limited to playing on the small balcony of the apartment. Often these children were not allowed even to play in the playgrounds below, because, as one mother said, "I can't keep my eyes on him all the time, up here on the 10th floor; and he might get into trouble with some of the bad kids that live in this project."

Another mother said, "I tell her she can't walk through this neighborhood. It isn't safe. Especially she is *not* to play in the elevators or on the stairs of this building. That means she can watch television, and she can do her school work, and she can wait for me or her daddy to take her out. Of course I don't get out much because of the younger kids. . . ."

One interviewer reported an extreme case in one of these families: "There are four children all under 5, and a baby. Each time I arrived, all four were lined up on the bed, watching television and not moving. I couldn't get even the oldest one to respond to me, even after several visits and after I tried repeatedly to bribe him with candy. I couldn't lure him from the fixed position on the bed."

Middle-class families, on the other hand, some of whom lived within several blocks of the same housing project, described the activities of their 10-year-olds quite differently.

She has to check in after school, of course, but then she usually goes down the block to play with her friend . . . or else the two get on their bicycles. (Interviewer: Where do they go?) Oh, around the neighborhood. Sometimes they ride over to the lake. They have to stay on the streets, of course, and they have to be home by five o'clock. They don't go into any deserted areas. But they're sensible by this age, and I don't worry. Then one day a week she takes the bus after school and goes to her piano lesson . . . and on Saturdays she goes down to the Art Institute for her art class. . . .

The Social Life Space

As is already clear from this discussion, it is not the physical aspect of the life-space itself, but the objects and the people included in it that are the primary concerns of the educator—the variation or complexity of experiential opportunities, the extent of social and intellectual stimulation provided, and the degree of psychological constraint and freedom. These characteristics vary not only with the age of the child, but also with the family and the type of community.

Constraints Within the Family

The degree of restraint or freedom placed upon the child's life space will vary from one family to the next, and may, as already indicated, be related among other factors to the social class of the family. Maas, for instance, found that lower-class children were subject to rigid parental control and punishment while children from working-class and lower-middle-class homes experienced more flexible and equalitarian relationships within the home, felt more free to disagree with parents, and regarded the world as a more "open" place. The latter children had more self-confidence; the world seemed to them a relatively safe place. On the other hand, the lowest-class children felt less psychological freedom than the others, and in their relations with other people, especially with peers, they tended to retain the excessively dependent relations they had formed earlier with their fathers (Maas, 1951).

We shall have more to say about socialization within the family in the next chapter, but it is clear that the degree of freedom a person perceives in the social world depends on the kind of social relations he has experienced in his family.

The Atmosphere of the Neighborhood

The neighborhood also plays its part. In a village or suburb, the neighborhood is likely to provide a relatively friendly, familiar, and free atmosphere for children. As already illustrated, in a city slum or public housing project, on the other hand, many parents see the neighborhood as containing moral as well as physical dangers for the child. Those neighborhoods in which social disorganization is prevalent—poor housing, transiency, dirty streets and alleys, over-crowding—are the neighborhoods of highest delinquency rates. Many families, like those quoted, fear the effects of the neighborhood upon their children, restrict the child's life space, and keep him under close supervision.

Variation by Type of Community

A child brought up on a farm has a relatively wide physical space to live in, but the life space may be a simple one in social complexity. There are relatively few people, and they may be rather similar in kind.

On the other hand, the life of children in a rural community is likely to be bound up closely with that of the adults; this may provide richness and variation of social experience. For instance, the book *Children of the Cumberland* (Lewis, 1946) describes the life of children in a rural Tennessee community, where the child shares in almost every activity of the adult—work and leisure, household chores, weddings and funerals, church meetings and town meetings. While the life of these children has a placid quality as compared with life in a metropolis, yet their life also has a certain complexity because of the closer relations with adults.

Barker, Wright, and their associates have been engaged in research along these lines of describing the psychological and social environments of children (Barker and Wright, 1954). One of their first studies was reported in the book entitled *One Boy's Day* (Barker and Wright, 1951), where, in a midwestern village of 725 people, Raymond, a seven-year-old boy, was followed through a typical day, from the time he woke in the morning until he went to bed at night. Raymond's physical life space, that day, consisted of nine square blocks, and all his physical movement occurred within a radius of two and a half blocks. He had that day some kind of personal contact with twenty-four adults, and he played, briefly or for a longer time, with twelve children varying in age from one to eleven. In his classroom at school were twenty-seven other pupils, all quite similar to him in religion, skin color, and social class.

Raymond's day may be contrasted with the more varied day of a seven-year-old who lives in a mixed residential area on the south side of Chicago. Jerry walked five blocks to a big school where he was one of a thousand pupils. On the way to school he passed stores, taverns, and restaurants; he crossed a busy street where a policewoman directed traffic. After school his mother took him in the automobile to his friend's home a mile away so that the boys could play together and then downtown to pick up his father. On the way they passed beaches, factories, a railroad roundhouse, a slum area, a new housing project, then the skyscrapers of the Loop.

In this typical day, Jerry experienced a greater variety of objects and physical settings than Raymond. While he probably did not have actual face-to-face dealings with more people than Raymond, the people were more varied. The forty children in his schoolroom, for instance, were of different races, religions, and social classes. There are more social contrasts in his life space than in that of Raymond.

Wright, Deeble and Ragel (1957) found that six- and seven-year-old children in a small town and in a medium-sized city of 23,000 did not differ much with regard to the amount of acquaintance they had with neighborhood families. The older children differed considerably, however. The greatest range of acquaintance was in the children of the small town. The city children were not only less acquainted with neighbors, in general, than small-town children; but, in addition, their acquaintance tended to be more focused upon peers. That is, they knew more about the children and the pets in their neighborhoods than about the adults; and proportionately more so than small-town children.

These findings tend to corroborate the general impression that children in small communities tend to interact with adults and to participate in adult activities more than do children in cities. What this means for the child's psychological and social development is not yet clear. One child may gain added security from knowing his adult neighbors; another may feel less autonomy and freedom as his anonymity becomes less.

COMPARISON OF SMALL TOWNS IN ENGLAND AND IN AMERICA. Not all small towns, of course, will provide the same ecological setting, nor will they have the same effects upon the child's or adolescent's social participations. Barker, for instance, applied his techniques of measurement in a small English town, Yoredale, that was similar in many respects to Midwest, Kansas, the small American town he had studied earlier. He found some striking differences in the extent to which the residents of different ages participated in the social life of the community and in the settings in which social interaction occurred (Barker, 1960). He compared the numbers of people involved in various "behavior settings" (a behavior setting is a place outside the home where certain expected patterns of activities and social interaction take place, even though the particular persons change from one time to another— for example, behavior settings in which residents of Midwest spent relatively great amounts of time are such places as a grocery store, a drug store, the post office, a school classroom, the church, and so on); and compared the extent to which residents of varying ages are engaged in "responsible positions" (a responsible position means a position in a behavior setting that is essential to the effective functioning of the setting—for example, proprietors and clerks of stores, chairmen and soloists at entertainments, presidents and secretaries of clubs, and so on).

Barker found major differences between the American and the English communities. Yoredale's population was 1,300; Midwest's, 700. In proportion to its size, Yoredale had half as many behavior settings as Midwest; and within those settings, fewer responsible positions. In a year's time, Midwest provided and required more than three times as many responsibilities of each of its residents, on the average, as Yoredale required. Particularly striking differences existed with regard to the adolescent age group. Adolescents in Midwest filled 3.5 times as many responsible positions in community settings during a year as did Yoredale adolescents. "On the average, every Midwest adolescent acts in a play, works in a store, teaches a Sunday school class, plays in a basketball league game every three weeks; Yoredale adolescents occupy such positions every eleven weeks." Barker related these findings to the educational system in the following terms:

> The Midwest and Yoredale systems for educating children are congruent with these facts about the settings of the communities. According to the Midwest theory of education, children are prepared for adulthood by participating to the maximum of their abilities in the regular behavior settings of the town along with adults; it is of particular value to children to undertake important and responsible roles even before they can discharge them with complete adequacy. This is exactly what Midwest behavior settings require: personnel to discharge important and responsible functions, even if this is done with considerably less than perfection. School behavior settings are considered important in Midwest education, but they are thought to function best along with regular community settings.

According to the Yoredale theory of education, children are prepared for adulthood by removing them from the community settings and placing them in special, reserved school settings under the direction of experts who, over a period of time, are able to prepare children for entrance to the normal life of the town's behavior settings. School settings are the unique and almost complete means of educating children, and it is one of their particular values that when they are in school behavior settings, children do not disturb community settings until the requisite skills and responsibility have been imparted to them so they can take their parts smoothly. This again is exactly what Yoredale behavior settings are able to require: protection from incompetent personnel, who may disturb the desired smoothness of operation.

It would be extremely difficult to exchange the educational systems of the two towns. Many Midwest community settings which would be crippled by the *removal* of children would in Yoredale be disrupted by their presence. In fact it appears that the towns could not tolerate such a shift without a major transformation in the whole community system. (Barker, 1960, p. 47.)

The School

Except for the allusions to English-American differences in educational theories, we have thus far omitted any direct reference to the school in discussing the child's life space. We shall comment on the school setting, the climate of the classroom, the differences between small and large schools, and other related topics in Chapter 8, "The School as a Social System"; and again, in Chapter 18, "The Teacher in the Classroom."

At this point, however, it may be said that it is the specific job of the school to widen the life space of the child. The school does so first through its curriculum, by teaching the child a whole array of facts about the world he lives in, and by introducing him to the wide variety of skills, both intellectual and social, that are necessary for full participation in society. The school's function in this respect is so taken for granted that we often define education itself in terms of "widening the child's horizons" or of "enlarging the child's view of the world."

Exercises

1. What are some of the goals of socialization in American society? What kinds of personal and social traits would you say our society attempts to produce in its members?

2. Give an example from your own experience (preferably, experience within the classroom) where identification was important in understanding a child's behavior.

3. Select any one group of which you are a member. What are some of the formal or informal ways used by the group to inculcate loyalty in its members?

4. Describe a child whose socialization experiences you regard as inadequate. What can be done to re-socialize him, or to provide compensatory social experience?

5. Describe two school situations that tend to restrict the child's life-space. Be specific. Describe two school situations that tend to enlarge the child's life-space.

6. Ask several children you know (preferably of the same age) to trace on a map the area with which they are familiar. Using crayons, one color can be used for streets covered every day; another color for streets covered as often as once a week; another color for streets and places visited once a month. How much variation do you find from child to child?

7. Ask several children (or adolescents) to write a diary-account of their activities on a typical school day (or a weekend). Ask them to describe everything they do, from the time they get up in the morning to the time they go to bed. Compare their reports for similarities and differences. What insights do you gain concerning the life-space of each child?

Suggestions for Further Reading

1. For a well-written account of the socialization process, read Chapters 6, 7, 8, and 9 in *Child Behavior and Development* by Martin and Stendler. See also the chapter, "Sociological Correlates of Child Behavior," by Clausen and Williams in the NSSE Yearbook, *Child Psychology*.

2. Television, comic books, radio and movies are important aspects of the culture that operate on the child. The chapter by Eleanor Maccoby, "Effects of the Mass Media," in Hoffman and Hoffman's *Review of Child Development Research* is a good overview of this topic.

3. The Negro adolescents described in *Children of Bondage* by Allison Davis and John Dollard were followed up twenty years later and described in an interestingly written book, *The Eighth Generation,* by

John H. Rohrer and Munro S. Edmonson. Problems of identification and identity are stressed throughout.

4. For the full description of one day in the life of a seven-year-old boy (the boy Raymond, mentioned in this chapter), read *One Boy's Day*, by Roger G. Barker and Herbert F. Wright.

5. The book of readings, *Education and Culture*, edited by Spindler, contains a number of interesting selections on the American culture and how it is transmitted to children in the school situation. See especially Chapters 7, 8, and 9 by Spindler and by Lee.

6. For general information and for varying points of view on socially disadvantaged children and the causes of their disadvantage, read Riessman's *The Culturally Deprived Child;* or Bloom's *Stability and Change in Human Characteristics;* or Bloom, Davis and Hess, *Compensatory Education for Cultural Deprivation*. A variety of publications have recently become available describing practicable programs for socially disadvantaged children and youth. Some of these are: "Programs for the Educationally Disadvantaged," U.S. Office of Education; *Promising Practices for the Culturally Deprived*, Great Cities Program for School Improvement; *Educating the Culturally Deprived in the Great Cities*, The Phi Delta Kappan; *Education in Depressed Areas*, edited by Harry Passow.

7. "Adult Status of Children with Contrasting Early Life Experiences" has recently been published as a Monograph by Harold M. Skeels. It is the complete account of the whole study which was cited in this chapter.

6 / The Family and the School

We have said that at birth the child's behavior is not truly "human," but that it becomes so as a result of social interaction and social learning. In the first years of life it is within the family that this "humanizing" proceeds. The family acts to teach the child the culture and subculture. The child not only learns the overt behaviors, he learns also the social, moral, and economic values: how children relate to adults, and how men relate to women; how to curb his aggressiveness and yet to cultivate his competitiveness; how to develop loyalties and how to seek for self-achievement. The overall expectancies and way of life of the group are transmitted through the family. Ethnic, religious, racial, and social groups maintain their differences through time to the extent to which different families provide their offspring with distinctive patterns of thought and action.

The family functions also to "prepare" a child for school and, thereafter, to influence his attitudes toward school.

The Family as a Social Institution

The family as a social institution has undergone marked changes over the past hundred years, changes that are highlighted by the contrast of a frontier family of 1850 with an urban family of today. The frontier family was almost a self-contained unit of economic production. Father, mother, and children shared in the tasks of producing the economic goods and services required by the family. Today the typical urban

149

father works in an office or industrial plant located at some distance from the home; mother and children are not involved in his work; food, clothing, shelter, and most of the other economic goods and services required by the family are produced outside the family setting. The modern urban family remains the unit of economic consumption but is no longer the unit of economic production.

Many frontier families provided all the education their children ever received. Today, formal education, as well as many types of informal education, have been taken over by the school and other agencies. The young child (particularly if he lives in the city) can now learn social skills in the nursery school as well as in the home; the young person is most likely now to learn his vocation in a trade school or professional school, not from a parent nor a master to whom he has been apprenticed.

Even the function of character building, once regarded as the primary responsibility of the family, has been taken on more and more by non-family agencies such as the church, the school, and special youth-serving organizations such as the Boy Scouts and Girl Scouts, the 4-H clubs, Future Farmers of America, the YMCA and YWCA.

The modern family is also characterized by a high degree of mobility, social and geographic. There is a constant attempt to improve the material standards of living, often accompanied by efforts to maintain or improve the social position of the family. There is also a great deal of physical moving about; from one house to another, from one part of the country to another. This geographical transiency is found not only among low socioeconomic groups, such as migrant agricultural workers or Negroes who move from south to north; it is also present to a marked degree among middle-class groups, as witnessed, for example, by the movements of young business executives from one community to another at various stages of their careers, or by the movement of older people from farms to cities and towns, and from cold climates to warm.

Despite the historical changes and the loss of some of its functions, the family has lost none of its importance as the primary socializing agency in the life of the child. It is the individual's first and most influential social system and provides him with his most influential social training situations.

The Family as a Social System

As a social system the family obviously differs markedly from other social systems or social organizations in which an individual participates at various times in his life. Compared with the play group, the school group, or the work organization, the family is a smaller and more closely-knit system; relationships are intimate and face-to-face; the old and young are related in a well-defined hierarchy of status; and while its members will change somewhat through the years, the family provides the individual with a primary group membership that endures throughout his life.

There is great diversity among American families when they are viewed as social systems, and there is no single pattern that characterizes "the" American family.

The modern middle-class family, for example, is becoming increasingly democratic in its relationships, with a growing sense of equality between child and parent and between husband and wife. At the same time the family is a social system in which responsibilities and privileges for each member are well-defined and well-differentiated. Each person fills a definite social role (the role of husband, father, wife, mother, child, or sibling) in which behavior is determined to a large extent by the role expectations established by the large groups to which the family belong. Thus, in the typical German family, at least until very recently, the father was the undisputed authority figure; while in a rural Negro family in America, it was usually the mother who was the authority figure. In many families of low socioeconomic level, the mother shares with the father the role of breadwinner, while an older child may act during the day in the role of mother to the younger siblings.

Social Class Differences in Family Organization

We have indicated that different social classes in America have somewhat different ways of life: different behavior, values, attitudes, different goals and expectations. Nowhere are these differences so clearly seen as within the family setting. The family, furthermore, as compared with other social institutions, is most intimately bound up with the social structure. Not only are class differences clearly reflected in family patterns, but the family reinforces and modifies the social class structure in a direct way. This is true because any given family trains its offspring in its own way of life. While there is much social mobility from one class to another, middle-class families, by and large, train their children in middle-class ways; working-class families train their children to lead working-class lives. Thus our social-class system produces wide variations in family life, and these, in turn, maintain the social-class system.

While the differences in family life between various social classes are many, we shall illustrate only a few. It should not be assumed, from the descriptions to follow, that all families at a given social-class level are alike. There is not only a great range of difference from individual family to individual family; there are also group differences *within* social classes related to ethnic, religious, geographic factors; and differences between families in which the father is employed in an entrepreneurial setting and those in which he is employed in a bureaucratic setting (Miller and Swanson, 1958).

Parental Roles in the Middle-Class Family

The "typical" middle-class family is organized primarily around the father-husband. The family lives where the husband's job dictates (secondarily, where the children's schooling dictates); the father is expected to act, in fact as well as by law, as the custodian over wife and children. As the economic provider, the father is responsible, legally, financially, and morally, for the welfare of other family members—he is the "head of the family." In the words of Talcott Parsons, a leading sociological theorist, the father-husband plays primarily an "instrumental" role in the family. That is to say, he is the person responsible for maintaining the family's position in relation to the outside world, and he copes with the extrafamilial environment (Parsons and Bales, 1955).

There has been a considerable change in the social role of the father within the last several decades, a change which is often described as a decline in role. Absent from the home for the greater part of the day, the father is less involved in the everyday details of child-rearing and child-disciplining than the mother.

To say that the social role of the father is a declining one is not, however, an evaluation of the importance of the father as compared with the mother in the life of the child. The comic-strip, TV, and radio image of the middle-class father as bumbling and ineffective is distorted. The father is a strong identification figure, and his influence in the formation of the child's personality is not to be measured by the actual number of hours he spends in the home. Today's father has less responsibility for discipline; but as he has become less authoritarian in relationship with the child, he has also become a major source of acceptance and affection (Bronfenbrenner, 1961). There is also evidence that it is primarily the behavior of the father, rather than that of the mother, that accounts for the differential effects of parental behavior on the two sexes; and that paternal authority and affection are especially important and salutary for boys (Bronfenbrenner, 1961; Burton and Whiting, 1961; Hoffman, 1961). It is the *social role* of the father, not his psychological influence then, that has declined in urban families over the past hundred years.

It is the wife-mother who bears the responsibility for maintaining integrated relationships within the family, who is primarily concerned with the expression of emotions and discipline—in other words, the one who, in Parsons' terms, plays the "expressive" role (Parsons and Bales, 1955). The role of the wife, furthermore, reflects the general change in the role of women that has been taking place in America over the past hundred years. The greater freedom of women, politically, economically, and socially; their better education; the labor-saving devices in the home and the trend toward outside employment for wives—all these are reflected in the wife's role in our middle-class urban family, where she is increasingly viewed as an equal partner with the husband.

Variations Among Families

We have chosen to focus attention here upon parental roles for, like many other aspects of family life, these roles differ markedly from one social-class level to another as well as from one ethnic or religious group to another. As we shall see, differences in parental roles bear directly upon the school.

We have already described some of the other variations in family life when in Chapter 1 we described different social classes. In Chapter 9 there are descriptions of family patterns as they are found in an upper-middle-class suburb (Crestwood Heights); a working- and lower-middle-class suburb of mixed ethnic and religious composition (Levittown); and a Puerto Rican lower-class neighborhood in New York City.

The fact that great variations exist in family life in America cannot be over-emphasized; nor the fact that schools face a wide range of different tasks in a wide range of communities. At the same time, a problem of particular urgency to educators is presently that of providing improved education for the so-called "disadvantaged" child of low socioeconomic status, the child found most frequently in the inner city of the metropolitan area and the child who is most frequently Negro. A contrast in parental roles, therefore, can be usefully drawn between the "typical" middle-class family just described and the "typical" Negro working-class family. It must be emphasized that in the description to follow the conditions of family life reflect *social-class* factors, not racial factors *per se*. It happens that most lower-class families in American cities today are Negro, and this fact brings with it certain additional problems of family disorganization due to the particular history of the Negro in America; but the same general conditions prevail in lower-class white families as in lower-class Negro families.

The Negro Working-Class Family

Sociologists throughout this century have made many studies of the Negro in the United States. They have agreed that the Negro family differs in certain important ways from the white American family as well as from the families of various European ethnic groups. To a considerable extent these differences are due to the fact that, under slavery, the Negro family hardly existed. Negro slaves could not legally marry; Negro men and women who were living together could be separated and sold separately, as could their children. There was no legal protection for the family as a unit.

After the emancipation of the slaves, most Negroes continued to live in the rural South, where they developed a simple folk culture and a simple family structure. Women continued to have the dominant role in the family, as they had had before emancipation. The Negro male was greatly restricted in his access to jobs, to rights as a citizen, and to other initiatives exercised by white men.

After World War I and through the 1920's there was a substantial migration of Negroes to the northern cities, and it soon became evident that the working-class Negro family would not stand up as a stable structure in the urban setting. Professor Franklin Frazier, the Negro sociologist, wrote in 1939:

First, it appears that the family which evolved within the isolated world of the Negro folk will become increasingly disorganized. Modern means of communication will break down the isolation of the world of the black folk, and, as long as the bankrupt system of southern agriculture exists, Negro families will continue to seek a living in the towns and cities of the country. They will crowd the slum areas of southern cities or make their way to northern cities where their family life will become disrupted and their poverty will force them to depend upon charity. . . .

The impact of hundreds of thousands of rural southern Negroes upon northern metropolitan communities presents a bewildering spectacle. Striking contrasts in levels among these newcomers to modern civilization seem to baffle any attempt to discover order and direction in their mode of life. (Frazier, 1939, p. 487, p. 298.)

Frazier's prophecy is supported by a mass of facts about Negroes in urban areas. In 1965 for example, a report on the Negro family prepared by a unit of the U.S. Department of Labor, drew attention to a compelling set of facts showing that, while the average white family had achieved a high degree of stability, the family structure of working-class Negroes, by contrast, was highly unstable and in many urban centers was approaching breakdown (U.S. Department of Labor, March, 1965).

The report presented considerable evidence that the Negro community was dividing between a stable middle-class group, that was steadily growing stronger and more successful, and an increasingly disorganized and disadvantaged working-class group.

Thus, nearly a fourth of Negro women living in cities who had ever married were divorced, separated, or living apart from their husbands (the rates were highest in the urban northeast). In the decade between 1950 and 1960, while the proportion of fatherless families held constant for white families, the percent had risen by a sixth for nonwhite families. It was estimated that only a minority of Negro children reaching the age of 18 had lived all their lives with both parents. In 1965, furthermore, fourteen percent of all Negro children were receiving Aid to Dependent Children (public assistance), as compared to two percent of white children; and it was estimated that, over their childhoods, the majority of Negro children were at one point or another on public assistance.

The relative breakdown of the Negro working-class family has been traced historically from the days of slavery through the hazardous periods of the Reconstruction and the appearance of Jim Crowism, to the spread of poverty and unemployment among Negro males, enhanced by urbanization and technological advances in the two decades since World War II, a period during which the economic plight of urban, unskilled and poorly educated Negroes grew steadily worse.

Unemployment and Family Structure

The impact of poverty on family structure is a primary factor, even though the effects of unemployment on the family, and particularly on

the male, are little understood. Unemployment, for whites and nonwhites alike, has on the whole been treated as an economic phenomenon
by social scientists, with almost no recent attention paid to social and
psychological consequences.

In 1940, however, Edward Wight Bakke had described the effects
of unemployment on family structure in terms of six stages of adjustment. Although the families studied were white, the pattern is probably
a general one that applies to Negro families as well.

The first two stages end with the exhaustion of credit and the entry
of the wife into the labor force. The father is no longer the provider and
the elder children become resentful. The third stage is the critical one of
beginning a new day-to-day existence. At this point two women are in
charge:

> Consider the fact that relief investigators or case workers are normally
> women and deal with the housewife. Already suffering a loss in prestige and
> authority in the family because of his failure to be the chief bread winner,
> the male head of the family feels deeply this obvious transfer of planning for
> the family's well-being to two women, one of them an outsider. His role is
> reduced to that of errand boy to and from the relief office. (Bakke, 1940, p.
> 212.)

If the family makes it through this third stage it is likely to survive,
and the rest of the process is one of adjustment. The critical element of
adjustment is not welfare payments, but work.

Work is precisely the thing the Negro family head has not received
over the past generation. In 1963, a prosperous year, 29 percent of all
Negro men in the labor force were unemployed at some time during the
year, almost half of them out of work for 15 weeks or more.

The Department of Labor report cited above documents the relationship between unemployment and increased numbers of marital separa-
tions; and between unemployment and the rate of illegitimate births.
During times when jobs were reasonably plentiful, the Negro family
becomes stronger and more stable. As jobs become more difficult to find,
the stability of the family becomes more and more difficult to maintain.
The facts are well known that in urban areas where there are high rates
of unemployment, illegitimate births, and broken homes, there are also
high rates of school dropouts, juvenile delinquency, and other forms of
social pathology.

FATHER ABSENCE AND SCHOOL PERFORMANCE. We shall return shortly
to a discussion of the relations between family and school, but at this
point it should be pointed out that there seems to be a direct association

between the absence of the father and the child's school performance. Deutsch and Brown (1964) found not only a direct relationship between social class and IQ, as many other studies have shown, but also a relationship between father's presence and school grades *within* social classes. For both girls and boys, the IQ's of children with fathers in the home were higher than those who had no father in the home. Whether or not this is a cause-and-effect relationship is difficult to determine, but as Table 6.1 indicates the actual proportion of nonwhite boys who are enrolled in school is related, at all ages, to whether or not one, both, or neither parent is present in the home. So also, as seen in Table 6.2, the percent of nonwhite boys who are one or more grades retarded in school is related to the presence of the father.

Table 6.1 Percent of Nonwhite Males Enrolled in School, by Age and Presence of Parents, 1960

Age	Both parents present	One parent present	Neither parent present
5 years	41.7	44.2	34.3
6 years	79.3	78.7	73.8
7 to 9 years	96.1	95.3	93.9
10 to 13 years	96.2	95.5	93.0
14 and 15 years	91.8	89.9	85.0
16 and 17 years	78.0	72.7	63.2
18 and 19 years	46.5	40.0	32.3

Source: 1960 Census, *School Enrollment,* PC (2) 5A, table 3, p. 24. Reprinted in U.S. Department of Labor, March, 1965, p. 37.

Table 6.2 Percent of Nonwhite Males Enrolled in School Who Are 1 or More Grades Below Mode for Age, by Age Group and Presence of Parents, 1960

Age group	Both parents present	One parent present	Neither parent present
7–9 years	7.5	7.7	9.6
10–13 years	23.8	25.8	30.6
14–15 years	34.0	36.3	40.9
16–17 years	37.6	40.9	44.1
18–19 years	60.6	65.9	46.1

Source: 1960 Census, *School Enrollment,* PC(2) 5A, table 3, p. 24. Reprinted in U.S. Department of Labor, March, 1965, p. 38.

A final fact will highlight this relationship. In a study of Negro and white dropouts in Connecticut high schools in 1959, it was found that only 29 percent of the Negro male dropouts discussed their decision to drop out of school with their fathers, compared with 65 percent of the white males (38 percent of the Negro males were from broken homes). In fact, 26 percent of the Negro males did not discuss this major decision in their lives with anyone at all, compared with only 8 percent of white males.

Family Preparation for School

In a sense, the family can be said to "launch" the child into the school environment; how well the child will do in school will depend in large part on how well his family has prepared him.

It has long been observed that children from lower socioeconomic groups provide by far the greater share of a school's behavior problems, academic failures, and dropouts. These phenomena were explained away in earlier periods as due, first, to lower native intelligence of these children; and second, to lack of concern on the part of their parents. Today, we know that neither of these explanations is adequate.

Parents of all classes now realize the importance of education; more and more jobs require specific technical skills and a general educational background that will permit people to adapt quickly to technological changes. As late as 1951, Stendler reported that families of the lowest class placed little value upon education; but as the unskilled jobs traditionally held by these people have declined in number, attitudes have changed. Particularly among the poorest Negroes, who have seen opportunities for their race suddenly develop—opportunities now closed to them through lack of education—schooling is becoming highly prized. Unskilled people who would have considered education economically useless only a few years ago are now eager for more education, if not for themselves, for their children.

It became quite clear during the 1960's that a massive effort must be mounted to assist children of low socioeconomic status (and thus, mainly Negro children) to do better in school. The question was not whether or not to make such an effort, but *how* to do it. The answer centered around the relative importance of the family and the school in the mental development of the child.

Factors Which Determine School Achievement

There are four factors which determine the level of achievement of a child in school. One is the inborn ability of the child. Another is the kind of family life or family training he experiences. A third is the quality of the schooling he receives. The fourth is his self-concept or aspiration level which grows out of his family and school experience. After several years of school experience, the child himself can determine how hard he shall work in school and toward what goals.

Inborn or biological differences of intelligence exist, but between individuals, not between large social or racial groups. Inborn differences in intelligence exist among children in a single family; and every school class of 30 children includes 30 different levels of intellectual potential.

Once a child is born the society influences his development in two ways: through the family factor and through the school factor. A very good family experience can operate so that a child with only average inborn ability does well in school. A very good school can operate so that a child with only average innate ability does well; and it can operate also to compensate a child for a poor family background.

Since the late 1950's studies of the relations between family factors and mental development have led to a revision of earlier beliefs about the relative importance of family and school, with greater emphasis being given to the family factor. As already mentioned in the preceding chapter, research on the cognitive development of children summarized by Bloom (1964) points to the family as the major influence and to the preschool years as the crucial ones for mental development.

In recent years efforts have been made to determine some of the specific ways in which different family experiences affect a child's development and behavior; for it is clear that social class differences in these factors are present when the child first enters school. Hess and Shipman (1965) have summed up the results of a number of observations on this problem as follows:

Children from deprived backgrounds score well below middle-class children on standard individual and group measures of intelligence (a gap that increases with age); they come to school without the skills necessary for coping with first grade curricula; their language development, both written and spoken, is relatively poor; auditory and visual discrimination skills are not well developed; in scholastic achievement they are retarded an average of two years by grade six and almost three years by grade eight; they are more likely to drop out of school before completing a secondary education; and even when they have adequate ability, are less likely to go to college. (Hess and Shipman, p. 869.)

The likely explanation for these differences is that different families create environments that influence children's intellectual growth and educational motivation in different ways. Thus, when one parent ignores his child's questions and another parent makes a point of reading to his child every day, the first has created an environment that mitigates against learning; the second, one that promotes further learning.

DIFFERENCES IN LANGUAGE ENVIRONMENT. The presence or absence of adequate parental techniques for helping the child understand his world or cope with complex situations may have permanent effects. Bernstein (1961, 1962) has analyzed the language used by working-class and by middle-class children, and he has found considerable differences. Children of both classes learn adequately the language of ordinary conversation, which is grammatically simple, uses stereotyped expressions, and does not permit precise statement of ideas or emotions, but relies upon gestures, inflection, and further explanation to make meaning clear. Bernstein calls this language "public," or "restricted." Middle-class children learn, in addition to the "restricted" language, what Bernstein calls the "formal" or "elaborated" language—the grammatically complex language of the schoolroom, which permits precise expression and provides greater potentiality for organizing experience than the "restricted" language. The child who learns only the "restricted" language, in Bernstein's view, is limited in his ability to learn new things and to interact with other people because his language restricts his ability to organize experience. The child who masters the "elaborated" language possesses a tool which permits expression of complex ideas and distinctions between feelings and ideas.

In an effort to understand why some children learn a more elaborate language than others, Hess and Shipman (1965) studied the ways in which mothers teach their own four-year-old children. They found that the techniques used by mothers vary by the amount of education the mothers have had—and thus also by social class. The middle-class mothers, as compared with the working-class mothers, talked almost twice as much to their children in teaching them, and used more abstract words, more adjectives, more complex grammar, and longer sentences. Furthermore, they more frequently gave explicit instructions, let the child know what was expected of him, and praised him for his accomplishments.

The children from the middle-class homes learned much better than the children from the working-class homes; and the middle-class children were more frequently able to explain correctly the principle behind the task they had learned.

These investigators suggest that homes which produce children who are, from the educator's point of view, educationally disadvantaged, are homes that are "status oriented," or oriented toward control of the child by ascribed roles. In such homes, a child is expected to obey his parent because children *should* obey parents. "Status-oriented families present the rules in an assigned manner, where compliance is the *only* rule-following possibility. In these situations the role of power in the interaction is . . . obvious, and coercion and defiance are likely interactional possibilities" (Hess and Shipman, p. 872). Middle-class families, on the other hand, are likely to be "person-oriented"; the feelings and desires of the child are taken into account, and explanations are given to him. This procedure requires a more elaborate language and permits responses from the child other than simple obedience. For example:

A child is playing noisily in the kitchen with an assortment of pots and pans when the telephone rings. In one home the mother says, "Be quiet," or "Shut up," or she issues any one of several other short, preemptory commands. In the other home the mother says, "Would you keep quiet a minute? I want to talk on the phone."

In one instance the child is . . . asked to attend to an uncomplicated message and to make a conditioned response (to comply); he is not called upon to reflect or to make mental discriminations. In the other example the child is required to follow two or three ideas. He is asked to relate his behavior to a time dimension; he must think of his behavior in relation to its effect upon another person. He must perform a more complicated task to follow the communication of his mother in that his relationship to her is mediated in part through concepts and shared ideas; his mind is stimulated or exercised (in an elementary fashion) by a more elaborate and complex verbal communication initiated by the mother. (Hess and Shipman, 1965, p. 872.)

The second mother has required her child to think about his behavior and to take the needs of others into consideration. A child who is consistently taught in this manner is likely to enter school with the capacity to choose among alternatives and to reflect before he acts. On the other hand, a child who is taught merely to obey is likely to be impulsive rather than reflective.

ATTITUDES TOWARD LEARNING. Children grow up, not only with different language environments but with different attitudes toward school and school achievement. Frankie, a four-year-old enrolled in an experimental reading-readiness program for children from improverished fatherless families, was a difficult child from the outset, aggressive, restless, and with an unusually short attention span. The mother, interviewed in the slum apartment where she lived with Frankie and two younger babies, pointed to the stout leather belt that she kept handy, and said:

"I don't have to use it so much any more. Just two or three times a week. I can give him a certain look, and he knows what I mean." She controlled his behavior also by his fear of the "bogeyman"—a fearful creature which came in the window and stood over him when he had been "bad."

When the interviewer asked how important it was to her for Frankie to do well in school, the mother said, "Very important. Very important! I tell him, I say, 'Frankie, when you go to school, I want you to learn,' I say. 'because it's important.' I say, "You do what the teacher tell you to do, you hear, when I send you to school, 'cause I want you to go to school and learn—you learn good, see? And if I get any reports on you from your teacher, I'm going to spank you good, see? That's what they got teachers for, to teach you . . . and you have to pay attention, see?' Frankie is smart, he's very smart. Only he just won't pay attention. Even though I whips him all the time."

It should be stressed that Frankie's behavior cannot be laid to his mother's lack of concern that he do well in school. She had gone to considerable effort to get him enrolled in the preschool program, and she was highly aware of the advantages education would bring. Parents such as Frankie's mother seldom are equipped, however, to help their children to succeed in school.

To illustrate this point further, we present the response of another mother who, when asked how she would prepare her four-year-old boy for school, answered:

First of all, I would remind him that now he was big enough to go to school and that we were proud of him. Then I would tell him that he was going to school to learn, that his teacher would take my place, and that he would be expected to follow instructions. Also that his time would be spent mostly in the classroom with other children, that he would enjoy it, and that any questions or any problems that he might have he could consult with his teacher for assistance. [Anything else?] No, anything else would probably be confusing for him at his age.

The attitudes of the two mothers just quoted are not isolated cases, but illustrate the fact that differences in the types of punishment used by parents and in the types of behavior they punish are reflections of actual differences in values between social classes. To quote just one study that supports this generalization, Kohn (1959, I, II), in a study of the values and use of authority by lower- and middle-class parents in Washington, D.C., found that lower-class mothers used physical punishment in an attempt to change behavior which they did not consider respectable and thus to fit their children to the mold of respectability. Middle-class mothers, on the other hand, placing the highest value on internal standards and controls, used a calculated holding-out and withdrawal of affection to create the pressures needed to change the child's behavior. In deciding whether or not to punish a child's misbehavior, middle-class parents tend to consider the child's motives and feelings; while working-class parents focus on the act itself. The middle-class child is likely to be punished for loss of self-control; the working-class child, for disobeying the parent.

The Family Factor Versus the School Factor

In asking how the school can improve the educational outcomes for disadvantaged children Deutsch comments in different words upon the same point made by Hess and Shipman:

In general we have found that lower-class children, Negro and white, compared with middle-class children, are subject to what we've labeled as "cumulative deficit phenomenon," which takes place between the first and fifth grade levels. Though there are significant socioeconomic and race differences seen in measured variables at the first grade level, it is important to note that they become more marked as the child progresses through school. While we can accept that some of this cumulative deficiency is associated with inadequate early preparation because of corresponding environmental deficiencies, the adequacy of the school environment must be in question: in a model system, one should except linearity in cognitive growth. (Deutsch, 1965, p. 80.)

Deutsch and others feel that socially disadvantaged children need compensatory education at the preschool level, and thus they are proponents of Operation Head Start, which in 1965 began a massive pre-kindergarten program for disadvantaged children with financing under the Economic Opportunity Act. However they feel that the schools must do a much better job once the disadvantaged child actually enters school, and that special efforts must be prolonged if they are to be effective.

As mentioned in the preceding chapter, it is still uncertain what balance of effort should be placed on preschool efforts and on efforts with school-age children. If stress is laid on the preschool years, this emphasizes the family factor and seems to imply that the lower-working-class family, and especially the Negro working-class family, is inadequate for rearing children in a complex urban society. If stress is placed on work with school-age children, this emphasizes the school factor and implies that society has failed in its job of educating lower-working-class children and that it is primarily the schools that should be improved.

When stress is placed upon the family factor, some persons see an inference that Negroes themselves are to blame, even though these persons also recognize that society, through slavery and racial discrimination, is responsible for the Negro working-class family. Emotions become aroused. Some Negro leaders and some civil rights workers, as well as some whites who are emotionally identified with the working class, tend to charge the schools with the responsibility for present defects in the achievement of Negro as well as other working-class children; while some educators and some social scientists see most of the difficulty as being rooted in the Negro working-class family, and look to other economic and political institutions of the society to remedy the situation. In the late 1960's, efforts to improve the situation for disadvantaged children were proceeding in a context of emotional tension, since various groups held different interpretations of the basic causes and therefore of the basic solutions to the problem.

Those who emphasized the family factor wished to expand preschool classes for socially-disadvantaged children, educational work with their mothers and fathers, spread of birth-control knowledge among lower-working-class people, and a variety of forms of assistance and support through social workers. For this group, the school system could go on with its present programs for school-age children, making improvements such as smaller classes and remedial instruction for disadvantaged children.

Those who emphasized the school factor were demanding new forms of education, not merely more of the old forms. They called for new and radical changes in the schools and asked that the schools find ways of teaching lower-working-class children. Among this group was Kenneth Clark, the eminent Negro psychologist who played a strategic role in marshalling the evidence for the Supreme Court decision of 1954 to end segregation in the public schools. Clark has called for school experimentation on a broad scale, insisting that educational compensation can and must be accomplished through the schools.

Another proponent of school reform is Frank Riessman, a psychologist who is especially critical of what he calls the "middle-class emphasis" of the schools. He believes that children from working-class families have certain positive qualities and learning abilities that are overlooked by most educators; and that these children, in contrast to middle-class children, have a mental style that is physical and visual rather than aural; content-centered rather than form-centered; externally-oriented rather than introspective; problem-centered rather than abstract-centered; inductive rather than deductive; spatial rather than temporal; slow, careful, patient, persevering (in areas of importance) rather than quick, clever, facile, flexible. (Riessman, 1962, p. 73, p. 80.) He points out that the education of working-class children should take account of these characteristics and build upon them, saying, "We must be careful not to try to make these children over into replicas of middle-class children. The educational system should be pluralistic enough, broad enough, to find a place for a variety of mental styles."

As yet Riessman has not pointed to empirical evidence that working-class children are better than middle-class children in the characteristics mentioned. Probably most students of human development would agree that children of stable working-class families (upper-working-class) are slightly below children of middle-class families on a number of mental abilities and are less disadvantaged with respect to the characteristics mentioned above than they are in other mental skills which require more vocabulary knowledge and more abstract reasoning ability. At the same time the child of lower-working-class families may be far below the children of upper-working-class families in all these positive traits.

The educators who use conventional methods and "more of the same" when working with disadvantaged children remain unconvinced that they should make radical changes. They want to know what changes are being suggested, and they ask for evidence that new methods would work better than existing methods.

The basic disagreements will probably be resolved in the next few years as educators experiment with a variety of ways of helping the socially disadvantaged child and as social scientists learn more through research about the mental development of children.

In summary, the family and the school operate always together in socializing the child. While most families expect their children to work conscientiously at school tasks, to obey the teacher and follow her example, and to conform to school expectations, still family-school relations vary from one setting to the next, especially around social-class differences. There is general agreement that thus far the schools have fallen short of succeeding with lower-working-class children.

The child is the product of his family and, figuratively speaking, "brings his family with him into the schoolroom." At the same time the child becomes also the product of the school, and eventually he "takes the school with him into the family." The relative influence of the family factor and the school factor in the mental development of the child remains unclear; it is also not clear how the interaction between the school and the family can be improved to insure long-run advantages for all types of children.

Exercises

1. Pick two or three children whose families are likely to be very different. Pay a visit to each home. What were the most striking differences you observed? What were the most striking similarities?

2. As a teacher, have you ever had a pupil whom you did not like? What were some of the things about the child that offended you or "rubbed you the wrong way"? Make a list of those items. Thinking now of yourself and of that child in terms of social class, which of the items on your list are "class" points, characteristics that offend you because of your own social-class background is a different one from the child's? (If you are not a teacher, reverse this situation and describe one of your former teachers whom you did not like.)

3. It is sometimes said that by the time a child enters school it is "too late" to make any real changes in his personality. A teacher may say, especially of a lower-class child, "What's the use trying? I can't undo what the family has done." Do you agree with this point of view, generally speaking? Why or why not?

4. Describe a child you have known who illustrates your point of view about the importance of family training as stated in answer to the preceding question. Describe a different case—one who is an exception or one

who illustrates the contrary point of view about the importance of family training.

5. Interview the parents of three or four children whom you know to investigate the methods of child-rearing that have been used. What similarities and what differences do you find?

Suggestions for Further Reading

1. For an interestingly written account of how the family acts to produce differences in personality between children of different social classes, read *Father of the Man* by Allison Davis and Robert J. Havighurst.

2. *The Changing American Parent* by Daniel R. Miller and Guy E. Swanson and *Patterns of Child Rearing* by Robert R. Sears, Eleanor E. Maccoby, and Harry Levin are reports of two recent large-scale studies of child-rearing practices. For an interesting account of how methods of child rearing have changed in America in the past hundred years, read Chapters 9 and 10 in *Childhood in Contemporary Cultures,* edited by Margaret Mead and Martha Wolfenstein. See also the article by Urie Bronfenbrenner, "Socialization and Social Class Through Time and Space," in *Readings in Social Psychology* by Eleanor E. Maccoby, which is an analysis of the findings from various studies of child rearing over the past 25 years.

3. There are a number of good textbooks on the family as a social institution. *A Modern Introduction to the Family* by Bell and Vogel is an especially good one; also the third edition of *The Family* by Burgess, Locke and Thomes.

4. *Family Worlds* by Hess and Handel describes five different families, each treated as a case study. It also introduces new ways of observing and interpreting family interaction.

5. For more information on the social and economic conditions of the lower-working-class Negro family, read the famous "Moynihan Report" which appeared as a booklet (which stirred a major controversy in 1965 and 1966) published by the U.S. Department of Labor, entitled *The Negro Family: The Case for National Action.* See also *Marriage and Family Among Negroes,* by Jessie Bernard. Frazier's book, *The Negro Family in the United States,* while written some time ago, remains a classic in the field.

6. For description of family life in various ethnic groups, see the readings suggested under #7 at the end of Chapter 2. And for family-life differ-

ences in various social-class groups, see #5 and #6 at the end of Chapter 1.

7. In *Society and Education: A Book of Readings* (Havighurst, Neugarten, and Falk) there are four selections which deal with various aspects of family socialization: The paper by Bronfenbrenner describes some of the ways that new child-rearing practices may be having profound effects upon the personalities of children; the article by Hess and Shipman describes a study of patterns of communication between mothers and their children, and shows how these patterns differ in different social classes; the Rosen study deals with family structure and the transmission of values; and the Cervantes' article illustrates how family socialization processes affect the child's school performance and how school dropouts tend to come from families where there are few close relationships between family members.

7 / The Peer Group and the School

The child grows up in two social worlds. One is the world of adults: his parents, teachers, club leaders, the store clerks, friends of the family, and the policeman. The second is the world of his peers or age-mates: his friends, play groups, clubs and gangs, and school groups.

The Nature of the Peer Group

For any given child, of course, "the" peer group means a succession of specific groups of children with whom he interacts, just as "the" family is, for any given child, one particular family. Peer groups are of many different kinds—from the informal play group to the organized Scout troop or organized gang, from the clique of three or four members to the wide school group—and the average child will interact with a variety of particular peer groups as he grows up. Each group has its own rules, implicit or explicit; its own social organization; and its own expectations for group members.

While there is great variation from one group to another, we may speak of the peer group in general terms, much as we do the family or the school. From this broad point of view, the peer group of the child and the adolescent constitutes a world of its own with its customs, traditions, manners, and even, at times, its own language.

The adult is always, to a greater or lesser degree, excluded from the peer group of the child and adolescent. At the one extreme, a peer group may be in open conflict with adults, as in a delinquent gang in a slum

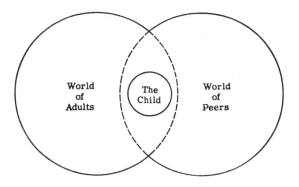

Figure 7.1 The child lives in two worlds.

neighborhood whose activities may be in express defiance of community standards of law and order; or as in groups of adolescents whose standards of dress, speech, and behavior, while by no means delinquent, nevertheless come into conflict with the expectations set by parents. The situation in which a teen-age boy or girl argues with his parents that, "The other kids stay out until midnight, why can't I?" has its countless variations. Yet the variations are on the same theme, that of reconciling two sets of expectations: one set from the world of one's peers, the other from the world of adults.

At the other extreme is the situation in which the peer-group expectations are in full accord with adult expectations and are even a direct outcome of adult planning, as in a neighborhood play group formed under the watchful eyes of mothers; or a Boys Club organized through a settlement house, or an urban renewal project; or a high school Hi-Y group meeting under the leadership of a respected teacher. Even in such situations, the adult is to some measure excluded, with youngsters reserving certain areas of communication and interaction to themselves. The child or the adolescent feels comfortable with age-mates in a way that he is not comfortable with the adult, however acceptant and understanding the adult may be. There are always certain thoughts, values, and behaviors that youngsters share only with other youngsters.

That the peer group constitutes a social world of its own is well known and accepted by most parents and teachers. Yet the importance of the peer group as a socializing agency is less often recognized. Unlike the family and the school, the peer group is not a formalized, institution-alized agent of society. It has no legal definitions, no formally ascribed functions or duties. Yet it pervades the life of the child to a greater extent as he grows older, and it performs increasingly important functions in teaching him the ways of his society.

The Peer Group as a Learning Situation

In the adult world the child is always in a position of subordinate status. In the peer world, he has equal status with others and he learns from persons who are not removed from him by wide differences in age, maturity, or prestige. Deference and respect for authority are largely irrelevant issues. The child with his peers is in a position where he is relatively free to express his own attitudes, judgments, and critical faculties. He is relatively free to explore personal relationships and to test himself out against others.

Furthermore, learning in the peer group, as compared with learning in the family, usually occurs in a less emotionally charged setting. A child's age-mates are relatively unconcerned about what he gains or fails to gain from the social situation. There is, at least in the early years, a lack of awareness that the social situation is a learning situation; and, even as such awareness develops in later childhood and adolescence, the "teachers" lack emotional investment in the outcomes. While there are exceptions, as in tightly knit cliques or gangs, social interaction and the learning that results take place in relatively neutral settings. The child or adolescent is not committed, as it were, in the way he is committed to his family—or even as he is committed to the same classroom teacher for a relatively long period of time.

One of the special characteristics of the peer group is the transitory quality of relationships. The average school-age child forms one or two close friendships and becomes a member of a small play group that he thinks of as "his" group. These relationships may be intense, but not necessarily long-lasting. An eight-year-old for example, may suddenly switch his allegiance from one child to another and report to his family that it is now Richy, rather than Don, who is the paragon of all virtues. A twelve-year-old girl said, in similar vein, "I used to think Ellen and Nancy and I would always be friends. We spent a lot of time together, and did our homework together, and all. But now Ellen seems kind of silly, and we get into a lot of arguments. So I've become friendly with Kathy and Jill, and I like them lots better. They're my best friends now."

There are, of course, long-enduring friendships formed in childhood. Still, unless he lives in a relatively isolated setting where he has so few age-mates that he is forced always into the company of the same group, the average child moves about in the world of his peers. He forms new relationships and breaks old ones as his own levels of social and emotional maturity shift in relation to others, as his interests change, and as his needs for new social experiences change. This transitory quality of relationships occurs within the peer group as a concomitant of what we have called the lack of emotional commitment.

A third differentiating characteristic of the peer group as a socializing agency is that its influence tends to become more rather than less important with the advancing age of the child. Unlike the family, whose influence becomes less monopolistic with time, the peer group becomes more influential. The eight- or the ten-year-old wants to do things "like the other kids do." By the time he is sixteen this desire may become an obsession. In adolescence, the peer group takes a certain precedence in many ways over any other group that influences the individual.

Functions of the Peer Group

As a socializing agency, the peer group serves the child in a number of ways. Adults generally expect the peer group to teach a child how to get along with others, as witnessed by the distress of parents and teachers over a child who is not accepted by other children and who is therefore denied many opportunities for social learning.

Teaching the Culture

While a peer group may be said to have a subculture that is particularly its own (a point to which we shall return presently), it nevertheless reflects the adult society and reinforces most of the values held by the adult society.[1] A child learns through his peers the prevailing standards

[1] The distinction should be drawn between an organized gang and other types of peer groups. The gang may be defined as an organization of preadolescents or adolescents that does not relate itself positively to adult leadership. A gang may or may not engage in delinquent behavior, but in the eyes of most adults gangs are undesirable because they are at least potentially antisocial, if not actually so. The efforts of most social agencies in dealing with gangs are directed toward the

of adult morality—competition, cooperation, honesty, responsibility— which, while they may at first be child-like versions, become adult-like with increasing age.

The peer group teaches children their sex roles, building upon, but changing and elaborating the earlier teaching of the family. A child learns from his peers what behavior is acceptable and admired in a boy, and what is accepted and admired in a girl. Thus the peer group is a powerful agency in molding behavior in accordance with current versions of manhood and womanhood.

The peer group is also an important source of information in areas other than social relations. Our modern sophisticate, aged ten, has obtained much of his up-to-the-minute knowledge of outer space and satellites from television, it is true; but it is after discussion with his agemates that the information takes on value and becomes part of his intellectual equipment. It is the peer group that often decides what knowledge is important, and what is not.

Certain areas of teaching and information-giving have become the special province of the peer group: for instance, to teach a child by actual experience how rules are made, how they can be changed and, concomitant with this, an understanding of the individual's responsibility in a group situation. It also has been left to the peer group, by and large, to impart sex education to the child. (The latter situation is now changing, as the family, the school, and other institutions are taking responsibility for sex education.)

The peer group teaches also the adult subculture of which it is a part. Ethnic, religious, social class, and regional subcultures are transmitted through the peer group. A child who grows up in the slums of Chicago learns from other working-class boys and girls, as well as from his family, the working-class way of life. The same is true of a child in the middle or upper class. Similarly, interracial schools develop parallel social systems for Negroes and for whites that correspond to the parallel social systems in the adult world. In most cases, the peer group acts to reinforce as well as to elaborate the teaching of the family inducting the child into his society and into a given position in the society.

---

transformation of gangs into "groups" by providing adult leadership and thus to guide their activities into socially acceptable channels. While gang activity is receiving a great deal of publicity recently in a period in which juvenile delinquency is regarded as an increasingly grave social problem, it must be kept in mind that only a small proportion of children or adolescents are ever members of a gang. We are omitting, therefore, the organized gang from this discussion of the peer group. See Chapter 13 for further discussion of the gang.

Social Mobility

The peer group also operates, in many cases, to teach social mobility. A working-class boy or girl who, through an organized youth group or through the school, becomes friendly with middle-class boys and girls, learns from them new ways of behaving. He may be encouraged to acquire the values and goals of his new friends.

The opportunity for working-class children to become acquainted with middle-class children is most often found within the school. Many educators, recognizing the power of age-mates in aiding social mobility, use this as a strong argument in favor of heterogeneous schools. They feel that one of the ways the school can help to foster mobility is to bring children of varying social backgrounds together in the same classrooms; and thus to provide the opportunity for working-class children and adolescents to learn from age-mates, as well as from adult school personnel, a middle-class way of life.

In a study which bears this out, it was found that a student's desire to attend college, and the likelihood that he would actually get into college, were both strongest if the student's best friend planned to go (Alexander and Campbell, 1964). The friend's influence was more important than the family's desires or the family's socioeconomic position.

Providing New Social Roles

In addition to its function of transmitting the wider culture, the peer group provides opportunities for new role behavior. The child raised in an autocratic family may find himself for the first time in a group in which democratic relationships are the rule; or the child raised in a democratic family may find himself in a group with a strong and dominating leader. Not only do members learn new roles of leader and follower, but a peer group usually provides, too, for other differentiations in role. One child becomes the "idea-man" for the group; another becomes the clown; another, the scapegoat; another, the slave; and so on. Peer groups often offer a wide arena to the child for social experimentation.

Other Functions

The peer group serves still other functions. It helps the child to achieve independence from adults. In giving him group support, it bolsters him in his dealings with adults, gives him a feeling of strength and solidarity with others like himself. Within the peer group the child finds new models of behavior, other persons not too far removed from himself in age or experience, whom he can imitate and with whom he can identify.

The Growing Influence of the Peer Group

While the peer group operates informally, as we have said, its influence has grown more important over the last hundred years in America. There are a number of factors involved. Since more and more children and adolescents live in urban rather than rural settings today, since the number of youth organizations of all types has grown, and since adolescents spend increasingly more years in school rather than at work, children and adolescents are thrown together in groups of age-mates to an ever-increasing extent.

In the modern urban society adolescents play a relatively insignificant part. Their labor is not required in economic production, and they remain in positions of economic dependence upon the family for longer and longer periods. As adolescence tends to be prolonged, and as youth are excluded from participation in the adult society, young people turn more and more to the peer group for recognition. In return, the peer group takes on an increasingly larger role in the socialization process.

Adolescent Values

The importance which the peer group assumes for the adolescent has been recently documented by James Coleman (1961, II) in a study of the student bodies in eleven different high schools. Even though the schools were carefully picked to reflect a wide range of differences in terms of the size of the community and the social-class backgrounds of the students, there was considerable agreement on major values from one adolescent group to the next as expressed in responses to questionnaires. Thus, for boys, the importance of being a "brilliant scholar" was secondary to being a "star athlete" in all schools in the study; and, for girls, it was less important than being an "activities leader." For both sexes, it was better to be popular than to be intellectually outstanding.

Coleman summarized his data, at one point, in the following terms: "Despite wide differences in parental background, type of community, and type of school, there was little difference in the standards of prestige, the activities which confer status, and the values which focus attention and interest. In particular, good grades and academic achievement had relatively low status in all schools" (Coleman, 1959, p. 338).

Along the same lines, Tannenbaum (1962) investigated students' reactions to a list of over 50 personal and social traits (e.g., "cheerful," "kind," "serious,") and found that the most acceptable classmate appeared to be one who loves fun, gets along well with others, has good physical health, and is personally attractive. He is bright and conscientious and proud of his school work, but he is not a "brain" or a "walking dictionary" and does not brag about his marks or complain about never knowing enough.

In a further analysis, Tannenbaum had students in different high schools assign the traits to eight hypothetical student types that possessed, in various combinations, the characteristics of being studious or not studious, brilliant or average, athletic or non-athletic. The second analysis revealed that it apparently makes little difference to a student's popularity to be brilliant, as long as he is sports minded, participates in many athletic activities, and spends no more time studying than most students.

It appears that, within the adolescent society while no special social stigma is attached to intellectual brilliance, neither is there any special value attached to it. There are, however, stigmas attached to disinterest in sports and to an excessive and apparent zeal for study.

Is There an Adolescent Subculture?

Although the stress on academic achievement in the 1960's may be operating to change adolescent values, the findings of investigators like Coleman and Tannenbaum confirm the impressions of some adults who have worked with adolescent groups. It is findings such as these that have led some observers to speak of an adolescent subculture in much the same way as they speak of ethnic, religious, or social class subcultures.

We must ask, however, if the adolescent subculture is in reality so different from that of the wider society. Is there indeed a peer culture separate from the adult culture, one that operates at cross-purposes with adult school personnel? Sociologists have taken opposite positions on this question, and, in truth, there is not a great deal of empirical evidence to substantiate one or the other interpretation. In the Coleman study, mentioned previously, it was suggested that adolescents have a value system that is relatively independent of the adult because adolescents are influenced primarily by their friends rather than by adults. Yet in that same study, when 400 teachers were asked if they would rather see the brilliant student, the athletic star, or the extra-curricular activities leader elected president of the senior class, the large majority chose the leader of extra-curricular activities. This suggests that the teachers' values were not so different from the adolescents', and that the separation between the adult and the adolescent cultures is not so great as has often been implied.

Similarly, in the Tannenbaum study 100 graduate students in education were asked to rank the student types in terms of the kinds of children they themselves would like to have. These educators ranked the brilliant types higher than the average, but, like the high school students, they also tended to favor the non-studious and the athletic types (Tannenbaum, 1962).

It may be that students' and adults' views are closer than many investigators have thought. Perhaps the teachers were reacting against academic one-sidedness rather than against academic achievement; but it may also be that school personnel encourage the athlete rather than the scholar. The differences between the school culture and the adult culture are, therefore, by no means clear.

Two other studies should be mentioned in this connection. One by Brittain (1963) indicated that whether or not an adolescent is influenced by his friends or by his parents will depend on what issue is involved. Peers are more influential in deciding some things, like what course to take in school; but parents are more influential when, for instance, a girl decides which of two boys to date. A study by Epperson (1964) showed that when adolescents were asked whose disapproval would make them feel most unhappy, parents' or friends', 80 percent said parents. Furthermore when pre-adolescent children were compared with adolescents in this respect, it was concluded that adolescents are no more estranged from adult culture than are younger children.

All in all, then, the evidence for an adolescent subculture is questionable, at least in the terms we have been discussing here. In light of the emergent bureaucratic orientation in the United States, with the emphasis on "getting along," the adolescent who stresses the importance of popularity may be reflecting directly the values of the adult.

More important, however, is the fact that adolescents may not be repudiating the adult culture so much as they are showing strain in learning to accommodate to it. Parsons, for example, suggests that indifference to school work does not represent alienation from adult cultural values, but perhaps the opposite:

In general I think that an important part of the anti-intellectualism in American youth culture stems from the *importance* of the selective process through the educational system rather than the opposite . . . the general trend of American society has been toward a rapid upgrading in the educational status of the population. This means that, relative to past expectations, with each generation there is increased pressure to educational achievement, often associated with parents' occupational ambitions for their children. To a sociologist this is a more or less classical situation of anomic strain, and the youth-culture ideology which plays down intellectual interests and school performance seems to fit in this context. The orientation of the youth culture is, in the nature of the case, ambivalent. . . . One of the reasons for the dominance of the anti-school *side* of the ideology is that it provides a means of protest against adults, who are at the opposite pole in the socialization situation. In certain respects one would expect that the trend toward greater emphasis on independence, which we have associated with progressive education, would *accentuate* the strain in this area and hence the tendency to decry adult expectations. (Parsons, 1959, pp. 312–313.)

Status in the Peer Group

Most parents and teachers are aware occasionally that the qualities which give a youngster high status in the eyes of his companions may be different from the qualities they themselves consider important. The following example, although unusual, illustrates this point:

The elementary school in which I teach (school population about 700 pupils) has, in addition to regular classrooms, several "ungraded" classrooms, three for boys and three for girls. The Hanley School is composed of 70 per cent Negroes and 20 per cent Italian-Americans. The remaining 10 per cent is composed of various nationalities including Mexican and Puerto Rican children. We have heterogeneity at Hanley, not in economic status, but in race, religion, and nationality.

Leadership among pupils is not based on intellectual attainment, but on age, size, and knowledge of sex. These factors seem to grow and thrive in our ungraded sections, since these children may not be graduated until they are at least fifteen and a half years old and have reached an achievement level of at least fourth grade. *These* children become the models of behavior for our much younger school population in the regular grades. This results in an atmosphere where these ungraded pupils are not penalized for their I.Q.'s (below 80), but are instead admired for their muscular, social, and sexual precocity. The ungraded leader cannot compete academically, but physically he has no peer. A leader is tough—he might not be able to read or write well, he may have the vocabulary of a hoot owl, but if he's tough, who cares?

There are some other interesting factors. In the ungraded sections, girls take cooking and sewing. As class projects, they cook their own breakfasts—orange juice, milk, wheatcakes, sausages, and so on, with the food being provided by the Board of Education. Since many of the children in the regular grades come to school without breakfast, this aspect of being in an ungraded room seems like paradise. The girls also take up sewing, again with materials provided by the school, and make their own clothes, putting on a fashion show at Easter time. The rooms in which these girls work are large and the enrollment is small—not exceeding 20 pupils in one group—and the class atmosphere is informal. The younger children in the regular grades, sitting at immovable desks and working haphazardly at academic tasks, see the ungraded rooms as the "Elysian fields."

But do these ungraded boys and girls at Hanley see themselves as they are seen by the regular-grade children? During the last few weeks I have asked, during conversations with these ungraded children, if they would like to be in the regular grades; and out of the total number asked, over 90 per cent answered "Yes." By and large they felt stigmatized by being placed in the ungraded sections—that it was unfair, that they were "as smart as anybody." Though they enjoyed their work in woodshop and kitchen, still the regular classroom with its routines, its discipline and strict order, its emphasis on academic achievement, was the greener field. There is a kind of phantasy that if someone were placed in an ungraded room and then succeeded so well academically that he were returned to a regular grade, then that person would feel something like "Ulysses returned to Ithaca." (I might add that where we have returned pupils to the regular grades from ungraded, they are more conscientious and less inclined to be school problems, and they seem to shun their old acquaintances in the ungraded section. It is a policy at our school that once a child is taken from the ungraded and placed in the regular grades, he is not returned. This is because of the far-reaching emotional effects this replacement would have on the child.)

I have focused my observations mainly on the ungraded sections because most of the teachers in our school feel that the pupils in the ungraded sections are the instigators, conspirators, and the reasons for most of our problems in school. The basis of my focusing so much attention on the ungraded is not to distort the situation as it exists, but rather to point out the fact that the ungraded pupils, who in the eyes of many of the teachers are just vegetables, are in reality the models and leaders of the school; they are the ones who are followed and imitated by pupils in the regular grades.

One more interesting point. In checking our records, I find that where truancy is involved, pupils of the regular grades are truant many more times than the ungraded pupils. This is, I believe, due to the fact that these ungraded children—who would be lost in the shuffle if they were competing with children their own age in high schools—have an important stake in school. Their status as leaders in the elementary school is not taken lightly. They find untold satisfaction in the position of being socially successful.

While this example illustrates how a group of children may operate on certain values that are different from those of adults, it would be a mistake to conclude that such differences are either more common or more important than the *similarities* between the social values of children and adults. The characteristics that make for success in most peer groups are generally the same that make for success in adult groups—courage, good sportsmanship, loyalty to the group, and the ability to strike a balance between conformity and individuality.

Nevertheless, as children grow up, factors which to them seem "accidental" may play a significant role in determining their status in the peer group. The boy whose physical maturation occurs early, for example, has a definite advantage over late-maturing boys. Among girls, on the other hand, early maturers are at a disadvantage in sixth grade but at an advantage in junior and senior high school (Faust, 1960).

Social-Class Factors

The peer group also reflects the social-status structure of the wider society. Social-class differences not only operate in the adult society but operate also in the society of children and adolescents.

The first study of social-class differences in the child's society was made in Jonesville. There Neugarten found that fifth- and sixth-grade children (all of whom were together in the same school), when asked who were their best friends, most often named children above them in social class, then, second, children from their own social class. Few choices were made downward in the social scale, with the result that most working-class children were chosen only by others of their own social status. Similarly, as regarded reputation, children ascribed favorable personality traits to children of the higher social classes; and unfavorable personality traits to the children from lower social classes. There was a consistent relationship between social class and reputation: as one moved up the social scale, from lower-working to upper-middle class, children received consistently higher proportions of mentions on favorable characteristics and consistently lower proportions on unfavorable ones.

Among tenth- and eleventh-graders in Jonesville, social-class differences were also clearly operative, but in somewhat more complex ways. Here, where a large proportion of working-class children had already dropped out of school, adolescents also chose upward or horizontally on the social scale, but seldom downward, in selecting their friends. Adolescents of upper social status, while less uniformly regarded by their classmates in favorable terms, were nevertheless in the limelight so far as social visibility is concerned. Working-class adolescents were rarely mentioned, either positively or negatively (Neugarten, 1949).

Subsequent studies have shown similar findings as regards the influence of social class upon the child's and the adolescent's social groups. Thus, Hollingshead, studying adolescents in Elmtown, found that clique relationships reflected the social-class position of the adolescents' families (Hollingshead, 1949); and Stendler, studying the children of Brasstown, found that while young children crossed social-class lines in choosing their school associates, their general tendency was to choose out-of-school friends from within their own social class (Stendler, 1949).

Social Class and Skin Color

In the typical school in the mid-1960's, friendship groups do not frequently cross racial barriers, it appears. For this reason, students who comprise very small racial minorities may be particularly dependent upon the formal social activities of the school.

Gottlieb and Ten Houten (1965) found that, in three high schools in a northern city, racial composition of the school strongly affected the extracurricular activities as well as the prestige ratings of activities for Negro students. In the school where Negroes constituted less than five percent of the student body, they participated primarily in the highly structured, school sponsored extracurricular activities such as sports, vocational clubs, and band and chorus—activities that do not require a great amount of personal interaction. The Negroes in this school placed considerable emphasis on being good students and participating in student government in order to achieve leadership; though they participated in sports, they did not give sports a high leadership ranking.

In the school where Negroes constituted almost half of the student body, a separate social system had developed parallel to that of the white students. Fewer Negro students thought it a prerequisite for leadership to be a good student, but being an athlete and being a party-goer received higher ratings than in the first school. The Negro students were not as dependent upon the formal activities of their school as were the Negroes in the first school, although their memberships were still heavily concentrated in the structured activities. In this school, there was greater consensus between white and Negro students on what activities were important for leadership.

The third school was 99 percent Negro, and the Negroes tended to rank a larger number of activities and memberships as important for leadership, indicating that they were no longer concentrating their energies in a small number of extra-curricular activities. The tiny minority of white students, on the other hand, was concentrated in a few school-sponsored groups—much the same as were the Negroes in the first school.

When the students were asked to rate the activities and the personal qualities that gave status in their friendship groups, it was found that race had little relationship to their responses, since, in all three schools, the friendship groups were racially segregated. Although in the first school, because they were so few in number, about a fifth of the Negro students made friendship choices across racial lines, on the whole the Negro students were less likely to make friendship choices with whites than whites were with Negroes. Within each racial group, girls were less likely than boys to make cross-race choices.

Social class may, in some instances at least, outweigh skin color as a factor that influences children's perceptions of each other. Weddington (1958) carried out a carefully designed study of the ways in which 7-year-olds and 10-year-olds assigned favorable and unfavorable traits. A picture technique was devised in which white and Negro individuals of obviously middle- and lower-class were presented in pairs, and the child was asked, "Which of these two people is more honest? Smart? Noisy?" and so on. The children assigned traits more in terms of social class than in terms of color. While this study differs from the others just described in that it focuses not on actual friendship choices, but upon what are probably children's stereotypes, nevertheless such stereotyped perceptions probably play a role in the child's interaction patterns.

The extent to which awareness of social-class differences operates in the minds of children and adolescents may be expected to vary not only with age, but with type of community. Sargent, in studying Ventura, a California community of about 18,000 population, found less class consciousness and fewer class distinctions among adults than in cities in other parts of the country. Correspondingly, among fifth- and sixth-grade children, repeating the same approach as was used in Jonesville (see p. 180), he found less of a trend among children to differentiate along social-class lines. Table 7.1 shows the differences between Jonesville and Ventura children.

Table 7.1   Social Class and Children's Reputations in Two Communities

	Jonesville *Grades 5–6* *(all in 1 school)*		*Ventura* *Grades 5–6* *(3 schools)*	
	PERCENT OF CHILDREN	PERCENT OF VOTES RECEIVED ON FAVORABLE TRAITS	PERCENT OF CHILDREN	PERCENT OF VOTES RECEIVED ON FAVORABLE TRAITS
Upper-middle	6	19	16	20
Lower-middle	17	27	45	47
Upper-working	62	50	34	30
Lower-working	15	4	5	3

Source: Sargent, 1953 (adapted).

The extent to which social-status and racial differences are reflected within peer groups may also be expected to vary with the school setting. In a school that draws children from a relatively narrow range of social classes, class lines within the school group may be minimal. At the same time, the pupils may feel themselves clearly marked off from other groups in the wider community; as in one school in an all upper-middle-class neighborhood, where a first-grader reported to the visitor, "Well, you see, it's going to be Christmas pretty soon, and our school is making presents for poor kids. Every room is making presents, and then they'll all be put in a big truck, and somebody will drive the truck over to where those people are, and then those poor kids can have these things and have some fun."

In a school whose pupils come from a variety of backgrounds, the so-called heterogeneous school, social-class lines within the school group may be relatively clear-cut, as in Jonesville; or relatively blurred, as in many a school where there is an explicit policy of minimizing social-class as well as racial factors among pupils, and where the policy is successfully implemented.

The "Ins" and the "Outs"

In any group of children or adolescents that persists through time, just as in any group of adults, there grows up a system of differentiation between members and a hierarchy of prestige. The values which serve as a basis for this differentiation may, as we have seen, be the same or different from those of the adult culture; they may follow social-class or racial lines; and they may be based on special abilities or attributes. Within any school population several different groups may form. Thus in a typical high school one can find the "leading crowd," the "brains," the "wild-ones," and the "average-guys." Among these groups an informal hierarchy will exist so that everyone will know which group has the greatest prestige and which the least. However, the members of any one group, the "Ins," so to speak, while recognizing this hierarchy, will be able to maintain among themselves a certain security in their group membership. The group, with its common values, gives the individual an identity and a sense of belonging.

Not all students, of course, are members of groups; some never become identified with any particular clique, but remain on the fringe, perhaps with one or two friends, perhaps not. These are the "Outs," and their marginal positions may have deleterious effects. Some of these individuals may have no need for group association; but for others, this lack of group identity will affect self-confidence and may retard the normal process of social and emotional development.

For example, Schmuch (1963) found that elementary-school children who saw themselves as being well-liked by their classmates, whether they actually were or not, were more likely to view themselves positively and to utilize their abilities than were children who saw themselves as being disliked.

In the Coleman (1961, II) study it was found that, compared to those girls identified as being in the "leading crowd," those girls who were not so identified stated more often that they wanted to be someone other than themselves. Also, in an analysis of other data collected in the same survey, Johnstone (1961) found that students who were members of the "leading crowd" spent more of their leisure time in the consumption of mass media in some way related to the activities or values of the group, whereas the others spent the majority of their leisure time in solitary pursuits or in pursuing the mass media within the family setting.

The Peer Group and the School

The school is expected to help the child to bridge the gap between his child's world and the adult world. This is, in one sense, the express function of the school as a socializing agency. While this is also a function of the family, the important difference between school and family in this respect is that the school deals with children and moves them along toward adulthood, not as individuals, but as groups. Consequently, the influence of the school upon the individual child is always mediated in the setting of the peer group. It is from this point of view that the school and the peer group are inextricably bound together in their influences upon the child.

The Effect of the Peer Group on the Student

It is well recognized that the extent to which a child or an adolescent succeeds in meeting the school's expectations has an important and direct bearing upon his status in the peer group. It is usually a good if not brilliant student who holds a position of leadership among his age-mates. It is usually the adolescent who is popular with teachers who is also admired by his fellows. There are many exceptions, of course. There is the "brain" or "the grind," neither of whom tends to be popular with age-mates. There are groups in which it is mandatory that anybody who is on the "in" must be scornful of the school and rebellious toward the teacher. In general, however, most peer groups value the same attributes in children that are valued by the school. Even the youngsters in the ungraded sections of the Hanley school, as described earlier, wanted to be "regular" and wished they were successful by the school's criteria.

It is equally true, at the same time, that the child's status in the peer group has an important and direct bearing upon his progress in school, as illustrated in the following case history:

The community of Farwest is a suburb of a large city in one of the western states. It is surrounded on all sides by upper-class suburbs but is, itself, a composite of lower-middle- and upper-working-class people.

The Japanese-Americans in Farwest comprised a sizable minority. For the most part the heads of families were gardeners by vocation who had chosen to live in Farwest because of its strategic proximity to the residential districts that provided them with employment.

There were two Japanese language schools in the community: one connected with the local Buddhist church; the other, the *Gakuen* (Japanese for "school"), supported by the non-Buddhists (most of them members of two Japanese Christian churches) who were interested in preserving a part of their culture. The *Gakuen* provided facilities for students from age six on, although few youths pursued their studies in the Japanese language beyond high school age.

As a group, the Japanese in Farwest were accepted as an industrious and sober people. A large percentage owned their own homes, and the criminal and delinquency rate was extremely low compared to the other minority group (Mexican-American) and compared to the community as a whole.

The Seito family was typical: the father was a gardener, four of the five children attended the *Gakuen,* and three children attended the larger of the two Christian churches. The eldest son was still in high school, and Mr. Seito was hard put to provide for his family on a gardener's income.

Sadao was the third of five children. He was slight of build and, although all five children tended to be so, he was the least athletic of the lot.

"Sad," an almost inevitable nickname, spent many blissful hours in the local public library within walking distance of his home. Sad was a fast reader, and the librarian soon came to recognize him because of the frequency with which his card was filled up and exchanged.

Play time was limited. After public school, he went home to pick up the *Gakuen* textbooks and proceeded to language school. Homework meant even less time for recreation.

Although Sad was not athletic, he made up for this deficiency by his proficiency in the classroom. Indeed, in his first year at the *Gakuen* he became an honor scholar. Scholarship is prized highly among the Japanese, and this achievement by one of their sons was something of which Mr. and Mrs. Seito were proud. In public school he had managed to distinguish himself in the same manner. In fact, by the end of the fifth year in school, Sadao had already skipped three half-grades.

The principal of the public school decided that Sadao should be transferred to another school at the beginning of the sixth grade. The new school was located near the university in one of the upper-class residential districts. It was a training school for teachers, and the bulk of the students were children from the families who lived in the neighborhood. The transfer meant daily travel on a bus, an added expense that the Seito family could ill afford, but one that they nevertheless met, given the honor that was involved.

The school had graded classes in the traditional style, and two special groups for gifted children, known as the Junior Special and Senior Special classes. Sadao began the new school year in the latter group.

The curriculum of the special classes was quite different from that of the traditional school. It was foreign to Sadao, literally as well as figuratively. French was introduced in the sixth grade. Free composition meant freedom of movement as well as freedom of thought. During this hour one could wander about the schoolgrounds at will so that one could become inspired to write poetry or essays. The music hour meant listening to programme music instead of "singing from the same old songbooks." Scientific principles were demonstrated by projects; for example, huge paper ballons were constructed and filled with gases escaping from the school incinerator to demonstrate the lighter-than-air principle.

The curriculum posed its problems, but they were not of paramount importance to Sadao. Since he was the first Oriental to attend the school, his classmates had probably been well instructed as to how to act toward him, or more likely, how not to act toward him. Even so, although the class was not unfriendly, it was difficult for Sadao to be accepted until he had shown in some manner that he deserved it.

Sadao's initial reaction to his new environment was not the same as that of most students transferring to a new school. Not only were there no familiar faces, but his was the only face in school that was not white. Although he had been outfitted with new clothes for the school year, it did not take long for him to become aware that he could not match the dress of his new classmates. Their clothes did not look so different from his, but they did not wear out so quickly and they were almost never soiled.

He lacked the necessary prowess to distinguish himself during the gym period, although he did manage to escape the fate of Dewey and Bernie who suffered the indignities of "We don't want him on our side" or "We don't want any girls."

Sadao experienced many unpleasant hours in his first few weeks in school. He could not tell his parents that he wished to return to his old school for they would have chastized him for his foolish attitude. This was an honor that he had to live up to. So he tried to do so in the only way he could—scholastically.

Strangely enough it was the new curriculum that provided him with his first social success. During the French lesson the teacher praised Sadao on the facility with which he was learning a second language. With a "Good, nothing—it's perfect" air he announced that it was actually a third language. This intrigued his classmates and during recess they crowded around for a lesson in Japanese.

After the ice was broken Sadao did not find the sledding quite so difficult. He was not physically aggressive, but he was the intellectual equal of his peer group. When he committed a faux pas, he was quick to perceive it and seldom repeated it.

There were other reasons, too. Sad was a link with an outside world to which the members of the class had not been exposed. For example, the magnets that he brought to school and gave to his friends (for a nominal fee) were much stronger and larger than the toy magnets bought in stores. They were obtained at home from his friends and from junkyards.

But Sad's attempts to win group favor led him into trouble. One day the group had been engaged in baiting Hall, "the Hog," and Sadao had joined in the sport. Hall hadn't been able to retaliate in the past, but now he could because Sad, too, was vulnerable. As the jibes became more personal between Hall and Sad, the crowd egged them on to fight. Too late the pair realized their position. To preserve honor, they exchanged blows. Hall slipped and fell to the ground. Sad leaped to pursue his advantage. He was stopped immediately by cries of "Hey, he's down!" "You can't hit a man when he's down." "Hey, that's not fair!" The crowd was suddenly turned against Sad. He was bewildered, for that's the way things were done in all the fights he had ever witnessed before. . . .

Sad managed to gain notoriety in class one day quite unwittingly. The teacher had been pleased with the performance of the group, and the last few minutes of a class hour was devoted to joke-telling. When it was Sad's turn to contribute, he confidently related a story that he knew had been hugely successful at home. Unfortunately, he did not quite understand what he was saying. At first, the guffaws of the older boys gave him a flush of elation. This was quickly replaced by a sinking feeling when he observed the shocked look on the faces of the girls, and the teacher told him that the classroom was not the place for that type of joke. . . .

When Sadao had finished two years at the school, he realized he had only been invited to one private social gathering in all that time. He decided he wanted to leave the laboratory school. At home he explained that there were certain people with whom you could associate and certain others with whom you could not. His parents reluctantly agreed, especially since they could not really afford the expense involved. . . .

Sadao's case is one in which early academic promise came to an unrewarding end. Back in the public schools, he worked hard at being inconspicuous. He took the college preparatory program and achieved an adequate, but not brilliant, record. After working a year he entered the local branch of the state university; but the pressure of class work, the necessity of a part-time job, and his lack of a clear notion of what he wanted to do mitigated against success. He dropped out after a year; and, after army service, he found a job in the postal service.

Although this case illustrates many aspects of the relations between ability, social class, and education, it is a particularly telling illustration of the power of the peer group. For although a number of factors operated in this case—school personnel who failed to follow through, lack of personal guidance, and economic pressures—it is nevertheless fair to say that, had Sad's relationships to the other children in the laboratory school been more rewarding, his career might well have been different.

Educators must reckon with the fact that the child and the adolescent have two sets of expectations to meet; the expectations set by the peer group may be as important as any set by adults in understanding school success and failure. Many boys and girls drop out of school, not for lack of academic ability or for failure to meet the school's requirements, but for failure to gain acceptance in the peer group.

Exercises

1. Are there any learning experiences offered by the peer group that could *not* be offered by other socializing agencies? Explain.

2. Give an example, from your own experience, in which the peer group's standards of behavior for a child (or adolescent) were at variance with adult standards. What did the child do to resolve the conflict?

3. Thinking back over your own experience as a school child, were children in your elementary school more or less democratic as regards social-class differentiations than your high-school group? Cite examples.

4. Describe briefly a case in which a boy or girl dropped out of school before graduating. How did the attitudes of his classmates toward him affect his decision to leave school? Was there anything the school might have done to change the situation for him?

Suggestions for Further Reading

1. The influence of the peer group is treated in most textbooks on child and adolescent development. See for example Chapter 12 in Martin and Stendler's *Child Behavior and Development*. See also the Chapter by Campbell, "Peer Relations in Childhood," in *Review of Child Development Research*, edited by Hoffman and Hoffman.

2. What the child learns from the peer group is discussed more fully in Chapters 5 and 9 in *Human Development and Education* by Robert J. Havighurst.

3. Jean Piaget, in *The Moral Judgment of the Child*, describes how children learn through games (and thus through the agency of the peer group)

how rules are made and changed, and how children move through various stages of maturity in the development of moral judgment. See especially Chapter 1.

4. For further discussion of the effects of social class upon children's evaluations of one another, read *Children of Brasstown* by Celia B. Stendler, or the excerpt from that book that appears on pp. 244–247 in *Social Foundations of Education* by William O. Stanley, *et al.* Read also Chapter 5 in *Democracy in Jonesville* by W. Lloyd Warner and associates and Chapter 9 in *Elmtown's Youth,* by August B. Hollingshead. *Street-Corner Society* by William Foote Whyte is an interesting account of life in an Italian slum and the influence of peer groups upon individual boys.

5. Edgar Friedenberg in his interestingly written little book, *The Vanishing Adolescent,* sounds a note of caution for those who would like to increase adult controls over adolescents. Friedenberg views adolescent conflict with adult society as necessary if the adolescent is to mature and become independent.

6. *The Adolescent Society* by James S. Coleman describes in non-technical language a study of the students in ten different high schools, and the implications for education of the differences between adult and adolescent values.

7. The paper by James Coleman in *Society and Education: A Book of Readings* (Havighurst, Neugarten, and Falk) advances the thesis that the adolescent subculture dominates the school environment and operates against academic achievement; while the social influence of the adolescent peer group is shown by Alexander and Campbell to extend to college. The early study by Neugarten, reprinted in this book, was one of the first to gather evidence showing the influence of social class upon the friendship patterns and reputations of children and adolescents. In the same book, the paper by Gottlieb and TenHouten discusses the relationships between Negro and white students and shows how the racial composition of the peer group affects the activity patterns of adolescents of both races.

8. A number of books dealing with adolescent or youth culture appeared in the early 1960's. See, for example, the issue of *Daedalus* called *Youth: Change and Challenge.*

8 / The School as a Social System

Like the family or the peer group the school is one of society's agents which socializes the child and transmits the wider culture. At many other places in this book we deal directly or indirectly with the school as a socializing agency: for example, in Chapter 14, where one of the implicit themes is the way the school socializes both white and nonwhite children and affects the relations between racial and ethnic groups in the community; or in Chapters 17 and 18, where the attention is upon the various roles of the teacher. At this point, however, we shall view the school as one of the important social *settings* within which the child participates. The school may be viewed as a self-contained social system with a unique organization and unique patterns of expectations for its members.

The Culture of the School

The school has a subculture of its own—a complex set of beliefs, values and traditions, ways of thinking and behaving—that differentiate it from other social institutions. The function of the school is education; and all the personnel of the school, from the kindergartener to the high-school senior, from the office clerk to the superintendent, are present to further that function. This sets the overall tone of the school, and defines certain limits on activities and social interactions. Education in the school, as compared with that in the family or in the peer group, goes on in relatively formal ways; and even those activities that are least formal (as

in children's play at recess or the adolescent's participation in extracurricular activities) are evaluated in terms of their contribution to the
learning situation. Groupings are formed, not on the basis of voluntary
choice, but in terms of aptitudes for learning and teaching.

Furthermore, the school is concerned primarily with motivating the
child to achieve, as Parsons (1959) and others have pointed out. In the
classroom the child enters a group comprised of his age-mates in which,
except for differences by sex, there is initially no formal basis for
differentiation of status. Differentiation develops gradually according to
achievement. In the elementary school, achievement proceeds along two
lines; the first is the "cognitive," or the learning of information and
skills; the second is what Parsons calls "moral" or social—learning
respect for the teacher, consideration of fellow-pupils, good work habits,
initiative, and responsibility. In the secondary school, the emphasis is
upon types, rather than levels, of achievement. With its variety of
subject-matter, personnel, and activities, the high school offers the
student a wider range of status; and the student makes increasingly
differentiated choices along both the cognitive and the social axes of
achievement.

Elements of School Culture

The culture of the school contains, of course, a great many different
elements: the physical plant itself with the objects and physical settings
it provides for both children and adults; the curriculum with its great
variety of ideas and facts; the persons who make up the school
personnel and the ways in which they interact; and the moral values and
principles that pervade the school setting. Without describing all the
features of the school culture, a few will serve to illustrate that the
school has a culture of its own, different from that found in other parts
of society.

Waller, in describing the culture of the school, has said:

Teachers have always known that it was not necessary for the students
of strange customs to cross the seas to find material. Folklore and myth,
tradition, taboo, magic rites, ceremonials of all sorts, collective representa-
tions, *participation mystique,* all abound in the front yard of every school,
and occasionally they creep upstairs and are incorporated into the more
formal portions of school life.

There are, in the school, complex rituals of personal relationships, a set
of folkways, mores, and irrational sanctions, a moral code based upon them.
There are games which are sublimated wars, teams, and an elaborate set of

ceremonies concerning them. There are traditions, and traditionalists waging their world-old battle against innovators. There are laws, and there is the problem of enforcing them. . . . There are specialized societies with a rigid structure and a limited membership. . . . There are customs regulating the relations of the sexes. All these things make up a world that is different from the world of adults. . . . (Waller, 1932, p. 103.)

While the paragraphs just quoted deal with special features of the school culture as they are found among children and adolescents, it is also true that there is a corresponding special culture for adults. There are explicit rules and implicit expectations regarding the ways in which teachers relate to pupils, parents, administrators, and each other. Just as there are rules about smoking, so also there are specific expectations regarding dress, speech, and eating behavior. There are rules to follow when a pupil is tardy or returns after an absence. There are expectations about what a pupil may or may not say to a teacher; and what a teacher may or may not say to a pupil. Whether children line up and march into class, as in Mrs. Gordon's fifth grade in the McManus school, or whether they enter the building in informal groups, as in Miss Bond's Forest Park school (see Chapter 1), procedures become institutionalized. Every adult and every child soon becomes aware that certain behaviors are appropriate and other behaviors are inappropriate within the school.

Compared with other social institutions, the school has its own rituals and ceremonies involving both children and adults. There are the school assemblies, the athletic events, and the graduation ceremonies; there are the school songs, school insignia, school colors, and school cheers. All these are an accepted part of the culture of the school.

The orientation of the American school is predominantly that of the middle class. There is strong emphasis upon the character traits of punctuality, honesty, and responsibility. Respect for property is stressed. There is a premium upon sexual modesty and decorum. While both competitiveness and cooperation are valued to varying degrees, there is always stress upon mastery and achievement. These middle-class values are expected to be binding upon both children and adults.

Formalism

The formality of the school is well exemplified in the extent to which rights and duties are distributed according to age. While the family, the peer group, and other social groups are also age-graded systems (ones in which younger and older members enjoy different privileges and obliga-

tions), it is the school that is the most age-graded of all social institutions. Not only does age-grading operate in formal aspects of the
school—with six-year-olds placed in the first grade and ten-year-olds
placed in the fourth grade, and with each grade group having a different
curriculum and a different teacher—but it operates also in more informal ways. Thus, in most elementary schools a child must have
reached seventh or eighth grade before being eligible to help out in the
principal's office or to act as a traffic patrol boy. In most secondary
schools, a boy or girl must be a junior or a senior to participate in
certain extracurricular activities. This emphasis upon age-grading is, of
course, reflected in the social evaluations made by students themselves.
Not only does the first-grader long to be a second-grader, but the
freshman longs to be a senior.

Time itself is formalized in special ways within the school. The day
is divided into periods, and every person is expected to be in a given
place, engaged in a given activity, at every period of time. The week is
divided into school days and nonschool days, and some activities occur
on Mondays, others on Fridays.

Authority rests with the adult personnel of the school, and children
are in clearly subordinate positions. This is to be seen in the very way in
which the physical space of the school is arranged. There are usually
certain rooms in the building set aside for teachers; cloakrooms, wash-
rooms, and lunchrooms may be divided, with certain space used by
teachers and other space by children. Within the typical classroom the
teacher's desk occupies a special part of the room.

The right to privacy is also differentially assigned. In most schools,
for instance, the teacher may inspect the child's desk at will, but the
teacher's desk is kept locked.

That children are clearly subordinated to the authority of adults
may be a necessary feature of the school, and the extent to which this is
carried out may be more or less desirable; in any case, it is a characteristic of most schools.

There are a number of schools and school systems in the United
States in which formalism has been reduced. There are schools, for
example, in which age-grade lines are not strictly drawn: as when six-
and seven-year-olds are grouped together into a "primary" section,
rather than into a first and a second grade; or when older children are
grouped on the basis of physical and social maturity, rather than on the
basis of age alone, in such activities as physical education or extra-
curricular activities; or when special-ability groupings may include boys
and girls who vary in age by three or four years.

Some schools have dropped the formal system of letter grades and "report cards" as methods of evaluating student progress, and have substituted informal written reports. Others have broken down the traditional lines between school subjects, giving longer periods of the school day to "basic curriculum," "social studies," or "language arts."

Some schools, both at the elementary and secondary levels, are experimenting in other ways with time, space, student activities, rules, and regulations. Student government is one of the means used to help boys and girls share in the authority system of the school and to decrease the social distance between teachers and students. Other extra-curricular activities have a similar effect in reducing formalism.

Bureaucratization

Not only is the school system a formally-organized institution, but it is becoming more and more bureaucratized, as are other organizations in the modern society. Bureaucracy involves increasing specialization of work, and at the same time coordination of the specialized activities into a functioning whole. Among other processes, bureaucratization involves the centralization of authority and the standardization of work routines. Corwin, in describing the growth of bureaucracy in the schools, says,

Standardization is based on rules, which represent the extention of central authority into the routine work situation. In schools, rules are specifically stated in terms of curriculum outlines and study guides by which course work is regulated. They also use other record-keeping devices such as taking attendance and requiring periodic progress reports from teachers. Much administrative routine consists of applying rules to particular cases. The persistent reference of bureaucrats to rules routinizes even the most dramatic work problems that confront an organization and contrasts with the tendency of clients to view their problems as exceptional. For example, when a parent comes to the teacher complaining that Johnny was treated unfairly at grading time she probably believes that her problem is very different from that of other parents, but the teacher will see her as a typical parent. (Corwin, 1965, p. 39.)

Given the growth in school populations and the economy that is gained from larger organizations, bureaucracy and centralization are becoming characteristic of school systems everywhere. Callahan (1962) has described the cult of efficiency that grew up in American school systems in the first half of this century, and the way in which business principles were taken over by educators. This trend is still apparent in the tendency of some educators and some laymen to measure the efficiency of a school system in terms of the numbers of pupils, classes, and teachers in relation to costs. The stress on efficiency and increased bureaucratization adds to the formalism of the school as a social system.

Variations in School Culture

Not only do individual schools have different insignia, songs, and symbols, but they differ in less tangible ways. In one school the relationships between teachers and pupils are unusually intimate and friendly; in another, unusually formal. One school has an atmosphere of regimentation; another emphasizes individual differences between pupils. In one school, competition is played up; in another, it is played down. A special history and tradition often develops. In one case, students may feel fierce pride in their school and its accomplishments. In another, there may be a feeling of resignation among both children and adults, as if mediocrity is all that can be expected in any school endeavor.

The culture of the school has a profound effect upon what children and adolescents learn and the ways in which they learn. There is a saying that children learn not what is taught, but what is "caught." Much of what is caught (attitudes toward learning, toward authority, values of right and wrong, and so on) comes not from the formal curriculum but from the pervading culture of the school.

Relevant here, for example, is the study by Coleman (1959, 1960) with regard to the impact of the adolescent subculture upon academic achievement. In various midwestern high schools, students gave highest priority to athletics, other school activities, and social popularity rather than to academic achievement. The implication is that there is conflict between adolescent and adult value patterns within the school. Schools undoubtedly vary in the extent to which this is the case. However, in a school in which the football player or cheerleader is given more prestige than the scholar, students are "catching" certain attitudes from their peers which may offset the attitudes they are catching from their teachers.

In this same connection, a study of eight different high schools in the San Francisco–Oakland Bay area provided good evidence that the ethos of a given school affects the academic achievement and occupational aspirations of its students in measurable degree (Wilson, 1959). The eight schools varied considerably with regard to the proportion of students who came from different occupational levels and showed differences in regard to the climate of values that prevailed. It was found that in schools that were predominantly lower status (the majority of fathers were manual workers), the proportion of *middle*-class boys who planned to go to college was significantly lower than in schools of predominantly middle-class students. Congruently, a lower-status boy attending a school in which the majority of his classmates were middle class (their fathers were upper-level white-collar or professional workers) was more likely to plan to go to college than if he attended a school in which the majority of his classmates were working class. The investigator interpreted these findings as evidence that the school milieu and peer-group norms can significantly modify the effects of social class in influencing the adolescent's values.

In any case, the culture of the school must be taken into account in understanding how the school functions as a socializing agent and what it is the school teaches. It is clear, furthermore, that the culture of the school must be defined as incorporating the attitudes and values of students as well as of teachers.

The School as a Social Organization

The school has not only a culture of its own, but a social organization of its own. Within the school a pattern of social relations develops that is not only unique but which persists through time, so that the pattern is not radically changed even when different individuals enter it or leave it. In other words, the individuals who make up the social system of the school act in certain social roles, and relate to each other according to the dictates of their role positions. Persons may move in and out of given role positions, but the roles themselves stay the same. This can be demonstrated, for instance, in the degree to which communication occurs between various members of the school staff and the ways in which a communication structure becomes established. Although communication patterns will vary in stability from school to school and from time to time within the same school, there is a considerable degree of continuity based on role expectations.

In this connection, Charters (1957) described a method for measuring the stability of the communication structure. Each member of a school staff was asked to write down the names of other staff members with whom he had talked regularly about school affairs during the past several months; and to indicate the frequency of these contacts. Where both members of a pair mentioned each other, a communication bond was said to exist.

Data of this type were gathered in a university laboratory high school one spring. Among the 30 staff positions in the school, or rather among the 435 possible pairs, there were 64 communication bonds. Persons in the same teaching specialty were far more likely to be linked by communication bonds than were persons who had been in the school for the same number of years or even persons who shared the same office.

Following an unusually high turnover of teachers that summer, parallel data were obtained in the autumn. Because more than half the staff members had changed between the two periods, bonds between faculty positions rather than the actual persons were used to compare the communication structures at the two different times. Of the total 435 possibilities, counting both bonds present and bonds absent, change had occurred in only 18 percent. Charters thus described the *stability* of the communication structure—independent from the individuals who occupied the structure—as being 82 percent. He concluded, furthermore, that the stabilizing force of teaching specialty in large measure compensates for the disruptive force of personnel turnover. (In other words, two teachers of English will tend to communicate regularly, whether or not one or both is new to the school.)

There have been other studies of communication patterns in the school and of how these are related to formal organization, job definitions, and role relationships. Berner (1957), for example, showed that official lines of communication within the school were more effective when they followed the informal communication structure. In one investigation of 11 schools of varying size, it was found that the smaller schools were superior to the larger ones with regard to communication and group cooperation (Shapiro, 1958). Various factors, then, related to both formal and informal interaction patterns, size of school, and composition of students, will be involved in creating the social organization of particular schools.

The Social Structure of the School

The school may also be viewed as a social structure in which various groups are related according to a system of rank and prestige.

In broadest outline, the school as a social system has four main levels of rank within it. At the top of the structure is the school board making school policy, selecting the chief administrator, and deciding on school expenditures. The school board acts as the agent of the wider community. It acts also as employer in relation to school administrators and teachers and has authority over the structure as a whole.

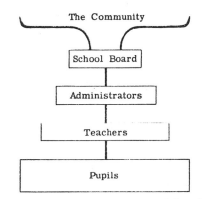

Figure 8.1 The formal structure of the school.

The second main level is that of school administrators, superintendents, principals, and supervisors. Although there are differences in rank within this group, school administrators are expected to act in positions of responsibility and authority over teachers. The role of the administrator has sometimes been described as that of the middle-man between school board and teacher. While this is true in some respects, it is also true that administrators and teachers together are employees in a system in which the employer is the school board.

The third level in the structure is composed of teachers: regular classroom teachers at elementary and secondary levels, various special teachers, and various nonteaching specialists such as guidance workers, social workers, school nurses, and psychologists who are regular members of the school staff. There are subdivisions within this level, with some groups of teachers occupying higher ranks than others (we shall return to this point presently); but teachers as a group are subordinate to school administrators and are, in turn, in positions of authority over students.

The fourth and bottom level of the structure is composed of students, the "clients" whom the school serves.

The Flow of Authority

This four-level structure characterizes the formal aspects of the school organization. While this structure is always present, the real power structure of a particular school may in actuality depart from it in one respect or another. In most schools the principal exercises authority over teachers; yet in some schools a particular teacher or small group of teachers may have disproportionate influence over the principal and may constitute the real authority on some issues. It happens, occasionally, as in certain small communities, that a teacher who has resided in the community all her life and is well-known to members of the school board may have special influence with the board.

Situations like the ones mentioned, where the true power structure within a school does not coincide in all details with the apparent structure, are not infrequent. Yet, in general, authority flows in only one direction within the school structure, downward from school board to student.

While authority flows downward, interaction of varying types occurs within the school structure in both horizontal and vertical directions, and the quality of interaction is an important influence upon the behavior of administrators, teachers, and pupils alike. In the sections to follow, we shall look more closely at certain types of interaction that occur within the social system of the school: interaction between school board and superintendent; between administrator and teacher; between teacher and teacher; and between pupil and pupil. The interaction between teachers and pupils is discussed more fully in Chapters 17 and 18.

Interaction Between School Boards and Superintendents

In one of the few empirical studies in this area, Gross (1958) interviewed at length over 100 school superintendents in Massachusetts as well as over 500 members of their school boards. On the whole the two groups tended to think well of each other. Approximately half the superintendents felt their school boards were doing an "excellent" job; and about half the members of school boards gave their superintendents a rating of "excellent" (another 40 percent gave ratings of "good").

At the same time, Gross found a certain amount of disagreement between the groups regarding their respective rights and obligations in terms of such matters as hiring teachers, dismissing teachers, handling teacher grievances, and selecting textbooks. In general, superintendents, more frequently than their school boards, felt that the superintendent should have total responsibility in these matters. School boards tended to reserve these matters to themselves.

About one out of five superintendents in this study, when listing their major role problems, said that school boards constituted a major obstacle to carrying out their jobs in a professional manner. The underlying reasons for this were varied: sometimes the superintendent thought a particular board member saw himself as filling a political patronage job; sometimes it was the board member's lack of concern for educational problems. At other times, it was because the board member interfered with the administration of the schools in what the superintendent regarded as inappropriate ways (as in bypassing the superintendent and giving directions directly to one of the superintendent's subordinates).

The role of the superintendent in relation to the school board and to the community is taking on new saliency in the late 1960's as problems of racial integration, the concept of the community school versus the "four-walls" school, and compensatory education for disadvantaged children are becoming more pressing. We shall return to this point in Chapter 11 in discussing the role of the superintendent in the relations between the schools and other social systems in the metropolitan community.

Interaction Between Teachers and Administrators

Relations between administrators and teachers are especially important in determining the general atmosphere and the general morale that characterizes a given school. Most administrators are persons who come into a school from outside, rather than persons who have moved up in the same school from the level of teacher to principal. While a person from outside is often thought to be in a position of greater freedom in dealing with subordinates, this policy often creates special problems in schools.

An extreme example is one that occurred in a large city system, where the policy is to assign principals according to merit, sidestepping either formal or informal consultation with the teachers of the school to which assignment is made. Here a principal, a Negro, was assigned to a school where all the teachers were white and where all the pupils were Negro. Although the principal tried in every way he knew to win the support of his teachers, the special problems in the situation were insuperable. One small group of teachers asked immediately for transfers to different schools, in the meantime taking pains to sabotage the principal's efforts. As might be expected, there were repercussions throughout the whole school, not only upon the principal, but upon all teachers and pupils alike.

In the more typical situation, where interaction between administrators and teachers is constructive, the morale of the school is likely to be high. An extreme example of this kind exists in the same city system. A school located in one of the worst slum sections of the city has a principal who is known throughout the system as being an unusually fine administrator. While the children are known to be among the most difficult of all to teach, this principal has built up a staff of devoted teachers, a staff that has acquired an enviable reputation for doing an outstanding job against formidable odds. There is a long waiting list of teachers who have asked to be transferred to this school. In a large city school system, where there is a complicated hierarchy of administrators, teachers do not usually have face-to-face interaction with the superintendent or with other top ranking administrators. Except for teacher-principal and teacher-supervisor, interaction becomes increasingly formal and impersonal; and communication occurs mainly by written memoranda and directives from "the downtown office." This increased social distance between teachers and top administrators in large systems is reflected in a study of 16 midwestern schools of varying size (Hunter, 1959). Greater discrepancies were found in large schools than in small ones between teachers' perceptions of the superintendent and the superintendent's self-perceptions. Nevertheless, the teacher's view of "the administration" is important in large cities as well as in small ones.

Teachers' Attitudes Toward Administrators

Teachers are likely to put interaction with administrators as one of the most influential factors in determining their overall satisfaction or dissatisfaction with their jobs.

In a nationwide study involving over two thousand teachers in forty-three states, one of the significant findings was the close correspondence between teachers' ratings of their superintendents, principals, and supervisors and the extent of their satisfaction with the school system in which they were working (Chase, 1951). Those teachers who were enthusiastic about their jobs gave high ratings to the superintendent's leadership; those who were dissatisfied with their positions rated his leadership as poor.

In the same study, teachers were asked to estimate the importance of various factors in contributing to their general satisfaction with their jobs. The most frequently-mentioned factor (mentioned by over 88 percent of teachers) was dynamic and stimulating leadership by the principal.

The importance of the interaction between principal and teacher is corroborated by other studies, such as one of elementary teachers in Chicago, where the principal was considered the most important single factor in making a "good" school (Wagenschein, 1950); and in a study by Bernstein (1959) where there was a significant relationship found between teacher morale and the teacher's perceptions of the principal.

Probably the essential factor in determining whether or not a teacher will think of the administrator as good or bad lies in the extent to which the administrator is meeting the teacher's expectations of leadership. These expectations will vary from one group of teachers to the next. Still, there are certain role-expectations for administrators that are commonly held.

Administrators are expected to support the teacher in matters of discipline. In a study of Chicago teachers the expectation was prominent in their statements that "the principal should protect the teacher's authority in dealing with both parents and children, no matter who is right" (Becker, 1951). Another study of Illinois teachers reports a similar finding (Yarbrough, 1949). Other important role expectations are that the principal should allow the teacher considerable freedom in her choice of methods and materials in teaching, and although he should offer advice he must always respect the teacher's rights.

Chase points out that the concept of the principal as a superdisciplinarian who bolsters the teachers' authority was emphasized in schools of low morale where teachers obviously felt insecure and frustrated. Teachers in high-morale schools, on the other hand, had a different concept of the principal's role, one that emphasized such things as the principal's helpfulness in solving problems of instruction and pupil adjustment, democratic administration, friendliness and interest in the teacher's work, and respect for her competence (Chase, 1951).

The teacher-administrator relationship is directly or indirectly affected by the school's relations with parent groups in the community. The following incident, is a dramatic illustration of this point:

The Samuel Slater School is an elementary school located in an area of *de facto* segregation in a large northern metropolitan city. Because of the residential patterns, seventy-one per cent of the school population is Negro, the remainder almost all Puerto Rican. Mr. Fields, the principal, has worked in this area for fourteen years. Each year he has faced the problem of teacher turnover. This year fifteen new, totally inexperienced teachers have been assigned to the school.

Mr. Fields anticipated that, with rare exception, his new teachers would be young white women who have had very little if any first hand acquaintance with conditions in a Negro and Puerto Rican neighborhood. He assumed that many had never been exposed to poverty or the breakdown of family to be found in the community to which they had been assigned. Thus, in an effort to cushion the shock he felt the young teachers might suffer upon meeting the children of this community, he sent a letter to his faculty, which said in part:

> Welcome back from vacation time. I hope that you have recharged your batteries and are ready for the challenges of the coming academic year. . . .
>
> Our school receives many special services such as smaller registers, more money per child, and teacher specialists. Why do we get these special services?
>
> Our children, for the most part, come from homes that are usually disadvantaged. That means that, compared with middle class homes, they are poorer financially, academically, socially. Specifically, many of our children are on welfare. We serve over 500 free lunches daily. The school lunch is the best meal they get.
>
> Many of our children have no father at home. There can be no organized family activities. There is lacking a male image. The mother is so busy with her brood that the individual child is lonely. He has no conversation with the mother or other adults. He is unaccustomed to listen. In fact, living in a noisy atmosphere, he has a high hearing level, i.e., he shuts out most noises and sounds in self-protection. Hence he is not going to hear his middle class teacher who speaks quietly, until he has been trained to do so by his teacher who has this as one of her conscious, specific aims. . . .
>
> Furthermore, there is lack of encouragement at home to achieve. Families on welfare for the third generation lack academic drive.
>
> The physical situation at home may be deplorable. Cold flats, no hot water, peeling paint and falling plaster, vermin, overcrowding— these are the characteristics of the homes of some of our children. For

such children, school is an oasis from squalor. You will find that your attendance is highest on the coldest days, for school is clean and warm. . . .

One purpose of this letter is to help you rid yourself of certain misconceptions: not "all slum children are slow learners." Actually, "underprivileged have just as wide a range of abilities as middle class kids." Hence, you must not have the idea that your role is chiefly custodial. That if you keep them quiet and in their seats that you have earned your salary; you haven't. Mere custodians are taking their checks under false pretences. You have a license as a teacher. That is your job—to teach—to teach with all these difficulties in mind, to try to compensate for their handicaps. If you are indifferent to their academic achievement or lack of it, they will continue to be indifferent for their poor environment and minority group status are not their fault. Nor is it yours. But it *is* your responsibility to plan your work with these facts in mind. . . .

Your first days will be devoted to training in routine; mechanical aspects of the classroom must be mechanized. You will see to it that the children are clean, that every child's hair is combed, and that every boy has a necktie on.

There are certain basic academic skills that you will stress. These are:

1. Listening
2. Reading
3. Expression of ideas
4. Mathematics

Through our P.T.A. we are going to try to instill a greater sense of responsibility in some of our parents. We will try to get them to understand the importance of:

1. Cleanliness
2. Proper dress
3. Punctuality
4. Attendance—unless ill
5. Care of school property
6. Neat, clean, complete, accurate notebooks
7. Academic achievement

From you the teachers I expect:

1. Punctuality
2. Careful preparation
3. Functioning on a level above that of the children
4. "Know how to call to the man which has lain dormant within the soul of the child."

There are many other things I could say, but this letter is much too long already. Hence, I shall say no more at this time.

But I do pledge you on behalf of the three supervisors our complete cooperation and aid. Their activities will be not only in the school, but in the community at large too, for there are certain responsibilities that the community must assume and not purge itself of a sense of guilt by criticizing the schools.

Mr. Fields, wishing to let the parents know how the school was helping new teachers do a better job, sent a copy of the letter to the president of the Parent Teachers Association.

At the P.T.A. executive board meeting held that week, Mrs. Post, the president reported the communication from the principal. Several of the board members immediately became infuriated. Discussion and anger at the principal became the subject of the entire meeting, and an unofficial committee was formed by several executive board members to see the principal to demand an apology.

When the committee called upon him, Mr. Fields was absolutely astonished. Indignant at what he considered an unjustified response by the parents to his sincere efforts to improve the school, he informed the parents that he had intended no harm and saw no need to apologize.

Angered by the principal's refusal to apologize, the parents' committee began to circulate a petition in the neighborhood of the school calling for his ouster. (Fuchs, 1966, pp. 3–4.)

Interaction Among Teachers

Among the teachers of any school both a formal and an informal social organization emerges that regulates behavior and in which individual teachers occupy positions of varying degrees of prestige. On the formal side, there is an organization that relates to the duties that teachers perform outside their regular classroom teaching. There may be committees—one responsible for curriculum, one for social activities, one for disciplinary problems—each with its chairman. Certain teachers may be responsible for supervising study halls; others, for supervising the lunchroom. In an elementary school there is likely to be one teacher who acts as assistant to the principal and who often enjoys an added measure of prestige over other teachers. In a large high school there may be departmentalization according to subject matter, with one teacher acting as department head. These and other factors are involved in creating a formal organization among the teachers of a particular school, an organization in which rights and duties are differentially assigned.

There is also, however, an informal organization that operates to influence social interaction. The informal organization is often one in which distinctions between teachers are unrelated to school duties but operate nevertheless to form a hierarchy of prestige.

FACTORS RELATED TO PRESTIGE. One factor is seniority. Teachers who have longer experience or who have been in a given school for a greater number of years usually occupy favored positions. Administrators are likely to give them preference over younger and newer teachers in a number of ways. Age itself is often a factor, and many older teachers expect younger ones to defer to them.

Another factor that operates in most school systems is related to the age of the children being taught. High-school teachers, whether or not they are being paid higher salaries, and whether or not they have had more formal education, tend to be regarded as being somewhat higher in the social system of the school than are elementary teachers. Teachers who "move up in the system" usually move from elementary to high school, and not vice-versa. The eighth-grade teacher often enjoys more prestige than the first-grade teacher; the teacher of Senior English, more than the teacher of Freshman English.

Subtle factors of prestige operate in the particular subject matter being taught, with teachers of "academic" subjects often taking precedence over others. In many schools, the teacher of English ranks above the teacher of bookkeeping, the mathematics teacher above the shop teacher, and so on. This factor is often related to matters of social class, since it is usually boys and girls of upper social-class levels who are enrolled in college-preparatory subjects, and boys and girls of lower social levels who are enrolled in vocational subjects. Thus teachers often consider it somehow "better" to teach one group of students than another. This basis for teacher rankings is also related to the values that are current within the teaching group itself, where it is sometimes thought that history, for example, is more difficult to teach than typewriting; and that the history teacher is therefore of higher intellectual ability or cultural refinement.

The subtle rankings that go on among teachers themselves may or may not coincide with the ranks accorded teachers by the wider community. Thus it may be the teacher of agriculture or the athletic coach who may enjoy the highest esteem in the community but who, in the eyes of fellow-teachers, occupies a position of low prestige in the teacher hierarchy.

In a large city, one school may be regarded as "better" than another, either because of the economic level of the neighborhood in which the school is located or the tradition that it is a school of unusually high academic standards.

CLIQUES AND FRIENDSHIP GROUPS. Teachers, just as any other group, form friendship cliques and these clique relations may affect the day-to-day operation of the school. Sometimes one clique of teachers will seem to dominate school politics; sometimes there will be friction between groups.

The following illustration, written by a teacher, is of a school in which interaction between teachers was only superficially democratic:

To a casual observer, there is a spirit of good will and cooperation at the Fulview Elementary School. The teachers smile at each other in the halls, they exchange chit-chat about relatively unimportant things, they discuss pupils and their progress and a host of other things that come up in a regular school day. But only a person who has not seen the more intimate groupings at lunch, at teachers' meetings, at school banquets, or when teachers leave the building, can entertain the notion that all is well at Fulview.

There are various factions based on race, ethnic groups, age, interests, and experiences. For instance, although there are no formal restrictions involved in where lunch should be eaten, the white teachers, irrespective of cliques, eat in one place and the Negro teachers eat in another. There are cliques, to be sure, within each group, but there is a solidarity based upon color. Although the white teachers and Negro teachers may go home in the same direction, one may drive past the other who is waiting for a street car.

There is a strong Irish Catholic faction who stick together on many basic issues. This is partly so because they share church interests. For example, one might walk up to this group and hear about a funeral, a confirmation, a mass, a wedding, or an encyclical from the Pope with which they are all familiar. Many of these teachers have taught side by side for years. They know much of the history of the school, they have worked under different administrators together, they have visited each other in their homes, they know each other's grandchildren. So this division is not one based on religion and ethnic group alone, but one that came into being because of similarity of memories and experiences.

There is another group of teachers, a younger group that includes two Jewish, one Polish, and one Italian girl. Clothes, social affairs, movies, television, and books are the subjects of their conversations.

The adherence to cliques and groups was aggravated when the assistant principal, the eighth grade teacher, was appointed acting principal. Her special friends were invited into the "inner sanctum" (the office) to talk at any time of the day. Some teachers thought she was showing favoritism, some of those in her own clique became envious, and some thought she was carried away with her new position. There was ill feeling, tempers flared, and general morale was low.

This was the situation into which our new principal came. His ambition to reorganize the school in light of new educational theory made matters more acute, for he implied that things were in a terrible mess, that his predecessors were to blame, and that many of us teachers were in a professional rut. To the Irish Catholics, the fact that he is Jewish constitutes two strikes against him. To the older teachers, the fact that he is young counts against him.

Things are going from bad to worse, and the whole situation seems unhealthy. I fear some of the attitudes attendant on the situation are detrimental to the children. I ask myself, How well are we teaching democratic living?

The next example is that of a school in a small town where the problem was between old teachers and a newcomer.

A few years ago, I accepted my first teaching position in a small community near my home town. The position appeared particularly challenging because it combined kindergarten and grade school music teaching.

When school started I found that most of the other teachers were older women. They taught largely by traditional methods and looked with suspicion upon "new" ideas.

Being new to the system, inexperienced in teaching, and worst of all, young, I had real problems in being accepted by the teaching staff. We were even further divided by our different views about teaching. As a kindergarten teacher, the staff rather expected that my ideas would be different (since you don't really *teach* in kindergarten!). But it was through my activities as the grade-school music teacher that our differences became pronounced.

One of the duties of the music teacher was to take responsibility for a Christmas program. The first year I suggested that we attempt to put on an original program, because it would provide more learning situations for the children than published material. This idea was considered impractical. That year the school presented a popular operetta, according to precedent.

The second year I was determined to utilize my ideas, and once again suggested that the children do their own show. After several weeks of discussion, during which no agreement was reached, I exercised my responsibility and planned a program myself. The plan was intended to foster the children's creativity with a minimum amount of teacher dictation; and second, to be one in which all the two hundred children in the school would have some part. The program theme was Christmas-around-the-world. Each room chose a country to study; folk music from that country was selected, and dialogue was prepared based on national customs. Each group made costumes and props for their ten-minute presentations.

From the beginning, the majority of teachers felt that the program could not possibly be successful. Many objections were raised, many compromises made, and unfortunately, many creative efforts of the children were not utilized. But I saw to it that every child participated.

There was no doubt that the parents enjoyed the final production, probably because every child took part. There were many favorable comments from both parents and children. Among the teachers, however, nothing about the program was said in my presence. Not until the following May, five months later, did one of them remark, "Well, that was quite a Christmas program. Are you gratified?"

It was clear that most of the barriers between myself and the other teachers still existed. This was essentially the reason why I decided to look for a different position, why today I am teaching in a school where I feel more in accord with the general school philosophy. No teacher can do a good job of teaching when she's considered an outsider by the other teachers.

Interaction Among Students

There is always a social organization among the students of any school, one that has its own system of rank and prestige, and one in which different students have quite different patterns of activities.

SIZE OF THE SCHOOL. The size of the school itself has been found to make a difference. Barker and his associates (1962), in comparing the social and intellectual environments of small high schools (35 to 151 students) and one large high school (2287 students) within the same state, found that the students in the small schools were more likely than those in large schools to participate actively in extracurricular activities and to hold positions of importance both in their schools and in the community. The students in the small schools, furthermore, were more likely to report satisfactions relating to the development of competence, to being challenged, to engaging in important activities, and to achieving more cultural values. Students in the large school were more likely to report satisfaction dealing with vicarious enjoyment, with large-entity affiliation, with learning about their school's members and affairs, and with gaining "points" for participation.

The students in the small schools had, as well as more opportunity, more pressure put upon them to participate—the small schools had much the same variety of positions to be filled as did the large school, but fewer students to fill them.

SOCIAL PRESTIGE HIERARCHIES. Social class background, as we have discussed it in an earlier chapter, operates to greater or lesser extent in creating a system of prestige among students (Neugarten, 1949). Athletic ability is an important factor in most high schools, with football and basketball players occupying privileged positions. Participation in extracurricular activities, physical attractiveness, personality attributes —all these are factors that combine to produce a system in which certain students are at the top of the social hierarchy while others are at the bottom.

This social-prestige hierarchy can be seen especially among adolescents. There are some who "rate" and some who do not.

Whatever the bases of rank, a social organization grows up among students that gives rise to a status system of its own.

Gordon (1957), for example, made a detailed study of the social system of the high school in a midwestern suburban community referred to as Wabash. By using a composite index of social status within the school, he placed each of the 576 students within the social network; then proceeded to show how students' behavior was related to their positions. The index of social status was based upon three factors: school grades; participation in formal student organizations; and sociometric status, or the number of times the student was chosen as a "best friend" by other students.

One of Gordon's major propositions was that most adolescents are oriented primarily toward fulfilling the expectations of the informal group, their peers, and toward gaining prestige within their social system. He showed how the informal social organization, the friendship and clique pattern, was closely related to participation in formal student organizations and how the prestige value assigned to the various formal organizations differed.

Thus, of the 50 different organizations in Wabash High, the seniors assigned the top ranks to Student Government, Varsity Basketball, Varsity Football, National Honor Society, Cheer Leaders, and Crest Coronation (Yearbook Queen's Court). The lowest ranks went to the Roller Skating Club, the Outdoor Club, the Pencil Pushers (creative writing), the Riding Club (horseback riding) and the Knitting Club. Directly related to the ratings of the organizations was the prestige assigned to their various offices. Competition to fill these offices, Gordon says, was a major preoccupation for a majority of students.

The student who belonged to a sufficient number of prestigious organizations and filled a sufficient number of offices warranted the title, "big wheel." For boys, the sources of this status were primarily athletic achievements, although by extreme effort, achievements in other than athletic activities might be combined to produce the "big wheel." The label itself denoted a pattern of expected behavior as well as a particular status in the eyes of the group.

One 12th-grade boy, a self-styled "big wheel," said: "Everyone enjoys privileges but none intends to take advantage of them, although I feel that sometimes I do. I am a necessary member of the choir, and I am afraid that I take advantage most of the time. I'm constantly absent or late to class.

"Today was a typical example. At 1:07 I strolled into class without a word and took my seat. I thought Andrews wouldn't say anything, but he stopped and asked me for an excuse. I gave my usual answer of, 'Why, am I late?' He says, 'Are you late? Seven minutes!' To this I just said, 'Oh, do you want me to get an excuse?' He gives up and we go on singing without my giving any sort of reason for being late.

"If I am just a minute or less after the bell, I just nod to him as I go in and he lets me go. What are the kids' reactions? They all think it's a big joke. Some girls come out with, 'big wheel.'

"Who are the 'big wheel' seniors? I think I am one, since I have carried on many more activities than anyone else. . . ." (He then goes on to name some 20 different athletic and other activities in which he has participated in his junior and senior years.)

Girls were "big wheels" too, and the most prized . . . status of all was formalized in the position, Queen of the Yearbook. The Queen was crowned in a public ceremony called the Yearbook Coronation, the major social function of the year.

The social careers of the 12th-grade girls were climaxed with the election of the Queen who was selected by a school-wide vote from a slate of nine candidates nominated by the senior boys. The eight candidates who were not chosen Queen served as Maids of the Queen's Court.

The Queen's throne was a slippery place, made so by the intense competition for the office. . . . Functioning as a model for behavior among girls throughout the school, the office of Queen was highly selective in the social type that achieved it. Its behavioral counterpart, the "Queen Role," integrated a complex set of expectations centered in the primary values of the adolescent female sex role: beauty, approved dress, moral character, democratic personality, scholastic achievement, exercise of influence, and school service. . . .

Girls "hoped" to be Queen, but they definitely worked to "make the

Coronation Court" as hard as boys worked to make the basketball team; girls differed in their covertness rather than in the intensity of their striving. Because of the hidden nature of the struggle, it was regulated only by informal rules and expectations which operated as a highly unstable control over the competition and as a source of tension among girls who were presumed to be candidates.

An 11th-grade girl said, "In my Freshman year I attended Waterville High School, . . . but in my sophomore year when I came to Wabash, one of the first things that I noticed was the girls in my class and their desire to be on the Court.

"The first day at school I heard a discussion of who would be on the Coronation Court. Various girls were named, so I thought I was as likely a candidate as any of them. So a girl friend and I set out to be popular.

"This friend and I gave pajama parties to help make the girls like us. When the day was over, we would get together and add up our progress. Such things were included: what older boys had asked us for a date, or had talked to us? If any popular boy in our class talked to us or acted interested, what things could we do or say that would attract favorable attention from him? . . . Then we tried to join every club we could, so it would look like we had done a lot for the school. . . . We also tried to become cheer-leaders. . . .

"Later that year I met and started going with Bob Hires and I decided to stop this silly act as I wanted to be myself and have Bob like me. . . . When I decided to be myself instead of some real popular girl and a big flirt, I had more friends. . . . I suppose that if I could be on the Coronation Court it would be nice but I would not act like some girls in my class for anything. There are in the large clique some girls who would stop at nothing to get on the Court. . . ." (Gordon, 1957, pp. 62–73.)

In Wabash High School, Gordon describes a single overall prestige system. In other schools, the social interaction between students seems more differentiated. Clark, for example, has described three adolescent subcultures to be found within the typical comprehensive high school: the first he calls the "fun" subculture—the sports, cars, dating, beauty queen value-pattern, with a derogation of intellectual values; the second, the "academic" subculture—the serious students who are more oriented toward their studies and to academic extra-curricular activities than to anything else, sometimes called by others, the "grinds" or "curve-raisers"; the third, the "delinquent" subculture—the students who rebel against the school and the adult value pattern, and who want to get out of school, the group who, in some slum schools, have the switchblade knife as their symbol. A fourth type of student Clark described as being marginal to all three orientations—these are the "faceless" students who never speak up, who go unnoticed during school hours, who show apathy and withdrawal (Clark, 1962).

The School as a Web of Social Interaction

From the above discussion it is clear that interaction between persons within the same general level of the school structure or between persons of two different levels affects the organization as a whole. Often it is the quality of the interaction between administrators and teachers or between teachers and teachers or between teachers and pupils that accounts for the degree of success or failure that a given school achieves.

The superintendent who enjoys the full support of his school board may undertake innovations that will have beneficial effects upon all teachers and pupils in the school system. If his relationships with the school board are strained, effects may also be noticeable throughout the entire school. Similarly, the interaction between administrators and teachers will make itself felt upon pupils, and the quality of teacher-pupil relations will affect teacher-administrator relations.

Whether a school shows a complex or a simple organizational pattern among students themselves, student interaction tends to be self-contained, and there is always a clear dichotomy between student and adult roles.

This dichotomy seldom poses problems at the elementary-school level, but it sometimes creates difficulties at the high-school level. The problem seems to arise, not when the distinction is clearly maintained, but when, for some reason, it becomes blurred. Thus Stinchcomb (1965) points out that those students who claim adult status in one or another way—for example, some students who devalue school and value early marriage and work—tend to be the students who rebel against the school expectations. This is, perhaps, another way of saying that the typical high school imposes a childlike status upon the adolescent and operates to prolong his immaturity; and that the typical high school functions smoothly to the extent that the dichotomy between adolescents and adults is maintained.

In summary, then, the school is a complex web of social interaction, with various types of interaction going on simultaneously, each affecting the whole, and each having at least an indirect influence upon the child.

Exercises

1. Describe a situation in which clique formations within a student body had a disruptive effect upon school procedures. Be specific.

2. Describe the social organization among the teachers in a school or college with which you are acquainted. (One in which you have been a student or a teacher.) Is there any cleavage between groups? Upon what bases are cliques formed?

3. Give an example of how administrator-teacher relationships affected the students of a given school.

4. What, in your opinion, is the most sensitive spot in the interactional system of the school? Why?

Suggestions for Further Reading

1. Willard Waller's book, *The Sociology of Teaching*, although written some time ago, is nevertheless an excellent treatment of the school as a social system. Excerpts from the book appear on pp. 70–89 in *Social Foundations of Education*, by William O. Stanley *et al.*

2. *School Culture* by Hilda Taba reports studies made in several school systems of student participation in school activities and of the dynamics of group life within the school. While the focus of these studies was upon the improvement of human relations, the book points up some of the tremendous variation that exists in the culture of American schools and how this culture impinges upon the life of the student.

3. Read C. Wayne Gordon's *The Social System of the High School* for more details of the social organization that exists within Wabash High School. The book contains much illustrative material.

4. Joseph Fichter, in *Parochial School,* gives a detailed analysis of an urban Catholic school. He describes various aspects of the culture of the school, its social organization, and its relations to the wider community.

5. For an interesting description of the subtleties of intended and unintended communications between teachers and other persons in the school system, and the kinds of "fronts" teachers put up, read Chapter 10, "Interpersonal Relations in Education," in Corwin's book, *A Sociology of Education.*

6. Read Parsons' article in *Society and Education: A Book of Readings* by
    Havighurst, Neugarten, and Falk for a description of the classroom as
    a social unit and the way the classroom group socializes the child. Both
    the paper by Coleman and the paper by Gottlieb and Ten Houten, in
    the same book, illustrate different aspects of the school as a social
    system by describing the relations of the peer group to the school and
    by demonstrating how the racial composition of a particular school
    affects the patterns of activities of both Negro and white adolescents.

7. Read Chapter 4, "The Child of the Slum in Educational Space and
    Time." in Eddy, *Walk the White Line,* for a graphic description of the
    school as a formal social system.

8. Read Chapter 12, "The Role of the School Administrator," in the book
    of readings, *Education and Culture,* edited by Spindler.

PART 3

THE SCHOOL IN
THE COMMUNITY

The chapters which constitute Part 1 of this book dealt with the school in the social structure of a modern democratic society. Here, we shall return to a consideration of the relation of the school to society, but from a different set of perspectives. We shall ask, first, what is the proper role of the school in the local community; then, given the growth of metropolitan communities, how does the school relate to the local community which has become the whole metropolitan area; finally, how does the school relate to other social institutions and social systems within the metropolitan community?

9 / The Community School

Ever since the evolution of human society brought the school into existence as a specialized agency for the socialization of the young, questions have been raised about the proper relations between school and community. Three general answers or points of view have been posited. The first is the traditional one, so called because it was the prevailing one in America up through the nineteenth century. According to this view, the school should be walled off from the problems of the local community and should limit itself to teaching essential mental and vocational skills. The other two answers, "the school as a model of the community," and "the community school," have emerged within the present century. According to the latter two views, the school has broader functions that bring it into close relations with the surrounding community.

What Is a Community?

In assessing these views, it is necessary to consider two rather different meanings of the term "community." While the school is located in the local community, it is also preparing children for life in the wider national and international community. The difference between the two uses of the term is perhaps made clearer by a distinction between "primary" and "secondary" communities.

A *primary community* is one in which people are related by face-to-face association and cooperation. It is often said of such a community

that "everybody knows everybody else." While this may not be completely true, it is true that everybody can see face-to-face anyone with
whom he is likely to have significant dealings. In this kind of community, people usually feel that they have common interests and that they
can trust one another.

A *secondary community* is one in which people are related indirectly by trade and business connections or by belonging to the same
religious, professional, or economic group. People in secondary communities are interdependent, but they seldom or never meet each other
face-to-face. The big city is a secondary community, as is a state, a
region, or a nation. The world is becoming a community, more than ever
before, but only on the secondary level.

School curricula and school activities are related both to the local
primary community and to the wider secondary community. Although
educators must constantly keep in mind the relationship of a good
school to both primary and secondary aspects of the human community,
the three conceptions of the school listed above refer to the school's
relation to the local community.

A. The Traditional School

When the school is seen to have only the highly specialized job of
training children's minds and teaching them intellectual and vocational
skills, it becomes separate from the community. This point of view,
overstated somewhat for the sake of contrast, is that the school should
do its job just as the municipal water works does its job. It should work
quietly, inconspicuously, and efficiently, and it should limit itself to its
special functions. According to this view, to ask the school to do other
things, such as teaching children to develop good social relations with
one another or to form good food habits, would be like asking the
municipal water works to do the job of the police department. The best
possible education is seen as taking place when children study lessons
that are chosen for their value as mental discipline; or for the information that will be useful in adult life. These lessons may or may not have
anything directly to do with the immediate local community surrounding
the school.

The traditional school, in one variation or another, is the type with
which most adults are familiar. Emphasis is placed upon school sub-

jects, with most of the time divided between reading, writing, and arithmetic in the lower grades, and between language, mathematics, science, and social studies in the higher grades. Teachers are expected above all to be expert in their subject-matter fields and in teaching methods; and emphasis is placed upon academic ability as the child's only avenue to school success.

Figure 9.1 The traditional concept of school-community relations.

Most schools in America have moved a long way from the traditional point of view, even though many of the values inherent within it are still recognized and sought after, and even though the point of view still has vigorous proponents. A large part of the ever-continuing controversy over the American school system revolves about this concept that the school has its special and limited functions of providing intellectual training and that any deviation from this goal is undesirable.

Thus Bestor, one of the champions of this position, points out that in the nineteenth century the public-school curriculum was radically reorganized, abandoning the classics as the foundation of education, and replacing them with science, mathematics, and history, subjects more relevant to a society that had become secularized, industrialized, and scientific in outlook. Outlining the fundamental disciplines and the fundamental areas of knowledge that had been agreed upon by the end of the nineteenth century as constituting effective education, he goes on to say, "It was a curriculum not for the year or the decade, but for the century that was about to commence." Arguing that American education has gone astray within the last few decades as it has moved from this curriculum, he says:

The next quarter century can redress the failures of the last if we as educators will take up again conscientiously and unitedly the business that was left unfinished a generation ago, when we began to allow educational faddists to sidetrack the schools into a succession of unprofitable, anti-intellectual programs, ranging from the "child-centered schools" to "life-adjust-ment education." (Bestor, 1955, p. 52.)

Or, in another instance, he says:

If the nation is to survive and remain strong, we must have an educa-tion system that is thoroughly up-to-date. The way to bring our public schools up to date is not to experiment with substitutes for intellectual training, but to find ways of teaching the fundamentals more thoroughly than ever before, and to an ever-increasing proportion of all the students in our schools. Our object, after all, is to produce educated men and women, not to reward our youngsters with a diploma for merely growing up. (Bestor, 1957, p. 8.)

There are many, educators and non-educators alike, who share Bestor's view of the function of the school and who oppose contrasting views that the school should be a model of the community or that the school should share in all aspects of community life.

B. The School as a Model of the Community

A second possible relation of school and community is one in which the school is a simplified model of the community. According to this view, children learn how to live as adults by learning first to live within the school community. John Dewey's first school was like this, and he said of it,

The School of Education wishes particularly, then, the cooperation of parents in creating the healthy moral tone which will render quite unneces-sary resort to lower and more unworthy motives for regulating conduct. The cultivation of a democratic tone, an *esprit-de-corps,* which attaches itself to the social life of the school as a whole, and not to some clique or set in it. . . . We hope you will remember that a school has a corporate life of its own; that, whether for good or bad, it is itself a genuine social institution—a community. (Dewey, 1904, p. 452.)

He said further:

When the school introduces and trains each child of society into membership within such a little community, saturating him with the spirit of service, and providing him with the instruments of effective self-direction, we shall have the deepest and best guarantee of a larger society which is worthy, lovely, and harmonious. (Dewey, 1915, pp. 27–28.)

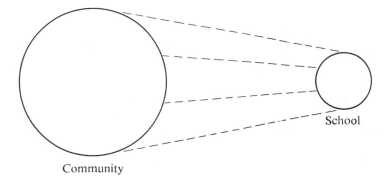

Community

Figure 9.2 The concept of the school as a model of the community.

The Elementary School Level

In a school of this kind the pupils have a busy and varied day. It is considered good for children to eat and play together as well as work together, and to share a wide range of activities. The elementary school of this type is likely to have a garden tended by the children, and pets in the classrooms or in shelters on the school ground. The kindergarten or first grade may have a miniature store, made out of paper cartons, where pupils can buy, sell, and make change right in their own classroom. As the pupils grow older they take responsibility for organizing much of their own work. They form committees to carry out class projects. They organize parties and start clubs. When classes are over they may have a period of supervised after-school play that keeps them off the streets and out of the city playgrounds, and confines their choice of playmates to their schoolmates.

The High School Level

At the high school level, this type of school often has an effective student government that has a good deal of power to deal with school activities, athletics, and often with minor problems of discipline. The high school tends to be a social unit, with its own parties and entertainments. Such a school usually offers a good program of dramatics and music. (This type of school occasionally takes the form of a boarding school with large grounds and sometimes a farm, where pupils do a share of the daily work.)

The following account is an illustration of a school in which opportunities are provided for a variety of work experiences, not in the outside community, but within the school.

The seventh and eighth grade children in the Ann J. Kellogg School, Battle Creek, Michigan, have the opportunity to choose work as an elective subject. This includes child care, cafeteria, library, office, and maintenance work. . . .

Counselors, who are helping children plan their programs, often advise them to choose child care. These classes provide situations calling for dependability, originality, the ability to understand and tolerate persons other than their kind, and a willingness to take directions from adults with whom they work.

The assistants work with special primary, special intermediate (mentally deficient), Braille, visual hearing, orthopedic, cardiac, epileptic and other types of exceptional children.

The experiences with child care are not merely of a routine nature consisting of waiting upon the handicapped. Quite to the contrary, the child has the opportunity to develop a keener sense of appreciation and to assist in creative work of all kinds: music, dramatics, and art. Tact, patience, and a wholesome attitude are required in this work. The assistants learn to exercise qualities of leadership without becoming dictators. . . .

Throughout the day students take care of the library. Here the child who enjoys the atmosphere of the library learns to catalog, classify, and service books to the students of the school. Many children are skilled in the use of reference materials and have a wide background of reading at their command; they are able to help other children find materials readily. It is necessary that library assistants exercise qualities of poise and dependability and learn to meet the public easily.

Boys working in the cafeteria spend from one to two hours daily there under capable direction learning to do a variety of tasks, such as cleaning tables, carrying trays, serving, kitchen work. These boys must be willing to work, take orders easily and be neat in their appearance. Children who choose cafeteria work find themselves in a most democratic situation and in almost every instance have made a fine adjustment to problems that arise. . . .

Boys and girls help in maintenance work and in keeping the building attractive inside and out. The student association is at present engaged in planning a definite work program in which each child and group takes the responsibility for certain tasks about the building. This work is not designed to take the place of that done by the regular maintenance staff, but is planned to give boys and girls a sense of responsibility, duty, orderliness, and service toward the social group to which they belong. Art work, showcases, bulletin boards, reading centers, plants, displays of all kinds are sponsored in every group. . . . Boys who choose to assist in maintenance work help care for the appearance of the gym, lobbies, and locker rooms.

The work program in our school has been an effective means of teaching that "service above self" is desirable and satisfying to the child. It has unconsciously developed in the child a sense of group responsibility not only to the handicapped but to society as a whole. . . . It has served to help develop the individual's worth to society and to make him an effective member of his social group. (Englund and Fuller, 1945, pp. 59–60.)

In schools of this type, it is expected that children and adolescents will be better citizens of the community because they have learned the lessons of democratic community life within the school itself, lessons that are appropriate to the *school* community and to children living and working together.

C. The Community School

A third relation between the school and the community is one that offers the closest structural unity possible, with the school operating directly as an agent for community betterment, and with pupils, either children or adults, taking part in community activities. This is the *community school* as it has developed in the United States since 1930.

Figure 9.3 The concept of the community school.

The Community as the Basis of Education

People who think about education in broad terms, as a process of teaching children the concepts and attitudes of their society, and of teaching them how to behave in their social, civic, and economic relations, tend to think of the whole community as an educative agent. From this point of view, the school alone cannot do the job of education, nor can the school and family together. Education is the result of living and growing up in a community.

Joseph K. Hart, writing about the nature of education in a democracy, and the role of the community in providing the most effective setting, said:

The democratic problem in education is not primarily a problem of training children; it is the problem of *making a community* within which children cannot help growing up to be democratic, intelligent, disciplined to freedom, reverent of the goods of life, and eager to share in the tasks of the age. A school cannot produce this result; nothing but a community can do so. (Hart, 1924, p. 383.)

Because the community is so important in the education of children, educators are interested in finding the best combination of school and community experience for educational purposes.

There are two broad characteristics of the *community school:* (1) It teaches children to discover, develop, and use the resources of the local community. (2) It serves the entire community, not merely the children of school age.

The Community School in a Rural Setting

These features are seen clearly in a number of community-school experiments first undertaken in small rural communities. For example, in the late 1930's the Sloan Foundation supported educational ventures in rural communities in Kentucky, Florida, and Vermont, aimed at improving diet, housing, and clothing (Henderson and Nutter, 1942; Morrill, 1945; Olson and Fletcher, 1946; Seay and Meece, 1944). Children were taken off the standard readers and arithmetic books that had been traditional in those schools and were given new reading material dealing with nutrition, housing, and clothing. At the same time projects were started within the schools. In Kentucky, children were taught to eat new foods. Gardens were planted; tomatoes were grown and introduced into the diet; goats were raised to produce milk. In Florida, a small model home was built out of local building materials. Children learned these new practices at school, then took them home to their parents; and parents were drawn into the school setting.

The Community School in an Urban Setting

If the community school were only a rural phenomenon, it would have limited usefulness in a society that is steadily growing more urban. It appears, however, that big cities also make use of the community school concept. The Flint, Michigan, public schools, for example, have developed a community-school program that could be adapted to fit any industrial city.

Although the community-school program in Flint, an automobile manufacturing city, began during the Depression of the 1930's, it has gained momentum since then and is now a regular part of the program of the Flint Public Schools. The program started with the use of the schools in the evenings and on weekends for providing recreation and diversion for men out of work and their families. When full employment returned, the program became even more popular. Most of the elementary schools are open evenings and Saturdays. All of the 20 or more elementary schools built since 1950 have a "community wing" consisting of a community room, a kitchen, a gymnasium, and an auditorium.

A visitor may observe the following:

Neighborhood elementary schools that are busier on almost any evening than during the day; 500 youngsters attending junior high school on Saturday mornings of their own accord to acquire skills they haven't found time for during the regular school week; an elderly woman going back to high school (one of 3,000 persons enrolled each year in adult high school education); a family reupholstering dad's easy chair in the school's arts and crafts room (part of 35,000 enrolled annually in 776 adult education courses); community players rehearsing their next production in the auditorium of an elementary school; a school person making neighborhood calls.

The Flint community school also provides the facilities for regular sessions of the neighborhood Teen Club (one of 43 such groups with a card-carrying membership of 13,000); for 7,000 children on tot lots during the summer; for meetings in the community room of men's clubs, P.T.A.'s and various other organizations; for square dances for parents, teen-agers and the younger ones, and other recreational activities held in the large gymnasium; for a Christmas party attended by 700 adults in a school with an enrollment of only 500. (Buehring, 1958, p. 36.)

The urban community school has one or both of two characteristics. First, as illustrated in Flint, the school is made to serve the educational, cultural, and social needs of its immediate local community.

The second, a more controversial characteristic and one that most often applies to the whole school system of a community rather than to one or another particular neighborhood school, occurs when the school takes part in the reshaping and renewing of the urban community. It adopts attendance or districting policies which are aimed at serving the purposes of urban renewal. If one of the purposes of urban renewal in a given community happens to be that of maintaining racial balance in the schools, then the urban-community-school system adopts practices that work toward racial balance. If another of the purposes is to reduce dropouts from high school and to reduce youth unemployment, then the urban-community school develops a program of work experience, remedial teaching, or other methods to serve those purposes.

The urban community school cooperates with non-school agencies in urban renewal. If it appears that parents and citizens of middle income are becoming concerned about educational standards in the city schools and are thinking of moving to the suburbs, the urban community school attempts to act constructively by involving those parents and other citizens in discussions and decisions about school policies and practices.

Urban Community Schools and Administrators

The urban community school which takes on a more controversial characteristic by participating in community development depends for its existence upon school administrators who can analyze and understand the communities they serve; and it also depends upon school policies which allow flexibility, so that school practices and school curricula can be deliberately varied from one area of the city to the next.

We shall have more to say about school superintendents in Chapter 11, but at the local neighborhood level a community school ideally involves educators who not only understand the community but also identify with it emotionally. In this respect, there is relatively little difficulty in establishing a community school in urban middle-class neighborhoods, such as in Crestwood Heights, to be described below. But emotional identification is a great deal to ask in neighborhoods where the middle-class teacher confronts the working-class child or the child who differs from him markedly with regard to culture, ethnicity, or race. In most instances of the latter type, therefore, as Saltzman (1963) has pointed out, the school's success will depend less upon virtuoso performances of its most talented and sympathetic teachers and will depend more upon becoming recognized as an agency that cares about the neighborhood and its children and one that can translate this concern into action.

In this connection, the role of the school principal is crucial. The principal must be flexible and willing to work with community needs more than with bureaucratic prescriptions. Saltzman suggests that a particular urban school should be planned long before the architect begins the design of the school building itself; that key school staff members (the principal, community coordinator, guidance coordinator) should be selected two years before a new community school is opened; that they should be free to study the community and to participate actively in planning the new school in collaboration with other agencies and citizens' groups (agencies such as the Urban Renewal Authority, the social welfare agencies which expend public funds in the area, and the health and welfare council).

Where the problem is not one of a new school, but of making an existing school more community oriented, then Saltzman suggests at least an advance selection of a new principal (or the temporary release of the assigned principal) to allow him at least six months, free of school responsibility, for studying the community and designing a community-school program.

The Four-Walls School

The alternative to the community school in the city system may be called the "four-walls" school. It focuses attention upon doing the best possible job of teaching every boy and girl who comes into the school, whoever he is, whatever his color, nationality, or IQ. It minimizes any activities which might "distract" school personnel from this task. This means building good school buildings, equipping them well, and staffing them with well-trained teachers. It means making clear to parents and interested citizens that the schools are run by professionals who know their business and who do not need help from other people in the community. It means keeping the schools "out of local politics." In contrast to the community school, it means relatively limited coopera-tion with other social institutions, public and private. The school may ask help from public aid and public health agencies, but the help must fit in with school policies and programs.

The four-walls type of school system works for efficiency, economy, and high educational standards, and attempts to free the teacher to do the best possible job under conditions that maximize his independence from outside groups. The community outside the school is regarded as introducing problems of undesirable complexity for school personnel, and the attempt is made to keep the boundary between community and school clearly defined and respected lest tensions arise to interfere with school operations.

Schools in Differing Metropolitan Neighborhoods

In the next chapter we shall examine some of the facts of urbanization upon our society, and point to the rapid social changes which center around the development of the metropolitan area as the geographic and economic unit of social organization. At this point, however, we shall focus upon school-community relationships as these vary from one type of neighborhood to another *within* the metropolitan area.

As already implied, the school is more congruent with some communities than others; and the concept of the community school is more easily implemented in some neighborhoods within a metropolitan complex than in others. Elizabeth Eddy (1967), has aptly illustrated some of this variety in her descriptions of family-school relations in three metropolitan subcommunities, each of different ethnic and socioeconomic composition. The descriptions are based, in turn, upon community studies recently completed in each community (Seeley, Sim and Loosley, 1963; Dobriner, 1963; and Padilla, 1958).

Crestwood Heights

An upper-middle-class suburb of Toronto, the population of Crestwood Heights is approximately 17,000, about equally divided between Jews and Gentiles. It is a community of single, spatially separated, one-family homes in which the "massive centrality of the schools . . . makes the most immediate physical impact on any outside observer." Schools and homes together "assert the community as a physically organized entity, as a psychological reality, and as a social fact."

The school buildings, whether they stress the modern, clean lines of the functional design, or the hominess of a Georgian country house set off by greensward and shrubbery, are thus an integral part of the landscape, a bridge between the homes, where the children are, and the wider community. The physical facts of school architecture mirror impressively the social facts. The school dominates the social scene; and in the structure of child-rearing, the major industry of Crestwood Heights, the school is all important.

The family pattern of Crestwood Heights is common among upper-middle-class suburbs in North America. Deriving its status from the male's occupation, it is a family of parents and children (usually two), isolated from other relatives and living alone in their own home. The larger kinship group is separated geographically from one another and usually meets only on ritual occasions. This isolation of the individual family unit "acts to decrease the ability of the family to transmit traditional patterns of behavior, which might otherwise be absorbed from close contact with, for instance, grandparents."

Oriented towards the future, the family views the task of child rearing as that of equipping the child "as effectively as possible in the present with all available means for his later solitary climb to better and more prosperous worlds lying far ahead in time."

Children are viewed as individuals who are learning to become adults capable of functioning independently. The child's time is divided between home and peer group activities, the latter coming to occupy more of his time as he leaves home for school and other institutions. Within the family, the child is "the promise of the future, the family's main ostensible justification for existence, and the target of the whole elaborate socialization process of Crestwood Heights, which . . . will gradually dissolve all close ties between him and his parents, and often between him and his brothers and sisters as well."

For families in Crestwood Heights, the public world of work is directly related to their way of life. Achievement in job and career is the means by which family life is validated. Further, the school is welcomed as an aid in the necessary task of socialization which must occur if the child is to continue the cultural line of social mobility.

In Crestwood Heights, the establishment of the school system occurred when the community itself was founded. The schools have largely contributed to community growth because their reputation attracts young couples. In turn, the growth of the community has necessitated the expansion of the schools and their continued qualitative improvement so that today they incorporate and sometimes lead in "all the marked changes in educational theory and its application which have occurred throughout the North American continent."

As the school has come to play an ever greater role in the preparation necessary for a career, it has come to occupy a position of considerable power and responsibility, with little competition from elsewhere in the important areas of academic and vocational achievement. The school "begins to parallel the career pattern of the adult, particularly that of the male, in that it now absorbs more and more of the personality of the child in a productive, workmanlike process, leaving fewer and fewer private areas and less and less opportunity for alternative institutions to exert an influence on character development in the direction of fun or enjoyment unsubordinated to the demands of a career."

Through the Home and School Association, "the most important voluntary association in Crestwood Heights," the school and parents have a common meeting ground in which agreements may be reached on the allocation of functions between home and school in the socialization of children for maturity and success. The chief activity of the Association is parent education; at home and school meetings it is not uncommon for parents to ask teachers for advice in the task of child-rearing. As the school has taken over more of the responsibility of socializing the child, the parents "are now viewed by the school somewhat as junior partners in the business of preparing children for material success in temporal life."

Levittown

In contrast to Crestwood Heights, Levittown, Long Island, is a "mass-produced suburb" within which, between 1947 and 1951, fifteen thousand families settled into Cape Cod homes built on open farmlands. From the beginning Levittown has been primarily populated by migrants from New York City, with smaller proportions of residents moving in from Nassau County or outside New York State. It is a suburb of "the first move for outward-migrating families whose primary concern is to find a suburban house within their modest financial means." In ethnic composition, the population is almost exclusively white, with about a third being foreign born or first generation native born. The religious distribution is 47 percent Catholic, 18 percent Jewish, 24 percent Protestant, and 11 percent other.

The vast majority of males are white-collar or blue-collar workers, thus making the suburb one predominantly composed of working- and lower-middle-class families. As Levittown's white-collar workers' incomes rise, however, they tend to move out of this suburb into one more compatible with their need for more space and their changing life-style. During the past decade this has resulted in a population increase among those in blue-collar occupations and a decrease among those in white-collar occupations. In the main, white-collar workers commuted into the city, while blue-collar workers found employment in the manufacturing and industrial firms that have moved into the suburban zone.

The model working-class family has been described as "integrated and cohesive." Its members are Catholic and attend church regularly. Ideally they would prefer to send their children to parochial school but it is full, so their children attend the public school.

They believe in a "good" education for their children, but look askance at the educational "frills" some of their more exuberant and generally more prosperous neighbors constantly propose. They are tired of the rising tax rate, and wonder where it will end. Many of the working-class husbands never completed high school, but they expect their children to do so.

Attitudes towards college are more ambivalent and summed up by one father as follows:

College? Well, that is something else. Not for the girl. For the boy, maybe. Might take something in business administration at this Nassau Community College. I don't know. It costs a lot to keep a kid in college these days.

For the white-collar middle-class families, Levittown is only a temporary watering place on the road to better things. Social mobility occurs as a result of the husband's rise in the occupational structure. The working-class husband, on the other hand, is not typically upward mobile, and "if the family income increases, it is through cooperative union activity rather than individual achievement."

In recent years, the schools of Levittown have faced a period of crises due to a rapidly expanding school population as well as differences of opinion among residents about the type of education needed in today's world. Between 1947 and 1960, the Levittown school enrollment increased from 40 to over 18,000; the number of school buildings from 1 to 15; the number of teachers from 2 to 678; and the tax rate rose from $0.73 per $100 of assessed valuation to $6.45 in 1962. The lack of taxable industry and the paucity of business property has caused the financial burden of school support to fall upon the home-owner. This burden has become more onerous as the percentage of working-class persons has increased, and in recent years the state has assumed an increasing role in financing the schools.

Controversy over allegedly "Communist" propaganda in the schools, the separation of church and state, and school construction have wracked the town, and over the years, the situation within the schools has been steadily deteriorating. The early 1960's witnessed the development of a Placement Bureau within the Levittown Teachers' Association as an aid to helping teachers locate elsewhere, petitions for the removal of two school board members, the resignation of the school superintendent, and a request from the Teachers Association for an investigation of the situation by the NEA.

Dissident citizens groups have emerged. One, the Information and

Education Committee (IEC) opposed a proposed school construction program in 1958:

> The IEC stands for a traditional and conservative approach to education. It is opposed to what it terms "frills" in the public school system. It stands for larger classes rather than increased building. Generally it opposes the employment of additional staff members and advocates the reduction of special services such as guidance counselors and psychologists. It hews to a basic "three R" view of education and its primary concern seems to be economy in order to hold the tax rate in check.

In opposition to the IEC is the Better Education League (BEL) and the District Five Education Association (EA). These groups "stand for smaller classes, more buildings, and extension of extracurricular services and activities." Of the groups, the IEC is often identified as a Catholic group, whereas the BEL is viewed as a Jewish group.

Although many of Levittown's citizens believed the cause of the school controversy to be rooted in differing views about public school education among religious groups, these were only the overt dimension of the conflict. Covertly, ethnic and social-class factors played the greater role. Catholics comprised the bulk of the working-class population; Protestants and Jews were largely middle-class:

> In the case of Levittown's working-class and still ethnically bound Catholic population, the values of education and the importance of education as an instrument of upward mobility and social status are not yet fully perceived. This relative lack of interest with only partial commitment to middle-class educational standards and values is then superimposed over the marginal economic position of Levittown's Catholic population, and the answer to Catholic conservatism stands revealed. Not only is there some doubt on the part of the working-class population in Levittown regarding education as the middle-class sees it, but they have been called upon to spend an extraordinary amount of money, particularly when one considers their modest income levels, to get the schools even to their present state. . . . If you are doubtful about the importance of schooling in the first place, you could not reasonably be expected to pay for other people's educative "frills"— particularly when you can't afford them anyway.

Eastville

The cultural gulf separating Crestwood Heights and Levittown is great, but that between Crestwood Heights and Eastville is even wider. Located in New York's East Harlem, Eastville is a slum occupying a twelve block area, "which is flanked by new housing developments, a hospital, warehouses, city housing projects, garages, and a more prosperous and well-preserved neighborhood where businessmen, skilled and white-collar workers dwell." Eastville itself is described as "one of New York's darkest niches of poverty and blight," and the 1950 census revealed that most of its buildings were more than fifty years old. Among its several ethnic groups, many are Puerto Ricans, who have appeared in increasing numbers ever since World War II.

For Hispano children living in Eastville, family life and values vary according to how recently their parents have migrated from Puerto Rico. In general, more recent migrants are less permissive and more fearful of the dangers of the big city. . . .

Parenthood attaches special duties and obligations to men and women. A man who has children expects to be given preference when looking for employment, for he must work to support his children, though in practice he will probably spend proportionately more on himself than on his family. This emphasis on the family as the center of an adult's obligations is cultivated from early childhood. Success and achievment on the part of the individual are encouraged only as ways by which he can help his family. In turn, the individual who does not succeed can expect to receive help from his family. Individuality and self-assertiveness are not as highly prized socially as are dependency and reliance through mutual obligations.

Among Hispanos, boys are raised to be men of character, who like to work hard, have acquired an education that helps them secure a job, assume responsibility for their parents in their old age, stay out of trouble and become good parents and persons of respect. Girls are trained to be modest and virtuous, to acquire an education in the event they need to work, and to care for a home. Fundamentally tied to the home, the girl is not to be on the streets unless she is attending to business matters. She too is taught to help in the care of aging parents unless this would interfere with her own family.

Within the family, the child has a subordinate role, which is distinct and separate from that of adults. Children have no voice in family matters even if they are directly related to them. They are taught to be obedient, for obedience is the "hallmark of respect." Because the father is the dominant authority in the family, the greatest respect and obedience are owed to him, and he has the primary disciplinary power. Beatings, scoldings and withdrawal of privileges are used to discipline recalcitrant children and in the attempt to teach them that they have violated the respect due to parents.

The schools attended by Eastville children are large units in New York City's educational system. Young children of recent migrants will probably not have attended nursery schools or formal play groups prior to entering school. Reluctance to turn children over to strangers is great, and potential criticism of the way children are being brought up is feared by the parents. When children are six or seven, however, even those who are recent migrants are entered in school. Frequently they are escorted to and from elementary school so that they may be protected from "bad" influences. Girls, particularly, are regarded with a protective eye by their mothers.

Parents view their children as the means through which "they can achieve many of their own aspirations in life, particularly those of social and economic improvement." Formal education is highly regarded, and "ignorance is considered bad, and something one should be ashamed of." Knowledge is good both as an asset for success and as an indication of one's own worth.

Before starting school, children will know something about it from parents and older siblings. They may even have played with notebooks and pencils, and they often have some knowledge of arithmetic as a result of running errands to the store. It is only the rare child, however, who will be able to follow simple instructions in English or even in Spanish. At home, children hear a mixture of both and thus enter the school without a mastery of either language.

> With a home background in which literacy is not high to begin
> with and where what there is, is mostly in a foreign tongue, where
> ways of living are different even from those of neighbors, recent mi-
> grant children, particularly those who had no previous schooling in
> Puerto Rico, are ill-prepared for what they encounter in school in
> New York. There they are expected to converse in grammatical Eng-
> lish and to meet standards of behavior that are not in agreement with
> those of their parents nor even those of their socioeconomic class. For
> all Hispano children, attending school is the beginning of their inten-
> sive, directed training in becoming American. Placed within this insti-
> tutional framework, they are exposed to new social situations for which
> neither the neighborhood nor their preschool experiences have pre-
> pared them.

For the parents, the school teachers and other school personnel represent powerful authorities of a higher social class and prestige. Relationships between parents and school are limited and often a source of discomfort to parents, who may feel they do not have the proper clothes to wear, cannot speak English adequately, or that their ability as parents will be criticized. The parent-teacher association is small, and does not include leaders from the neighborhood as active participants. These and other reasons often keep parents away from the school in reply to formal written messages to attend a conference or meeting.

Parents, however, do not define the role of the school as that of encouraging beliefs and behavior which conflict with the family. Teachers and school authorities are expected to report on the child's behavior to the family. If these reports are negative, however, parents often view them as critical of their methods of child-rearing and become defensive about the child. They may then punish the child for casting a poor reflection on themselves as parents. Further misunderstandings with the school may arise as a result of the child's lack of proper clothing or money for school needs and the placing of family business ahead of school responsibilities.

If a parent needs a child to do errands, take care of other children, accompany him when he has to go somewhere, or act as interpreter, the child must then miss school. While a child is doing his homework he will perhaps be asked to run errands, or a parent or some other adult may speak to him intermittently, expecting him to obediently reply. This, despite the fact that outside reading or assignments are desirable from the parents' point of view, since they keep the children busy and quiet in the home and are considered evidence they are learning. (On the other hand, however, it is held that too much studying or reading is detrimental to the child's health, because too much weakens the brain and a person may go crazy from over studying.) In the same room where a child is doing his homework, a television show or a radio program may be playing, and friends and relatives may have dropped in for a casual chat. Living conditions thus combine with the low evaluation given whatever a child does (even that which involves the highly prized education) to make for interruptions and lack of privacy in studying.

Many children of migrants leave school as soon as they pass the age when compulsory schooling is required. Some leave as a result of "beatings by teachers and attacks on the part of other students." Others are needed as income producers in the family. In contrast to those who leave, are those who are supported and encouraged by parents to complete high school. A small number enter college after the completion of secondary school, but this must be done at their own expense, for "graduation from high school is considered to terminate the parents' obligation to their children, after what is viewed as a long hard stretch to prepare them to earn a living, and thus, in part, to assume the responsibilities of adulthood and marriage." (Eddy, 1966).[1]

The schools of Crestwood Heights, Levittown, and Eastville differ greatly, not only in socioeconomic and ethnic composition, with the accompanying differences in educational values, school practices, and school curricula, but also in the degree to which they represent the concept of community school. In many ways, even though the school in Crestwood Heights does not attempt to change the community, nor to serve community members other than the children themselves, it comes nearest of the three systems to being a community school, for it operates in close collaboration with the community and fulfills the functions of the school as that community defines those functions. In Levittown, the

---

[1] From *Walk The White Line,* by Elizabeth M. Eddy. Copyright © 1965, 1967 by Elizabeth M. Eddy. Reprinted by permission of Doubleday & Company, Inc.

school suffers from the conflicts between religious, ethnic, and social-class groups in the community; it has not been effective in breaching the differences or in welding the groups together to create a more harmonious community. In Eastville, the school stands apart from the community, and misunderstandings between school personnel and parent groups lead to ineffective functioning of the school in the lives of both children and parents.

Exercises

1. Think of a local community that you know well. What are two or three ways in which the school could actually assist the community?

2. Of the three types of schools described in this chapter, do you favor one over the others? Why? Explain your reasons.

3. List and analyze the work of the agencies and organizations that serve the children of a particular school grade in a particular community. Which ones fit in well with the school program? Which ones tend to compete with the school?

4. Compare the role of the teacher in a "traditional" school with the role of the teacher in a "community school." How are they the same? How are they different?

5. Look carefully at the program and the public policy statements of your own school system and decide whether it is, on the whole, a four-walls or a community school. Evaluate the program of the school in the light of the distinction made in this chapter between the two types of schools.

6. Study the content of the course of study in your city to see how the history and government of the local community is taught. Organize a teaching unit for pupils which deals with the metropolitan area as the unit. Choose a particular grade level, such as third grade where pupils might be studying the local community, or eleventh grade, where community civics is being studied.

Suggestions for Further Reading

1. Read Chapter 12, "Contrasting Conceptions of the Social Role of the School," in *Social Foundations of Education* by William O. Stanley *et al.,* for a concise presentation of various points of view regarding the proper place of the school in the community. To contrast in more

detail the arguments for the traditional school on the one hand and the community school on the other, read Arthur Bestor's *The Restoration of Learning* and Elsie Ripley Clapp's *Community Schools in Action.*

2. *This Happened in Pasadena* by David Hulburd, written in journalistic style, tells the story of what happened in one school system when a small group of citizens began an attack upon it. Bruce Raup's book, *Education and Organized Interests in America,* although written some time ago, is a revealing account in more general terms of how various groups bring pressures to bear upon the schools.

3. There is a large body of literature on the community school and its development. *The Use of Resources in Education,* by Elsie Ripley Clapp, for example, is an account of work carried on over a seven-year period in two public rural schools, one in Kentucky and one in West Virginia. *These Things We Tried,* by Jean and Jess Ogden, describes educational work with adults in three rural communities in Virginia. For a survey of the major writings about community schools, see *The Community School,* 52nd Yearbook of the National Society for the Study of Education, Part II, especially Chapters 3, 4, 5, and 17. See also *School and Community* by Edward G. Olsen.

4. The article by Saltzman in *Society and Education: A Book of Readings* (Havighurst, Neugarten, and Falk) describes some of the ways in which the concept of the community school can be implemented in an urban setting. In the same book, the selection by Corwin discusses the relations between school and community in terms of the power structure of the community; and the selection by Carter discusses some of the problems in communication between voters and their schools.

5. Read Chapter 7, "The Clash of Class Interests in School Politics," in Vidich and Bensman, *Small Town in Mass Society,* for an interesting account of the relations between the school board, the principal of the high school, local businessmen, and farmers in a small rural community in New York State.

10 / Metropolitan Development and Educational Problems

The community of the future is the metropolitan area—a complex of central city, suburbs, industrial areas, highways, parks, and open spaces that are bound together by economic and cultural ties. Metropolitan development brings with it a host of educational problems. In this chapter the relationships between the school and the community and the relation of educational policy to social policy will be explored with special reference to the metropolitan community.

Forces Causing Urbanization

Urbanization and technification are the most characteristic aspects of modern society. Urbanization is the process of making people into city-dwellers. "Technification" is a word we shall use to denote the process whereby machines and natural resources of energy are employed to increase production. Until 1800 the people of even the most powerful and up-to-date societies were mainly engaged in getting food and fuel from the land—some 80 percent of the working population were tillers of the soil, or sheep and cattle tenders, or fishermen, or foresters. Then the growing technification of society enabled fewer and fewer people to raise more and more food, until, today, less than 10 percent of the working force in the United States produces enough fuel and food to provide a high standard of living for all the population.

The farm, the home, the office, as well as the workshop, have all been technified, and with this process has come increasing urbanization.

Larger and larger proportions of the population have come to live in cities. From 1880 to 1960 the proportion of Americans living in towns and cities of 2,500 or more increased from 30 percent to over 70 percent. This growth in urbanization is shown in Table 10.1.

Table 10.1 Growth of Urban Population in the United States

YEAR	Distribution of urban population (by percent)		
	PLACES OF 2,500 AND OVER	PLACES OF 100,000 AND OVER	METRO-POLITAN AREAS
1790	5	—	—
1810	7	—	—
1830	9	2	—
1850	15	5	—
1870	26	11	—
1890	35	15	—
1910	46	22	46
1930	56	30	54
1950	64*	29	59
1960	70*	29	63

* Current U.S. Census definition of "urban" adds about 5 percent to number based on pre-1950 definition.

Source: U.S. Census of Population: 1960, Selected Area Reports. Standard Metropolitan Statistical Areas. Final Report PC(3) 10, p. 1.

Growth of Metropolitan Areas

The cities themselves have spread out to include within their economic and social nets smaller communities or suburbs and sections of open country. This growth has been facilitated by the automobile and the highway, which have made it relatively easy for people within a radius of ten or twenty miles to travel quickly from one part of a metropolitan area to another.

By 1950 a "standard metropolitan area" had been defined in the United States Census and had become a significant unit of population. A metropolitan area includes a central city or cluster of cities and the surrounding area that is functionally related to the central city. In the Census a city of 50,000 or more is counted as a central city of a standard metropolitan area (SMA); and the unit includes the whole county surrounding this city, plus any contiguous county that is economically and socially integrated with the central county. A number of SMA's contain two or more cities, such as Minneapolis-St. Paul, New York-Newark-Jersey City, and San Francisco-Oakland-Berkeley-Richmond.

There were 212 metropolitan areas in 1960, with 112 million, or 63 percent of the population. Although metropolitan units as a whole gained 24 percent between 1950 and 1960, central cities gained only 8 percent, while the suburban areas gained 47 percent. In fact, some of the central cities actually lost population. Of the 225 central cities included in the SMA's of 1950, 72 lost population, while 153 gained. Of the five cities with populations of one million or more, only Los Angeles gained. Among cities that lost population were Boston, St. Louis, Detroit, Minneapolis, Washington, Philadelphia, Cleveland, Chicago, Cincinnati, Baltimore and New York, with losses ranging from 15 to 3 percent. While the 225 central cities as a group moved up from 51 million in 1950 to 56 million in 1960, their suburban areas expanded with almost explosive effect from 36 million to 53 million.

Metropolitanism and the Schools

Two-thirds of the school children and school teachers in the United States are located in metropolitan schools. Although the problems of the metropolitan area and of life in the city are subject to many investigations, research is just beginning on the educational problems posed by metropolitan development.

Metropolitanism refers not only to economic and social processes that go on in the metropolitan area, but also to an emerging way of life which is neither urbanism nor suburbanism. It is a way of life in which people come to feel at home in the complex metropolitan area; to enjoy the cultural facilities of the central city; to be responsible as a citizen for the welfare of the whole metropolitan area; and to be able to live comfortably at various stages of the life cycle in one or another section of the metropolitan area.

The growth of the metropolitan area and the changing character of the school system can be described in five stages: the medium-sized city, the industrialized city, the growth of suburbs, the appearance of the metropolitan complex, and urban renewal.

The Medium-Sized City

A small trading center grows over a period of years to a medium-sized city of 25 to 50 thousand. Enough geographical stratification occurs in this period to give rise to differentiation among elementary schools along socioeconomic lines. One or more "poorer" schools appear, where educational motivation and educational achievement are inferior as compared with schools in "better" parts of the city. People who can afford it and who are concerned about the education of their children try to avoid living in the districts of the "poorer" schools.

During this period there is only one public high school, drawing a cross-section of youth in terms of ability, educational motivation, and socioeconomic status.

The Industrialized City

As Handlin (1959) illustrates in his detailed account of the growth and development of New York City, if the medium-sized city is located in a strategic place with respect to transportation, raw materials, or markets, it attracts large numbers of in-migrants and it becomes an industrial and commercial center of several hundred thousand. By this time the areas near the center of the city become industrialized, or the dwellings deteriorate and their owners move away from the center to more peripheral areas of the city. Slum areas develop, and choice residential areas appear on the outskirts of the city.

During this period the schools take on the qualities of the areas in which they are located. Some elementary schools become entirely lower-class in character; others, middle-class. At the same time, a number of high schools are built, generally to serve youth from given geographical districts which contain eight or ten elementary schools. The single comprehensive high school serving all kinds of youth is now replaced by high schools with contrasting socioeconomic compositions. Some schools get a reputation for college preparation; others begin to specialize in vocational education.

The Growth of Suburbs

By the end of World War I a number of American cities were moving into a third stage, with the appearance of choice residential suburbs, at first strung out along the railway lines that led into the city. These suburbs are exclusive residential areas, expensive to live in, with greater "living space" and with superior schools provided at no greater cost to the taxpayer than in the central city. These suburbs are heavily upper-middle-class, with fringes of upper-class and of lower-middle-class residents. Their schools, elementary and secondary, are homogeneous along socioeconomic, racial, and ethnic lines.

During this phase, which, for cities already industrialized by 1920, lasted from World War I to World War II, some of the suburbs developed well-known public schools along "progressive" lines. Known throughout the educational world are the school systems of Winnetka, Bronxville, Manhasset, Shaker Heights, Clayton and Pasadena. Despite the fact that the people in these suburbs were known to be politically conservative, in educational matters they were progressive; and their schools tended to retain many of their progressive features during the conservative reaction in education that followed World War II.

Since the suburb is a part of the metropolitan complex, the fact that it draws mainly middle- and upper-class people results in an increase in the proportion of lower-class population who live in the central city. As population expands, and as more persons move into metropolitan areas, the working-class areas of the central city expand, creating obsolescence and reduced monetary values in former middle-class residential areas. Slum areas expand. The area of solid middle-class residences becomes smaller and is often cut up into small islands within lower-class areas.

The Appearance of the Metropolitan Complex

At the close of World War II there was a shift toward greater complexity within the metropolitan area. While the suburbs grew much more rapidly than the central cities, suburban growth consisted of two contrasting patterns. First, the pre-war pattern of the migration of middle income people from the central city to the suburbs was intensified. This pattern dominated until the mid-1960's. At the same time, a new and offsetting pattern appeared of working-class migration to the suburbs. The result has been greater stratification within the total metropolitan area by income and by skin-color.

Increased Socioeconomic and Racial Stratification

As the total population of a metropolitan area grew larger, the people became more stratified or segregated in terms of social class, ethnic, and racial composition. By the mid-1960's, individual schools were more homogeneous with respect to these factors than they had been before World War II.

The proposition that segregation of the population by social class, ethnicity, and race is increasing may need further clarification, since obviously there are current trends opposed to stratification and segregation. The growth of working-class suburbs and the development of islands of middle-class housing within the inner city have reduced the extent to which large areas are homogeneous and have reduced the size of neighborhoods which are wholly working-class in composition. We shall return to this point presently in discussing urban renewal, but the evidence is that overall: (1) The percent of all middle-class children who attend schools in which 80 percent or more are middle-class has increased since 1920. (2) The percent of all working-class or blue-collar-family children who attend schools in which 80 percent or more are working-class has also increased since 1920. Data from the Detroit area illustrate this generalization.

According to a study of incomes of families in Detroit and its suburbs, conducted as part of the Detroit Area Study of the University of Michigan (1960), the median income per family in the Detroit metropolitan area was related to the distance the family lived from the central business district. For families living within six miles of the central business district, the median income rose 3 percent between 1951 and 1959, to a total of $3,800; but the cost of living rose 12 percent. Thus in 1959 the median family in this area had less "real income" than the median family who had occupied this area eight years earlier. Families living further out, between the six-mile radius and the city limits, gained 18 percent in median income and reached $6,000, which gave them a small gain in real income. Meanwhile, families living in the Detroit suburban area gained 47 percent in median income, reaching $7,200.

Thus the central part of the city grew poorer during this decade, while the suburbs grew richer. Or, in other words, the central part of the city became more solidly working-class in composition while the suburbs became more middle class. This was due to the movement of middle-class people out of the central city.

Changing School Enrollment

A similar process is going on in other large cities. Some of its effects on schools can be seen by looking at what happened in a particular elementary school in a northern industrial city between 1955 and 1961.

Leibnitz School in 1955 was attended by 1,250 pupils coming mainly from lower-middle- and upper-middle-class families of German, Dutch, and Swedish origin. The district was situated about seven miles from the city center, and close to transportation lines. Parents of some of the pupils had attended the same school.

Then came a period of rapid change. Some of the three-story apartment buildings were cut up into smaller units and rented to southern white and Negro families who were moving into the city in large numbers. By 1960 the school enrollment was 2,400. The school was running on a double-shift schedule, with one group of children coming in the morning to one shift of teachers, and another group coming in the afternoon to a new shift of teachers.

Transiency at the Leibnitz School is calculated at 70 percent, which means that 1,900 pupils transferred in or out of the school during the year from September, 1960, to June, 1961. At times of heavy turnover the children waiting to transfer in or out are seated in the auditorium, in some cases with their parents; in some cases, without. One clerk sits at a desk on the stage and processes transfers and records from incoming children; another clerk sits on the opposite side of the stage and processes papers for the out-going children.

The records of transfers out during the past several years show that most of the children leaving the school have transferred to schools farther out from the city center, or in the suburbs.

Not only is there increased economic stratification of school populations, but also increased racial and ethnic segregation. In the northern cities all Negro neighborhoods come into being, and the school enrollments inevitably reflect this fact. For instance, the 1958 report of New York City's Superintendent of Schools (New York City, 1959) showed a net loss of 15,000 white pupils per year for the preceding five years, pupils who had moved out to the New York suburbs. Negroes formed

20 percent of the school enrollment, and Puerto Ricans, 15 percent. Of 704 public schools, 455 had 90 percent or more of their pupils of one group, either Negro or white or Puerto Rican (Morrison, 1958). Only one in five schools could be said to be "integrated" in the sense that it had more than 10 percent of pupils who did not belong to the majority group for that particular school.

In Pittsburgh, the trend toward increased racial segregation in the public schools is well documented. According to the annual report for 1965 by the Pittsburgh Board of Public Education, the percentage of Negro children increased from 14 to 36 percent in the twenty-five years from 1940 to 1965. This trend was similar to that of other large cities, where in the same 25 years, the enrollment of Negro children jumped from 9 to 51 percent in Chicago; from 8 to 47 percent in New York; and from 14 to 54 percent in Philadelphia. Negro pupils comprised nearly 90 percent of the enrollment in Washington, D.C. in 1965.

In Pittsburgh the growing proportion of Negro pupils was increasingly enrolled in schools which were all or nearly-all Negro in composition, as shown in Table 10.2. While strictly comparable data have not

Table 10.2 Increasing Racial Segregation in Public Schools (Pittsburgh: 1950 to 1965)

	1950		1955		1960		1965	
	#	%	#	%	#	%	#	%
Number and percentage of elementary schools with 80% or more Negro enrollment	6	6%	8	8%	10	11%	15	17%
Number and percentage of secondary schools with 80% or more Negro enrollment	2	8%	1	5%	3	12%	4	16%
Percentage of all Negro elementary pupils enrolled in schools where 80% or more are Negro		45%		45%		53%		67%
Percentage of all Negro secondary pupils enrolled in schools where 80% or more are Negro		23%		36%		54%		58%

Source: Adapted from Pittsburgh Board of Public Education, 1965, pp. 10–11.

been made available for other large cities, there is evidence that the same trend is true in many other cities, and that despite increased efforts at integration, increased de facto segregation was occurring up through the mid-1960's.

Stratification in the Suburbs

While the socioeconomic stratification has proceeded within the central city, there has been a similar process in the suburbs since World War II. Even though most of the suburbs do not include the lowest socioeconomic group found in the central city, the suburbs too have become differentiated into communities which are predominantly upper-middle, lower-middle, or working-class.

The city dweller who aspires to a house in the suburbs will find that the amount of money he can pay for a house determines the type of suburb he will live in. If he is employed as a manual worker in an auto assembly plant or an electronics factory located 15 miles from the city, he is likely to make a payment on a two-bedroom bungalow in a real estate development in which there are hundreds of similar houses, all variants of one basic design, all on small lots with a plot of grass in front, a garage in the rear. He will live in a working-class suburb. If he is a lawyer with an office in the city he may buy a ranch-type house on a large lot in an area where all other houses are of similar size and cost, in a new section of a well-established upper-middle-class suburb that has a reputation for good schools and a good country club.

The New York metropolitan area shows this decentralized stratification more clearly than other centers, partly because of its size, and partly because it contains several large industrial cities, such as Jersey City, Bayonne, Newark, Paterson, Passaic, and Elizabeth, none of which is part of the central city of New York. Members of the lower-working class live in Manhattan, Brooklyn, the Bronx, and in the Jersey industrial cities. Craftsmen and foremen live out beyond the lower-working class and also in some of the residential suburbs such as Mineola on Long Island, Tuckahoe in Westchester County, and Roselle Park in Union County. The upper-middle and upper classes live in Manhattan (on the upper East Side), in Westchester County to the north, Nassau County on Long Island, and Essex and Bergen Counties in New Jersey.

Suburban stratification is partly due to the decentralization of industry that has gone on since World War II. Formerly there were a few small industrial cities around the fringes of big cities. For example, Chicago Heights, Harvey, Whiting and Gary grew up south of Chicago; Passaic and Elizabeth, outside New York City; and Alameda and Richmond, outside San Francisco. After the war various economic factors, as described by Vernon (1959), led to further decentralization of industry. "Light" industry such as the manufacture of electronic equipment, plastics, pharmaceuticals, airplanes and airplane parts became established in suburban areas. This in turn pulled workers from the central city into new working-class suburbs. These people are mainly skilled craftsmen and white-collar workers with relatively high incomes who, because they drive automobiles to work, are not dependent on public transportation. Examples of this type of community can be seen in various parts of the country: in the new suburbs northwest of Chicago; in North Kansas City; in Edwardsville and other suburbs across the Mississippi river from St. Louis; in some of the new suburbs in central Long Island; and in the northern and southern suburbs of Los Angeles.

Express highways leading into or around the city from one suburb to another permit new suburbs to grow up in the open spaces between the railroad lines which radiate out from the center city like the spokes of a wheel, each spoke with its own string of older suburbs.

At the same time, if there is a substantial Negro population in the metropolitan area, as is true in Chicago and Detroit, a few Negro working-class suburbs come into existence. Also when a large Negro slum area develops in the central city, Negro middle-class people find their way into mixed Negro-white middle-class residential areas in the central city, and into middle-class suburbs.

The Socioeconomic Ratio (SER)

In studying the facts of socioeconomic stratification and segregation, it is useful to employ a ratio of white-collar to blue-collar workers, a ratio that can be worked out for the families of children in a given school, or worked out from census data for the people who live in a particular school district or neighborhood. There are several ways of calculating such a ratio. In Table 10.3 the upper-middle-class occupations (UM) have been weighted twice as heavily as the lower-middle (LM); and in the other direction the lower or unskilled working-class occupations

(LW) have been weighted twice as heavily as the upper-working class (UW). The ratio thus becomes 2 UM + LM ÷ UW + 2 LW.

Looking at the socioeconomic ratio (SER) for the United States, we see that this ratio has been increasing since 1940, and especially since 1950. The numbers illustrate that the proportion of white-collar jobs in the American economy is increasing while the proportion of blue-collar jobs is decreasing.

Table 10.3   Socioeconomic Ratios for the United States and for Chicago

	USA	Chicago SMSA*	Chicago City	Chicago Suburbs	Chicago City	
					WHITE	NON-WHITE
1940	.66	.71	.69	.77	.75	.17
1950	.71	.77	.73	.86	.84	.18
1960	.82	.92	.69	1.28	.82	.25

* Standard Metropolitan Statistical Area.
Note on the Computation of the SER: This is a crude socioeconomic index, based on easily obtainable census data on occupations in the male labor force, aged 14 and over. The occupations are placed in four categories, as follows:

   A. Upper Middle Class (UM):
       Professional, technical and kindred
       Proprietors, managers and officials
       Farm owners and managers (one-fifth of total)

   B. Lower Middle Class (LM):
       Sales and clerical occupations
       Farm owners and managers (two-fifths of total)

   C. Upper Working Class (UW):
       Foremen, craftsmen and kindred
       Operatives and kindred
       Farm owners and managers (two-fifths of total)

   D. Lower Working Class (LW):
       Service workers, including private household workers
       Laborers, including farm laborers

The SER for the total Chicago Metropolitan Area shows a similar increase. At the same time, it is clear that socioeconomic stratification has been increasing between the central city and the suburbs. In 1940 the SER for the city of Chicago was slightly below that of Chicago's metropolitan area. By 1950, the Chicago city SER had increased from .69 to .73, but the suburbs had increased from .77 to .86. Clearly, the central city was lagging, and the flight of middle-class people to the suburbs was in full course.

The decade after 1950 saw even greater changes. The city of Chicago decreased in SER from .73 to .69, while that of the suburbs jumped from .86 to 1.28. The average socioeconomic level of the central city was decreasing in the face of a country-wide increase, and especially in the face of a sharp increase in the Chicago suburbs.

The racial aspect of this phenomenon can also be seen in Table 10.3. While the SER of white male workers in the inner city moved from .75 to .84 to .82 between 1940 and 1960, the SER for nonwhites (almost all of whom were Negroes) moved only from .17 to .18 to .25. Since the proportions of nonwhites in Chicago had increased meanwhile from 8.2 percent in 1940 to 22.9 percent in 1960 (not shown in the table), it was the in-migration of nonwhites with relatively low SER that caused a substantial part of the change in the city's overall SER.

Effects of Stratification on the Schools

The school achievement and the behavior of pupils in schools in the central city and in the suburbs reflect differences in socioeconomic levels. For example, as reported in the survey of the public schools of Chicago (Havighurst, 1964), Table 10.4 shows how the elementary schools in Chicago's 21 school districts reflect the socioeconomic status of the neighborhood in which they are located. The measure of socioeconomic status is based upon median family income and median level of education of adults in the various school districts. While there are a number of exceptions, the average IQ for the school, the performance of first-graders on a reading readiness test, and the achievement level of sixth-graders in reading and arithmetic (as measured by a standardized achievement test) are related quite closely to the socioeconomic rank of the families who live in the school district.

Similar findings emerged in a study made by Patricia Sexton (1961) in another northern industrial city. Sexton's data show that schools in lower income areas of the city had poorer records of achievement and intelligence and a higher rate of dropouts; while the schools in the higher income areas had a higher proportion of pupils at elementary and junior high levels chosen to participate in a program for "gifted" children and had more senior high school students going to college.

Table 10.4   Socioeconomic status, school achievement, and race
by school districts (Chicago, 1963)

Chicago school districts ranked by socioeconomic status[a]	IQ	Percent of first-grade pupils who were average or above on tests of reading readiness	Grade-level achievement of 6th grade in reading & arithmetic	Percent of elementary pupils who are Negro
1	111	75	7.5	0
2	104	74	6.8	37
3	112	89	7.8	0
4	108	74	7.4	7
5	101	67	6.4	77
6	107	78	7.1	1
7	107	74	6.8	0
8[b]	95	48	5.8	85
9[c]	94	44	5.8	48
10	109	85	7.2	0
11	109	79	7.2	16
12	96	48	6.0	67
13	93	47	5.7	100
14	103	65	6.7	1
15	99	52	6.3	69
16	91	41	5.5	92
17	89	33	5.4	81
18	92	45	5.5	96
19	93	45	5.6	61
20	90	42	5.5	100
21	90	34	5.3	81
City wide	99	55	6.2	

[a] The actual school district numbers are not shown here.
[b] This District contains the University of Chicago, where many children of higher socioeconomic status attend the University Laboratory School, a private school, and are thus not included in the public school population.
[c] This District includes the North Side "Gold Coast," where many children attend private schools.

Source: Havighurst, (1964), The Public Schools of Chicago, Table 2, p. 39 (adapted).

Differences in School Climates

There is a whole complex of relationships involving curriculum, student relations to teachers, relations between parents and teachers, and other aspects of the school climate which also reflect differences between school neighborhoods. The complex inner working of any school is affected by the neighborhood and by the types of children and parents the school serves.

In studying the elementary schools in the city of Chicago by means of interviews with teachers and principals and by observation of pupils, the staff of the Chicago School Survey (Havighurst, 1964) identified four types of schools: (1) "high-status schools"—generally found in high income areas, usually in neighborhoods at the edges of the city or in upper-middle-class suburbs; (2) "main-line schools"—usually located in areas where lower-middle-class families predominated; (3) "common-man schools"—located in areas where most of the families were stable working-class, both Negro and white; (4) "inner-city schools" located in slum areas of low-income, high-transiency families, both Negro and white, where rates of delinquency were high.

The four types were distinguished from each other by the nature of the academic program in the school, the attitudes of parents and pupils toward the teachers, the nature of discipline in the school, and the teacher's concept of her role. For example the "high-status" schools were those in which teachers felt the total academic climate was rewarding to the teacher, and where they felt they were really teaching almost all the time. The "inner-city schools" were those in which teachers said an academic climate was lacking, where children's behavior was frequently unrewarding to the teacher, and where they often felt that they were "not teachers, but policemen."

The schools were readily distinguishable not only by staff members of the Survey, but by teachers themselves. Doll (1965) found that Chicago teachers could decide relatively easily the type of school in which they worked by rating their school on ten different characteristics, two of which are shown on page 254.

The ten characteristics referred to curriculum and texts (as in Item #1 in the chart); the teaching role; attitudes toward non-academic duties expected of teachers; degree to which teaching emphasizes academics; student hostility; parents' attitudes toward school; students' and parents' respect for teachers; students' exposure to cultural experiences in their everyday lives; students' values; and school climate (as in item #2).

The choices made by teachers tended to fall consistently in one of the four columns for the ten characteristics. "High-status" schools were described most frequently by checkmarks in the first column; "main-line schools," by the second column; "common-man schools," by the third;

Check the statement which applies to your school:

1. Curriculum is enriched with extra work. Texts one year or more above grade level can be used.	Curriculum is used as planned. Texts at grade level can be used.	Curriculum is altered downward. Difficulty in the use of grade level texts.	Curriculum does not fit students' needs. Texts one to two years below grade level must be used in many cases.
2. Climate of school set by academically oriented pupils. Children with discipline problems can be easily handled within framework of the school. Discipline problems are mild.	Children with discipline problems are seldom leaders of student behavior but can exert influence in some cases. Discipline problems can be handled within the framework of the school.	Children with discipline problems may be leaders for some students and they sometimes upset academic classroom situations. Majority of discipline problems can be handled within the framework of the school; a few cannot.	Children with discipline problems are influential in setting climate of the school. Many children with discipline problems require the help of outside agencies such as police or Family Service.

and "inner-city schools," by the fourth. These relationships were not totally consistent, as might be anticipated, for the characteristics of any given school vary not only according to the socioeconomic level of the neighborhood, but also according to the manner in which the school principal sets the general tone of the school, and according to the relationships between individual teachers and between teachers and parents. Some "inner-city schools" were characterized by relatively high morale among teachers and by relatively infrequent discipline problems.

Thus, as is probably true in all cities, elementary schools in Chicago were found to vary markedly from one type of neighborhood to another; but they varied also according to other factors which make every school to some degree different from every other.

Socioeconomic Ratios in Various High Schools

In Figure 10.1 the social compositions of three typical high schools are shown. School A is a typical comprehensive high school in a town or small city which has only one high school; it therefore receives all the children of secondary-school age. The high-school population will not be distributed in the same way as the elementary-school population in this community because some of the high-school students drop out of school without graduating. Hence the actual SER is not .6, as it would be in a cross-sectional elementary school, but instead is approximately 1.0.

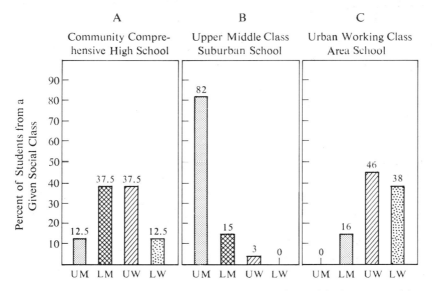

Figure 10.1 Socioeconomic types of secondary schools. Social class composition of various types of secondary schools.

School B is a high school in an upper-middle-class suburb, where there are very few working-class people. This type of school is sometimes called a "comprehensive" high school because it offers several curricula, including commercial and vocational courses, but it is not comprehensive in the sense that its students represent a cross-section of the American social structure.

School C is a high school where the SER is low, for the school serves a working-class area where there are no upper-middle- and only a few lower-middle-class families. In such an area there may be a majority of lower-working-class residents, but since their children tend to drop out of school early, the composition of the high school shows a preponderance of pupils from upper-working-class homes.

There is probably a critical point in the SER of most schools, a point at which middle-class parents are likely to become anxious and will consider removing their children from the school. This is not to imply that parents think in terms of the socioeconomic ratio itself; but rather that middle-class parents begin to fear the effects of the growing proportions of lower-class students upon their own children. They may fear a drop in the academic standards of the school, or changes in curricular offerings, or unwelcome influences upon their own children's motivations for school achievement.

It might be noted that such attitudes on the part of parents are not altogether unfounded. A study by Wilson (1959) supports the generalization that when student bodies vary in their proportions of middle and working class, students develop different educational and vocational aspirations. The study showed that in predominantly lower-status schools, *higher*-status children have lower educational and occupational aspirations than in predominantly higher-status schools, and in predominantly higher-status schools, *lower*-status children have higher aspirations than in predominantly lower-status schools. Wilson says, "The *de facto* segregation brought about by concentrations of social classes in cities results in schools with unequal moral climates which likewise affect the motivation of the child . . . by providing a different ethos in which to perceive values" (Wilson, 1959, p. 845).

The point at which a school becomes undesirable in the eyes of middle-class parents (the critical point in the SER) is subjective, depending upon the attitudes and experience of a particular parent, and depending also upon such factors as the tradition of the school, the racial composition of the school, the type of curriculum, and the quality of the teachers. However, there is consensus among middle-class parents on the question of when a school has become a "poor" school and when they begin to move out of the school district.

Secondary schools are more vulnerable than primary schools to desertion by middle-class parents when the status ratio reaches the critical point. In an upper-middle-class suburb the SER is very high. However, in the central city, the slums continually encroach upon high schools in formerly middle-class areas, and reduce the status ratio in such schools toward the critical point. At that point there tends to be a flight to the suburbs by middle-class families who have children of high-school age.

A High School in a Rapidly Changing Area

An example of what happens when the SER reaches the critical point is seen in the case of Benjamin Franklin High School, located in a large city. Franklin High School is situated in what was a middle- and upper-class area, some six miles from the center of the city. In 1910 this was the school with the best academic record in the city, sending a high proportion of its graduates to college, and winning most of the prizes for academic excellence on the part of its students. The school's SER in 1910 was probably about 1.5.

Between the two world wars many of the upper-class people moved out to suburbs, and some of the upper-middle-class residents took over the old upper-class mansions, while other upper-middles moved to a high-school district farther from the center of the city. Several areas of middle-class houses deteriorated, and some of the old, large apartment buildings were "converted" into small, low-rent apartments. A considerable number of lower-class people moved in. On one edge of the high-school district an area of old apartment buildings was turned over to Negro occupancy after the apartments had been "converted." By the beginning of World War II the SER of Franklin High was about .80.

Immediately after World War II, there was a further influx of working-class Negroes into a formerly middle-class area. However, there was also some new building of apartments, and some well-to-do Negroes began to buy the old upper-class mansions. The SER of Franklin High gradually dropped to .60 by 1955. With a large rate of dropouts of lower-class pupils in the ninth and tenth grades, this meant that the SER of the ninth grade was .35, while that of the twelfth grade was 1.5. The SER for the ninth grade was well below the critical point for middle-class parents, and they began to move away from the area when their children were ready to enter high school.

At about this time the community sensed that a crisis had occurred. An organization was formed by the middle-class people in the district whose goals were "community conservation" and urban renewal. With the aid of government funds, deteriorated houses were torn down and replaced by middle-class houses. The high school was reorganized on the basis of a multi-track program, with the upper track consisting of college-going (and largely middle-class) pupils, thus achieving a high SER for this sub-group. These measures partially stemmed the outflow of middle-class families, and brought some new middle-class families with young children into the area.

However, in the same high school district another area where there was no community conservation movement (the area served by the Leibnitz elementary school, already described) also "changed" sharply after 1955. Its graduates tended to force down the SER at Franklin High. At this writing there seems to be a close balance between the forces that, on the one hand, tend to make Franklin High into a slum school, and those forces, on the other hand, that will preserve it as a school with an academic ethos serving a community with a substantial proportion of middle-class families.

Socio-Educational Motivation

What most parents desire for their children is a school which stimulates students to do well academically, encourages them to finish high school and go to college, and at the same time offers something useful and interesting for children from all kinds of families. Looking for these things, parents try to sense the spirit or *ethos* of the school. The SER can be improved upon as a measure of school ethos by replacing the percentages of children from various social classes with percentages of children with certain kinds of socio-educational motivation. If the latter data are available, the substitution would allow for the fact that children of any one social class have a wide range of educational motivations.

It is possible to describe four levels of educational motivation, each level indicating the kind of occupational aspiration held by the individual as well as the probable educational level he will attain.

Table 10.5 gives data of this kind for the ninth grade of a high

Table 10.5   Socio-educational Motivation of Male Students in a Cross-sectional High School

Probable educational level	Characteristic occupational aspiration	Social class				
		UM	LM	UW	LW	TOTAL
College	Academically motivated; major white-collar career (A)	10	16	8	1	35
High school graduate	Minor white-collar career (B)	—	9	7	4	20
High school graduate or drop-out	Skilled blue-collar career (C)	—	5	20	5	30
Dropout	Socially alienated (D)	—	—	5	10	15
	Total	10	30	40	20	100

(SER = .6.3; Motivation Ratio = 1.50)

school which represents a cross-section of the American society. In this school the SER is 50 ÷ 80 or .63.

The SER can be replaced by a motivation ratio which is computed as follows: $(2A + B) \div (C + 2D)$ where the letters refer to the motivational levels shown in Table 10.5. In this case the motivation ratio is 90 ÷ 60 or 1.50. While this ratio is a better measure of the academic ethos of a high school than is the socioeconomic ratio, it requires so much more knowledge about the students that it is likely to be used less frequently than the SER.

Urban Renewal

During the 1950's the civil ills accompanying metropolitan growth caused a type of social action called urban renewal, which is the fifth stage of metropolitan development. At its minimum, urban renewal consists of tearing down the worst of the slums and building large blocks of public housing for low-income families. Beyond that minimum, urban renewal consists of planning the growth of metropolitan areas from the center out to the suburbs, with parks, shopping centers, libraries, churches, and schools organized to serve people where they live; and with industry, the central business district, and the centers of residence linked by fast, comfortable transportation, public and private. Billions of dollars are now being spent on bold new physical structures for shopping plazas, garden villages, high-rise apartment housing, and expressways.

Since, as already mentioned, more than two-thirds of American children go to school in metropolitan areas, and two-thirds of all teachers work in these schools, the schools can hardly be insulated from these momentous events. In fact, organization of school systems and the programs of schools are likely to be determining factors in the forms which urban renewal will eventually take.

There are two alternative approaches to the solution of metropolitan area problems. One is a process of adaptation to the existing present trends of metropolitan evolution; the other is a bold and fundamental effort at reversing some of these trends, and at designing and building the metropolitan area of the future with appropriate physical and institutional features. Both approaches require cooperation by the schools, and both approaches involve considerable changes in school programs and school organization. The twin functions of the school—to mirror the present community and to aid the community in achieving its goals—are simultaneously called into action.

Educational Adaptations to Existing Trends

The policy of adaptation to existing metropolitan trends assumes that the future structure of metropolitan areas will follow present trends. The belt of lower-class residential area around the center of the city will expand and grow wider. The flight of middle-class families to the suburbs will continue. Suburbs will increase in number and size and variety. Low cost public housing will gradually make a physical improvement in the deteriorated areas and will result in physical renewal of slums. Expressways will give automobile owners quicker and more comfortable access to all parts of the metropolitan area. The present trend toward residential segregation by socioeconomic status will continue, together with at least as much racial segregation as now exists. Only a few small counter-trends will be seen, such as the growth of working-class suburbs, and the construction of expensive apartment houses near the center of the city for well-to-do people who have few school-age children.

If this policy is followed, the major educational adaptations consist of attempts to provide educational stimulation and opportunity to the children of the slum areas, combined with an attempt to identify the abler children and to separate them into special classes in the school. This approach involves several procedures:

1. *A multi-track system* operates to separate children into several different groups according to learning ability and social status. This system has the effect of maintaining at least one sub-group with fairly strong academic motivation in a school located in a slum area or in a school threatened by encroaching slums. The children of higher social status tend to be placed in the superior group, which makes the school more tolerable for their parents. Although the value of homogeneous grouping in helping children to achieve according to the level of their intelligence is being repeatedly questioned, there is no doubt that teachers and parents alike favor a multi-track system in a school where the status ratio has fallen below the critical point. This is because the multi-track organization gives some assurance to concerned parents that their children will be given special help and special consideration.

2. *Enrichment programs* are developed for working-class children who achieve fairly well. This is a supplement to the multi-track program, and involves placing the more promising children in smaller classes, giving them special counseling and guidance, encouraging their parents to take more interest in their education, and giving them access to museums, libraries, theaters, and concerts. A widely-known example is the Higher Horizons program of Junior High School No. 43, Manhattan, and the George Washington High School of New York City (Hillson, 1963). This program has stimulated a considerable number of boys and girls to graduate from high school and to enter college who would not have done so if they had not received special attention. Financial assistance for college attendance is a necessary part of such a program.

Since the New York City project was undertaken, scores of similar projects have been developed for high school youth who are doing fairly well in school but who give evidence of being capable of doing superior work if they are stimulated and if high standards are set for them. A number of private schools and colleges offer special summer schools for such youth. Frequently a preference is given for Negro youth on grounds that there is more unrealized potential in this group than among white working-class youth who have not suffered from discrimination. Also, several public school systems have experimental scholarship fund programs which recruit potentially able youth in the early high school years and guide them toward college, with a promise of a college scholarship if they do well in high school.

3. *Enrichment programs for culturally disadvantaged children* are introduced at the kindergarten-primary level. A number of large cities are trying out a type of program that gives special assistance to children in the primary grades in slum schools, on the theory that many of these children lack stimulation from parents to read and to achieve well in school. These children fail to master the task of reading; they stumble along for the first few years in school, after which they become confirmed non-learners; and they tend to become social misfits in school during their adolescence. By putting specially-trained teachers into relatively small classes, by using a social worker or visiting teacher to bring the home and school into contact, and by giving these children a variety of enriching experiences, it is presumed that these children will get a better start in school and thus a better start in life.

As was discussed in an earlier chapter, the family environment is now seen as a major limiting factor in the cognitive development of perhaps 15 percent of children, mainly those from the lower-working class. Assisted by funds made available under the Economic Opportunity Act of 1964, and the Elementary and Secondary Education Act of 1965, most city school systems have now undertaken vast programs of "compensatory education" at the pre-school and kindergarten-primary levels.

4. *Work-study programs* can be developed for alienated youth. Under present conditions 15 percent of all children fail to grow up successfully through the avenue provided by the schools. They become non-learners, and after about the sixth grade they react to the school either with hostility or with apathy. In slum areas this proportion is likely to reach 25 or 30 percent. These children are alienated from the values of the school and other middle-class institutions. It is these boys and girls who make teaching so difficult at the seventh, eighth, and ninth grades, and who make the junior high school and the early years of senior high school so difficult for academically-motivated youth in schools where the socioeconomic ratio is below the critical point. A good deal of experimentation with work-study programs is now under way, programs which aim to give alienated youth, especially the boys, a chance to grow up satisfactorily through the avenue of work. (These programs are described in Chapter 13.)

5. *Long range city and suburban developments.* If present trends continue, it appears that educational programs in the central city will be increasingly aimed at providing opportunities for working-class youth in relation to their abilities and needs, while the suburbs are likely to be the scene of experimentation with ideas and materials aimed at higher standards of educational performance for middle-class youth. The suburbs are likely to continue to have more money to spend on the schools than will the central city, and the predominantly middle-class orientation of suburban parents will make them responsive to proposals for the use of new methods, new kinds of school buildings, and new types of school programs.

Fundamental Urban Renewal

Many individuals, including some educators, are not satisfied with accepting the present trends of metropolitan development and with adapting school programs to meet them. They believe that the civic problems of metropolitan growth call for fundamental urban renewal. These people—the prophets of urban renewal—are proposing new enterprises that will require substantial educational changes.

THE GOALS OF URBAN RENEWAL. Urban renewal has the goal of restoring physical areas of comfortable middle-class living in the central city and also of establishing areas of comfortable, slum-free lower-class living. Beyond this, urban renewal has a social goal of making the whole metropolitan area a good place for all kinds of people to live. The leaders of urban renewal often speak of their goal as that of increasing the range and amount of choice people have among good ways to live.

Among the specialists in city planning there is much discussion of the physical structure of the metropolitan area. It is generally agreed that there should be *decentralization* of residential areas, each area being self-contained with respect to the ordinary needs of social living— shopping facilities, schools, libraries, and churches. One type of arrangement is the *galaxy* in which the constituent cities are spaced more or less evenly over the territory, with a network of highways and transportation lines leading to the areas of specialized activity such as industrial sites, airports, freight docks, and financial centers. Another possible type is the many-pointed star or wagon wheel, with residential areas radiating out from a central business district, with industry located in certain sectors of the star, and with transportation routes leading out from the center and crisscrossing with other transportation routes which form concentric circles around the center.

In all cases there seems to be agreement on two matters: 1) that the metropolitan area should consist of residential areas which are relatively complete in themselves for the ordinary needs of family and cultural life; and 2) that many of these residential areas should contain cross-sections of the social structure, with people of the upper, middle, and working classes living in the same area. In particular, it is planned that many of the residential areas near the central business district should be populated by middle-class as well as working-class people.

A number of large cities have embarked on major programs of slum clearance with the aim of restoring cross-sectional communities within the central city. For example, Chicago has such areas to the south, southwest, and northwest of the central business district. St. Louis has the Mill Creek Valley District, southwest of the city center. New York City has several such areas, including one north of Columbia University. In these and other metropolitan areas the slum buildings have been cleared, and land has been made available to private builders for apartment buildings and single-family residences to sell or rent to people who can afford to pay substantial prices.

The future of these developments is still uncertain, however, and further urban renewal is likely to be postponed until such experiments are evaluated. A major question is whether middle-class people with children will move into these renewal areas. This will depend, in turn, on their attitudes toward the schools. These people may want new, modern school buildings; and in many cases they will get them because the old buildings are obsolete. More important, they are likely to want assurance that the SER of the schools will be maintained above the critical point. This assurance may be possible in relation to elementary schools which serve relatively small areas; but not in terms of secondary schools which may serve both a renewal area and a large neighboring working-class area. The secondary school is likely to be the crucial element of the school system which will make or break programs of urban renewal.

Educational Programs for a Transition Period

It appears, now, that a number of metropolitan areas are ready for fundamental programs of urban renewal that will have the cooperation of suburban and central city governments. Such programs will need to provide for a transitional period of perhaps twenty years, during which time the planned metropolitan organism can emerge from the present metropolitan chaos. During this period the local communities can gradually become organized and separated from other communities by green belts, parks, and open spaces; and they can be linked together by a system of highways and open transportation routes.

Certain educational policies will have to be adopted for the transitional period, policies aimed at stopping the flight of middle-class people from the central city, and aimed at building self-contained communities of 50,000 to 200,000 people which are cross-sections of the social composition of the entire area. Some policies would be temporary, while others would become relatively permanent. Some of the principal policies might be these:

1. For the central city at large, a set of *regional selective high schools* would be created which would be generously selective on the basis of intelligence and school achievement, to be open to the top third of the high school age group. Admission to these high schools would be con-

trolled so that no school would have less than 50 percent white students, and every school would have a status ratio higher than .6. By the end of the transition period, these schools would change in character and probably become comprehensive high schools which would serve their local communities and would be open to all high school pupils of the area.

These selective high schools would probably be necessary as part of a transition program in order to retain present groups of middle-class families and to attract other middle-class families to the central cities. The region served by such a high school would be two or three times as large as the usual high school district so that enough students would be available for an academic type of school.

The notion of a set of selective high schools is repugnant to some educators, especially some who are interested in expanding the educational opportunities for Negro youth. Because many Negro adolescents are now hindered by social disadvantages in their earlier years, they might not qualify for such selective schools. The educators opposed to selective high schools even for a temporary period would like to see more of the multi-track programs now to be found in many big-city high schools. However, the multi-track program in a predominantly working-class school does not attract large numbers of middle-class children, for their parents generally prefer selectivity in the admission policy. Since these are the parents who tend to move from the city to the suburbs if they feel the high school does not meet their needs, and since such moves tend to threaten the eventual success of fundamental urban renewal, it is probably wise to create a set of selective high schools in the central city as a transitional "holding" strategy.

2. A set of *general high schools* would be maintained with strong commercial and vocational training programs not available in other types of schools. By the end of the transition period these general high schools would probably merge with the selective schools into comprehensive high schools that would serve all the adolescents in their local communities.

3. A set of *work-study centers* would be created at the junior high school level for boys and girls who have demonstrated inability to profit from the regular academic high school program. These centers should be located in junior and senior high schools, although they run on their own class schedule. They should enroll 10 to 20 percent of the school population at the ages 12 to 16. They should grow smaller in enrollment

in future years, as the elementary schools improve their educational programs.

4. Special attention should be given to enrichment programs *at the kindergarten-primary level* to children from inadequate homes so as to give these children as good a start in school as possible, thus reducing the numbers who would later go into the work-study centers.

5. A set of *regional junior colleges* would be established and located in such a pattern that there would eventually be one in each local residential community.

6. An *adult education program* on an area-wide basis, using junior colleges and branches of the public library, would be aimed at exploiting the educative potential of all types of people.

This chapter can be summarized by saying that metropolitan development as it has occurred in United States in the past 60 years has made it more difficult for boys and girls to get a good education. The schools have been handicapped by the growing economic and racial stratification within the metropolitan area. Fundamental urban renewal can recreate high educational standards within the city, but urban renewal, if it is to succeed, depends upon substantial changes in present-day educational organization and policy.

Exercises

1. Trace the history of the standard metropolitan area you know best. In which of the five stages is it?

2. Compute the SER of a school that you know. In which direction is the ratio moving? What do you predict will be the SER of this school five years from now?

3. How are the schools governed in the metropolitan area you know best? What problems do you see ahead in educational policy for this area?

4. Describe the steps being taken for urban renewal in a metropolitan area, and discuss the relations you think the schools should have to urban renewal in this area.

5. Write a paper on the various planning agencies that exist in your SMSA with special emphasis on educational planning and its relation to the government planning.

6. Write a report on public housing in your area and discuss its contribution to making the area a more or less desirable place to live.

7. If you live in a city of less than 50,000, study it and its county as an example of tension between urban and rural styles of life. How do the schools fit in? Do they tend to work toward urbanization?

Suggestions for Further Reading

1. There are a number of recent books dealing with the growth of metropolitanism and the problems of the city. A general discussion can be found in *The Exploding Metropolis*, by the Editors of *Fortune*, which was published as a paperback. The book by Bollens and Schmandt, *The Metropolis* is particularly relevant, as is also *The Anatomy of a Metropolis* by Hoover and Vernon, and *The City is the Frontier*, by Abrams. *Metropolis, 1985* by Raymond Vernon is one of a series describing the New York Metropolitan Region Study. Jean Gottmann's *Megalopolis* gives a striking account of metropolitan development in the chain of urban areas that stretches from Boston to Washington, D.C.

2. An interesting set of readings about suburban life will be found in *The Suburban Community* edited by William Dobriner. Compare this book with *The Exurbanites* by Auguste C. Spectorsky.

3. The American metropolis is rather different in its history and structure from the great cities of other parts of the world. To see the range in types of cities, the following books are useful: *The Urban Community: A World Perspective* by Nels Anderson; *The City* by Rose Hum Lee; *Images of the City* by Anselm L. Strauss, and *The City in History* by Lewis Mumford.

4. For a discussion of some of the issues involved in urban redevelopment, read the paper by Marris in *Society and Education: A Book of Readings* (Havighurst, Neugarten, and Falk). A provocative book by Jane Jacobs is *The Death and Life of Great American Cities*. Mrs. Jacobs believes that much of modern physical city planning is destructive of the values of neighborhood life. She argues for more attention to *social* rather than *physical* factors in urban renewal.

5. *The Schools and the Urban Crisis*, edited by August Kerber and Barbara Bommarito, is a useful collection of readings in urban sociology and related educational issues.

6. A good description of the educational problems of the great city is to be found in James B. Conant's *Slums and Suburbs*.

7. Various programs are now being tried to improve the educational opportunities of disadvantaged children and to enlist the active cooperation of parents. Promising practices found in 20 schools located in depressed residential neighborhoods of 5 large urban school districts are described in the bulletin, "School-Home Partnership in Depressed Urban Neighborhoods," by Gene C. Fusco.

11 / School Systems and Other Social Systems in the Metropolitan Area

In the preceding chapter we discussed the metropolitan area as the community of the future and considered some of the educational problems that have arisen as a result of metropolitan growth. In this chapter we deal again with this topic, but we shall now discuss the school system as one of the many social systems that interact in creating and controlling processes of social change.

Social System Defined

To the sociologist the concept, *social system,* is useful in studying social structure and social organization. A social system is a network or system of social interactions—or, more strictly, a system of the *actions* of individuals—organized to carry out one or more essential tasks of society. The principal units of the system are roles and constellations of roles (Parsons and Shils, 1952). The educational system is one among many social systems, such as local government, business organizations, social welfare agencies, and churches. It is a set of roles and role constellations which has been devised for the purpose of systematically teaching children and adults a variety of information, skills, and attitudes that people are not likely to learn efficiently in the family or in work situations. A police system, to take another example, is a set of

269

roles and role constellations designed to protect order and to enforce the law.

When there is social change, various social systems alter their functions and alter their relations with each other. Thus we are accustomed to describing changes over the last 100 years in the functions of the family, and the relations between family and the school; or in the relations between the church and the school; or government and school.

Role Analysis

To understand how a school system operates, one may study its various functions, its sub-systems, and the roles of which it is composed. Students of school administration sometimes make such studies using the method of systems analysis. Getzels (1963), for instance, has pointed out that one can study the school system in this way, quite independent of the particular persons who fill the roles; that is, by studying how teachers carry out their teaching responsibilities, how they relate, say, to pupils, to other teachers, and to administrators; and similarly, to study the principal, the superintendent, and the school board, all in terms of the way in which these roles are performed. Such a study would provide a picture of how the school operates as a social system and how the system maintains itself, even though different individuals move in and out of particular roles. This type of analysis has been illustrated briefly in Chapter 8 of this book.

Similarly, one may study the interactions *between* social systems in terms of role analysis: how, for instance, the high school principal or the superintendent relates to the chief of police in the community, to the mayor, to the chairman of the Board of Health, to ministers, to representatives of the Chamber of Commerce; how teachers generally relate to other institutional representatives; and so on. Any social system "relates" to any other by the interactions of the people who fill the roles in the two systems.

We shall return to a role analysis later in this chapter, after discussing inter-system relations in somewhat more abstract terms. We shall take the metropolitan area as the unit for analysis, for this unit is large enough to provide an elaboration of sub-systems within the educational system and to include all the other principal social systems with which the educational system interacts.

Relations Among Educational Sub-Systems

The educational sub-systems of a metropolitan area consist of the various public school districts in the area: the system of Roman Catholic schools, the system of Lutheran schools, other church-related school systems such as the Christian schools and the Seventh-Day Adventist schools, and the independent private schools.

These sub-systems have had a tradition of working separately. However, in the 1960's needs for cooperation were becoming apparent among the public school districts, and also between public and private schools.

Cooperation Among Public School Districts

Among public school districts a variety of shared educational projects have made their appearance, including television, special schools for handicapped children, junior colleges, and in-service teacher training programs. Most of this cooperation is presently taking place among suburban districts, without the participation of the central city district; but in some instances it involves all the districts within the metropolitan area.

The first steps are often taken by volunteer and non-official groups which meet to study the problems of a metropolitan area and to plan for possible cooperation among schools.

The PACE Association, established under the auspices of the Greater Cleveland Association Foundation, is a case in point. A committee of citizens made a five month study of the school needs of the whole county, and then published a Plan for Action by Citizens in Education (PACE, 1963).

The report points out, among other things, that: inequalities among Cuyahoga County's school districts are so vast that they cannot possibly be justified by a community which believes in equal opportunity. In one favored district, 60 professionals serve a thousand children; libraries, laboratories, and swimming pools are numerous; more than $800 is spent annually to educate each child. But in less fortunate districts, only about 40 professionals serve the same number of children; the elementary schools have no libraries, and $400 is available each year for each child. Similar disparities occur in all aspects of education: housing, facilities, personnel, programs, services.

The major recommendation was that the Cuyahoga County Superintendents' Association, parochial school leadership, and the present informal group of Cuyahoga County school board presidents should launch a thorough county-wide study of cooperative programs and services.

The concluding recommendation in the report was that "A continuing tax-exempt Greater Cleveland Citizens Committee should be formed which, over the next seven years will: (1) work with existing organizations to review this Plan for Action and help to carry out its recommendations; (2) foster a climate of opinion which demands quality elementary and secondary education for all Cuyahoga County children; and (3) provide a badly needed and long awaited county-wide mechanism for the many citizens who want to work in the best interests of all the schools."

The first step in some metropolitan areas may be to create an area-wide organization such as a metropolitan area planning commission, followed soon thereafter by the creation of a metropolitan education authority. The functions assumed by the education authority might include planning new suburban school districts; administering a basic state aid fund so as to help equalize educational opportunity for all the children; administering an area-wide educational research and evaluation council; administering programs of special education for the entire area; maintaining a public university, including a teacher-training institution; recruiting and selecting teachers; administering a teachers' pension system; administering an educational television station.

In some instances voluntary cooperation among school districts has taken the form of a study council or a superintendents' study group in which a local university works with the school superintendents of the area. This may lead to a more formal arrangement for voluntary cooperation, such as the Educational Research and Development Council of the Twin Cities Metropolitan Area, Inc.

The superintendents of the Minneapolis–St. Paul area, together with members of the School of Education at the University of Minnesota, formed the Council in 1963. It consists of 35 public school districts in the seven-county metropolitan area, schools which serve 44 percent of all the pupils in the state of Minnesota.

During the first three years of the Council, a number of research studies have been completed on the organizational climate and structure of schools, school output measures, program evaluation, and school staffing, and surveys dealing with finance and taxation problems and school expenditures. The Council has also undertaken various developmental activities including workshops for teachers and administrators, programs for the mentally retarded children in the area, and the utilization of computer methods in school record and school accounting systems.

Another example of metropolitan cooperation is the "federation" plan adopted in Toronto, Canada in 1954 which is an area-wide government that includes thirteen municipalities. One part of this government is a metropolitan school board which provides school sites and buildings and makes uniform per-pupil payments to the eleven locally-elected school boards, which in turn operate the elementary and secondary schools in their areas.

The creation and development of a metropolitan area authority may lead to the joining together of certain small suburban districts in units large enough to support a good elementary-secondary system. It may also spur the central city board of education to work with other branches of the city government in defining the local communities in accordance with their specific goals of urban renewal, as well as encouraging cooperation with citizens' groups in the local communities.

Cooperation Between Public Schools and Church Schools

Cooperation between the public school and church school systems has taken various forms over the years. Because of the American tradition of separation between church and state, there have long been laws against public support of church-operated schools. For this and other reasons, the several church school systems (the so-called parochial schools) have tended to operate in isolation from the public schools. At the same time patterns of collaboration have grown up with regard to religious instruction independent of instruction in the other areas of school curriculum.

THE ISSUE OF RELIGIOUS INSTRUCTION. A number of Protestant churches offer a week-day program of religious classes which usually meet one period a week in the latter part of a school day. In some communities the Roman Catholic Church gives similar instruction to pupils from public schools. Sometimes the children leave the school building and go to their own churches for this instruction; at other times they remain in school and are instructed by teachers provided by the church. In some communities, a group of churches have banded together to employ teachers who teach an inter-denominational religion; and the instruction is given in the regular school classroom. There are a variety of such "released-time" arrangements, in which those children who do not attend the religious classes are provided for in some other way by the school, often by being placed in a study hall. The "released time" program was first put into practice in 1914 in Gary, Indiana. The program spread so that by 1950 it included some 2,000,000 children in more than 2,000 communities.

This type of week-day religious instruction in the public schools and on school time, but with varying degrees of church responsibility, has been a matter of controversy in America. Some people have opposed it on the ground that it infringes the constitutional principle of separation between church and state.

In 1948 the United States Supreme Court passed down a decision on a test case involving a "released-time" program in Champaign, Illinois, in which children were taught religion in the school buildings and on school time by teachers employed by some of the local churches. Attendance records in the religious classes were reported to the school authorities. Children who did not attend the classes were required to sit in study hall during that period. It was argued by attorneys in this case that the minority of children who would not attend the religious classes would be ridiculed by the other children who attended these classes. For this reason, it was argued the existence of the religious classes meant in effect that the state, through the school, would be putting pressure on children to take part in a church program, and that the state would thus be supporting the church.

The Supreme Court ruled that this particular form of church and school collaboration is unconstitutional; and, in so ruling, said:

Religious education so conducted on school time and property is patently woven into the working scheme of the school. The Champaign arrangement thus presents powerful elements of inherent pressure by the school system in the interest of religious sects. The fact that this power has not been used to discriminate is beside the point. Separation is a requirement to abstain from fusing functions of Government and of religious sects, not merely to treat them all equally. That a child is offered an alternative may reduce the constraint; it does not eliminate the operation of influence by the school in matters sacred to conscience and outside the school's domain. The law of imitation operates, and non-conformity is not an outstanding characteristic of children. The result is an obvious pressure upon children to attend. (U.S. Reports 333 U.S. 227.)

As a result of this Supreme Court ruling, some "released-time" programs of religious education have been abandoned. Most of them, however, were retained but were carefully kept within limits so that the school could not fairly be accused of putting pressure on children to attend. The Court of Appeals in New York State held in 1951 that a "released-time" program was constitutional if the children whose parents so desired were dismissed from school to get religious instruction elsewhere.

Stanley (1961), in reviewing the situation with regard to church-school relationships, said:

> At the end of the nineteenth century most informed educators would have said that the major questions of church-school relationships were settled. But there is no doubt that they have now been reopened. Many of the forces at work are not new. The religious pluralism of the American people, the democratic and constitutional doctrine of religious freedom, the belief that education must be based on some moral and social philosophy— these forces were as evident in 1900 as they are today. But they have been augmented by other factors which, if not wholly new, have made their weight felt in recent years. The increased proportion of Roman Catholics in the total population, the rising cost of education, the insistent pressure for federal aid to education, the spectacular rise of neo-orthodoxy among Protestants, the widespread uneasiness about the moral foundations of American society, and the growing anxiety engendered by the world crisis all have contributed to the revival of the state-church-school problem.
>
>   . . . It is apparent that, apart from agreement on prohibition of teaching a particular sectarian doctrine, there is no consensus in theory or in practice about the place of religion in the public schools. What is clear is that there is a considerable, and perhaps growing, body of opinion in Catholic, Protestant, and even Jewish circles that the public schools must recognize the importance of religion in the American way of life. (Stanley, 1961, pp. 91, 93.)

THE EFFECTS OF THE ELEMENTARY AND SECONDARY EDUCATION ACT OF 1965. A new chapter in the history of relations between public schools and church-supported schools began in 1965, with the passage of the Elementary and Secondary Education Act. This bill represented a workable compromise in the effort to get federal aid for general education that had been discussed for thirty years. Previous bills had lost out in Congress due to the opposition of Congressmen who generally opposed expansion of federal government activities as well as the opposition of Congressmen from big-city districts where there was a large proportion of Roman Catholics. The latter group of Congressmen was not opposed to federal aid to education in principle, but they represented districts in which many Roman Catholic parents were opposed to paying extra taxes for support of the public schools while they also had to pay for the education of their own children in parochial schools.

The 1965 Act authorized a substantial amount of federal aid to church-supported education and thus won the votes of big-city Congressmen. Essentially, the Act provides aid to the *education of children,* whatever schools they may attend. The assistance must be given *through the public schools,* but not necessarily *in the public schools.*

Title I of the Act provides money (about 50 percent of the previous per-pupil expenditures in the state) to improve educational programs for children from low-income families. The following two paragraphs from Section 205 of the Act specify that a public educational agency may receive federal money provided the State Department of Education determines, among other things:

(2) that, to the extent consistent with the number of educationally deprived children in the school district of the local educational agency who are enrolled in private elementary and secondary schools, such agency has made provision for including special educational services and arrangements (such as dual enrollment, educational radio and television, and mobile educational services and equipment) in which such children can participate;

(3) that the local educational agency has provided satisfactory assurance that the control of funds provided under this title, and title to property derived therefrom, shall be in a public agency for the uses and purposes provided in this title, and that a public agency will administer such funds and property. (United States, 89th Congress, 1965, pp. 4–5.)

The leaders of public schools and private schools are now working together to answer such questions as the following: How is the state to spend this money on improving the education of children who are in private schools? Most of these children will be found in Catholic schools. Should the public school system employ teachers and assign them to Catholic schools to reduce class size? Should the public school system employ social workers, nurses, and other personnel and assign them to parochial schools? Should the public schools provide instruction in certain subjects for these children under a "shared time" or dual enrollment program?

In addition to the provisions of Title I, Titles II and III of the Act provide for approximately $200 million per year of expenditure *through* the public school system, to assist the education of children, regardless of the school they attend and regardless of their family income level. Title II provides money for textbooks, library books, visual aids, and other teaching materials, to be *loaned* to private schools by public schools. Title III provides for the support of supplementary educational centers, which will offer educational assistance to pupils regardless of their school membership. The centers may provide classes and services for gifted and for handicapped children, counseling services, and other enrichment programs. Also, the centers may make equipment and the services of specialized personnel available to private schools. Public school authorities and private school authorities may be jointly responsible for the direction of these centers.

Thus the period from 1965 to 1970 is one in which public and church-supported schools are learning to cooperate. This is being done more easily in some states than in others; several states have laws which make it almost impossible for public schools to give *any* assistance to pupils in private schools. These laws are now undergoing critical study and revision.

THE QUESTION OF "SHARED TIME." The Act is giving a good deal of impetus to programs of dual enrollment or "shared time," which is an arrangement whereby a pupil is enrolled and regularly attends a public school part of the time and a private school part of the time. Though this practice is an old one in a few communities (Pittsburgh has had it for fifty years), it has been promoted lately as a means whereby the expanding Roman Catholic schools can meet the expense of their growing enrollments. By teaching pupils only certain subjects, and permitting them to study other subjects as regular students in public schools, the parochial schools can operate at less expense.

Thus the trend of social forces is to push the public and church school systems closer together, and to create new patterns of cooperation within the educational sub-systems of the metropolitan area.

Inter-system Relations in the Metropolitan Area

In order to study relations between educational and other social systems which operate in a metropolitan area, the social systems can be divided into two categories, *critical and supporting* systems. The distinction is a loose one. A supporting system is one which performs its functions in a routine, efficient manner, and is not undergoing major change in its functions: for example, the water department in an ordinary city. The critical systems at any given time are those faced with new demands or new functions because the community is changing. If, for example, the water supply runs low, due to drought, population growth, or other circumstances, as was the case in New York in 1965, the water department quickly becomes a critical system. Also, if the water department is asked to take on a new function, such as that of preventing dental caries among the population through fluoridation of the water supply, this change of function may become controversial in some communities so that the water department may become a critical system.

In the following list, those systems designated as critical are those presently concerned with pressing social problems:

CRITICAL SOCIAL SYSTEMS (and some of their sub-systems)

> Educational systems (public school districts; system of Roman Catholic schools, other church-related schools; independent, private schools; teachers' organizations)
>
> Government systems (city, county governments; special districts; court systems)
>
> Welfare agency systems (Welfare Council, Bureau of Public Assistance, private charities; settlement houses; youth-serving organizations such as YMCA, Scouts, Boys' Clubs)
>
> Economic systems (banks, department stores, industrial corporations, Chamber of Commerce, AFL-CIO Council, real-estate board)
>
> Culture Agency systems (Public library, museums, TV and radio stations, park districts)
>
> Transportation Systems (Rapid transit; airport; department of streets; expressway systems)
>
> Church systems (Church Federation, Roman Catholic Diocese, area or city-wide organizations of specific religious denominations)
>
> Civic organization systems (Civil Rights organizations, foreign-policy organizations, League of Women Voters, Urban League, Citizens' Schools Organizations)

SUPPORTING SYSTEMS

> Health maintenance systems (Board of Health, medical societies, hospitals)
>
> Communication (newspapers, TV and radio, telephone systems)
>
> Public service systems (Fire, police, water departments; Commission on Human Relations)
>
> Political Organizations
>
> Sociability systems (Country clubs, "service" clubs, lodges)

Certain social systems operate effectively when they operate relatively independently. Again, the water supply system is an example. It performs a technical and mechanical function, which is clearly defined; and it is seldom called upon to cooperate with other systems. On the other hand, the educational system is an example of one that must cooperate with other systems, because its functions are complex and similar to the functions of other social systems.

School and Library Systems

For example, the school and the library systems have overlapping functions which are worked out in various ways in different communities. The story of school and library cooperation in the City of Chicago is a good example. Much of the early part of the story is told by John A. Vieg (1939) who studied the schools of metropolitan Chicago in the 1930's.

In 1910 there were no school libraries in Chicago. At that time the Chicago Public Library provided a large number of fifty-book collections on long-term loan to classrooms in the schools. During 1916–17 the Library set up libraries in six high schools and maintained them for a short time, then closed them.

After several years, a formal cooperative agreement was made by which the Chicago Public Library provided books, magazines, supplies; selected librarians and supervised them; and the Chicago School Board paid the salaries of the librarians. This agreement continued from 1923 until 1937, when thirty-eight high schools and two junior college branches had libraries under this plan. There were no elementary school libraries during this period, but the classroom loan collections were continued. Although the cooperative agreement was in effect for more than a decade, there was some dissatisfaction. For example, the 1935 annual report of the Chicago Public Library says that the services of the librarians were not fully appreciated by the schools.

After 1937, the Board of Education assumed the cost of books and magazines and later took over the selection and supervision of librarians. A complete library system that included almost all of the elementary schools was established in the Chicago Schools during subsequent years. Thus the school libraries became integral parts of the school system, though the long-term loan collections from the Public Library continued in the elementary schools on a declining basis, with 32,000 books out on loan in 1962.

In this case the new function (school libraries) was introduced into the school system through inter-system cooperation, and then the cooperation was gradually discontinued as the school system took over the responsibility.

School and Social Work Agencies

With regard to a different social function, the history of cooperation has been quite different:

> For years before the Depression of the 1930's the Chicago Schools had a significant social welfare function. The schools provided services to immigrant, non-English-speaking families. This was generally done informally by school principals and teachers working in areas of the city with large immigrant populations. Some schools had "fresh-air classrooms" for children with tuberculosis. The attendance officers in many cases worked with families who needed help. In 1927 the Chicago schools began to employ "visiting teachers" to work with maladjusted children and their families. There were 17 visiting teachers in 1931, but these positions were abolished as an economy measure shortly thereafter.
>
> During the Depression Decade of the 1930's the social welfare system of the city expanded, due to social security and welfare legislation, and became a large system of public and private agencies with a growing and self-conscious professional staff. Efforts since 1950 to bring social workers back into the Chicago Public Schools have had little success, and cooperation between the two systems has not been established, even though many people recognize the need for such cooperation.

Many other school systems are now employing school social workers or visiting teachers, often after a period of cooperation with a social welfare agency which provides and pays the social workers. Currently, in the 1960's, there is a good deal of experimentation with home-school coordinators, who are people with some social work training and who are located on the staff of the school. There is also some experimentation between public schools and child-care or nursery school agencies to provide preschool classes for socially disadvantaged children. Gradually, as the schools learn how to make use of social workers and nursery school teachers, and if the need for such workers in the schools continues, the schools in the big cities will probably develop social work and nursery school sub-systems of their own.

The "Independent" School System

For many years, it was a basic principle among school administrators that the school system should be protected from invasion by other social systems. Professor Strayer of Columbia University, the most influential leader among school administrators during the period from 1920 to about 1945, repeated frequently what he wrote in his report on the Chicago School Survey in 1932, "It is always a mistake for the schools to be organized so that agencies other than a board of education are responsible for the administration of vital and indispensable services in the schools" (Strayer, 1932, p. 145).

This principle of school administration may be interpreted broadly to mean that the schools should control the administration of all services they perform—even the new and marginal services such as the school lunch program, recreation services in city parks, job placement of students taking part in work-experience programs, delinquency-prevention programs, transportation of pupils. Yet in these and other programs, other social systems have an interest, and their personnel may not cooperate if the school system is regarded as aggressive or uncooperative.

In the present decade there are problems of cooperation in many metropolitan areas between school systems and social welfare agencies, recreation agencies, police and youth-serving agencies, and transportation systems. Frequently the local city government is responsible for social systems which might cooperate with a school system. As the city government becomes increasingly responsible for a program of *positive welfare of the city*, it comes very close to the activities of the school system; and the mayor or the city manager may wish to cooperate in particular with the superintendent of schools. At the same time, such city government agencies as the police department, public housing authority, department of human relations, park department, are often seen by the school administrator as sources of trouble for him. He may feel that cooperation with them will involve him in "local politics."

A push for cooperation between city government and school government has become more pronounced since about 1950 with the advent of federal legislation and federal funds for urban renewal. Civic improvement, under the conditions of the 1950's and 1960's, was obviously tied up with improvement in the city schools. The schools, however, were suffering generally. They were overcrowded as a result of the post-war population boom; their buildings were aging; and many of their best pupils and teachers were being lost to the growing suburbs.

Role of Federal Government

Early in the 1960's, the federal government stepped in with substantial funds aimed at improving the quality of the city's population as workers, parents, and citizens. The Manpower Development and Training Act, the Vocational Education Act of 1963, the Economic Opportunity Act, and the Elementary and Secondary Education Act of 1965 all pumped money from Washington into the city school systems, and all aimed at improving the quality of city life. These funds stretched the functions of the school system into forms of more direct service to the city. Education was seen increasingly by civic leaders as serving to improve the city, not only through its effects on the mind and character of the pupils, but also through its effects on the economic system and the social structure of the city. The school system became an instrument for attracting and holding desirable groups of people within the central city, for stabilizing racially integrated neighborhoods, and for solving or holding in check the problems of an alienated and economically marginal minority of slum dwellers.

A contemporary leader among school administrators, Professor Roald Campbell of the University of Chicago, called on school superintendents and school boards to be more cooperative with city government. Speaking at the 1965 White House Conference on Education he said:

> . . . Americans have long thought that education should be removed from politics; hence school government, particularly at the local level, has been more or less independent of city government. Some city councils can adjust the school budget, many cannot. Some mayors or city councils name the school board members, many do not. Even where city government influences school board selection and school budget allocations, seldom does city government play any role in establishing the program of the schools. The courts have often sustained the point that school boards are created by the state, that the state has delegated to such boards powers necessary for the operation of the schools, and that board members are state, not city, officials.
>
> Thus, there is historical and legal precedent for the feeling of independence found in school board members and administrators. Unfortunately, this feeling can get in the way of cooperation with other agencies when the problems require collaboration. The matter is further compounded when representatives of each of the other agencies also exhibit similar feelings of independence, as is often the case. The situation often gets worse while the agencies that might help waste their energies over jurisdictional self-justification. . . .
>
> All of this suggests that local government, particularly in our cities, needs serious reexamination. In that process we ought to assess the relationship of school and other special government to general government. Clearly, we need to insist on political responsibility in both general and school government. (Campbell, 1965.)

Cooperative Planning by Social Systems

In a time of social change there is a premium on planning for the future. Innovation is necessary, and planned innovation gives better results than haphazard innovation. The planning that is needed depends, of course, on the particular social system. With changes in the numbers of people living in the different parts of a metropolitan area, there is need for planning of new school buildings, churches, libraries, shopping centers, sewer lines, water pipes, and expressways. With changes in the numbers of people in various occupations there is need for planning of occupational training programs and of employment services.

The opportunities and the needs for planning are greater than in the past for at least two reasons. First, the pace of social change is now so rapid that failure to plan is tantamount to failure of a system to function. Second, although the vast amounts of federal government money now available are being used in ways that are largely determined at the local and metropolitan area levels, the federal government itself requires a plan before releasing money to local government systems. This money goes into urban renewal, public housing, education, manpower training, highways, health and retirement insurance, and cultural activities. For instance, recent additions to the Federal Highway Act required every population area of 50,000 or more to produce a transportation plan by July 1, 1965, in order to be eligible for federal highway money. The government is also making "planning grants" under the Economic Opportunity Act and other acts to enable local and metropolitan units to plan programs before asking for funds to support them.

Among private business and private social, cultural and religious systems planning is the accepted procedure. The National Council of Churches has a planning agency. The welfare council of a metropolitan area has a planning staff. The board of trustees of a privately supported college assigns a planning function to the president of the institution and often appoints a committee of the board to assist him. The church federation of a large metropolitan area usually has a planning officer. Every large industrial or business concern has a planning staff.

During a period of rapid social change it is necessary to have both inter-system and intra-system planning. The following are examples of the need for inter-system planning that involves the school system.

Employment of Youth

Technological change has made the employment of juveniles less and less efficient from the economic point of view. The economic system no longer employs large numbers of youth as they reach the legal school-leaving age. At the same time, the secondary schools are not performing efficiently the function of educating the kinds of youth who in the past dropped out of school and went to work. The result is a serious youth problem, which is not being handled efficiently by either of the two systems.

Recognizing the problem, the federal government has supplied money for new kinds of vocational training for youth who are not being served by orthodox vocational schools, and has set up major programs under the Job Corps and the Neighborhood Youth Corps. What social system should receive these federal funds and take on this new function?

Some school systems are slowly and haltingly developing Urban Youth Programs to give work experience and to find employment for those youth who are marginal to the labor force and marginal to the school. Some welfare agency systems such as the YMCA are working at the same task; and other youth-serving organizations are setting up work experience and job-finding programs. Also, some private business firms are accepting government contracts to operate Job Corps centers to train out-of-school and unemployed youth. Thus at least three social systems are experimenting with a new function. It is too soon to tell which system can operate best for this purpose, but the channels of inter-system planning should be kept open during this period of readjustment of function.

Furthermore, after a year or two of work training or work experience, the unemployed and marginal youth will be discharged onto the labor market at the age of 18 or 19, looking for work. Who will employ them? The state employment offices, which are welfare agency systems, have had difficulty placing these youth in the past. Some new way of carrying out the function of providing jobs for youth under 21 may have to be devised in the current decade. This situation requires inter-system planning between the economic systems of employers and employment service, with possibly a government public works agency coming into the picture.

Pre-School Classes

Another form of inter-system planning is needed in the area of compensatory education for socially disadvantaged children of pre-school age. If further experience shows that the cognitive development of such children will be markedly improved by pre-school education, and that programs such as "Head Start" which began in 1965 are effective, there will be federal and state money to pay for such classes. Will this new function be taken up by the public school system, by public and private welfare agency systems, or by private schools which specialize in this function?

Site Selection and Building Planning

The school system has traditionally planned its own expansion with regard to new sites and buildings. In recent years there has been some inter-system planning between the school system and park systems to bring schools into juxtaposition with parks. Now, with major programs of physical urban renewal underway, the city planning agency and the school planning agency have new reasons to cooperate. This is especially important where the goals of urban renewal include the maintenance and stabilization of racially integrated neighborhoods. The actual location of a new school may be crucial to the stabilization of an integrated residential area; just as new public and private housing projects will radically affect school attendance patterns. It appears mandatory that school building planning be carried on cooperatively between the school system and the housing systems of the community.

Salient Roles in Changing Social Systems

It was said earlier in this chapter that the interactions between social systems can be studied in terms of role analysis. Let us see how this generalization applies within the context being developed here regarding problems of cooperation between schools and other social systems.

The educational system includes, among others, the following roles:

Administrator
Teacher
Non-professional staff member
Board of Education member
Student
Parent organization member
Civic organization member

Each of these roles represents a pattern of behavior which, if a school system is to be successful, is geared smoothly into all the other roles in ways that enable the school to perform its functions efficiently and at the same time to provide satisfaction for the people who fill the roles.

The social changes occurring in metropolitan areas are causing many of these roles to undergo rapid redefinition. There are accompanying strains in role performance; and in some city school systems, accompanying dissatisfactions. The social changes which have disarranged the functions of the school system have also demanded changes in the patterns of behavior which, in an earlier day, were defined as appropriate for the various roles. For example, the teacher's role is different, if she teaches socially disadvantaged children, from what she learned her role should be when she was teaching docile children who were ready learners. Similarly, the principal of an inner-city school has a different role from the one he may have learned earlier as principal of a school in a middle-income area. The administrator who has overall charge of a changing system needs a different set of skills and attitudes than the administrator of a stable system in which the school carries out only traditional functions.

At the present time, in changing metropolitan areas, there are two roles that are particularly important not only in relation to each other but also in relation to representatives of other social systems: the role of the superintendent and the role of board-of-education member. With regard to other social systems, the role of civic-organization member is a particularly salient one.

The Superintendent's Role

Traditionally, the superintendent's role has consisted mainly of the following behaviors:

1. To discuss matters of policy with the Board of Education generally as a mentor. In most instances, to be careful to yield to the

Board in the making of decisions, once having helped to clarify various policy alternatives and their consequences.

2. To select assistant administrators and to divide the work of administration among them.
3. To draw up the annual budget, and present it to both the Board and the public.
4. To represent the school system in relations with the public—to explain school policies, to hear suggestions and complaints, and to persuade the public that the schools are performing their functions well or that school personnel are working wisely on the problems they are facing.
5. To represent the Board of Education in negotiations with teachers and non-professional personnel regarding salaries and working conditions.

In the contemporary situation in most big cities, the role of the superintendent has three additional major components:

6. To understand the society in which the school operates—its social systems and sub-systems—and to strive to work out agreement with the other systems on allocation of functions.
7. To plan for development of the school system, encouraging innovation and evaluation.
8. To analyze the tensions in the community that affect the schools, and to work to reduce these tensions by assisting diverse groups to communicate with one another and to achieve a peaceful *modus vivendi.*

The Board Member's Role

The board member's role involves the following:

1. To represent the public interest with regard to the school system.
2. To formulate general policy with respect to the curriculum, methods of teaching, organization of the system into sub-districts, placing and building of schools, employment and working conditions of personnel, discipline of students, etc.
3. To conduct independent and continuing scrutiny of the performance of the school system.
4. To determine the financial needs of the school system and to work with appropriate government agencies to secure the needed funds.

The Civic Organization

The civic organization, for the purposes of this discussion, consists of any organization of citizens who have an explicit interest in the school system. Some organizations are city- or area-wide. Some represent a particular segment of the population, such as businessmen, or religious leaders, or residents of a given local community or neighborhood. (The Parent-Teacher Association may be considered a civic organization, though its special interest in the schools and its relationship to local schools give it special importance.)

The role of a member of a civic organization includes the following kinds of behavior:

1. To study the school system and attempt to understand its functions and its capabilities.
2. To formulate the educational needs of the particular section of the community which it represents, or of the entire community.
3. To communicate with other organizations, and attempt to arrive at consensus regarding school policy.
4. To support the Board of Education in its plans for financial support of the schools.

During a period of rapid social change and consequent social conflict, the tendency is for civic organizations to form pressure groups and to promote particular group interests. Thus the years after 1960 have seen the rise of scores of pressure groups in every big city, which express their own needs as they see them. For example, Negro parents organize to obtain better schools for their children; taxpayers' groups, to keep taxes down, or parents in a middle-class neighborhood, both Negro and white, to protest the redrawing of school boundaries which will bring lower-class children into their local schools.

Role Relations

In the big city it is inevitable that the roles of superintendent and board member overlap to some extent. In every city, the board works out its own arrangements with the superintendent, to provide appropriate separation of duties and maximum accommodation to the particular points of view (and particular personalities) involved.

The members of the school board are usually sensitive to the attitudes of the community or certain sections of the community. They are likely to seek ways of meeting the desires of the public by adjusting the school program here and there and by effecting compromises between various pressure groups. They may find themselves dealing with a superintendent who defines his role in primarily the same terms, and who devotes much of the time working with them in adapting policy in the light of total community needs and in promoting good relations with other social systems in the community. On the other hand, the board may find itself at odds with a superintendent who holds to a more traditional definition of his role; who regards himself as the educational expert; and who concentrates his efforts on problems *within* the school system and its sub-systems, rather than upon the relations of the educational system to other social systems of the community.

The growth of pressure groups, furthermore, while it is a natural social process (and to some degree, desirable) carries with it no method of making decisions. The pressure group may separate itself off from the decision-making function; it may assume that a body, such as the board of education, makes the decisions, and that its own role is to present its case persuasively to that decision-making body, even going to extremes in doing so.

If a city consists of warring factions with respect to school policy and program, it is unlikely that the superintendent and the board of education can work together in full harmony. The board members will be differentially sensitive to the various pressure groups. The superintendent may ally himself, more or less consciously, with certain factions in the city.

To illustrate how the roles of school superintendent, school board member, and civic-organization member interact, the following two hypothetical cases have been constructed:

Both cities A and B are large metropolitan centers, both plagued with the problems of the central cities that have been described in preceding chapters. There is not much difference between the two cities in size, complexity, percentage of Negroes, delinquency rates, or educational levels of the adult population.

In city A, the superintendent has had a wide variety of experience, including classroom teaching, a principalship, a superintendency in a small city, and a superintendency in a high-income suburb.

Superintendent A is a student of his community. He spends a great deal of time talking with community leaders, and in becoming acquainted with a wide variety of people, encouraging them to tell him freely what they think of the schools. He speaks frequently at public gatherings.

In his relations with the teachers' union, he strives to get the union on his side in matters of educational policy; and to convince the union that he does all he can to further the economic interests of teachers. Recently he announced a policy of rotating experienced teachers into the inner-city schools serving children of low-income families. This plan was announced after lengthy discussion with the union, and was not resisted by them, even though it required experienced teachers to give up some of their seniority privileges.

In his relations with community leaders, Superintendent A has encouraged the school board to appoint a Citizens' Commission on the Public Schools, and has made changes in his budget to provide the Commission with money to employ staff and to undertake evaluative studies. The Commission, which includes some board members, has issued two reports within the past three years; and most of its recommendations have been adopted by the board and put into effect by the superintendent. An assistant superintendent works especially on problems of racial integration in the schools, as was recommended by the Citizens' Commission.

The school system works closely with the other social systems in the area, including the city's Commission on Human Relations and the Youth Bureau of the city government.

In city B, the superintendent has a wide variety of experience, similar to that of Superintendent A, including classroom teaching, high-school principalship, and superintendency in several smaller cities.

Superintendent B started by concentrating on a new building program to meet the needs of the rapidly expanding school population, and on improving the quality of education in the schools. He spoke a few times before businessmen's groups, but generally begged off from public appearances, leaving, as he said, the speech-making to those who enjoy it.

His relations with the teachers' union are not cordial, even though he has been successful in getting pay raises that have kept teachers' salaries in his city among the highest in the country. At one point he announced a plan that would tend to keep experienced teachers in the inner-city schools. This plan was not discussed with the teachers' organizations before it was announced; and, somewhat to the surprise of the superintendent, it met such vociferous opposition from teachers that the Board of Education refused to adopt it.

Superintendent B is usually too busy to listen to the various groups of parents and citizens who come to talk with him. Instead, he has appointed a public-relations officer who supervises the publication and distribution of well-designed and profusely-illustrated reports on various aspects of the school program.

As tensions arose in the city over racial segregation, Superintendent B announced that the school's task was to provide top-quality education for all the children, wherever they were to be found, but that it was not the school's task to take an active part in reducing *de facto* segregation, since the latter was something outside the school's control. Perhaps as the unwitting result, he became the hero of the groups who were opposed to integration in the schools.

The Board of Education, like other groups in the city, became divided. One group became openly antagonistic to the superintendent; another tended to follow him without question. The Board members became uncertain as to their appropriate roles. Some members began to study the controversial questions intensively, then to criticize the methods of the superintendent and his staff. Sub-committees of the Board were formed to look into specific problems of the operation of the schools. These committees were regarded by the superintendent as usurping his functions as executive.

The school system in city B has come to be regarded by representatives of other social systems as uncooperative. In programs aimed to prevent school dropouts, in delinquency prevention programs, and in pre-school programs, the public school system has either taken a dominant position or has declined to participate. A movement to use women as volunteers in inner-city schools was recently discouraged by the superintendent.

Thus the roles of board members, superintendent, and civic-organization members have become confused in city B; the superintendent has become a controversial figure; and pressure groups continue to protest.

Conclusions

For the next decade there is bound to be tension and conflict in the metropolitan area over school policies and practices, because solutions to new problems must be worked out by people who have different attitudes and different conceptions of their roles. The board of education, the superintendent, and various civic organizations must adapt their roles to the changing situations.

The superintendent is probably the key figure. He needs to understand the whole complex of social systems and sub-systems in the metropolitan area; and he needs to develop his own role as one which promotes communication and cooperation among the systems. This is difficult for the superintendent whose training has disposed him toward working for efficiency within his own sub-system of teachers, pupils, and administrators, and to guard jealously these sub-systems from the encroachment of other systems.

Civic organizations will need to combine the functions of special pleading for special interest groups with that of seeking to communicate with other groups. The small number of community-wide civic organizations will have special responsibility to promote communication among the more narrowly-based groups and to help them take a responsible part in decision-making. Probably a big city should develop *regional education councils* to serve this purpose, bringing the local civic associations and parent-teacher organizations together within a region where there are certain common interests and problems which are different from those in other regions of the big city.

The delicate art of operating a school system in a period of rapid social change will need to contain action which maintains communication and decision-making with other cooperating systems; which accepts new functions as they are demanded by the changing social situation; and which maintains flexibility within the educational system for new roles to emerge.

Exercises

1. Study and report on the performance of two persons in important roles in a school system. How do their performances relate to the nature of the roles they fill? How do their personalities lead them to fill their roles in unique ways?

2. Study the relations between the school system and some other social system in your metropolitan area where there has been cooperation. What has happened in this connection?

3. How do the public and private educational systems in your area co-operate? What are some of the problems?

4. If a "shared time" or dual enrollment plan is operating in your community, pay it a visit and find out how it is working. For background, you might read the U.S. Office of Education Bulletin entitled *Dual Enrollment in Public and Non-public Schools,* by James E. Gibbs, Carl J. Sokolowski, August W. Steinhilber, and William C. Strasser, Jr.

5. Make an analysis of the public school systems in your metropolitan area. To what extent and in what ways do they cooperate? Has there been any consolidation of school systems? Is there now any talk of consolidation of school systems?

6. Study the relations between civic organizations, the superintendent, and the board of education in your community. How well do you think the various roles are being filled?

Suggestions for Further Reading

1. For a study of the problems of a big city school board in working out its functions in relation to those of the superintendent, read the book by Joseph Pois entitled *The School Board Crisis: A Chicago Case Study*.

2. For a summary of examples of cooperation among systems in metropolitan areas, read Chapter 13, "The Cooperative Approach," in Bollens and Schmandt, *The Metropolis*.

3. For an analysis of the relations between personality factors and role structure in an educational system, read Jacob W. Getzels, "Conflict and Role Behavior in the Educational Setting."

4. The paper by Anderson and Powell in *Society and Education: A Book of Readings* (Havighurst, Neugarten, and Falk) states the pro's and con's on the question of permitting children to be simultaneously enrolled in a public school and in a religious school; and thus relates to the discussion in the present chapter of the relations between subsystems in the educational system.

5. Chapter 9. "Church, State and School" in *Social Foundations of Education* by William O. Stanley *et al.* is an excellent discussion of questions about religion and the public schools.

PART 4

THE SCHOOL IN THE
WIDER SOCIETY

$\it{12}$ / Education, Population, and Economic Trends

In the preceding section of this book we have been discussing the school in the context of the local community, defining the community as neighborhood, town, city, or metropolitan area; and we have looked at some of the ways in which the school relates to other social institutions within that context. In this section we take a somewhat different perspective of the relations between education and society and consider how, within the context of the wider society, changes in population, in economic and technological developments, in relations between ethnic and racial groups all bring about a continually changing set of functions for the educational system.

Population Growth

The American population doubled in size every thirty years from 1800 to 1920; then at the beginning of the 1930's the growth curve began to lose its upward thrust. It was predicted that the population would level off at about 153 million by 1980, and would thereafter remain constant or even decrease somewhat. Since the populations of several European countries had already leveled off or were showing declines by 1930, it seemed quite probable that the American population would eventually do the same.

However, after a decade of stability, the American population again began to increase rapidly. By 1950 it had grown to 151 million, by 1960 to 179 million, and by 1965, to 196 million, far exceeding earlier predictions (U.S. Bureau of the Census, Population Estimates, P

25 Series, December, 1965). It is generally agreed today that the increase in the U.S. population will continue into the next century.

Education is influenced by, but also influences, population change. Increased population has the obvious effect of producing greater numbers of children to be served by the school. At the same time, education gives people the technological skills by which they are able to produce more goods and therefore to support more lives. Education also functions to teach people how to reduce death rates (thus to increase the population) and how to control birth rates (thus to control population increase).

As shown in Figure 12.1 birth rates and death rates (the annual numbers of births and deaths per thousand people) are both lower in the last half-century than in the early 1900's. Both are rather stable in the 1960's with only slight fluctuations around 23 per thousand for the birth rate and 9 per thousand for the death rate. Since death rates have been

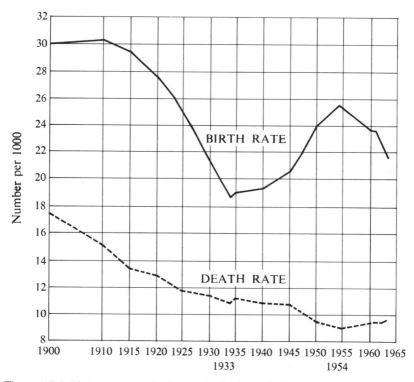

Figure 12.1 Birth rates and death rates in the United States, per 1,000 inhabitants. (Data from Dewhurst and associates, 1955, and from Statistical Abstract, 1964).

below birth rates in the United States, there has been a natural increase in overall population.

Effects of Increased Productivity

While there are many factors that influence the size of individual families, the birth rate for the country as a whole appears to be mainly a result of the interaction of two factors: (1) economic productivity and (2) knowledge of birth control.

Productivity has increased so greatly that the average worker today produces in one hour as much as the average worker in 1850 produced in six hours (Dewhurst and associates, 1955). From the years 1909 to 1964, the productivity of non-farm workers had increased three-fold (U.S. Bureau of Labor Statistics, 1965). This increase in productivity has occurred in agriculture as well as in industry. Increased productivity in industry at first tended to decrease the birth rate, because as machines replaced human labor the economic value of having large numbers of children in the family was reduced. Children, unlike adults, could not handle machines, and their labor was not needed. With the spread of information regarding birth control, the number of children per family decreased, first in the cities, and later on the farms.

During the past two decades, however, the increase in productivity of urban workers has tended to increase their birth rates, through raising their incomes and standards of living and, consequently, their ability to support children. A major part of the upswing in birth rate since 1940 can be attributed to the rising standard of living in America.

World Population Growth

The substantial growth of population in the United States since 1950 has been paralleled by similar growth rates in most other countries. In Europe, where it appeared before World War II that population was becoming stationary, there has been a new wave of population growth. Russia's population is growing as rapidly as that of the United States. China's vast population is growing probably at about the same rate. But the greatest rate of population increase is found in the "underdeveloped countries" where, until the twentieth century, a high death rate had partially offset a high birth rate and had thus kept the population at a slow rate of growth. With the coming of modern health practices in areas such as sanitation and disease prevention, the death rate has dropped sharply in these countries while the birth rate has remained high, thus providing for a very rapid rate of natural increase. In Latin America, for example, the rate of natural increase of population is between 2.0 and 2.5 percent per year, while the analogous rate of natural increase for the United States is about 1.5 percent per year.

A country with a natural increase rate of 2.5 percent a year will double its population in about 30 years, while a country with a rate of 1.5 percent requires about 50 years to double its population.

The data from various countries add up to a phenomenon of world population growth which is becoming a source of grave concern to many people. It took thousands of years to reach the one-billion mark in world population, a mark reached about 1825. The second billion was reached only a hundred years later in 1925; and the third billion, only 35 years later, in 1960. If present rates continue, it will reach four billion by 1975.

This "population explosion," as it has been called, has led to the possibility that the numbers of people may increase faster than the food supply, and that consequently the world's standard of living will go down. One group of experts believes that this danger is imminent and that birth-control measures must be adopted on a world-wide scale to prevent it. Another group believes that scientists and technologists will find ways to increase the food supply as rapidly as the population increases. Whichever point of view proves to be right, it is true that an underdeveloped country which doubles its population in 30 years must double its production of food and other essential goods in the same period of time, just to keep its standard of living from going down. This is what Mexico has been able to do after hybrid corn was introduced into Mexican agriculture; the food supply increased dramatically. Other countries have actually lost ground during the present century due to the imbalance between population increase and production increase.

Even the most productive countries face an impossible situation if they continue to increase their population at their current rates. Thus, the United States, after 650 years at the present rate of growth, would have one person for every square foot of land—hardly enough to stand on, and certainly not enough to sleep on, or to live on.

The effect of world population growth on the schools is two-fold. First, it is forcing an enormous expansion of primary and secondary education in the presently underdeveloped countries and a substantial expansion in the more industrialized countries. Second, the problems of population growth, food supply, and population control are becoming a part of the school curriculum as subjects about which every intelligent citizen should have knowledge.

Changes in Age Distribution

Since 1850 there has been a marked shift in the age distribution of the American population, as shown in Figure 12.2. In the first half of the nineteenth century there was a large proportion of young children in the population and a very small proportion of persons over sixty. In recent decades the distribution has changed, and the proportion of adults has increased markedly. Roughly speaking, 52 percent of the population

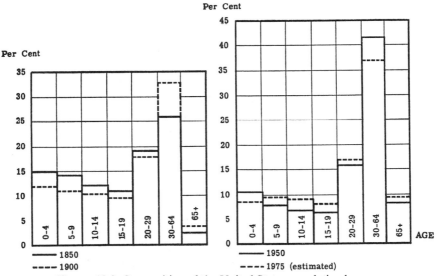

Figure 12.2 Composition of the United States population by age.

were under twenty in 1850, 44 percent in 1900, and 38 percent in 1960. This means that there are more adults to do the work of the society. Children and adolescents have been freed from the necessity of working and have been given more time that can be used for education.

Table 12.1 shows what has happened in terms of school and college enrollments. At first, children remained in school until the age of fourteen, then until sixteen; then more and more remained through high school graduation at seventeen or eighteen. Finally, since 1920, there has been a great popular movement into the colleges.

Table 12.1   Secondary School and College Enrollments in
Relation to Total Age-Groups

Year	Number enrolled in secondary schools per 100 persons 14–17 years of age	Number graduated from secondary schools per 100 persons 17 years of age	Resident degree-credit students per 100 persons 18–21 years of age
1889–90	7	3.5	3.0
1899–1900	11	6.4	3.9
1909–10	15	8.8	5.0
1919–20	32	16.8	7.9
1929–30	51	29.0	11.9
1939–40	73	50.8	14.5
1949–50	77	59.0	26.9*
1955–56	84	62.0	27.6
1959–60	86	65.0	31.1
1961–62	90	70.0	32.5
1963–64		77.0†	33.8
1964–65	93		

* Includes a half-million veterans of the armed services, almost all of whom were over 21 years of age.

† Probably high, due to fluctuation of numbers of 17-year-old youth from year to year.

Source: U.S. Office of Education, *Digest of Educational Statistics, 1965.*

By 1965, over 75 percent of the youth of America were graduating from high school, and half of this group were entering college. Thus, in 1963–64, approximately 34 percent of all American youth aged 18 to 21 were enrolled in college, taking courses for degree-credit. (We shall return later in this chapter to the discussion of growth in college enrollments.)

These proportions are far higher than in any other country; so much higher, that educators in other countries find it difficult to believe that American standards of work in secondary schools and universities are as high as their own. American educators, on the other hand, point to these figures as proof that America offers greater educational opportunity than other countries; and that there is a huge reservoir of human ability that can be developed to far greater extent than has been attempted in any other country. (For further discussion of this point, see Chapter 4, p. 108.)

Immigration

The American population and, in turn, the American educational system has been affected in a major way by great streams of immigration throughout the nineteenth and twentieth centuries.

Once the United States had been formed and the new nation had begun to grow, this country became a haven for the poor and the persecuted. The severe economic depression which followed the Napoleonic Wars in Europe brought many dispossessed people to America. Immigration from the British Isles consisted generally of poor but industrious people who were looking for better economic opportunities. The great Irish famine of the 1840's resulted in a large fraction of the Irish population emigrating to America. The political upheavals of Germany after 1848 caused many Germans to emigrate, some of them middle-class people.

Jewish immigrants came from all over Europe, seeking both religious freedom and economic opportunity. Swedes, Norwegians, and Danes came in large numbers after 1850, and for fifty years French people migrated into New England from French Canada. Then came Finns, Lithuanians, Estonians, Letts, Poles, Bohemians, Russians, and Hungarians. By 1910 the tide of immigration was running strongly from South and Southeastern Europe; and between 1900 and 1914 Italians, Bulgarians, Rumanians, Yugoslavs, Greeks, Armenians, and Portuguese brought the total of immigrants to an average of almost a million a year.

Meanwhile after the Gold Rush of the nineteenth century, Chinese, Japanese, and, later, Filipino and Hawaiian immigrants had been entering the western part of the continent; and later, as the southwest developed, there was an influx of Mexicans.

Most of these people from Europe and the Orient came without knowledge of English and with few useful occupational skills. Education for them consisted at first of "Americanization" classes in which they learned both English and enough of the American form of government to meet citizenship requirements. Night schools were established in the cities by the public schools and by settlement houses. The children attended the public and parochial schools, learning American ways they could not learn at home, and learning occupational skills. Many of these children went on to college, to prepare for better jobs than those of their fathers.

Figure 12.3 shows the numbers of immigrants who came to the United States during each decade from 1820 to 1960, and it shows the great drop in the numbers after World War I when restrictive legislation was adopted. This legislation aimed at reducing the numbers of immigrants, particularly those from countries that were not in the north and

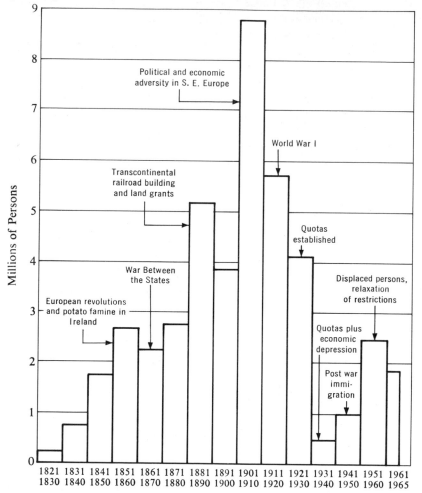

1961-1965, from U.S. Bureau of Census Population Estimates, P 25 Series, Dec. 1965.

Figure 12.3 United States immigration, 1821–1965 (1921–1950 adapted from the National Education Association, December, 1951, p. 141; 1951–1960 taken from Statistical Abstract of the United States, 1961, p. 93; 1961–1965, from U.S. Bureau of Census Population Estimates, P 25 Series, Dec. 1965).

west of Europe. The depression of the 1930's further discouraged immigration.

After World War II there was an upswing in immigration which lasted until 1952, when new restrictive legislation was passed by the Congress. Another upswing began in 1957 after counteractive legislation was adopted. Additional restriction-easing legislation was introduced in 1958 and 1959 and this, coupled with the large number of European displaced persons wishing to enter this country, made the immigration in the decade of the 50's one-and-a-half times greater than in the preceding decade. (Approximately two and one-half million immigrants entered the United States from 1951–1960, compared to one million from 1941–1950.) More than one million immigrants entered the United States in the four-year period 1961–64.

In 1965 Congress passed legislation which, when it takes effect in 1968, will eliminate the "quota" system based on national origins; although the total number of immigrants allowed into this country each year will not increase, persons will no longer be admitted on the basis of their nationality.

Migrations Within United States

Although immigration has been greatly reduced since World War I, America's expanding industry has continued to demand workers, with the result that there has been large-scale movement of people *within* the United States. Workers were found among the southern Negroes, the Mexicans, and the Scotch-Irish and English people from the hills of West Virginia, Tennessee, Kentucky, Missouri, and Arkansas. These people have streamed to the cities of the industrial North. The vast industrial developments on the West Coast and in the South and Midwest, have brought into the cities not only more Negroes and more Mexicans but also a stream of Puerto Ricans from outside the borders of the United States. Together with several hundred thousand displaced persons coming from the Baltic countries, these latter groups are repeating the patterns of their nineteenth-century predecessors, learning English, and generally trying to work their way into good jobs as their children learn American ways in the schools.

The problems faced by the schools in helping rural Americans adapt to urban ways of life and in helping foreigners become Americanized have been touched upon in earlier chapters in this book. We shall return to these problems again in a following section of this chapter.

Differential Rates of Reproduction

Another population phenomenon of significance for the educational
system is the fact that birth and death rates vary with socioeconomic
status. This variation is due to several factors. Death rates tend to be
lower for people of high socioeconomic status because such people can
afford better food, care, and medical attention than can people of low
socioeconomic levels. Birth rates tend to be higher for people of low
socioeconomic status, because these groups are less likely to make use
of birth-control methods and because, especially if they are rural people,
they still regard a child as an economic asset. Their children frequently
quit school by the age of sixteen and help to support the family.

Crude birth and death rates are not as accurate a basis for measuring population change as is the net reproduction rate (the number of
female births in a given period compared to the number of female
births within a similar interval of time in their mothers' generation). A
net reproduction rate of 1 means that for every 100 females born in a
certain year, there will be, when these women have grown up and passed
the childbearing age, exactly 100 girl babies. A country with a long-term
net reproduction rate of less than one is losing population (unless there
is immigration to offset the deficit in births). This was the case, for
example, in Sweden for some years after 1930. In the United States, as
shown in Table 12.2, the reproduction rate fell below one for a brief

Table 12.2   Net Reproduction Rates in the United States

Year	Net reproduction rate
1905–1910	1.34
1920	1.25
1930	1.08
1930–1935	0.98
1935–1940	0.98
1943	1.23
1947	1.51
1950	1.44
1954	1.65
1959	1.72
1960	1.72
1961	1.70
1962	1.63

Source: Taeuber and Taeuber, 1958; Statistical Abstract of the United States, 1964.

period, but not long enough to cause an actual decrease in population. Table 12.2 also shows that the net reproduction rate fluctuates from year to year, so that it is more meaningful to consider the net reproduction rate averaged over a period of several years.

Rates of Reproduction and Social Mobility

In the United States, as in almost all modern industrial societies, there has been an inverse relation between fertility and such socioeconomic factors as education of parents and occupation of fathers. Estimates of the net reproduction rates of various occupational groups have been made on the basis of birth rates occurring about 1940. These show that professional workers were at that time failing to reproduce their numbers by a very considerable margin. They were producing only about 75 children for every 100 adults in their generation. The same was true of business owners and executives. On the other hand, unskilled workers were producing about 125 children per 100 adults. Farmers and farm laborers were the most prolific of all.

Table 12.3 cites a set of estimated net reproduction rates for the five social-class groups with which we are familiar. The estimates in Part A of the table are based on what is known about differential fertility in the period 1920–1940; the estimates in Part B of the table, for the period 1950–1975.

THE PERIOD 1920–1940. It will be seen that in the period 1920–1940 the upper and upper-middle classes were not fully reproducing their numbers, while the lower-middle class was barely doing so. This set of facts has had a considerable influence on the degree of upward social mobility presently existing in the United States and, therefore, has special relevance for the educational system. When the higher-status groups do not reproduce themselves in a society, they leave vacant spaces behind them after each generation, spaces that will be filled by people moving up from lower-status levels. (See Chapter 2, page 64, for more discussion of this point.)

Table 12.3 also gives a calculation of the degree of upward mobility that results from the differential fertility in the various social-class groups. On the average, from 1920 to 1940, the society as a whole had a net reproduction rate greater than 1 (about 1.09); thus for every 100 adults in the population, there were 108.7 in the next generation.

Table 12.3 Relations Between Natural Population Increase, Differential Fertility, and Upward Mobility (Estimates)

Social Class	Number in Every 100 Adults	Net Repro-duction Rate*	Number in Next Genera-tion If No Mobility Occurs	Number Needed in Next Genera-tion	IF PROPORTIONS ARE TO REMAIN THE SAME:	
					Number Who Must Be Mobile from Each Class†	Percent of Upward Mobility from Each Class‡
			A. FERTILITY CONDITIONS EXISTING 1920–1940			
Upper	3	.80	2.4	3.3	0	0
Upper-middle	8	.80	6.4	8.7	0.9	14
Lower-middle	30	1.00	30.0	32.6	3.2	11
Upper-working	39	1.15	44.9	42.4	5.8	13
Lower-working	20	1.25	25.0	21.7	3.3	13
Total	100		108.7	108.7	13.2	12

B. FERTILITY CONDITIONS LIKELY TO EXIST, 1950–1975

Upper	3	1.0	3.0	3.4	0	5
Upper-middle	8	1.0	8.0	9.1	0.4	5
Lower-middle	30	1.05	31.5	34.3	1.5	9
Upper-working	39	1.20	46.8	44.6	4.3	9
Lower-working	20	1.25	25.0	22.9	2.1	8
Total	100		114.3	114.3	8.3	7

* Net reproduction rates are based on estimates from available data on differential fertility. The net reproduction rate in the 1920–40 period was such that for every 100 adults in one generation, there would be 108.7 in the next generation. In the 1950–55 period, the rate had increased markedly, but over the 1950–75 period a conservative estimate is that the net reproduction rate will be 114.

† The computation of the "number who must be upward mobile from each social class" is made as follows in Table 12.3A: there would be 2.4 upper-class people in the next generation out of a total population of 108.7 if no mobility occurred. But if we assume that enough mobility occurs to bring the upper class back to 3 percent of the total, then there must be a mobility of 0.9 from the upper-middle class, in order to bring the number of upper-class people to 3.3 (or 3 percent of 108.7).

In turn, the upper-middle class which made up 8 percent of the adult population will produce only 6.4 persons. But there must be 8.7 upper-middle-class people out of a total of 108.7 to restore the upper-middle class to 8 percent of the population. This requires an addition of 2.3 persons from the lower-middle class, plus another 0.9 to fill the places of those upper-middle people who have been mobile into the upper class. Thus the lower-middle class must provide 3.2 mobile persons, 11 percent of its number. And so on.

‡ In reading this table it is important to remember that these figures refer only to that degree of social mobility that results from differential fertility. There are other causes of upward mobility not taken into account here. Thus, there is a considerable degree of downward mobility that is offset by upward mobility. As many as 10 percent of people are downward mobile as much as one class level in their lifetime, and therefore as many as 10 percent of people must be upward mobile to balance them.

For the purposes of this calculation, it has been assumed that the percentage distribution of people in the various social classes remains unchanged from one generation to the next, and that there is no downward mobility. (In actuality, this table underestimates the degree of upward mobility for at least two reasons: (1) there is some downward mobility that is offset by upward mobility, and (2) the economic and occupational structure of American society is changing in the direction of enlarging the upper-middle class, thus creating more places to be filled in that class in each generation.)

According to this calculation, there is presently a minimum upward mobility of about 12 percent, due alone to differential fertility rates. (Present rates of mobility are based on fertility rates of the 1920–1940 period since the infants born in that period constitute the present generation of adults.) About one in eight persons (13.2 in every 109) will therefore move up one step on a five-step scale of social status during his lifetime. The degree of mobility is about equal among the four groups who can be upward mobile.

The educational consequence of differential fertility in the United States is that schools and colleges are called on to help prepare boys and girls for the upward mobility that must occur. Not only do boys and girls need training in engineering, law, medicine, science, business administration, theology, and teaching, but also the schools and colleges help these boys and girls learn the manners and the attitudes of the higher-status groups.

THE PERIOD 1950–1975. This picture changes somewhat when, as in part B of Table 12.3, we base our computations upon differential fertility as it is likely to exist over the period 1950–1975.

Since the close of World War II, it has become evident that a considerable part of the increase in birth rate is due to an increase in numbers of children born to families of middle- and high-economic status. More middle- and upper-class girls are marrying, they are marrying younger, and they have more children. While the women of the working classes, especially farm women, have also increased their birth rates, the fertility of these women has not increased as much as the fertility of middle-class women.

Table 12.3 B gives conservative estimates of the net reproductive rates of the several social classes during the 1950–1975 period. The fertility rates of women of the various social classes are only estimates; but if present trends continue, there will be a considerable lessening of the degree of social mobility caused by socioeconomic differential fertility.

According to Table 12.3 B, the amount of upward mobility due to differential fertility may, by 1980 or 1985, be reduced to about half of what it is at present (since present rates of mobility are based upon fertility rates of the 1920–1940 period).

Differential fertility is, of course, only one factor in determining overall rates of mobility. The possible reduction due to differential fertility may be at least partially offset by a general increase in the proportion of people in higher-status occupations during the next few decades, a point to which we shall return shortly. The rates of mobility will also depend upon whether or not the American economy continues to expand. A factor which may operate to decrease rates of mobility in the future is the fact that an abnormally large group of young people will reach adulthood during the 1970–1980 decade. As this number increases, unless there is a corresponding increase in the number of upper-status occupations, there will be larger numbers of young people competing for high-status occupations. This will work in the direction of lowering the rate of upward mobility, with consequent effects upon the schools.

Effects of Population Changes and Economic Trends
upon the Schools

Changes in population size and distribution, when combined with changes occurring in the economic sphere, have produced a new set of educational problems for America that are especially significant when seen in historical perspective.

The Great Depression of the 1930's

After a hundred and fifty years of almost continuous economic expansion, the American economy suffered a decade of near paralysis, now known as the Great Depression of the 1930's. Nothing like it had been known in America, where previously the periodic "panics" and business cycle depressions had been partially relieved by the opening up of new

land to homesteaders and by the general onward sweep of industrialization.

So severe was the depression in this country that 20 percent of
workers were unemployed for several years, industrial production fell to
55 percent of its 1929 level, prices plummeted, and farm mortgages
were defaulted to the extent of billions of dollars.

The depression brought the marriage rate to its lowest point in
many years. This tended to reduce the birth rate, which was cut further
by the unwillingness of many married couples to have children during
such bad times. People came to think the United States economy had
reached the height of its productivity in the 1920's before the depression. The most to be hoped for in the '30's, they believed, was a
checking of the downward trend and the establishment of what would be
an indefinite period of stationary business and industrial production,
with the population leveling off and eventually decreasing.

In 1933 the situation was so desperate that a quarter of a million
boys went "on the road," scrounging a living wherever they could find it.
America awoke to the fact that it had a youth problem.

At this time the Civilian Conservation Corps was created with
government funds to put boys into camps where they could do useful
work, get vocational training, and at the same time send home 20
dollars a month from their 30 dollars pay. Shortly afterward, the
National Youth Administration was created to provide work projects in
high schools and colleges whereby needy youth could earn enough to
pay their school expenses.

EFFECTS ON THE SCHOOLS. During this period, the schools and colleges
took on a major new function, that of custodial care of youth. Since
there was little or no work available for youth, boys and girls were
encouraged to stay in school, aided if necessary by government scholarships and work projects. The idea was to keep young people out of
trouble—in cold storage, as it were—until society could find a use for
them.

Many boys and girls were uninterested in academic work, but
remained in school because there was nothing else to do. Some schools
and colleges took this situation as a challenge and tried to find ways of
interesting these students in educational activity. These institutions
made a contribution to the modern general education movement. They
attempted to create forms of education that would help young people
become better citizens, parents, and users of leisure time, regardless of
their socioeconomic status or their occupational goals.

School curricula were generally modified in the direction of greater participation by pupils in the planning and evaluating of their work. Teaching aids in the form of motion pictures, radio, and more vivid reading materials were introduced into the schools.

During the depression, teachers' salaries were generally reduced and salary checks were often delayed because there were no funds in city and county treasuries. Nevertheless, teaching jobs were much sought after by people who had some training or experience in teaching but who had been employed in business or industry. For many people there was more security in teaching than in depression-ridden business. Soon there was overcrowding in the teaching profession, and young people were not encouraged to enter it. For ten years after 1932 the intake of young teachers was small; and the total number of elementary and secondary school teachers stayed nearly constant from 1930 until 1950. After 1950 the post-war increase in birth rate raised the school enrollments rapidly and created a vast demand, first for new elementary-school teachers and then for secondary-school teachers. Thus, by the mid 1960's there was a large group of teachers in the age range 25–40 and a relatively small group over 40.

Post-War Economic Expansion and Population Growth

Beginning with World War II and continuing thereafter, the American economy has experienced an enormous expansion. This has meant nearly full employment, high wages, and a generally increasing economic standard of living. It has also meant increasing numbers of positions in executive and professional occupations, especially in the areas of science and health.

At the same time, the great increase in birth rate flooded the schools with children. Since there had been little or no building of new elementary schools between 1930 and 1950, the schools were crowded to overflowing after 1950. Many city elementary schools had to go on "double shift," with one group of children and teachers occupying classrooms in the morning and another group in the afternoon. There was a surge of new school construction, at first of elementary schools and then of secondary schools.

The swelling of school enrollments greatly enlarged the cost of education to the community. With the numbers of elementary and secondary school children having remained relatively constant at about 28 million in the years from 1940 to 1950, the numbers jumped to 31 million in 1955 and to 42 million in 1965 (U.S. Office of Education, 1965). To meet these increased costs, most states have increased their payments from state funds to local school districts.

TEACHER SHORTAGES. Every year since 1948 there has been a greater need than the year before for new teachers at the elementary level. This need has increased as school enrollment increased from 1955 to 1965 and has extended into the high schools and colleges.

Table 12.4 shows how the percentages of teachers in the total population aged 20–64 have varied since 1900. From 1900 to 1950, the percentage was relatively constant at 1.2 to 1.4 percent of the adult population; then it took a sharp rise, and was estimated at 2.05 in 1965. This constitutes a 50 percent increase in the proportions of teachers from 1950 to 1965.

Table 12.4   Percentage of the Population 20–64 Who Are Teachers

Year	Elementary and Secondary School Teachers	College and University Teachers
1890	1.22	.04
1900	1.18	.06
1910	1.14	.07
1920	1.25	.08
1930	1.32	.11
1940	1.25	.14
1950	1.18	.22
1955	1.34	.25
1960	1.70	.31
1965	1.91	.37
1970	1.92*	.39*
1975	1.91*	.38*

* Estimated by the authors.

Source: U.S. Office of Education, *Digest of Educational Statistics, 1965.*

EFFECTS ON COLLEGES AND UNIVERSITIES. The direct effect of the low birth rates of the 1930's and of the high birth rates in the 1940's has been to create an abnormally small college-age population in the years from 1950 to 1960, then an abnormally large college-age population after 1960. Table 12.5 shows how the age group 15–19, the group supplying the colleges, fluctuates from 1900 to 1975.

Table 12.5   Distribution of the Population by Age-Groups, 1900–1975

Year			Age Group					Total (thousands)
	−5	5–9	10–14	15–19	20–29	30–64	65+	
			(in percent)					
1900	12.1	11.6	10.5	9.9	18.4	33.4	4.1	76,094
1910	11.6	10.6	9.9	9.8	18.8	35.0	4.3	92,407
1920	10.9	10.8	10.0	9.0	17.5	37.1	4.6	106,466
1930	9.3	10.2	9.8	9.4	16.9	38.9	5.4	123,077
1940	8.0	8.1	8.9	9.4	17.2	41.7	6.8	131,954
1945	9.3	7.8	7.7	8.4	17.0	42.2	7.5	139,928
1950	10.7	8.8	7.3	7.0	15.8	42.2	8.1	151,677
1955	11.1	10.4	8.1	6.8	13.6	41.6	8.5	165,248
1960	11.3	10.4	9.4	7.4	12.1	39.8	9.2	179,323
1965	10.7	9.9	9.9	8.9	13.0	38.5	9.1	193,643
1970	9.9	9.8	9.8	9.2	14.9	37.0	9.4	208,199
1975	10.7	9.5	9.0	9.1	16.4	35.6	9.7	225,552

Source: Data for 1900–1960 are taken from Bureau of the Census reports. Projections are taken from the U.S. Bureau of the Census, November, 1958. These projections assume that fertility will decline from the 1955–57 level to the 1949–51 level by 1965–70, then remain at this level to 1975–80.

Reflecting the population changes were manpower shortages in the age-group 20–29, shortages that grew more severe until 1965. This group of young adults has been called upon to furnish the new recruits to four rapidly expanding professions—engineering, scientific research, nursing, and teaching—as well as to supply the demands of all other professions in a growing population. It is estimated that the numbers of people in these four occupations increased by 40 percent between 1955 and 1965, while the size of the 20–29 age group increased by only 11 percent. Thus, young people in this period were under great pressure to attend college and to take jobs in the occupational areas where shortages existed.

These factors produced greatly increased college enrollments after 1955. In addition, there is the more general factor that increasing *proportions* of young people have been entering college over the past 100 years. As we have seen, approximately 34 percent of the age group were in college by 1960, and approximately half of these were graduating from a four-year course. These proportions changed very little between 1960 and 1965. One of the major questions now confronting higher education is whether the proportion of young people entering college will go on increasing after 1965 or whether this proportion will stabilize. In either case, there will be an increase in college enrollments due to the increase in the absolute size of the college-age group.

Since the colleges are so full, there may be less effort on the part of high school and college educators to urge young people to go to college. Those with the most determination and motivation, combined with adequate scholastic aptitude, will get into college while those who are less motivated will not.

EFFECTS ON MOBILITY RATES. Those young people with less motivation for college are likely to continue to come from working-class homes. With the motivation factor working against them, working-class youth will also be at a disadvantage due to the competition from increasing numbers of youth from middle-class and upper-class families. As these high-status groups move closer toward a reproduction rate of one, as shown earlier in Table 12.3 B, there will be less room for lower-status youth to move up into higher ranks.

Thus it is possible that the conditions that favored a high degree of social mobility in the years from 1920 to 1960 may give way to conditions favoring a lower degree of mobility. Educational opportunity will remain the principal means of social mobility, but there may also be less educational opportunity.

On the other hand, if the people who make educational policy decide to do so, they can maintain the present degree of educational opportunity by expanding the enrollments of colleges and universities to take all applicants who meet present standards, and by seeing to it that scholarship assistance is provided for all those who need it. Another factor that may work for continuing educational opportunity in the future is a continuing rise in the income of the American working class, enabling more working-class people to finance their children through college.

If only the present degree of educational opportunity is maintained after 1965, there will probably be a considerable amount of competition among college graduates for positions in the professions and business. The present shortages may give way to surpluses after 1975.

Population Movement and the Schools
in Metropolitan Areas

The movements of population within metropolitan areas produce a variety of educational problems. In many metropolitan areas of the United States, especially the largest (and excluding metropolitan areas in the western part of the country), there has been a shift in the distribution of population, with approximately half the people now living within the central city and half living in areas outside the central city.

Whenever the central city has reached or approached its population limit, it has become subject to a loss of middle-class residents, a lowering of its socioeconomic ratio, and a set of internal population movements that create special problems for the public schools. This has been true, for example, in Boston, New York, Philadelphia, Washington, Baltimore, Buffalo, Cincinnati, Cleveland, Detroit, Chicago, St. Louis, and Kansas City.

Population Shifts Within the Central Cities

Another type of population movement in metropolitan areas is the in-migration of Negroes and their concentration within the central cities. This trend is shown in Table 12.6 which gives the proportion of the

Table 12.6   Proportion of Population in SMSAs* That Is Nonwhite: 1900–1960

Year	Percent in SMSAs* who are nonwhite	Percent in Central City who are nonwhite	Percent outside Central City who are nonwhite
1900	7.8	6.8	9.4
1910	7.3	6.9	8.1
1920	7.2	7.3	7.0
1930	8.1	9.0	6.4
1940	8.6	10.1	6.0
1950	10.0	13.1	5.7
1960	11.7	17.8	5.2

* Standard Metropolitan Statistical Areas.

Source: U.S. Bureau of the Census. U.S. Census of Population: 1960. *Selected Area Reports. Standard Metropolitan Statistical Areas.* Final Report, PC(3)-1D.

population living in metropolitan areas that is nonwhite and shows differences in proportions of nonwhites in central cities and in suburban areas over the past sixty years.

Since Negroes coming into the big cities have settled mostly in segregated residential neighborhoods, the central cities have developed large areas of segregated Negro residence with schools that have consequently become all Negro, especially elementary schools. Furthermore, the rapidity of Negro in-migration, the general inability of these new families to pay high rents, and the widespread practice of residential segregation that limited their dispersion throughout the metropolitan area have resulted in a close concentration of Negro population, much denser than that which characterized the same neighborhoods earlier. Another important fact is that the Negro in-migrants have tended to be relatively young men and women who were just starting their families.

As a consequence, after about 1950 the Negro areas of the large cities experienced a very rapid increase of child population which soon overcrowded the schools in these areas. By the early 1950's schools which had formerly stood partially empty in many of the central cities were full to overflowing with Negro children.

Meanwhile, other sections of the central city fared differently. Some areas near the center of the city became so run down that slum-clearance projects removed whole blocks of tenements, often leaving a school district with only half as many dwellings and empty schools. Some areas of stable European ethnic composition, especially Poles and Italians, maintained their populations, as the younger generations took over homes from their parents. Schools in such areas stayed comfortably full. In still other areas on the outer edges of the central city occupied by middle-class people, the school-age population decreased as grown children left the area, generally to establish their own homes in suburbs. Thus the schools in the latter areas lost enrollment and stood with as many as a quarter of their rooms empty.

All these movements of population were taking place during the 1950's and 1960's. At the same time, the total school enrollment of the central city was increasing, due to the post-war birthrate increases and due also to the in-migration of Negro families who were at the height of their child-bearing cycle. These factors created problems of housing school children. Some schools in the crowded Negro areas went on double-shift, at the same time that other schools in nearby areas stood partially empty.

Locating New School Buildings

Most cities met this situation by building new schools in the areas of overcrowding, which meant new schools in the Negro segregated areas. Occasionally, also, a new school was built near the outskirts of the city, where there was still some vacant land for new houses.

The situation in the period from 1960 to 1965 was about what is shown in the schematic map of Figure 12.4. The map does not represent a real city, but it represents the general pattern found in most of the big northern cities. As this figure shows, new schools have been built in the Negro area and at the southern corners of the city where there is some new housing. Some schools in the middle-class areas of white residence are completely filled and some are partly empty. The areas of European ethnic composition have schools comfortably filled. There are a few partly empty schools in slum areas. These areas are waiting for urban renewal, and the school buildings will then be reconditioned or torn down.

The coming of the "Negro Revolution" has inspired some of the Civil Rights advocates in these cities to propose that a measure of integrated schooling be achieved by sending Negro students into the underpopulated schools which are presently populated mainly by white children. This proposal would save money for the school system, it is argued, and at the same time it would promote integration.

Most school boards responded to this suggestion by establishing an "elective transfer" plan which permitted a pupil to transfer from an overcrowded school to an underpopulated one, if he provided his own transportation. A few cities, including New York City, provided bus transportation for children who wished to transfer. Others, of which Kansas City is an example, made transfers mandatory by assigning all the children in certain blocks of overcrowded school districts to be carried by bus to underpopulated schools, where they become regular members of the receiving schools.

At the same time, as already mentioned, most cities built new schools in the neighborhoods where the schools were overcrowded, often against the wishes of Civil Rights leaders. The boards of education generally argued that the "neighborhood school policy" was a good policy and that it dictated the building of new schools wherever the excess population lived. Furthermore, the board could generally show that the majority of Negro parents favored the building of new schools for their children near home, even if they were segregated, as preferable to a plan of transporting their children to distant, integrated schools. Differences of opinion on these matters constituted a source of great tension in many cities, with headline stories in the newspapers appearing almost daily.

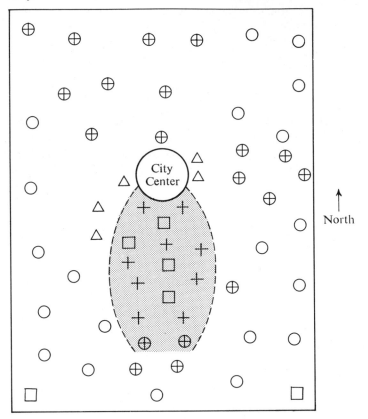

Shaded area is occupied by Negroes.

⊕ School comfortably full.

△ School at 75 percent capacity in a decaying area of inner city.

○ School at 75 percent capacity in old middle class area.

☐ New school built since 1955.

✛ Overcrowded school

High status areas are Northeast and Southwest.

Stable ethnic (European) areas are Northwest and East.

Figure 12.4 School building occupancy in a big city after the population shifts of 1950–60.

The Age Distribution of Negro Parents

To complicate an already complex situation, the publication of figures showing the numbers of Negro and white pupils in the public schools (publication of which was insisted on by Civil Rights leaders) showed that in northern cities Negro school enrollments were growing very rapidly during the 1960's, while the numbers of white pupils tended to decrease. City after city passed the 50 percent mark of Negro enrollment in the elementary schools, even though the total Negro population in these particular cities was 25 percent or less. Many white children attended parochial or other private schools, increasing the proportion of Negro children in the public schools.

The natural but mistaken tendency of many people was to infer that the proportions of Negro children in the public schools would go up and up; and the tendency was to encourage white parents to move out to the suburbs if they were worried that their own local school lay in the path of what they believed to be an advancing Negro residential area.

The true situation might have been clarified by a demographer who knew the age distribution of the in-migrant Negro adults after World War II. For example, Table 12.7 shows the age characteristics of non-white females in Chicago and Kansas City in 1950 and 1960. (Chicago passed the 50 percent mark in Negro elementary school enrollment in 1965, while Kansas City reached 42 percent in that year.) The 1950 data show a sharp increase in the numbers of young Negro women aged 20–24 compared with the numbers aged 15–19. The 25–29 age group was even larger. These numbers reflect the in-migration of young Negro women to the city around 1950. By 1960, however, this phenomenon had largely passed, with the group aged 20–29 being no larger than that aged 10–19.

Thus the young Negro women who migrated into these and other big cities around 1950 had borne most of their children during the ensuing 15 years, and they had added a large but short-term component to the Negro school population. This is shown clearly in Table 12.7; the school-age population for the 5–9- and 10–14-year-olds is much larger for 1960 than it is for 1950. This short-term component will have spent its effects during the 1960–1970 decade, after which the Negro school population will probably stop increasing rapidly and may actually decline. A glance at the table shows also that after 1980 there should be a further spurt in Negro births, as the girls born in 1955–65 begin to bear children. But by that time there may be other population move-

Table 12.7   Age Characteristics of Nonwhite Females in Two
Metropolitan Areas: 1950 and 1960

	Chicago		Kansas City	
	PERCENT OF TOTAL		PERCENT OF TOTAL	
	1950	1960	1950	1960
0–4	10.3	15.0	8.5	14.7
5–9	7.4	11.8	6.6	11.0
10–14	6.4	8.4	6.0	8.0
15–19	6.2	6.2	6.0	6.1
20–24	9.7	7.6	8.6	6.5
25–29	11.3	8.0	9.7	6.8
30–34	9.7	8.4	9.0	7.7
35–39	9.2	7.6	9.1	7.3
40–44	7.6	6.2	7.8	6.2
45–49	6.6	5.2	7.5	5.4
50–54	5.0	4.3	6.2	4.7
55–59	3.5	3.8	4.6	4.4
60–64	2.5	2.7	3.5	3.5
65–69	2.2	2.1	3.5	3.2
70–74	1.2	1.4	1.8	2.2
75+	1.2	1.5	1.7	2.4
20–44	47.5	37.8	44.2	34.5
Total No.	265,000	436,000	29,166	43,935

Source: U.S. Census Vol. 1, 1950 and 1960.

ments which will counteract this effect, so that projections beyond 1980
are presently little better than guesswork.

What should a board of education do about building new schools,
transporting Negro children to underpopulated schools, and adopting
plans to promote integrated school experience, based on this kind of
demographic knowledge? A thorough study of the demographic data
available in each metropolitan area might provide plans which are both
more economical and which will contribute more to integration than
plans to concentrate new school construction in presently-existing Negro
residential areas.

Technology and Occupational Trends

The change in America from an agricultural to a modern industrial
country has been marked not only by profound shifts in population but
also by profound shifts of occupations. As Table 12.8 shows, over 70

percent of gainful workers were employed in agriculture in 1820; but only 9 percent in 1960. Meanwhile the proportions of workers engaged in manufacturing rose from 12.2 to 32.5 percent, and those in trade and transportation rose from 2.5 to 32.5 percent. Even more important for its educational consequences has been the increase in professional and government white-collar workers, from 2.8 to 19 percent. Thus the occupations requiring least formal schooling have tended to decrease in numbers while those requiring the most schooling have increased.

Table 12.8   Percentage Distribution of Gainful Workers by Industry Group, 1820–1960

Year	Agri-culture	Mfg. and Mechan-ical Pursuits	Trade and Transp.	Domestic and Personal Service	Public and Profes-sional Service	Mining
1820	71.9	12.2	2.5	10.0	2.8	0.3
1840	68.6	14.6	3.8	9.6	2.7	0.3
1860	59.7	18.4	7.4	9.5	2.9	1.6
1880	48.9	24.1	12.2	9.3	3.5	1.5
1900	36.8	27.0	18.7	10.6	4.2	2.0
1920	26.1	30.6	24.9	10.1	5.0	2.6
1940	18.8	28.0	28.7	8.9	12.1	2.0
1950	12.5	32.0	32.5	6.2	13.7	1.7
1960	8.8	31.5	32.5	7.0	19.0	1.2

Source: Thompson, W. S., 1953, *Population Problems,* 4th edition, New York: McGraw-Hill Book Company, p. 390. 1960 estimates based on U.S. Department of Labor, October, 1961.

More specific than these overall trends are such facts as these: Since 1870 the numbers of professional persons in science and technology have increased over eightyfold. The proportion of the labor force defined as professional and technical increased from 6.7 percent in 1940 to 10.9 percent in 1959. Employment of scientific and engineering staff by industry increased 8 percent per year in just the 3-year period between 1954 and 1957.

At present automation and the use of computers, the two processes which together have been called "cybernation," are having further profound effects upon the American occupational structure—some not altogether predictable given the rapidity with which the changes are proceeding. Some economic analysts predict huge reductions in proportions of blue-collar workers, as the machines take over more and more of the skilled as well as the unskilled jobs, with consequent piling-up of white-collar and technical jobs and growing rates of technological unemployment. Other analysts think the long-run effects of cybernation will be, not to produce large-scale reduction of manpower needs nor a great shift in the balance between work and leisure for most workers, but to produce new types of jobs at about the same rate as old ones are destroyed. In either case, the present trend of increased *proportions* of white-collar, technical and professional workers is likely to continue.

The increases in proportions of professional and technical workers have meant an enormous increase in the numbers of college graduates, particularly those holding master's and doctor's degrees, as can be seen in Table 12.9.

Table 12.9   Numbers of People in the United States Earning
Various Degrees in Higher Education

| | *Degree Earned* | | |
YEAR	BACHELOR'S OR FIRST PROFES- SIONAL	MASTER'S DEGREE	DOCTOR OF PHILOSOPHY OR SCIENCE
1869–70	9,371	0	1
1879–80	12,896	871	49
1889–90	15,539	1,009	135
1899–1900	27,410	1,583	369
1909–10	37,199	3,771	420
1919–20	48,622	4,301	564
1929–30	122,484	15,043	2,225
1939–40	186,500	26,731	3,290
1949–50	432,000	58,000*	6,633*
1954–55	288,000	58,000	8,500
1959–60	392,000	74,000	9,829
1961–62	417,846	85,000	11,622
1963–64	499,000	101,000	14,490
1964–65	525,000	111,000	15,300

* These numbers are unusually large due to a "piling up" of veterans of the armed services whose training had been delayed.
Source: U.S. Office of Education, *Digest of Educational Statistics, 1965.*

A hundred years ago it was a social luxury for many youth in their teens to go to high school and college. Today it is a social necessity, as society's demands for highly-trained young people have increased so markedly.

Effects of Occupational Trends on Youth Employment

The revolution in manufacturing technology caused by cybernation is having other profound effects upon the young men and women in the age group 16 to 20. It is reducing the numbers employed in the working force and causing young people to stay longer in school since they need more knowledge and skills than formerly in order to hold the jobs that are now available.

At the same time that more young people are extending their education and going to college, a group of *marginal* youth is also being created, youth who are not in school, not at work, and not married. This group has become the object of increasing concern to society because it is larger and more visible than in previous decades. In earlier times many out-of-school youth lived in rural or semi-rural areas where they secured unskilled jobs fairly easily on the farms, or in the towns, or, in the case of girls, at domestic service. With increasing urbanization of the population, the marginal youth group increased in size in the cities. If members of this group became involved in delinquent acts, this behavior was widely advertised.

National unemployment figures showed that during the 1950's the rate of unemployment among youth aged 16 to 20 was about twice as high as for older age groups. The American economy was reducing its supply of unskilled jobs, and the numbers of "juvenile jobs" or jobs for young people at less than adult pay rates was decreasing drastically.

By 1960, when some 35 percent of youth were dropping out of high school, only about half of them were able to get and to hold steady full-time jobs. The census of 1960 showed that 11 percent of boys and 18 percent of girls aged 16 through 20 were not in school, not at work, and not married. These were averages over a five-year age span, and they overstate the level of employment at ages 17 and 18.

This problem group increased in absolute size during the 1960's due to the effects of the increased birth rates of the post-war years. In 1960 there were 12.6 million youth aged 16 through 20 (born 1940–44); in 1965 there were 16.1 million (born 1945–49); and in 1970 there will be 18.1 million (born 1950–54). Putting the problem another way, 30 million young people under the age of 25 will enter the labor force during the decade of 1965–1975. Of these it is estimated that 10 million or 33 percent will have some college education, and another 11 million or 37 percent will complete high school. This leaves 9 million or 30 percent who will not complete high school. This is a much larger number of dropouts than were produced during the 1950's.

The Schools and Marginal Youth

The decade of the 1960's is seeing the society turn increasingly to the schools as a means of solving the problems of marginal youth. It appears that the economy will not absorb these young people while they are in their teens, for they lack the knowledge, skills, and maturity to make themselves employable.

The simplest procedure is to extend the period of compulsory school attendance to 17 or 18. This has been talked about, and bills have been introduced in several state legislatures to raise the legal school-leaving age. However, up to 1966 none of these bills had become law. The opposition to the bills came largely from school administrators and school teachers, who argued that most school dropouts have done poorly in school and would not be using their own time or the money of society efficiently by staying longer in school.

On the other hand, the proponents of raising the school-leaving age argue that society has a responsibility to young people which it must meet either through providing jobs for them or through education. If the private sector of the economy cannot provide a sufficient number of jobs, then some other agency of society must provide useful and growth-promoting experience. The school is the natural social agency to undertake this task. If the schools cannot do it, then the society must create another agency to perform this function. Another agency might be a state-supported youth authority, responsible for out-of-school and unemployed youth up to a certain age.

The Federal Government and Marginal Youth

The federal government has acted positively with respect to marginal youth through two major laws: the Manpower Development and Training Act and the Economic Opportunity Act.

The Manpower Development and Training Act is aimed at the vocational training and retraining of people who are unemployed and who lack the skills and knowledge needed for steady employment. The federal government will pay to public and private agencies the cost of vocational training for people over 17 who are unemployed. The vocational skills that are taught are generally rather simple and non-technical. People are trained for jobs such as janitors and maintenance men, service station attendants, restaurant workers, and taxicab drivers. They are paid a maintenance allowance during the training period. This program is available for men and women of all ages, and a number of young people over 17 have enrolled.

More directly aimed at assisting marginal youth are some programs under the Economic Opportunity Act of 1964. Three specific programs, aimed either at keeping young people in school and college or at giving them vocational training, were in effect in 1966 and are presently being adapted and modified on the basis of experience.

1. WORK-STUDY PROGRAMS IN COLLEGES. Colleges may develop work programs to give part-time employment to college students. The work-projects are socially useful but do not have commercial value and do not displace people from employment. Such projects as the following are involved: assisting professors on research projects, tutoring socially disadvantaged children, and improving library service.

2. THE JOB CORPS. Under the terms of the Economic Opportunity Act, the federal government makes contracts with private industrial corporations or universities and other non-profit agencies which provide for the administration, staffing, and maintenance of training camps and other residential training centers for out-of-school and unemployed youth aged 16 through 20. Each training center provides maintenance and spending money for enrollees who are also paid a relatively small stipend which they can assign to their families.

The locations of Job Corps projects are either in unused government facilities such as abandoned army forts and camps, state parks, or unused hotels and similar facilities in cities. The training program of a particular center tends to specialize in a set of closely related jobs that do not require high school diplomas but do require serious study and systematic training. Examples are business office jobs, food service jobs, auto mechanics and service station jobs, and beauty shop jobs.

An applicant for the Job Corps is interviewed and tested by the state employment services. From there he is sent to the center at which the training program seems best for his particular abilities. Applicants are also screened with respect to their family backgrounds and their behavior. While records of relatively minor delinquency will not bar an applicant, major delinquency is a valid reason for rejection. By the beginning of 1966 there were some 15,000 young men and women enrolled in these centers, and the numbers were increasing.

The record of the Job Corps is a matter of concern to people interested in marginal youth. Even though the screening of applicants keeps out the ones with major delinquency and with severe educational retardation, those who enter the centers are necessarily marginal and not well adjusted to society. Many of these young people are likely to get into trouble in the centers both academically and socially. As an institution operating independently of conventional school systems, the Job Corps may conceivably show the way to successful programs for marginal youth. On the other hand, the Job Corps may fail in many cases for the same reasons the school system has failed with these young people.

3. NEIGHBORHOOD YOUTH CORPS. The Neighborhood Youth Corps program is much more extensive and less expensive than the Job Corps. It consists of work-experience in the local community for youth aged 16–20 under the auspices of school systems and other non-profit agencies. The work must be socially valuable but must not displace anyone in an existing job. For example, young people may work in city parks, in school cafeterias, or in the offices of local government, assisting those who are regularly employed there. To be eligible for assignment, a young man or woman must come from a low-income family.

The Neighborhood Youth Corps is partly aimed at keeping young people in school. It does not give systematically-planned vocational training, though it attempts to aid marginal youth in developing habits of punctuality and of cooperation with other workers, as well as giving them a limited amount of vocational skill.

The Neighborhood Youth Corps challenges the secondary schools to develop a meaningful school program for these young people at the same time that they are working in the Corps.

OTHER PROGRAMS. A number of city, state, public, and private agencies have worked with marginal youth for some time, though not on a scale large enough to meet the need. For example, many state employment services had special staff working in the placement of out-of-school youth before the Economic Opportunity Act was passed. Also, many local welfare agencies and youth-serving organizations had job-training and placement programs, as did some city school systems.

Thus, the federally-aided projects of the mid-sixties are an outgrowth of work that was going on in the preceding decade; some of that work, in turn, was related to programs for assisting jobless youth which grew out of the depression decade of the 1930's.

In summary, the relations between education and society are being transformed as the result of the two sets of factors discussed in this chapter: first, overall growth of population and changing rates of reproduction in various social-class, racial, and ethnic groups; second, the great expansion of the American economy with the attendant revolution in technology and the growth of cybernation, and with the accompanying new patterns of migration from rural to urban centers, and within urban centers themselves. These changes in the society are creating some of the major problems with which the schools will be grappling in the late 1960's and 1970's, problems which range from the general to the specific: for example, from planning for growth in school enrollments and in teacher recruitments, to deciding the location of new school buildings to keep pace with rapidly-shifting population changes within given metropolitan areas; from meeting society's needs for increased proportions of technical and professional workers, to providing meaningful educational experience for the increasing numbers of marginal youth who presently drop out of school but do not find work in the changing job market.

Changes in population and changes in the economy interact with other types of social change (some of which are discussed in the chapters to follow) to create a new social context in which the educational system operates.

Exercises

1. State departments of education make surveys and forecasts of the school-age population to aid local school boards of the state university in making future plans. If your state has such a report available, obtain a copy. What will be the future needs for schools in your own community? What will your state university need to do?

2. One of the interesting things about recent population trends is the increase in numbers of children in middle-class families. What effect will this have upon the education of middle-class children? What effect will it have upon their parents' attitudes about education?

3. Under present immigration policies, the number of foreign-born children in the schools is lower than it was before 1920, but there is a major immigration from Puerto Rico and a major migration of Negro working-class people from the South to the northern industrial cities. What should be the functions of the schools in relation to these groups? What are the similarities and differences, compared to the schools' functions in dealing with immigrant groups prior to 1920?

4. In your own community, what plans exist for the location of new school buildings? What do you think the effects will be upon integration?

5. What proposals are being made in your state about compulsory education beyond the age of 16? Who favors and who opposes the raising of the age limit?

6. How have the federal government funds for assistance to marginal youth been used in your community? What have been the successes and what have been the failures?

Suggestions for Further Reading

1. For a stimulating discussion of current and future population trends in relation to manpower needs and to education, read the report of the Educational Policies Commission of the National Education Association, *Manpower and Education.*

2. The National Manpower Council made an extensive study of women's employment patterns and the nation's need for women workers; and in the book *Womanpower,* recommended policies for the more effective use of women in the labor force.

3. A wealth of factual information about the social and economic characteristics of the nation is to be found in the Twentieth Century Fund Report, *America's Needs and Resources: A New Survey* by J. Frederic Dewhurst and associates. Read also the pamphlet by Michael, *Cybernation: The Silent Conquest.*

4. To obtain background information on the population history and the present structure of population in the United States, any one of the following books is a good reference: *Population Problems* by Paul T. Landis and Paul K. Hatt; *Population Problems,* 5th ed., by W. S. Thompson and D. T. Lewis; *Length of Life* by Louis I. Dublin, Alfred J. Lotka, and Martin Spiegelman; *The Population of the United States* by Donald J. Bogue; and *The Changing Population of the United States* by Conrad and Irene Taeuber.

5. The paper by Michael in *Society and Education: A Book of Readings* (Havighurst, Neugarten, and Falk) is a provocative discussion of technological innovations in American society and of the likely effects of cybernation (the use of computers and automation). Also, the paper by Rice analyzes current occupational trends in America and the new relations between education and the world of work; and the paper by Miller argues that the expansion of educational opportunities will be of value only if it goes hand-in-hand with the expansion of the economy.

13 / Juvenile Delinquency and the Schools

From 1948 to 1963 cases of juvenile delinquency taken to the courts increased about 150 percent while the youth population rose about 40 percent. There have been similar increases since 1950 in Sweden, Austria, Greece, Finland, Australia, New Zealand, Japan, the Philippines, and England. Much of the delinquency is committed by gangs of boys, and in most countries special names have been coined for members of such gangs. In the United States they are *Hoods,* in England *Teddy Boys,* in Germany they are called *Halbstarke,* in France *Blousons Noirs,* in Australia and New Zealand *Bodgies,* in Japan *Mambo Boys,* in Russia and Poland *Hooligans,* in Italy *Vitelloni,* and in South Africa the whites are *Ducktails,* the colored are *Skollies* and the native Africans are *Tsotsies.* In all the countries that are urbanized and industrialized, juvenile delinquency is believed to be an actual or a potential problem of great magnitude.

Concern over juvenile delinquency has been shown in the United States Congress, with hearings held by committees of both Houses and a substantial report issued by a committee of the House of Representatives (U.S. 86th Congress, 1960). The Chief of the Children's Bureau reported that under the conditions of the late 1950's one boy in five came into juvenile court on delinquency charges at some time during his adolescence.

The most useful way to look at juvenile delinquency is to regard it as an abnormality of growth. A boy or girl who becomes delinquent is failing to grow up in the way expected of a normal youth in America. The growth of boys and girls—moral, as well as mental—is as much a concern of the school as it is of the family. Consequently the relation of delinquency to schooling must be explored to see whether the school can in some way be used to reduce this form of social pathology. First, however, we shall consider in detail some of the factors related to juvenile delinquency.

The Definition of Juvenile Delinquency

Juvenile delinquency in the strict sense refers to acts forbidden by law that are committed by children of the age range 10 to 18. Since many and probably most children commit such acts at one time or another, it is necessary to qualify this definition. Juvenile delinquents will refer here to youth brought into court on delinquency charges and found guilty. These may be called "adjudged delinquents."

A very large number of youth are apprehended by the police; in 1962 over 2,000,000 between 10 and 17 years of age were apprehended. Two-thirds of these were released by the police with warnings to the youngsters and to their parents. Over 850,000, however, were brought into court as "alleged delinquents" and almost all of them were judged to be delinquent. A fraction of this number were actually committed to an institution such as a reform school; a larger number were released on probation; and an even larger number of cases were adjusted or held open without specific action.

The offenses for which boys and girls are apprehended are very often minor in nature. Boys of 11 or 12 may do some mischief to property in the neighborhood and may be warned by the police. Boys and girls of legal driving age may be arrested for breaking traffic laws. In 1962 there were about 300,000 traffic cases handled by juvenile courts and 550,000 juvenile delinquency cases of other kinds, making up the total number cited above. The actual number of children involved was 750,000, because some were arrested more than once during the year.

About 20 percent of the youth arrested were charged with serious offenses, as follows: burglary, 12 percent; automobile theft, 7 percent; robbery, 1 percent; aggravated assault, 1 percent; criminal homicide, 0.1 percent. In the early 1960's juveniles, rather than adults, were responsible for most of the auto thefts, about half of all burglaries, and half of all larceny cases. The peak ages for arrests of youth are 16 and 17.

Delinquency rates are about three times higher in the cities than in rural areas.

Factors Related to Juvenile Delinquency

In the search for causes, a number of factors have been found to be statistically related to delinquency. These factors may not be *causes* of delinquency, but they are elements in a complex of factors or a pattern that is found together with delinquency.

Socioeconomic Status

Rates of delinquency are highest in the lower-class areas of the larger cities. For instance, in Chicago from 1958 to 1961, eight of the city's 75 community areas produced 42 percent of the official court cases of male juvenile delinquency. Four of these areas produced 28 percent of the cases. This general picture has not changed much in the 1960's, and similar situations exist in New York and other large cities.

In the smaller cities, there is the same relationship with social class. For example, Table 13.1 shows the relation between social class and

Table 13.1   Delinquency and Social Class in River City

| Social class | Boys classified as delinquent: by category | | | | |
	I (MOST SERIOUS)	II	III	IV (LEAST SERIOUS)	ALL BOYS IN AGE COHORT
Upper and upper-middle	0	1	0	2	22
Lower-middle	2	2	4	14	64
Upper-working	5	6	7	19	91
Lower-working	9	9	5	11	70
Total	16	18	16	46	247

delinquency among boys in River City. In this midwestern city of 43,000, Havighurst *et al.* (1962) found that slightly over 20 percent of the boys had enough contact with the police to be placed into delinquency categories I, II, or III. Another 20 percent were on unofficial police records for such minor offenses as truancy, speeding in automobiles, faulty automobile brakes, breaking windows, or trespassing on property, offenses which are placed in category IV.

It is clear from this table that the more serious types of delinquency are heavily concentrated among working-class boys. Nevertheless, two out of three lower-working-class boys did not become delinquent and four out of five upper-working-class boys did not. Consequently living in a working-class family does not necessarily mean that delinquency will follow.

It is sometimes claimed that the findings of a concentration of delinquency among working-class boys are in error because the police are more likely to arrest a working-class delinquent than a middle-class delinquent. No doubt there is a tendency for offenses by middle-class boys to be settled informally by discussion between the police and the boy's parents, and this tends to reduce the numbers of middle-class boys brought to court. On the other hand, there is a great deal of working-class delinquency undetected by the police and therefore not reported in the official statistics. Probably the lower socioeconomic groups contain the great majority of boys who are repeatedly and systematically delinquent, as well as the bulk of delinquent gangs.

School Failure, Dropout, and Low Intelligence

The relation between school dropout and delinquency is well exemplified by the findings in the River City Study (Havighurst *et al.*, 1962). In River City all of the boys in delinquency category I, the most serious, dropped out of school without finishing high school, and most of them dropped out as soon as they reached the legally permissible age of 16. Fifteen of the 18 boys in category II and 13 of the 16 in category III also dropped out of school. In a New York City study covering a larger sample of delinquent youth in the 1950's, it was found that 95 percent of the 17-year-olds adjudged delinquent had dropped out of school, and 85 percent of the 16-year-olds were school dropouts.

On the other hand, two-thirds of the boys who drop out of school do not became officially delinquent. Thus dropping out of school does not mean that delinquency will result.

Failure in school is also related to delinquency. Most delinquents have a history of low or failing school grades. Again, however, failing grades in school is not a sure prediction of delinquency.

Low intelligence is sometimes claimed to be a cause of delinquency. It is proposed that people of low intelligence are likely to make mistakes of various kinds, and a delinquent act is one form of mistake. In discussing this proposition it is useful to distinguish among the various levels of low intelligence. Two or three percent of the population fall at the IQ level of 70 to 75 or 80. These children are usually placed in special classes for the "educable mentally handicapped." In general, if they find simple work to do, they make a fairly good adjustment in adolescence and adulthood. However, if they are educationally and socially neglected they are likely to get into trouble as they grow older. About 15 percent of children fall at IQ levels of about 75 to 90 and might be called "slow learners." Half to three-quarters of this group do passable work in school and grow up to be fairly competent adults. But the remainder of this group is likely to have difficulty.

In the River City Study, most of the severe delinquents were in the lowest quarter of intelligence; half of the boys considered by the school authorities to be severe discipline problems were in this group; sixty percent of the 75–90 IQ group dropped out of school before reaching eleventh grade. Members of this group were twice as likely to be delinquent as the other people in the age group.

Thus, the combination of school failure, school dropout, and inferior intelligence is a relatively strong predictor of delinquency.

Family Experience

All students of juvenile delinquency ascribe some causal effect to the family which neglects or rejects a child. For instance, Sheldon and Eleanor Glueck (1950, 1956) found the following five family characteristics to be closely related to delinquency:

> Overstrict, erratic or lax discipline of boy by father.
> Lack of supervision of boy by mother.
> Lack of affection of father for boy.
> Lack of affection of mother for boy.
> Lack of cohesiveness in the family.

On the basis of an interview with the parents or observation of the home situation it is possible to rate the family on these five characteristics. The Glueck Delinquency Prevention Scale was thus created. Later, in order to study the large numbers of father-absent homes, it was modified by omitting the factors relating explicitly to the father and rating on the following three factors: supervision of boy by mother; discipline of boy by mother; cohesiveness of family.

The usefulness of this scale has been tested by studying a group of boys who entered one or the other of two elementary schools in high delinquency areas of New York City (Craig and Glick, 1963, 1964). The boys were studied for 10 years. Thirty-three boys (11 percent) of the sample were predicted to become delinquent, and 28 of them did so. Of the 243 boys (81 percent) of the sample who were predicted to be non-delinquents, seven actually became delinquent. This is a good performance for a predictive measure, but the study shows that there is not a single characteristic, such as the nature of the family, which "produces" delinquency. Apparently delinquency is caused by a combination of factors, the most important being poor family relationships, low socioeconomic status, school failure, and below-average intelligence.

The Effects of War Experience

It is natural to look for a relation between war and juvenile delinquency, but no clear-cut conclusions can be safely drawn. On the one hand, there is the possible effect of the example of adults killing one another and committing acts of violence. Also the aftermath of a war in a defeated country is likely to be social disorganization, with juveniles growing up without parental or other forms of social control. On the other hand, war causes a nation to discipline itself—to put everyone to work, including juveniles, and causes people to sacrifice personal pleasure for the common welfare. The net result of war on rates of juvenile delinquency seems unpredictable, but there is some evidence of an increase in delinquency in the United States during both World War I and World War II.

Another possible effect of war is the development of a delinquency-prone generation of children because of the absence of fathers from the home during a crucial period of the children's lives. Some evidence on this point is provided in the English Ministry of Education report on youth (1959) which cites a study by Leslie T. Wilkins on the degrees of delinquency shown by various age-groups of English children who were temporarily separated from their homes and, in particular, from their fathers during World War II. His conclusion is that boys who passed their fourth and fifth years under war conditions show extremely high delinquency rates as adolescents. It is possible that this results from the absence of a masculine model in the home at the time in personality development when the boy's conscience is being formed and his patterns of social behavior established.

Economic Prosperity and Depression

Another factor that may have something to do with juvenile delinquency is the relative economic prosperity of the country. There is evidence (Teeters and Matza, 1959) that delinquency rates tend to be high during periods of prosperity and low during periods of economic depression. Possibly the high visibility of automobiles, luxury goods, and free spending during a period of prosperity leads boys who are relatively disadvantaged (working-class whites, Negroes, and Puerto Ricans, for example) to seek illegitimate means for securing those things they cannot readily obtain otherwise.

TV, Movies, and Comic Books

It has been claimed by some people that the prevalence in the mass media of scenes of killing and violence, together with the growing openness of sexual behavior and sexual symbols, have created models of behavior which young people tend to imitate (Wertham, 1954). For instance, from 1960 to 1965, in practically every "western" or adventure movie from Hollywood and in TV shows, there was a standardized fight sequence in which the "good guy" and the "bad guy" fought each other in the most brutal manner. The evidence is clear that most delinquents view these episodes and read sadistic and sexual comic books; still it is clear that many non-delinquents are also addicts of this form of amusement. Some experts argue that reading and seeing this kind of material has the beneficial effect of catharsis that is, of releasing destructive emotions which might otherwise be released in action. Although there is general agreement among intelligent adults (except among those who make money from this use of the mass media) that these programs are bad esthetically, there is no such agreement that they cause juvenile delinquency (United States, 86th Congress, 1960).

Sex Differences in Delinquency

In all societies for which delinquency data are available, boys out-number girls in the delinquency statistics by a ratio ranging between 4 to 1 and 10 to 1. There appears to be something in the personalities or the social roles of girls that makes it rare for them to engage in the types of delinquent behavior characteristic of boys. Girls do not do much fighting or stealing. Their most common offenses are incorrigibility, including truancy from school, and sexual misbehavior. An example of female delinquency that illustrates both of these qualities is the following:

> Sue was first picked up at the age of fifteen for hanging around down-town with a group of girls. A month later she was reported by her father for being truant, not coming home nights, and being unmanageable. She was married at sixteen but was reported to the police shortly afterward by her neighbors who complained of the filthiness of the apartment and the neglect of a small baby. On that occasion, the police found her in a tavern. Two months later she was brought in for soliciting men in a tavern.

To some extent a parallel to delinquency data is found in the rates of illegitimate births. This rate increased from 3.8 percent of live births in 1940 to 5.6 percent in 1961. In 1940, there were 8 illegitimate births per thousand unmarried teen-age girls. In 1961, there were 16 per thousand.

Delinquency as a Gang Phenomenon

Juvenile delinquency tends to be a male phenomenon; it also tends to be a group phenomenon. For instance, records in the juvenile court of Chicago show that 90 percent of the boys brought before the court for all offenses had one or more accomplices. The group nature of juvenile crime is not a recent development. A report issued in 1931 stated that, in over half the property offenses committed by juveniles in Chicago, three or more participants were known by the police to be involved.

Delinquent or semi-delinquent gangs of boys have been studied in the United States for at least 40 years. Frederic M. Thrasher (1936) described gangs in words which seem applicable today. He gave the following report in 1924 of gangs in El Paso, Texas.

> In the Mexican section of El Paso is a group of three or four hundred Mexican boys composed of from twenty to twenty-five gangs, each with its

separate leader. These gangs have been growing steadily for eight or nine years and now embrace a rather seasoned and experienced leadership in all sorts of crime. Eighty per cent of their members are probably under fifteen years of age; most of the older boys are under eighteen. Stealing, destroying property, and all kinds of malicious mischief are their chief activities. In fact, these groups are almost literally training schools of crime, and they seem to be related to each other in a sort of loose federation. For the most part, the boys do not go to school or do not work unless it be for an occasional day. Fifty of them have been sent to the state industrial school, eight are in jail, 25 or 30 are being especially investigated, and about 200 are under surveillance. These boys may be observed in their characteristic groupings every evening on street corners and in vacant lots and alleys. The park, which is their favorite meeting place, with its double rows of tall hedges, its trees and shrubbery, affords them a good place to hide and to conceal their delinquencies. (Thrasher, 1936, pp. 380–381.)

Rahm and Weber (1958) found similar gangs in El Paso in the 1950's and report that the origins of most of the gang names are lost in history. Some of them may have existed in the earlier period reported by Thrasher.

Since 1955 most of the studies of juvenile delinqency have focused on delinquent gangs and on delinquency as a characteristic of a deviant or *delinquent subculture.* Formation of close-knit groups of boys after the age of twelve is common in all social classes, but disadvantaged working-class boys appear to form groups which have great potential for aggressive and criminal behavior.

At the same time, the study of juvenile gangs in Chicago reported by Short and Strodtbeck (1965) presents evidence to indicate that delinquency is not the only or principal aspect of gang life. Comradeship and friendship are important values of gang participation. Some gang members show relatively little delinquent behavior; these members tend to be boys who do well in school and have high educational aspirations. Short found, in studying Negro working-class gangs, that the members with high educational aspirations and successful school work had an average of 0.9 police-recorded offenses, while those with low educational aspirations and poor school performance had an average of 4.0. Thus, gang membership itself does not necessarily mean delinquent behavior. High delinquency rates are much more apt to be associated with unsuccessful educational adaptions regardless of educational aspirations (in Clinard, 1964, p. 110). Cohen (1955), Cloward and Ohlin (1960), Miller (1967), Short and Strodtbeck (1965), and Yablonsky (1962) have described the gang as an instrument of a sub-cultural group which is disadvantaged in relation to the dominant group. We shall return to the question of delinquency as a sub-cultural phenomenon in the following discussion of the types and causes of delinquency.

Types and Causes of Juvenile Delinquency

Juvenile delinquency is not one simple manifestation of behavior but a complex phenomenon that takes a variety of forms and has a variety of causes. At the same time, three main categories of delinquency can be discerned, each with somewhat different causes.

1. Delinquency Due to Severe Personality Disturbance

There appear to be two types of delinquent behavior which are related to abnormal personality. One type consists of extremely aggressive and uncontrolled behavior, behavior that may even go as far as murder. Children who show such extreme behavior have little or no inner moral control. They have usually been raised by parents who neglected them and who failed both to love and to discipline them consistently. A person showing this type of behavior is often called a "psychopathic personality." This type is quite rare.

The other type of personality disturbance consists of a severe and pervasive anxiety which makes the child do strange things. In contrast to the type previously described, this child is over-inhibited and suffers from pangs of conscience or fits of anxiety for mild sins and even for imagined misbehavior (Hewitt and Jenkins, 1946; cited in Bloch and Flynn, 1956, pp. 157–175). The conscious or unconscious feelings of guilt cause this child to commit acts for which he is almost sure to be found out and punished, such as setting fires or compulsive stealing. This type of delinquency, also, is rare.

Since emotional disturbance is present to some degree in all people at one time or another, it is difficult to distinguish the delinquency that is due primarily to emotional disturbance from other types. Some experts see emotional disturbance as a component of all delinquency, while others regard such disturbance as rarely being the principal cause. In the discussion by Kvaraceus and Miller (1959), a distinction is drawn between the children who show little or no emotional maladjustment (this group is said to be 90 percent or more of the age group) and those who show such maladjustment. This latter group is divided into two categories, as is shown in Figure 13.1. The smaller subgroup is delinquent; the members of the larger subgroups show maladjustment by withdrawn or self-punishing behavior that is not considered delinquent. Thus, the number of boys who are delinquent primarily because of emotional disturbance is probably not more than three or four percent of the total groups of boys.

	Little or no PERSONALITY DISTURBANCE	Some or much PERSONALITY DISTURBANCE
Delinquent	Most delinquents	A few delinquents
Not delinquent	The average, well-adjusted boy	Maladjusted boys of the withdrawn or self-punishing type

Figure 13.1 Emotional maladjustment and delinquency in an average group of boys.

II. "Developmental" Delinquency

A second category of delinquency is sometimes called "developmental" and is regarded as common and normal behavior related to the conflicts and crises of adolescence. Most adolescent boys do some petty stealing or destroy some property, but their transgressions are infrequent, and they are seldom caught. When they are older, they look back on this behavior with mild feelings of guilt or amusement, and wonder why they acted so irrationally. If they are caught, they are seldom brought into court but are usually let off with a warning by the police or by the persons whom they have offended.

One way to estimate the amount of developmental delinquency is to ask young people of college age or of late high school age to report on their experience of delinquency. This has been done by several researchers who have used anonymous questionnaires. In general, they find that there is a great deal of mild delinquency which is undiscovered by the police, and that there is not as much difference between social classes as would appear from official statistics of police-recorded delinquency.

Some societies seem to have more developmental delinquency than others. This may be related to the various ways in which a society imposes its authority upon adolescents. Some countries have a great deal of organized resistance to the law or to political authority on the part of secondary-school and college students. In Japan, for instance, where the college generation must not only fight for admission to college, but where these students are rebelling against a centuries-old tradition, this type of delinquency is common (Rockefeller, 1960).

Developmental delinquency does not figure very heavily in the official statistics. However, the dividing lines between this and the other two types are hazy. The basic distinction between developmental delinquency and the other forms is that, for the young person, developmental delinquency disturbs but does not prevent growth toward adulthood, while the other types constitute severe obstacles to satisfactory social development.

III. Delinquency as a Sub-Cultural Phenomenon

The most common type of juvenile delinquency in the United States and other industrialized countries seems to arise from certain disjunctions in the society itself. People in power in the society regard certain types of behavior as undesirable and they label it "delinquent," although the same behavior may appear "natural" to other people who belong to special sub-cultural groups. From this point of view, delinquent acts are primarily carried out by subgroups of youth who are at odds with the value system of the greater society in which they live. In a sense these young people are alienated from society and, feeling rejected by the community at large, they do not wish to obey its rules.

Most sociologists see juvenile delinquency as resulting from the fact that many children grow up in a disadvantaged American sub-culture. Working-class boys and girls are more likely than middle-class to become delinquent because in their culture they readily learn to become delinquent.

There are several theories of delinquency as a sub-cultural phenomenon. They all rest upon the following propositions:

1. Delinquency is learned and generally occurs with other persons.
2. When delinquency is learned, the learning includes both motives and methods of committing crime.
3. Juvenile delinquency is one way of expressing needs and values, not in themselves delinquent, which are shared by all youth.

DELINQUENCY AS AN EXPRESSION OF WORKING-CLASS CULTURE. One of the theories of delinquency as a sub-cultural phenomenon explains it as a "natural" form of behavior for working-class boys. According to this theory, working-class boys grow up with standards of behavior which get them in trouble with the authorities who represent middle-class standards. Kvaraceus and Miller (1959) favor this theory and list the following characteristics of working-class culture which tend to get a boy in trouble with the authorities: high value placed upon toughness, outsmarting others, seeking excitement, maintaining one's autonomy, and attributing events to fate. In contrast, the middle-class culture places high value upon the following traits: achievement through hard work, responsibility, desire for education, respect for property, cleanliness, ambition, belonging to formal organizations, and ability to defer present pleasure in favor of future gratification.

The male gang is frequently found in working-class culture; the sub-culture provides the value system, teaches boys to become delinquent, and then fortifies their delinquency.

Since most working-class boys do *not* become delinquent, it is pointed out by Kvaraceus and Miller (1959) that not all working-class families have typical working-class values, and that some boys from working-class families learn middle-class modes of behavior in school, in church, or in recreational settings. With the aid of education, these boys move out of the working class. Many other boys accept the working-class culture but are not aggressive enough to become involved in serious delinquency, even though they participate with delinquents in many gang activities.

According to this theory, the boy who is *normally* socialized in working-class culture has a strong chance of becoming delinquent; but he will show little or no emotional disturbance. This is depicted in Figure 13.2, in which it is assumed that roughly 25 percent of delinquent boys have demonstrable emotional disturbance. How this proportion is distributed differently in middle- and working-class boys also is indicated.

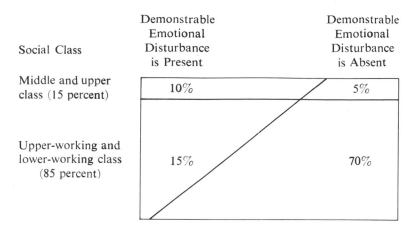

Social Class	Demonstrable Emotional Disturbance is Present	Demonstrable Emotional Disturbance is Absent
Middle and upper class (15 percent)	10%	5%
Upper-working and lower-working class (85 percent)	15%	70%

Note: It is assumed here that roughly 25 percent of delinquent boys have a "demonstrable" degree of emotional disturbance.

Figure 13.2 Emotional maladjustment in relation to social class among delinquent boys.

STATUS DISCONTENT. A second theory in which delinquency is viewed as originating in the social structure is the "status-discontent" theory of Cohen (1955). In this theory it is assumed that all or practically all boys have accepted most of the goals of *middle-class* society, but that some boys are unsuccessful in achieving these goals. All boys would like to have money, a job, and, as they grow older, a girl friend, then a wife and family. Most middle-class boys and many working-class boys make steady and sure progress toward these goals by doing satisfactory work in school, by getting along well in the school peer group, and by getting a job and earning money. These boys have adequate mastery of the means for achieving their goals.

However, a minority of boys—most of them from working-class families—do not have the intelligence, or the study habits, or the work attitudes, or the social skills that are necessary to achieve these goals legitimately. Because they have the same desires as their peers, they become discontented with their disadvantaged status. These boys then seek illegitimate means to get what they want. They turn to the delinquent gang for moral support and for guidance in ways to get money, excitement, power, and the feeling of masculinity. Being frustrated by the adult society around them, they may become hostile and aggressive toward that society, and they may vent their hostility by destruction of property and by attacks on law-abiding people.

These boys develop a "contra-culture" which denies the validity of middle-class standards. Their delinquent behavior is malicious, negativistic, hedonistic, non-utilitarian, and oriented toward independence from adult controls.

THE OPPORTUNITY STRUCTURE. A third theory emphasizes not the *inability* of working-class youth to measure up to middle-class standards, but the unfair or unequal distribution of *opportunity* between middle-class and working-class youth. Cloward and Ohlin (1960) argue that, if opportunity is not available by legitimate means, boys will band together in delinquent groups to seek illegitimate means of achieving their goals. There are three types of illegal behavior which they tend to follow, depending on the opportunities available to them. One type is crime. If boys live in a part of the community where adult criminals are available as models, where crime is organized, where they can become apprentices to the "syndicate," and where there are means of disposing of stolen goods, they form criminal gangs and engage in burglary and theft.

Another type of community may offer very little opportunity for successful crime. The police may be too effective, or the community may be so unstable that adult criminal organizations do not flourish. When the stability provided by legitimate or illegitimate organizations of power is not present, the frustrations of adolescent boys are likely to break out into gang warfare. This warfare gives boys status and feelings of masculinity and excitement, even though it does not give them money or property.

If neither of these types of delinquent behavior is available to frustrated youth, either because of police control or because community social controls operate effectively, they turn to a third form of delinquency which is essentially a retreat from the more aggressive modes of behavior. They turn to drugs or to an escapist type of drinking. Drug-addiction and drinking are not dependent upon gangs and gang organization.

IV. Delinquency as a Phenomenon of Idleness

Some sociologists view delinquency not as an outcome of a delinquent sub-culture but as the product of a social structure that fails to operate effectively to provide pathways of growth to adulthood. According to this view, it is the *absence* of a constructive social situation rather than the *presence* of a destructive social situation which is essentially responsible for much lower-class delinquency (Matza, 1964).

The great increase of juvenile delinquency since World War II may be more closely related to the growing numbers of unemployed and out-of-school youth than to any sub-culture that causes boys to become delinquent. Idleness leads boys into trouble. With nothing socially constructive to do, boys easily turn to theft, car stealing, and fighting. According to this view, if middle-class boys were out of school and out of work in large numbers, they, too, would show high delinquency rates.

Delinquency as Failure to Grow Up

All the types of delinquency discussed above can be viewed as results of failure to grow up normally. When a child is slow in gaining social maturity, he may behave in one of various ways. He may struggle to grow up and his struggle may take the form of delinquency. He may, on the other hand, give up the attempt; he may develop a sense of hopeless and helpless inferiority; or he may construct a world of daydreams in which he can imagine himself successful.

Where delinquency is the result of personality disturbance, the failure to grow up has usually taken place early in life, usually in the pre-school years. Because of failure to accomplish certain early tasks of social and emotional growth, the child either fails to form an effective moral conscience, or he becomes fearful, anxious, and guilt-ridden.

The developmental form of delinquency occurs during adolescence when a boy is suffering from a certain degree of frustration and of uncertainty in his attempts to establish an adult identity. The normal adolescent becomes aggressive at times, and his inner moral control may be thrown off balance. His delinquent acts disturb his growth but do not prevent it. As he grows up, he overcomes his temporary delinquency.

The form of delinquency which originates as response to the social environment arises as a boy fails to follow the rules of society by failing to do satisfactory work in school, failing to get a steady job, or by failing to get along well with his age-mates. As a result of this failure, he may seek illegal and socially undesirable substitutes for growth, such as the easy money that comes from stealing or the excitement and sense of masculinity that comes from fighting and from sexual promiscuity. The boy who came to be called Duke is a case in point:

Duke was the oldest of two boys born to his mother when she was living with her second husband. Deserted by this man when the boys were young, the mother supported the family partly by working and partly by receiving Aid to Dependent Children. Duke's IQ was about average as measured by an intelligence test, but he did poor work in school and had to repeat the sixth grade. He was regarded by his age-mates and by his teacher as a highly aggressive boy. His sixth grade teacher checked the following adjectives as descriptive of him: aggressive, alert, boastful, bossy, cruel, depressed, honest, loyal, revengeful, show-off, tease, touchy, vindictive.

As Duke grew older he became increasingly aggressive in school, until in the ninth grade he was being sent out of one class after another. Shortly after he reached his sixteenth birthday, he decided to quit school. One of his best friends had just been expelled, and another one had dropped out.

When asked by an interviewer how he felt after having been out of school several months, Duke said: "I'd rather be in. But when I quit I had a feeling that they were going to kick me out anyway. It was quit or get kicked out because of my bad behavior. I couldn't mind my teachers or they couldn't mind me; I don't know which. Anyway, I had mostly study halls when I quit. They kicked me out of science and social studies and algebra."

Duke's first brush with the law had come at the age of ten, when he and some other boys were brought before the police matron for putting their footprints in some freshly-laid cement. By the time he was sixteen he had an assortment of misbehaviors on the record, including stealing, fighting, and sexual offenses.

After he quit school at sixteen Duke loafed around town with his cronies, getting unskilled jobs for a few weeks at a time, and getting into various kinds of trouble. At seventeen, he enlisted in the Navy; but he was soon discharged. He came back into the community where he resumed his delinquent ways.

This boy's failure to grow up according to society's expectations was becoming clear by the time he was ten or eleven years old. He reacted to this failure by becoming aggressive, tough, and boastful. Unable to hold a job for any length of time, he stole in order to get money. Within his delinquent gang he was accepted as a leader, thus earning his nickname, Duke. His enlistment in the Navy marked another effort to grow up, but the enlistment did not work out. He did not have the stability or the self-discipline required by the Navy.

When reinterviewed at the age of nineteen, Duke seemed to be somewhat stabilized. At that time he was married and seemed to have become a steadier and more dependable person.

The Prevention of Delinquency

Any program for the prevention of delinquency is likely to be directed at a target group of youngsters who appear to be pre-delinquent. The first step, then, is to identify those who are most likely to become delinquent.

Methods of Identifying Pre-Delinquents

A method which has many advantages is the use of the Glueck Delinquency Prediction Scale mentioned earlier (see page 336) in which the family environment of the child can be assessed. This method might be used to locate the potential delinquent at as young an age as six and would permit the prevention program to start very early. However, the Glueck Scale requires an interview or observation with the parent or parents, preferably in the home. The process requires trained observers and is expensive and complicated to carry out in the average community, where the goal would be to screen many hundreds of families to identify the delinquency-prone children.

Somewhat less expensive methods can be used with boys who are as old as nine or ten, methods that depend on observation of the boy's behavior rather than on observation of the family. Kvaraceus and Ulrich (1959) describe several such methods for detecting delinquency proneness.

A method described by Havighurst *et al.* (1962) combined a sociometric test and a teacher-observation instrument to identify the boys in the fourth to sixth grades who showed the greatest aggressive maladjustment. This group was then studied to find which ones were doing unsatisfactory or failing school work. It was possible to identify about 14 percent of the age-group in the community, 28 boys, as being prone to delinquency. After following this group for ten years, it was found that 20 of the 28 boys did indeed become delinquent. In this instance, however, this method failed to identify another 20 to 30 boys who also became delinquent in the ten-year period.

It is probable that methods of this type are fairly good for discovering the typical boy who will become delinquent if not given special help. These methods are not likely to be useful, however, in discovering the boy whose delinquency has unusual causes; and they are especially inadequate for discovering the pre-delinquent who is characterized by anxiety and fearfulness.

Methods of Preventing Delinquency

For a delinquency-prevention program that might start as early as the first grade, it might be possible to use the observations of kindergarten teachers to pick out a group of boys who show various kinds of behavior disturbance (not only aggression). Visits might then be made to the homes of the boys so identified, visits that would serve as a basis for a prediction made by the Glueck Scale. This procedure might not be as efficient or economical as methods applied later in a boy's life, but it would probably serve to identify those youngsters who show a high probability of some form of maladjustment (though not necessarily delinquency), all of whom would benefit from special attention at this early age.

Since the causes of delinquency are multiple, it is natural that a variety of procedures has been proposed for its prevention. The report of the U.S. Congressional Committee studying juvenile delinquency summarizes in the following terms the various types of programs and the theories of causation underlying them:

Programs specifically established to prevent delinquency by treatment of incipient offenders vary widely in plan and underlying theory of causation and cure. Among the favored assumptions as to what will help are the following:

Having an adult friend or sponsor who will stick to the delinquency-prone boy or girl through thick and thin and will secure needed services in his behalf will render the child less likely to become delinquent.

Delinquency-prone children can be identified by teachers at an early age (the schools know all the children and their ways, it is said) and referred for treatment to either a particular agency set up for the purpose or to the ongoing service agencies.

Delinquency results largely from disturbances in the parent-child relationship; hence, these disturbances should be recognized by all services (health, schools, day nurseries, police, etc.) that have contact with the families, and prophylactic measures should be taken.

Delinquency frequently results from or is a sign of emotional disturbance, and this disorder can be remedied by individual or group therapy.

Delinquency results largely from a breakdown in the cohesiveness of neighborhoods and in the controls exercised by parents and neighbors. A reduction in delinquency can be secured by restoring these lost or diminished social attributes and functions.

The chief source of delinquent conduct and the chief bearers of the delinquent tradition in slum areas are certain of the established street-corner clubs or gangs. Direct work with these groups is required to carry them fairly peacefully through the tumultuous years of adolescence, to teach them democratic ways of conducting their organization, and—perhaps—to break the chain of transmission of delinquent customs.

The usual social and mental health services of a community are not effective in delinquency prevention because they do not operate in concert and are inadequately staffed, quantitatively and qualitatively.

Delinquency can be reduced by assuring that all intellectually capable children, even though they are handicapped by language and culturally impoverished homes, should learn to read well and acquire other basic intellectual skills.

Lack of opportunity for paid work is an important factor in juvenile delinquency, partly because denial of a chance to earn money puts an adolescent in a childlike status and does not permit him to progress smoothly toward adulthood. (United States, 86th Congress, 1960, p. 27.)

Methods Used by Schools

Kvaraceus and Ulrich (1959) describe a variety of programs which are being used or have been used in schools as a means of preventing or controlling delinquency. If one views delinquency as primarily a consequence of failure to grow up successfully, there are two types of school programs which seem most promising: one is conducted in the primary grades of school; the other, at the junior high school age.

A PROGRAM FOCUSED ON READING INSTRUCTION. In the underprivileged or slum areas of the cities, it is well known that a relatively high proportion of boys and girls fail to do satisfactory work in the first grade; this means that they fail to learn to read. Some school systems set up a third semester of the first grade for these children; or they provide a summer school session for such children after they have finished the first grade; or they attempt to identify these children in kindergarten or early in the first grade in order to give them special instruction from the outset, as well as to help the parents do a better job for encouraging reading in the home.

This approach has received a good deal of attention in the last few years, on the theory that a great deal of later maladjustment can be prevented by spending a little more money on children at the beginning of their schooling. (Probably a distinction should be made, here, between children of any social class who have reading difficulties due either to biological inadequacy or emotional problems, and children of certain working-class families who lack stimulation and example at home. It is the latter group that is being discussed here.) In the Head Start program which began in 1965, federal funds are being used by many school systems to provide compensatory educational experiences to children beginning at age four, even before they enter school.

The reasoning behind programs focused on reading instruction is this: For the young child in school the crucial task is to master the art of reading so that he can use reading as a tool for later mental development. It seems likely that "mastery" of the reading task should occur at a six- or seven-year age level. The child who achieves this mastery then goes on to read more complex material as he grows older, more or less as a matter of course. But the child who does not master the reading task at the six- or seven-year age level stumbles along in the second grade, and later tries to keep up with the class but falls further and further behind.

This child may be passed from one grade to another on the basis of a "social promotion" policy until he reaches the fifth or sixth grade. By this time, he is doing so poorly that he practically *must* fail to be promoted. But failure and repetition of a grade do not help him, since his difficulty began long ago. Thus school becomes more and more an arena of failure and frustration. The child may react with aggression and hostility, or with apathy. The child who reacts with aggression soon acquires a reputation for being a trouble-maker in the school and community. He ceases learning anything useful in school and drops out just as soon as he is allowed to do so.

The crucial failure of growth here is a failure to learn to read at the age of six or seven. The school might meet the needs of these children by discovering them early, putting them in relatively small groups with specially trained teachers, working closely with their parents, and continuing to give them special attention until they master the reading task.

A WORK-STUDY PROGRAM. A second point at which the school program might be focused to overcome growth failure is at the junior high school level. This is usually the time when boys who have not found the school a satisfactory place for growth become a serious problem to teachers due to their aggression, hostility, and refusal to try to learn what the school tries to teach.

There have always been boys of this type, but in the past they have generally dropped out of school at age fourteen or even earlier and have sought to grow up through the avenue of work. As recently as 1920 this alternative pathway was freely available to city boys as well as to farm boys in the United States. At that time, 58 percent of boys between fourteen and seventeen were employed full-time or part-time. But in 1961, only 25 percent of boys in this age group were employed at all, either full-time or part-time. During this forty-year period the proportion of boys employed full-time decreased from an estimated 30 percent to 3 percent. The American economy with its emphasis on mass production and automation has steadily reduced the number of jobs at unskilled levels and has nearly discarded the practice of employing boys full-time. Many employers make it a practice not to hire anyone below age eighteen. Child labor legislation, adopted when there was danger of exploiting juvenile workers, now makes it difficult to hire boys and girls aged fourteen to eighteen even for the most desirable kinds of work. Thus, unemployment rates are very high among boys who have dropped out of school.

Most of the proposals for delinquency prevention at the junior high school level include some type of work experience as a means of getting the boy started again on the path of growth. There is hardly a big city school system that does not have some form of work-study program for youth at ages 16 or older. Examples are programs in St. Louis, Detroit, Chicago, New York, Philadelphia and Kansas City. These are programs for boys (and sometimes for girls) who would not be eligible for regular vocational education programs.

The need for a work-based or vocation-oriented school program for youth not served by the conventional vocational educational program has been recognized by the U.S. Congress in the Vocational Education Act of 1963. Money has been provided through this Act to support experimental and demonstration school programs aimed to help youth for whom the conventional vocational education is not effective.

It is generally agreed that the work-study program should commence as early as possible, and certainly by the age of thirteen or fourteen. Yet part-time jobs are exceedingly scarce for youth at these ages, and especially for youth with poor behavior records and poor school records. Consequently, some kind of "sheltered" work experience as part of the school program may be indicated, where the work done by the boys is socially useful, even though at first it may not be done for private employers. A plan for such a work-experience program is now being tried out in Kansas City. It begins with boys in the eighth grade identified in the way described earlier. These boys are placed in a work-study program; half their time goes into work experience, and half into a specially adapted course in basic subjects such as English, arithmetic, and history. The work-experience part of the program has three stages:

STAGE I. Age 13–15. Boys are placed in a work team supervised by a Work-Supervisor. They do socially useful work three hours a day in parks, school grounds, alleys, forests, or in a school workshop. They are graded on basic work attitudes and skills such as punctuality, cooperation, ability to follow directions, and efficiency.

STAGE II. Age 15–17. Boys graduate from Stage I into this stage when they are ready for part-time individual jobs with private employers where they receive pay at juvenile rates. They are placed in jobs by an Employment Coordinator-Supervisor, and they are evaluated periodically.

STAGE III. Age 16–18. Boys leave school for full-time jobs. The Employment Coordinator-Supervisor helps them get jobs and keeps in touch with them until they appear to be firmly established. They may go to a continuation school or an evening high school.

It is expected that these boys will feel less alienated from society as they become more successful in school and as they see themselves making progress toward adulthood through the avenue of work. The work-study program, it is hoped, will provide the following benefits:

1. It will make school more rewarding. The boy is then likely to make more effort to be successful in school, thus becoming more orderly and controlled in his behavior.
2. It will reduce the amount of punishment for school failure and bad behavior, thus reducing the intensity of the boy's aggression toward society and its institutions.
3. It will bring success for productive work behavior, thus making unproductive behavior less attractive to the boy.
4. It will bring a stable male figure—the Work Supervisor—into the boy's life in such a way that the Work Supervisor may become an object of identification and a model for the boy.

There are some objections to this type of program. The chief one is that it aims to prepare a group of boys for unskilled or at best semi-skilled adult jobs in a society in which the proportion of such jobs is decreasing. The boy who enters this kind of program cannot expect to graduate from high school, and he may suffer thereafter from his lack of formal education.

The objection that there may not be enough jobs in a modern economy for boys of this type is discussed in a statement published by Phi Delta Kappa, the honorary educational fraternity (Havighurst and Stiles, 1961). Through its Commission on Juvenile Delinquency and the Schools, this organization has proposed that society should create such jobs, even if it costs money to do so. If the principle is followed that every child has a right to an education fitted to his needs, then work experience may have to be provided by public funds for some boys and girls, just as courses in mathematics, science, and foreign languages are provided for others. The local school board may have to subsidize work-experience programs just as it subsidizes programs of instruction in other areas.

The Phi Delta Kappa Commission believes that if work experience of this type becomes a part of the school program, it will require the support of employers and of labor unions, because a category of *juvenile jobs* will be created which may compete with *adult jobs* and which may not be economically efficient. Employers may need to make some sacrifice of efficiency; and labor unions may need to give up some of their control over jobs.

The Kansas City work-study program, as well as a dozen or more others that start with work experience for junior high school youth, has been described in a case-book edited by Burchill (1962). It must be said that none of these programs has yet proved so successful that it can serve as a model for nationwide adoption. For example, on the basis of preliminary results, the Kansas City project has produced only partial success. After the first four years of the project, the experimental group of boys (those who began the work-study program in the 8th grade) were only slightly better adjusted to school and society than their control group (those who were just like them at the beginning of the study, in the 8th grade, but who followed the conventional school program). The experimental group stayed in school somewhat longer than the control group and had more paid work experience, but they did not have less police-recorded delinquency than the control group. It appeared that possibly one-fourth of the boys in the work-study experiment profited markedly. They learned to perform well at work and were located in stable jobs by the age of 17 or 18. But the other three-fourths were no more clearly moving toward adulthood than the control group.

Projects with a Broader Community Base

During the 1960's the United States Congress has been sufficiently disturbed about the increase in juvenile delinquency to pass the Delinquency Control and Prevention Act. This provides funds for several major community programs to combat delinquency. The most widely publicized and the largest of these is New York City's *Community Mobilization for Youth*. In this program there has been a concerted and cooperative effort to attack all the probable causes of delinquency: social workers serve families, group workers serve juvenile gangs, work experience programs are provided, and school programs are aimed at reducing the number of dropouts.

The Economic Opportunity Act of 1964 is aimed against poverty and the correlates of poverty—illiteracy, unemployment, and juvenile delinquency. Consequently, a large part of the anti-poverty program has been to provide work experience with related training for youth who are out of school and unemployed, and for youth who need both money and work experience while in school and college. Two programs (which have been described in Chapter 12) have been directed toward assisting youth from groups where delinquency is high: youth who are out of school and not working; and youth who are on the verge of dropping out of school.

The first, the *Job Corps* program is designed for out-of-school boys and girls who might profit from a program aimed at teaching the skills that normally come with high school graduation. These boys and girls are sent from their home towns to centers where specialized training is offered. The boys and girls are given the type of training for which they seem best fitted on the basis of aptitude tests. The program is not specifically aimed at delinquency reduction. Boys or girls with a police record for serious crimes are not admitted.

The second, the *Neighborhood Youth Corps* program, operates on a far larger scale to provide employment for boys and girls who are expected to attend school while working part-time. The young people are employed at socially valuable work but do not compete with workers in already established jobs.

Thus, the anti-poverty programs for youth operating in the mid-1960's represent a massive attack on idleness through the creation of jobs and of job-training opportunities. Since the programs are limited to the age-group 16 through 20, they have only indirect bearing on juvenile delinquency at younger ages. However, if a large group of 16- and 17-year-olds is taken off the street corners and given a chance to do socially constructive work, its example may influence younger boys and girls.

While the long-range outcome remains to be seen, these programs are large enough in scope to make an impression on the delinquency statistics for the period from 1965 to 1970. The programs represent an assumption of responsibility by society for a group of young people who are socially maladjusted, whether these young people are delinquent or not. The results of these programs will help to answer the question of the source of delinquency: whether it arises from social situations characterized by idleness, failure at school, and lack of constructive activity; or whether it is the product of a special sub-culture that characterizes working-class urban youth.

Exercises

1. Read what you can find on delinquency among girls. What differentiates it from delinquency among boys?

2. Read several newspaper accounts of delinquent gangs and try out on these descriptions the Cloward and Ohlin theory of "differential opportunity." Does the theory explain the types of delinquency found in these gangs?

3. Find an example of a work-experience program for pre-delinquent or delinquent boys; describe and evaluate it.

4. Some of the programs under the Economic Opportunity Act of 1964, notably the residential *Job Corps* program, have been severely criticized in some quarters, and have received unfavorable press reports. Read accounts of one or more of the Job Corps projects. Try to get a well-balanced view of what actually happened, what the program consisted of, what kinds of youth were served, and how well the program succeeded. Compare this type of program with the *Neighborhood Youth Corps* projects in your own community.

5. Have you seen any semi-delinquent gangs composed mainly of middle-class boys? What was their "hang-out"? In what respects was it similar to or different from a working-class gang?

Suggestions for Further Reading

1. Compare the theories of delinquency causation in *Delinquent Behavior* by William D. Kvaraceus and Walter B. Miller, *Delinquent Boys* by Albert K. Cohen, and *Delinquency and Opportunity* by Richard A. Cloward and Lloyd E. Ohlin.

2. A more psychological and less sociological treatment of delinquency than the one given in this chapter can be found in writings of psychiatrists and psychologists, especially W. Healy and Augusta Bronner, *New Light on Delinquency and Its Treatment;* Fritz. Redl, in *New Perspectives for Research on Delinquency;* and August Aichhorn, *Wayward Youth.*

3. The theory of delinquency as a natural product of life in the slum area of a city is developed by Clifford R. Shaw and Henry D. McKay in their book, *Juvenile Delinquency and Urban Areas.*

4. Recent books with empirical data as well as theoretical discussions of nature and causes of delinquency include: Marshall B. Clinard, ed. *Anomie and Deviant Behavior;* David Matza, *Delinquency and Drift;* Walter B. Miller, *City Gangs: An Experiment in Changing Gang Behavior;* John M. Martin and Joseph P. Fitzpatrick, *Delinquent Behavior;* and James F. Short, Jr. and Fred L. Strodtbeck, *Group Process and Gang Delinquency.*

5. There are many government pamphlets on juvenile delinquency. A folder describing these publications will be mailed on request from the Superintendent of Documents, U.S. Government Printing Office, Washington 25, D.C. Of special interest is the report of a research symposium on *The Role of the School in Prevention of Juvenile Delinquency,* edited by William R. Carriker.

6. Recently a number of communities have begun to use work-study programs in city schools as a means of preventing delinquency among alienated youth. Programs in Philadelphia, Kansas City, Rochester, N.Y., and other cities are described in *Work Experience Programs,* prepared by the "Commission on Juvenile Delinquency and the Schools" of Phi Delta Kappa, the professional education fraternity, and edited by Burchill.

7. Read Glaser's paper in *Society and Education: A Book of Readings* (Havighurst, Neugarten and Falk) for a review of the major theories of the causes of delinquency. In the same book, the selections by Hammer and by Heise provide descriptions of life in disadvantaged urban areas

where delinquency rates are high. Erdman Palmore's report on his study of "Factors Associated with School Dropouts and Juvenile Delinquency among Lower-Class Children" and the Havighurst and Stiles statement prepared for the Phi Delta Kappa Commission on the Role of the School in the Prevention of Juvenile Delinquency are also reprinted in this book of readings.

14 / Social Integration and the Educational System

The People of the United States are:

- 100 million, Anglo-Saxon
- 20 million, Teutonic
- 19 million, Negro
- 12 million, Irish
- 12 million, Slavic
- 7 million, Italian
- 6 million, Scandinavian
- 4 million, Polish
- 4 million, Latin-American
- 1 million, French
- ½ million, Oriental
- ½ million, Finn
- ½ million, Lithuanian
- ½ million, Greek
- ½ million, American Indian

The people of the United States are:

- 100 million Protestant
- 50 million, Roman Catholic
- 5½ million, Jewish
- 3 million, Eastern Orthodox Catholic
- 1¾ million, Mormon
- ½ million, Christian Scientist

Not only the United States, but every modern society includes groups who feel themselves different from and, to some degree, in competition with other groups. To a certain extent such intergroup competition is not unhealthy for a society, for each group tries to make life more rewarding for its members. Such competition may, however, result in prejudice, discrimination, and conflict which, if carried to extremes, may undermine the welfare of the society as a whole.

The Problem of Intergroup Relations

The United States today is faced with the problem of intergroup conflict, a problem that exists in various forms and various degrees of intensity. There are conflicts between economic groups, such as management and labor; and between religious groups, such as fundamentalists and modernists within Protestant denominations; and between different denominations. Some Americans of one skin color look down upon people of other skin colors. Some Americans are hostile to people of a different nationality and may try to prevent them from moving into their neighborhoods and encroaching on what they consider their own territory.

Intergroup conflict is reflected in the schools, as illustrated in the following account written by a teacher in a metropolitan high school:

The "Hebes" and the "Dagoes" were the two major groups of students in the high school to which I was first assigned. During my seven years in this job I had many opportunities to observe both groups.

There were many differences between them. The first reflected an attitude toward school. Most of the Jewish students respected the school. It was a means to further advancement, and graduation was to be achieved at any sacrifice. Most Jewish students took the college preparatory course, and only a small number dropped out of high school. On the other hand, school for most Italian students was something to be endured, and many of them dropped out as soon as the law allowed. For the most part they took the commercial and shop courses.

This difference in attitude about the school itself tended to cause other differences. Many of the informal activities were dominated by one group or the other. The basketball teams were preponderantly Jewish, probably because basketball was a major activity in the Jewish boys' clubs of the neighborhood. As manager of the assembly hall, I had charge of two groups, the stage hands and the ushers. The stage hands were mostly Italian boys, and the ushers were Jewish. Try as I might, the groups remained essentially unchanged until I left the school.

All of these differences added up to a running conflict. Jewish students voted for the Jewish candidates. Since the Italians were in the minority, this meant offices were held mostly by Jewish students. This caused resentment among the Italians, who retaliated in subtle or direct ways. Sometimes the conflict became open, with gang fights in or near the school.

The observance of religious holidays also accented differences in the two groups. At first the Jewish students, most of them coming from religious homes, observed many of the religious holidays by staying home. To "get even," the Italians then insisted in observing many of the less important Catholic holy days. The result was a loss of much school time by both groups.

Integration of the two groups was never achieved, due partly to the lack of any real program or plan at the school. The differences were accepted as inevitable by the administrators and teachers who did little other than learn to live with them. Jews and Italians grew up and left school, still maintaining their prejudices and still having little understanding of each other.

Unlike the instance just described, many schools are learning how to deal with such conflicts within the schools and are recognizing that the schools can reduce the intensity of intergroup conflicts within the society. Before taking up educational procedures, let us look at the problem in broader terms and find the ways in which solutions are being sought in society.

Solutions to Intergroup Conflict

There are two solutions of the problem of intergroup relations which are acceptable in a democratic society: the first is integration, biological and/or social; the second is democratic pluralism. Other solutions, such as destruction of the weaker group, or forming a caste-like society in which lower castes must accept a menial status, are not acceptable to most Americans.

Biological and Social Integration

Biological integration means a fusion of racial and cultural groups through widespread intermarriage. Social integration means the mixing of various racial and cultural groups through association in business, education, government, and cultural affairs. An example of both biological and social integration is found in Brazil, where there were originally three distinct racial and cultural groups, the Indians, the Portuguese, and the Negro slaves from Africa. For four centuries there was a great deal of intermarriage as well as a great deal of miscegenation that was not sanctified by the marriage ceremony. While today a large fraction of the population is apparently unmixed Caucasian, including German and Italian immigrant groups of the nineteenth and twentieth centuries, the Brazilians are largely of mixed racial background. An important cultural fact (although it operates informally) is that anyone who has any evidence of "white blood" is defined as being "white." Brazil is said to have gone further than any other modern nation in biological integration, and Brazilians are officially proud of their racially mixed society.

In the early years of slavery in the South of the United States, there was also a great deal of miscegenation. White slave-owners often took Negro women as concubines. As a consequence, the majority of American Negroes are of so-called "mixed blood" today. After the end of slavery the process of biological integration between white and Negro slowed down, and it is not regarded now as generally desirable by either white or Negro people, though there are a small number of successful mixed marriages. Certain American Indian tribes, on the other hand, have intermarried freely with whites and Negroes. Finally, there has been a great deal of intermarriage between various nationalities in the white group. Despite these types of biological integration, it is accurate to say that social integration has proceeded much further than biological integration in the United States.

Democratic Pluralism

In a society characterized by democratic pluralism, the various groups settle down to an amicable coexistence, each group keeping its culture fairly intact and intermarrying little or not at all with other groups. If equal respect and equal opportunities and privileges are accorded to all groups, a condition of democratic pluralism may be said to exist. This has been the situation in Switzerland, with its French, German, and Italian cantons; and it is developing in New Zealand between the whites and the Polynesian Maoris.

There is a certain degree of democratic pluralism in the United States, where Catholics, Protestants, and Jews live amicably with one another while preserving their religious differences, and where various racial and ethnic groups preserve certain features of their own cultures at the same time that they have equality of economic and political rights.

It seems probable that the United States is working out a combination of social integration and pluralism that will secure some of the advantages of both solutions.

The tendency toward social (but not biological) integration is seen in such social characteristics as the development of a standard public-supported education which teaches common technical skills and political values; the growing conformity in tastes, seen in the mass consumption market and in the wide appeal of the mass media (newspapers, radio, motion pictures, and television); widespread social and geographic mobility; and the growing equality of educational opportunity for the youth in various racial and socioeconomic groups. The privileges and opportunities of American life are increasingly open to people of all groups.

A common culture is spreading through the United States. By combining the former diversity of culture traits, and by developing new and unique cultural forms, the American society is moving toward greater social integration.

On the other hand, there are strong elements of democratic pluralism that are at least holding their own in the American scene today. Most powerful in the maintenance of diversity are the religious and ethnic cultures. Conservative Jewish groups generally work for pluralism in religious and social matters and the Roman Catholic Church is a power for religious pluralism as well as for plural systems of schools and colleges. Ethnic groups that tend to preserve cultural differences include the Italian, Polish, Indian, and Spanish-American groups. (The American Negro, by contrast, with no special culture to promote other than the standard American one, tends to work for social integration.)

The United States seems to be moving, then, toward both goals: social integration is the goal in political and economic aspects of life, as well as in intellectual, artistic, and literary areas; democratic pluralism is the goal as regards religion and certain cultural and family values that various ethnic groups are encouraged to preserve.

Education and Intergroup Relations

The educational system mirrors the intergroup relations that exist within the society. For instance, the American system of parochial schools existing side by side with public schools reflects the fact that there is religious diversity in American society. Furthermore, the existence of nonsectarian private schools reflects a hierarchical social structure producing social diversity, and that many people of upper social classes want their children to associate in school with children of their own class.

Intergroup diversity is also reflected in the content of the school program and in the administrative policies of the school. Most American schools teach something of the history, the customs, the holidays of various national groups. Cooperation or conflict between racial, ethnic, and religious groups is reflected within a given school in the ways in which teachers relate to each other and to their pupils, and in the ways in which a social organization forms among pupils. In some schools, there are distinct cleavages between Negro and white students, between Polish and Italian, or as we have already illustrated, between Jewish and non-Jewish; and such cleavage affects the morale of the school as a social unit. Differences between social classes, as we have also seen earlier, are pervasive in their influence upon school policy and school organization. The school, in a variety of ways, reflects the pluralism that exists within the American society.

On the other hand, the educational system is also a means for promoting social integration and for improving intergroup relationships. This is being exemplified anew in the 1960's by the fact that segregation of Negro children in public schools is being abandoned, and educational opportunities for Negro as well as other minority groups are being equalized.

The Negro Revolution

Although there are other groups in America that have long been discriminated against, such as the Mexican-Americans in the southwestern part of the country, Negroes have been subjected to more discrimination than any other minority group in America. They have suffered discrimination in jobs, housing, the use of hotels, restaurants, buses and railway trains, as well as in education. Despite these disadvantages, Negroes have made great economic and social gains in the last quarter-century, as discrimination is being rapidly reduced.

To understand the presently changing position of Negroes in the United States and the role of the educational system in influencing the rate of change, a historical context is necessary.

The Historical Setting

For five centuries, from 1450 to about 1950, the Caucasian West Europeans and North Americans dominated the world through their superior technology applied to material production and warfare. On this basis the Caucasian race established itself as superior to the other races.

Only at the beginning of the twentieth century did a colored nation (Japan) defeat a white nation (Russia) and become a world power. During the second half of the century China has grown in power and constitutes the great enigma in international relations around which the strategies of the white nations turn. India during the twentieth century established herself as a moral force in the parliament of nations. After World War II the once dark continent of Africa developed a set of independent nations which slowly learned to live and work together toward the goal of bringing economic and political influence to bear on the rest of the world. Among the colored peoples of the world, only the indigenous peoples of South, Central, and North America did not rise to power during the twentieth century. They were too much integrated into a white-dominated society, or too much subordinated, or too much isolated to assert themselves politically as nations of colored people.

In this sense the twentieth century marks the close of the white man's dominion. In the twenty-first century, if color will mean anything at all, the white man will have to come to terms with his minority status in terms of numbers and with his changed status in terms of political and economic power.

What has been called the *Negro Revolution* in the United States started in the early 1960's, and became a national movement in 1963, when two hundred thousand Negro and white Americans marched to the Lincoln Memorial in Washington to demonstrate the urgency of action for political and economic equality for Negroes.

On June 4, 1965, the President of the United States, Lyndon B. Johnson, speaking to the graduates of Howard University, said:

Our earth is the home of revolution.

In every corner of every continent men charged with hope contend with ancient ways in the pursuit of justice. They reach for the newest of weapons to realize the oldest of dreams; that each may walk in freedom and pride, stretching his talents, enjoying the fruits of the earth. . . .

But nothing in any country touches us more profoundly, nothing is more freighted with meaning for our own destiny, than the revolution of the Negro American.

In far too many ways American Negroes have been another nation:

deprived of freedom, crippled by hatred, the doors of opportunity closed to hope.

In our time change has come to this nation, too. The American Negro, acting with impressive restraint, has peacefully protested and marched, entered the courtroom and the seats of government, demanding a justice that has long been denied. . . .

We seek not just freedom but opportunity—not just legal equity but human ability—not just equality as a right and a theory, but equality as a fact and as a result. (Johnson, 1965.)

Among the social forces that have brought the Negro Revolution into existence are urbanization, new patterns of geographical mobility, and the growth of Negro leadership.

URBANIZATION. In 1910, 73 percent of Negroes were living in rural or semi-rural conditions; in 1960, 73 percent were living in towns and cities of 2,500 or more, and 50 percent of these were living in cities of 50 thousand or more. Under rural conditions most Negroes were farmhands or share-croppers, getting a bare subsistence from the soil. Under urban conditions most Negroes are factory or service workers, and many are members of labor unions. Many are voters, many have incomes vastly greater than when they lived in rural conditions, and many are now in a position to influence history.

MIGRATION TO THE NORTH. Together with urbanization, migration from the South to the North and West has occurred. Table 14.1 shows how

Table 14.1 Nonwhite Population Trends in the Big Cities
(Percent of the city's population)

	1920	1940	1960
New York	2.7	6.1	14.0
Chicago	4.1	8.2	22.9
Philadelphia–Camden	7.4	13.0	26.4
Los Angeles–Long Beach	2.5	3.9	12.2
San Francisco–Oakland	1.1	1.4	14.3
Detroit	4.1	9.2	28.9
Boston	2.2	3.1	9.1
Pittsburgh	6.4	9.3	16.7
Washington, D.C.	25.1	28.0	53.9
Atlanta	31.3	34.6	38.3
Birmingham	39.3	40.7	39.6

Note: Nonwhite includes orientals, who are present in noticeable numbers in San Francisco and Los Angeles, but not in other cities on this list.

the proportions of Negroes have changed in the populations of major cities. The northern cities including Washington, D.C. had slow increases between 1920 and 1940, then very rapid increases between 1940 and 1960. The southern cities have stayed about the same. Since 1960 the northern and westward migration of the Negro has continued, but at a somewhat slower rate.

GROWTH IN NEGRO LEADERSHIP. Organizations to support the Negro Revolution have grown in strength and in number since World War II. The principal pre-war organizations were the National Association for the Advancement of Colored People (NAACP) and the Urban League. Later came the Congress of Racial Equality (CORE), and the Southern Christian Leadership Conference (SCLC), organized by Dr. Martin Luther King. These organizations are not aligned with any political party; their political programs are aimed at obtaining civic, economic and educational opportunity for Negroes.

THE NEGRO REVOLUTION AND THE AMERICAN WAY OF LIFE. It is characteristic of the leadership of the Negro Revolution that it seeks to make the fruits of democracy as available to Negroes as to other groups. Because the American Negro does not try to promote any other culture than the American culture, the Negro Revolution is a movement which seeks to join, not to destroy, the American way of life.

The Problem of "The Negro Role"

Full participation in the American way of life has been more difficult for the Negro to attain than for other minority groups because his skin color makes him so highly visible. Although other ethnic groups were not as easily distinguishable, they too had to wait and work their way slowly into the American social structure. The Irish, Swedes, Poles, and Italians have all had this experience, even though each group has had a different history and each has moved up in the social structure at a different rate of speed. In the middle of the nineteenth century, for instance, the Irish immigrants were called "shanty Irish," job advertisements often carried the cryptic phrase NINA (No Irish Need Apply), and much of the crime and social pathology of urban centers was concentrated among the Irish. Later there were the "dumb Swedes," and after the Swedes had moved up the socioeconomic ladder, the "Polacks" took their place as objects of discrimination.

The stereotyped expression applied to an ethnic group means that a certain social role has been ascribed to the group. People in this group are expected to fit this stereotype, and they sometimes do, since there is a strong social pressure to behave in accordance with an assigned role. The role of a "lazy dull-witted Negro" is imposed on many Negroes, some of whom live up to it. If a Negro is supposed to be lazy and shiftless, he may find it easy to behave this way as a child and, later, as a man. The positive roles that are ascribed to Negro youth are presently those of athletes and entertainers. Negroes are expected to be especially good at basketball, football, boxing, and running, or at singing and dancing. These expectations sometimes help Negro boys and girls in school but they do not help them to become scholars.

One of the basic obstacles to the Negro's full participation in the American way of life is his assignment to the old stereotyped Negro role. The role must be changed to one which connotes success in urban industrial society. The image of the Negro must become one that encourages Negro children to work hard in school, to set high educatonal and vocational goals for themselves, and to become confident of their ability to do anything that people of another color can do.

The role of a lazy, shiftless, and dull person has been fostered by racial segregation and by economic, political, and social discrimination against Negroes. The positive role that must come requires integration in economic life, political life, and especially in the schools.

Already large numbers of Negro children are successfully learning the new role. The growing numbers of Negro middle-class people, of Negro college graduates, of Negro businessmen and professional workers, including school teachers, show that the positive role is being acquired. As the numbers of these people grow, the old stereotype will disappear, just as the unfavorable stereotypes of other ethnic groups have disappeared.

Desegregation in the Schools

The greatest barrier to democratic pluralism in the case of the Negro has been the segregated schools that existed in some states. This system generally (although there are a few exceptions) denied Negro children educational opportunity equal to that of white children. When the United States Supreme Court in 1954 declared segregated schools to be unlawful, a major step in a series of improvements in the status of Negroes was taken.

The Supreme Court decision rested in part upon the interpretation of the evidence that segregation had damaging psychological effects upon Negro children, even when the school facilities themselves were "equal" to those of white schools. The consensus of social scientists studying the effects of segregation on Negroes is that it has been an obstacle to their competence in an urban, industrial, democratic society. This conclusion is based on the following propositions which have been supported by research in the social psychology of race relatons (Pettigrew and Pajonis , 1964; Katz, 1964.)

1. Negro children become aware of their skin color before they reach school age.
2. Most Negro children are taught by their parents that they cannot expect to be treated as equals by most white people.
3. Many Negro children (mostly in the lower socioeconomic group) are taught by their parents or grandparents that they have "bad blood" and are born inferior to white people.
4. When they enter and attend a segregated school, most Negro children are taught to feel that theirs is a poor, inadequate school.
5. Many Negro children are taught by their parents and teachers that the Negro tends to be lazy and ignorant.
6. Many Negro children come to look upon themselves as inferior; they accept and adopt the "Negro role."
7. Many teachers, both white and Negro, look upon Negro pupils as inferior and lower their standards of expectation when they meet Negro students. They give good school grades for performance to which they would give poor grades in the case of a white student. They maintain lower standards in the school than they would if they were in an all-white school, or a mixed school.
8. In order to overcome or avoid an inferior self-concept, the Negro child should:
   a. Have experience with white children in which he is obviously superior a part of the time and inferior a part of the time;
   b. Have this experience as early as possible in his life;
   c. Have this experience under a biracial school staff.
9. Negro students should be taught in interracial learning situations so that they will have a basis for effective performance later in interracial work situations.

Rates of Desegregation

Given the rapidly changing position of the American Negro, all the propositions listed above may not continue to be valid, but for the next decade, at least, one of the major problems of American education will be the desegregation of schools. There are two aspects to this problem— that of *de jure* segregation and that of *de facto* segregation. The first is the problem of southern states where state laws have long prevented white and Negro children from attending the same schools. The second is the problem of industrial cities mainly in the North, where, because most Negroes live in segregated housing areas, many schools have been attended entirely by Negro children.

When the U.S. Supreme Court in 1955 ordered the southern states to proceed with desegregation of their schools "with all deliberate speed," there was at first a period of rapid change in seventeen southern and border states. Within two years, 3,008 out of 9,015 school districts in these seventeen states had at least some white and some Negro children attending desegregated schools. The border states complied with the Court order most readily, and the major cities of these states, which earlier had maintained separate schools for Negroes, changed with relative ease. This was true of Baltimore, Nashville, Louisville, St. Louis, and Kansas City.

In the Deep South, and in certain of the larger cities, notably New Orleans and Little Rock, the process of desegregation went more slowly and resulted in open conflict at times. Integration of schools in the South continued to move slowly until 1965. The U.S. Office of Education reported that, at the beginning of the 1965 fall term, at most 7.5 percent of Negro pupils in the Deep South were attending schools with white children. In Mississippi, it was less than one-half of one percent.

Integration is moving somewhat more rapidly now, proceeding as part of a complex process of social and political readjustment prodded by the passage of the Civil Rights and the Economic Opportunity Acts of 1964, and the Elementary and Secondary Education Act of 1965. (We shall return to these points later.)

The Pros and Cons of School Integration

For the most part Negro parents who have been successful in socio-economic terms believe in integration to such an extent that they seek to live in integrated residential areas and to send their children to integrated schools. There are, however, two groups of Negroes who do not favor integration so strongly. One is the Black Muslim group, which favors completely separate schools and other forms of separation between whites and Negroes. Besides this active and aggressive minority group, there is a large and relatively inarticulate group of Negro parents who feel that their children are at a disadvantage in an integrated school and would rather have "better" segregated schools. It is difficult to estimate the size of this latter group. They are probably most numerous in the South, where there are reports that some Negro parents have petitioned the authorities to allow their children to attend all-Negro schools near home rather than to send them to integrated schools farther from home. (In some cases in these integrated schools the white children have a higher socioeconomic status, and they do so much better work in school that the Negro children are made to feel inferior.) There may be some of this group in the North and West, but they have not been vocal; and in these sections of the country the Negro community has generally supported the leaders of the Civil Rights movement in asking for integrated schools.

It is useful to explore the evidence and the arguments in favor of segregated Negro schools for Negro pupils. One widely quoted publication by Clairette P. Armstrong and A. James Gregor argues that integrated schools cause psychological damage to Negro pupils because such schools tend to 1) make Negro inferiority in school achievement evident to Negro pupils; 2) emphasize the superiority of white culture; 3) cause Negro children to be rejected by white children; and 4) fail to provide Negro models of achievement and authority. These authors conclude that "biracial school experience during a critical developmental period may well play a significant part in the shaping of certain defensive patterns in Negro personality development" (Armstrong and Gregor, 1964). In short, they propose that Negro children are happier and mentally more healthy in all-Negro schools.

On the other hand, the people who favor school integration point out that the argument just given assumes that disadvantaged people are happiest in the conditions with which they are familiar: poverty, lower-class status, ethnic ghetto life, illiteracy. To keep these people happy would be to prevent social or economic progress—a position which most persons would find untenable.

Nevertheless, Negroes in integrated or biracial situations probably are less comfortable today than they are in segregated or uniracial situations. There is some evidence that Negro students in an all-Negro school are better adjusted to school life than Negro students in an interracial school (Pugh, 1943). At the same time, it is pointed out that these students may be purchasing comfort now at the price of later discomfort, when they find themselves at a disadvantage in competing in interracial situations.

The proponents of integration argue that segregation means oppression of the Negro. Pupils should be taught in environments similar to those in which they will later be required to perform. Thus the school should be racially balanced, and the balance should start as early as possible in the life of the child. The proponents of integration argue further that the separate Negro school may protect a system of low standards for Negro pupils. In this event, it becomes an instrument of human oppression. By assigning the "Negro role" of inferiority to both pupils and teachers in segregated Negro schools, segregation makes it "easy" to be a Negro; if Negroes are to make progress, it should be as difficult to be a Negro pupil or teacher as it is to be a white pupil or teacher.

Educational Policies for Negro Youth

There are three different policies regarding the education of Negro pupils. All three are often found operating simultaneously in schools in various parts of the country:

COMPENSATORY EDUCATION FOR SOCIALLY DISADVANTAGED PUPILS. Under the Elementary and Secondary Education Act of 1965 and the Economic Opportunity Act of 1964, large amounts of federal government funds are going into compensatory education for children of low-income families. These funds will pay for better school programs for many Negro pupils, even though at least half of all Negro families will not qualify for such educational programs because their incomes place them above the poverty level. The advantage of the compensatory education concept is that it attempts to compensate the socially disadvantaged child for handicaps that are due to inadequate family training. (See Chapter 6.)

MAINTAIN THE SAME STANDARDS FOR ALL PUPILS. This policy is based on the assumption that much of the retardation of Negro children in school is due to practices which allow them to get along in school without exerting themselves. It is claimed that teachers who hold the stereotype of the "lazy ignorant Negro" do not expect Negro children to learn as much as they expect white children to learn, and that they do not work as hard at teaching Negro children. It is also claimed that segregated schools do not provide adequate books and equipment to teach Negro children effectively. This policy places the blame for poor school achievement of Negro pupils on the school and urges the school to raise the standards of work expected of Negro pupils.

This policy is generally tied to a policy of integration, on the premise that high standards can be more easily maintained in an integrated school than in a segregated Negro school. The disadvantage of this policy is that the family factor tends to be ignored. It tacitly assumes that the experience of a child in the family makes little difference in his school work, and that the differences between children in school achievement are due either to innate biological differences or to differences in what the school does for them.

CREATE AS MANY INTEGRATED SCHOOLS AS POSSIBLE. This policy is based on the assumption that segregated schools are undesirable, and that a variety of devices should be used to increase the numbers of pupils who attend integrated schools. This is now official policy in many school districts, and the several federal educational assistance laws are being interpreted to require as much integration *as possible* where federal funds are to be used.

Strong policy statements on integration have been issued by the boards of education and the superintendents of several major cities, notably New York, Detroit, Pittsburgh and Philadelphia, as well as by the New York State Commissioner of Education. Other educational authorities have been more cautious in their public pronouncements. Southern cities have understandably been very cautious, even though schools in the South are now officially desegregated, and there are no longer any public schools in the United States legally and officially designated as schools for Negroes only or for whites only.

At the same time, *de facto* segregation rules in all big cities due to residential segregation of Negroes. As pointed out in Chapter 10, the actual numbers of Negro children attending schools which are in fact segregated (90 percent or more Negro attendance) are increasing or at least not decreasing markedly during the 1960's.

How Does the School System Promote Integration?

The years since 1954 have seen a wide variety of experiences with integration in the schools. Some programs have gone smoothly, while others have been stormy. The degree to which integration has been accomplished is related to the particular school situation, to the attitudes of the local public, and to the performance by the school staff. There are four types of situations:

1. Schools Where Negroes Are in the Minority and There Is Little Probability of Rapid Increase of Negro Population

This situation exists in many suburban communities, and in small and medium-sized cities which have not recently expanded. In this situation, integration has been relatively uneventful.

An example is the middle-class suburbs of Baltimore where a relatively small number of Negroes live. When desegregation came, a number of Negro children transferred from Banneker Elementary School (all-Negro) to Halethorpe (all-white) and then went on to Catonsville Junior High (all-white). A school principal wrote the following report:

We have the highest percentage of Negro pupils at Halethorpe School of any school in the county, 30 out of 245, but integration has been accomplished without any friction. I can't tell how we have solved our problems, for they have been practically non-existent. I attribute this to the fact that the Negroes at Halethorpe are a very fine group, above the average economically. No one could object to them on the grounds of cleanliness, behavior, habits, or language. Secondly, our teachers were ready and willing to accept them.

I can't prescribe any solution to problems. I shall simply tell the story of integration in our school.

The morning after the Supreme Court handed down its historic decision in May, 1954, as my seventh graders were settling down for work, one asked, "What do you think of what the Supreme Court decided yesterday? Do you think Negroes will come to school here at Halethorpe?"

My answer was simply, "Well, not while you are here. I'm rather sure, however, that before you get through at Catonsville there will be Negroes in your classes." The sixth graders were rather excited. After a few minutes their teacher entered the discussion with, "There is really only one thing for you to worry about. Be sure your work and behavior is as good as theirs when they get here." In the second grade there was considerable talk to which the teacher contributed, "We must be sure not to teach them any bad habits." That was all. The teachers had calmly and simply let the children know they accepted the fact and expected no evil to come of it.

It so happened that our P. T. A. met that night. After the meeting a sixth grade father approached me and asked, "Do you think any Negroes will enter Halethorpe?" My answer was, "I imagine so. After all, there are a good many living on the other side of the Boulevard." He then came back with, "I'll be very sorry to do it, but when a Negro child enters here, I'll have to withdraw my boys." I told him that would be his privilege. He would be perfectly free to enter them in any private school he cared to. When the Negro children arrived this September, this gentleman's older boy had gone on to Catonsville Junior High where he has not yet been faced with the problem. His third grade boy has four Negroes in his class, but I have had no request for Barry's transfer. A major operation suffered by the father during the summer may have caused his pocketbook to influence his mind. And, too, it may have mellowed him. Be that as it may, that one threat in May, 1954, to withdraw a child if non-segregation became a fact was the only one I ever heard.

In June of 1954, a mother of considerable influence and with Southern forebears came to me and said, "Do you think we might get up a petition requesting that Negroes not be entered in our school? Would you sign it?" My reply was, "Of course not. My job is to teach children. I have taught some white ones in my time that I could have cheerfully petitioned someone to remove, but I didn't. Why should I launch a petition against some little children about whom I know nothing objectionable?" If that petition ever went any further, I never heard of it. Occasionally during the school year 1954–1955 a parent would voice some concern to me about what would happen. I always tried to reassure them by reminding them of the fact that the Negroes in Halethorpe were a fine group. No reports of disturbance ever came from their section of the community, and whenever I saw any of the children or young people going along Ridge Avenue to the bus they were always behaving decorously.

Then came the registration days of this September. Mr. Driver had told me at the principals' meeting that about 18 had indicated their intention of transferring from Banneker to Halethorpe. An hour went by that morning of September 1st. No Negroes came. About 10:30 four (Negro) mothers arrived with their children. Our clerk registered them with the same courtesy she extends to everyone. In no way did she treat them any differently. Teachers passing in the hall spoke as casually to them as though there were nothing new in the situation. One little nine-year-old had to wait some time while the younger ones were being registered. A teacher carrying books across the hall asked him to help her. When they left, one mother said to me, "Thank you. This has been easy." There had doubtless been as many, probably more, fears in their minds as in the minds of the whites. During the afternoon and the next day the others came. Ten beginners brought the expected 18 up to 28. After school had been open three days two others came, two who had not signed up for transfer. Their reason was that they had been placed in an annex at Banneker. I suspect they had heard that the other 28 had been accepted just as any other new children were.

In no way at work or play have we been able to see any difference in the way the white children treat the Negroes. One fifth grade white boy was brought in by a Safety Officer before 9 o'clock on the first morning for using an unseemly descriptive word not to, but about "those little blacks" as he termed them. The teacher to whom he was taken gave him a little lecture on the importance of being "white" on the inside. She ended by telling him she would rather have in her class a little boy with a black skin and a "white" heart than one with a white skin and a "black" heart. We have had no other incident of that nature. (Giles, 1959, pp. 89–91.)

Another example of smooth integration is the working of the "Princeton Plan" in some (but not all) situations. Named after Princeton, New Jersey, where it has been carried out successfully, the plan consists of grouping two or three formerly segregated schools into a single attendance unit; sending all the children of certain grades to one school; and sending all the children of other grades to another school. This has worked successfully in situations where the socioeconomic status of the white and Negro groups are rather similar, and where there is no great probability of an expanding Negro population.

2. *Schools Where There Is a Good Prospect of Stabilized Interracial Residence in the Area*

In areas where there is a racial balance and the attitudes of the residents favor integration, the school system can take steps to maintain racial balance in each school within some such range as 30 to 70 percent *white*. This can be done by modifying attendance rules to allow or to encourage children to attend schools outside their immediate neighborhood; and by modifying school boundaries. Sites for new buildings can be chosen to serve areas of stable interracial residence.

3. *Schools in Segregated Negro Residential Areas*

If a Negro residential area becomes large enough to cover a dozen or more elementary school and one or more high school attendance areas, it is very difficult to work toward integrated schooling. Several methods have been tried or proposed in such situations.

Open Attendance. This is now the rule in several cities. Under this arrangement a student can attend any school in the city if there is room for him and if he provides his own transportation. Some cities provide free transportation. While the definition of an "open" school varies greatly from city to city, in general, open attendance in these respective cities has resulted in only some three to six percent of Negro youth leaving segregated Negro schools and going to schools with a white majority. This policy has also permitted a few white children to leave schools that were predominantly Negro and go to schools which are all or nearly all white. It seems clear that the great majority of Negro parents will persist in sending their children to the nearest school, even though it is an all-Negro school. Many cities today have severe over-crowding in schools in Negro residential areas at the same time that empty classrooms exist in some schools in white residential areas. In these cases the board of education may transport Negro pupils to all-white schools as a means of relieving the overcrowding. Much useful experience is being gained concerning viable forms of integrated school-ing as the result of these transportation programs. Many of these programs are meeting difficulties, often due to the different levels of achievement between newcomers who come from low-income families and the local pupils who come from middle-income families.

TRANSPORTING CHILDREN AS A DIRECT MEANS OF ACHIEVING INTE-GRATION. This is advocated by some civil rights groups. This may take the form of providing free transportation for Negro children under a free-choice open-attendance plan. A drastic procedure would be to transport Negro and white pupils to schools according to a plan which would produce integrated schools throughout the city, a plan which would involve transporting some white children to previously all-Negro schools and some Negro children to previously all-white schools. Such a plan has not been seriously considered thus far by any board of education, but it has been viewed as a possible danger by some groups who oppose integration in principle. These groups have sought to influence the community against more conservative forms of integration by claiming that, if the first steps toward integration are taken, the more drastic steps will follow.

PARTIAL VERSUS MONOLITHIC INTEGRATION. It seems clear that inte-gration of schools is closely tied to integration of residential areas. The integration plans which are working most successfully are following a slow, step-by-step method in which local community sentiment deter-mines the speed and extensiveness of integration. The schools work closely with city planning agencies and with urban renewal and public housing agencies. They attempt to anticipate population changes and to adjust school attendance rules to the present and future residential pattern of the city in such ways as to promote integration.

4. Schools Where There Has Formerly Been Legal Segregation

It might be expected that integration would come especially slowly in places where legal and formal segregation of Negro pupils existed up to the 1954 Supreme Court decision. This was hardly the case, however, in the border cities such as Baltimore, Washington, Cincinnati, Louisville, St. Louis, and Kansas City. Though these cities have relatively large Negro populations and large areas of segregated Negro residence, they have moved rapidly toward integration. Furthermore, there has been somewhat less controversy in these cities than in cities farther north where *de facto* segregation has been supported by custom and by attitude.

Farther south, beyond the "border states" integration has gone much more slowly, and by the mid-sixties, had not gone beyond the "token" stage in many communities. The extent of integration in the schools depends largely on the extent to which local sentiment is favorable to integration. On this point there is much variation, with some states much more ready to make changes than other states; and with some cities more ready than others within the same state. Texas has moved more rapidly than Louisiana, for example; and the city of Atlanta is more acceptant of integration than most other cities and towns in Georgia.

It is also a matter of importance who serves on the local board of education and who fills the roles of mayor and chief of police. This is illustrated by the differences between New Orleans and Atlanta a few years ago. At about the same time both school systems were declared to be "integrated" and a few Negro pupils entered previously all-white schools. In New Orleans, a picket line formed outside an elementary school every day for several months, while a solitary Negro girl attended first grade, and while only a handful of white pupils attended the school. The little Negro girl was escorted to and from school every day by a United States marshal, and she was taunted and threatened by the pickets. In Atlanta, where a dozen Negro pupils entered high schools that had been all-white, there were no picketing, no marshals, and no violence.

The school systems were essentially the same in the two cities: public opinion was against integration in both cities; and the school

boards, in their formal actions, behaved similarly in ordering integration. Presumably, however, the mayor, the police chiefs, and school
board members filled their respective roles differently in the two cities,
especially with regard to enforcing the law and preventing disorder. A
series of decisions by these strategically-placed individuals led to quite
different outcomes: decisions which involved encouraging or discouraging
the formation of picket lines, preparing or failing to prepare school
personnel for the forthcoming changes, and accepting or refusing local
responsibility for enforcing the law. It was not the roles themselves that
made the difference, but the people who filled the roles. These people, in
turn, probably reflected the attitudes of powerful civil leaders who were
filling their own roles differently in the two instances.

The Courts and De Facto Segregation

Since the Supreme Court Decision of 1954 there have been a number of
court cases dealing with *de facto* segregation, which was not declared
unconstitutional by the 1954 decision. In general these cases have been
instituted against school boards to force them to take steps toward
school integration in the face of residential segregation. Since 1962 there
have been a number of lawsuits in states outside the South which raise
the following questions:

Do school boards have an affirmative duty under the equal protection
clause of the Fourteenth Amendment to eliminate or reduce racial imbalance
when the imbalance has not been caused by deliberate action of local or state
authorities?

Are the constitutional rights of Negro pupils infringed by *de facto*
segregation which results when a school board, in good faith, adheres to a
neighborhood school policy?

Are the constitutional rights of *white* pupils violated when school
boards take racial factors into account in drawing school boundary lines or
in adopting other plans to reduce racial imbalance in the schools? (NEA,
1954.)

As of 1965, the court decisions in such lawsuits have varied. In
Gary, Indiana, the Federal District Court held that there is nothing in the
law requiring the school to change boundaries when those boundaries
had originally been conscientiously constructed with no purpose of
segregating the races. This decision has been followed by the federal

courts in several subsequent cases, with the U.S. Supreme Court refusing to review these cases.

Other federal courts have decided differently when Negro families claimed that the strict neighborhood school policy violated their constitutional rights. In Manhasset, New York, all Negro elementary-school children, together with a few white children, were enrolled in one of the district's three elementary schools. The court held that the maintenance of neighborhood school attendance lines (by which all Negro elementary school children were separated from 99 percent of white children), coupled with an inflexible no-transfer policy was equivalent to state-imposed segregation in violation of the Fourteenth Amendment. The school board was ordered to discontinue its no-transfer policy with respect to the children in these schools.

The California Supreme Court made a similar ruling in the Pasadena case in 1963. It held that, where there is racial imbalance in the school owing to residential segregation, the right of children to equal opportunity for education and the harmful consequences of segregation require school boards, in so far as is reasonably feasible, to take steps to alleviate the racial imbalance in the schools regardless of the cause.

In New York and New Jersey, the courts have upheld the actions of school boards in fixing boundary lines of schools so as to produce an ethnic balance among students. The New York Court of Appeals distinguished between an *obligation* on the part of the school board to reduce *de facto* segregation and the *right* (not the duty) of the school board to correct racial imbalance. The court held that an otherwise reasonable and lawful zoning plan does not become unlawful because racial factors were taken into consideration. The U.S. Supreme Court declined to review the case. Other New York and New Jersey courts have held that the school board is not prohibited from taking race into account in changing school boundary lines, in carrying out school pairing plans and open enrollment plans designed to correct racial imbalance, and in reducing or eliminating *de facto* segregation in the public schools.

THE MASSACHUSETTS LAW. In 1965 the State of Massachusetts went further than any other state had yet gone by passing a law "providing for the elimination of racial imbalance in the public schools." The law states:

It is hereby declared to be the policy of the commonwealth to encourage all school committees to adopt as educational objectives the promotion of racial balance and the correction of existing racial imbalance in the public schools. The prevention or elimination of racial imbalance shall be an objective in all decisions involving the drawing or altering of school attendance lines and the selection of new school sites. . . .

Whenever the state board of education finds that racial imbalance exists in a public school it shall notify in writing the school committee or regional school district committee having jurisdiction over such school that such finding has been made. The school committee shall thereupon prepare a plan to eliminate such racial imbalance and file a copy of such plan with the board. The term "racial imbalance" refers to a ratio between non-white and other students in public schools which is sharply out of balance with the racial composition of the society in which non-white children study, serve, and work. For the purpose of this section, racial imbalance shall be deemed to exist when the percent of non-white students in any public school is in excess of fifty percent of the total number of students in such school.

Said plan shall detail the changes in existing school attendance districts, the location of proposed school sites, the proposed additions to existing school buildings, and other methods for the elimination of racial imbalance. Said plan shall also include projections of the expected racial composition of all public schools. Any plan to detail changes in existing school attendance districts, the locations of proposed new school sites and proposed additions to existing school sites and proposed additions to existing school buildings with the intention of reducing or eliminating racial imbalance, must take into consideration on an equal basis with the above-mentioned intention, the safety of the children involved in travelling from home to school and school to home. Said plan may provide for voluntary co-operation by other cities and towns in rendering assistance and in making available facilities to effectuate said plan.

No school committee or regional school district committee shall be required as part of its plan to transport any pupil to any school outside of its jurisdiction or to any school outside the school district established for his neighborhood, if the parent or guardian of such pupil files written objection thereto with such school committee. . . .

The school building assistance commission shall . . . increase the amount of grants for schoolhouse construction to sixty-five percent of the approved cost, whenever the board of education is satisfied that the construction or enlargement of a schoolhouse is for the purpose of reducing or eliminating racial imbalance in the school system and so notifies the school building assistance commission. (Commonwealth of Massachusetts, 1965.)

This law can have far-reaching effects on schools in Negro ghettoes which have more than 50 percent Negro pupils. It could require a widespread application of the Princeton Plan, and it could bring about a major revision of the "neighborhood school" concept.

Thus it appears that, as a minimum, school boards will be legally free to develop policies and practices aimed against *de facto* segregation, and they may in some states be required to develop such practices. The maintenance and creation of integrated schools has thus become the business of public education.

Exercises

1. What are the principal intergroup conflicts (economic, ethnic, religious, or racial) in your community? In your school or college? Interview a member of each of the groups in question and obtain their views regarding the ways in which conflict could be alleviated.

2. If you were to teach a classroom of children with mixed nationalities, how would you go about reducing cultural barriers?

3. Work out a teaching unit for elementary or high school on *The Negro in American Life*. What books and pamphlets would you assign students? What topics would you suggest for individual projects? How would you treat contemporary Negro protest movements?

4. Investigate a school which has had a successful program of racial integration. Talk with some of the teachers and parents as well as the principal. Analyze the reasons for success.

5. Investigate a school in which efforts at racial integration have been unsuccessful. What are the reasons for failure?

Suggestions for Further Reading

1. Three articles in the book, *Society and Education: A Book of Readings* (Havighurst, Neugarten, and Falk) provide interesting elaborations of some of the issues of segregation and desegregation in American schools. The paper by Gottlieb and TenHouten illustrates how differing racial compositions within the school affect not only the relationships between Negro and white students, but also the total activity patterns of each racial group. The article by Wolf is a case study of *de facto* segregation in a midwestern city. Howe's article describes a social experiment in education, the Mississippi Freedom Schools established in the summer of 1964, which was an attempt to provide intensive supplementary education for Negroes outside the regular school system.

2. For reports on recent studies and for various points of view on the problems of the disadvantaged Negro, read Silberman, *Crisis in Black*

and White; Clark, *Dark Ghetto;* or Pettigrew, *Profile of the Negro-American.* See also *Youth in the Ghetto,* by Harlem Youth Opportunities Unlimited, Inc.

3. School-community crises with regard to integration have been analyzed by school survey teams working in large cities, such as Odell's *Educational Survey Report* on the Philadelphia Schools; or Havighurst's *The Public Schools of Chicago: A Survey Report.* See also the report of the Commission on School Integration, entitled *Public School Segregation and Integration in the North;* and Klopf and Laster, *Integrating the Urban School.*

4. Smith's book, *They Closed Their Schools,* tells the story of the closing of public schools in Prince Edward County, Virginia, an extreme example of a community which attempted to avoid, then delay, school integration. The story is told in the personal terms of the people involved.

5. Read the booklet entitled "Equality Through Integration," a report on Greenburgh School District No. 8. It describes the ways in which a New York school district, located 25 miles north of New York City, was transformed from one that was segregated and inferior to a model of integrated and quality education. The booklet is distributed by the Anti-Defamation League.

6. For a comprehensive and clearly-written review of the research literature on the effects of desegregation on the intellectual performance of Negroes, read the article by Irwin Katz, "Review of Evidence Relating to Effects of Desegregation on the Intellectual Performance of Negroes," *American Psychologist,* 1964.

7. In 1965 the United States Office of Education commissioned a major study of how Negro children and youth get along in schools in various parts of the country. This study was directed by Professor James S. Coleman, a sociologist at Johns Hopkins University. It has been published under the title, *Equality of Educational Opportunity.*

15 / The Educational Enterprise

in the Changing Society

Given the changing society with its growth in population, its expanding economy, cybernation, metropolitanism, a changing social-status structure, and new relations between racial and ethnic groups, it is inevitable that there are simultaneous major alterations in the organization of the educational enterprise.

Increasing Size of Operating Units

Throughout this century, the individual school, the school system, the college, and the university have all grown bigger. This reflects not only the urbanization of the country, but also the conviction among educators that a big school is better than a small one. As the one-room school is disappearing, so also is the small school district. In the first nationwide survey of local school districts in 1932, the United States Office of Education found 127,244 public school districts (see Table 15.1). The midwestern farm states had thousands of small districts, usually each with three citizens serving as school trustees. Consequently, at that time these states had more members of school boards than they had school teachers. The numbers fell steadily to fewer than 30,000 in 1964. More than 3,000 of these districts in 1964 were "non-operating"; this means they did not operate schools but confined their duties to the collection of tax funds to pay tuition for their children to attend school in neighboring districts (see Table 15.2).

Meanwhile, the average school district increased in school attendance. As Table 15.2 shows, the number of school systems with 1,200

Table 15.1   Changes in School Districts Since 1930

	1931–32	*1961–62*	*1964–65*
No. of Public School Districts	127,244	35,555	28,814
No. of Public School Systems		37,019	29,391
No. of Public Schools	270,000	107,000	
No. of 1-teacher Schools	143,000	13,333	
Total Public School enrollment below college level	26,300,000	38,253,000	42,784,000
Average Enrollment in Systems	202	1,030	1,450

Sources: Biennial Surveys of Education—U.S. Office of Education; and U.S. Office of Education, *Digest of Educational Statistics, 1965.*

Table 15.2   Size of Public School Systems

No. of Pupils in System	*Number of School Systems*		
	1951–52	*1963–64*	*1964–65*
25,000+	58	143	146
12,000–24,999	97	293	307
6,000–11,999	265	774	778
3,000–5,999	611	1,599	1,608
1,200–2,999	1,600	3,522	3,562
600–1,199	3,000	3,210	3,187
300–599	4,400	2,663	2,641
150–299	5,047 ⎫		
50–149	7,902 ⎬	15,559	13,762
1–49	34,400 ⎭		
Non-operating School Districts	10,000	3,942	3,400
Total	67,380	31,705	29,391

Source: U.S. Office of Education, Progress of Public Education in the United States; Annual Reports, *Digest of Educational Statistics, 1965.*

or more pupils has more than doubled in the last decade. This results partly from the sharp rise in school enrollments after 1952, when the post-war birth rate began to affect the schools. Many school systems passed the 1,200 mark in enrollment even though their towns or cities did not show much increase of population. While the number of large school districts with 25,000 or more pupils has increased, the most rapid growth is in systems of 1,200 to 12,000, reflecting the growth of small and medium-sized cities, especially in suburban areas.

Consolidation of rural elementary schools together with the growing urbanization of the country slowly increased the size of high schools. The average high school had 87 students in 1900; 234 in 1930; and 460 in 1960.

Colleges and universities grew in even more striking fashion. In 1900 the average size of 977 colleges and universities was 243 students. By 1930 the average was 780, and by 1962 it was 2,010. During this period the number of small institutions varied considerably, but there was a steady growth in medium-sized and large institutions. By the autumn of 1961, there were 85 universities each with 10,000 or more degree-credit students.

Evaluation of School Size

When the members of President Eisenhower's Commission on National Goals recommended that the number of school districts should be reduced to 10,000 by 1970, they were saying, in effect, that the one-room school should disappear altogether. Consolidation of school districts will continue to the point where in the near future there will hardly be a school system with less than 300 pupils.

At the other end of the scale it is difficult to predict the future size of the large school systems. Certainly more cities will reach a size where they have more than 25,000 pupils (the number of such cities doubled between 1950 and 1960); but the suburbs will continue to grow, and their medium-sized school systems will drain off some of the city's school population. Probably some sort of metropolitan area school district will develop, responsible for a hundred thousand to a million pupils. If so, it is doubtful that this kind of district will operate under one central administration as does the big-city district today. More probably there will be a decentralization of administration into districts with 10 to 25 thousand elementary and secondary school pupils. There is likely to be a continued search for the optimum size of a school district.

THE HIGH SCHOOL. High schools will continue for a time to grow to a larger average size through the elimination of smaller schools. However, it is doubtful that schools with less than 500 pupils will disappear, as has been urged by James B. Conant (1959). A community of some 6 to 10 thousand is required to provide pupils for a four-year high school of 500 pupils. Communities smaller than 6,000 are not likely to disappear, nor are they likely to give up their own local high schools. Probably a number of devices for introducing outside help for the more advanced high school students in small communities will be developed instead, devices such as television, teaching machines, and short-term courses of a special nature. Regional vocational high schools will probably come into being to serve more than one rural county.

A recent study of a small high school compared with a large one challenges the recommendations made by Conant. Barker *et al.* (1962) studied the actual participation of students in various high school activities outside the regular classroom, and found that the average student in the small school took greater part in musical activities, dramatics, school clubs, journalism, and athletics. Furthermore, while the large school presumably offers a number of special or advanced courses not available in a small school, and while it may have a better library, its classes may be larger and be conducted in such a way that a student gets little personal contact with the teacher.

THE COLLEGE AND UNIVERSITY. At the level of higher education the average school size will no doubt increase, but to a limited extent. The number of universities with more than 10,000 students on a single campus is not likely to grow very much since no one seems to be in favor of huge student bodies. To maintain efficiency as well as economy the large public universities will probably continue to sub-divide into branches in different locations or into systems of coordinated institutions, following the trend in this direction already established in the past decade.

Another reason that average size will not increase very much is that colleges with enrollments as low as 200 seem to be viable. Quite a number of liberal arts colleges of 200 to 500 students are doing very well in the 1960's, meeting the expectations of faculty as well as those of students and alumni, and many of these colleges will not try to increase in size. In 1962, the 481 Protestant church-related colleges had an average enrollment of 782; and the 334 Roman Catholic colleges averaged 1,057 in enrollment.

Increasing Financial Investment in Education

During the current century there has been a great increase in the funds spent on education.

Traditionally, American schools have been financed locally. Even though the states had responsibility for a system of public education, they generally passed this responsibility on to the local community—town, township, or county. In the field of higher education the states were slow to move, though most of them were supporting a university by 1900.

In 1929 public school education was supported 75 percent by local school districts. Then local schools began to be supported from state funds, with federal funds limited to assisting vocational education. By 1962, local districts were paying only 55 percent of the cost of public elementary and secondary education; the states were paying 40 percent; and the federal government, 5 percent.

The relation of educational costs to national product is shown in Table 15.3. Approximately three times as much of the national product was spent on education in 1960 as was spent in 1900. In relation to

Table 15.3   Cost of Education in the United States, 1900–1964
(In Millions of Dollars, Current Prices)

School Year	Elementary Schools	Secondary Schools	Colleges and Universities	Total	Gross National Product (In Billions of Dollars)	Percent of GNP
1899–1900	233	19	40	292	17	1.66
1929–30	1,950	750	535	3,233	104	3.1
1959–60	12,590	5,435	6,616	24,700	483	5.1
1963–64	24,900		11,000	35,900	585	6.1
1964–65	26,900		12,100	39,000	623	6.3

Note: The gross national product is for the calendar year in which the school year commences.

Sources: U.S. Office of Education, *Digest of Educational Statistics, 1965,* and Schultz, 1960.

dollars of constant purchasing power, the resources allocated to education were multiplied twenty times between 1900 and 1956. According to many economists this was an investment in the development of human capital that paid very good dividends (Schultz, 1960, 1963). People obtained more education; they become more efficient producers, increased their own earning power, and increased the productivity of the economy in which they worked. With about six percent of the gross national product now going into education, the United States invests relatively more in education than most other countries.

Research and Development

In any catalogue of major social changes of the twentieth century the emergence of "research and development" stands out as an important phenomenon. While some industrial corporations have maintained research laboratories for several decades, the amount of money spent on research in this country hardly reached a billion dollars a year in 1940.

It was during World War II that the federal government began to spend large sums of money on research and development for military purposes. This federal program has been continued and expanded since the war into three categories:

1. Basic research—fundamental scientific investigation aimed at increasing knowledge.
2. Applied research—knowledge applied to a practical objective.
3. Development—designing and testing of new products and processes.

In relation to the Gross National Product, national expenditures on research and development grew from 1.02 percent in 1950 to 2.78 percent in 1960, and to an estimated 3 percent in 1964.

While private industry has done far more research and development work than either government or universities, the universities have been rapidly increasing their basic research programs, supported in the main by federal funds. The research budget of American universities was 4 percent of their total expenditures in 1940 as compared to 20 percent in 1960. This research is being carried out in some 10 percent of the institutions of higher education.

Research and Development in Education

The success of American industry since World War II in using research and development to increase productivity and efficiency has caused educators to think along the same lines. Following the patterns of government support for research in other fields, in 1960 the United States Office of Education (through its Cooperative Research Program) and the National Science Foundation were devoting millions of dollars annually to research and development in school and college curricula.

It is difficult to estimate the amount of research and development money spent specifically in the field of education, since it is difficult to draw a line between education and other fields such as mental health or vocational development and rehabilitation. However, the best estimates are that no more than five million dollars a year was being spent on educational research in 1930, including stipends for graduate students for research in education. Very few universities had budgets for educational research; and there were only a few experimental or laboratory schools where a part of the budget could be charged to research and demonstration.

From 1930 to World War II it is doubtful that the annual expenditure on educational research increased very much. There were several private foundations supporting research in education, but the total money spent on such programs did not exceed two million dollars a year during this period.

After World War II several private foundations began spending more money in educational research and development, notably the Ford Foundation. Still the annual expenditure probably did not surpass ten million dollars a year until after 1955 when the federal government came into the field and when support for educational research and development shifted. The federal government began to allocate substantial funds for educational research, and congressional committees, rather than educators, have had direct control over the areas to be supported. This fact would probably have produced more discontent among educators had the amounts spent on educational research and development not multiplied at the same time. Priorities have tended to go to education in the physical sciences; then to mathematics and foreign languages. The social sciences have been lower on the list of priorities, and the humanities lowest of all, although significant federal support in the last two areas is beginning to appear.

The pattern of support may change as studies of the effects of federal government support on higher education become more numerous and their findings become better known. With the establishment by Congress of the National Humanities and Arts Foundation, government support of education will certainly increase in the fields of arts and humanities.

One trend which counteracts the influence of the federal government in education is the growth of research and development departments in local school systems. Most cities of a hundred thousand or more now have a professional research and development staff to help the local schools adopt new practices and put new policies into effect. The Committee on Instruction of the National Education Association has recommended that local school systems devote one percent of their annual budgets to this purpose. Where the local school system is too small to support a research department, a county office may be established; or the state department of education may develop a state-wide research and development program for the smaller school systems.

The Federal Government and Education

Up to the 1950's federal support of education was slow and limited largely to support of vocational education. As already indicated the government plunged into the support of education and of educational research after 1955. In 1963 Congresswoman Edith Green, Chairman of the House Special Subcommittee on Education, reported that the federal government's education activities cost $2.2 billion in fiscal 1962, or seven percent of the total national outlay for education, public and private (Green, 1964, p. 15). Soon thereafter came new legislation to increase the federal expenditures. The Higher Education Facilities Act of 1963, the Vocational Education Act of 1963, the Manpower Development and Training Act, the expanded National Defense Education Act, the Higher Education Act of 1965, and the Elementary and Secondary Act of 1965 all added new money for education, while expanded budgets for the National Science Foundation, the National Institutes of Health, and the National Aeronautic and Space Administration provided large additional sums for research and training of researchers. By 1966 the federal government was spending some $4.5 billion on education and research in educational institutions, or 13 percent of the total national bill.

Except for support of vocational education, none of this money was for basic support of established school or college programs. Instead, it was for expansion of educational services, for improvement of education, and for direct support to graduate and undergraduate students.

By 1966 it was possible to describe an emergent policy on federal aid and participation in education. The federal government was assisting education in the following ways:

1. INNOVATION AND IMPROVEMENT. The government seems now to be ready to work through a number of different programs of educational research and development, with money administered by the United States Office of Education, or the National Science Foundation. For example, four major centers of educational research and development were founded in the early 1960's at Harvard, the University of Pittsburgh, the University of Wisconsin, and the University of Oregon. Continuing along this line, the Education Act of 1965 provided one hundred million dollars to give initial support to a number of regional centers for educational research and development. It is likely that thirty to forty such centers will be established by 1970.

2. TRAINING OF PERSONNEL. Money for the advanced training of various specialists is fairly readily supplied by the federal government. Most of this money goes for training research workers in the natural sciences, but substantial sums have also been provided through the United States Office of Education and the National Defense Education Act for training school counselors, and for the re-training of classroom teachers in science, mathematics, foreign languages, and work with handicapped children.

3. EDUCATION OF THE UNDERPRIVILEGED AND THE HANDICAPPED. Provision will continue to be made by the federal government for education and rehabilitation of physically handicapped people; retraining of people who have lost their employment through automation; education of adult illiterates; work-experience and related education for unemployed youth; compensatory education for pre-school and school-age children from socially disadvantaged families. It also provides funds for research on the causes of mental deficiency.

4. COLLEGES AND UNIVERSITIES. At the level of higher education the federal government has given direct support to both public and private universities and colleges through programs of scholarships and fellowships, through direct grants and loans for buildings, and through grants

for research. By 1962 the federal government was supplying 25 percent of the total income to colleges and universities. Almost half of this federal support goes for research projects and research facilities. An additional fourth goes to students in the form of training grants or fellowships.

Agencies of Federal Aid

The principal agencies for federal aid to education are the United States Office of Education and the National Science Foundation, with the National Humanities and Arts Foundation as a potentially strong future organization. One of the important problems of government policy during the next five years is to work out an efficient division of labor and responsibility among these agencies.

THE NATIONAL SCIENCE FOUNDATION. For 1964–65 the National Science Foundation received $420 million, its largest budget to that date. The bulk of this money goes to universities for the support of research and training in the sciences. However, a considerable sum goes to projects for the improvement of education in secondary schools in the sciences and mathematics. The NSF has supported the secondary school programs of the Physical Sciences Study Committee, the Biological Sciences Curriculum Study, the Chemical Education Materials Study, the Chemical Bond Approach Project, and the School Mathematics Study Group.

THE UNITED OFFICE OF EDUCATION. Since 1955 the United States Office of Education has been administering large funds under the National Defense Education Act, the Vocational Education Act of 1963, the Higher Education Facilities Act, and the Elementary and Secondary Education Act of 1965. In addition, the USOE administers the Cooperative Research Program in which grants are made to universities for research on educational problems. These grants were first limited to problems of mental retardation, then expanded to research on gifted children, and later extended to cover a variety of aspects of education, including international comparisons of educational methods and educational efficiency. The Office of Education has become a larger source of funds for educational experimentation than such private foundations as the Ford Foundation, the Kellogg Foundation, and the Carnegie Corporation.

Policy Makers in Education

Although the responsibility for public education resides in the fifty states, each an autonomous authority in educational matters, power has been delegated in most states to the trustees or members of the boards of education in local or county districts. In the United States there is a greater degree of local community responsibility for education, both for financial support and for determination of educational policy, than is true of any other modern nation.

Local School Boards

School trustees are usually elected by the voters of the local district, but occasionally they are appointed by the mayor or some other public official. In the vast majority of urban school districts, the members of the school board have been upper-middle-class men and women.

In recent years there have been certain changes in the socioeconomic composition of city school boards. It is becoming fairly frequent to have one or two representatives of organized labor on the school board. In small cities the labor representative may be a blue-collar worker. In the larger cities the labor representatives are likely to be union officials who have themselves been working men but who are now living in middle-class neighborhoods, receiving middle-class salaries, and sending their children to college. At the same time, several studies made in the late 1950's in various parts of the country indicated that, in general, school boards were made up increasingly, rather than decreasingly, of persons from upper socioeconomic levels (Albert, 1959; Caughran, 1956; Eaton, 1956; Teal, 1956).

In general, members of school boards attempt to represent the entire community as well as they know how. For example, a study of the records of 172 board members in twelve western cities from the period 1931–1940 showed "little or no relationship between certain social and economic factors and school board competence" as judged by a panel of professional educators who studied the voting records on educational issues (Campbell, 1945). Nor does the high social status of school board members generally seem correlated with conservative attitudes toward education. In some instances, no relationships were found between these two sets of factors; in other instances, higher educational and occupational levels of school board members were associated with the relatively liberal attitudes. ·

Government Controls

The state governments exert control over the public educational system through various legislative actions. For example, by establishing licensing laws requiring that a teacher meet certain educational requirements, the state government controls the admission of people to positions as teachers in public schools.

A more direct control of educational policy is exerted by a government if it requires certain political beliefs of those who teach in the schools. For example, the German Nazis in 1937 required all teachers in the schools of Germany to become members of the Nazi party; and in the Soviet Union teachers are required to subscribe to communist political views. In the United States there has been no requirement of membership in any political party or of agreement with any particular political philosophy, but there has occasionally been a requirement of nonmembership in certain unpopular organizations. For instance, in 1826 when there was strong feeling against the Masons in certain parts of the country, the Antimasonic Party was formed, and it grew so strong in the state of New York that it was practically impossible for a member of the Masons to hold a state job or to be elected to state office. In the period after 1945, several states passed laws requiring nonmembership in the Communist Party or in the organizations that were designated by the Attorney General as subversive. One effect of such requirements is to bar from teaching a few people who may hold subversive political views. Another effect is to bar from teaching a larger number whose political and economic views, when judged a few years earlier or a few years later, might be seen neither as subversive nor dangerous, but merely as unpopular or nonconformist.

State governments exert direct control over the content of education in public schools by laws that require or forbid the teaching of certain subjects. For instance, many states have laws that require the teaching of civics or government and American history. Many states require their schools to teach the alleged harmful effects of tobacco and alcohol; some have laws forbidding the teaching of the theory of biological evolution.

In general, however, the degree of legislative control over the content of education has not been great in the United States, and the selection of curricular content has been left largely to educators.

NATIONAL VS. STATE RESPONSIBILITY. The period from 1930 to 1965 saw a steady growth of participation and financial support by the federal government in the process of urbanization and metropolitanization, and in the conduct of public business, including education.

At the same time there was a general reluctance to accept this trend without exploring other alternatives, one of which was to build up the competence of state government and other state institutions to meet emerging social needs on a decentralized basis. In the field of education there was an influential group that favored the build-up of state departments of education and other state agencies. For example, after making a national study of teacher education, James B. Conant (1963) argued for state autonomy and initiative in the planning of educational development, with informal cooperation among the states. Among political scientists there is a general agreement that emerging needs will be better met by strengthening and modernizing state governments than by greater reliance on the national government.

Since about 1955 there has been active interest by representatives of state and national government in working out more efficient state government performance with respect to metropolitan area problems and with respect to state-wide planning (Council of State Governments, 1962; Advisory Commission on Intergovernmental Relations, 1961). While education has not been singled out as a specific area in need of state government attention, the general revival of state government enterprise has affected education. A number of states have established commissions to survey educational needs at the higher education and the common school levels, and are reorganizing their state departments of education to take the lead in improving local and county school systems. The 1965 Elementary and Secondary Education Act provided funds to assist state departments of education.

If the state educational organizations succeed in leading metropolitan areas to more effective internal cooperation, in helping rural school districts to consolidate efficiently, and in helping small city school systems to modernize, they are likely to be given popular support as well as liberal federal financing. In this case, the role of federal government is likely to be limited to providing financial support of education through the states, rather than undertaking more direct support of education.

"Public Interest" Groups

Educational policies are formed by various groups who are officially or unofficially appointed to act in the public interest. One such group that holds major responsibility for educational legislation is the state legislature. Another is a commission of laymen or educators appointed to study an educational problem and to make recommendations.

Inevitably, the trustees and officers of the great educational foundations exert an influence on education by their support or non-support of various educational programs, experiments, and demonstrations.

Finally there are the parents' organizations and the laymen's organizations such as the National Association of Parents and Teachers, and the Citizens Committee on Public Schools. These groups, like the others mentioned here, usually have upper-middle-class leadership and predominantly middle-class membership. In some instances they may be unaware of lower-class values and consequently may fail to take them into account; but there is very little conscious espousal of the interests of any one social class. The people who make decisions in education tend to think of themselves as trustees for the entire society.

Growth of National Educational Organizations

As the American educational system developed during the nineteenth century, it became clear that the schools and colleges were not to be administered or controlled by the national government. The common schools were left to local responsibility, except for the maintenance of minimum standards by state officials. Only a few states such as Massachusetts and New York used state departments of education for stimulation and coordination. Higher education was largely in the hands of private groups. One could hardly speak of *an* American system of education.

At the same time, the need for coordination on a national or regional scale was recognized, and voluntary organizations appeared in large numbers shortly after the turn of the century. The emergence of these organizations is shown in Table 15.4. The great majority of these associations are national in scope. They signify a sense of national unity which came into being without any pressure from the national government. (Most of these organizations, however, have set up their national offices in Washington, D.C.)

Table 15.4   Emergence of National and Regional Organizations
in Education

Name	Date of Initiation
National Education Association	1857
American Association of School Administrators	1865
Regional Accrediting Associations of Colleges and Secondary Schools:	
New England Association	1886
Middle States Association	1887
North Central Association	1895
Southern Association	1895
Northwest Association	1917
Western Association	1948
College Entrance Examination Board	1900
Association of American Universities	1920
National Catholic Education Association	1904
Association of Urban Universities	1914
Association of American Colleges	1900
American Federation of Teachers	1916
American Council on Education	1918
American Association of Teachers Colleges	1918
Progressive Education Association	1919
American Association of Junior Colleges	1920
American Association for Adult Education	1926
Council of Chief State School Officers	1928
Educational Policies Commission	1934
National Teacher Examination Service	c. 1940
National Commission on Teacher Education and Professional Standards	1946
American Association of Colleges for Teacher Education	1946
American Personnel and Guidance Association	1952

THE NATIONAL EDUCATION ASSOCIATION. The first of the voluntary
organizations, and the largest of all, was founded in the nineteenth
century. The National Education Association became the organizational
center of the public school interests of the country. Practically from its
beginning it has concerned itself with the quality and content of
education, and through a series of commissions it has made most of the
major pronouncements about educational policy that have been made in
this country.

Based in a loose way on state education associations, the NEA
consists more of a federation of *functional* organizations than of state

organizations. They include: the Association of Elementary School Principals; Association of Secondary School Principals; Association for Supervision and Curriculum Development; National Council of the Social Studies; National Association of Science Teachers; Association for Higher Education; Association for Childhood Education.

THE AMERICAN COUNCIL ON EDUCATION. Parallel in its influence to the National Education Association is the American Council on Education, which is made up of public and private institutions and organizations.

The Council was founded in 1918, at the same time that the National Research Council and the Social Science Research Council were formed, primarily to assist the government in organizing the resources of universities for the conduct of World War I. The war was over before much was accomplished, but the three Councils remained in existence. The two science councils attracted support from such private foundations as the Rockefeller Foundation and the Carnegie Corporation, and together with the American Council of Learned Societies became the representatives of scholarship in the United States. The American Council on Education, on the other hand, did not at first attract much support from foundations or from universities. Not until the Depression of the 1930's forced the institutions of higher education into a measure of national cooperation did the American Council find its function. By 1940 the ACE filled a secure place in the national scene as the representative of both public and private supported higher education.

The Federal Government and Educational Policy-Making

With the growing strength of the NEA, the ACE, and other national organizations, government agencies were kept in a relatively weak position as far as policy-making goes, even though the government agencies were spending large sums of money in the fields of education and research. By 1945 the non-governmental organizations were well stabilized, as far as their internal relationships and functions were concerned. Then came the post-war period with its enormous expansion of education and with its problems of educational policy. These problems affected and stimulated all educational organizations, and made them more sensitive to national needs and policies. Since 1960, the federal government has supported two major educational policy-making bodies, the National Science Foundation and the U.S. Office of Education, neither of which had a policy-making function four years earlier. With the responsibility of allocating large sums for educational research and development, the choices made by these agencies of what to support are bound to have an influence on educational policy. Some of the policy questions now directly affected by federal government action are:

What directions should vocational education take in the light of contemporary trends in the labor force?

What should educational agencies do about unemployed youth in the age range 16–21?

Should public education extend downward below age five for children of socially disadvantaged families?

How should science and mathematics be taught in the elementary and secondary schools?

What proportion of college-age youth should go to college?

Should the federal government concentrate aid for scientific research and training in a small number of leading universities, or should the government deliberately assist average universities to improve their research and training programs?

According to the report by Representative Edith Green (see page 392) there were in 1963 forty-two government agencies and departments involved in educational activities. Some of these programs overlap and some are administered with little or no knowledge of other similar government programs. Mrs. Green proposed:

1. Creation, within the executive branch of the government, of an Inter-agency Council on Education to coordinate the educational activities of all Federal agencies and departments.
2. Creation of a nonlegislative Joint Congressional Committee on Education in order to provide the Congress with an overall picture of Federal educational activities and education needs.
3. Combining the Office of Education and the National Science Foundation, the only two agencies of the Federal Government whose primary concern is education. (Green, 1964, pp. 28–29.)

Another proposal is that the National Science Foundation should take responsibility for higher and graduate education, while the Office of Education should take responsibility for elementary and secondary education. The coming of the National Humanities and Arts Foundation, although welcome to most educators, will further complicate the picture with regard to policy-making.

The stronger non-governmental organizations are now adjusting to the emergence of policy-making activities within the federal government.

As the National Science Foundation, the National Institutes of Health, and the Office of Education allocate large sums of money, they are drawn inevitably into the act of making policy. They find, however, that policy is already being made by educational institutions acting in voluntary associations. Thus there is presently a balance of power in policy-making between federal agencies and voluntary educational associations. It is difficult to predict how this balance will swing during the coming decades. A strong tradition supports the voluntary associations, and they are equipped by organization and leadership to perform the function of policy making. On the other hand, the federal government's responsibility is growing greater and federal agencies are likely to push for a larger role in policy-making.

Exercises

1. Study the composition of the board of education in your local community. How are its members selected? Do they adequately reflect the various socioeconomic, ethnic, and racial groups in the community? How do these factors affect their decisions on education?

2. How does your state department of education influence or control the quality of education in the local communities? Does the state help the educational process in the local communities? How?

3. How has your state responded to the demand for expanded higher education? Is there a state system of colleges and universities? How is it organized? What recent developments have taken place?

4. Give several reasons why you think that the federal government should take a *more* active role in education. Give several reasons why you think the federal government should take a *less* active role in education.

Suggested Readings

1. Francis Keppel, one of this country's most effective Commissioners of Education, stayed in office less than four years. His book, *The Necessary Revolution in American Education,* depicts his view of the functions of the federal government in the field of education.

2. The United States Office of Education publishes annually a *Digest of Educational Statistics.* During the rest of this term, read the most re-

cent edition to learn what kinds of information you may expect to get from this source.

3. The play, *Inherit the Wind,* by Jerome Lawrence and Robert E. Lee, is a fictionalized account of an actual situation in which school curricula were affected by social and governmental controls.

4. Several articles in *Society and Education: A Book of Readings* (Havighurst, Neugarten, and Falk) show the effects of the wider society upon education. The articles by Corwin and by Robinson discuss pressure groups and their relation to the schools. Campbell and Bunnell analyse the impact of national programs upon the schools. The paper by Donald Michael speculates upon the possible effects of technological innovations on people's lives and their value patterns in the next two decades.

PART 5

THE TEACHER

16 / The Social Origins

of Teachers

The Choice of Teaching as an Occupation

There are many different factors involved in choosing an occupation. For some persons teaching may be regarded as a highly respectable occupation, one that will increase the individual's prestige in the community. For others, it may be seen as an opportunity to lead a life of service. For still others, teaching may be seen primarily as an occupation that offers short working hours, long vacations, and long-term security.

Psychological Factors

In general, one set of factors is psychological in nature. Individuals have different psychological needs, some of them conscious, some of them unconscious, that may be met in the teaching situation. One man or woman has a need for affection that is gratified by relating to children; another may have the need to wield power over others. Another, having formed a strong identification with a teacher in his own childhood, may have always longed to be a teacher. Another has a strong love of a particular subject and is happiest when teaching and learning about English literature, science, or woodworking.

Social Factors

The psychological factors are always intimately related in terms of both cause and effect, to social factors. In a family where one or both parents are teachers, the child may have been influenced from his earliest years toward the choice of teaching as an occupation. In another family, where parents have had little schooling themselves, there may be parental pressure to select teaching as the best route to a better life. Some persons, in deciding to enter the teaching field, are strongly influenced by peers; others are influenced by teachers or other adults. A middle-aged woman, for example, seeing other women at work, may go back to teaching when her own children grow up and leave home.

Interaction of Factors Determining Choice

Some persons select teaching as their occupational goal relatively early in life and plan their college years accordingly. Others make their decision relatively late, and seem—at least, from a superficial point of view—to enter teaching almost by accident. This is often the case with the wife of a graduate student who goes into teaching for a few years as a means of helping her husband through school.

   Whatever the particular factors that operate in any individual case, there is always a variety of psychological and social factors interacting to produce a vocational choice, as is illustrated in this man's case:

   As far back as I can remember I was interested in mechanical devices and enjoyed working with tools. At first I worked with simple things such as toys, roller skates, and bicycles, forever taking them apart and repairing them. As I grew older my interest centered on more complex machines. I worked with electricity and electrical gadgets. About 1920 radio was becoming important. For several years my main interest was radio.

   When I was fifteen years old I became intensely interested in automobiles and their repair. At this point my father and mother began to object. They could not tolerate the grease and dirt I brought home after working on a car. They were also worried about the dangers involved when working on these heavy machines. My father was a businessman and he felt that I belonged in business with him when I had finished school.

   "Why do you want to become an auto mechanic? No one in our whole family has ever been a mechanic! Manual labor is not what we want you to do," they stormed. They cited as examples some of the mechanics and tradesmen we knew, and I must admit some of them were pretty rough characters. But this did not deter me. I worked part time after school in a neighborhood garage.

   By the time I graduated from high school I had definitely decided that automechanics was my future. My parents were furious.

   "Why don't you go to college like your two brothers did?" they demanded. "Don't you want to be somebody?"

I guess I was pretty obstinate because instead of going to college I got a full-time job as a mechanic. After about a year my enthusiasm began to wane. I still was interested in automobiles, but the working conditions of thirty years ago were poor. I found that I could not tolerate these drawbacks: (1) The people I had to work with used foul language. (2) There were many heavy drinkers on this job. (3) The physical strain was great. My hands were a mess. I couldn't possibly keep them clean, and I was embarrassed when I went out on a date. (4) The dangers were many. Several times I nearly lost a finger. (5) There was little security.

I knew that I would have to do something else; yet I wanted to remain in the automotive field because I still found it the most interesting. The answer was not long in coming. I met a young high school teacher who taught shop in the city school system. HE pointed out that I could probably be placed as an auto-shop teacher if I could meet the requirements. I went to the Board of Education and was told what I would have to do to become a shop teacher. I registered at the University and started my preparation. My parents were happy again. I too was happy because now I could work with people like myself and still use my interest and skills to best advantage.

Within society as a whole, there are economic and social factors that influence persons in their choice of teaching as an occupation. One is the need for teachers. As the need increases, more effort is made to recruit teachers through high school and college "career orientation" programs and career counseling, through radio and television programs, through books, newspapers, and magazines. In times of economic depression teaching offered greater opportunities for economic security than other occupations, despite low salaries. In times of economic expansion, teaching may offer relatively less opportunity for economic advancement than other occupations. In the present decade, with the growth of international aid programs, such as the Peace Corps, and government programs to combat poverty, many persons elect teaching as an effective means of serving underdeveloped or underprivileged groups and helping to bring about social change.

Other factors are related to marriage and birth rates. As the birth rate increases, more teachers are needed. At the same time, as persons are now marrying at earlier ages and having children at earlier ages (the median age of marriage for women in America has been dropping, and is now 20), many young women do not enter the teaching field who in another period might have done so.

Another of the social factors related to the choice of teaching as an occupation is that of social status. Teaching is more or less attractive to persons of different social levels; and the teaching profession in America has drawn, at different periods of time, different proportions of people from various social backgrounds.

Increasing Heterogeneity in Social-Class Origins

In the decades prior to 1920, teachers were recruited in large numbers from middle-class urban families, and from rural families of upper-middle and lower-middle class. Relative to the general population, persons who entered the teaching field had large amounts of formal schooling and more often than not were persons who regarded teaching as a calling. In those years, teaching was one of the few occupations available to respectable and educated women; as the schoolmaster made way for the schoolmarm, a sizable number of teachers were women from upper-middle-class and upper-class backgrounds. While teaching has always offered an avenue of opportunity for certain groups of young people, especially rural groups, the overall proportion of teachers who came from lower-status levels was probably smaller some decades ago than at present.

As America became increasingly urban; as the educational system mushroomed, with greater need for teachers, with the growth of teacher-training institutions, and with an increasing proportion of young people obtaining college educations; and as more occupations became available to women, the social composition of the teaching profession changed.

A number of studies have been made of various groups of teachers and of various groups of students preparing to be teachers. While these studies show that there is considerable variability according to the region of the country and according to the size and the type of college attended, nevertheless they indicate that a large group of teachers is still drawn from business and professional families and that significant proportions come from farm families and from skilled laborers' families. The overall majority, however, is coming increasingly from lower-middle and upper-working classes.

A few such studies may serve as illustrations: As early as 1927, in a study of students attending midwestern teachers' colleges, it was found that over half came from working-class and farm backgrounds (Whitney, 1927). By 1939, Elsbree, in his book *The American Teacher,* was describing teachers as being predominantly lower-middle class in origin (Elsbree, 1939). In 1941, Greenhoe's study of over 9,000 public-school teachers, selected as a national sample, showed 38 percent whose fathers were farmers, 26 percent whose fathers were engaged in small businesses, 18 percent whose fathers were day-laborers, and only 4 percent whose fathers were professional men (Greenhoe, 1941). In 1948, a study of seniors in education at the University of Michigan showed a bare majority coming from white-collar families (Best, 1948). In 1950, studies of students in a teachers' college in Chicago showed a majority coming from lower-middle-class families (Valentine, 1950; Wagenschein, 1950).

In more recent years, there has been a further increase in the heterogeneity of social backgrounds, with the most pronounced changes being a drop in the number of teachers from farm families (although teachers' colleges outside the large cities still show a large proportion of farm youth) and an increase in the number from urban working-class homes.

Table 16.1 shows the distribution by age and family origin of a national sample of teachers drawn in 1960–61. Of the total group, about 27 percent came from farm families and 30 percent from blue-collar families (i.e., their fathers were unskilled, semiskilled, or skilled workers). However, these proportions are quite different in different age groups. For example, of the oldest teachers, those aged 56 and over,

Table 16.1   Distribution of teachers by father's occupation and by age

OCCUPATION OF TEACHER'S FATHER	Ages 56 or older	Ages 46–55	Ages 36–45	Ages 26–35	Age under 26	Total
Farmer	39.2%	34.5%	28.7%	13.9%	20.3%	26.5%
Skilled or semi-skilled worker	14.4	22.8	24.0	27.9	23.6	23.4
Managerial or self-employed	23.6	18.7	21.7	24.6	21.9	22.0
Professional or semiprofessional	11.8	13.8	14.7	13.6	20.3	14.5
Clerical or sales worker	9.1	5.2	6.0	9.2	6.3	7.1
Unskilled worker	1.9	5.0	4.9	10.8	7.6	6.5
	100.0%	100.0%	100.0%	100.0%	100.0%	100.0%
Number reporting	263	464	387	509	237	1,860

Source: National Education Association, April, 1963, p. 16 (adapted).

almost 40 percent came from farm families; while of the youngest teachers, those under age 26, only 20 percent came from farm families.

These figures are for the country at large. Differences exist between large school systems and small. In the largest school systems, the proportion of teachers who come from farm families is much lower and the proportion from urban working-class families is much higher than the national averages. As can be seen from the detailed listing of fathers' occupations of teachers in the Chicago public schools in 1964, less than five percent came from farms, while almost half came from working-class homes (see Table 16.2).

Table 16.2   Occupations of fathers of Chicago Public School teachers (percentages)

Category	Elementary school	High school
Farm laborer	0.5	0.5
Laborer, not farm	5	4
Farm renter	0.5	0.5
Semiskilled worker	12	9
Skilled worker	14	16
Foreman and similar	17	14
Office worker	5	6
Store clerk	1	1
Farm owner	3	4
Small business owner	16	17
Salesman of insurance, etc.	6	5
School teacher	4	4
Doctor, lawyer, other professions	12	13
Business manager or owner	5	6
Number	6,930	3,713

Source: Havighurst, 1964, p. 417.

Social Mobility Among Teachers

The social origin of a teacher is not, of course, synonymous with his social status as an adult. It is one thing to describe the social status of the families from which teachers come; another thing to describe the social status that teachers occupy once they have become established in the teaching profession.

Factors Affecting Social Status

When judged in terms of social participation, the social status of the teacher will vary to some extent, depending upon a number of factors—his social origin, the community in which he teaches, the extent and type of his social interactions, the extent to which he participates in community affairs, and so on. A teacher who comes from a working-class family and who teaches in the same city in which he was born may continue to participate almost entirely with working-class people and may, by this criterion, be said to have remained in the working class. A woman teacher in a small southern city who comes from an upper-class family may continue to occupy an upper-class position in the community. A young woman who goes to a small midwestern town may remain isolated from the rest of the community, so that it would be difficult on the basis of social participation to decide what position she occupies within the social structure of the community.

While there are occasional exceptions of these kinds, by and large most teachers in America see themselves as middle-class people; they participate with others of the middle class and hold middle-class attitudes and values.

Frequency of Mobility

Since teachers are overwhelmingly middle class it follows that a large proportion are upward-mobile persons, with many having moved up from lower-middle to upper-middle status and many having moved up from working-class backgrounds. McGuire and White (1957), for example, estimated the frequency of mobility among Texas teachers at about 44 percent. It was found that the least mobility occurred among Texas teachers from upper-middle-class families who were reared in small towns, while the greatest proportion of mobility occurred among those born in the country or in large cities. The same finding has emerged from studies in Michigan and in Kansas.

It is likely that mobility occurs more frequently among teachers in metropolitan areas than among teachers in small towns. In this connection the data on Chicago teachers have been regrouped in Table 16.3,

Table 16.3   Socioeconomic backgrounds of teachers in Chicago
(percentages)

	Elementary school			High school		
Socioeconomic group of father	MALE	FE-MALE	TOTAL	MALE	FE-MALE	TOTAL
Professional & managerial	20	27	26	25	36	29
Clerical & small business	20	26	25	24	30	27
Skilled worker, foreman, & similar	33	31	31	30	24	30
Semi-skilled & unskilled	27	16	18	21	10	14
Number	720	4,430	6,930*	1,123	1,250	3,713*

* Includes counselors, adjustment teachers, nurses, assistant principals, and other nonclassroom teachers.

Source: Havighurst, 1964, p. 418

with fathers' occupations categorized into four socioeconomic levels; and with the data for male and female teachers shown separately. This table shows that the proportion of all Chicago teachers who have been upward mobile is probably more than half, since an overall majority came from families of skilled and unskilled workers, levels that are below that of public-school teaching. This table shows also that teachers from working-class families were somewhat more likely to be teaching in elementary schools than in secondary schools—the higher the level of instruction, the higher the level of socioeconomic background of the teacher. (The table shows also that more men than women had achieved mobility through the teaching career. The differences in career lines between men and women teachers is a point to which we shall return in this and later chapters.)

Perceived Social Mobility

Up to now we have called teachers upward mobile if their fathers' occupations were at a socioeconomic level below that of teaching. This is quite different from saying that teachers themselves feel that they have been socially mobile. There is evidence, however, that teachers do indeed perceive a social ladder. Colombotos (1962) asked the high school teachers in a large industrialized suburban community to place their parents and then themselves into one of five social classes. The results are shown in Table 16.4.

Table 16.4   Subjective Intergenerational Mobility of Teachers: Social Class Background as Perceived by the Respondents

Present social class compared to that of parents	Men				Women			
	UPPER MIDDLE	LOWER MIDDLE	UPPER WORKING	LOWER WORKING	UPPER MIDDLE	LOWER MIDDLE	UPPER WORKING	LOWER WORKING
Higher than that of parents	10	39	62	73	13	32	56	90
The same as that of parents	71	56	34	27	72	63	44	10
Lower than that of parents	19	5	4	0	15	5	0	0
Total %	100	100	100	100	100	100	100	100
(number of respondents)	(48)	(112)	(104)	(49)	(48)	(78)	(32)	(10)

Source: Colombotos, 1962, p. 67 (adapted).

From this table it can be seen that those teachers who described themselves as coming from lower-middle- or upper-middle-class backgrounds were most likely to see themselves as having the same social position as their parents had; while teachers who saw themselves as coming from working-class families were most likely to see their present social class as higher than that of their parents. For this latter group, then, a teaching career has brought with it social advancement.

There is, furthermore, some evidence that ambitious working-class youth are more likely to enter teaching than other professions of comparable status. Colombotos, to test this supposition, compared the social-class backgrounds of the men teachers in his sample with a sample of industrial staff experts (men whose positions required a college degree). He found the teachers were somewhat more likely to have come from working-class backgrounds.

Teaching Compared to Business Careers

It is not known why teaching might be favored over business by mobile working-class youth. We surmise that at least two factors are involved: First, the teacher is often the first professional with whom working-class children have had continued contact and perhaps for this reason teaching will seem more attainable than less visible positions in business such as accountant, lawyer, or purchasing agent. Second, a business career is frequently furthered by older men who take an interest in sponsoring an able young employee. A young man who lacks acquaintance with business executives may more readily choose a career that depends primarily upon his ability to do college work and to pass civil service examinations.

There is other evidence (see Table 16.5) that suggests that people of different social origins are somewhat differently oriented toward teaching and plan their careers differently. The Colombotos data showed that men from upper-middle-class backgrounds were seldom interested in leaving classroom teaching for an administrative position. Among men from working-class backgrounds, on the other hand, as many wished to advance through the educational administrative hierarchy as wished to remain in the classroom. It is likely that most of the upper-middle-class men were attracted to the profession because they wished literally to teach, while many of the working-class teachers chose teaching as a means to an administrative position.

Table 16.5   Teachers' Career Plans by Social Class Background

Career Plans	Men				Women			
	SOCIAL CLASS BACKGROUND				SOCIAL CLASS BACKGROUND			
	UPPER MIDDLE	LOWER MIDDLE	UPPER WORKING	LOWER WORKING	UPPER MIDDLE	LOWER MIDDLE	UPPER WORKING	LOWER WORKING
To leave education for a job in something else	6% (3)	7% (8)	6% (6)	6% (3)	2% (1)	6% (5)	3% (10)	0%
To advance in education . . . principal, superintendent, supervisor, coordinator	17 (8)	22 (24)	30 (30)	45 (22)	2 (1)	2 (2)	0	0
To leave teaching, raise a family, then return to teaching	0	0	0	0	35 (17)	23 (18)	39 (13)	18 (2)
To leave teaching, raise a family, and *not* return to teaching	0	0	0	0	20 (10)	13 (10)	12 (4)	9 (1)
To stay in teaching	77 (37)	71 (79)	64 (65)	49 (24)	41 (20)	56 (44)	46 (15)	73 (8)
Total (number of respondents)	100% (48)	100% (111)	100% (101)	100% (49)	100% (49)	100% (79)	100% (33)	100% (11)

Source: Colombotos, John L. *Sources of Professionalism: a study of high school teachers.* U.S. Office of Education Cooperative Research Project No. 330. Ann Arbor: department of Sociology, University of Michigan, 1962. Page 68.

417

The differences among the women teachers were less striking. Those with working-class backgrounds were, however, more likely to think of teaching as a full-time career, and less likely, if they planned to leave teaching to raise a family, to think of retiring altogether. It is possible that this last difference is due primarily to economic reasons.

Relatively few women in this study showed interest in achieving mobility through a career; and of this sample, only three, all of middle-class background, expressed an interest in moving into an administrative position. The typical woman teacher, no matter what her background, saw her teaching career as beginning and ending in the classroom.

The actual frequency of upward mobility among teachers cannot be definitely established for the country at large, but the evidence is that the frequency is high, with as many as two or possibly three of every five teachers having experienced a move of at least one level in a five-level social structure. It is likely that the frequency of upward-mobile persons in the teaching field has been increasing in the past fifty years and will continue to increase so long as there is a growing demand for teachers.

Social Origin as a Factor in Teaching Performance

It is important to know something of the social origin of any given teacher if we are to understand his performance in the teaching role. In this connection, however, we must look at social origin in relation to personality. It has been said, for instance, that social origin is the single most important fact in predicting a teacher's behavior. This is a gross oversimplification. Although a given teacher's social origin may have had an important influence upon his personality, it is virtually impossible to cite generalized effects that would be true for all teachers of any single origin.

For example, a teacher who comes from a middle-class family is not necessarily ineffective in dealing with working-class children. Some middle-class teachers, coming from fairly relaxed home environments, may emerge as adaptive personalities who readily take on the color of their social surroundings. For them it would be relatively easy to get along sympathetically with children and parents quite different from themselves. In another group, for whom a rigid upbringing had the effect of inculcating a tendency to panic when faced with the strange or unusual, prejudices may be easily aroused. Some of these persons drift toward treating with disdain children or parents who are of different races, religions, nationalities, or economic circumstances.

Middle-Class Backgrounds

Mrs. Gordon, whom we described earlier (see Chapter 1) is a woman of middle-class background who obtains her major satisfactions in dealing with working-class children. She feels she is doing an important and successful job in helping them become better Americans; she searches out those who have special abilities, helping them to develop their talents and to become upward mobile.

Another teacher from a middle-class background might react very differently from Mrs. Gordon. Louise Carson, for instance, said of herself:

Considering my family background, I am definitely a middle-class person with typical middle-class values. My parents are college graduates, and both parents have always been active in organizations such as Kiwanis, Girl Scouts, PTA, and the like. They have felt the responsibility of maintaining a stable, secure home, and instilling an appreciation for the "finer things in life" in their children.

In spite of being rather sheltered from other classes of people, I am certain that I was influenced by my parents and teachers in being tolerant, fair, and feeling civic responsibility. These latter attitudes are probably the only factors which "saved" me when I graduated from college full of grand ideas and found myself teaching children in a slum neighborhood. Disregarding the racial difference (although I must admit that the first glance at my class of nearly fifty Negro children was a shock, since I had never before had so many Negro people near me at one time), I was stunned more by seeing so many shabbily dressed and dirty children. . . .

The impressions of my very first day of teaching are still vivid. I saw a girl from the eighth grade who was several months pregnant. At first I thought she was just a very young mother bringing her child to school, but I found out that she was a thirteen-year-old pupil. (When she appeared in this obvious condition she was immediately withdrawn from school.) In discussing this with the older teachers at lunch, I learned that during the previous semester the upper ungraded class had had a baby shower for one of the girls who had been forced to leave school for the same reason. The teacher explained that she allowed the class to have the party to "help soothe their feelings, since they thought it was very unfair that the girl couldn't finish the semester just because she was having a baby." I was shocked at this teacher, too, and I felt more confused than ever.

My other experiences that first day of school included listening to a dialect that was almost incomprehensible and to language that was shocking (most terms I had never heard before), and watching one seven-year-old boy emerge from the dressing room without any clothes on. When I went back with him to see that he dressed, I found that his underwear was filthy and ragged. It was held together with a large rusty safety pin that the boy claimed had been sticking him.

I tried—I really tried my best. I remembered how I had to be tolerant, and how these were just children who didn't know any better. I remembered how I wanted to be a teacher, and how I wanted to succeed on my first assignment. But I simply couldn't take it. I applied for a transfer after a few weeks, deciding that I had to get into a different school or withdraw from teaching altogether. I did stick it out for the rest of that year, but I never could overcome my feelings. It seems to me, in retrospect, that I spent all my time breaking up fist-fights and "butting" sessions, trying to retrieve stolen objects, and pretending not to hear the remarks that made me blush. . . .

I've been in a middle-class school since then, and I'm happy with teaching now. But I still feel guilty and somehow ashamed of myself. I wish I could have been different. But at the same time, a person has to be honest with herself, and has to be comfortable in what she's doing, or she can't do anything at all. . . .

It is, of course, not only middle-class teachers dealing with lower-class children who can provide us with varying examples of how social origin and personality interact in influencing teaching behavior. Some teachers have difficulty in working with children whose families are of higher social levels than their own.

It may be recalled that Miss Bond, teaching in the exclusive Forest Park suburb (see Chapter 1), felt uncomfortable with parents of her fifth-grade pupils. Another example of this general type is to be seen in the following paragraphs, taken from a longer account written by a teacher entitled "Analysis of a Failure."

Last year I was a teacher in a private school for boys in a large city. Despite my pleasant anticipation of the job, and my desire to be a better teacher than I had been in my first five years, I found myself very unhappy with the situation. . . .

The students came from families of wealth. A few athletes were there on scholarships, but in the elementary school almost all the children came from socially prominent families. Most of these boys transferred to eastern boarding schools in the ninth or tenth grade. The high school was therefore smaller, with many new students from somewhat less socially secure families admitted to fill the gaps. There were no Negro students. Jewish students were admitted, but kept below a certain percentage in each grade and in the school as a whole. This percentage was not disclosed, not even to the faculty. . . .

I was hired by the Headmaster. The first interview that I had with him perhaps set the tone for the year to come more than I realized at the time. My credentials from the teachers' agency were already before him. Rather than evaluating me as a person, he seemed to be basing his decision on the prestige value of the institutions at which I had been trained. The facts that I had graduated from a well-known eastern college, that I had taught at Quaker boarding schools, and that he had a high regard for the Quaker educators he had known, seemed to be enough. I can only suppose that he had some vague hopes that I would help give the school some atmosphere of "easternness" that both he and the parents prized. I, on the other hand, expected to be evaluated as an individual trying to be a good teacher. . . .

I felt uneasy with my students; their habits and values were different from mine. This in turn was a factor in the difficulties I had in the classroom. The majority expected me to keep strict order and to be explicit about what they should study, how they should study it, how they should write down what they knew, and so on. I had never been authoritarian in my teaching, and I was probably even less so that year as a result of the graduate work I had done the year before. I did not wish to become authoritarian. I wanted to interest the boys in the subject-matter. But for them, school, and later college, were merely stepping stones to social and business success in the adult world. They intended to learn enough to get into a good college, but no more; and in the meantime they could try to enjoy school by playing the game with the teacher. Her role was to keep order; theirs, to disrupt it. . . .

I had very little contact with parents. I did see them *en masse* at the two or three evening meetings of the parent-faculty organization and at the spring Carnival where they made $14,000 in one evening to buy new equipment for the school. The off-hand way many parents treated us teachers made the cartoon seem quite real, in which the mother says to the principal, "I can't understand why the teachers can't get along with Johnny; all the other servants can." I felt far removed from parents in terms of values and standard of living. I found I did not want to become like them, although I probably envied and resented their wealth . . . and I think they had no desire for me to be a model for their children. . . .

All of us—myself, the students, the parents, the Headmaster—were glad to see the year come to an end and to find me moving on to a different teaching job. . . .

The range of teaching behaviors in middle-class Negro teachers is probably as great as among white teachers. Some enjoy teaching working-class children, Negro or white; others do not; some become active civil rights workers; others stay aloof from problems of Negro-white relations.

William Jones came from a Negro family which was well regarded in the community. His father was a post office clerk; his mother had been a maid for a fashionable white family. Their home life conformed to general middle-class standards. They were proud of themselves and of the church and fraternal organizations to which they belonged. Their social life was confined largely to Negro friends.

The family plans included college education for the three children. Choice of occupation had been carefully discussed in terms of employment possibilities. William had wanted to be an engineer, but it was the 1940's and the idea was vetoed on grounds that there were no jobs for Negro engineers. Teaching was his second choice. At college he joined a Negro fraternity and attended social events with this group.

After graduation he became a science teacher in a school in an almost solidly Negro district. The pattern set by his parents seemed good to him, and he followed their example. In his quiet way he did a good job of teaching. He was regarded by students and fellow-teachers as a steady influence in the school. He enjoyed his life and hoped that students would sense the advantages of the path he had chosen. His own rewards were a comfortable home, a good family of his own, and a respected position. He served on several boards and committees, and was active in raising funds for Negro colleges in the South.

Not all his associates approved of Mr. Jones, however. Those who were concerned about such issues as civil rights and fair employment opportunities for Negroes called him an "Uncle Tom." This made him angry because he regarded himself as race conscious and he belonged to groups like the Urban League. He condemned the "hot heads" who were "always shooting off their mouths." He was even more contemptuous of the Negroes who were docile or servile toward whites, however. He felt that the existence of solidly Negro areas was a good thing; if these did not exist, he doubted if he would have found so good a teaching job. He liked the Negro community because of his good position within it. Mostly he wanted to be left alone to live his life in what had become a family tradition. (Adapted from Stiles, 1957, pp. 51–52.)

Working-Class Backgrounds

Among teachers coming from lower-status families, we also see differing patterns. One, for example, tortured by inner feelings of inferiority, may regard his origin as a thing of shame to be lived down. Another, having a powerful identification with father and older siblings, may so conduct himself as to retain and exemplify his family's social rank, and in so doing ally himself with pupils and parents of similar origin. A third, imbued with strong achievement drives, may seek to deny his origin by accepting middle-class standards and by being unusually strict, if not actually punitive, against the children and parents from whose ranks he sees himself as having risen by dint of self-denial. These illustrations, of course, do not by any means exhaust the possibilities.

Jim Mallory is an example of a teacher who has moved a long way up the social ladder, and whose flexible personality has made him unusually successful:

Jim Mallory was born in 1917 in the state of Washington. His family's income was derived mainly from fruit picking, and each member was responsible for some aspect of the family endeavor. It was often Jim's lot to do the cooking, family wash, mending, and the making of clothes for the entire family. Since the Mallorys lived in a tent much of the time, it was also his job to erect the tent at the fruit picking locations and to "keep house" in any and all aspects.

Because fruit picking was seasonal work and the father was not too steady a provider, responsibility for food and money often fell on the shoulders of the children. At one time Jim spent five hours each evening setting pins in a bowling alley at a nearby army base. If he told the soldiers he was hungry they would bring him food from their mess hall. This food plus the money earned from pin setting was for a time the sole family subsistence.

When Jim was sixteen he joined the army but was given a medical discharge a year later. He stayed with his family for about two weeks subsequent to his discharge, and then stowed away on a fruit truck and went to Texas. There he got a job and enrolled in a junior college. After two years, he entered a large university in a pre-law curriculum. World War II interrupted his college work, but he received his bachelor's degree shortly after the war. He then went into graduate work in psychology, where he specialized in counseling and guidance. He became an avid student of "non-directive" counseling and "student-centered" teaching, finding this general approach in keeping with his implicit world-view. He is never so delighted as when he is discussing the conflicting values of American culture, especially those of the middle-class in general and of school administrators in particular.

Jim's values are apparent in his attitudes toward his own children. They are allowed to solve their own personal and social problems, and the limits on their behavior are kept to the absolute minimum. This attitude is not always approved by his neighbors and colleagues, but it poses no special problems in Jim's eyes. . . .

Jim has been a successful teacher in high school and is now one of the most popular and admired teachers on a college faculty. His unique teaching methods in the classroom, and his sympathy and permissiveness in the counseling situation—his ability to give the student a sense of worth—this combination is one that appears strongly to almost all his students. . . .

Alice Davis is another kind of teacher:

Alice Davis grew up under the care of her grandmother, a Negro woman who did "day work" for middle-class white families. Alice was born when her mother was 18 years old and unmarried. The baby was given to the grandmother to rear, and the mother worked in a factory until she married at 20. This marriage did not last, and she married another man, who left her after two more children were born. She thereupon applied for Aid to Dependent Children and lived on this money with her three children and with two others that were born later.

Alice never lived with her mother, but she often saw her on Sundays. She remembers that her grandmother warned her not to play with her half-brothers and sisters and kept telling her that her mother was "not fit to bring up children." The grandmother spent evenings reading to Alice and always took her to church on Sunday.

Alice found school a wonderful place. She learned to read promptly and was the favorite of her teachers. After school she went to a neighborhood center where there was a club leader whom she liked very much. This woman kept in touch with Alice and encouraged her to finish high school and go on to the local teachers college. Alice was never so proud of herself as when she got her diploma, and looked down at her grandmother, sitting in the audience and smiling.

Alice teaches now in a working-class school. The children are all Negro and they come to school fairly regularly and behave themselves when they are in her class. She runs her room strictly and punishes her pupils for the least infraction of rules. She gives out homework and insists on its being done. She often tells her children that they are lucky to have such a good school and that they must work hard to show their appreciation. She will not tolerate lying or copying.

About a fourth of her pupils come from homes where there is no father present. She is especially strict with these children and will not accept anything but the most conscientious work from them. To those who do well she devotes much time, and she gets them properly enrolled in church groups and in settlement houses. Those pupils who do not do well in school find her a merciless taskmaster. When she meets physical resistance or active hostility from such a pupil, Alice becomes so anxious that she sometimes gets sick. Her principal has learned to help her with a few such children each year by removing them to a class of another teacher who can tolerate this kind of behavior better than Alice.

Personality as a Determining Factor

Each individual's personality will determine, then, the effects of his social background on his teaching behavior. There is a wide range of personality patterns within each social class and in each ethnic and racial group. Even though some modes of child-raising and some personality patterns are more typical of one group than another, in each group there is a wide variety. No social class and no racial or ethnic group is barren of adaptive individuals, or of well-adjusted men and women of strong conscience, or of adventuresome pioneers.

At the same time, from the range of individuals who grew up in each social group, teaching probably draws only a fraction. The sample may be differently constituted for each type of social origin. Thus, from less well-situated economic groups teaching may be expected to draw a good number of ambitious, striving people. By contrast, the upper-class boy or girl with a strong achievement drive is unlikely to choose teaching as a career. From the middle-classes, education probably draws many social young people who feel most at ease with other middle-class people. In the slum areas and working-class districts, the educational profession would seem more attractive to relatively isolated youngsters who set themselves apart from the bulk of their classmates.

Social origin may have a different influence upon a teacher's behavior during his first years of teaching than at a period later in his career. Thus a person who had felt teaching represented a step upward in social prestige might gradually find childhood friends who had made other choices gaining greater income or higher position; he might eventually feel he had made a poor occupational choice.

The effects of social origin may take different forms in the older teacher than in the newcomer to the profession. A special case exists where population change has altered the type of child a school serves. Thus, we have the experience of teachers who were drawn to a school in a "good" neighborhood and stayed in that school while the surrounding area turned into a slum. For a middle-class teacher with strong latent prejudices, this can be a demoralizing experience.

In summary, then, factors related to social origin interact with personality factors in influencing a teacher's behavior. It is also evident that both in turn are influenced by the particular school setting in which the teacher finds himself.

Teachers, like the members of any other occupational group, tend to move about until they find the setting in which they are comfortable and productive. While we shall have more to say in a later chapter about the degree to which there is movement in the teaching profession (Chapter 19), at this point it is relevant to note that movement from one school to another is only partially determined by such factors as salary, the quality of administration, or the quality of the physical school plant. More important factors may be those that relate to the social and personal characteristics of the teacher.

Teachers as a Heterogeneous Group

We have seen that teachers presently represent a wide range of social-class origins. There are other ways in which teachers are an increasingly heterogeneous group. There are more Catholic and more Jewish teachers in public schools than in earlier years, not only in large cities, but also in smaller communities. There is more diversity in marital status. Not only have the barriers against married women rapidly disappeared in all parts of the country, but there are more divorced persons being employed as teachers. There are more teachers who are mothers, especially in the present period when numbers of older women are returning to the teaching field. There are more male teachers than there were a few decades ago. (In 1965, there were slightly more men than women high school teachers.)

There is a greater diversity of ethnic and racial backgrounds. Since World War II, for instance, there has been a substantial flow of Japanese men and women into teaching positions in western and midwestern cities, and teachers of Japanese ancestry abound in Hawaii. Puerto Ricans are now coming into the profession in noticeable numbers.

The Negro group is different from the other ethnic groups in the teaching profession due to the segregated school system in the South and in some border states prior to 1954, which created a substantial group of Negro teachers in Negro schools. The largest group of Negro teachers is still to be found either in the South teaching in *de facto* segregated Negro schools or in inner-city schools in metropolitan areas in the North and West, although they are relatively highly represented also on the teaching staff in border cities such as Kansas City, St. Louis, Louisville, Washington and Baltimore. In 1965, 28 percent of the public-school teachers of Kansas City were Negroes compared with about 18 percent Negroes in the city population. In Chicago in 1966 only 32 percent of the teachers were Negro although more than half of the pupils were Negro.

In the country at large the assignment of Negro teachers is largely to schools with a predominance of Negro pupils, but this practice is slowly changing. For example, Philadelphia in 1965 worked out an arrangement between the teachers' union and the school administration whereby 40 white teachers went into schools that were mainly Negro in pupil and staff composition, while 40 Negro teachers transferred to schools that were mainly white. Detroit in 1965 announced a "balanced staff" policy, saying that it is educationally desirable for children in all schools to come into contact with teachers who are young and old, male and female, Negro and white; and the Detroit school administration worked out a plan with the teachers' organizations for teacher assignment and transfer that would work toward the goal of a balanced staff.

Effects on Teacher-Pupil Interaction

The growing diversity of teachers, and plans such as Detroit's balanced staff mean that American school children are coming into contact with a greater variety of adult personalities. Among other things, there are now more teachers, especially at the secondary level, who know first-hand the attitudes and values of working-class children, and who know the problems of the Negro child. Of the total number of teachers encountered by a child as he goes through school, he is now likely to meet a greater range of types and to experience a greater range of interpersonal relations with teachers.

Effects on Teacher-Teacher Interaction

The greater heterogeneity also affects the interaction between teachers. In many schools, new problems are created as the attitudes of older teachers come into conflict with those of younger. The following account illustrates this point.

There has been considerable change in education during my twenty-five years of teaching at North High School. When I came here to teach in the 1930's I was very much impressed with the social status of the teachers and the very high caliber of students. The Botony and Zoology courses that I was to teach were organized on a near-collegiate level. . . . There were honor clubs in every subject; and students and teachers stayed many hours after school doing club work. . . . Pupils trained for scholarship examinations. At that time probably a greater percent of students from North went to colleges and universities than from any other high school in the city. The principal and the assistant principal were both Ph.D.'s from top universities. The teachers were remarkably able scholars. To illustrate, Mr. A was a real southern gentleman; Miss B was a foreign diplomat's daughter who was as much at home in European countries as in the United States. Miss C came from a line of well-known educators. Mr. D was the author of several textbooks used in high schools all over the country. Miss E was a native Parisian who had been decorated by the French government for her work. Miss F had a doctorate in science. And so it went, right on through our faculty.

Most of these early teachers have left now, either through retirement or death. The teachers who followed were different. There are many more now who come from teachers' colleges; who have never traveled; some, but fewer, are from families of educators. They come from a different social class, and they reflect it in their teaching and social attitudes.

The older teachers get separated from the younger and newer ones. Respect for experience has dwindled. Many of the newer teachers will not take charge of clubs after school. They refuse to do extra work. They call us old-fashioned and resent the fact that we are willing to give a bit more than their idea of a day's work. All they seem to be interested in is shorter hours and more pay. Many frown on homework for pupils because it means more work for the teacher. And as they take over lunchroom duty and corridor discipline, they act more like policemen than like teachers.

This teacher is giving a personal view that is undoubtedly biased by an age differential between her and her colleagues, as well as by a social-class differential. Nevertheless, differences and possible conflicts are bound to occur among teachers as heterogeneity increases in the teaching profession.

Heterogeneity of teaching staff within a given school is likely to be greater in large cities than in smaller communities; even though it is increasing to some extent in small school systems, too. Due to employment policies, the differences between teachers in small communities arise less often from ethnic or racial differences than from differences in religion, age, and marital status.

Effects on Teacher-Administrator Interaction

There are also new problems arising in the interaction between teachers and administrators, as described in the following passage:

As the teaching force becomes more diversified, new attitudes toward professional relationships enter the picture. An administrator "of the old school" may like to think of teaching as a profession after the model of the medical practice of three decades ago. At that point there was a spirit of "noblesse oblige" as expressed in donated time to clinics for "the poor." Realistically, in the field of medicine this tradition has wilted. However, emotional belief in its existence as an ideal for educators is very strong. The administrator who embraces this ideal in his own professional life is often upset by the appearance of what he would term unprofessional attitudes toward demands upon teachers' time and towards supervisors.

The repeated condemnation of the American Federation of Teachers by superintendents' groups is only one aspect of this clash in values. Actually, the differences find expression in a multitude of ways. The teacher familiar from home experience with such ideas as overtime premium rates, portal-to-portal pay, and the like, may precipitate resistance to programs calling for visits to homes "on your own time," or even to unpaid supervision of extra-curricular activities. Recently a survey of the hours worked by Detroit teachers showed that the group which devoted extraordinary amounts of time to professional activity was preponderantly made up of older teachers. Similarly, the traditional labor suspicion of supervisors and of "company men" may enter relationships between the teachers and anyone from "the downtown office." There must be no over-simplification of these trends. It would be unwarranted to assume that the attitudes mentioned above have a simon-pure, one-to-one relation to social origins. Actually, many status-conscious teachers of labor origin are hostile to teachers' unions and exemplify what they see as a contrasting "professional attitude." Some teachers from white-collar backgrounds have stronger pro-labor attitudes than many union members in factories. (Wattenberg *et al.,* 1957, II, pp. 63–64.)

As teachers are coming to represent more of a cross section of the American population, this heterogeneity affects school-community relations. In some communities new problems are created as when powerful groups in the community, who have regarded teachers as a special elite, look with disdain upon any move that diversifies the teaching personnel. In other situations there are new bonds created between school and community as teachers appear who can, in a figurative sense, "speak the same language" as parent groups. While there will be great variation in this regard from one locality to the next, in overall terms it would appear that the greater heterogeneity of teaching personnel is producing new opportunities for communication between school and community.

Exercises

1. How did you decide to become a teacher? How was your decision re-lated to factors in your own social background?

2. Persons who enter the teaching profession are today more heterogeneous in terms of social origins than were past groups. What effects is this likely to have, when one thinks of the school as an agency affecting social mobility? Do you think the effects will be to increase mobility or to decrease it in the society at large? Why?

3. Select a teacher whom you know. Describe how his social background is affecting his teaching behavior.

4. Describe a situation in which differences in the social backgrounds of the teacher and the parent had an effect upon the child's learning. What was the effect upon the child?

5. Describe a situation in which interaction between a teacher and the principal, or the teacher and a supervisor, was influenced by factors relating to their social origins.

6. Make a study of the social origins of the people in your college class, or the teachers in your school. How many come from rural backgrounds? How many social classes are represented in the group? How many ethnic groups? Religious groups?

7. If you have friends or colleagues who are Negro teachers, describe their attitudes toward teaching socially disadvantaged children. Can you relate differences among them to differences in their personalities?

Suggestions for Further Reading

1. See the selections by Wattenberg and by Doherty in *Society and Education: A Book of Readings* (Havighurst, Neugarten, and Falk) for further discussion of the social origins of teachers and the relations between social-class origin and teaching performance.

2. For questionnaire studies of the characteristics of public school teachers, see *The American Public School Teacher,* 1960–61, published by the Research Division of the NEA: and Chapter 16 and Appendix A of Havighurst's *The Public Schools of Chicago.*

3. For an interpretation of the place of the teacher in American society, read Barzun's *The Teacher in America.* Caplow's *The Academic Marketplace* is a description of some of the problems in the teachers' position in higher education (colleges and universities).

17 / The Social Roles
of the Teacher

A social role is the pattern of behavior that is expected of all people who fill a certain position in society. Policemen, even though they are all different individuals, have a certain set of behaviors in common, and our society has a set of common expectations about their behavior. Thus we speak of the social role of the policeman; and, in the same way, of the social roles of mother or father or pupil or teacher.

Every person fills a whole set of social roles. A teacher assumes the roles of worker, husband or wife, parent, church member, club member, and citizen. In describing the social roles of teachers, however, we shall not deal with the various roles occupied by teachers as persons, but instead with the various roles occupied by persons when they are teachers.

The role of teacher is made up of a cluster of sub-roles, some that refer primarily to the teacher's behavior in relation to the wider community, and others that refer primarily to the teacher's behavior in relation to pupils. In real life the sub-roles are neither separate nor distinct, but for purposes of analysis we may focus our attention upon one after another.

The Teacher in the Community

The concept of role, as we have indicated, involves both behavior and expectations regarding behavior. To ask, "What is the teacher's role in the community?" is at least in part to ask, "What are the social expectations that the community has of the teacher?"

Various Images of the Teacher

There have been at different times in history different images of the
school teacher in American society: the strict schoolmaster, bending
over the heads of perspiring pupils, rod in hand; the Puritanical schoolmarm, straitlaced and humorless; the absent-minded professor; and in
Waller's terms, the sacred object:

> For some reason, the school has become almost equally with the church
> the repository of ideals. The teacher, like the minister, possesses a high
> degree of social sacredness. He must be a little better than other men; it is
> therefore better if he does not smoke, and he certainly must not drink. In
> fact, he must be the master of all the negative virtues. It is his part to enjoy
> the finer things of life, literature, art, and the best music. He must likewise
> be interested in all good causes, that is, in all such causes as do not upset
> important vested interests in the community. . . . Like the minister, the
> teacher excites very real reverence and people regard him as slightly ridicu-
> lous. (Waller, 1942, p. 217.)

There were positive as well as negative images of the teacher: the
revered scholar; the self-sacrificing idealist; the sympathetic advisor of
youth. Margaret Mead, for example, offers the following description:

> . . . when the American hears the word "schoolteacher" . . . the
> image will be something like this. He will think of a grade school teacher
> who teaches perhaps the third or fourth grade; this teacher will be a woman
> of somewhat indeterminate age, perhaps in the middle 30's neither young nor
> old, of the middle class and committed to the ethics and manners of the
> middle class world. In the emotional tone which accompanies the image
> there will be respect, a little fear, perhaps more than a little affection, an
> expectation that she will reward his efforts to learn and conform, and a spate
> of delighted memories of those occasions when he himself perpetrated feats
> of undetected mischief. . . . (Mead, 1951, p. 5.)

Whatever the prevailing image of the teacher at different times and
at different places, it has always contained contradictory elements.
Furthermore, as the society has increased in complexity, the images of
teachers have increased in variety. As teachers have become a more
heterogeneous group of people, the stereotypes about teachers are being
broken down and discarded; and it has become increasingly difficult to
generalize about "the" image of the teacher held by Americans. Whiteford (1955) and Barkley (1956), for example, found that both school
administrators and high school students held rather different images of

the "typical" woman teacher, depending upon her subject. Thus, Whiteford found that all teachers were seen as conscientious, capable, resourceful, and poised; but in addition, social studies teachers were described as democratic, academic, intellectual and well read; while home economics teachers were described as orderly, wholesome, and appropriately dressed.

Ascribed Social Status of Teachers

It is by and large true that teachers as a group have been awarded somewhat less social status than other professional groups in America. In Warner's ranking of occupations according to social prestige, the public school teacher ranks lower than the other professions (Warner, Meeker, and Eells, 1960). In a list of ninety occupations, North and Hatt reported that teaching in 1947 ranked thirty-sixth, not far above the average for all occupations (North and Hatt, 1949); and a repeat study in 1963 indicated that no real change in prestige of teaching has occurred (Hodge, Siegel, and Rossi, 1964). When judged in terms of level of education required, or in terms of income earned, teaching does not compare favorably with other occupations. In these ways, the society may be said to hold an image of the teacher that is not commensurate with teachers' claims to full professional status and recognition.

This situation is partly due to the unresolved question in the minds of many Americans as to whether or not the public school teacher should be regarded as a professional person in the same way that a lawyer or a physician is regarded. On the one hand, this question may be answered affirmatively, since teaching is a legally recognized and regulated occupation; one that requires a high level of intellectual and social competence; and one that has its own professional organization that develops standards of competence—criteria commonly used to distinguish occupations from professions.

On the other hand, the question is often answered negatively, since the teacher's social role is less specialized than that of other professionals. The teacher acts as a surrogate of the society in socializing children, and in this sense teachers perform a role more similar to that of parents than to that of professionals. Their responsibility is to all children, not to the selected few who need a specialized service. Teachers, accordingly, are regarded as public servants in a quite different way from other professional persons.

Herein, then, lies part of the ambiguity with which teachers are regarded in the society: They are experts with a professional know-how of their own; yet they are also, in their role of public servant, subject to the dictates of public opinion.

The teacher's role in the community involves a number of different sub-roles, only a few of which can be discussed here.

The Participant in Community Affairs

Since the teacher is an educated person and possesses certain skills that are useful in conducting the affairs of the community, teachers have been in demand for church work (teaching Sunday school classes, singing in the choir), for volunteer jobs with the Red Cross and other welfare organizations, and for other useful community services. Vidich and Bensman have characterized teachers as being, in this respect, "a replacement pool for spare talent as it is needed for various organizational jobs." (Vidich and Bensman, 1958, p. 270.) This role has, however, been circumscribed; it is usually limited to the "safe," noncontroversial community affairs and to activities to which little prestige is attached. There is likely to be resistance and criticism, especially in small towns, if the teacher takes an active part in politics or starts a business "on the side." Women teachers in many communities find it difficult to be accepted in the more prestigious women's clubs. The few men teachers who are accepted in the service clubs of the community are usually principals or superintendents or athletic coaches.

In a study of over 1,100 teachers in 66 communities in Pennsylvania, Buck (1960) found that one-third participated in community organizations at or above the rate of top business and professional people (the latter group has consistently ranked highest, as compared with other occupational groups, with regard to participation in community affairs), and 80 percent had participation scores higher than the average for white-collar workers. Rates of participation were approximately the same in large as in small communities.

Because a majority of the teachers had grown up in homes where community participation was low, the implications are that many teachers change their life styles to meet the expectation that the teacher will take part in community life beyond the school.

More recently, in a nationwide sample, four out of every five teachers were found to be active in one or more organizations, and over two-thirds of the active members belonged to one or more groups besides church. The amount of time spent in organizational work was considerable, given the average work week of over 47 hours reported by these same teachers. Teachers spent close to two hours a week, in organization work not counting attendance at religious services. Table 17.1 shows the proportion that were active and non-active members of various types of organizations. The table indicates that at the present time there is little administrative pressure upon teachers to join outside organizations, other than teachers' associations. Religious affiliation is the most usual type of membership, a fact that was pointed out also by Ryans (1960) in summarizing his findings from an elaborate study of teachers' characteristics.

Community Leadership

Such findings say nothing regarding the quality of the participation or the extent to which the teacher is a powerful person in the community. Studies made in 1940 by Cook and Greenhoe (Cook and Cook, 1950) showed that teachers participated in community affairs, but not as leaders.

While the picture with regard to community participation may be changing as teachers, like other professional groups, become more actively concerned over civil rights, efforts to eliminate poverty, and other national and international problems, it is unlikely that the overall picture concerning organizational leadership will be reversed. As the number of teachers from lower-middle and working-class levels increases, teacher participation in community life may well be more varied; and the number occupying leadership positions in the community, positions typically held by upper-middle-class people, is likely to be proportionately smaller.

There are, of course, various factors that interact to produce this pattern of participation, only one being the prevailing attitude in the community as regards the teacher's qualifications for leadership. Another factor that operates to curtail the teacher's participations, especially in political and economic affairs, is the expectation that the teacher as a public servant should remain neutral on controversial issues. Possibly this is the reason why only two percent of the teachers in the NEA sample of 1960–61 (the sample reported in Table 17.1) had ever run for public office and less than seven percent were active workers in a political party. (NEA, April, 1963.) In many communi-

Table 17.1   Teacher Membership in Religious, Civic, or Other
                  Organizations

Type of organization	Active member and workers	Inac- tive member	Not a member	Feel administra- tive pressure to take part[a]
Teachers association	54.1%	40.7%	5.2%	13.0%
Church or synagogue	53.2	34.0	12.8	0.5
Youth-serving group	15.8	5.4	78.8	0.3
Fraternal or auxiliary group	14.7	17.9	67.4	0.1
Political party organi- zation	6.6	24.2	69.2	0.4
Women's group	20.1	11.5	68.4	0.1
Men's service club	13.4	6.2	80.4	0.2
Other organizations	24.1	12.7	63.2	0.4
Number reporting	a	a	a	1,852

[a] For all types of organizations, except women's group and men's service club, columns 2, 3, and 4 are based on the number 1,881, and add horizontally to 100%. For women's group the number is 1,291; for men's service club, 590.

Source: National Education Association, April, 1963, p. 27 (adapted).

ties, teachers are barred by state law or by local requirement from participation in political activities. These restrictions often stem from the desire to protect the teacher from political influence. In other instances, they stem from the assumption, still unproved, that the teacher who participates in partisan politics loses his objectivity in teaching.

Other factors are derived from the teaching situation itself. One of these is the teacher's relative inability to control large blocks of time, as compared, for example, with other professional men or business executives. It is one thing, in terms of time required, to teach a Sunday School class; another thing, to organize and direct a Community Chest drive. In some instances, limited finances may operate against certain types of community participation.

While there are many individual exceptions, there is little evidence that teachers as a group are straining for fuller civic participation. Not only are teachers influenced by community tradition in this respect, but there has been, in general, little in their professional training that prepares them for community leadership.

The Sociological Stranger

At the same time that teachers are expected to participate in the community, there has been the contrasting social expectation that teachers will be "sociological strangers" in the community. The teacher has often been regarded as a person who is in, but not of, the community, one who seldom sinks roots into the community.

This role of the stranger has, again, resulted from various factors. One is the expectation that teachers are a group apart, with cultural interests and cosmopolitan tastes that differentiate them from the community at large. Another is the desire to maintain the neutrality of the teacher—the theory that he will be more objective in his teaching if he is neither too well acquainted with the families of his pupils nor too much involved in local problems. Another is the view of the teacher as the sacred object or the idealist or the social reformer, whose sights are set upon goals that transcend the immediate and the present; the theory that, should he become too closely identified with the local community, his effectiveness would be diminished.

Another set of factors stems from the fact that, traditionally, teachers have been a transient group, not usually committed to the particular community in which they find themselves. Many teachers move from one community to another in search of new experience, better salaries, or better working conditions. This transiency is true of teachers in large cities as well as those in small towns, since the city teacher tends to move from one school to another and, as is still true, often teaches in a different neighborhood from the one in which he lives. Teacher placement policies are such that young teachers are often specifically advised, after completing their training, not to return to their home communities to teach.

Factors both general and specific operate in given situations to increase or to decrease the degree of social isolation of the teacher. The following account is an illustration of how the situation of the rural teacher has varied from one time to another. It is reported here at some length since it points out many of the broad social changes that have occurred in the United States over the past several decades and shows how these social changes have affected the role of the teacher in the community.

Although the role of the teacher in our society has changed remarkably in the past twenty-five years, probably the role of the teacher in the one-room country school has undergone the greatest transformation. My account is based upon a community that is located in Minnesota, populated chiefly by small farm owners and by tenant farmers. My mother taught in this community from 1927 through 1931, and I myself attended a rural school there from 1939 through 1944, and I have remained in touch with this community ever since.

Forty years ago, the school was the focal point of virtually all non-church-centered social activities. The teacher served as a social leader. Her position was as important to the teenager and young adult as it was to the school-age child and his family. This unique role can be attributed to a number of factors. The school was a convenient, and often the only, center for social affairs. It was a roomy, centrally located, easily accessible, and inexpensive meeting place. Very few forms of entertainment were readily available to the inhabitants of a rural community at that time. Consequently, it fell to the teacher, as sovereign of the school, to organize and lead various types of social activities for groups of varying ages. . . .

The rural school teacher was seldom originally a member of the community in which she taught. Few farmers could afford to send their daughters away to school for the necessary training; therefore most of the teachers came from families living in towns or cities where teacher-training centers were located. Since not enough positions were available in town and urban schools to accommodate these teachers, and also since training was required for rural school teachers, these girls accepted positions in towns or cities. This factor also tended to keep teachers from becoming permanent members of a rural community. Most schools refused to employ married teachers, hence providing another barrier to the chance of a teacher's establishing herself in a community. . . . In general, the position of the rural school teacher of forty years ago was that of an active, highly respected, socially indispensable, but nevertheless temporary, member of the community. She was the social leader and organizer.

By the early 1940's, this picture had changed drastically. Nearly half of the rural schools in this area were closed, given the paucity of pupils and the relative ease of transporting pupils to the neighboring towns. Farms had grown larger, given the improvements in machinery and methods of farming. Families had become smaller. Instead of the eight or ten children that were common in my mother's day, the average family had only three or four. With urbanization, children had left for the cities and more and more farms were being operated by only an older couple.

A change in educational standards had also affected the rural school. Whereas earlier the completion of the eighth grade had been the educational goal, by the early 1940's a large percentage of the members of this rural community at least entered high school.

Perhaps even more fundamental was the disintegration of the small, closely knit community. Recreation facilities, movies, and high schools tended to draw young people away from their immediate communities. Better automobiles, trains, and buses facilitated social intercourse over larger areas. The nucleus of the small, self-contained community—the rural school —was no longer needed.

The one-room school became a burden rather than an asset to the community. Replacement of worn-out buildings was costly and, during the war years, practically impossible. Replacement of textbooks and other equipment was also difficult. Improved roads and school-buses made transportation of children to town schools relatively simple. In fact, since the buses had long been transporting high school students, why not send elementary school students to town schools, too?

There was, furthermore, the difficulty of hiring good teachers at reasonable salaries. Few girls were willing to take a position in a rural school, a post that seemed solitary, dull, and highly undesirable when other employment was available. Educational requirements for certification had become nearly equal for rural and urban schools, and fully qualified teachers who could find employment elsewhere were extremely hesitant to accept a job in a rural school. The members of the community no longer saw the teacher as a particularly valuable part of the social structure, and hence were unwilling to pay the salary that would have made the job attractive. An established member of the community or of a neighboring community might accept such a job because she need not move to a new community and make new friends.

The two women who taught in the school district during the years when I was a student there were fairly typical of the teachers to be found in the rural schools of this community during the early 1940's. Miss L. was a teacher who had been retired for a number of years. Because of the acute shortage of teachers at that time, she had been asked to teach in our school, a small school that could not afford to offer the salary that would have attracted a younger and perhaps better qualified person. Miss L. had taught my father the three R's some thirty years before she became my teacher.

Mrs. M. lived on a small farm. Now that her daughter was in high school, she welcomed the opportunity to return to her profession and lead a more active life. Each morning and evening, she drove the fifteen miles between her home and the school.

Less than ten percent of the rural schools that were in operation 30 to 40 years ago exist today. In those few that do still exist, however, we can detect some change during the past ten years in the function of the teacher. The tendency for the teacher to be a permanent resident of the community or of a nearby community still remains. However, in addition to married women, younger girls are once more accepting positions as rural school teachers. As more of the children in this rural community go on to college, a greater proportion are also qualified to become teachers. Some wish to return to their homes and are glad of the opportunity to teach in a school in their immediate community.

A perhaps more striking change is the apparent recapture of a social function by the rural school teacher. The school has again become a cultural center. PTA units have been formed. Mother's Clubs and gardening and literary societies have sprung up. The teacher has become an active participant, if not an actual organizer, of such groups. The school has once again become a social center for at least one part of the community, the mothers.

Several factors help explain this phenomenon. Modern time-saving conveniences for the home are becoming widespread in this community and women have more time to engage in cultural activity. The educational level of the women in the community is constantly being improved; consequently, they are more likely to take an active interest in PTA and cultural groups. And the few rural schools that do remain are looking more and more to the urban school as an example. Since such activities are widespread in urban schools, it is understandable that they are being initiated also in rural schools.

Although, compared to ten years earlier, the teacher's role is an expanding one, it is not the role of social leader that it was twenty-five years ago.

This description illustrates how changing economic and social conditions can affect the teacher's role. In rural Minnesota the present-day teacher, compared to earlier years, is no longer the social leader in the community—but neither is she the sociological stranger.

The role of stranger is probably a declining one for teachers in various other parts of the country as well. In a study of Detroit teachers in the 1950's, the overwhelming majority of younger teachers were native Detroiters (Wattenberg et al., 1957, I). In Chicago in 1963, 70 percent of the elementary and 69 percent of the high school teachers had grown up in Chicago. Another five percent of each group had grown up in a big city (Havighurst, 1964). A nation-wide sampling of teachers in 1960 showed that over 80 percent identified with their communities and one-third had lived in the community in which they were teaching since childhood (NEA, April, 1963). The teacher's role of "stranger" is on the decline, furthermore, as teachers are becoming a more heterogeneous group, and as they can no longer be singled out as a group separate and apart from the community in terms of social origins, family patterns, or educational and cultural interests.

Given the present situation of teacher supply and demand, it is to be expected that more and more teachers will gravitate toward communities in which they feel at home. At the same time, public attitudes are changing, and there is a breaking down of stereotypes about teachers. Both factors are working in the direction of helping teachers to be of, as well as in, the communities in which they live.

Table 17.2 Responses of a Nation-Wide Sample of Teachers to Questions Concerning Sense of Identity with the Communities* in which They Live During the School Year (N = 1,869)

Response	Percent responding
I am living in my home community where I have lived since childhood	33.2
Although I came here as an adult, I now feel that I belong	50.9
Although I have been here for some time, I do not feel identified with the community	4.6
I have been here for too short a time to expect to feel identified with the community	11.3

* Town, city, or other unit of population.

Source: National Education Association, April, 1963.

Other Community Roles of the Teacher

As is evident from the preceding sections, there are various sub-roles that constitute the role of the teacher in the community in addition to *community participant* and *sociological stranger*. We have already mentioned briefly the teacher as *sacred object,* as *social reformer,* and as *public servant*. We may list several others that are usually of importance in describing the teacher's behavior, although it should be kept in mind that any such list is not exhaustive, that the sub-roles are not mutually exclusive, and that terms other than the ones given here might be equally descriptive.

The teacher is the *surrogate of middle-class morality*. Parents often expect the teacher to be a better model of behavior for their children than they are themselves. Although parents may smoke, drink, and gamble, they want the teacher to avoid any behavior that they think might be bad for children to imitate. In this respect parents may be following a sound principle, for the teacher, especially the young teacher dealing with adolescents, is often a more effective model for youth than is the parent. As a consequence, the teacher is expected to practice the personal virtues of the middle class—correct speech, good manners, modesty, prudence, honesty, responsibility, friendliness, and so on. At the same time, certain other middle-class virtues, such as competitiveness, striving for financial rewards, or independence of authority, are less likely to be valued in teacher behavior.

The teacher is also expected to be a *person of culture,* with more refined tastes than the general population. He is expected to be widely read and widely traveled and to be sophisticated in outlook.

The teacher is a *pioneer in the world of ideas,* the seeker for truth. While this role is more often accorded to college professors than to public-school teachers, still there is a tradition in America that educators as a group should be explorers in the world of knowledge, should be leaders in formulating the values and ideals of the society, and should work for the continual improvement of the society.

Teachers are expected to be not only fountainheads of knowledge but also *experts in regard to children,* a source of information and guidance with respect to the best methods of child rearing and the understanding of child development.

Conflict in Role Expectations

Certain of these sub-roles are contradictory, of course. The cautious and colorless public servant is not the bold adventurer in the world of ideas. The full participant in community affairs is not the neutral and objective stranger.

In a study of role-conflict in the teaching situation Getzels and Guba (1955) found the major problems to lie in three areas. The first was related to the socioeconomic role, where teachers are expected to maintain standards of tastes and living that are sometimes out of reach in terms of the salaries they receive.

The second was in the citizen role, where teachers often see restrictions placed upon them in respect to public and private conduct. The teacher may, for example, be required to participate with more vigor in church affairs than his neighbors, but with less vigor in political matters.

The third was in the role of expert or professional, where, although the teacher is expected to have expertness in his particular field of competence, community groups may nevertheless dictate classroom content and procedures that are at times in opposition to the teacher's best professional judgment.

This study was based upon the reports of teachers in midwestern rural, suburban, and private, church-affiliated schools, and did not include teachers in large city systems. In large cities, these problems probably occur less often. There may be conflict, not only among the roles themselves, but also between certain role behaviors and self-concept. The teacher, for example, who sees himself as a cosmopolitan person—one who has seen Paris, who has a store of wordly wisdom—may be irked by the demands put upon him to be the conservative example for children. Similarly teachers who, as a group, place such high premium upon professional status, responsibility, and freedom in their work may well find it difficult to conform to the role of safe and colorless public servant. In a large-scale study by Chase (1951), freedom to plan one's own work was rated as the most important potential source of satisfaction by teachers.

Yet the apparent contradictions in roles should not be over-emphasized. In the first place, the teacher is not different from other people in being faced by a variety of social expectations and a variety of roles to fill. The same type of analysis that has been made above can also be made for other occupational groups, and many of the same sub-roles would emerge. The physician also is expected to be a cosmopolitan person at the same time that he is a surrogate of middle-class morality.

Teachers are in a particularly sensitive relation to the community because they are dealing with the community's children. They are, accordingly, under more constant public scrutiny than other groups, and may well have developed a greater degree of self-consciousness. It does not follow, however, that teachers have more complex or more conflict-laden roles to perform in the community than do other professionals.

In the second place, the presence of contradictory demands does not necessarily produce personal conflict. The teacher, like any other person, fills a variety of roles at different periods of the day or at different periods in his life. The teacher can be, in some respects, the participant—in other respects, the stranger. Most teachers, like most other people, work out a successful integration of their various role expectations.

Role Perceptions

We have implied that people hold much the same views of the roles of the teacher and how these roles should be filled. A study of teachers' roles undertaken in the Kansas City area (Biddle, Rosencranz, and Rankin, 1961; Biddle, Twyman, and Rankin, 1962; Rosencranz and Biddle, 1964) demonstrates, however, that these assumptions are not necessarily correct. In this study, samples of teachers, parents, pupils, school supervisors, school board members, principals, school superin-tendents, and university undergraduates (about half of whom were education majors) were questioned concerning how they expected teachers to behave in a series of situations. They also were asked how they thought teachers, school officials,, and "people in general" felt about teachers.

The results showed that, although there was general agreement that teachers conformed to the role of *surrogate of middle-class morality,* there were some sharp differences as well as inconsistencies regarding certain aspects of the teacher's role. For example, parents saw teachers as desiring to avoid participation in the Parent-Teachers Association; while teachers, in fact, said they wished to attend and that they did attend PTA. School officials, as well as parents, saw teachers as wanting to speak out on various social and civic issues (but, presumably, saw teachers also as being silent on such issues). Teachers, on the other hand, attributed to school officials and to parents a desire for teachers to keep quiet. In fact, teachers said they did not speak out in violation of their own norms (Rosencranz and Biddle, 1964, p. 257).

Of perhaps more importance, however, were the findings that all types of respondents felt that "people in general" made unreasonable demands upon teachers; and that "people in general" were more conservative than they themselves were in these regards. School officials, as the representatives of the public, were also thought to expect more than is necessary from their teachers and thus to precipitate conflict within the school system. The students (of whom half were in education) were less aware of such conflict than the other community respondents, but they held even more extreme views of the restrictive and oppressive nature of "the public" and of school officials.

Although this study was limited to one midwestern metropolitan area, it nevertheless suggests that teachers, administrators, and teachers-to-be in many respects attempt to meet public expectations that in fact do not exist. Efforts on the part of administrators and teachers to find out what the public really thinks might relieve teachers of some of the community pressures they feel, and might in this way help make the profession more attractive.

The Teacher in the School

If we shift our focus from the teacher's role in the community to the teacher's role within the school setting, we may describe the latter also as a set of sub-roles.

There are, first, the roles that describe the teacher in relation to other adults in the school system. Thus, as we have said in an earlier chapter, the teacher is in the role of *employee* in relation to the school board. He is also in the role of *subordinate* to the principal, of *advisee* to the supervisor, of *colleague* to his fellow-teachers. That these roles are not always performed smoothly has been illustrated at earlier points in this book. The older teacher whose idea of the job of the teacher conflicted with the ideas of the younger and newer teachers (p. 427), and the young music teacher who had trouble being accepted by older teachers (pp. 209–210) are having difficulty in filling the role of colleague.

Within the network of adult interaction, the teacher is in some respects in the role of *follower;* in other respects, in the role of leader or innovator. It is, however, the teacher's roles in relation to pupils that we wish to consider in more detail.

Mediator of Learning

The teacher's main role in relation to pupils, indeed the most significant of all his roles, is that of *mediator of learning.* In this role, he transmits knowledge and directs the learning process. In somewhat different terms, the main role of the teacher is to induce socially valued change in his pupils. This is at once the crux of the teaching profession and the most important criterion of the teacher's success.

In contrast to the other roles that we shall discuss presently, it is in the role of mediator of learning that the teacher tends to be most sure of himself. What is to be taught and how it is to be taught are the teacher's main stock in trade. Most of his professional training has prepared him for this role: his courses in curriculum, in methods, and in educational psychology. It is also within this role, as contrasted with others, that the teacher's behavior is the most highly ritualized and formalized. There are rules to follow and a structure within which to work. Subject matter can be defined and divided, lesson plans can be followed. There are well-defined criteria for measuring success in this role: the child can be tested and graded; and the teacher's own success is often measured in terms of the pupil's progress.

Disciplinarian

It has been said that if the teacher is to be successful in this role of facilitating learning, he must dominate the classroom situation.

He must make the students learn, and therefore he must dominate
them. He must be able to present a topic in such a way as to elicit as much
spontaneous interest as he can. When the attention of the class wanders, he
must be able to bring it back to the subject at hand, by persuasion if possible,
by force if necessary. If the ever-present covert resentment of school routine
breaks out into open rebellion, the teacher must know how to quell it. In
short, he must know how to play the role of domination. (Waller, 1942, pp.
207–208.)

Domination, in the terms just described, may or may not be an
integral element in the role of mediator of learning; but there is no
denying that the teacher must keep some kind of order in the classroom
if he is to teach, and that a second role that teachers occupy in relation
to pupils is the role of *disciplinarian*.

It is this role that seems to present the most problems, especially
for beginning teachers. Some complain that nowhere in their professional training were they prepared for the real problems related to
maintaining order in the classroom. "Even though I had my share of
practice teaching," says one young woman, "and even though there were
other problems in my first year of teaching, it was my total unprepared-
ness in knowing what to do about discipline that was my big nightmare."

Keeping order is generally easy in a high status or a conventional
type of school, but it may be very difficult in an inner-city school that
serves deprived children. Some teachers end a day with the feeling that
they have used up most of their energy just in keeping order and that
they have not had time for much real teaching. The problem of the
teacher in such a situation is illustrated in the following paragraphs:

Fighting: howling and tearing at each other in the halls. Raw emotion,
all on the surface. Corridor fighting needles the children in the room. Anything goes. "I went home for lunch and there wasn't no lunch, the gas was
off. Virgil wouldn't let me in the lunch line, then he laid for me, beat me
when I got back!" "That's all right, you hog all the food. I'll take y'on again
if y'come on, come on!" "I ain' giving it back. It ain't yours." "I'll getcha,
Bucky Blackie, I'll come back and getcha. I said you could have it yesterday,
give it back, I didn't say today." "Hatchet Head! It ain't hardly yours it's
Vernon's and he stoled it." And almost every child leaves in the morning
with something gnawing him. Vernon is eleven and has eight brothers and
sisters. Mrs. Weiss tells me this mother just returned from the hospital with a
baby and at noon I say, "I hear you have a new baby brother, Vernon." He
stares me straight in the eye, tears starting into his. *"I do not,"* he answers.

Mutual misery, mutual attack. Some cry all day; stay out in the hall
crying, won't come in and can't tell you why. Malcolm: "Teacher, Reggie's
hurtin' on Donald." Donald (hastily, scared): "No he isn't, teacher."

I put a problem on the board—a rather long one—turn around, and two children are bleeding, three are on top of them, fingers stabbing at eyes. The whole thing has been completely silent. Pieces of skin ripped off a cheek. A little girl is crying with her coat over her head.

Choking gutteral noises outside—not loud. In the corridor a third-grade girl, low-slung, stocky, is slugging a fifth-grade boy. Her eyes are cloudy; she drives her fists at him, "——off, buddy," but he gets her head and beats it against the wall. My kids rush to the door behind me, Reggie's eyes gleaming. But for once it looks so deadly, most kids are scared. The boy and girl are ringed. A boy says, *"She turnin' him on,* let her get what he give her. She gotta learn to defend herself." The boy is socking her in the throat. (Greene and Ryan, 1965, pp. 170–171.)

In another city, an eighth-grade teacher said,

The emotional problems that these kids have are beyond the scope of the schools. For example, I had problem reports on about ten pupils in my room, and I can't get them out of the room. They use profanity; they're antagonistic. Each moment I have to spend just sitting on them. To tell you the truth, they get to the seventh and eighth grade and the teachers just can't handle them. It's not that we don't understand the reasons for their behavior. Sure, we understand the reasons for their behavior. Even though we have all the understanding in the world, the behavior in the classroom hinders the teacher and this is the most important part.

In only some classrooms, of course, does the problem of discipline take the acute forms just described; but the role of disciplinarian troubles teachers in other types of situations as well. Sometimes the problem arises out of different expectations held by students and teacher, as in the case described in Chapter 16, where the teacher in the private school found herself faced by a group of boys who expected her to be authoritarian, contrary to her own expectations. Sometimes it arises when teachers object to the very requirement that they impose discipline, and when they see this role as interfering with their main tasks.

Whether a teacher is strict or lenient is not so much the issue; in more general terms it is the problem of role definition: How is the teacher to regard himself in the role of disciplinarian? What is desirable and what is undesirable behavior in the role? Questions such as these seem to be a main source of preoccupation among teachers, especially in schools that serve the so-called socially disadvantaged child.

Parent Substitute

A third role in interacting with children is that of *parent substitute*. This role comes to the foreground especially in the behavior of most primary teachers: helping the child with his clothing, comforting him, showing affection, praising or censuring various types of social and emotional behavior. The role is also present to greater or lesser degree in dealing with older children and adolescents.

The role of parent substitute has received increasing attention in recent years. The male teacher probably acts as often in the role of father as does the female teacher in the role of mother. One of the reasons that men have been urged to enter the teaching profession in greater numbers, especially at the elementary levels, is the belief that children stand to benefit from the presence of both father and mother figures in the school setting.

Judge

The teacher acts also in the role of *judge*. He has authority and he maintains discipline; he gives out grades and he promotes or does not promote the child. The role of judge is never confined, however, to the area of learning and academic progress. It carries over into many other aspects of the child's behavior. The teacher decides what is right and what is wrong, what is good and what is bad in social interaction between child and teacher and between child and child.

As a biology project, the class had set some seeds to grow, and we had put the dishes in a dark place in the basement. One day, we went down to check. There were several dishes on the floor that at the time seemed to have no owners—at least their owners had seemed to lose interest in the sluggishly germinating seeds. I asked whether one of these owners would like to give up his dish so that Jim, who had been absent, could have his own project, too. No one immediately volunteered, but Jim turned to me and said, "Here's one that doesn't belong to anyone."

"You're sure?" I questioned, looking around for an owner to claim it.

"Sure, it's O.K.," said Jim.

"O.K.," I told him and began showing him how to prepare the dish. Just as he finished and had the seeds and blotting paper well wetted down and carefully fitted into the dish, Arthur accosted him.

"That's my dish," he cried belligerently.

"It is not, it's mine," retorted Jim.

"That's my dish, Miss Troller," Arthur cried, turning to me.

"Jim told me it didn't belong to anyone," I replied. "We found it with nothing in it and no one would claim it."

"It's mine, and I want it," pouted Arthur.

"Well, you can't have it," replied Jim. Arthur looked at me, and I made it clear I was going to uphold Jim's claim. Arthur's face fell, he hunched his shoulders in the manner of a man unfairly beaten, and left the room. A short time later, upon returning to the classroom, I found Arthur huddled with dejection in a chair far across the room from where the other boys were working. He appeared disillusioned and thoroughly uninterested in participating further in the class. I inquired about his isolation.

"You gave him my dish!" he accused me. I reiterated that Jim and I had acted in good faith and that this, therefore, was not a case of stealing. Eventually Arthur's antipathy subsided, and he rejoined the group activity, but every once in a while reminding me that I had given his dish away.

There are more colorful terms that have been used to describe the behavior of teachers as judges or disciplinarians. Thus Redl and Wattenberg have described the roles of the teacher as being, at times, that of the *referee,* or *detective,* or *policeman* (Redl and Wattenberg, 1951).

Confidante

Somewhat opposed to the roles of disciplinarian and judge is the role of friend and *confidante.* Teachers are expected to be the friends of children; to be so supportive that children will place trust and affection in the relationship; to be so sympathetic that children will confide in them.

Surrogate of Middle-Class Morality

We have spoken in the preceding section of the teacher's role in the community as a *surrogate of middle-class morality.* This is a role that the teacher is expected to uphold, not only in his personal life outside the school, but particularly in his relations with his students. This role, as any other, stems not only from the expectations held by parents and other adults in the community, but also from the expectations held by teachers and students themselves.

I took my boys one day to the Garfield Park Conservatory. We visited the Desert Room, which was full of cactuses. Many of the boys tried to find out how much the burrs on the cactuses hurt, and I neither approved nor disapproved of their attempts. Ronnie, however, gave me a few uncomfortable glances when he noticed the signs, "Do not touch or damage plant material."

Later, we were in the Palm Room, and I had given a brief résumé of plant evolution. I tried to illustrate relatedness among plants by pointing out that the cycad looked like both a palm tree and a fern, making specific comparisons to the palm growing next to the cycad and the ferns that were growing at our feet. I turned the fern leaves over to look for spores, but there were none on these particular specimens. Remembering that a Boston fern at the door had very obvious spores, I walked the boys over to look. Turning the leaf over so the brown spots were visible, the boys remarked, "Oh, yeah!" and seemed a little impressed.

As we walked toward the door to the Jungle Room a few minutes later, Ronnie read aloud one of the several signs in the conservatory, "Do not touch or damage plant material."

"How come we were touching the plants when the sign said definitely not to?" he asked. Floyd, Eugene, and Alton looked at me quizzically.

"Yes, that's right," I answered him ambiguously.

"Well, how come you were touching the plants?" he demanded.

I told him it was permissible for the boys to do it occasionally when they were in a class with me and had a good purpose in doing so. Ronnie could not accept this as a valid excuse. Alton, Bernard, and André, however, supported my contention by going into action at once. They resumed examination of everything in sight. From then on Ronnie kept warning the boys about the signs; and I kept feeling more uncomfortable. There were a few specimens I wanted the boys to see more closely; so I continued as previously. The boys who were not walking near me seemed impressed by Ronnie's warnings and they made a point of not handling the plants any further. Those who stayed near me followed my own example, and continued to handle the plants gently.

Ronnie could not understand my attitude, and my behavior obviously distressed him more and more until we left the greenhouse.

Individuality in Role Performance

Any given teacher will fulfill varying role expectations in a unique manner. One teacher will stress the role of disciplinarian above all others; a second will see himself primarily in the role of friend and counselor to children; a third will attempt to eliminate all but the role of mediator of learning. For every teacher, factors of personality, factors related to social origin, and factors present in the particular school setting will interact to produce comfort in one role, discomfort in another.

Not only will every teacher work out his own pattern of behavior, but individuality will even go so far as to create new and unusual roles for the teacher. This may be seen in the case of Miriam Goldman, where a unique combination of personal and social factors was involved in producing the role of gang leader:

Miriam was born to a mobile upper-working-class family. Her immigrant parents owned a small dry goods store on the lower East side of New York, and the family lived in an apartment above the store. Her parents believed in hard work, education, and social improvement. This caused her home environment to be at sharp variance with the neighborhood culture.

Miriam was the last of eight children, physically unattractive and sensitive in temperament. In an otherwise close family unit she soon won the position of ugly duckling. Frustrated by lack of parental and sibling warmth, she became hostile to the world. Her defensive aggressiveness, quick temper, and "hard" behavior, made her an accepted leader of a neighborhood gang. The new behavior patterns that she learned coincided with her deepest personality drives. Miriam's resentment of her family led to increasingly antagonistic behavior. She continued to be frustrated by lack of personal recognition; jealousy and bitterness made her more of a fighter and less acceptable to her family.

Upon graduation from high school, an uncle sent her to teachers college. He believed that her sharp mind and keen sense of humor could, in a better environment, overcome her present difficulties. Through her college friendships she joined a clique of intellectuals. She married and had a child, only to be deserted by her husband a few months later.

Faced with the need to support a son, Miriam turned to teaching. She was given an assignment teaching delinquent boys in a lower-working-class public school. This situation was one that provided challenge, utilized her skills, and rewarded her personality traits. In her own words, she "found herself."

Her social background enabled her to understand working-class motivation. She understood the obstacles to learning—how the slum child fears being taken in by the teacher or of being a softie, and, how studying can be considered a disgraceful activity.

Discipline was the major problem. At first the boys tested her by pulling knives, threatening and physically molesting her. She responded with courage, humor, and fierce anger. In time she won the respect of the class leaders. Her aggression, quick tongue, and caustic wit made her acceptable to these boys. Miriam became a most effective teacher in this situation. To a degree she won the position of older female leader of a male gang. She could then move ahead to teaching, and to the attempt to awaken dormant intellects in these boys.

Role performance is, as we have seen, greatly influenced by various personality factors. One of these factors is age. The relation between age of teacher and age of pupil is a variable that has diverse ramifications in role performance. On the one hand, the teacher grows older while the age of his pupils tends to remain the same (as with the teacher who continues to teach in the fourth grade, year after year). Unlike the family situation, where change goes on in both parent and child simultaneously, the difference in age between teacher and child tends to increase with length of teaching experience. This affects more than one of the teacher's roles.

While there are a great many exceptions, it is usually the younger teacher, for example, who has more difficulty in the role of disciplinarian than does the older teacher. The younger teacher may also have greater difficulty, both with pupils and with parents, in being accepted as an expert in dealing with children. Peterson (1964), however, found that older women high school teachers, unless they had begun their careers with students very different from themselves, looked back with nostalgia to the time when there was little difference in age between themselves and their students. The older teacher may find increasing social distance between himself and his students and may accordingly have greater difficulty in filling the role of confidante or counselor.

It is likely that the relationship between the teacher's age and his teaching success varies tremendously, depending upon the needs of a particular group of children and the types of persons who can serve them as models.

Fulfilling the Roles of the Teacher

Age, sex, marital status, social-class background, and personality configuration all have their influence upon the ways in which teachers fill their roles; all will influence the extent to which role conflict is produced. Just as there may be conflict between various role expectations for the teacher in the community setting, so also there may be conflict between various role expectations for the teacher in the school setting. To act in the role of judge is often to decrease the teacher's effectiveness as mediator of learning; to act in the role of disciplinarian may be contrary to the teacher's role of confidante.

Yet here, as before, the important point is not so much the presence of conflict, but the resolution of conflict and the integration of varying role expectations. Waller, who differentiated between what he called the authoritative role of the teacher, on the one hand, and the personal roles of the teacher, on the other, stated this point well:

> When we analyze the classroom activities of a good teacher, we find that he alternates the authoritative role with personal roles, and *lengthens and shortens the rubber band of social distance* with consummate art [italics ours].

The good teacher makes such adjustments as we have described without reflection and almost without awareness. As if by a sort of instinct, he knows when to be cold and distant and when to be warm and personal, when to tighten up and when to relax, when to pat a boy on the back and when to be ruthlessly severe. He also knows what kinds of classroom deviations he must suppress as likely to disrupt equilibrium and threaten control and what kinds he can afford to tolerate. He knows when to enforce his rules and when to look the other way. But it is not really instinct that guides him, nor yet reason; it is habit. From a thousand trials and a hundred errors, from a thousand crises met and mastered, he has gained the sort of unreflective wisdom that is better than conscious principle as a guide to action, better because it acts quicker and more surely. In other words, the good teacher has so completely absorbed the teacher's roles that his personality is perfectly adjusted to the classroom situation. It has become as natural and easy for him to teach and to control a class as to breathe or eat his dinner. Only when the teacher has attained this complete adjustment of his personality to his job can we say that he has really learned his art. (Waller, 1942, pp. 212, 214.)

Exercises

1. Describe briefly two or three instances in which you or a teacher you know behaved toward the class in such a way as to fit the role of "surrogate of middle-class morality."

2. What do you think is the single most important role for the elementary school teacher to fulfill? Why?

3. Many educators see their role as maintainer of the status quo so far as the social class system is concerned. Do you think this is a proper role for the educator? Why, or why not?

4. Select any two of the roles discussed in this chapter and describe how
    they have created a conflict for you at one time or another. What
    happened? How did you resolve the conflict?

Suggestions for Further Reading

1. Margaret Mead, the well-known anthropologist, presents a stimulating
    discussion of the role of the teacher and of the place of the school in
    American society in a little book called *The School in American Culture.*

2. Read Chapters 10 and 13 in *Mental Hygiene in Teaching* by Fritz Redl
    and William Wattenberg for further discussion of the teacher's roles in
    dealing with classroom groups. See also "The Teacher's Roles," by
    Willard Waller (Chapter 10, in *Sociological Foundations of Education,*
    by J. S. Roucek and Associates); or "Role Functions of the Teacher in
    the Instructional Group," by William Clark Tron, Chapter 3 in the
    NSSE 59th yearbook, *The Dynamics of Instructional Groups.*

3. The paper by Getzels in *Society and Education: A Book of Readings*
    (Havighurst, Neugarten, and Falk) describes some of the contrasting
    roles which the teacher must assume and which produce inevitable
    conflicts. Also in this book of readings is a report by Biddle, Twyman,
    and Rankin on their investigation into the relationship between the role
    of the teacher and recruitment into the profession. The chapter by
    Peterson in this book gives insight into how teacher relationships and
    roles are affected by age.

4. A recent bestseller is the humorous book by Bel Kaufman, *Up the
    Down Staircase,* which describes the ups and downs of an inexperienced
    high school teacher in a large urban school trying to meet administrative
    directives as well as students' expectations as she reformulates her
    concept of the teacher's role.

18 / The Teacher in
the Classroom

The teacher is the key figure in the educational system. It is the teacher's behavior in the classroom situation that must eventually be the focus of our attention if we are to understand how society through its agent, the school, and, in turn, the school through the person of the classroom teacher, influences the lives of children. The issues we have discussed in previous chapters of this book—how family, school, and peer group interact in the socialization process, how the school promotes social mobility or social stability, how the teacher himself is influenced by social forces—take on reality in terms of particular teachers interacting with particular children.

From one point of view, we shall be elaborating here upon our preceding discussion of the teacher's roles in relation to pupils. In this chapter, however, we shall direct our attention to three aspects of the teacher's behavior in the classroom: how the teacher acts as a socializing agent, how various styles of leadership used by the teacher affect the behavior of children, and how the teacher relates to the peer group that constitutes the classroom group.

The Teacher as a Socializing Agent

There are countless examples that could be used to illustrate how teachers act to socialize children.

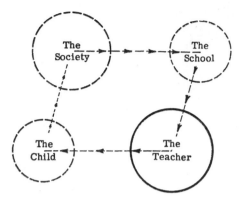

Figure 18.1 The teacher is the key figure in the interaction between society, school, and child.

Here is an observation made in a fourth-grade class:

"SPELLING BASEBALL"

The children form a line along the back of the room. They are to play "spelling baseball," and they have lined up to be chosen for the two teams. There is much noise, but the teacher quiets it. She has selected a boy and a girl and sent them to the front of the room as team captains to choose their teams. As the boy and girl pick the children to form their teams, each child chosen takes a seat in orderly succession around the room. Apparently they know the game well. Now Tom, who has not yet been chosen, tries to call attention to himself in order to be chosen. Dick shifts his position to be more in the direct line of vision of the choosers, so that he may not be overlooked. He seems quite anxious. Jane, Tom, Dick, and one girl whose name the observer does not know, are the last to be chosen. The teacher even has to remind the choosers that Dick and Jane have not been chosen. . . .

The teacher now gives out words for the children to spell, and they write them on the board. Each word is a pitched ball, and each correctly spelled word is a base hit. The children move around the room from base to base as their teammates spell the words correctly. With some of the words the teacher gives a little phrase: "Tongue, watch your tongue, don't let it say things that aren't kind; butcher, the butcher is a good friend to have; dozen, twelve of many things; knee, get down on your knee; pocket, keep your hand out of your pocket, and anybody else's. No talking! Three out!" The children say, "Oh, oh!"

The outs seem to increase in frequency as each side gets near the children chosen last. The children have great difficulty spelling "August." As they make mistakes, those in the seats say, "No!" The teacher says, "Man on third." As a child at the board stops and thinks, the teacher says, "There's a time limit; you can't take too long, honey." At last, after many children fail on "August" one child gets it right and returns, grinning with pleasure, to her seat. . . . The motivation level in this game seems terrific. All the children seem to watch the board, to know what's right and wrong, and seem quite keyed up. There is no lagging in moving from base to base. The child who is now writing "Thursday" stops to think after the first letter. and the children snicker. He stops after another letter. More snickers. He gets the word wrong. There are frequent signs of joy from the children when their side is right. (Henry, 1963, pp. 297–298.)

What is the teacher actually teaching in this situation? First, of course, spelling itself; and the corresponding value that to spell correctly is an important skill in American life. There are, however, many other values and attitudes being taught. The child may learn it is bad to say unkind things; he may wonder why he should keep his hands out of his own pockets, and he may be anxious lest the teacher should suspect that he wants to put his hands in other people's. He learns that the teacher upholds morality; at least, a certain type of morality. The most important part of the lesson, inadvertent though it may have been on the teacher's part, is perhaps the lesson of competitiveness: that it is serious to fail, important to succeed, that the society disapproves of slow people and rewards fast ones.

While competitiveness and self-assertion are important values in American society, so also are conformity and docility. Here are a few examples of how docility is inculcated in children by getting them to give the answers the teacher wants:

In a second-grade classroom, the children have been shown movies of birds. The first film ended with a picture of a baby bluebird.
TEACHER: Did the last bird ever look like he would be blue?
The children did not seem to understand the slant of the question, and answered somewhat hesitantly: Yes.
TEACHER: I think he looked more like a robin, didn't he?
CHILDREN (in chorus): Yes.

A fourth grade art lesson. Teacher holds up a picture.
TEACHER: Isn't Bobby getting a nice effect of moss and trees?
Ecstatic Ohs and Ahs from the children. . . .
(Later) The art lesson is now over.
TEACHER: How many enjoyed this?
Many hands go up.
TEACHER: How many learned something?
Quite a number of hands come down.

TEACHER: How many will do better next time?
Many hands go up.

In the same fourth grade classroom, the children have just finished reading the story "The Sun, Moon, and Stars Clock."
TEACHER: What was the highest point of interest—the climax?
The children tell what they think it is. Teacher is aiming to get from them what she thinks it is, but the children give everything else but. At last Bobby says: When they capture the thieves.
TEACHER: How many agree with Bobby?
Hands, hands, hands. (Henry, 1955, II, pp. 34–35.)

The children in these situations are learning to look to the teacher for cues, rather than to think for themselves. As they learn to give the expected responses, they are learning to be docile.

These examples are typical of everyday occurrences in which the teacher acts, in indirect ways, to transmit prevailing social values and expectations. Instances like these occur, although in less simple and less quotable forms, in higher as well as in lower school grades. A somewhat different example is one in which the teacher gives a lesson in interracial tolerance:

Richard returned to school after having been kept out for four months by his father who disapproved of the fact that there were Negro children in our school. The boy returned because of a court order, but he came with considerable hostility. Although he was successful in concealing his hostile feelings in the schoolroom, he formed cliques to fight the Negro children on the playground.

At home he reported to his father how he was attacked daily by groups of Negro children. The father was enraged and came to school to complain. We decided that the children would be observed in secret in order to get a true picture of the situation.

The first day of observation proved rewarding. A group of boys joined Richard and they ambled over to a group of Negro children who were playing marbles. Richard pushed Kenneth, a Negro boy, while his companions kicked the marbles over the playground. There was a tussle until the teacher on duty interfered.

Their escapade was reported to their home room and both sides had a chance to explain what had happened.

"Richard and his gang pushed Kenneth and kicked our marbles around."

"I did not. You and your gang are always jumping us and we gotta fight," retorted Richard.

Aside, Richard was told that he had been seen, and it was known that he had started the fight. He admitted that this was true.

Finally the entire group was taken into the discussion. It was a delicate subject, but a necessary one. It so happened that one little girl named Donna volunteered to say that her father wanted her to go to our school because he felt that his daughter should know Negro children. He did not want his child to be prejudiced. Other children related stories that helped to build up good feeling.

It turned out well. The Negro children learned that hostile feelings existed only among a few, but that most of us liked them. The white children became conscious that the Negro children had a problem, and they offered their sympathy. The culmination was unexpected. Richard openly apologized to the children and promised that he would not fight them again. We had no further problems in this area for the rest of the semester.

In this instance, the teacher has taught at least two lessons in addition to the lesson in interracial understanding: one, that the guilty person must not shift the blame to an innocent person; second, that group discussion is an effective means of solving problems.

The following is an example taken from a guidance lesson in a fourth-grade class for the intellectually gifted in a slum school in New York City. The school was dedicated to helping lower-working-class children enter into middle-class ways of life and was deliberately trying to train these children for a separation from the private world of the family to the public world outside of the school.

Mrs. Smith, the teacher, now asks the class the following question. "A couple of weeks ago, what did you do about taking photographs?" A child replies, "First, the man told us to smile." Mrs. Smith says, "Yes, true. Where did your preparation for the picture start?" A child says, "You had to make sure you were dressed properly." A second child says, "You had to comb and brush your hair." A third child replies, "You had to ask your mother whether she wanted you to take the photograph."

Mrs. Smith accepts all of these answers and comments that they are very good. "What you have told me, children, comes under the heading of GROOMING." As she speaks, she writes this word on the blackboard in capital letters. She asks the children to pronounce the word, which they do in unison. She asks them if they have ever used that word before, and many of the children indicate that they have. Mrs. Smith now writes the following heading on the blackboard: "For a *good photograph* we need." Under the heading, she prints the words, *grooming, washing, dressing, combing,* and *smiling.*

Turning back to the class, she inquires, "What part of you does not show in a photograph?" A child answers, "The shoes on your feet." The teacher replies that, "They would show on a full-length photograph of you."

Another child says, "Your intelligence." Mrs. Smith says, "Good. That has to do with what, children?" "With your mind," answers another child.

On the blackboard Mrs. Smith writes MENTAL PHOTOGRAPH in capital letters. Next to these words, she writes the words, *teacher, yourself,* and *parent.* She now explains to the class that these three groups have some idea of your mental photograph.

Meantime Mrs. Smith has written the numbers 1 and 2 under the words MENTAL PHOTOGRAPH. She then continues the lesson by saying, "Under a good physical photograph, if you wish, you could comb your hair, brush your hair and have good grooming. You would then have a good flat photograph of yourself. What is the part that you play in building a good mental photograph of yourself?" Robert, one of the children in the class, says, "Try to do the best you can. The teacher will ask you to do something and you try to do it anyhow even if it is hard." Mrs. Smith asks, "What is a word which means trying to do the best you can?" "Studying," replies Robert. The teacher says, "Good. That might cover it, but let's use the word *effort.*" She goes to the blackboard and writes the word *effort* next to the number 1 under the MENTAL PHOTOGRAPH. "Robert," she says, "touched on something else—good studying." She puts these words next to the number 2 under the words MENTAL PHOTOGRAPH. (Eddy, 1965, 1967.)[1]

The above examples have been selected, not because they illustrate desirable or undesirable behavior in teachers, but because they illustrate the point that the teacher, with or without awareness, and in direct or indirect ways, transmits not only information and knowledge, but also a wide variety of cultural values and attitudes. It is in this sense that the teacher is a potent socializing agent in the life of the child and adolescent.

Leadership in the Classroom

As implied earlier, the teacher is the authority figure in the classroom, whether or not his authority is exercised in formal or informal ways, and whether or not the situation created for students is relatively repressive or relatively permissive. While it is always inherent in the teaching situation that the teacher acts in the roles of authority figure and group

[1] From *Walk The White Line,* by Elizabeth M. Eddy. Copyright © 1965, 1967 by Elizabeth M. Eddy. Reprinted by permission of Doubleday & Company, Inc.

leader, teachers show considerable variation in the ways in which they fill the leadership role.

Teaching Styles

As one watches teachers in different classrooms, one can see that each teacher has a style of his own. It is as if he has a model in his mind of what the classroom should be like, and acts in ways to make the classroom conform to this image. Thelen has described in colorful terms a number of models that teachers seem to use:

(1) *Socratic discussion.* The image is of a wise, somewhat crusty philosopher getting into arguments with more naive people. The issues discussed are known to both parties, and the arguments are primarily to clarify concepts and values.

(2) *The town meeting.* The image is of a group of citizens meeting together to decide on courses of action required to solve problems.

(3) *Apprenticeship.* The image is of a young person's life being "taken over" by an older person. The apprentice identifies with and imitates the master. According to this image, the child is in school to learn how to be like the teacher.

(4) *Boss-employee, or army model.* The image here is of a teacher who has a higher status than pupils, and who has the power to reward or punish. He tells others what to do and how to do it; then sees that it gets done; and finally, evaluates how good a job he thinks it is. According to this image, the relationship between teacher and pupils need not be harsh or unfriendly, but it is necessary that the subordinate be dependent upon the "boss."

(5) *The business deal.* This is essentially the "contract plan" in which the teacher makes the best deal he can with each individual student and consults with him as the work proceeds.

(6) *The good old team.* The image is of a group of players listening to the coach between quarters of the football game.

(7) *The guided tour.* The image here is of a group of interested children following closely behind a mature guide, who, from time to time, calls their attention to objects he wants to tell them about. He gives information, stories and opinions; he also answers questions. He maintains order, and sees to it that the number of children who arrive home equals the number who set out in the morning. (Adapted from Thelen, 1954, pp. 36–39.)

Certain of these models are obviously more realistic than others; and certain ones will be appropriate in some situations, but not in others. Each will produce a different effect upon group interaction.

Types of Leadership

Among the earliest studies of styles of leadership that seemed to have relevance for educators were those carried out by Lewin, Lippitt, and White, in which boys' clubs were exposed to leaders who used democratic, *laissez-faire,* or authoritarian methods. The interactions of club members showed consistent differences under the various styles of leadership (Lippitt and White, 1943). Under democratic leaders, for example, group morale was highest; comments phrased in terms of "we" rather than "I" were more frequent; there was more friendly sociability. Intergroup aggression was highest under authoritarian leaders. While the boys spent more of their time actually "working" when the leader was authoritarian, their work tended to stop and the group tended to disintegrate as soon as the leader left the room. These findings point to the importance of the adult's behavior in influencing the social and emotional climate for the group as a whole.

Using a different approach, Cunningham and her associates identified five general patterns of interaction between teacher and pupils in first, fourth, and eighth grade classrooms:

(1) "Adult rule, child obedience," in which the teacher seems to act on the assumption that he holds absolute authority and that pupils should respond unquestioningly with the demanded behavior.

An extreme example of this type of leadership is the following: "Miss Armstrong was, to the best of our knowledge, a sincere teacher attempting to carry out her functions as she deemed necessary. In one observed period of sixty minutes she issued forty orders, from 'Class, come to attention!' to 'John, put your pencil away!' Approximately 50 per cent of her verbal interaction with the class, as classified by the observer, took the form of directives, such as 'David, take question four!' 'Mary, read the next paragraph!' or of the type exemplified by the earlier statements. An additional 30 per cent might be classified as directives, though in question form, such as 'Why did you do that?' or 'Where is Boston?' Another 10 per cent was classified by the observer as dictums, such as 'That's right!' or 'Correct!' The remaining 10 per cent of her verbal comment was put into a miscellaneous grouping and included such statements as 'John, are you listening?' and 'Do you understand?' " (Cunningham and associates, 1951, pp. 25–26.)

(2) The planless "catch-as-catch-can" pattern, in which the teacher makes no attempt to control or organize the group. (While this pattern is relatively infrequent, it occurred most often when teachers who used the first pattern felt they were "loosening the reins" for brief intervals.)

(3) The pattern in which the teacher works with individual students in planning their work; emphasis is upon individual attention and individual initiative, but group interaction is curtailed. (4) The pattern of adult-directed group planning, where group interaction is allowed for, and where children plan their activities within the boundaries set by the teacher. (5) The pattern of group self-management through group planning.

Here again, pupil behavior seemed to vary in relation to the style of leadership employed by the teacher. Under the "adult rule, child obedience" pattern, for example, there were two kinds of reactions in pupils: docile obedience or open hostility. Under the "catch-as-catch-can" pattern, the reaction of pupils seemed to be confusion, insecurity, and keen competition for power.

Gordon and Adler (1963), using still another method, studied modes of teacher leadership derived from questionnaires given to pupils in a large urban grade school to gauge the amount of emphasis the teachers placed upon authority, performance, and expressivity. The teachers whose pupils showed the most favorable gains in learning, compliance, and classroom order were those who were perceived by their pupils as stressing performance, seldom relying upon authority, and placing average stress upon expressivity. Teachers who were rated low on stressing performance and low on expressivity but high on authority had pupils who gained in knowledge and were compliant, but who also had low morale and poor class order and who did little voluntary work.

Teacher-Student Interaction

Another approach to the study of teaching style is that of analyzing student and teacher interaction in terms of small units of behavior. Such an approach permits study of pupil behavior and teacher behavior at the same time; and therefore reveals certain aspects of the classroom climate as well as of teaching style. The studies of Anderson and his co-workers of "dominative" and "integrative" behavior of different teachers in the actual classroom situation were among the first of this type (Anderson and Brewer, 1945, 1946; Anderson, Brewer, and Reed, 1946).

Dominative contacts by teachers included: calling to attention; giving warnings or reminders; making gratuitous judgments for a child; lecturing; refusing, denying, or contradicting (with explanations); punishing (including sending child out of room, keeping him after school, depriving him of specific material, or an activity or privilege); giving approval or disapproval of required work; and granting permission. *Integrative* contacts included: extending invitation to child; helping to define, redefine, or advance a problem; giving approval of spontaneous or self-initiated behavior of child; questioning of possible, though not expressed, interest of child; and admitting responsibility for own act that is inconvenient, unjust, or unfair to another, or admitting own ignorance or incapacity.

The findings from the Anderson studies have most recently been summarized as follows:

First, the dominative and integrative contacts of the teacher set a pattern of behavior that spreads throughout the classroom; the behavior of the teacher, more than that of any other individual, sets the climate of the class. The rule is that, when either type of contact predominates, domination incites further domination and integration stimulates further integration. The teacher's tendency spreads among pupils and persists even when the teacher is no longer in the room. Furthermore, that pattern a teacher develops in one year is likely to persist in his classroom the following year with completely different pupils.

Second, when a teacher has a high proportion of integrative contacts, pupils show more spontaneity and initiative, voluntary social contributions, and acts of problem solving.

Third, when a teacher has a high proportion of dominative contacts, the pupils are more easily distracted from school work and show more compliance to, as well as rejection of, teacher domination. (Flanders, 1964, pp. 204–205.)

From this series of investigations, it is evident that the teacher's behavior influences pupil behavior; and that, together, teacher and pupils create a classroom "atmosphere" or "climate" which is more or less favorable for teaching and learning.

Verbal Communication in the Classroom

Flanders and his associates (Amidon and Flanders, 1961, 1963; Flanders, 1960, 1964) have studied classroom climate and made observations in terms of the verbal communication that occurs during lesson time in 16 seventh-grade social studies classes and in 16 eighth-grade mathematics classes. The teachers taught a specially-developed two-week unit of study that was flexible enough so that it did not hamper individual teaching style. The classrooms were observed at the beginning, at the middle, and at the end of the two-week session, and in each observation session the classroom talk was classified at three-second intervals.

The teachers were characterized as "direct" if they preferred teaching methods that restricted student freedom of participation (lecturing, giving directions, criticizing or justifying authority) and as "indirect" if they preferred methods that expanded student freedom of participation (accepting student feelings, praising or encouraging, accepting or using ideas of students, asking questions).

At the end of the unit the pupils were given an achievement test to determine what they had learned and how well they could apply their new knowledge and skills. Contrary to what one might expect, the pupils with the more indirect teachers learned the most, whether they were studying mathematics or social studies. Analysis of the findings indicated, however, that the essential difference between the most successful and the least successful teachers lay not in the fact that the most successful used the most indirect methods (and the least successful the fewest indirect methods), but that the teachers who used the most indirect methods had at their command a wider *range* of techniques, and changed methods more frequently than did the teachers who used the most direct methods.

Leadership styles vary not only in tone, but in terms of range, so to speak. One teacher will emphasize his relationship with the group as a whole, aiming his directives, questions, and comments more often to the whole group than to individual boys and girls.

Sources of Information on the Classroom Group

In relating to the classroom group, the teacher utilizes not only his general knowledge of groups as a socializing force upon children and adolescents, but he also uses his knowledge of the social network, the dynamics of interaction, and the values and attitudes of the particular group before him. After the first few weeks of the school year, every teacher knows something of the social organization that exists within his classroom and makes use of this information in dealing with the group.

The teacher obtains his information in various ways. One is by his own observation: noticing the friendship patterns that exist, determining who seem to be the isolated members of the group, who seem to be the ones sought after by the other children, and so on.

In many instances, the teacher obtains a relatively comprehensive and accurate picture in these ways. In many other instances, however, he obtains only a partial, if not an incorrect, picture. Possible distortion arises from several sources. The first stems from the very fact that the teacher is an adult and thus necessarily views boys and girls from an adult point of view. To some extent, he obtains only an outsider's view of the child's world.

Another factor is that the teacher's information is usually limited to only certain types of observation and to information obtained from only certain members of the group. In the busy round of his activities, the teacher is seldom able to make systematic observations of group behavior or to see a sufficient variety of social situations. His observations tend to be limited to what goes on within the schoolroom itself, or the immediately surrounding areas such as the playground, the corridors, the lunchroom.

For these reasons many teachers find the use of sociometric techniques an important aid in obtaining better understanding of the social network that exists within the classroom.

Sociometric Methods

The sociometric method most frequently used in the classroom situation consists, in its simplest terms, of asking each child to say with whom he would like to sit or work on a committee or whom he would choose for a similar type of school interaction. These choices are then related to one another in systematic fashion so as to obtain a picture of the entire structure of relationships that exists within the group.

THE SOCIOGRAM. Most often the results are shown graphically in what is called a sociogram (see pages 470–471). The *sociogram* shows each child's position in the group in terms of the choices he receives and the choices he makes. It also shows the overall network—if the group is tightly or loosely structured; if there are few or many isolates (children who receive no choices); if there are few or many "stars" (children who receive a disproportionately large number of choices); if there are few or many mutual choices; if there is one or more cliques (where three or four members choose each other but do not choose persons outside the sub-group); if there are certain types of cleavages that exist, say, between boys and girls; and so on.

A sociogram can yield important new information to the teacher.

In the first place, it offers a means of checking the teacher's own evaluations against those of the pupils. Thus one teacher reports:

> I learned a lot from the sociogram of my class. As I had expected, Marianne was popular with the other children, and Fred was an outcast. I was right, too, about some of the others. Still it was a real surprise to find that Ronald, whom I had thought of as a leader in the group, was chosen by only one other boy in the room; and Nancy, who seems to me so quiet and colorless, is one of the best-liked children in the group. I saw at once that my own judgments were being made on different grounds than those used by the children themselves; and I saw also that I must find out what the children's judgments were based upon, if I was to handle the group wisely.

This teacher's comment is by no means unusual, as is shown by a large number of formal and informal studies based upon sociometric methods in classroom settings. To mention but two examples, a study by Bonney showed that teachers often award official leadership roles to boys and girls who possess no leadership in the eyes of the group, and to rely on children who have little influence with their peers for communication of the teacher's ideas and values (Bonney, 1947). Moreno found, furthermore, that, while kindergarten teachers could predict with 65 percent accuracy which children in their classes were the most popular, by the seventh grade, teacher's averages had dropped to 25 percent (Moreno, 1934).

Social Dynamics of the Classroom

Implicit in the teacher's comments quoted above is the fact that the sociogram itself is only the first step in helping the teacher understand the social dynamics of the classroom group. It tells who is and who is not chosen; it does not tell why. Another teacher, after interviewing each boy and girl in her class to find out the reasons underlying their choices, describes her new insights. She had predicted that one girl, Estelle, would be highly chosen. "She was intelligent; she could do a remarkable amount of work (for me and for them) in a short time; she was always handy when I needed her." Yet Estelle turned out to be unchosen, and in comparing the children's picture of Estelle with her own, the teacher says:

> What a contrast! I saw a girl who appeared to be quiet, who agreed easily to do anything *I* wanted her to do, who was a model student as far as her teacher was concerned. Her classmates showed her as a child frustrated

in all her attempts to join a group of teen-agers, disturbed and upset because
she knew she was unwanted, displaying a bad disposition as a result of her
frustration, joining in friendship with another girl who had a bad reputation
because no one in her own group would accept her, and bringing upon
herself further condemnation because of that very act of friendship.

Immediately I realized the possible effect of what I had been doing on
Estelle's social position. Instead of keeping her out of the limelight until I
could help her adopt behavior that was more socially acceptable, I had been
constantly calling on her to assist those who, as I know now, wanted no
assistance from her. I had been putting her in a position that invited
rejection. (Taba and Elkins, 1950, p. 5.)

It is not only in terms of the positions of individual boys and girls
that the sociogram gives useful information. The teacher deals essentially with the classroom group as a *group,* and not as an aggregation of
individuals. Although individual boys and girls influence the behavior of
the group as a whole, and although individual positions are one of the
indices of group cohesion, still there are other aspects of group interaction that are of equal or greater importance.

Sociometric Structures

Sociometric structures in different classroom groups frequently are
similar. Thus, in primary grades (where sociometric choices are obtained orally, rather than in writing) the structure usually shows chains
of one-way choices (A chooses B; B chooses C; C chooses D) and few
mutual choices. At higher grade levels, clique formations are more
frequent. Boy-girl cleavages seem to vary with age, with fewer intersex
choices in the lower school grades, and with more intersex choices in
grades six through twelve. Certain studies have shown cleavages that
follow racial and religious lines; others that show cleavages between
children of different social class backgrounds. Still, in the wide literature
on sociometry, the more striking thing is not the *similarities* in sociometric structure from group to group, but rather the great *variation* that
exists between groups and the change that occurs from time to time
within the same group within the same school year.

The group structure that is found in a given classroom at any given
time is the result of a great variety of factors: the personalities of
individual children; the presence of newcomers in the group; the extent
to which cleavages exist between ethnic, racial, and religious groups in
the community at large. The administrative policies followed by the

school are also important, such as the extent to which the school uses homogeneous grouping according to ability; the extent to which boys and girls have separate clubs and separate classes; the extent to which the school generally encourages or discourages social class differentiations.

Classroom Climate and Sociometric Structure

More important than any of these factors, however, is the social and emotional climate that prevails within the classroom itself. The climate is in many ways directly affected by the teacher's own behavior. In a classroom, for example, where the teacher gives certain students authority over others, the structure of choices and rejections may show the effects. In a group where children hold the teacher in especially high regard, his own choices among the group will be reflected in the children's choices. In a group where the teacher is not so highly regarded, children may reject those whom the teacher seems to favor.

The fact that the social and emotional climate of the classroom will affect the sociometric structure within the group is well illustrated in the following two sociograms, in which the same group is shown in September and again in April of the same school year. These sociograms are based on seating preferences; students were asked to write on a card the names of three people whom they wanted to sit next to, then to write the name of anyone whom they preferred not to sit next to.

This was an eighth grade group in a public elementary school, a school located in a lower-class neighborhood in an eastern city. Of the twenty-five students, eight were new to the school. Nine were boys; sixteen were girls. In terms of religious affiliation 13 were Protestant, 11 were Catholic, and one was Jewish. Ethnic backgrounds included Lithuanian, Polish, Russian, German, French-Canadian, Scotch, Irish, Italian, Swedish, and English. Only one student was of upper-middle class; ten were lower-middle; eleven, upper-working; and three, lower-working.

The teacher, with the help of a consultant in intergroup education, planned and carried out a special program aimed at the improvement of human relations. By organizing social studies, literature, and guidance into one sequence the teacher had two and one-half hours with the group each day. She organized reading and discussion around topics which concerned the students—family relations, siblings, problems of growing up, peer relations. Emphasis was put on the ethnic backgrounds of American people, problems of minority groups, and upon historic documents dealing with individual rights and democratic equality. Students were encouraged to express their feelings as well as their ideas, and to analyze the causes and

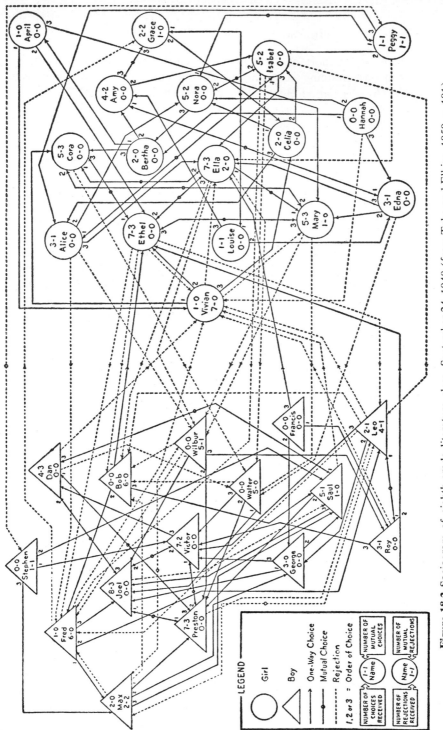

Figure 18.2 Sociogram of eighth-grade literature class, September 24, 1948 (from Taba and Elkins, 1950, p. 191).

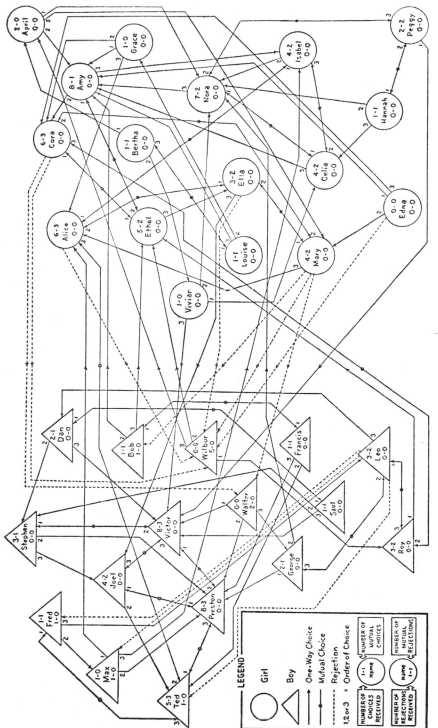

Figure 18.3 Sociogram of eighth-grade literature class, April 29, 1949 (from Taba and Elkins, 1950, p. 192).

consequences of incidents in their own lives as well as those found in the books they read.

Group planning was used whenever possible. Students were combined and recombined sociometrically into committees and study groups. These groups were made up to preserve existing networks while extending them gradually, and by combining skills for maximum mutual help and inter-action.

While the group changed in many desirable ways, the change was evidenced also in the sociometric findings. The teacher reported: "The series of sociograms gave me tangible evidence of shifts toward broader and more harmonious relations.

"The most dramatic change was the reduction of general hostility. From September to May rejections were reduced from forty-three to eleven. Early in the year only three boys chose girls, no girls chose boys, and the large number of boy-girl rejections, twenty-four, suggested a virtual cleavage. By the end of the year there were fifteen boy-girl choices and only eight rejec-tions, five of them concentrated on one boy, Wilbur.

"In September there were three rather intimate groups, two of them practically closed, with no choices going out. While intimate clusters ap-peared in April also, their personnel changed and none of them was closed. The number of completely unchosen children dropped from six to three. In addition, there was a distinct reduction in the hostility that centered on certain individuals. Vivian, who was at first one of the most highly rejected children, received not even one rejection on the second sociogram. In the early part of the year, no matter what that child did or said, it was held against her. This was also true of other students: Fred, Walter, Bob, Leo, although not to so marked a degree. Wilbur was the only boy for whom life became no more comfortable at school. For the rest, life in school must have become a good deal more pleasant and satisfying." (Adapted from Taba and Elkins, 1950, pp. 190–93, and Taba, 1955.)

Uses of Sociometric Data

The foregoing example is an unusual one in that a number of factors— administrative arrangements, the curriculum itself, teaching methods, the presence of an expert consultant—all combined to produce a situa-tion in which group structure was modified in desirable ways. In more typical situations, where the teacher may be more limited in his control over administrative and curricular policies, the outcomes may be less striking. Still sociometric findings in themselves may be used to produce beneficial results. Most teachers, for instance, notice desirable changes in group morale when they simply make new seating arrangements, or new committee groupings, on the basis of the students' choices.

Sociometric methods can be used successfully in situations in which the teacher knows relatively little about his students, as in the first weeks of the school year. Groupings made on the basis of students' choices are as successful with high school students as with elementary students; and in special subject-matter classes as well as in regular homerooms. Thus shop teachers have reported excellent results when boys were assigned to work-tables according to their choices for partners; gym teachers have used student choices in assigning locker space and in drawing up teams for group games; and so on.

We have been discussing two related aspects of the use of sociometric methods. In the first, the teacher uses sociometry as an aid in understanding the existing social network within the classroom, in order that he may work more effectively with the peer group. In the second, the teacher uses sociometry as an aid in modifying the network and in bringing about certain changes within it that he considers desirable. In the latter connection, it should be emphasized again that although a sociogram can tell the teacher a good deal about the network of relationships that exists within the class, it cannot, in itself, show the reasons underlying the structure. To understand why children choose as they do, the teacher must look to other sources of information—the values and attitudes boys and girls express in classroom discussions, what they reveal of themselves in essays or in autobiographical accounts; what they say of each other in interviews with the teacher; their family backgrounds; and so on. Neither does the sociogram itself offer any answers about what the teacher should or should not do to modify the existing network of relationships. For example, Reger (1963) has reported two instances of failure by teachers and staff to make effective use of sociometric information. In the first instance, the most unpopular boy was deliberately given a job greatly envied by his peers in an attempt to enhance his status and make him more acceptable to the group. Subsequent sociometric tests, however, showed that he remained the most disliked boy in the group. At the same time, a very popular but shy and passive boy was put in charge of group safety at street crossings. He took his new responsibilities seriously, became extremely "bossy," and rapidly lost popularity.

These two examples demonstrate that the teacher does not necessarily make a rejected child more popular by singling him out for attention (although he may, by increasing the child's self-confidence, enable him to win acceptance for himself). Similarly, in deciding that a given clique should be broken up, or that the influence of a particular boy or girl is too pervasive in the group as a whole and should be mitigated, the teacher must proceed with considerable caution. Acting upon only the best intentions, teachers have sometimes attempted to modify the social relationships between children, only to find that the intervention resulted in hindering, rather than helping, the situation. In deciding what to do on the basis of sociometric findings, the teacher must bring to bear all his knowledge of individual children in the group and all his skill in human relations.

The Importance of the Classroom Climate

Having considered some of the techniques by which teacher-student and student-student interaction can be judged, we turn to a study in which several different methods were used to determine the characteristics of classroom climates.

Connor (1960) selected the "best" and the "worst" classrooms for study by giving the students in eight primary schools in an English urban area a questionnaire for measuring adjustment to school. It included such questions as these:

Does the class 'play up' when the teacher leaves the room?
Are you so keen on your work that you always try your best?
Have you ever been strapped by a teacher?
Are you afraid when you don't finish your work?
Does your teacher have lots of fun with you?
Would you work just as hard if there were no tests?
Does the teacher make you feel foolish?
Are you sometimes not sure what to do next in class?

All the selected classes were observed; the number of social contacts of each child was recorded; and the quality of interaction between teacher and students was rated in terms of interest, enjoyment, emotional rapport, physical tension, social relations, and reactions to orders. A sociometric test was used to measure group cohesiveness, and a peer ranking test to measure peer reputation.

The differences between classrooms were greater than the differences between schools in this study. The classrooms with "good" climates were those in which the relationships between teacher and children were warm and friendly and the pupils were relaxed. They confided in the teacher and generally behaved well. The peer groups were cohesive, with few "stars" and few isolated children. In these classes the children were well adjusted to school and had favorable attitudes toward school. The classrooms with "poor" climates, on the other hand, were those in which pupil-teacher relationships were distant and formal and the pupils frequently were aggressive and competitive. The peer group was more fragmented, and there was less interaction among pupils. In these classes, the children were poorly adjusted to school and held relatively negative attitudes toward school.

Connor did not measure the amount of learning that occurred in "good" and in "bad" climates, but his conclusions make it clear that he sees a close relationship between classroom atmosphere and amount learned:

> There is little doubt . . . that in general the school surroundings, the home backgrounds of the pupils, as well as individual personal attributes of pupils and teacher, have their influence, but it is the interaction of these in a dynamic classroom situation that has more immediate relevance for the teacher and the learning process. . . . Important end products (of a good climate) are good rapport between teacher and pupils, a reasonably permissive atmosphere, a "socially well-balanced" classroom, and a healthy attitude to school in general. (Connor, 1960, p. 249.)

Exercises

1. Give an example of how a middle-class teacher became a model for a working-class child. What did the teacher do? What did the child do? Be specific.

2. Give an example at the high school level in which a teacher promotes conformity in a group of students. Be specific. Give an example in which the high school teacher promotes competitiveness.

3. Describe an instance in which a teacher used autocratic leadership. Was it the most effective approach, under the circumstances? Why, or why not? Now describe an instance in which a teacher used democratic leadership. Was it the most effective approach in that situation? Why or why not?

4. Describe an instance in which a teacher worked against, or at odds with, the peer group. What was the outcome? If the teacher had behaved differently, would the outcome have been different?

5. It has been said that the typical teacher in a middle-class school directs the hostility of children toward one another and away from himself;

whereas in a working-class school he behaves in such a way as to promote the solidarity of the peer group by focusing their hostility upon himself. Do you agree or disagree with this statement? Why?

Special Exercise I

Analyze the interaction between a teacher and a class, using the method described below, developed by Amidon and Flanders (1963). Use a tape recorder so that you can listen back as many times as necessary in categorizing the verbal communication. (Because only verbal behavior is observed, you may analyze *your own* teaching methods by making a recording of one of your own class periods.)

Verbal behavior is recorded in small units as will be demonstrated presently. All verbal interaction is categorized first as either "teacher talk" or "student talk." Teacher talk is classified as either direct influence (limiting freedom of response) or as indirect influence (maximizing freedom of response); student talk, according to whether it occurs in response to the teacher, or is initiated by the student. There are 10 categories in all, as shown in Table 18.1.

The observer (or the teacher, working from a tape recording) writes down every 3 seconds, in sequence, the numbers of the categories that best correspond to the interaction occurring in the classroom. Each change in category is recorded; and if no change occurs within 3 seconds, the category number is repeated. The observer makes his judgments according to the teacher's effect upon his pupils (that is, the effect of restricting or expanding their freedom) rather than according to the teacher's *intent*. For example, a portion of a fifth-grade social studies lesson was observed and recorded as follows:

> The teacher says to the class, "Boys and girls, please open your social studies books to page 5." (Observer classified this as a 6, followed by a 10 because of the period of silence and confusion as the children try to find the page.) The teacher says, "Jimmy, we are all waiting for you. Will you please turn your book to page 5?" (Observer records a 7 and a 6.) "I know now," continues the teacher, "that some of us had a little difficulty with, and were a little disturbed by, the study of this chapter yesterday: I think that today, we are going to find it more exciting and interesting." (Observer records two 1's, reacting to feeling.) "Now, has anyone had a chance to think about what we discussed yesterday?" (Observer records a 4 for a question.) A student answers, "I thought about it, and it seems to me that the reason we are in so much trouble in Southeast Asia is that we haven't really had a chance to learn to understand the ways of the people who live there." (Observer records three 8's.)
>
> The teacher responds by saying, "Good, I am glad that you suggested

Table 18.1 Summary of Categories for Interaction Analysis

TEACHER TALK	INDIRECT INFLU- ENCE	1. * ACCEPTS FEELING: accepts and clarifies the feeling tone of the students in a nonthreatening manner. Feelings may be positive or negative. Predicting and recalling feelings are included. 2. * PRAISES OR ENCOURAGES: praises or encourages student action or behavior. Jokes that release tension, not at the expense of another individual, nodding head or saying "um hm?" or "go on" are included. 3. * ACCEPTS OR USES IDEAS OF STUDENT: clarifying, building, or developing ideas or suggestions by a student. As teacher brings more of his own ideas into play, shift to category five. 4. * ASKS QUESTIONS: asking a question about content or procedure with the intent that a student answer.
	DIRECT INFLU- ENCE	5. * LECTURING: giving facts or opinions about content or procedure; expressing his own idea; asking rhetorical questions. 6. * GIVING DIRECTIONS: directions, commands, or orders with which a student is expected to comply. 7. * CRITICIZING OR JUSTIFYING AUTHORITY: statements intended to change student behavior from nonacceptable to acceptable pattern; bawling someone out; stating why the teacher is doing what he is doing, extreme self-reference.
STUDENT TALK		8. * STUDENT TALK-RESPONSE: talk by students in response to teacher. Teacher initiates the contact or solicits student statement. 9. * STUDENT TALK-INITIATION: talk by students, which they initiate. If "calling on" student is only to indicate who may talk next, observer must decide whether student wanted to talk. If he did, use this category.
		10. * SILENCE OR CONFUSION: pauses, short periods of silence, and periods of confusion in which communication cannot be understood by the observer.

Source: Amidon and Flanders, 1963, p. 12.

that, John. Now let me see if I understand your idea completely. You have suggested that if we had known the people better in Southeast Asia, we might not be in the trouble we are in today." (This is classified as a 2, followed by two 3's.) "Jim, what would we need to know about the people in Southeast Asia in order to understand them better as John has suggested?" (Observer records a 3, not a 4, because the question is constructed on the ideas and concepts suggested by a pupil.) (Adapted from Amidon and Flanders, 1963, pp. 25–26.)

After the class session is over the observer places a 10 before and after the series of numbers, arbitrarily assuming that the class began and ended with silence. He then records the frequency of the numbers by placing tallies in a 10 by 10 matrix to represent *pairs* of numbers, so that the row indicates the first number of a pair and the column, the second. For the example given above, the first pair is 10 (silence before class) and 6, and is recorded by placing a tally in the cell formed by row 10 and column 6. The second pair, 6, 10, is recorded in row 6, column 10; and so forth. Each number, except the first and last, is thus used twice. (For more detailed instructions, see Amidon and Flanders, 1963.)

The completed matrix (see Figure 18.4) yields much valuable information concerning how the teacher uses class time. To illustrate, column totals are given in the figure for a class period for which 150 interaction units were tallied. A total of 150 tallies is used here for illustrative purposes only. In actual practice it is difficult to interpret a matrix that has fewer than 400 tallies (400 represent about 20 minutes of teaching).

During this particular period the teacher talked 70 percent of the time (the sum of percents for columns 1 through 7), the students, 28 percent of the time (the sum of percents for columns 8 and 9). These figures correspond very closely to what is found in the average classroom. (According to Flanders' "two-thirds rule," someone is talking two thirds of the time; two thirds of that time it is the teacher who is talking; and two thirds of the time he is talking the teacher is using direct influence.)

The total number of tallies in columns 1–4 divided by the number of tallies in columns 5–7 gives the ratio of indirect to direct teacher influence. A ratio of less than 1 classified this teacher's teaching as direct (about 70 percent of the teachers studied by Flanders and his associates used primarily direct methods).

Within the matrix, the presence or absence of large numbers of tallies in certain regions gives clues to teaching style. The area marked A gives evidence of the teacher's use of student ideas and acceptance of student feelings. Area B represents amount of emphasis upon direct authority and a concentration of tallies in this area may indicate discipline problems or a rejection of the teacher's authority. Area C represents student talk that is stimulated by the teacher; area D, sustained student interaction without interruption by the

Columns (second no. of pair)

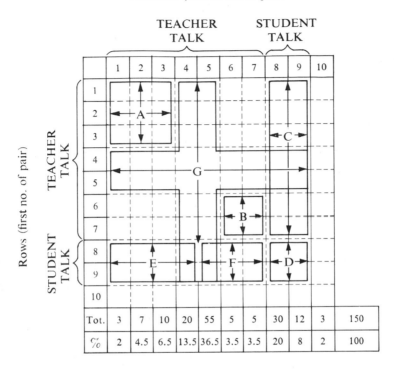

Note: In identifying cells, row number is given first, e.g., cell
4-8 refers to the cell at the intersection of row 4 and column 8.

Figure 18.4 Flanders interaction matrix.

Source: Amidon and Flanders, 1963, pp. 28–36; Medley and Mitzel, 1963, p. 273.

teacher. Areas E and F indicate the manner in which the teacher responds
to statements by his students: tallies in area E show direct responses; tallies
in F, indirect responses. The cross-shaped area G indicates emphasis on
subject matter.

Make a matrix like the one shown here and record your data. Study the
matrix.

Now make a second matrix, based on observation of a different teacher.
What have you learned about the teaching styles of the two teachers? In
which matrix was there more pupil talk? What caused more pupil talk in one
situation, compared to the other? Which teacher was the more effective, do
you think? Why do you think so?

Special Exercise II

Design and use a sociometric test on a group of children. If you are presently teaching, use your own classroom group. If you do not have a classroom group available, choose another group with which you have contact, such as a Sunday School class, a recreation group, or a club you are sponsoring.

There are two major purposes of this exercise: (1) to understand how sociometric tests are used and what kinds of information they yield—in short, to understand the test as a research tool; and (2) to gain information about the particular group of children you are studying. Be sure you choose a *meaningful* situation for the children, and one which can be acted upon afterward (for example, do not ask for choices in seating arrangements unless seating arrangements have some importance to the children, and unless you can actually rearrange the seating once the choices have been made). Be matter-of-fact and casual in your approach. Be sure that the children do not see or find out the results. Ask only for choices (and not for rejections). For instructions on how to use sociometric methods, one or another of the following references will be useful (they duplicate one another to a large extent):

Jennings, Helen Hall, *Sociometry in Group Relations.* Washington, D.C.: American Council on Education, 1948.

Northway, Mary L., and Lindsay Weld, *Sociometric Testing: A Guide for Teachers.* Toronto, Canada: University of Toronto Press, 1957.

Smith, Walter D., *Manual of Sociometry for Teachers.* Ann Arbor: Child Development Laboratories, University of Michigan, 1951.

Horace Mann-Lincoln Institute of School Experimentation, *How to Construct a Sociogram.* New York: Bureau of Publications, Teachers College, Columbia University, 1947.

Thorpe, L. P., and others, *Studying Social Relationships in the Classroom: Sociometric Method for the Teacher.* Science Research Associates, Inc., Chicago, 1959.

Before undertaking to use the sociometric technique, it is well to keep in mind certain cautions. The following paragraphs are taken from *How to Construct a Sociogram,* pages 11–12:

The investigator who employs sociometric techniques should be aware of their limitations. A few of these limitations are noted below:

A. Validity. The responses of individuals in the group are only as valid as is made possible by the degree of morale of the group and the degree of rapport of the teacher with the group. If there is resistance to making responses, or to signing names to responses, it is unlikely that the results will be valid, and thus the sociogram is not worth the paper on which it is made, and certainly not worth a teacher's time to chart it.

B. Reliability. There is considerable evidence that group structure is quite fluid in groups of young children. The structure becomes more stable as the age of children in the group increases, but a teacher should avoid the assumption that the charting at any one time is sufficiently reliable as a measure over a period of time.

C. Scope. It must be realized that the way in which basic material is collected tends to force responses. . . . A sociogram based on a statement of three friends cannot tell us the general friendship tone of an individual. . . .

D. It should be clearly recognized that a sociogram merely points to opportunities for further study and does not give final answers. For example, so many factors operate in determining group structure that extreme caution should be employed in using sociograms as a measure of any one experience in before-and-after application. Any such application should be supplemented by careful observations recorded as anecdotes.

E. A sociogram is a professional instrument to be used by professional people. If it is used as a mere "popularity contest" or to reinforce a teacher's prejudice for or against certain individuals, it is better that no sociograms be made. Although some investigators feel that sociograms may be used as educational devices in work with parents and pupils, it is urged that extreme caution be employed in using the result of any sociometric devices with groups which have difficulty in maintaining an objective, professional point of view toward the data.

II. Draw the sociogram, and study the pattern of interaction it shows.
   Answer the following questions:
   1. What appears on the sociogram that you had expected to find?
   2. What appears that you did *not* expect?
   3. What cleavages are there?
   4. Once you have carried out your agreement with the children, do you plan to do anything further to influence the social relationships within the group? If so, what? Be specific. How do you justify these plans?

Suggestions for Further Reading

1. The chapter by Withall and Lewis, "Social Interaction in the Classroom," in the book edited by Gage, *Handbook of Research on Teaching,* is an excellent review of the findings from various studies of teacher-pupil interaction. See also the chapter by Medley and Mitzel, "Measuring Classroom Behavior by Systematic Observation," in the same book.

2. For further reading on the classroom as a social group, read Chapter 4, "The Class as a Group," in *Educational Psychology: A Book of Readings,* edited by Arthur P. Coladarci. Included here, for instance, is a description by Lewin, Lippitt, and White of how the space of free movement varies for boys according to type of adult leadership.

3. A recent yearbook of the National Society for the Study of Education, *The Dynamics of Instructional Groups,* is devoted to group processes in the classroom. The chapters by Jacob W. Getzels and Herbert A. Thelen, Gale Jensen, Jack R. Gibb, David H. Jenkins, and Ned A. Flanders (chapters 4, 5, 6, 8, and 9) are especially relevant.

4. Gronlund's book, *Sociometry in the Classroom,* is a full treatment of sociometric methods. Chapter 4, "Typical Sociometric Patterns," is included in *Society and Education: A Book of Readings,* edited by Havighurst, Neugarten, and Falk.

5. Sections 4, 5, and 6 of the book, *Readings in the Social Psychology of the Classroom,* edited by Charters and Gage, include a number of studies of teacher-student interaction in the classroom, including studies of classroom management, the control of hostility and the relief of anxiety over examinations.

19 / The Career of
the Teacher

In this chapter we shall approach the teacher's career from three somewhat different, although related, points of view: the patterns to be found in the career line itself; the economic status of the teacher; and the professionalization of teaching that has occurred.

The Career Pattern

In viewing the career pattern of the teacher we may look first in broad outline at the salient features that distinguish teaching from other occupations and professions.

The teacher's clients are his pupils, and the school as a whole is built around the teacher-pupil relationship. The teacher has also a secondary, or indirect, group of clients, the parents of pupils. Beyond these, the teacher's immediate contact is with colleagues and with administrators. Thus, the teacher's relationships are primarily with four groups of people—pupils, their parents, fellow-teachers, and administrators.

The teacher works in an organization that is relatively bureaucratic. At the same time, the separateness of each classroom makes direct and continuous supervision impossible, and the teacher is himself in an administrative position. Although there is a great degree of structure and routine in the work setting (with time, space, and duties allotted in regular and scheduled ways), the routinization is in terms of the administrative system and not in terms of relationships with clients.

Compared with other occupations (although not with other professions) teaching involves a relatively long period of preparation, followed at once by full membership in the profession. A teacher takes on full status with his first regular teaching assignment, and, while informally he may be regarded as a novice for a few years by his older and more experienced colleagues, there is no formal period of apprenticeship once the first job placement is made, nor is there a period when participation and responsibility are only partial.

For the classroom teacher (omitting administrators or college teachers), the career is not, as in another occupation, characterized by movement from one to another level in a hierarchy. While it is true that many men and women who enter the teaching field move from classroom to administrative levels, or to affiliated professional service positions such as school psychologist or master teacher, the majority of teachers remain at the level of classroom teaching for the full length of their careers. Progress for most teachers is measured by relatively small and regular increments attained with age and experience—choicer assignments, more autonomy, more security, more salary, more prestige—but all these gains are within the same hierarchical level within the school structure.

Entering the Field

We have already spoken of the fact that persons choose to enter the teaching field for a great variety of reasons and that these reasons influence subsequent career patterns. Thus the person for whom entrance into teaching constitutes a clear and major step in upward social mobility may not exert himself greatly to move upward within the teaching hierarchy. In another case, the opposite may be true. In a third instance, the person who enters teaching with a strong sense of mission and dedication may be concerned with moving from one position to another primarily in terms of finding the place where he can be of greatest service to children. For many teachers, the initial decision was to enter college rather than to enter teaching, and a teacher-training institution, being conveniently located and relatively inexpensive, was chosen. Those who enter the teaching field in this way may have careers quite different from those who had a different entry.

Initial Adjustment

Having once chosen to become a teacher, and having obtained the requisite preparation, the teacher enters the second major phase of his career when he takes his first regular teaching position. For many persons, the first teaching experience requires considerable readjustment in personal and social life (Shaplin, 1961). Many beginning teachers experience what has been called "reality shock." Louise Carson, described in Chapter 16, is a good example of a young woman who found herself in a situation at marked variance with her preconception of the teaching role. In large cities, where beginning teachers are often assigned to "poorer" schools, the reality shock, when it occurs, often arises from problems encountered in dealing with disadvantaged children and parents, or from encountering the more hardened orientations of older teachers and administrators (Wagenschein, 1950).

This phenomenon of reality shock does not occur in all cases, of course. The persons, for example, who come from families of educators and who have considerable advance knowledge of the teaching career (and this is a large number) may find relatively little for which they are unprepared. The teacher who begins his career in the same type of community in which he was reared, whether small town or city neighborhood, may similarly make the transition into teaching smoothly and uneventfully.

Nor does reality shock necessarily come at the beginning of the teaching career. In a study of experienced high school teachers in Kansas City, for instance, it occurred for many not at the point of their first teaching job but at the point of entering the large city system. There the major readjustment was due to (1) the failure to anticipate the lack of community recognition given teachers in a large city; (2) the more impersonal tone of the interaction between teacher and pupil: and (3) the problems of paper work and clearance of routines that are involved in the larger and more bureaucratic system (Peterson, 1956).

Commitment to the Profession

Becoming committed to teaching as a career occurs at various times and to varying degrees for different people. To take a commonplace example, men tend to have different career orientations from women and thus evaluate teaching from a different point of view—not only when

they make their initial choice of occupation, but at successive points
along their career lines.

This everyday observation is documented in a study of 545 secondary school teachers in a large industrial metropolitan area (Colombotos, 1962). As shown in Chapter 16, Table 16.5, seventy-five of the
women in that study said they expected to leave teaching at some time in
order to raise a family. Of this group, 50 planned to return to teaching
and 25 did not plan to return. Eighty-four of the men, but only three of
the women planned to continue in the field of education but to move
from classroom teaching into some other area of education.

Some persons seem to drift into teaching; only later do they
become strongly committed to it. Others select teaching as a career
while still in high school and plan every move carefully. Miss Allison,
for example, the daughter of a school superintendent in a small midwest
town, had decided at an early age to become a teacher. She completed a
B.A. degree before taking her first teaching job, taught in a small town
high school for one year, then moved to a small city for one year, then
entered a large city system at the age of twenty-four. She says, "Going
into the profession wasn't just an impulsive thing, with me. I haven't
been like many teachers I know, moving from one place to another. I
improved myself with every move."

Another teacher, by contrast, is Miss Thorburn, a teacher now in
the same city high school as Miss Allison. Miss Thorburn, who also
grew up in a small town, took her first teaching job in a one-room rural
school, as soon as she finished high school. She moved after two years to
another rural school; then to a small town of 2,000 population; then to
a second, and a third small town. After eight years, she moved to a
small city of 10,000; and after several more moves within communities
of approximately the same size, entered the large city system at the age
of forty. "I've done a lot of moving around," she says, "and I'm not
always sure why. I wasn't even sure for a long time if I really wanted to
stay in teaching. Oh, one thing I've gotten out of it, of course, is different kinds of experience. I taught in Colorado, and in Texas, and in
Wisconsin. And I went to several different universities in the summers
before I finished my bachelor's degree."

For those who enter teaching without strong commitment in advance, it has happened more frequently than not that the major commitment occurs after several years of experience and when the teacher is in
the age range of thirty to forty. While the timing of this commitment is
affected by a variety of influences, an important factor in the past has
stemmed from the fact that most people who entered the teaching field
were young unmarried women. By their mid-thirties many had married

and left the profession. Those who had not married or withdrawn from the field for other reasons tended, at this age, to commit themselves to teaching as their life-work.

It is likely that this "age of commitment" varies more now, since the persons who are teachers are now a more varied group of people and especially since women are no longer forced to choose between marriage and a career.

There is, on the other hand, a strong pressure for early commitments stemming from another source, that of increasing professionalization. The requirements for entering the teaching field are rising, they are becoming standard from state to state, and the teacher's education is becoming increasingly "specialized." As a result, movement in and out of the teaching field tends to diminish. Some people have deplored this situation, for, as Riesman has pointed out, ". . . we have all seen what has happened to teaching when the teachers' colleges and professional bodies forced those who entered it to make a career commitment, which has meant expulsion from teaching of those gifted amateurs from whom it could be a way-station on the road to something else. . . ." (Riesman, 1955, p. 232.)

The trend toward early commitment was in some measure counteracted in the 1950's when the shortage of teachers was particularly acute. At that time the schools recruited a large number of broadly educated persons holding the bachelor's degree, who had had no thought of preparing for teaching while doing under-graduate work.

During periods of teachers shortages, then, persons enter the field who have not had prior commitments to teaching. Teacher training institutions have facilitated their entry by developing intensive summer-school courses and fifth-year professional training programs, such as the Master of Arts in Teaching (MAT) program. Still, as professionalization continues, the long-term trend is to increase the pressures for early commitment to the field.

Movement Along the Career Line

Although the large majority of teachers does not move from the general level of classroom teaching, there is considerable movement within that level: geographical movement, where the teacher goes from one community to another; movement from one grade level to another (usually from elementary to high school); and movement from one school to another within the same city system.

THE TRADITIONAL CAREER LINE. The traditional career for a school teacher was to start teaching in a rural school after one or two years of post-high school preparation. After a few years the teacher went back to college and completed a four-year course; then went to work in the schools of a small city. Often the line of progress was from grade school to high school as well as from small town to larger town.

Peterson (1956, 1964) studied the careers of women school teachers in the Kansas City school system. In the early 1950's the Kansas City system had been stable in numbers for a decade, as had other cities, due to the low birth rate of the 1930's; and like other central cities, Kansas City had adopted a policy of employing only experienced teachers. Thus in 1953, of the women high school teachers, 78 percent were over 40 years of age. The general direction of the career movement for these teachers had been from smaller to larger towns, from grade school to high school, from lower to higher salaries, from unstable to stable teaching conditions, from poorer to wealthier communities.

Unmarried rural-reared teachers typically began teaching in a country school near their home at the age of seventeen or eighteen; moved to a small town school after about two years of experience and some additional education in summer school; secured a B.S. in education at about the age of twenty-four; made two additional moves to large schools in larger towns; entered the Kansas City system at about the age of thirty-one; moved twice within the Kansas City system; secured their current placement within the city system at the age of thirty-five; and, in the course of continued summer school education, received an M.A. degree at about the age of thirty-eight.

Table 19.1   Average Age at Time of Major Occupational and Educational Transitions (Unmarried Women High-school Teachers in Kansas City)

Place of origin	Num- ber	Took Her First Posi- tion	Com- pleted B.S. Degree	First Teaching Posi- tion in Kansas City	Took Current Posi- tion	Com- pleted M.A. Degree	Current Age
Rural	9	18	24	31	35	38	48
Small Town	13	22	25	31	35	35	57
Urban	13	23	23	27	34	35	51

Source: W. Peterson, 1956, p. 76 (adapted).

The unmarried teachers from small towns, as Table 19.1 indicates, followed much the same path. However, they tended to be somewhat older when they began teaching, because they often did some other kind of work in their home towns before going to school. Since many of the rural girls looked upon country school teaching as a way of earning money for further education, there is some similarity between country girls and town girls in this respect. There were, among unmarried teachers from the smaller towns, several who, like rural girls, began teaching in a country school when out of high school, saving their money for further education.

The early career phases of unmarried urban-reared teachers are noticeably different from the others. As a rule, urban-born teachers completed their degrees before beginning to teach, taught in small town schools for a much shorter period, and entered the urban system when younger. They were not, however, much younger than teachers from small towns and farms in moving to present positions within the city system, perhaps because "settling" within the city system is more closely affiliated with age. (Peterson, 1956, pp. 75–77.)

An alternative career line existed in a few large cities, mainly in the East. Here the teachers were more likely to come from working-class and lower-middle class families in the central city. They went from the local high school to a municipal teachers' college or university and then began teaching in the city schools. After a two- or three-year probationary period they secured tenure and began looking for a school that was conveniently located near the area in which they wanted to live. They would transfer once or twice until they found a school where they liked the principal, the pupils, and the neighborhood. A subgroup, of course, worked for promotion to administrative positions.

THE CONTEMPORARY CAREER LINE. Since 1950 a new career line has developed for teachers in metropolitan areas. The majority come from the central city and attend a local teachers' college. Upon securing a bachelor's degree and a teaching certificate, they start teaching in the central city system. The central cities have been actively recruiting new teachers since about 1955 when the post-war birth rate increases swelled school enrollments.

Many teachers secure a master's degree through part-time study. Those who want to be administrators then start preparing for examinations and get a variety of teaching experience. The others look for a school assignment that will be best for them.

The beginning teacher runs the risk of being assigned initially to an unsatisfactory school, since schools that have many vacancies and no teachers requesting transfer to them are those in which something is "wrong." Schools in the lower socioeconomic areas tend to be such "transfer vacuums." Havighurst (1964) found 11 percent of the teachers in Chicago's slum schools had only one year of teaching experience, while only 16 percent had more than 16 years' teaching experience. In contrast, in upper-middle-class schools only 2 percent of the teachers had been teaching only a year, while 58 percent had more than 16 years' experience. A few teachers found teaching in the slums a rewarding and challenging experience, but most had, through the transfer system, moved on to "better" schools.

There are, of course, a variety of reasons why teachers request transfers. Havighurst found only 16 percent of elementary and 12 percent of high school teachers wishing to transfer because of dissatisfaction with pupils or with the local community. The most frequent reason given was personal convenience—distance from home, for example. A teacher may also transfer for reasons of professional advancement; for example, to gain experience in another type of school, or a better position; or a teacher may be dissatisfied with his principal, or with certain aspects of his assignment that he feels mitigate against professional service. Nevertheless, more teachers request transfers from slum schools than from other schools in Chicago.

This career line leads increasingly often to a suburban school system. Since the suburbs have been growing rapidly they cannot secure many teachers who were born in suburbs. They recruit from the central city or from the towns or cities outside the metropolitan area.

Thus there has developed a teacher career line which remains entirely within a metropolitan area. More and more teachers are following their entire professional lives within a particular metropolitan area, teaching in a wide variety of schools in the area.

The Economic Status of the Teacher

One way of appraising the teaching career is to compare it with other occupations and professions in terms of financial rewards. Teaching as an occupation has a variety of appealing features, many of them intangible. Nevertheless, to examine the economic aspects of teaching is one of the few tangible ways to gauge the attractiveness of the teaching career, as well as to assess the importance of the teacher's function in the eyes of the community at large.

Teachers' Salaries

Teachers' salaries, in general, have been increasing markedly in recent years. From 1939 to 1960 the average annual salary of all classroom teachers increased 269 percent. For the ten years 1949–1959, the percent of salary increase for teachers (73 percent) was greater than that for employees in manufacturing (69 percent); or for all wage and salary workers (60 percent) (NEA, May, 1960; March, 1961 II).

Salaries must be considered in relation to the purchasing power of the dollar. (Purchasing power is measured by indexes that show the change in prices from one specified date to another. Most commonly used is the Consumer Price Index of the U.S. Bureau of Labor Statistics.) Where comparisons are based upon changes in "real" purchasing power, it has been shown that there was a half century, from 1904 to 1953, in which deterioration occurred in the relative purchasing power of educators as compared to industrial workers and other occupational groups; but in the decade of the 1950's this deterioration ended (Tickton, 1961).

There are a variety of factors operating, of course, to produce this change. One is the shortage of teachers, the need to attract qualified persons to the teaching field rather than to lose them to other occupational fields. Another is that teachers have shown an increasingly higher quality of preparation over the years, and these higher standards have gained fuller public recognition.

While teachers' salaries are often compared either with those of doctors and dentists or with those of industrial workers, it is more pertinent to make comparisons with other occupational groups from whom approximately the same level of preparation is required. Table 19.2 gives such comparative data. The table shows that starting salaries paid to teachers are still considerably lower than those paid to persons in other occupations requiring similar amounts of college training and experience.

Efforts to obtain professional-level salaries for professionally-trained teachers have been intensified over the past few years; and while results are uneven, advances have been made in some school systems beyond the levels shown in Table 19.2. The National Education Association in 1964–65 surveyed 2,033 school systems with enrollments of 3,000 or more students; and 53 highly selected suburban districts with enrollments between 1,000 and 3,000 students. Of this sample of school systems, 338 had provisions of a minimum of $5,400 or more for a

Table 19.2   Salaries of Jobs in Industry and Education Requiring
                  Comparable Amounts of Experience and Training, 1964

Starting Salaries for Jobs Requiring a Bachelor's Degree

IN BUSINESS AND INDUSTRY		TEACHERS IN PUBLIC SCHOOLS	
Mechanical Engineers	$7,620	Buffalo	$5,100
Chemists	7,260	Albany	5,000
Humanities & Social Sci-		New York City	5,300
ences	6,144	Washington, D.C.	5,350
Accountants	6,636	Los Angeles	5,500
General Business Trainees	6,360	Chicago	5,350
Marketing and Distribution	6,192		

Starting Salaries for Jobs Requiring a Master's or Professional Degree

IN BUSINESS AND INDUSTRY		TEACHERS IN PUBLIC SCHOOLS	
Physicists	$9,132	New York City suburbs	
Mathematicians	8,868	such as Garden City,	
Chemists	8,604	Great Neck, Manhasset,	
Mechanical Engineers	9,180	and Scarsdale ..	$6,000–6,200
Business Administration ..	7,776	New York City	6,425

Sources: Annual salary figures in business and industry computed by the authors
from College Placement Council data in their *Salary Survey, Final Report,* June,
1965.
    Salary figures for teachers in public schools from National Education Asso-
ciation, October, 1964.

beginning teacher with a bachelor's degree, *or* a maximum of at least
$9,500 for a master's degree, *or* a maximum of $11,000 or more for
the highest preparation recognized. In 107 of the 338, all three criteria
were met. It is true that very few persons qualify for the maximum
salaries (usually the Ph.D. degree or 7 years' training); and it is true
that most of the 107 school systems were located in suburban communities in large metropolitan areas, chiefly in the Los Angeles, Chicago, San
Francisco, and New York areas. Still this survey indicates that changes
are taking place in the direction of increased remuneration for teachers
(NEA, December, 1964).

Salaries and Teacher Turnover

Another useful method is to compare average annual salary for teachers
and for *nonsupervisory* professionals in industry. In 1960–61, such
professionals received an average salary 31 percent higher than that of

classroom teachers. It should be recalled, however, that relatively few teachers have had the long years of experience attained by those in other fields. Turnover in the teaching profession is far higher than in most other professions. For example, in the one year 1962–63 the rate of turnover for large school systems was almost 12 percent, a rate that would probably have been greater if it had been based upon turnover in all schools in the country (NEA, August, 1964). In a study of persons receiving teaching certificates from colleges and universities in the San Francisco Bay Area, it was found that only three-quarters actually became school teachers; of those who did, only 60 percent of the women and 79 percent of the men were still teaching five years later (Carlson, 1962).

This high turnover means that, as compared with other professions, fewer teachers have long experience; thus, fewer qualify for top-level salaries. In 1962–63, of all teachers on single salary schedules, only about six percent of those with a bachelor's degree and about eleven percent of those with a master's degree were receiving the maximum salary for their level of preparation (NEA, February, 1965, p.9).

Salaries and Other Occupational Factors

Teaching salaries must be considered, not only in overall comparisons with other occupational groups, but also in terms of their relation to other factors *within* the teaching profession.

Omitting administrators and college teachers, the difference that used to exist between elementary and secondary school teachers is disappearing as the single salary schedule is becoming the standard practice in school systems. Thus by 1954–1955, 96 percent of all school systems in communities over 2,500 in population were using salary schedules; of these, 98 percent were using the single schedule, one where salary is based upon training and experience and is not affected by grade level taught, by sex, or by marital status.

As standards are being raised for elementary teachers, and as all but a few of the states require a bachelor's degree for an elementary-school certificate, the salary difference between elementary and high-school teachers has narrowed. In 1950 the average annual salary of elementary-school teachers was 82 percent of that of high-school teachers; by 1964, it had increased to 93 percent (NEA, February, 1965, p. 6).

Differences exist between small and large communities. Teachers in the largest school systems once enjoyed a great advantage in salary over their colleagues in smaller systems; yet in recent years it has been teachers in small communities who have enjoyed the greatest gains, so that the gap is narrowing. In 1964–65, beginning teachers in school systems with over 100,000 pupils received salaries that were on the average only six percent higher than those of beginning teachers in schools of 1,200 to 2,999 pupils (NEA, October, 1964, p. 5). There are still substantial differences between salaries paid in the very largest and in the very smallest school systems, however, reflecting the inability of the smallest districts to employ fully qualified teachers.

There are also wide salary variations among the different regions of the United States, with the far West and the Mideast showing higher averages than the Southeast or the Great Plains areas. Part of these regional differences is due to the larger number of very small school districts in the less industrialized areas that accept partially prepared teachers.

Another factor is the length of time it takes the average classroom teacher to arrive at the maximum salary in the salary schedule. This period is now usually eleven or twelve years at the bachelor's degree level, thirteen or fourteen years at the master's level or above (NEA, December, 1964, p. 5).

In the 1950's, in an attempt to overcome teacher shortages, greater salary increases were given to beginning teachers than to experienced teachers, thus reducing the difference between minimum and maximum salaries within a given salary class. Beginning in 1960, however, while both minimum and maximum salaries were increasing, higher percents of increase were scheduled for experienced rather than for beginning teachers. Many cities also added salary classes for higher levels of preparation for those beyond the master's degree and gave greater salary recognition for experience.

At the moment, salary schedules for teachers still operate to make the teaching profession different from such other occupations as law and medicine. In the latter, after long initial periods of relatively low income, the largest economic gains tend to come in the middle and late years of the occupational career. While teachers do not typically have the long period of apprenticeship or the "early career phase" that is characteristic of many other professional groups, neither do they have the relatively large increments of income in their later years of teaching.

There has been a good deal of discussion in recent years over modifying salary schedules by adopting quality-of-service or "merit" provisons. Such plans attempt to reward the superior teacher by accelerating his movement up the salary scale, by placing him in a special, better-paying category, or by paying him a bonus. On the whole, merit plans have proved difficult to administer, and many school systems have never implemented them or have abandoned them, largely because of difficulties in evaluating performance and because of the resentment and misunderstanding they created among the professional staff (NEA, March, 1961 I). Teachers' organizations on the whole have taken the position that such provisions are unfair and demoralizing to the profession.

Working Hours and Working Conditions

The number of hours of work per year by teachers was increasing in the fifty-year period, 1904 to 1953 (the greatest increase occurred prior to 1930), in contrast to industrial occupations where the number of hours of work was decreasing significantly. A survey made by the NEA in 1960–61 showed that teachers on the average were required to be on duty a little less than seven and one half hours a day (excluding duty-free lunch periods), or about 37.5 hours a week for from 36 to 40 weeks per year. Out-of-class work, however, brought the average work week to 48.5 hours for elementary school teachers and to a little less than 46 hours for high school teachers. Although accurate information is lacking for other professions, teachers' working hours may not be unfavorable when compared with those of social workers, librarians, and similar professional groups, especially when considering the long summer vacations.

Non-Wage Benefits

Non-wage benefits, or so-called "fringe benefits," are another important factor in economic status. Here the teaching profession has made marked gains in recent years. In at least three-fourths of the states, for instance, there are now tenure provisions that apply to at least some of the teachers of the state. Although the laws vary considerably in the protection they provide against dismissal, demotion, or reduction of salary, they nevertheless offer considerable security to an increasing proportion of teachers. Teachers in large city systems still have a decided advantage in this respect over teachers in small communities, since most large cities provide tenure that is wider in coverage and that offers a greater degree of protection than that provided in the state at large. Other security features such as pension plans and retirement plans also are growing in number at both local and state levels.

At the same time, fringe benefits have lagged as compared to those of other occupational groups. Pension and welfare funds, insurance, and other such benefits have increased much more rapidly for other groups, so that while the trend is for increased economic security for teachers, both teachers' salaries and non-wage benefits are far from equal to those of similarly-qualified personnel.

Professionalization

Criteria for Professionalization

Because there are varying definitions of a profession, there are differences of opinon concerning the degree to which education can properly be regarded as a profession. Usually the following criteria are used for an occupation to be considered a profession; (1) it requires high skill and intellectual effort; (2) it requires extensive formal education; (3) it involves primarily the exchange of service or advice in return for a fee or a salary, rather than the sale of goods for profit; (4) it has acquired traditions of group dignity and resistance to commercialism. In applying these particular criteria, there can be little question that public school teaching is a profession.

Another way to look at the question of professionalization is in terms of how the work of a professional person differs from that of a non-professional. Because teachers are, for the most part, public employees who are not self-employed or remunerated on the basis of fees rather than salary (the traditional position of, say, physicians or attorneys) a more salient comparison is with other similarly-qualified personnel who are employed in large organizations. Table 19.3 shows the differences between a non-professional position in a large bureaucratic organization (such as that of cashier in a bank) and a professional position (such as that of resident physician or industrial scientist) according to the characteristics of the two types of work.

According to this analysis, the work of the professional as compared to the non-professional is less standardized, less centralized, and more specialized; the emphasis is upon the uniqueness of the client (in the case of the teacher, the primary client is the child); there is responsibility for policy decisions; and the work depends primarily on

Table 19.3   Differences Between Bureaucratic and Professional Positions

Bureaucratic	*Professional*
1. High degree of standardization: (a) stress on uniformity of clients' problems (b) personnel treated interchangeably (c) highly specific and uniform rules and work procedures	1. Low degree of standardization: (a) stress is upon uniqueness of clients and (b) of skills of personnel (c) diffuse and alternative rules and procedures
2. Decision-making is highly centralized: (a) little responsibility of employees for decision making (b) primary responsibility to the organization and the administration	2. Decision-making is decentralized: (a) responsibility of professional employees for making policy decisions (b) primary loyalty to clients and colleagues rather than to the organization
3. Specialization is task-oriented: (a) based primarily on practice or experience (b) involves primarily the accomplishment of a set of tasks (c) stresses efficiency and technique	3. Specialization is client-oriented: (a) based primarily on theoretical knowledge rather than practice (b) stresses competence in aiding clients rather than efficiency or technique

Source: Corwin, 1965, pp. 229–247 (adapted to table form by the authors).

competence in aiding the client rather than upon the worker's efficiency or techniques.

From this point of view, it is somewhat less clear, whether or not classroom teaching is to be regarded as a profession. Most of the time the teacher is on his own in the classroom and is generally free to develop his own teaching techniques. At the same time, he is bound to a standard curriculum, his work is evaluated by an administrator or administrative staff, and, as an employee, he is obligated to implement the policies of the administration and the board of education, policies which, in the typical case, he had little or no voice in determining.

The Professional Organization

Still another criterion for a profession is that there be a responsible association to set standards for admission and exert control over members, based upon a code of ethics and a concept of competency. This criterion, too, is becoming applicable to the teaching profession through the growth of the National Education Association (whose membership includes school administrators as well as classroom teachers), and various other local, state, and national organizations of teachers. According to the *NEA Reporter,* (June 18, 1965, p. 4) the estimated number of instructional staff in American public elementary and secondary schools was over 1,800,000 in 1964–65. Of this total, over 90 percent were members of state teachers' associations affiliated with the NEA; and over 50 percent held membership directly in the national organization.

The NEA, with its 33 departments and its various commissions and committees, performs a variety of services aimed not only toward improving public education generally but also toward enhancing teaching as a profession. Among its activities it provides opportunities for growth in teaching competence through conferences, publications, and consultant services; it has developed a code of ethics for teachers (*NEA Handbook,* 1965–66, pp. 66–68); and it has established an agency, the National Commission on Teacher Education and Professional Standards, to work with college personnel in conducting the national accreditation program in teacher education, and to develop a program in matters of recruitment, selection, and advancement of professional standards.

On the other hand, the NEA has only very recently moved to limit its active membership to qualified professionals. Before August, 1964, active membership was open to "any person actively engaged in educational service." Since that date, new active members must be qualified for full certification, must possess at least a bachelor's degree, and must be "actively engaged in educational work of a professional nature." (The status of old active members who are less qualified remains unchanged.)

While the new standards reflect the NEA's views concerning minimum requirements for teaching, the organization does not set minimum standards for employment. This matter rests with state boards; thus the NEA does not act to control entry into teaching. Neither does the NEA have the power to discipline teachers for professionally unethical conduct. In these ways, education is said to fall short of being a full-fledged profession.

Other Criteria

There are still other criteria for professionalization. Lieberman (1956, 1960) points out, for instance, that teaching is similar to other professions such as medicine, law, pharmacology and accountancy, in that there are state boards which have responsibility for certification or licensure. Unlike those for other professions, however, these boards are composed of lay persons and not of professionals. As a matter of fact, professional educators are frequently excluded by law from membership on state boards of education. It should be pointed out that this situation, whereby the control of education is in the hands of laymen rather than professional educators, is one which educators themselves have encouraged. For instance, the NEA's position on this point for many years was the following:

We recognize the distinction between the lay control of education and the professional administration of our schools. We believe that the highest type of professional service in the offices of state superintendents or state commissioners of education, of county superintendents of schools, and of city superintendents of schools can be secured by the selection of all such administrative officers by lay boards of education elected by the people. (NEA, 1921, p. 27.)

Trends Toward Increasing Professionalization

In recent years teachers' organizations have become much more energetic. The *New York Times,* in January, 1964, noted:

A resurgence of militancy among the nation's public school teachers marked the year of 1963. There was mounting evidence that teachers are no longer content to rule only the classroom to which they are assigned. They want a hand in the assignment and a voice in the policy that controls their professional lives. They are not asking to run the schools, but they want their views heard and heeded.

An Office of Education bulletin, in commenting that this new militancy continued to mount during the spring of 1964, said:

New terms have evolved for the educator's vocabulary—strikes, sanctions, mediation, professional negotiation, collective bargaining, appeal, and arbitration.

The growing importance of the teacher organization as a vigorous, articulate, and forceful element in the improvement of working conditions for teachers is well recognized. Today's teachers are interested and increasingly active through their organizations in such matters as civil rights, academic freedom, manpower needs, and international affairs. Quite recently they have become vitally concerned about their rights and responsibilities in participating in the development of the policies and regulations which determine the conditions under which they work. (Steffensen, 1964, p. 2.)

For one thing, teachers' organizations have been asserting the right of professional educators to a voice in determining educational policy at both the state and the local level. In 1959 a special task force of the NEA's National Commission on Teacher Education and Professional Standards began drafting recommendations for further professionalization of teaching (the New Horizons Project). The final report of this group said:

A clear distinction must be drawn between the public's responsibility for decisions on education as public policy and the public's relation to execution of that policy. When it comes to determining the means for accomplishing purposes agreed upon by the public and the profession, the public should, with complete confidence, give autonomy to the profession. (Lindsey, 1961, pp. 22–23.)

The Representative Assembly of the NEA passed in 1962 two resolutions that read in part:

The National Education Association insists on the right of professional associations, through democratically selected representatives using professional channels, to participate with boards of education in the determination of policies of common concern, including salary and other conditions of professional service. . . .

The National Education Association believes that, as a means for preventing unethical or arbitrary policies or practices that have a deleterious effect on the welfare of the schools, professional sanctions should be invoked. These sanctions would provide for appropriate disciplinary action by the organized profession. (NEA Handbook, 1962–63, p. 64.)

These resolutions have provided the basis for the development of new procedures known as *professional negotiations* and *professional sanctions*.

PROFESSIONAL NEGOTIATIONS are a form of collective bargaining, although many educators disavow the latter term. Negotiations are carried on according to formalized procedures between the local teachers' association and the school board about matters of joint concern (NEA, 1963, p. 10). There are provisions for mediation through professional educational channels, should the association and the board fail to reach agreement. Teachers' salaries and other aspects of economic welfare have, of course, long been topics for negotiation. A new development, however, is the insistence that teachers, by right of their professional status, should have a say in determining matters which have hitherto been regarded as resting solely within the province of the school boards and administrative staff, matters such as qualifications for employment, class size, and special services.

In the summer of 1962 the first known professional negotiation agreement based upon the NEA resolution was adopted and by spring, 1965, nearly 400 other school systems had followed suit (*NEA Journal,* 1962, Vol. 51, No. 8, pp. 28–30; 1965, Vol. 54, No. 5, pp. 30–31).

PROFESSIONAL SANCTIONS are viewed by NEA-affiliated organizations as the ultimate weapon for correcting unsatisfactory conditions. They are applied, generally speaking, somewhat as follows:

A local association, unable to persuade the school board to correct what it feels are unsatisfactory conditions for professional service, requests the state education association to investigate. If the state association's investigating committee agrees with the local association, it will make recommendations to the school board and allow it a reasonable length of time to meet them. If the board does not comply, the state association will publicize the matter, refuse the school district the use of its placement service, and sanction certain procedures by the local association to enforce compliance. Such steps might include the refusal to renew contracts or the withholding of certain services by the teachers. The state association might even rule that it would be professionally unethical for teachers to accept positions in that district.

The following report from an NEA periodical, *The Urban Reporter,* shows the conditions which the NEA felt must be met before sanctions against the state of Oklahoma could be lifted in 1965:

The two major corrective steps taken by Oklahoma legislators and voters between July and September made the removal of sanctions possible. On July 30, reversing its previously adamant hold-the-tax-line position, the state legislature approved a 25% increase in state support for common and vocational education plus a public referendum on amending the constitution to permit raising the property tax ceiling by ten mills. On September 14, Oklahoma voters, who had repeatedly defeated school tax measures by huge majorities in the past . . . also evidenced a reversal of previously held views. They went to the polls and supported raising the property tax ceiling by a 2 to 1 vote of approval.

. . . Oklahoma's 25,000 teachers had courageously joined forces to win meaningful improvements in educational services for children as well as in their own hard-pressed situation. Before sanctions could be lifted, those teachers were entitled to concrete evidence that at long last the message had gotten through to the public, some indication that public support could be won and could be anticipated in the future. (NEA, *The Urban Reporter,* October, 1965.)

In a corollary move the NEA in 1963 revised its code of ethics so that it now reflects the expanded role of present-day professional teachers' organizations. The old code had stressed the responsibility of the teachers for improving the quality of education and for increasing the situations in which teachers exercise professional judgment.

Teachers' Unions

The current drive toward increasing professionalization involves two parallel aspects: the demand of all professional educators (teachers, special staff, and administrators) for more professional autonomy; and the demand of classroom teachers for the right to influence policy within the particular school systems in which they are employed.

Disagreement exists regarding the best means of reaching these objectives. Some educators feel that the NEA is moving satisfactorily and is providing good leadership. Others, such as Lieberman (1956, 1960), have felt that only a newly strengthened professional organization can do this job, and that a necessary first step is the reform and merging of teachers' organizations (i.e., a merger between the NEA and the teachers' union, The American Federation of Teachers). Other educators feel that teachers' unions are the only effective agents in producing a change in status for teachers.

There is considerable disagreement around the more general issue of teachers' unions. There is, on the one hand, the point of view that classroom teachers would do best to align themselves with all other persons professionally engaged in the field of education, to regard themselves as professionals in something of the pattern of doctors, lawyers, or social workers; and to work in this way toward improving the status of teaching as a profession. This is, in oversimplified terms, the position of the NEA.

On the other hand, the point of view has been put forth that classroom teachers would do best to regard themselves as employees, to see their interests as different in some respects from those of school administrators; to organize in the same way workers in other fields have done; and to affiliate with organized labor in America. This, again in oversimplified terms, is the position taken by teachers' unions.

There has been a growth of teachers' unions in recent years, especially in large cities. While some are independent unions, most are locals of the American Federation of Teachers. The AFT, affiliated with the American Federation of Labor-Congress of Industrial Organizations (AFL-CIO), grew in membership from 61,000 in 1961 (Megel, 1961) to 110,000 in 1965 and in the one year 1964–65, eighty-two new locals were chartered (AFT Officers' Reports, 1965, pp. 4–5).

Like the NEA-affiliated teachers' organizations, teachers' unions have been attempting to negotiate on topics beyond the traditional ones of salaries and fringe benefits. Thus, for example, in 1962, the New York City teachers' union established a committee to develop a plan for making recommendations on school and class size, teacher specialists, integration, staff and community relationships, and instructional materials and techniques. The plan has been a basis for joint teacher-administration planning (Bleeker, 1965, pp. 5–6, 19–20).

Unions have also endeavored to improve their ability to gain their demands; in 1963 the AFT rescinded its no-strike policy and recognized the right of locals to strike under certain circumstances. There followed a threatened strike of New York teachers in 1963 and of Chicago teachers in 1965, with generally favorable outcomes for the union. (For instance the 1965 Chicago strike threat was partially settled by provision for an election in which the Chicago Teachers' Union hoped to establish itself as the sole bargaining agent for the teachers.) In 1964–65, six AFT locals used the strike as a weapon in negotiations with school boards.

Many teachers, feeling that the NEA and the AFT serve complementary rather than contradictory functions, have belonged to both. As these organizations have broadened their programs, however, their services to their members have become more similar. That is, while their theoretical positions and their terminologies are different, impartial analyses of their activities have not revealed clear-cut differences at the practical level: differences, for example, between professional negotiation and collective bargaining or between professional sanctions and strikes (Steffensen, 1964, pp. 54–57; Kratzmann, 1963). While at the present time competition between the NEA and the AFT appears to some observers to be sharpening, it remains to be seen whether the movement toward enhanced professional status will be weakened by the conflict between these organizations.

It should be pointed out that, because teachers are presently demanding the right to influence policy, it does *not* follow that teachers did not influence policy in the past. In small schools the principal is more likely than not to confer with his teachers before coming to a decision or before presenting his views to the school board, and the teachers are more likely than not to recognize that they have had a part in making decisions. However, as school districts have consolidated and urban school districts have mushroomed, administrators have come more and more to rely upon their own staffs for information and advice, and classroom teachers have found themselves more and more isolated from the administration. The present movement is, therefore, in part an attempt to replace the earlier informal lines of communication typical of the small school system with formal ones that can function in large bureaucratic school systems.

Certification and Accreditation

Growth in professionalization has been accompanied by a rise in the standards of teacher preparation. In 1940, 11 states required the bachelor's degree for teaching at the elementary level, and 40 states required the degree for the secondary level. By 1964 the number of states (including Puerto Rico and the District of Columbia) had risen to 46 and 52 respectively. At the same time, despite a shortage of teachers, the proportion of teachers holding emergency certificates (signifying less than minimum requirements) declined from a high of fifteen percent in 1946–47 to six percent in 1962–63 (Armstrong and Stinnett, 1964).

Certification requirements have recently been severely criticized both by persons outside the profession and by persons within it (Conant, 1963; Kinney, 1964; Koerner, 1963; Lieberman, 1960; and Lindsey, 1961).

Kinney (1964) has pointed out that, since the teachers' professional organization does not control entry into the profession, certification by state boards of education has had to serve two separate functions. The first is to define who is eligible for the various positions

within public schools in the state, and, by changing certification requirements from time to time to meet the practical situation, to provide
enough teachers for all the classrooms in the state. The second function
is to determine from the professional point of view who is and who is
not qualified to teach. In the case of other professional groups, the
second function is usually performed by the professional organization
and the state acting jointly. The latter is the case with physicians, whose
license to practice, although granted by the state, rests upon definitions
of competence established by the medical profession. Kinney believes
that professional competence must be determined and controlled by the
profession, and that this must be done through strengthened teachers'
organizations.

Authorities responsible for certification in the various states, acting
upon the advice of members of the teaching profession, have nevertheless begun to add measures of teaching competence to certification
requirements; and the NEA through coordinated activities at the national level, through affiliated state associations, and through the National Council of Accreditation of Teacher Education is working to
improve professional education and certification requirements.

Despite a continuing shortage of teachers, there has been steady
improvement in teaching standards over the past two decades. The
greater responsibility for improvement that the profession is assuming
will undoubtedly hasten the process.

Achievement of Full Professionalization

Hughes (1958) has discussed professions as occupations which possess
both a *license* and a *mandate* from the larger society—*license* being defined as the successful claim to carry out certain activities which others
may not perform, and to do so in exchange for remuneration; and *mandate* being defined as the right to determine what is the proper conduct of
others toward these activities. The steps by which an occupation that
functions within an institution, such as teaching, reaches the status of a
profession may be said to be these:

(1) Some members of the occupational group begin the movement
towards professionalization by organizing their membership and defining
more precisely its relationships with other occupations and with laymen in
the functioning of the institution. (2) Curriculum for the training of practitioners is developed and standardized by the efforts of a body set up to
accredit training efforts and to certify qualified practitioners. (3) The cur-

riculum is incorporated into the university and is further standardized, with bachelors and, later, graduate degrees awarded. (4) A corps of persons specializing in the training of future practitioners develops, and research is conducted. (5) The prerequisites for practicing the profession multiply, resulting in the necessity for a firm and early commitment to the occupation on the part of the would-be practitioner. (6) *Infra dignitate* occupational duties are assigned to non-professionals (that is, in this case, that teachers will only teach; and other persons will correct papers, counsel students, and keep discipline). (7) The service rendered becomes esoteric; that is, the client has some idea of the results he wants but is in no position to judge the quality of the service he receives. (8) The group attempts to keep judgments of competence within the circle of colleagues. (9) Society grants the occupational group a mandate—to tell laymen what is good and right for the individual and for society in this particular area.

Teaching has more or less completed the first four steps in this process, and has at least part of the characteristics of steps 5 and 6. It is not likely that the profession will ever come to be regarded as esoteric. As Phenix (1960; cited in Lindsey, 1961, p.31) has pointed out, the teacher does not, unlike the lawyer or the doctor, perform for his client some service the client cannot do for himself. Instead, he works with his client to develop in him the skills that the teacher himself possesses. The public therefore has greater familiarity with the teacher's craft than with the doctor's or the lawyer's—and this familiarity is undoubtedly one factor that makes attainment of full professional status difficult for teachers. Perhaps in summary it may be said that in Hughes' terms teaching possesses a license but not a mandate from the public; and that teaching is rapidly moving toward, but has not yet reached, full professional status.

Exercises

1. What tenure provisions for teachers are there in your state? In your city? Describe in detail.

2. What are your views regarding teachers' unions? What are their advantages, and what are their disadvantages?

3. Choose two classroom teachers who have had outstanding career lines. Describe the careers of each. What was the reason underlying each move the teacher made?

4. Read the Code of Ethics of *The Education Profession* formulated by the National Education Association (pp. 66–68 in the *NEA Handbook,*

1965–66). What do you consider the most important points in the code? Why?

5. Read the platform of the National Education Association (pp. 51–55 in the *NEA Handbook, 1965–66*). Then read the little pamphlet called "Questions and Answers about the American Federation of Teachers" which can be secured from American Federation of Teachers, 716 N. Rush Street, Chicago, Illinois, 60611.

Suggestions for Further Reading

1. See *Education as a Profession* by Myron Lieberman for a discussion of the issues and of the forces operating for and against professionalization. See especially Chapters 9, 10, 11 that deal with teachers' associations and teachers' unions; and Chapter 13 that deals with professional ethics. See also his 1960 book, *The Future of Public Education*.

2. The book, *Society and Education: A Book of Readings* (Havighurst, Neugarten and Falk) includes three papers which deal with different aspects of professionalization: Steffensen describes the growing militancy among teachers by describing seven case histories of teachers' conflicts with their school boards; the article by Winick describes the reactions of New York City teachers to a strike called by a teachers' union; and the reading by Stinnett describes some of the factors that lie behind the current movement toward professionalization of teaching.

3. Recent books describing teachers' reactions to inner-city schools are *Up the Down Staircase* by Bel Kaufman, and *The School Children,* by Greene and Ryan.

4. The chapter, "Teachers as Professional Employees," Chapter 8 in Corwin's *A Sociology of Education,* is a penetrating discussion of various issues in professionalization, and makes the point that a fundamental tension exists between the professional and the bureaucratic principles of organization that teachers are expected to follow.

Bibliography

ABRAMS, CHARLES (1965), *The City is the Frontier*. New York: Harper & Row, Publishers. (p. 267)

ADVISORY COMMISSION ON INTERGOVERNMENTAL RELATIONS (1961), *Governmental Structure, Organization, and Planning in Metropolitan Areas: Suggested Action by Local, State, and National Governments*. Washington, D.C. (p. 397)

AICHHORN, AUGUST (1935), *Wayward Youth*. New York: The Viking Press, Inc. (p. 358)

ALBERT, FRANK R., JR. (1959), "Selected Characteristics of School Board Members and Their Attitudes Toward Certain Criticisms of Public School Education." Unpublished doctoral dissertation, University of Mississippi. (p. 395)

ALEXANDER, C. NORMAN, JR., and ERNEST O. CAMPBELL (1964), "Peer Influences on Adolescent Aspirations and Attainments," *American Sociological Review*, 29, 568-75. (p. 174)

AMERICAN FEDERATION OF TEACHERS (1965), "Officer's Reports to the AFT Convention," unpublished multilith document. (p. 503)

AMIDON, EDMUND J., and NED A. FLANDERS (1961), "The Effects of Direct and Indirect Teacher Influence on Dependent-prone Students Learning Geometry." *Journal of Educational Psychology*, 1961, 52, 286-291. (p. 464)

AMIDON, EDMUND J., and NED A. FLANDERS (1963), *The Role of the Teacher in the Classroom: A Manual for Understanding and Improving Teachers' Classroom Behavior*. Minneapolis: Paul S. Amidon & Associates, Inc., 1963. (pp. 464, 476-479)

ANDERSON, C. ARNOLD (1961), "A Skeptical Note on the Relation of Vertical Mobility to Education," *American Journal of Sociology*, LXVI, 560-570. (p. 70)

ANDERSON, HAROLD H., and HELEN M. BREWER (1945), *Studies of Teachers' Classroom Personalities. I: Dominative and Socially Integrative Behavior of Kindergarten Teachers*. Applied Psychology Monographs No. 6. Stanford, Calif.: Stanford University Press. (p. 463)

ANDERSON, HAROLD H., and JOSEPH E. BREWER (1946), *Studies of Teachers' Classroom Personalities. II: Effects of Teachers' Dominative and Inte-*

grative Contacts on Children's Classroom Behavior. Applied Psychology Monographs No. 8. Stanford, Calif.: Stanford University Press. (p. 463)

ANDERSON, HAROLD H., JOSEPH E. BREWER, and MARY F. REED (1946), *Studies of Teachers' Classroom Personalities. III: Follow-up Studies of the Effects of Dominative and Integrative Contacts on Children's Behavior.* Applied Psychology Monographs No. 11. Stanford, Calif.: Stanford University Press. (p. 463)

ANDERSON, NELS (1959), *The Urban Community: A World Perspective.* New York: Holt, Rinehart, & Winston, Inc. (p. 267)

ARMSTRONG, CLAIRETTE P., and A. JAMES GREGOR (1964), "Integrated Schools and Negro Character Development: Some Considerations of the Possible Effects." *Psychiatry,* 27, 69-72. (p. 372)

ARMSTRONG, W. EARL, and T. M. STINNETT (1964), *A Manual on Certification Requirements for School Personnel in the United States.* Washington, D.C.: National Commission on Teacher Education and Professional Standards, National Education Association of the United States. (p. 504)

ASTIN, ALEXANDER W. (1962), "An Empirical Characterization of Higher Educational Institutions," *Journal of Educational Psychology,* 53, 224-235. (p. 107)

———— (1964), "Some Characteristics of Student Bodies Entering Higher Educational Institutions," *Journal of Educational Psychology,* 55, 267-275. (p. 107)

BAGDIKIAN, BEN H. (1964), *In the Midst of Plenty: The Poor in America.* Boston: Beacon Press. (p. 38)

BAILEY, WILFRID C. (1953), "The Status System of a Texas Panhandle Community," *Texas Journal of Science,* 5, 316-331. (p. 15)

BAKKE, EDWARD WIGHT (1940), *Citizens Without Work.* New Haven: Yale University Press. (p. 156)

BARKER, ROGER G. (1960), "Ecology and Motivation," *Nebraska Symposium on Motivation, 1960,* Marshall R. Jones, ed. Lincoln: University of Nebraska Press. (pp. 145-146)

BARKER, ROGER G., and HERBERT F. WRIGHT (1951), *One Boy's Day: A Specimen Record of Behavior.* New York: Harper & Row, Publishers. (pp. 143, 148)

BARKER, ROGER G., and HERBERT F. WRIGHT (1954), *Midwest and Its Children: The Psychological Ecology of an American Town.* New York: Harper & Row, Publishers. (pp. 15, 99, 143)

BARKER, ROGER G., HERBERT F. WRIGHT, JACK NALL, and PHIL SCHOGGEN (1950), "There is no Class Bias in Our School," *Progressive Education,* 27, 106-110. (p. 94)

BARKER, ROGER, et al. (1962), *Big School — Small School: Studies of the Effects of High School Size Upon the Behavior and Experience of Students.* Department of Psychology, University of Kansas. (pp. 210, 388)

BARKLEY, MARGARET K. (1956), "The Concept of the Home Economics

Teacher Held by High School Students." Unpublished doctoral dissertation, University of Illinois. (p. 432)

BARZUN, JACQUES (1954), *The Teacher in America.* Garden City, N.Y.: Doubleday and Company, Inc. (p. 430)

BECKER, H. S. (1951), "Role and Career Problems of the Chicago Public School Teacher." Unpublished doctoral dissertation, Department of Sociology, University of Chicago. (p. 203)

BELL, NORMAN, and EZRA VOGEL (1961), *A Modern Introduction to the Family.* New York: The Free Press. (p. 167)

BENDIX, REINHARD, and SEYMOUR LIPSET (1953), *Class Status and Power: A Reader in Social Stratification.* New York: The Free Press. (p. 37)

BERDIE, RALPH F., WILLIAM L. LAYTON, THEDA HAGENAH, and EDWARD D. SWANSON (1962), *Who Goes To College?* Minnesota Studies in Student Personnel Work, No. 12. Minneapolis: University of Minnesota Press. (pp. 96, 107, 120)

BERELSON, BERNARD (1960), *Graduate Education in the United States.* New York: McGraw-Hill Book Company. (p. 120)

BERGER, BENNETT M. (1960), *Working Class Suburb.* Berkeley and Los Angeles: University of California Press. (p. 38)

BERNARD, JESSIE (1966), *Marriage and the Family among Negroes.* Englewood Cliffs, N.J.: Prentice Hall, Inc. (p. 167)

BERNER, MARSHALL K. (1957), "Development of Procedures and Techniques for the Analysis of the Relationships Between the Formal Organization of High School Systems and the Informal Communication Structures Within These Systems." Unpublished doctoral dissertation, University of Illinois. (p. 198)

BERNSTEIN, B. (1961), "Social Class and Linguistic Development: A Theory of Social Learning," *Education, Economy and Society,* A. H. Halsey, J. Floud, and C. A. Anderson (eds.). New York: The Free Press. (p. 160)

——— (1962), "Linguistic Codes, Hesitation Phenomena, and Intelligence," *Language and Speech,* 5, 31-46. (p. 160)

BERNSTEIN, MILDRED R. H. (1959), "A Study of Teachers' Role-Expectations and Role-Perceptions of a Principal, Superintendent and Board of Education, and the Relationship Between Convergence and Divergence of Role-Expectation and Role-Perception and Teacher Morale." Unpublished doctoral dissertation, New York University. (p. 203)

BEST, JOHN WESLEY (1948), "A Study of Certain Selected Factors Underlying the Choice of Teaching as a Profession," *Journal of Experimental Education,* XVII, 201-259. (p. 411)

BESTOR, ARTHUR (1955), *The Restoration of Learning.* New York: Alfred A. Knopf, Inc. (pp. 221, 239)

——— (1957), "The Education Really Needed for a Changing World." *Harvard Educational Review,* 27, 1-8. (p. 221)

BETTELHEIM, BRUNO (1959), "Feral Children and Autistic Children," *American Journal of Sociology,* LXIV, 455-467. (p. 124)

BIDDLE, BRUCE J., HOWARD A. ROSENCRANZ, and EARL F. RANKIN, JR.

(1961), *Studies in the Role of the Public School Teacher,* Vol. 5. Columbia, Mo.: Soc. Psychol. Lab., University of Missouri. (p. 443)

BIDDLE, BRUCE J., J. PASCHAL TWYMAN, and EARL F. RANKIN, JR. (1962), "The Role of the Teacher and Occupational Choice," *School Review,* 70, 191-206. (p. 443)

BLEECKER, TED (1965), "New York City's Effective Schools Make History," *American Teacher Magazine,* 49, No. 4. (p. 503)

BLOCH, HERBERT A., and FRANK T. FLYNN (1956), *Delinquency: The Juvenile Offender in America Today.* New York: Random House, Inc. (p. 341)

BLOOM, BENJAMIN S. (1964), *Stability and Change in Human Characteristics.* New York: John Wiley & Sons, Inc. (pp. 130, 148, 159)

BLOOM, BENJAMIN S., ALLISON DAVIS, and ROBERT D. HESS (1965), *Compensatory Education for Cultural Deprivation.* New York: Holt, Rinehart, and Winston, Inc. (p. 148)

BOGUE, DONALD J. (1959), *The Population of the United States.* New York: The Free Press. (p. 330)

BOLLENS, JOHN C., and HENRY J. SCHMANDT (1965), *The Metropolis.* New York: Harper & Row, Publishers. (pp. 267, 293)

BONNEY, MERL E. (1947), "Sociometric Study of Agreement Between Teacher Judgments and Student Choices," *Sociometry,* X, 133-146. (p. 467)

BRIM, ORVILLE G., JR. (1958), *Sociology and the Field of Education.* New York: Russell Sage Foundation. (p. 94)

BRITTAIN, CLAY V. (1963), "Adolescent Choices and Parent-Peer Cross Pressures," *American Sociological Review,* 28, 385-391. (p. 177)

BROGAN, DENIS W. (1944), *The American Character.* New York: Alfred A. Knopf, Inc. (p. 93)

BRONFENBRENNER, URIE (1960), "Freudian Theories of Identification and Their Derivatives," *Child Development,* 31, 15-40. (p. 134)

——— (1961), "The Changing American Child — A Speculative Analysis," *Merrill-Palmer Quarterly,* 7, 73-84. (p. 153)

BUCK, ROY C. (1960), "The Extent of Social Participation among Public School Teachers," *Journal of Educational Sociology,* 33, 311-319. (p. 434)

BUEHRING, LEO E. (1958), "New Pattern: Community Schools," *The Nation's Schools.* January. (p. 227)

BURCHILL, GEORGE, ed. (1962), *Work-Study Programs for Alienated Youth: A Casebook.* Chicago: Science Research Associates. (pp. 355, 358)

BURGESS, ERNEST W., HARVEY J. LOCKE, and MARY MARGARET THOMES (1963), *The Family.* Third Edition. New York: American Book Co. (p. 167)

BURTON, ROGER V., and JOHN W. M. WHITING (1961), "The Absent Father and Cross-sex Identity," *"Merrill-Palmer Quarterly,* 7, 85-95. (pp. 134, 153)

CALLAHAN, RAYMOND E. (1962), *Education and the Cult of Efficiency.* Chicago: University of Chicago Press. (p. 195)

CAMPBELL, ROALD F. (1945), "Are School Boards Reactionary?" *Phi Delta Kappan*, 27, 82-83, 93. (p. 395)

———— (1965), "Community Extension," pp. 155-62 in *White House Conference on Education*. Washington, D.C.: U.S. Government Printing Office. (p. 282)

CAPLOW, THEODORE (1958), *The Academic Marketplace*. New York: Basic Books, Inc., Publishers. (p. 430)

CARLSON, RICHARD O. (1962), *Executive Succession and Organizational Change*. Chicago: Midwest Administration Center, The University of Chicago. (p. 493)

CARRIKER, WILLIAM R., ed. (1963), *Role of the School in Prevention of Juvenile Delinquency*. Cooperative Research Monographs No. 10, Washington, D.C.: U.S. Government Printing Office. (p. 358)

CAUGHRAN, ROY W. (1956), "A Study of the Socio-Economic Backgrounds and the Attitudes of Illinois Public School Board Members." Unpublished doctoral dissertation, Northwestern University. (p. 395)

CHARTERS, W. W., JR. (1957), "The Communication Structure of School Staffs." Paper given at meeting of the American Sociological Society, Washington, D.C. (p. 197)

———— (1963), "The Social Background of Teaching," Chapter 14 in *Handbook of Research on Teaching*, N. L. Gage, ed. Chicago: Rand McNally and Co. (p. 87)

CHARTERS, W. W., JR., and N. L. GAGE (1963), *Readings in the Social Psychology of Education*. Boston: Allyn and Bacon, Inc. (pp. 94, 482)

CHASE, FRANCIS S. (1951), "Factors Productive of Satisfaction in Teaching." Unpublished doctoral dissertation, Department of Education, University of Chicago. (pp. 203, 443)

CHINOY, ELY (1955), *Automobile Workers and the American Dream*. New York: Doubleday & Company, Inc. (p. 37)

CLAPP, ELSIE RIPLEY (1939), *Community Schools in Action*. New York: The Viking Press, Inc. (p. 239)

———— (1952), *The Use of Resources in Education*. New York: Harper & Row, Publishers. (p. 239)

CLARK, BURTON R. (1960), *The Open Door College: A Case Study*. New York: McGraw-Hill Book Company. (pp. 105, 107)

———— (1962), *Educating the Expert Society*. San Francisco: Chandler Publishing Co. (p. 213)

CLARK, KENNETH (1965), *Dark Ghetto: Dilemmas of Social Power*. New York: Harper & Row, Publishers. (p. 384)

CLAUSEN, JOHN A., and JUDITH R. WILLIAMS (1963), "Sociological Correlates of Child Behavior," Chapter 2 in *Child Psychology*, The 62nd Yearbook of the National Society for the Study of Education, Part I. Chicago: University of Chicago Press. (p. 147)

CLINARD, MARSHALL B., ed. (1964), *Anomie and Deviant Behavior*. New York: The Free Press. (pp. 340, 358)

CLOWARD, RICHARD A., and LLOYD E. OHLIN (1960), *Delinquency and Opportunity: A Theory of Delinquent Gangs*. New York: The Free Press. (pp. 340, 346, 358)

COHEN, ALBERT K. (1955), *Delinquent Boys: The Culture of the Gang*.
New York: The Free Press. (pp. 340, 345, 358)

COLADARCI, ARTHUR P., ed. (1955), *Educational Psychology: A Book of
Readings*. New York: The Dryden Press. (p. 481)

COLE, CHARLES C., JR. (1955), *Encouraging Scientific Talent*. A Report to
the National Science Foundation. New York: College Entrance
Examination Board. (p. 120)

COLEMAN, JAMES S. (1959), "Academic Achievement and the Structure of
Competition," *Harvard Educational Review*, 29, 331-351. (pp. 176,
196)

———— (1960), "The Adolescent Subculture and Academic Achievement,"
American Journal of Sociology, 65, 337-347. (p. 196)

———— (1961, I), *The Adolescent Society*. New York. The Free Press.
(p. 190)

———— (1966), *Equality of Educational Opportunity*. Washington, D.C.:
U.S. Government Printing Office. (p. 384)

COLEMAN, JAMES S., with the assistance of KURT JOHASSOHN and JOHN
W. C. JOHNSTONE (1961, II), *Social Climates in High Schools*. Cooperative Research Monograph No. 4, U.S. Office of Education. Washington, D.C.: U.S. Government Printing Office. (pp. 175, 184)

COLEMAN, RICHARD P., and BERNICE L. NEUGARTEN (1967), *Social Status
in the City*. New York: Atherton Press. (p. 18)

COLOMBOTOS, JOHN L. (1962), *Sources of Professionalism: A Study of
High School Teachers*. U.S. Office of Educational Cooperative Research Project No. 330. Ann Arbor: Department of Sociology, University of Michigan. (pp. 414, 415, 417)

COMMISSION ON SCHOOL INTEGRATION (1963), *Public School Segregation
and Integration in the North*. Washington, D.C.: National Association
of Intergroup Relations Officials. (p. 384)

CONANT, JAMES B. (1959), *The American High School Today*. New York:
McGraw-Hill Book Company. (p. 387)

———— (1961), *Slums and Suburbs*. New York: McGraw-Hill Book
Company. (p. 267)

———— (1963), *The Education of American Teachers*. New York:
McGraw-Hill Book Company. (pp. 397, 504)

CONFERENCE ON ECONOMIC PROGRESS (1962), *Poverty and Deprivation in
the United States*. Washington, D.C.: Conference on Economic Progress. (p. 38)

CONGER, LOUIS H. (1950), "Lack of Funds and Lack of Motivation as
Barriers to College Attendance in New York State." Report of a Type
A Project, Teachers College, Columbia University, New York. (p. 99)

CONNOR, D. V. (1960), "Behavior in Class Groups of Contrasting Climate."
British Journal of Educational Psychology, 30, 244-249. (pp. 474-475)

COOK, LLOYD A., and ELAINE F. COOK (1950), *A Sociological Approach to
Education*. 2nd Edition. New York: McGraw-Hill Book Company.
(p. 435)

CORWIN, RONALD G. (1965), *A Sociology of Education*. New York: Appleton-Century-Crofts. (pp. 94, 195, 215, 497, 507)

COUNCIL OF STATE GOVERNMENTS (1962), *State Responsibility in Urban Regional Development.* Chicago. (p. 397)

CRAIG, MAUDE M., and SELMA J. GLICK (1963), "Ten Years' Experience with the Glueck Social Prediction Table," *Crime and Delinquency,* July, 249-261. (p. 337)

———— (1964), *A Manual of Procedures for Application of the Glueck Prediction Table.* New York City Youth Board. (p. 337)

CUNNINGHAM, RUTH, and ASSOCIATES (1951), *Understanding Group Behavior of Boys and Girls.* New York: Bureau of Publications, Teachers College, Columbia University. (p. 462)

CUTRIGHT, PHILLIP (1960), "Students' Decision to Attend College," *Journal of Educational Sociology,* 33, 292-299. (p. 97)

DAEDALUS, *Youth: Change and Challenge* (Winter, 1962), *Journal of the American Academy of Arts and Sciences.* (p. 190)

DARLEY, JOHN G. (1962), "Distribution of Scholastic Ability in Higher Education." Unpublished manuscript, Center for the Study of Higher Education, University of California, Berkeley. (p. 96)

DAVIS, ALLISON (1948), *Social-Class Influences upon Learning.* Cambridge, Mass.: Harvard University Press. (p. 94)

DAVIS, ALLISON, and JOHN DOLLARD (1940), *Children of Bondage.* Washington, D.C.: American Council on Education. (pp. 37, 147)

DAVIS, ALLISON, BURLEGH B. GARDNER, and MARY R. GARDNER (1941), *Deep South.* Chicago: University of Chicago Press. (p. 36)

DAVIS, ALLISON, and ROBERT J. HAVIGHURST (1947), *Father of the Man.* Boston: Houghton Mifflin Company. (p. 167)

DAVIS, KINGSLEY (1947), "Final Note on a Case of Extreme Isolation," *American Journal of Sociology,* LII, 432-437. (p. 124)

DETROIT AREA STUDY (1960), *"Family Income in Greater Detroit: 1951-1959.* Ann Arbor: Survey Research Center, University of Michigan. (p. 245)

DEUTSCH, MARTIN (1965), "The Role of Social Class on Language Development and Cognition," *American Journal of Orthopsychiatry,* 35, 78-88. (pp. 130, 163)

DEUTSCH, MARTIN, and BERT BROWN (1964), "Social Influences in Negro-White Intelligence Differences," *Journal of Social Issues,* 20, 24-35. (p. 157)

DEWEY, JOHN (1904), "The Significance of the School of Education," *Elementary School Teacher,* 4, 441-453. (p. 222)

———— (1915), *School and Society,* 2nd Edition. Chicago: University of Chicago Press. (p. 222)

DEWHURST, J. FREDERIC, and ASSOCIATES (1955), *America's Needs and Resources: A New Survey.* New York: The Twentieth Century Fund. (pp. 298, 299, 330)

DOBRINER, WILLIAM M., ed. (1958), *The Suburban Community.* New York: G. P. Putnam's Sons. (p. 267)

———— (1963), *Class in Suburbia.* Englewood Cliffs, N.J.: Prentice-Hall, Inc. (pp. 38, 230)

DOLL, RUSSELL (1965), "Categories of Elementary Schools in a Big City." Unpublished Working Paper. University of Chicago, Department of Education. (p. 253)

DOLLARD, JOHN (1937), *Caste and Class in a Southern Town.* New Haven, Conn.: Yale University Press. (p. 37)

DRAKE, ST. CLAIRE, and HORACE R. CAYTON (1945), *Black Metropolis.* New York: Harcourt, Brace and World, Inc. (p. 37)

DUBLIN, LOUIS I., ALFRED J. LOTKA, and MARTIN SPEIGELMAN (1949), *Length of Life.* New York: The Ronald Press. (p. 330)

EATON, HAROLD E. (1956), "The Social Composition of and Attitudes Toward Educational Planning of County Boards of Education in West Virginia." Unpublished doctoral dissertation, University of Pittsburgh. (p. 395)

ECKLAND, BRUCE (1964), "Social Class and College Graduation: Some Misconceptions Corrected," *The American Journal of Sociology,* LXX, 36-50. (p. 97)

EDDY, ELIZABETH M. (1965, 1967), *Walk the White Line.* New York: Doubleday & Company, Inc. (pp. 216, 237, 459-460)

EDUCATIONAL POLICIES COMMISSION (1956), *Manpower and Education.* Washington, D.C.: National Education Association. (pp. 120, 330)

EELLS, KENNETH, *et al.* (1951), *Intelligence and Cultural Differences.* Chicago: University of Chicago Press. (pp. 17, 78)

ELSBREE, WILLARD S. (1939), *The American Teacher.* New York: American Book Company. (p. 410)

ENGLUND, GEORGIA YORK, and MIMMIE FULLER (1945), "Service Above Self," *School Executive,* 64, 59-60. (p. 225)

EPPERSON, D. C. (1964), "A Reassessment of Indices of Parental Influence in 'The Adolescent Society'," *American Sociological Review,* 29, 93-96. (p. 177)

FAUMAN, JOSEPH (1958), "Occupational Selection among Detroit Jews," pp. 124-137 in *The Jews, Social Patterns of an American Group,* Marshall Sklare, ed. New York: The Free Press. (p. 57)

FAUST, MARGARET SILER (1960), "Developmental Maturity as a Determinant in Prestige of Adolescent Girls," *Child Development,* 31, 173-184. (p. 180)

FICHTER, JOSEPH (1958), *Parochial School.* Notre Dame, Ind.: The University of Notre Dame Press. (p. 215)

FLANDERS, NED. A. (1960, 1964), "Teacher Influence on Pupil Attitudes and Achievement. Final Report, 1960." University of Minnesota, Project 397; U.S. Dept. of Health, Education, and Welfare. Cooperative Research Program, Office of Education. In Bruce J. Biddle and William J. Elena (eds.), *Contemporary Research on Teacher Effectiveness.* New York: Holt, Rinehart & Winston, Inc. (p. 464)

FLANAGAN, JOHN C. *et al.* (1964), *The American High-School Student.* Project TALENT Office, University of Pittsburgh, Pittsburgh, Penn. (p. 72)

FORTUNE, EDITORS OF (1957), *The Exploding Metropolis.* Garden City, N.Y.: Doubleday Anchor Books. (p. 267)

FRAZIER, E. FRANKLIN (1939), *The Negro Family in the United States.* Chicago: University of Chicago Press. (pp. 155, 167)

FRIEDENBERG, EDGAR Z. (1959), *The Vanishing Adolescent.* Boston: Beacon Press. (p. 190)

FUCHS, ESTELLE (1966), *Pickets at the Gates.* New York: The Free Press. (p. 206)

FUSCHO, GENE C. (1964), "School-Home Partnership in Depressed Urban Neighborhoods," Bulletin No. 20. U.S. Office of Education: U.S. Government Printing Office. (p. 268)

GAGE, N. L., ed. (1963), *Handbook of Research on Teaching.* Chicago: Rand, McNally & Co. (p. 481)

GALBRAITH, JOHN K. (1958), *The Affluent Society.* Boston: Houghton Mifflin Company. (p. 37)

GALLAHER, ART, JR. (1961), *Plainville Fifteen Years Later.* New York: Columbia University Press. (pp. 15, 16, 37)

GANZ, HERBERT J. (1962), *The Urban Villagers.* New York: The Free Press. (p. 68)

GARDNER, JOHN W. (1961), *Excellence.* New York: Harper & Row, Publishers. (p. 120)

GETZELS, JACOB W. (1963), "Conflict and Role Behavior in the Educational Setting," pp. 309-318 in *Readings in the Social Psychology of Education,* W. W. Charters, Jr. and N. L. Gage, eds. Boston: Allyn and Bacon, Inc. (pp. 270, 293)

GETZELS, JACOB W., and E. G. GUBA (1955), "The Structure of Roles and Role Conflict in the Teaching Situation," *Journal of Educational Sociology,* 29, 30-40. (p. 442)

GIBBS, JAMES E., CARL J. SOKOLOWSKI, AUGUST W. STEINHILBER, and WILLIAM C. STRASSER, JR. (1965), *Dual Enrollment in Public and Non-Public Schools.* Washington, D.C.: U.S. Office of Education. (p. 292)

GILES, H. HARRY (1959), *The Integrated Classroom.* New York: Basic Books, Inc., Publishers. (pp. 375-377)

GLASER, NATHAN, and DANIEL P. MOYNIHAN (1963), *Beyond the Melting Pot.* Cambridge, Mass.: The M.I.T. Press. (p. 68)

GLASS, DAVID V., ed. (1955), *Social Mobility in Britain.* New York: The Free Press. (p. 64)

GLAZER, NATHAN (1958), "The American Jew and the Attainment of Middle-Class Rank: Some Trends and Explanations," pp. 138-146 in *The Jews, Social Patterns of an American Group,* Marshall Sklare, ed. New York: The Free Press. (p. 57)

GLUECK, SHELDON, and ELEANOR T. GLUECK (1950), *Unraveling Juvenile Delinquency.* New York: Commonwealth Fund. (p. 336)

———— (1956), "Early Detection of Juvenile Delinquents," *Journal of Criminal Law, Criminology, and Police Science,* 47, 174-182. (p. 336)

GORDON, C. WAYNE (1957), *The Social System of the High School.* New York: The Free Press. (pp. 211-213, 215)

GORDON, C. WAYNE, and LETA McKINNEY ADLER (1963), "Dimensions of Teacher Leadership in Classroom Social Systems," Project No. 1084, The Cooperative Research Program of the Office of Education. Los Angeles: Department of Education, University of California. (p. 463)

GORDON, MILTON M. (1964), *Assimilation in American Life.* New York: Oxford University Press, Inc. (pp. 38, 68)

GOTTLIEB, DAVID, and WARREN D. TENHOUTEN (1965), "Racial Composition and the Social Systems of Three High Schools," *Journal of Marriage and the Family,* 27, 204-217. (p. 181)

GOTTMAN, JEAN (1961), *Megalopolis: The Urbanized Northeastern Seaboard of the United States.* Twentieth Century Fund. (p. 267)

GRAY, SUSAN W., and R. A. KLAUS (1965), "An Experimental Preschool Program for Culturally Deprived Children," *Child Development,* 36, 887-898. (p. 130)

GREAT CITIES' PROGRAM FOR SCHOOL IMPROVEMENT (1964), *Promising Practices from the Projects for the Culturally Deprived.* Chicago: Research Council of the Great Cities Program for School Improvement. (p. 148)

GREELEY, ANDREW M. (1963), *Religion and Career.* New York: Sheed and Ward. (p. 38)

GREEN, EDITH (1964), "The Federal Role in Education," in *Education and the Public Good.* Distributed by the Graduate School of Education of Harvard University. Cambridge, Mass. (pp. 392, 401)

GREENE, MARY FRANCES and ORLETTA RYAN (1965), *The Schoolchildren: Growing up in the Slums.* New York: Pantheon Books, Inc. (pp. 38, 446-447, 507)

GREENHOE, FLORENCE (1941), *Community Contacts and Participation of Teachers.* Washington, D.C.: American Council on Public Affairs. (p. 410)

GRONLUND, NORMAN E. (1959), *Sociometry in the Classroom.* New York: Harper & Row, Publishers. (p. 482)

GROSS, NEAL (1958), *Who Runs Our Schools?* New York: John Wiley and Sons, Inc. (p. 200)

HALSEY, A. H., JEAN FLOUD, and C. ARNOLD ANDERSON, eds. (1961), *Education Economy, and Society.* New York: The Free Press. (p. 120)

HANDLIN, OSCAR (1959), *The Newcomers.* Cambridge, Mass.: Harvard University Press. (pp. 68, 243)

HARLEM YOUTH OPPORTUNITIES UNLIMITED, INC. (1964), *Youth in the Ghetto.* New York. (p. 384)

HARRINGTON, MICHAEL (1962), *The Other America.* New York: The Macmillan Company. (pp. 30, 38)

HART, JOSEPH K. (1924), *The Discovery of Intelligence.* New York: King's Crown Press. (p. 226)

HAVIGHURST, ROBERT J. (1953), *Human Development and Education.* New York: Longmans, Green & Company. (p. 189)

———— (1960), *American Higher Education in the 1960's.* Columbus: Ohio State University Press. (pp. 110, 112)

———— (1964), *The Public Schools of Chicago, A Survey for the Board of Education of the City of Chicago.* Chicago: The Board of Education of the City of Chicago. (pp. 85, 251, 252, 253, 384, 412, 414, 430, 440, 490)

HAVIGHURST, ROBERT J., PAUL H. BOWMAN, GORDON F. LIDDLE, CHARLES V. MATHEWS, and JAMES V. PIERCE (1962), *Growing Up In River City.* New York: John Wiley & Sons, Inc. (pp. 17, 100, 334, 335, 349)

HAVIGHURST, ROBERT J., and H. G. MORGAN (1951), *The Social History of a War-Boom Community.* New York: Longmans, Green & Company. (p. 15)

HAVIGHURST, ROBERT J., BERNICE L. NEUGARTEN, and JACQUELINE FALK (1967), *Society and Education: A Book of Readings.* Boston: Allyn and Bacon, Inc. (pp. 38, 68, 168, 190, 216, 239, 267, 330, 358, 383, 403, 430, 454, 506)

HAVIGHURST, ROBERT J., and LINDLEY J. STILES (1961), "National Policy for Alienated Youth," Phi Delta Kappan, XLII, 283-291. (See also Havighurst, Neugarten, and Falk, 1967) (p. 355)

HEALY, W., and AUGUSTA BRONNER (1936), *New Light on Delinquency and Its Treatment.* New Haven, Conn.: Yale University Press. (p. 358)

HENDERSON, LEON W., and H. B. NUTTER (1942), "The University of Florida Project in Applied Economics," *High School Journal,* 25, 318-320. (p. 226)

HENRY, JULES (1955), "Docility, or Giving Teacher What She Wants," *Journal of Social Issues,* XI, 33-41. (pp. 457-458)

———— (1963), *Culture Against Man.* New York: Random House, Inc. (pp. 456-457)

HENRY, WILLIAM E. (1965), "Social Mobility as Social Learning: Some Elements of Change in Motive and in Social Context," in *Mobility and Mental Health,* Mildred B. Kantor, ed. New York: Charles C. Thomas. (p. 42)

HERRIOTT, ROBERT E., and NANCY HOYT ST. JOHN (1966), *Social Class and the Urban School.* New York: John Wiley & Sons, Inc. (p. 94)

HESS, ROBERT D., and DAVID EASTON (1960), "The Child's Changing Image of the President," *Public Opinion Quarterly,* 24, 632-644. (p. 135)

HESS, ROBERT D., and GERALD HANDEL (1959), *Family Worlds.* Chicago: University of Chicago Press. (p. 167)

HESS, ROBERT D., and VIRGINIA C. SHIPMAN (1965), "Early Experience and the Socialization of Cognitive Modes in Children," in *Child Development,* 36, No. 4, 869-886. (pp. 159, 160, 161)

HEWITT, LESTER E., and RICHARD L. JENKINS (1946), *Fundamental Patterns of Maladjustment: The Dynamics of Their Origin.* Springfield: State of Illinois. (p. 341)

HILLSON, HENRY T. (1963), *The Demonstration Guidance Project.* George Washington High School, New York: Board of Education. (p. 261)

HIMMELWEIT, HILDE T. (1961), "The Role of Intelligence in Modifying

Social Class Differences in Outlook," *Acta Psychologica,* 19, 273-281. (p. 53)

HODGE, ROBERT W., PAUL M. SIEGEL, and PETER H. ROSSI (1964), "Occupational Prestige in the United States, 1925-63," *American Journal of Sociology,* 70, 286-302. (p. 433)

HODGES, HAROLD M., JR. (1963), "Peninsula People: Social Stratification in a Metropolitan Complex," in *Education and Society,* W. Warren Kallenbach and Harold M. Hodges, Jr., eds. Columbus, Ohio: Charles E. Merrill Books. (pp. 19, 21, 23, 24, 30, 37)

HOFFMAN, LOIS W. (1961), "The Father's Role in the Family and the Child's Peer-Group Adjustment," *Merrill-Palmer Quarterly,* 7, 97-105. (p. 153)

HOFFMAN, MARTIN L., and LOIS W. HOFFMAN, eds. (1964), *Review of Child Development Research.* New York: Russell Sage Foundation. (pp. 147, 189)

HOLLINGSHEAD, AUGUST B. (1949), *Elmtown's Youth.* New York: John Wiley & Sons, Inc. (pp. 17, 86, 94, 181, 190)

HOLLINSHEAD, BYRON S. (1952), *Who Should Go to College?* New York: Columbia University Press. (p. 120)

HOOD, ALBERT B., and RALPH F. BERDIE (1964), "The Relationship of Ability to College Attendance," *College and University,* 39, 309-318. (p. 95)

HOOVER, EDGAR M., and RAYMOND VERNON (1959), *Anatomy of a Metropolis.* Cambridge, Mass.: Harvard University Press. (p. 267)

HUGHES, EVERETT C. (1958), *Men and Their Work.* New York: The Free Press. (p. 505)

HULBURD, DAVID (1951), *This Happened in Pasadena.* New York: The Macmillan Company. (p. 239)

HUNTER, OVID N. (1959), "The Relationship between School Size and Discrepancy in Perception of the Superintendent's Behavior." Unpublished doctoral dissertation, Washington University. (p. 202)

JACOB, PHILIP E. (1957), *Changing Values in College; An Exploratory Study of the Impact of College Teaching.* New York: Harper & Row, Publishers. (p. 120)

JACOBS, JANE (1961), *The Death and Life of Great American Cities.* New York: Random House, Inc. (p. 267)

JAYASURIA, D. L. (1960), "A Study of Adolescent Ambition, Level of Aspiration, and Achievement Motivation." Unpublished doctoral dissertation, London School of Economics, University of London. (p. 53)

JOHNSON, LYNDON B. (1965), Speech to Graduates of Howard University on June 4, 1965. (pp. 366-367)

JOHNSTONE, JOHN (1961), "Social Structure and Patterns of Mass Media Consumption." Unpublished doctoral dissertation, University of Chicago. (p. 184)

KAGAN, JEROME (1958), "The Concept of Identification," *Psychological Review,* 65, 296-305. (p. 134)

KAHL, JOSEPH A. (1953), "Education and Occupational Aspirations of 'Common Man' Boys," *Harvard Educational Review,* 23, 186-203. (pp. 102, 103)

——— (1957), *The American Class Structure.* New York: Holt, Rinehart & Winston, Inc. (pp. 12, 22, 25, 27, 28, 37, 62, 63, 67)

KATZ, IRWIN (1964), "Review of Evidence Relating to Effects of Desegregation on the Intellectual Performance of Negroes." *The American Psychologist,* XIX, 381-399. (pp. 370, 384)

KAUFMAN, BEL (1964), *Up the Down Stair Case.* New York: Avon Books. (pp. 454, 507)

KEPPEL, FRANCIS (1966), *The Necessary Revolution in American Education.* New York: Harper & Row, Publishers. (p. 402)

KERBER, AUGUST and BARBARA BOMMARITO (1965), *The Schools and the Urban Crisis: A Book of Readings.* New York: Holt Rinehart & Winston, Inc. (p. 267)

KIMBALL, SOLON T., and JAMES E. McCLELLAN (1962), *Education and the New America.* New York: Random House, Inc. (p. 94)

KINNEY, LUCIEN B. (1964), *Certification in Education.* Englewood Cliffs, N.J.: Prentice-Hall, Inc. (p. 504)

KLOPF, GORDON JOHN and ISRAEL A. LASTER, eds. (1963), *Integrating the Urban School.* New York: Teachers College, Columbia University, Bureau of Publications. (p. 384)

KOERNER, JAMES D. (1963), *The Miseducation of American Teachers.* Boston: Houghton Mifflin Company. (p. 504)

KOHN, MELVIN L. (1959, I), "Social Class and the Exercise of Parental Authority," *American Sociological Review,* 24, 352-366. (p. 163)

——— (1959, II), "Social Class and Parental Values," *American Journal of Sociology,* LXIV, 337-351. (p. 163)

KRATZMANN, ARTHUR (1963), "The Alberta Teachers' Association: a Prototype for the American Scene?" *Administrator's Notebook,* XII, No. 2. (p. 504)

KRAUSS, IRVING (1964), "Sources of Educational Aspirations among Working-Class Youth," *American Sociological Review,* 29, 867-879. (p. 54)

KVARACEUS, WILLIAM D., and WALTER B. MILLER (1959), *Delinquent Behavior: Culture and the Individual.* Washington, D.C.: National Education Association. (pp. 341, 344, 358)

KVARACEUS, WILLIAM D., and WILLIAM E. ULRICH (1959), *Delinquent Behavior: Principles and Practices.* Washington, D.C.: National Education Association. (pp. 349, 351)

LANDES, RUTH (1965), *Culture in American Education.* New York: John Wiley & Sons, Inc. (p. 38)

LANDIS, PAUL T., and PAUL K. HATT (1954), *Population Problems.* New York: American Book Company. (p. 330)

LANE, ROBERT E. (1959), *Political Life.* New York: The Free Press. (p. 136)

LAWRENCE, JEROME, and ROBERT E. LEE (1955), *Inherit the Wind.* New York: Random House, Inc. (p. 403)

LEE, ROSE HUM (1955), *The City*. Philadelphia: J. B. Lippincott Co. (p. 267)

LEWIS, CLAUDIA (1946), *Children of the Cumberland*. New York: Columbia University Press. (p. 143)

LIEBERMAN, MYRON (1956), *Education as a Profession*. Englewood Cliffs, N.J.: Prentice-Hall, Inc. (pp. 499, 502, 507)

———— (1960), *The Future of Public Education*. Chicago: University of Chicago Press. (pp. 499, 502, 504, 507)

LIEBERSON, STANLEY (1963), *Ethnic Patterns in American Cities*. New York: The Free Press. (p. 68)

LINDSEY, MARGARET (1961), *New Horizons for the Teaching Profession: a Report of the Task Force on New Horizons in Teacher Education and Professional Standards*. Washington, D.C.: National Commission on Teacher Education and Professional Standards, National Education Association. (pp. 500, 504, 506)

LIPPITT, RONALD, and RALPH K. WHITE (1943), "The 'Social Climate' of Children's Groups," Chapter 28 in *Child Behavior and Development*, Roger G. Barker, Jacob S. Kounin, and Herbert F. Wright, eds. New York: McGraw-Hill Book Company. (p. 462)

LIPSET, SEYMOUR M., and REINHARD BENDIX (1959), *Social Mobility in Industrial Society*. Berkeley and Los Angeles: University of California Press. (pp. 61, 63, 67)

LYONS, EUGENE (1966), *David Sarnoff*. New York: Harper & Row, Publishers. (p. 67)

MAAS, HENRY S. (1951), "Some Social-Class Differences in the Family System and Group Relations of Pre- and Early Adolescents," *Child Development*, 22, 145-152. (p. 142)

MACCOBY, ELEANOR E. (1958), *Readings, in Social Psychology*. New York: Holt, Rinehart, & Winston, Inc. (p. 167)

MARTIN, JOHN M., and JOSEPH P. FITZPATRICK (1965), *Delinquent Behavior: A Redefinition of the Problem*. New York: Random House, Inc. (p. 358)

MARTIN, WILLIAM E., and STENDLER, CELIA BURNS (1959), *Child Behavior and Development*. New York: Harcourt, Brace & World, Inc. (pp. 147, 189)

MATZA, DAVID (1964), *Delinquency and Drift*. New York: John Wiley & Sons, Inc. (pp. 347, 358)

MAYER, KURT (1963), "The Changing Shape of the American Class Structure." *Social Research*, XXX, 458-468. (p. 31)

MCARTHUR, CHARLES (1954), "Personalities of Public and Private School Boys," *Harvard Educational Review*, 24, 256-262. (p. 86)

MCCLELLAND, DAVID C., et al. (1953), *The Achievement Motive*. New York: Appleton-Century-Crofts. (p. 99)

MCCONNELL, T. R. (1961), "Problems of Distributing Students among Institutions with Varying Characteristics," *North Central Association Quarterly*, 35, 226-238. (p. 107)

———— (1962), *A General Pattern for American Public Higher Education*. New York: McGraw Hill Book Company. (pp. 112, 120)

McGuire, Carson, and George D. White (1957), "Social Origins of Teachers — Some Facts from the Southwest," Chapter 3 in *The Teacher's Role in American Society,* Lindley J. Stiles, ed. Fourteenth Yearbook of the John Dewey Society. (p. 413)

Mead, Margaret (1951), *The School in American Culture.* Cambridge, Mass.: Harvard University Press. (pp. 432, 454)

―――― and Martha Wolfenstein (1955), *Childhood in Contemporary Cultures.* Chicago: University of Chicago Press. (p. 167)

Medley, Donald M., and Harold E. Mitzel (1963), "Measuring Classroom Behavior by Systematic Observation." In *Handbook of Research on Teaching,* N. L. Gage, ed. Chicago: Rand, McNally & Company. (p. 479)

Megel, Carl J., and Administrative Staff (1961), *Report to the Convention of the American Federation of Teachers, Philadelphia, Pennsylvania.* Chicago: American Federation of Teachers. (p. 503)

Merton, Robert K., Leonard Broom, and Leonard S. Cottrell, Jr., eds. (1959), *Sociology Today.* New York: Basic Books, Inc., Publishers. (p. 94)

Michael, Donald N. (1962), *Cybernation: The Silent Conquest.* Santa Barbara, Calif.: Center for the Study of Democratic Institutions. (pp. 120, 330)

Miller, Daniel R., and Guy E. Swanson (1958), *The Changing American Parent.* New York: John Wiley and Sons, Inc. (pp. 152, 167)

Miller, Herman P. (1964), *Rich Man, Poor Man: The Distribution of Income in America.* New York: Thomas Y. Crowell Company. (pp. 29, 30, 38)

Miller, S. M. (1964), "Educational Strategies." Unpublished manuscript, Syracuse University Youth Development Center. (p. 130)

Miller, Walter B. (1967), *City Gangs: An Experiment in Gang Behavior.* New York: John Wiley and Sons, Inc. (pp. 340, 358)

Mills, C. Wright (1951), *White Collar.* New York: Oxford University Press, Inc. (p. 37)

Moorefield, Thomas E., and Robert J. Havighurst (1964), "Early Marriage and Social Mobility among Girls," *Journal of the National Association of Women Deans and Counselors,* XXVII, No. 4, 160-171. (p. 52)

Moreno, J. L. (1934), *Who Shall Survive?* Washington, D.C.: Nervous and Mental Disease Publishing Company. (p. 467)

Morrill, Maurice B. (1945), "Clothing, the Sloan Experiment in Vermont," *Clearing House,* 19, 429-431. (p. 226)

Morrison, J. Cayce (1958), *The Puerto Rican Study.* Brooklyn: New York City Board of Education. (p. 245)

Mumford, Lewis (1961), *The City in History.* New York: Harcourt, Brace & World, Inc. (p. 267)

Nam, Charles B., and Mary G. Powers (1965), "Variations in Socioeconomic Structure by Race, Residence, and the Life Cycle," *American Sociological Review,* 30, No. 1, 97-103. (pp. 32, 35)

NATIONAL EDUCATION ASSOCIATION (1921), *Addresses and Proceedings,* Vol. 59. Washington, D.C.: National Education Association. (p. 499)

———— (December, 1951), "Schools and the 1950 Census," *Research Bulletin,* 29, No. 4, Washington, D.C.: National Education Association. (p. 304)

———— (May, 1960), "Economic Status of Teachers in 1959-60," *Research Report* R8. Washington, D.C.: National Education Association. (p. 491)

———— (March, 1961 I), "Why Have Merit Plans for Teachers' Salaries Been Abandoned?" *Research Report* R3. Washington, D.C.: National Education Association. (p. 495)

———— (March, 1961 II), "Economic Status of Teachers in 1960-61," *Research Report* R4. Washington, D.C.: National Education Association. (p. 491)

———— (1962), *NEA Handbook for Local, State, and National Associations, 1962-63.* Washington, D.C.: National Education Association. (p. 500)

———— (1963), *Guidelines for Professional Negotiation.* Washington, D.C.: National Education Association. (p. 501)

———— (April, 1963), *The American Public School Teacher, 1960-61.* Research Monograph 1936-M2. Washington, D.C.: Research Division, NEA (pp. 411, 430, 435, 436, 440, 441)

———— (August, 1964), "Selected Statistics of Local School Systems, 1962-63," *Research Report,* R11. Washington, D.C.: National Education Association. (p. 493)

———— (October, 1964), "Salary Schedules for Classroom Teachers, 1964-65," *Research Report,* R13. Washington, D.C.: National Education Association. (pp. 492, 494)

———— (December, 1964), *Research Bulletin,* 42, No. 4. Washington, D.C.: National Education Association. (pp. 492, 494)

———— (1965), *NEA Handbook for Local, State, and National Associations, 1965-66.* Washington, D.C.: National Education Association. (pp. 498, 506)

———— (1965), *Research Bulletin,* "De Facto Segregation," 43, 35-37. Washington, D.C.: National Education Association. (p. 380)

———— (February, 1965), "Few Teachers Get Top Salaries," *Research Bulletin,* 43, No. 1, 9. Washington, D.C.: National Education Association. (p. 493)

———— (October, 1965), "Oklahoma Sanctions Lifted," *The Urban Reporter,* IV, No. 2. Washington, D.C.: National Education Association. (pp. 501-502)

NATIONAL MANPOWER COUNCIL (1957), *Womanpower.* New York: Columbia University Press. (pp. 120, 330)

NATIONAL SOCIETY FOR THE STUDY OF EDUCATION (1953), *The Community School.* Fifty-second Yearbook, Part II. Chicago: University of Chicago Press. (p. 239)

———— (1960), *The Dynamics of Instructional Groups.* Fifty-ninth Yearbook, Part II. Chicago: University of Chicago Press. (pp. 454, 482)

NEUGARTEN, BERNICE L. (1949), "The Democracy of Childhood," Chapter 5 in *Democracy in Jonesville*, W. Lloyd Warner and Associates. New York: Harper & Row, Publishers. (pp. 181, 211)

NEW YORK CITY (1959), *Sixtieth Annual Report of the Superintendent of Schools, School Year 1957-58*. Statistical Section. Brooklyn: Board of Education of the City of New York. (p. 246)

NICHOLS, ROBERT C. (1965), "The Financial Status of National Merit Finalists," *Science*, 149, 1071-1074. (p. 118)

NOEL, EDWARD WARREN (1962), "Sponsored and Contest Mobility in America and England: a Rejoinder to Ralph H. Turner," *Comparative Education Review*, 6, 148-151. (p. 65)

NORTH, CECIL, and PAUL HATT (1949), "Jobs and Occupations: a Popular Evaluation," pp. 464-473 in *Sociological Analysis*, Logan Wilson and William A. Kolb, eds. New York: Harcourt, Brace, & World, Inc. (p. 433)

ODELL, WILLIAM R. (1965), *Educational Survey Report*. Philadelphia: Board of Education. (pp. 75, 384)

OGDEN, JEAN, and JESS OGDEN (1947), *These Things We Tried*. University of Virginia Extension, 25, No. 6. (p. 239)

OLSEN, EDWARD G., ed. (1954), *School and Community*. Englewood Cliffs, N.J.: Prentice-Hall, Inc. (p. 239)

OLSON, CLARA M., and NORMAN D. FLETCHER (1946), *Learn and Live*. New York: Alfred P. Sloan Foundation. (p. 226)

PACE(1963), *Report by the Committee on a Plan for Action by Citizens in Education*. Cleveland: The PACE Association. (p. 271)

PADILLA, ELENA (1958), *Up from Puerto Rico*. New York: Columbia University Press. (pp. 68, 230)

PARSONS, TALCOTT (1959), "The School Class as a Social System: Some of Its Functions in American Society," *Harvard Educational Review*, 29, 297-318. (pp. 178, 192)

PARSONS, TALCOTT, and ROBERT F. BALES (1955), *Family Socialization and the Interaction Process*. New York: The Free Press. (pp. 152, 153)

PARSONS, TALCOTT, and EDWARD A. SHILS, eds. (1952), *Toward a General Theory of Action*. Cambridge, Mass.: Harvard University Press. (p. 269)

PASSOW, A. HARRY (1963), *Education in Depressed Areas*. New York: Bureau of Publications, Teachers College, Columbia University. (p. 148)

PETERSON, WARREN A. (1956), "Career Phases and Inter-Age Relationships: The Female High School Teacher in Kansas City." Unpublished doctoral dissertation, Department of Sociology, University of Chicago. (pp. 485, 488-489)

——— (1964), "Age, Teacher's Role and the Institutional Setting," Chapter IX in *Contemporary Research on Teacher Effectiveness*, Bruce J. Biddle and William J. Elena, eds. New York: Holt, Rinehart, & Winston, Inc. (See also Havighurst, Neugarten, and Falk, *Society and Education: A Book of Readings*.) (pp. 452, 488)

PETTIGREW, THOMAS F. (1964), *Profile of the Negro-American.* Princeton, N.J.: D. Van Nostrand Co., Inc. (p. 384)

PETTIGREW, THOMAS F., and PATRICIA J. PAJONIS (1965), "Social Psychological Considerations of Racially-Balanced Schools." pp. 87–108 in *Because It Is Right — Educationally; Report of the Advisory Committee on Racial Imbalance and Education.* Boston, Mass.: State Board of Education. (p. 370)

PHEARMAN, LEO T. (1949), "Comparisons of High School Graduates Who Go to College with Those Who Do Not," *Journal of Educational Psychology,* 40, 405-414. (p. 99)

PHI DELTA KAPPA (1963), "Educating the Culturally Deprived in the Great Cities," *Phi Delta Kappan,* 45, November. (p. 148)

PIAGET, JEAN (1932), *The Moral Judgment of the Child.* New York: Harcourt, Brace, & World, Inc. (p. 189)

PITTSBURGH BOARD OF PUBLIC EDUCATION (1965), "The Quest for Racial Equality in the Pittsburgh Public Schools," *The Annual Report for 1965.* Pittsburgh, Pa.: Board of Public Education. (p. 247)

POHLMANN, VERNON C. (1956), "Relationship Between Ability, Socioeconomic Status, and Choice of Secondary School," *Journal of Educational Sociology,* 29, 392-397. (p. 84)

POIS, JOSEPH (1964), *The School Board Crisis: A Chicago Case Study.* Chicago: Aldine Publishing Company. (p. 293)

THE PRESIDENT'S ADVISORY COMMISSION ON HIGHER EDUCATION (1948), *Higher Education for American Democracy.* New York: Harper & Row, Publishers. (p. 108)

PROJECT TALENT (1964), *The American High School Student.* Pittsburgh: University of Pittsburgh. (p. 95)

PUGH, R. W. (1943), "A Comparative Study of the Adjustment of Negro Students in Mixed and Separate High Schools," *Journal of Negro Education,* 12, 607-616. (p. 372)

RAHM, HAROLD J., and J. ROBERT WEBER (1958), *Office in the Alley.* Austin: University of Texas Printing Division for the Hogg Foundation. (p. 340)

RAINWATER, LEE, RICHARD P. COLEMAN, and GERALD HANDEL (1959), *Workingman's Wife.* New York: Oceana Publications, Inc. (p. 37)

RATHS, LOUIS E., and STEPHEN ABRAHAMSON (1951), *Student Status and Social Class.* Bronxville, N.Y.: Modern Educational Service. (p. 36)

RAUP, BRUCE (1936), *Education and Organized Interests in America.* New York: G. P. Putnam's Sons. (p. 239)

REDL, FRITZ (1956), "Types of Delinquents," pp. 58-62 in *New Perspectives for Research on Delinquency.* Helen L. Witmer and Ruth Kotinsky, eds. Children's Bureau Publication No. 356. Washington, D.C.: U.S. Government Printing Office. (p. 358)

REDL, FRITZ, and WILLIAM WATTENBERG (1951), *Mental Hygiene in Teaching.* New York: Harcourt, Brace, & World, Inc. (pp. 449, 454)

REGER, ROGER (1963), "An Attempt to Integrate a Group Isolate," *Journal of Educational Sociology,* 36, 154-158. (p. 473)

RIESMAN, DAVID (1955), *Individualism Reconsidered.* New York: The Free Press. (p. 487)

RIESMAN, DAVID, *et al.* (1950), *The Lonely Crowd.* New Haven, Conn.: Yale University Press. (pp. 21, 37)

RIESSMAN, FRANK (1962), *The Culturally Deprived Child.* New York: Harper & Row, Publishers. (pp. 148, 165)

ROCKEFELLER, JOHN D., III (1960), "Students of Japan," *New York Times Magazine,* June 5, p. 21+. (p. 343)

ROHRER, JOHN H., and MUNRO S. EDMONSON (1960), *The Eighth Generation.* New York: Harper & Row, Publishers. (p. 147)

ROPER, ELMO (1949), *Factors Affecting Admission of High School Seniors to College.* Washington, D.C.: American Council on Education. (pp. 99, 120)

ROSEN, BERNARD C. (1959), "Race, Ethnicity, and the Achievement Syndrome," *American Sociological Review,* 24, 47-60. (p. 58)

ROSEN, BERNARD C., and ROY D'ANDRADE (1959), "The Psychological Origins of Achievement Motivation," *Sociometry,* 22, 185-218. (p. 99)

ROSENCRANZ, HOWARD A., and BRUCE J. BIDDLE (1964), "The Role Approach to Teacher Competence," pp. 232-263 in *Contemporary Research on Teacher Effectiveness,* Bruce J. Biddle and William J. Ellena, eds. New York: Holt, Rinehart & Winston, Inc. (pp. 443, 444)

RYANS, DAVID G. (1960), *Characteristics of Teachers.* Washington, D.C.: American Council on Education. (p. 435)

SALTZMAN, HENRY (1963), "The Community School in the Urban Setting," in *Education in Depressed Areas,* A. Harry Passrow, ed. New York: Teachers College, Columbia University. (p. 229)

SANFORD, NEVITT, ed. (1962), *The American College: A Psychological and Social Interpretation of the Higher Learning.* New York: John Wiley & Sons, Inc. (pp. 107, 120)

SARGENT, S. STANSFELD (1953), "Class and Class-Consciousness in a California Town," *Social Problems,* 1, 22-27. (p. 183)

SCHMID, CALVIN F., and CHARLES E. NOBBE (1965), "Socioeconomic Differentials among Non-White Races," *American Sociological Review,* 30, 909-922. (p. 59)

SCHMUCH, RICHARD (1963), "Some Relationships of Peer Liking Patterns in the Classroom to Pupil Attitudes and Achievement," *School Review,* 71, 337-359. (p. 184)

SCHULTZ, THEODORE W. (1960), "Capital Formation by Education," *Journal of Political Economy,* 68, 571-583. (pp. 389, 390)

———— (1961), "Education and Economic Growth," Chapter 3 in *Social Forces Influencing American Education,* Sixtieth Yearbook, Part II, National Society for the Study of Education. (p. 109)

———— (1963), *The Economic Value of Education.* New York: Columbia University Press. (p. 390)

SEARS, ROBERT R., ELEANOR E. MACCOBY, and HARRY LEVIN (1957), *Patterns of Child Rearing.* Evanston, Ill.: Row, Peterson & Company. (p. 167)

SEAY, MAURICE F., and LEONARD E. MEECE (1944), "The Sloan Experiment in Kentucky." Bulletin of the Bureau of School Service, 16, No. 4. College of Education, University of Kentucky. (p. 226)

SEELEY, JOHN R., R. ALEXANDER SIM, and ELIZABETH W. LOOSLEY (1963), Crestwood Heights. New York: John Wiley & Sons, Inc. (See also Basic Books, Inc., Publishers, 1965). (p. 230)

SEXTON, PATRICIA (1961), Education and Income. New York: The Viking Press, Inc., (p. 251)

——— (1965), Spanish Harlem. New York: Harper & Row, Publishers. (p. 68)

SHAPIRO, DAVID F. (1958), "Relationship of High School Size to Staff Relations." Unpublished doctoral dissertation, Stanford University. (p. 198)

SHAPLIN, JUDSON T. (1961), "Practice in Teaching," Harvard Educational Review, 31, 33-59. (p. 485)

SHAW, CLIFFORD R., and HENRY D. McKAY (1942), Juvenile Delinquency and Urban Areas. Chicago: University of Chicago Press. (p. 358)

SHORT, JAMES F., JR., and FRED L. STRODTBECK (1965), Group Process and Gang Delinquency. Chicago: University of Chicago Press. (pp. 340, 358)

SHOSTAK, ARTHUR B., and WILLIAM GOMBERG, eds. (1964), Blue-Collar World. Englewood Cliffs, N.J.: Prentice-Hall, Inc. (p. 37)

SILBERMAN, CHARLES E. (1964), Crisis in Black and White. New York: Random House, Inc. (p. 383)

SKEELS, HAROLD M. (1966), "Adult Status of Children with Contrasting Early Life Experiences." Monograph of the Society for Research in Child Development, 31, No. 6, Serial 105. Chicago: University of Chicago Press. (pp. 132, 148)

SKEELS, HAROLD M., and H. B. DYE (1939), "A Study of the Effect of Differential Stimulation on Mentally Retarded Children," Proceedings and Addresses of the American Association of Mental Deficiency, 44, No. 1, 114-136. (pp. 130-132)

SMITH, BOB (1965), They Closed Their Schools: Prince Edward County, Virginia, 1951-64. Chapel Hill: University of North Carolina Press. (p. 384)

SPECTORSKY, AUGUSTE C. (1955), The Exurbanites. Philadelphia: J. B. Lippincott Co. (pp. 37, 267)

SPINDLER, GEORGE D., ed. (1963), Education and Culture. New York: Holt, Rinehart & Winston, Inc. (pp. 148, 216)

STANLEY, WILLIAM O. (1961), "Educational and Social Policy," Review of Educational Research, XXXI, 91-108. (p. 275)

STANLEY, WILLIAM O., et al. (1956), Social Foundations of Education: A Book of New Readings. New York: The Dryden Press. (pp. 94, 190, 215, 238, 293)

STEFFENSON, JAMES P. (1964), Teachers Negotiate with Their School Boards. Bulletin No. 40. Washington, D.C.: Office of Education. (pp. 500, 504)

STENDLER, CELIA BURNS (1949), Children of Brasstown. Urbana, Ill.:

Bureau of Research and Service of the College of Education, University of Illinois. (pp. 94, 181, 190)

——— (1951), "Social Class Differences in Parental Attitude Toward School at Grade I Level," *Child Development,* 22, 37-46. (p. 158)

STERN, GEORGE C. (1963), "Characteristics of the Intellectual Climate in College Environments," *Harvard Educational Review,* 33, 5-41. (p. 107)

STETLER, HENRY G. (1949), *College Admission Practices with Respect to Race, Religion, and National Origin of Connecticut High School Graduates.* Hartford, Conn.: State Interracial Commission. (p. 97)

STILES, LINDLEY JOSEPH, ed. (1957), *The Teacher's Role in American Society.* Fourteenth Yearbook of the John Dewey Society. New York: Harper & Row, Publishers. (p. 422)

STINCHCOMBE, ARTHUR L. (1965), *Rebellion in a High School.* Chicago: Quadrangle Books, Inc. (p. 214)

STIVERS, EUGENE H. (1958), "Motivation for College in High School Boys," *School Review,* LXVI, 341-350. (pp. 99, 100)

——— (1959), "Motivation for College in High School Girls," *School Review,* LXVII, 320-334. (pp. 99, 100)

STRAUSS, ANSELM L. (1961), *Images of the City.* New York: The Free Press. (p. 267)

STRAYER, GEORGE D. (1932), *Report of the Survey of the Schools of Chicago, Illinois,* Vol. III. New York: Bureau of Publications, Teachers College, Columbia University. (p. 281)

STRODTBECK, FRED L. (1958), "Family Interaction, Values and Achievement," Chapter 4 in *Talent and Society,* David C. McClelland, Alfred L. Baldwin, Urie Bronfenbrenner, and Fred L. Strodtbeck. Princeton, N.J.: D. Van Nostrand Co., Inc. (p. 58)

SUTHERLAND, ROBERT L. (1942), *Color, Class and Personality.* Washington, D.C.: American Council on Education. (p. 37)

TABA, HILDA (1955), *School Culture.* Washington, D.C.: American Council on Education. (pp. 215, 469-472)

TABA, HILDA, and DEBORAH ELKINS (1950), *With Focus on Human Relations.* Washington, D.C.: American Council on Education. (pp. 467-468, 469-472)

TAEUBER, CONRAD, and IRENE TAEUBER (1958), *The Changing Population of the United States.* New York: John Wiley & Sons, Inc. (pp. 306, 330)

TANNENBAUM, ABRAHAM J. (1962), *Adolescent Attitudes Toward Academic Brilliance.* New York: Teachers College, Columbia University. (pp. 176, 177)

TEAL, HAL C. (1956), "Attitudes of Selected School Board Members Concerning Problems Facing Public Education." Unpublished doctoral dissertation, University of Pittsburgh. (p. 395)

TEETERS, NEGLEY K., and DAVID MATZA (1959), "The Extent of Delinquency in the United States," *Journal of Negro Education,* 28, 200-203. (p. 338)

THELEN, HERBERT A. (1954), *Dynamics of Groups at Work*. Chicago: University of Chicago Press. (p. 461)

THOMPSON, W. S., and D. T. LEWIS (1965), *Population Problems*. Fifth edition. New York: McGraw-Hill Book Company. (p. 330)

THRASHER, FREDERIC M. (1936), *The Gang*. Second revised edition. Chicago: University of Chicago Press. (pp. 339-340)

TICKTON, SIDNEY G. (1961), *Teaching Salaries Then and Now — A Second Look*. New York: Fund for the Advancement of Education. (p. 491)

TURNER, RALPH (1960), "Sponsored and Contest Mobility," *American Sociological Review*, 25, 855-867. (p. 64)

UDRY, J. RICHARD (1960), "The Importance of Social Class in a Suburban School," *Journal of Educational Sociology*, 33, 307-310. (p. 84)

UNESCO *Courier*, 3, No. 6-7 (1950). Quotation occurs also in the *United Nations Bulletin*, 9, 105. (p. 79)

UNITED STATES BUREAU OF LABOR STATISTICS (January 29, 1965), *Indexes of Output per Man-Hour for the Private Economy, 1947-64*. Washington, D.C.: U.S. Government Printing Office. (p. 299)

UNITED STATES DEPARTMENT OF LABOR (October, 1961), *Employment and Earnings*. Vol. 8, No. 3. (p. 323)

UNITED STATES DEPARTMENT OF LABOR (March, 1965), *The Negro Family: The Case for National Action*. Washington, D.C.: U.S. Government Printing Office. (pp. 155, 157, 167)

UNITED STATES, 86TH CONGRESS (1960), *Report on Juvenile Delinquency*. Washington, D.C.: U.S. Government Printing Office. (pp. 332, 338, 350-351)

UNITED STATES, 89TH CONGRESS (1965), *Higher Education Act of 1965*. Hearings Before the Special Subcommittee on Education of the Committee on Education and Labor, House of Representatives. Washington, D.C.: U.S. Government Printing Office. (pp. 117, 276)

UNITED STATES OFFICE OF EDUCATION (1963), *Programs for the Educationally Disadvantaged*. Bulletin No. 17. Washington, D.C.: U.S. Government Printing Office. (p. 148)

UNITED STATES OFFICE OF EDUCATION (1964), *The 1963 Dropout Campaign*. Bulletin No. 26. Washington, D.C.: U.S. Government Printing Office. (p. 94)

UNITED STATES OFFICE OF EDUCATION (1965), *Digest of Educational Statistics*. Bulletin No. 4. Washington, D.C.: U.S. Government Printing Office. (pp. 302, 314, 324, 389)

UNITED STATES REPORTS, Vol. 333 (1948), *Cases Adjudged in the Supreme Court at October Term, 1947*, pp. 203-256. Washington, D.C.: U.S. Government Printing Office. (p. 274)

VALENTINE, EARL C. (1950), "The Occupational Expectations of Three Normal School Student Groups." Unpublished masters thesis, Department of Sociology, University of Chicago. (p. 411)

VERNON, RAYMOND (1959), *The Changing Economic Function of the Cen-*

tral City. New York: Committee for Economic Development. (p. 249)
——— (1961), *Metropolis, 1985*. Cambridge, Mass.: Harvard University Press. (p. 267)
VIDICH, ARTHUR J., and JOSEPH BENSMAN (1958), *Small Town in Mass Society*. Princeton, N.J.: Princeton University Press. (pp. 16, 239, 434)
VIEG, JOHN A. (1939), *The Government of Education in Metropolitan Chicago*. Chicago: University of Chicago Press. (p. 279)
VOLBERDING, ELEANOR (1948), "Out of School Behavior of Eleven-Year-Olds," *Elementary School Journal*, 48, 432-441. (p. 140)
——— (1949), "Out of School Living of Eleven-Year-Old Boys and Girls from Differing Socio-Economic Groups," *Elementary School Journal*, 49, 348-353. (p. 140)

WAGENSCHEIN, MIRIAM (1950), " 'Reality Shock': A Study of Beginning Elementary School Teachers." Unpublished masters thesis, Department of Sociology, University of Chicago. (pp. 203, 411, 485)
WALKER, CHARLES R., and R. H. GUEST (1952), *The Man on the Assembly Line*. Cambridge, Mass.: Harvard University Press. (p. 37)
WALLER, WILLARD (1932), *The Sociology of Teaching*. New York: John Wiley & Sons, Inc. (pp. 192, 215)
——— (1942), "The Teacher's Roles," Chapter 10 in *Sociological Foundations of Education*, J. S. Roucek and Associates, eds. New York: Thomas Y. Crowell Company. (pp. 423, 446, 453, 454)
WARNER, W. LLOYD (1953), *American Life: Dream and Reality*. Chicago: University of Chicago Press. (p. 37)
——— (1962), *The Corporation in the Emergent American Society*. New York: Harper & Row, Publishers. (p. 66)
WARNER, W. LLOYD, and JAMES C. ABEGGLEN (1955), *Big Business Leaders in America*. New York: Harper & Row, Publishers. (pp. 61, 67, 70)
WARNER, W. LLOYD, and ASSOCIATES (1949), *Democracy in Jonesville*. New York: Harper & Row, Publishers. (pp. 15, 17, 37, 190)
WARNER, W. LLOYD, BUFORD H. JUNKER, and WALTER A. ADAMS (1941), *Color and Human Nature*. Washington, D.C.: American Council on Education. (p. 37)
WARNER, W. LLOYD, and PAUL S. LUNT (1941), *The Social Life of a Modern Community*. New Haven, Conn.: Yale University Press. (pp. 17, 36)
WARNER, W. LLOYD, MARCHIA MEEKER, and KENNETH EELS (1960), *Social Class in America. new ed. New York: Harper Torchbooks*. (pp. 13, 17, 20, 37, 433)
WATTENBERG, WILLIAM, *et al.* (1957, I), "Social Origins of Teachers — Facts from a Northern Industrial City," Chapter 2 in *The Teacher's Role in American Society*, Lindley J. Stiles, ed., Fourteenth Yearbook of the John Dewey Society. New York: Harper & Row, Publishers. (p. 440)
WATTENBERG, WILLIAM, *et al.* (1957, II), "Social Origins of Teachers and American Education," Chapter 5 in *The Teacher's Role in American*

Society, Lindley J. Stiles, ed., Fourteenth Yearbook of the John Dewey Society. New York: Harper & Row, Publishers. (p. 429)

WEDDINGTON, RACHEL (1958), "The Relative Influence of Social Class and Color on the Stereotypes of Young Children." Unpublished doctoral dissertation, Committee on Human Development, University of Chicago. (p. 182)

WERTHAM, FREDERIC (1954), *Seduction of the Innocent.* New York: Holt, Rinehart, & Winston, Inc. (p. 338)

WEST, JAMES (1945), *Plainville, U.S.A.* New York: Columbia University Press. (pp. 15, 37)

WHITEFORD, EMMA M. B. (1955), Administrators' Stereotype of the High School Home Economics Teacher." Unpublished doctoral dissertation, University of Illinois. (p. 432)

WHITNEY, FREDERICK L. (1927), "The Social and Economic Background of Teacher College and of the University Students," *Education,* XLVII, 449-456. (p. 410)

WHYTE, WILLIAM FOOTE (1943), *Street-Corner Society.* Chicago: University of Chicago Press. (p. 190)

WHYTE, WILLIAM H., JR. (1956), *The Organization Man.* New York: Simon and Schuster, Inc. (p. 37)

WILSON, ALAN B. (1959), "Residential Segregation of Social Classes and Aspirations of High School Boys," *American Sociological Review,* 24, 836-845. (pp. 84, 196, 256)

WOLFLE, DAEL (1954), *American Resources of Specialized Talent.* New York: Harper & Row, Publishers. (p. 119)

WRIGHT, HERBERT F., CHARLES T. DEEBLE, and DAN M. RAGLE (1957), "Children's Acquaintance with Neighborhood Families in Communities Differing in Size." Paper read at meetings of the American Psychological Association, New York City. (p. 144)

YABLONSKY, LEWIS (1962), *The Violent Gang.* New York: The MacMillan Company. (p. 340)

YARBROUGH, JOSEPH W. (1949), "Morale is a Number of Things," *Illinois Education,* 38, 130-131. (p. 203)

ZAPOLEON, MARGUERITE W. (1961), *Occupational Planning for Women.* New York: Harper & Row, Publishers. (p. 120)

Index

Achievement motivation:
    and child-rearing practices, 159
    and social mobility, 58
Administrators (*see* School administrators)
Adolescent values, 175–176, 213
Age-grading, in the school, 193–194
American Federation of Teachers, 503–504

Biological development, of the child, 123–124, 126
Biological integration, of the society, 362–363
Birth-rates (*see also* Population): 298–300
    differential rates, 306–311
    and social mobility, 307–311
Boards of Education (*see* School boards)
Bureaucratization, in the school, 195–196

Career (*see* Teaching career)
Caste:
    Caste-like groups and social structure, 33–34
    definition, 33
    and intergroup relations, 362
Certification of teachers, 504–505
Child-rearing practices:
    in entrepreneurial and bureaucratic families, 152–153
    historical changes, 149–150
    social-class differences, 151–152
Churches and religious organizations, 273–277

Churches and religious organizations (*cont.*)
    church schools, 273–274 (*see also* Parochial schools)
    and public schools, 273–277
    "released time" programs, 273–275
College attendance (*see also* College enrollments):
    and financial ability, 97–98
    and intellectual ability, 96, 98
    motivation for, 99–103
    number who should attend, 108–109
    and propinquity to college, 98
    and race, 96–97
    and religion, 96–97
    scholarships, 116–118
    and sex ratios, 96
    and social status, 97–98
College enrollments (*see also* College attendance; School enrollments):
    changes in, 71, 301, 314, 316
    factors related to, 95–103
    and fluidity in the social structure, 97–118
    future, 111–118, 314–316, 327
    and manpower needs, 111–112
Colleges:
    composition of student bodies, 106–107
    control of, 396
    selectivity in admissions, 113–115
    types of, 104–107
Comic books, 338
Community school, the, 225–229
    characteristics of, 226